LEARNSMART ADVANTAGE WORKS

LEARNSMART

A	B	C	D	
30.5%	33.5%	22.6%	8.7%	4.7%

A	B	C	D	
19.3%	38.6%	28.0%	9.6%	4.5%

Without LearnSmart

More C students earn B's

*Study: 690 students / 6 institutions

Over 20%
more students pass the class with LearnSmart

*A&P Research Study

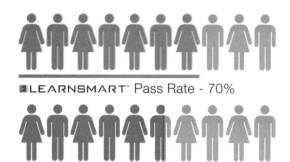

LEARNSMART Pass Rate - 70%

Without LearnSmart Pass Rate - 57%

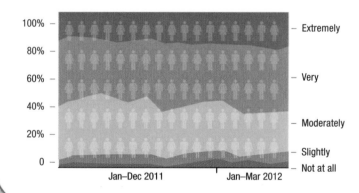

- Extremely
- Very
- Moderately
- Slightly
- Not at all

100%
80%
60%
40%
20%
0

Jan–Dec 2011   Jan–Mar 2012

More than 60%
of all students agreed LearnSmart was a very or extremely helpful learning tool

*Based on 750,000 student survey responses

> *AVAILABLE*
ON-THE-GO

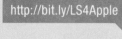

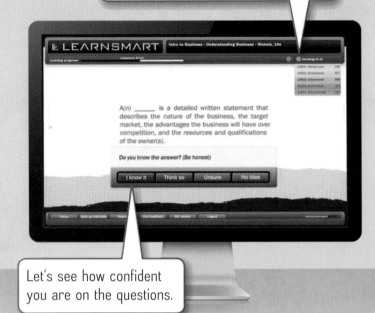

How do you rank against your peers?

Let's see how confident you are on the questions.

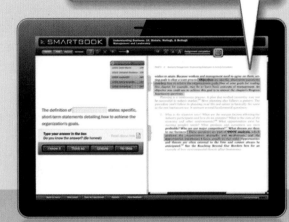

What you know (green) and what you still need to review (yellow), based on your answers.

COMPARE AND CHOOSE WHAT'S RIGHT FOR YOU

	BOOK	LEARNSMART	ASSIGNMENTS	
connect plus+	✓	✓	✓	LearnSmart, assignments, and SmartBook—all in one digital product for maximum savings!
connect plus+ Looseleaf	✓	✓	✓	Pop the pages into your own binder or carry just the pages you need.
connect plus+ Bound Book	✓	✓	✓	The #1 Student Choice!
SMARTBOOK Access Code	✓	✓		The first and only book that adapts to you!
LEARNSMART ADVANTAGE Access Code		✓		The smartest way to get from a B to an A.
CourseSmart eBook	✓			Save some green and some trees!
create	✓	✓	✓	Check with your instructor about a custom option for your course.

> Buy directly from the source at www.ShopMcGraw-Hill.com.

Business Driven Technology

SIXTH EDITION

Paige Baltzan

Daniels College of Business

University of Denver

BUSINESS DRIVEN TECHNOLOGY, SIXTH EDITION

Published by McGraw-Hill Education, 2 Penn Plaza, New York, NY 10121. Copyright © 2015 by McGraw-Hill Education. All rights reserved. Printed in the United States of America. Previous editions © 2013, 2010, and 2009. No part of this publication may be reproduced or distributed in any form or by any means, or stored in a database or retrieval system, without the prior written consent of McGraw-Hill Education, including, but not limited to, in any network or other electronic storage or transmission, or broadcast for distance learning.

Some ancillaries, including electronic and print components, may not be available to customers outside the United States.

This book is printed on acid-free paper.

2 3 4 5 6 7 8 9 0 DOR/DOR 1 0 9 8 7 6 5 4

ISBN   978-0-07-337690-5
MHID   0-07-337690-6

Senior Vice President, Products & Markets: *Kurt L. Strand*
Vice President, Content Production & Technology Services: *Kimberly Meriwether David*
Director: *Scott Davidson*
Senior Brand Manager: *Wyatt Morris*
Executive Director of Development: *Ann Torbert*
Development Editor: *Allison McCabe*
Digital Development Editor II: *Kevin White*
Senior Marketing Manager: *Tiffany Russell*
Director, Content Production: *Terri Schiesl*
Content Project Manager: *Kathryn D. Wright*
Media Project Manager: *Joseph A. McCarthy*
Senior Buyer: *Carol A. Bielski*
Design: *Matt Diamond*
Lead Content Licensing Specialist: *Keri Johnson*
Typeface: *10/12 Utopia*
Compositor: *Laserwords Private Limited*
Printer: *R. R. Donnelley*

All credits appearing on page or at the end of the book are considered to be an extension of the copyright page.

Library of Congress Cataloging-in-Publication Data

Baltzan, Paige.
    Business driven technology / Paige Baltzan, Daniels College of Business, University of Denver.—6th ed.
      pages cm
    Includes bibliographical references and index.
    ISBN 978-0-07-337690-5 (alk. paper)
    ISBN 0-07-337690-6 (alk. paper)
    1. Information technology—Management. 2. Management information systems. 3. Information resources management. 4. Industrial management—Technological innovations. I. Title.
HD30.2.B3575 2015
658.4'038—dc23

                                                                    2013041473

The Internet addresses listed in the text were accurate at the time of publication. The inclusion of a website does not indicate an endorsement by the authors or McGraw-Hill Education, and McGraw-Hill Education does not guarantee the accuracy of the information presented at these sites.

www.mhhe.com

In memory of Allan R. Biggs, my father, my
mentor, and my inspiration.
Paige

TABLE OF CONTENTS

Paige Baltzan

Paige Baltzan teaches in the department of Business Information and Analytics at the Daniels College of Business at the University of Denver. She holds a BS/BA specializing in Accounting/MIS from Bowling Green State University and an MBA specializing in MIS from the University of Denver. She is a coauthor of several books, including *Business Driven Information Systems, Essentials of Business Driven Information Systems, I-Series,* and is a contributor to *Management Information Systems for the Information Age.*

Before joining the Daniels College faculty in 1999, Paige spent several years working for a large telecommunications company and an international consulting firm where she participated in client engagements in the United States as well as South America and Europe. Paige lives in Lakewood, Colorado, with her husband, Tony, and daughters Hannah and Sophie.

The overall goal of the Technology Plug-Ins is to provide additional information not covered in the text such as personal productivity using information technology, problem solving using Excel, and decision making using Access. These plug-ins also offer an all-in-one text to faculty, avoiding their having to purchase an extra book to support Microsoft Office. These plug-ins offer integration with the core chapters and provide critical knowledge using essential business applications, such as Microsoft Excel, Microsoft Access, and Microsoft Project with hands-on tutorials for comprehension and mastery. Plug-Ins T1 to T12 are located on this textbook's website at www.mhhe.com/baltzan.

Plug-In	Description
T1. Personal Productivity Using IT	This plug-in covers a number of things to do to keep a personal computer running effectively and efficiently. The 12 topics covered in this plug-in are: ■ Creating strong passwords. ■ Performing good file management. ■ Implementing effective backup and recovery strategies. ■ Using Zip files. ■ Writing professional emails. ■ Stopping spam. ■ Preventing phishing. ■ Detecting spyware. ■ Threads to instant messaging. ■ Increasing PC performance. ■ Using antivirus software. ■ Installing a personal firewall.
T2. Basic Skills Using Excel	This plug-in introduces the basics of using Microsoft Excel, a spreadsheet program for data analysis, along with a few fancy features. The six topics covered in this plug-in are: ■ Workbooks and worksheets. ■ Working with cells and cell data. ■ Printing worksheets. ■ Formatting worksheets. ■ Formulas. ■ Working with charts and graphics.
T3. Problem Solving Using Excel	This plug-in provides a comprehensive tutorial on how to use a variety of Microsoft Excel functions and features for problem solving. The five areas covered in this plug-in are: ■ Lists ■ Conditional Formatting ■ AutoFilter ■ Subtotals ■ PivotTables
T4. Decision Making Using Excel	This plug-in examines a few of the advanced business analysis tools used in Microsoft Excel that have the capability to identify patterns, trends, and rules, and create "what-if" models. The four topics covered in this plug-in are: ■ IF ■ Goal Seek ■ Solver ■ Scenario Manager
T5. Designing Database Applications	This plug-in provides specific details on how to design relational database applications. One of the most efficient and powerful information management computer-based applications is the relational database. The four topics covered in this plug-in are: ■ Entities and data relationships. ■ Documenting logical data relationships. ■ The relational data model. ■ Normalization.

Plug-in	Description
T6. Basic Skills Using Access	This plug-in focuses on creating a Microsoft Access database file. One of the most efficient information management computer-based applications is Microsoft Access. Access provides a powerful set of tools for creating and maintaining a relational database. The two topics covered in this plug-in are: ■ Create a new database file. ■ Create and modify tables.
T7. Problem Solving Using Access	This plug-in provides a comprehensive tutorial on how to query a database in Microsoft Access. Queries are essential for problem solving, allowing a user to sort information, summarize data (display totals, averages, counts, and so on), display the results of calculations on data, and choose exactly which fields are shown. The three topics in this plug-in are: ■ Create simple queries using the simple query wizard. ■ Create advanced queries using calculated fields. ■ Format results displayed in calculated fields.
T8. Decision Making Using Access	This plug-in provides a comprehensive tutorial on entering data in a well-designed form and creating functional reports using Microsoft Access. A form is essential to use for data entry and a report is an effective way to present data in a printed format. The two topics in this plug-in are: ■ Creating, modifying, and running forms. ■ Creating, modifying, and running reports.
T9. Designing Web Pages	This plug-in provides a comprehensive assessment into the functional aspects of web design. Websites are beginning to look more alike and to employ the same metaphors and conventions. The web has now become an everyday thing whose design should not make users think. The six topics in this plug-in are: ■ The World Wide Web. ■ Designing for the unknown(s). ■ The process of web design. ■ HTML basics. ■ Web fonts. ■ Web graphics.
T10. Creating Web Pages Using HTML	This plug-in provides an overview of creating web pages using the HTML language. HTML is a system of codes that you use to create interactive web pages. It provides a means to describe the structure of text-based information in a document—by denoting certain text as headings, paragraphs, lists, and so on. The seven topics in this plug-in are: ■ An introduction to HTML. ■ HTML tools. ■ Creating, saving, and viewing HTML documents. ■ Apply style tags and attributes. ■ Using fancy formatting. ■ Creating hyperlinks. ■ Displaying graphics.
T11. Creating Web Pages Using Dreamweaver	This plug-in provides a tour of using Dreamweaver to create web pages. Dreamweaver allows anyone with limited web page design experience to create, modify, and maintain full-featured, professional-looking pages without having to learn how to code all the functions and features from scratch. The five topics in this plug-in are: ■ Navigation in Dreamweaver. ■ Adding content. ■ Formatting content. ■ Using cascading style sheets. ■ Creating tables.
T12. Creating Gantt Charts with Excel and Microsoft Project	This plug-in offers a quick and efficient way to manage projects. Excel and Microsoft Project are great for managing all phases of a project, creating templates, collaborating on planning processes, tracking project progress, and sharing information with all interested parties. The two topics in this plug-in are: ■ Creating Gantt Charts with Excel. ■ Creating Gantt Charts with Microsoft Project.

Unlike any other MIS text, *Business Driven Technology* discusses various business initiatives first and how technology supports those initiatives second. The premise for this unique approach is that business initiatives should drive technology choices. Every discussion in the text first addresses the business needs and then addresses the technology that supports those needs.

Business Driven Technology offers you the flexibility to customize courses according to your needs and the needs of your students by covering only essential concepts and topics in the five core units, while providing additional in-depth coverage in the business and technology plug-ins.

Business Driven Technology, 6e, contains 20 chapters (organized into five units), 12 business plug-ins, and 12 technology plug-ins offering you the ultimate flexibility in tailoring content to the exact needs of your MIS or IT course. The unique construction of this text allows you to cover essential concepts and topics in the five core units while providing you with the ability to customize a course and explore certain topics in greater detail with the business and technology plug-ins.

Plug-ins are fully developed modules of text that include student learning outcomes, case studies, business vignettes, and end-of-chapter material such as key terms, individual and group questions and projects, and case study exercises.

We realize that instructors today require the ability to cover a blended mix of topics in their courses. While some instructors like to focus on networks and infrastructure throughout their course, others choose to focus on ethics and security. *Business Driven Technology* was developed to easily adapt to your needs. Each chapter and plug-in is independent so you can:

- Cover any or all of the *chapters* as they suit your purpose.
- Cover any or all of the *business plug-ins* as they suit your purpose.
- Cover any or all of the *technology plug-ins* as they suit your purpose.
- Cover the plug-ins in any order you wish.

LESS MANAGING. MORE TEACHING. GREATER LEARNING.

McGraw-Hill *Connect MIS* is an online assignment and assessment solution that connects students with the tools and resources they'll need to achieve success.

McGraw-Hill *Connect MIS* helps prepare students for their future by enabling faster learning, more efficient studying, and higher retention of knowledge.

MCGRAW-HILL *CONNECT MIS* FEATURES

Connect MIS offers a number of powerful tools and features to make managing assignments easier, so faculty can spend more time teaching. With *Connect MIS*, students can engage with their coursework anytime and anywhere, making the learning process more accessible and efficient. *Connect MIS* offers you the features described next.

Simple assignment management

With *Connect MIS,* creating assignments is easier than ever, so you can spend more time teaching and less time managing. The assignment management function enables you to:

- Create and deliver assignments easily with selectable interactive exercises, scenario-based questions, and test bank items.
- Streamline lesson planning, student progress reporting, and assignment grading to make classroom management more efficient than ever.
- Go paperless with the eBook and online submission and grading of student assignments.

Smart grading

When it comes to studying, time is precious. *Connect MIS* helps students learn more efficiently by providing feedback and practice material when they need it, where they need it. When it comes to teaching, your time also is precious. The grading function enables you to:

- Have assignments scored automatically, giving students immediate feedback on their work and side-by-side comparisons with correct answers.
- Access and review each response; manually change grades or leave comments for students to review.
- Reinforce classroom concepts with practice tests and instant quizzes.

Instructor library

The *Connect MIS* Instructor Library is your repository for additional resources to improve student engagement in and out of class. You can select and use any asset that enhances your lecture. The *Connect MIS* Instructor Library includes:

- Instructor's Manual with
  - Classroom openers and exercises for each chapter
  - Case discussion points and solutions
  - Answers to all chapter questions and cases
  - Video guides–discussion points, questions and answers
- PowerPoint Presentations with detail lecture notes
- Animated step-by-step solutions to the Apply Your Knowledge problems, narrated by the author
- Instructor Course Guide–a topical organization of all the instructor content, material and resources available

Student study center

- The *Connect MIS* Student Study Center is the place for students to access additional data files, student versions of the PowerPoint slides and more.

Student progress tracking

Connect MIS keeps instructors informed about how each student, section, and class is performing, allowing for more productive use of lecture and office hours. The progress-tracking function enables you to:

- View scored work immediately and track individual or group performance with assignment and grade reports.
- Access an instant view of student or class performance relative to learning objectives.
- Collect data and generate reports required by many accreditation organizations, such as AACSB.

Lecture capture

Increase the attention paid to lecture discussion by decreasing the attention paid to note taking. For an additional charge Lecture Capture offers new ways for students to focus on the in-class discussion, knowing they can revisit important topics later. Lecture Capture enables you to:

- Record and distribute your lecture with a click of button.
- Record and index PowerPoint presentations and anything shown on your computer so it is easily searchable, frame by frame.
- Offer access to lectures anytime and anywhere by computer, iPod, or mobile device.
- Increase intent listening and class participation by easing students' concerns about note-taking. Lecture Capture will make it more likely you will see students' faces, not the tops of their heads.

McGraw-Hill *Connect Plus MIS*

McGraw-Hill reinvents the textbook learning experience for the modern student with *Connect Plus MIS*. A seamless integration of an eBook and *Connect MIS, Connect Plus MIS* provides all of the *Connect MIS* features plus the following:

- An integrated eBook, allowing for anytime, anywhere access to the textbook.
- A powerful search function to pinpoint and connect key concepts in a snap.

In short, *Connect MIS* offers you and your students powerful tools and features that optimize your time and energies, enabling you to focus on course content, teaching, and student learning. *Connect MIS* also offers a wealth of content resources for both instructors and students. This state-of-the-art, thoroughly tested system supports you in preparing students for the world that awaits.

For more information about Connect, go to **www.mcgrawhillconnect.com,** or contact your local McGraw-Hill sales representative.

Tegrity Campus: Lectures 24/7

Tegrity Campus is a service that makes class time available 24/7 by automatically capturing every lecture in a searchable format for students to review when they study and complete assignments. With a simple one-click start-and-stop process, you capture all computer screens and corresponding audio. Students can replay any part of any class with easy-to-use browser-based viewing on a PC or Mac.

Educators know that the more students can see, hear, and experience class resources, the better they learn. In fact, studies prove it. With Tegrity Campus, students quickly recall key moments by using Tegrity Campus's unique search feature. This search helps students efficiently find what they need, when they need it, across an entire semester of class recordings. Help turn all your students' study time into learning moments immediately supported by your lecture.

You can learn more about Tegrity by watching a 2-minute Flash demo at **http:// tegritycampus.mhhe.com.**

Assurance of Learning Ready

Many educational institutions today are focused on the notion of *assurance of learning,* an important element of some accreditation standards. *Business Driven Technology,* 6e, is designed specifically to support your assurance of learning initiatives with a simple, yet powerful solution.

Each test bank question for *Business Driven Technology* maps to a specific chapter learning outcome/objective listed in the text. You can use our test bank software, EZ Test and EZ Test Online, or in *Connect MIS* to easily query for learning outcomes/objectives that directly relate to the learning objectives for your course. You can then use the reporting features of EZ Test to aggregate student results in similar fashion, making the collection and presentation of assurance of learning data simple and easy.

AACSB Statement

The McGraw-Hill Companies is a proud corporate member of AACSB International. Understanding the importance and value of AACSB accreditation, *Business Driven Technology,* 6e, recognizes the curricula guidelines detailed in the AACSB standards for business accreditation by connecting selected questions in the text and/or the test bank to the six general knowledge and skill guidelines in the AACSB standards.

The statements contained in *Business Driven Technology,* 6e, are provided only as a guide for the users of this textbook. The AACSB leaves content coverage and assessment within the purview of individual schools, the mission of the school, and the faculty. While *Business Driven Technology,* 6e, and the teaching package make no claim of any specific AACSB qualification or evaluation, we have within *Business Driven Technology,* 6e, labeled selected questions according to the six general knowledge and skills areas.

McGraw-Hill Customer Care Contact Information

At McGraw-Hill, we understand that getting the most from new technology can be challenging. That's why our services don't stop after you purchase our products. You can email our Product Specialists 24 hours a day to get product-training online. Or you can search our knowledge bank of Frequently Asked Questions on our support website. For Customer Support, you can call **800-331-5094, email hmsupport@mcgraw-hill.com**, or visit **www.mhhe.com/support**. One of our Technical Support Analysts will be able to assist you in a timely fashion.

Walkthrough

This text is organized around the traditional sequence of topics and concepts in information technology; however, the presentation of this material is nontraditional. That is to say, the text is divided into four major sections: (1) units, (2) chapters, (3) business plug-ins, and (4) technology plug-ins. This represents a substantial departure from existing traditional texts. The goal is to provide both students and faculty with only the most essential concepts and topical coverage in the text, while allowing faculty to customize a course by choosing from among a set of plug-ins that explore topics in more detail. All of the topics that form the core of the discipline are covered, including CRM, SCM, Porter's Five Forces Model, value chain analysis, competitive advantage, information security, and ethics.

Business Driven Technology includes four major components:
- 5 Core Units
- 20 Chapters
- 12 Business Plug-Ins
- 12 Technology Plug-Ins

UNITS

BUSINESS PLUG-INS

TECHNOLOGY PLUG-INS

Format, Features, and Highlights

Business Driven Technology, 6e, is state of the art in its discussions, presents concepts in an easy-to-understand format, and allows students to be active participants in learning. The dynamic nature of information technology requires all students, more specifically business students, to be aware of both current and emerging technologies. Students are facing complex subjects and need a clear, concise explanation to be able to understand and use the concepts throughout their careers. By engaging students with numerous case studies, exercises, projects, and questions that enforce concepts, *Business Driven Technology* creates a unique learning experience for both faculty and students.

- **Logical Layout.** Students and faculty will find the text well organized with the topics flowing logically from one unit to the next and from one chapter to the next. The definition of each term is provided before it is covered in the chapter and an extensive glossary is included at the back of the text. Each core unit offers a comprehensive opening case study, introduction, learning outcomes, unit summary, closing case studies, key terms, and making business decision questions. The plug-ins follow the same pedagogical elements with the exception of the exclusion of opening case and closing case studies in the technology plug-ins.

- **Thorough Explanations.** Complete coverage is provided for each topic that is introduced. Explanations are written so that students can understand the ideas presented and relate them to other concepts presented in the core units and plug-ins.

- **Solid Theoretical Base.** The text relies on current theory and practice of information systems as they relate to the business environment. Current academic and professional journals and websites upon which the text is based are found in the References at the end of the book—a road map for additional, pertinent readings that can be the basis for learning beyond the scope of the unit, chapter, or plug-in.

- **Material to Encourage Discussion.** All units contain a diverse selection of case studies and individual and group problem-solving activities as they relate to the use of information technology in business. Two comprehensive cases at the end of each unit reflect the concepts from the chapters. These cases encourage students to consider what concepts have been presented and then apply those concepts to a situation they might find in an organization. Different people in an organization can view the same facts from different points of view and the cases will force students to consider some of those views.

- **Flexibility in Teaching and Learning.** While most textbooks that are "text only" leave faculty on their own when it comes to choosing cases, *Business Driven Technology* goes much further. Several options are provided to faculty with case selections from a variety of sources including *CIO, Harvard Business Journal, Wired, Forbes,* and *Time,* to name just a few. Therefore, faculty can use the text alone, the text and a complete selection of cases, or anything in between.

- **Integrative Themes.** Several themes recur throughout the text, which adds integration to the material. Among these themes are value-added techniques and methodologies, ethics and social responsibility, globalization, and gaining a competitive advantage. Such topics are essential to gaining a full understanding of the strategies that a business must recognize, formulate, and in turn implement. In addition to addressing these in the chapter material, many illustrations are provided for their relevance to business practice. These include brief examples in the text as well as more detail presented in the corresponding plug-in(s) (business or technical).

Visual Content Map

Visual Content Map.
Located at the beginning of the text and serving as a logical outline, the visual content map illustrates the relationship between each unit and its associated plug-ins.

Introduction

Information is everywhere. Most organizations value information as a strategic asset. Consider Apple and its iPod, iPod accessories, and iTunes Music Store. Apple's success depends heavily on information about its customers, suppliers, markets, and operations for each of these product lines. For example, Apple must be able to predict the number of people who will purchase an iPod to help estimate iPod accessory and iTunes sales within the next year. Estimating too many buyers will lead Apple to produce an excess of inventory; estimating too few buyers will potentially mean lost sales due to lack of product (resulting in even more lost revenues).

Understanding the direct impact information has on an organization's bottom line is crucial to running a successful business. This text focuses on information, business, technology, and the integrated set of activities used to run most organizations. Many of these activities are the hallmarks of business today—supply chain management, customer relationship management, enterprise resource planning, outsourcing, integration, ebusiness, and others. The five core units of this text cover these important activities in detail. Each unit is divided into chapters that provide individual learning outcomes and case studies. In addition to the five core units, there are technology and business "plug-ins" (see Figure Unit 1.1) that further explore topics presented in the five core units.

The chapters in Unit 1 are:

- **Chapter One**—Business Driven Technology.
- **Chapter Two**—Identifying Competitive Advantages.
- **Chapter Three**—Strategic Initiatives for Implementing Competitive Advantages.
- **Chapter Four**—Measuring the Success of Strategic Initiatives.
- **Chapter Five**—Organizational Structures That Support Strategic Initiatives.

Learning Outcomes and Introduction

Introduction. Located after the Unit Opening Case, the introduction familiarizes students with the overall tone of the chapters. Thematic concepts are also broadly defined.

Learning Outcomes. These outcomes focus on what students should learn and be able to answer upon completion of the chapter or plug-in.

Introduction

Decision making and problem solving in today's electronic world encompass large-scale, opportunity-oriented, strategically focused solutions. The traditional "cookbook" approach to decisions simply will not work in the ebusiness world. Decision-making and problem-solving abilities are now the most sought-after traits in up-and-coming executives. To put it mildly, decision makers and problem solvers have limitless career potential.

Ebusiness is the conducting of business on the Internet, not only buying and selling, but also serving customers and collaborating with business partners. (Unit Four discusses ebusiness in detail.) With the fast growth of information technology and the accelerated use of the Internet, ebusiness is quickly becoming standard. This unit focuses on technology to help make decisions, solve problems, and find new innovative opportunities. The unit highlights how to bring people together with the best IT processes and tools in complete, flexible solutions that can seize business opportunities (see Figure Unit 3.1). The chapters in Unit 3 are:

- **Chapter Nine**—Enabling the Organization—Decision Making.
- **Chapter Ten**—Extending the Organization—Supply Chain Management.
- **Chapter Eleven**—Building a Customer-centric Organization—Customer Relationship Management.
- **Chapter Twelve**—Integrating the Organization from End to End—Enterprise Resource Planning.

LEARNING OUTCOMES

9.1 Explain the importance of decision making for managers at each of the three primary organization levels along with the associated decision characteristics.

9.2 Classify the different operational support systems, managerial support systems, and strategic support systems, and explain how managers can use these systems to make decisions and gain competitive advantages.

9.3 Describe artificial intelligence and identify its five main types.

Unit Opening Case and Opening Case Study Questions

Unit Opening Case. To enhance student interest, each unit begins with an opening case study that highlights an organization that has been time-tested and value-proven in the business world. This feature serves to fortify concepts with relevant examples of outstanding companies. Discussion of the case is threaded throughout the chapters in each unit.

Opening Case Study Questions. Located at the end of each chapter, pertinent questions connect the Unit Opening Case with important chapter concepts.

UNIT ONE OPENING CASE

Apple—Merging Technology, Business, and Entertainment

This might sound hard to believe, but a bit more than a decade ago, Apple was on the brink of bankruptcy. Apple Inc., now back from near oblivion, is blazing a trail through the digital world with innovation and creativity that has been missing from the company for the past 20 years. The unique feature of Apple's competitive advantages is that they come from customers and users, not Apple employees. That's right; the company welcomes products created by consumers to sell to consumers, a trend new to business.

Capitalizing on the iPod

With millions of iPods in the hands of consumers, many people are finding ways to capitalize on the product. John Lin created a prototype of a remote control for the iPod and took his prototype to *Macworld,* where he found success. A few months later, Lin's company had Apple's blessing and a commitment for shelf space in its retail stores. "This is how Apple supports the iPod economy," Lin said.

In the iPod-dominated market, hundreds of companies have been inspired to develop more

OPENING CASE STUDY QUESTIONS

1. Explain how Apple achieved business success through the use of information, information technology, and people.
2. Describe the types of information employees at an Apple store require and compare it to the types of information the executives at Apple's corporate headquarters require. Are there any links between these two types of information?

Projects and Case Studies

Case Studies. This text is packed with case studies illustrating how a variety of prominent organizations and businesses have successfully implemented many of this text's concepts. All cases promote critical thinking. Company profiles are especially appealing and relevant to your students, helping to stir classroom discussion and interest.

Apply Your Knowledge Project Overview

Project Number	Project Name	Project Type	Plug-In	Focus Area	Project Level	Skill Set	Page Number
1	Financial Destiny	Excel	T2	Personal Budget	Introductory	Formulas	AYK.4
2	Cash Flow	Excel	T2	Cash Flow	Introductory	Formulas	AYK.4
3	Technology Budget	Excel	T1, T2	Hardware and Software	Introductory	Formulas	AYK.4
4	Tracking Donations	Excel	T2	Employee Relationships	Introductory	Formulas	AYK.4
5	Convert Currency	Excel	T2	Global Commerce	Introductory	Formulas	AYK.5
6	Cost Comparison	Excel	T2	Total Cost of Ownership	Introductory	Formulas	AYK.5
7	Time Management	Excel or Project	T12	Project Management	Introductory	Gantt Charts	AYK.6
8	Maximize Profit	Excel	T2, T4	Strategic Analysis	Intermediate	Formulas or Solver	AYK.6
9	Security Analysis	Excel	T3	Filtering Data	Intermediate	Conditional Formatting, Autofilter, Subtotal	AYK.7
10	Gathering Data	Excel	T3	Data Analysis	Intermediate	Conditional Formatting	AYK.8

Chapter One Case: The World Is Flat—Thomas Friedman

In his book *The World Is Flat*, Thomas Friedman describes the unplanned cascade of technological and social shifts that effectively leveled the economic world and "accidentally made Beijing, Bangalore, and Bethesda next-door neighbors." Chances are good that Bhavya in Bangalore will read your next X-ray, or as Friedman learned firsthand, "Grandma Betty in her bathrobe" will make your JetBlue plane reservation from her Salt Lake City home.

Friedman believes this is Globalization 3.0. "In Globalization 1.0, which began around 1492, the world went from size large to size medium. In Globalization 2.0, the era that introduced us to multinational companies, it went from size medium to size small. And then around 2000 came Globalization 3.0, in which the world went from being small to tiny. There is a difference between being able to make long-distance phone calls cheaper on the Internet and walking around Riyadh with a PDA where you can have all of Google in your pocket. It is a difference in degree that's so enormous it becomes a difference in kind," Friedman states. Figure 1.10 displays Friedman's list of "flatteners."

FIGURE 1.10

Thomas Friedman's 10 Forces That Flattened the World

1. Fall of the Berlin Wall	The events of November 9, 1989, tilted the worldwide balance of power toward democracies and free markets.
2. Netscape IPO	The August 9, 1995, offering sparked massive investment in fiber-optic cables.
3. Work flow software	The rise of applications from PayPal to VPNs enabled faster, closer coordination among far-flung employees.
4. Open-sourcing	Self-organizing communities, such as Linux, launched a collaborative revolution.
5. Outsourcing	Migrating business functions to India saved money *and* a Third World economy.
6. Offshoring	Contract manufacturing elevated China to economic prominence.
7. Supply-chaining	Robust networks of suppliers, retailers, and customers increased business efficiency.
8. Insourcing	Logistics giants took control of customer supply chains, helping mom-and-pop shops go global.
9. Informing	Power searching allowed everyone to use the Internet as a "personal supply chain of knowledge."
10. Wireless	Wireless technologies pumped up collaboration, making it mobile and personal.

Apply Your Knowledge. At the end of this text is a set of 33 projects aimed at reinforcing the business initiatives explored in the text. These projects help to develop the application and problem-solving skills of your students through challenging and creative business-driven scenarios.

Making Business Decisions

Making Business Decisions. Small scenario-driven projects help students focus on decision making as they relate to the topical elements in the chapters and plug-ins.

✳ MAKING BUSINESS DECISIONS

1. Improving Information Quality

HangUps Corporation designs and distributes closet organization structures. The company operates five different systems: order entry, sales, inventory management, shipping, and billing. The company has severe information quality issues including missing, inaccurate, redundant, and incomplete information. The company wants to implement a data warehouse containing information from the five different systems to help maintain a single customer view, drive business decisions, and perform multidimensional analysis. Identify how the organization can improve its information quality when it begins designing and building its data warehouse.

2. Information Timeliness

Information timeliness is a major consideration for all organizations. Organizations need to decide the frequency of backups and the frequency of updates to a data warehouse. In a team, describe the timeliness requirements for backups and updates to a data warehouse for

- Weather tracking systems.
- Car dealership inventories.
- Vehicle tire sales forecasts.
- Interest rates.
- Restaurant inventories.
- Grocery store inventories.

3. Entities and Attributes

Martex Inc. is a manufacturer of athletic equipment and its primary lines of business include running, tennis, golf, swimming, basketball, and aerobics equipment. Martex currently supplies four primary vendors including Sam's Sports, Total Effort, The Underline, and Maximum Workout. Martex wants to build a database to help it organize its products. In a group, identify the different types of entity classes and the related attributes that Martex will want to consider when designing the database.

4. Integrating Information

End-of-Unit Elements

⁕ UNIT CLOSING CASE TWO

Zillow

Zillow.com is an online ~~
renters, real estate agent~~
find and share informatio~~

⁕ MAKING BUSINESS DECISIONS

1. Improving Information Quality

HangUps Corporation designs and distributes closet organization structures. Th~~
operates five different systems: order entry, sales, inventory management, sh~~
billing. The company has severe information quality issues including missing,~~
redundant, and inc~~
house containing in~~
tomer view, drive bu~~
the organization ca~~
its data warehouse.~~

2. Information Tim~~

Information timelin~~

⁕ KEY TERMS

Analytical information, 86	Data-mining tools, 107
Attribute, 93	Data visualization, 112
Backward integration, 100	Data visualization tools, 112
Business intelligence dashboard, 112	Data warehouse, 105
	Dynamic catalog, 98
Business-critical integrity constraint, 97	Dynamic information, 98
	Entity, 93
Business rule, 97	Extraction, transformation, and loading (ETL), 105
Content creator, 98	
Cube, 106	Foreign key, 94
Content editor, 98	Forward integration, 100
Database, 92	Informing, 111
Database management system (DBMS), 92	Information cleansing or scrubbing, 108

Each unit contains complete pedagogical support in the form of:

- **Unit Summary.** Revisiting the unit highlights in summary format.
- **Key Terms.** With page numbers referencing where they are discussed in the text.
- **Two Closing Case Studies.** Reinforcing important concepts with prominent examples from businesses and organizations. Discussion questions follow each case study.
- **Critical Business Thinking.** Small scenario-driven projects that help students focus individually on decision making as they relate to the topical elements in the chapters.
- **Apply Your Knowledge.** In-depth projects that help students focus on applying the skills and concepts they have learned throughout the unit.
- **Apply Your Knowledge Application Projects.** Highlights the different AYK projects available at the end of the text that takes the MIS concepts and challenges the students to apply them using Excel, Access, and other tools.
- **Entrepreneurial Challenge:** This section offers an exciting running case that tasks the students with applying the MIS concepts to their own start-up business.

About the Plug-Ins

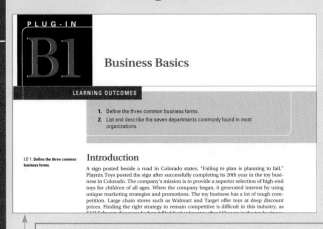

Management Focus. By focusing on the business plug-ins, your course will take on a managerial approach to MIS.

The plug-ins are designed to allow faculty to customize their course and cover selected topics in more detail. Students will read core material related to all of the plug-ins in the five units.

As an example, students will learn about various facets of customer relationship management (CRM) most notably in Chapter 11. However, customer relationship management has its own business plug-in. The CRM business plug-in gives both faculty and students the ability to cover CRM in more detail if desired. Likewise, students will receive an introduction to decision making in Unit 3. The Excel technology plug-ins allow coverage of decision-making tools such as PivotTables, Goal Seek, and Scenario Manager.

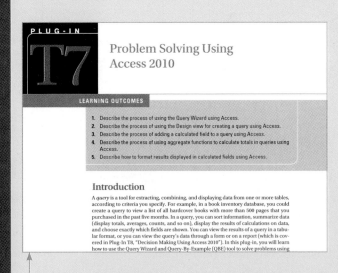

Technical Focus. If hands-on, technical skills are more important, include technical plug-ins in your MIS course.

End-of-Plug-In Elements

Each business plug-in contains complete pedagogical support in the form of:

- **Plug-in Summary.** Revisiting the plug-in highlights in summary format.
- **Key Terms.** With page numbers referencing where they are discussed in the text.
- **Two Closing Case Studies.** Reinforcing important concepts with prominent examples from businesses and organizations. Discussion questions follow each case study.
- **Making Business Decisions.** Small scenario-driven projects that help students focus individually on decision making as they relate to the topical elements in the chapters.

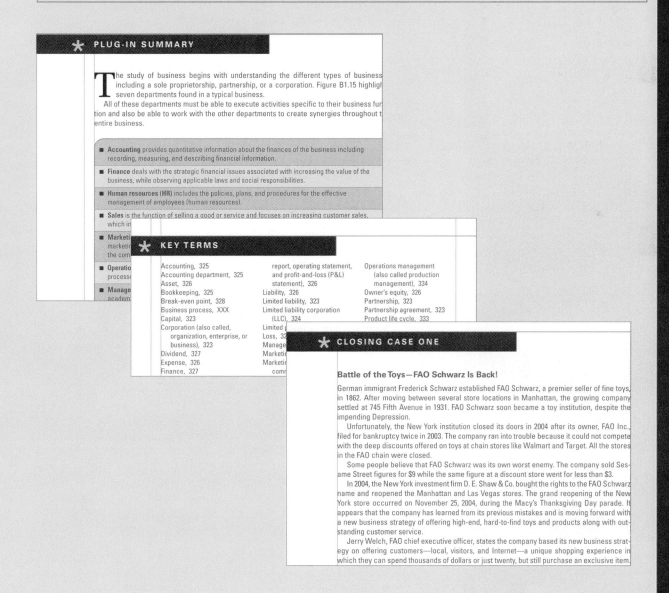

✳ PLUG-IN SUMMARY

The study of business begins with understanding the different types of business including a sole proprietorship, partnership, or a corporation. Figure B1.15 highligh[t] seven departments found in a typical business.

All of these departments must be able to execute activities specific to their business fun[c]tion and also be able to work with the other departments to create synergies throughout t[he] entire business.

- **Accounting** provides quantitative information about the finances of the business including recording, measuring, and describing financial information.
- **Finance** deals with the strategic financial issues associated with increasing the value of the business, while observing applicable laws and social responsibilities.
- **Human resources (HR)** includes the policies, plans, and procedures for the effective management of employees (human resources).
- **Sales** is the function of selling a good or service and focuses on increasing customer sales, which in
- **Marketi**[ng] marketi[ng] the com[
- **Operatio**[ns] processe[
- **Manage**[ment] academ[

✳ KEY TERMS

Accounting, 325
Accounting department, 325
Asset, 326
Bookkeeping, 325
Break-even point, 328
Business process, XXX
Capital, 323
Corporation (also called, organization, enterprise, or business), 323
Dividend, 327
Expense, 326
Finance, 327

report, operating statement, and profit-and-loss (P&L) statement), 326
Liability, 326
Limited liability, 323
Limited liability corporation (LLC), 324
Limited [
Loss, 32[
Manage[
Marketi[
Marketi[ng] comm[

Operations management (also called production management), 334
Owner's equity, 326
Partnership, 323
Partnership agreement, 323
Product life cycle, 333

✳ CLOSING CASE ONE

Battle of the Toys—FAO Schwarz Is Back!

German immigrant Frederick Schwarz established FAO Schwarz, a premier seller of fine toys, in 1862. After moving between several store locations in Manhattan, the growing company settled at 745 Fifth Avenue in 1931. FAO Schwarz soon became a toy institution, despite the impending Depression.

Unfortunately, the New York institution closed its doors in 2004 after its owner, FAO Inc., filed for bankruptcy twice in 2003. The company ran into trouble because it could not compete with the deep discounts offered on toys at chain stores like Walmart and Target. All the stores in the FAO chain were closed.

Some people believe that FAO Schwarz was its own worst enemy. The company sold Sesame Street figures for $9 while the same figure at a discount store went for less than $3.

In 2004, the New York investment firm D. E. Shaw & Co. bought the rights to the FAO Schwarz name and reopened the Manhattan and Las Vegas stores. The grand reopening of the New York store occurred on November 25, 2004, during the Macy's Thanksgiving Day parade. It appears that the company has learned from its previous mistakes and is moving forward with a new business strategy of offering high-end, hard-to-find toys and products along with outstanding customer service.

Jerry Welch, FAO chief executive officer, states the company based its new business strategy on offering customers—local, visitors, and Internet—a unique shopping experience in which they can spend thousands of dollars or just twenty, but still purchase an exclusive item.

Support and Supplemental Material

All of the supplemental material supporting *Business Driven Technology* was developed by the author to ensure you receive accurate, high-quality, and in-depth content. Included are a complete set of materials that will assist students and faculty in accomplishing course objectives.

Online Learning Center (www.mhhe.com/baltzan) The McGraw-Hill website for *Business Driven Technology* includes support for students and faculty. All supplements will be available exclusively on the OLC. This will allow the author to continually update and add to the instructor support materials. The following materials will be available on the OLC:

Video Exercises. Many of the videos that accompany the text are supported by detailed teaching notes on how to turn the videos into classroom exercises where your students can apply the knowledge they are learning after watching the videos.

Test Bank. This computerized package allows instructors to custom design, save, and generate tests. The test program permits instructors to edit, add, or delete questions from the test banks; analyze test results; and organize a database of tests and students results.

- **Instructor's Manual (IM).** The IM, written by the author, includes suggestions for designing the course and presenting the material. Each chapter is supported by answers to end-of-chapter questions and problems and suggestions concerning the discussion topics and cases.

- **PowerPoint Presentations.** A set of PowerPoint slides, created by the author, accompanies each chapter that features bulleted items that provide a lecture outline, plus key figures and tables from the text, and detailed teaching notes on each slide.

- **Sample Syllabi.** Several syllabi have been developed according to different course lengths—quarters and semesters, as well as different course concentrations such as a business emphasis or a technology focus.

- **Classroom Exercises.** Choose from over 30 detailed classroom exercises that engage and challenge students. For example, if you are teaching systems development, start the class with the "Skyscraper Activity" where the students build a prototype that takes them through each phase of the systems development life cycle. All classroom exercises can be found in the IM.

- **Image Library.** Text figures and tables, as permission allows, are provided in a format by which they can be imported into PowerPoint for class lectures.

- **Project Files.** The author has provided files for all projects that need further support, such as data files.

- **Cohesion Case.** The Broadway Cafe is a running case instructors can use to reinforce core material such as customer relationship management, supply chain management, business intelligence, and decision making. The case

Supplements:
- Business Driven Teaching Notes
- Online Learning Center
- Instructor's Manual
- PowerPoint Presentations.
- Sample Syllabi
- Classroom Exercises
- Image Library
- Project Files
- Internet Links
- Captivate Files
- Cohesion Case

has 15 sections that challenge students to develop and expand their grandfather's coffee shop. Students receive hands-on experience in business and learn technology's true value of enabling business. Please note that the Cohesion Case is not a McGraw-Hill product but a Baltzan direct product. The case can be found at www.cohesioncase.com.

- **Video Content.** More than 20 videos accompany this text and cover topics from entrepreneurship to disaster recovery. Video IMs are also available so you can turn the videos into engaging classroom activities.

McGraw-Hill Higher Education and Blackboard have teamed up. What does this mean for you?

1. **Your life, simplified.** Now you and your students can access McGraw-Hill's Connect™ and Create™ right from within your Blackboard course—all with one single sign-on. Say goodbye to the days of logging in to multiple applications.

2. **Deep integration of content and tools.** Not only do you get single sign-on with Connect™ and Create™, you also get deep integration of McGraw-Hill content and content engines right in Blackboard. Whether you're choosing a book for your course or building Connect™ assignments, all the tools you need are right where you want them—inside of Blackboard.

3. **Seamless Gradebooks.** Are you tired of keeping multiple gradebooks and manually synchronizing grades into Blackboard? We thought so. When a student completes an integrated Connect™ assignment, the grade for that assignment automatically (and instantly) feeds your Blackboard grade center.

4. **A solution for everyone.** Whether your institution is already using Blackboard or you just want to try Blackboard on your own, we have a solution for you. McGraw-Hill and Blackboard can now offer you easy access to industry leading technology and content, whether your campus hosts it, or we do. Be sure to ask your local McGraw-Hill representative for details.

Craft your teaching resources to match the way you teach! With McGraw-Hill Create, www.mcgrawhillcreate.com, you can easily rearrange chapters, combine material from other content sources, and quickly upload content you have written, like your course syllabus or teaching notes. Find the content you need in Create by searching through thousands of leading McGraw-Hill textbooks. Arrange your book to fit your teaching style. Create even allows you to personalize your book's appearance by selecting the cover and adding your name, school, and course information. Order a Create book and you'll receive a complimentary print review copy in 3–5 business days or a complimentary electronic review copy (eComp) via email in about one hour. Go to www.mcgrawhillcreate.com today and register. Experience how McGraw-Hill Create empowers you to teach *your* students *your* way.

ACKNOWLEDGMENTS

There are numerous people whom we want to heartily thank for their hard work, enthusiasm, and dedication on this edition of *Business Driven Technology*.

To the faculty at the Daniels College of Business at the University of Denver—Richard Scudder, Don McCubbrey, Paul Bauer, Hans Hultgren, Daivd Paul, Dan Connolly, and Ked Davisson—thank you. Your feedback, advice, and support is truly valued and greatly appreciated.

We offer our sincerest gratitude and deepest appreciation to our valuable reviewers whose feedback was instrumental.

Etido Akpan
Freed Hardemann University

Dennis Anderson
Bentley University

Kaan Ataman
Chapman University—Orange

Vikram Bhadauria
Southern Arkansas University

Utpal Bose
University of Houston—Downtown

Traci Carte
University of Oklahoma

Carey Cole
James Madison University

Charles DeSassure
Tarrant County College—SE Campus

Mike Eom
University of Portland

Ahmed Eshra
St. John's University—Jamaica

Deborah Geil
Bowling Green State University

Naveen Gudigantala
University of Portland

Saurabh Gupta
University of North Florida

Vernard Harrington
Radford University

Shoreh Hashimi
University of Houston—Downtown

Tracey Hughes
Southern Arkansas University

Keri Larson
The University of Alabama—Birmingham

Linda Lynam
University of Central Missouri

Michael Magro
Shenandoah University

Richard McMahon
University of Houston—Downtown

Don Miller
Avila University

Allison Morgan
Howard University

Vincent Nestler
University of California—San Bernardino

Sandra Newton
Sonoma State University

Ahmet Ozkul
University of New Haven

Susan Peterson
University of California—San Diego

Julie Pettus
Missouri State University

Gerald Plumlee
Southern Arkansas University

Pauline Ratnasingham
University of Central Missouri

Julio Rivera
University of Alabama—Birmingham

Thomas Sandman
California State University—Sacramento

Dmitriy Shalteyev
Christopher Newport University

Lakisha Simmons
Belmont University

Ron Sones
Liberty University

Nathan Stout
University of Oklahoma

Stephen Taraszewski
Youngstown State University

Sharon Testa
Merrimack College

John Wee
University of Mississippi

Chuck West
Bradley University

Melody White
University of North Texas

Benjamin Yeo
Chapman University

Zehai Zhou
University of Houston—Downtown

Business Driven Technology

*

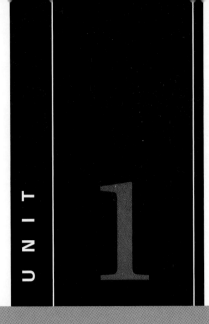

U N I T

1

Achieving Business Success

What's in IT for Me?

This unit sets the stage for diving into *Business Driven Technology*. It starts from the ground floor by providing a clear description of what information technology is and how IT fits into business strategies and organizational activities. It then provides an overview of how organizations operate in competitive environments and must continually define and redefine their business strategies to create competitive advantages. Doing so allows organizations to not only survive, but also thrive. Individuals who understand and can access and analyze the many different enterprisewide information systems dramatically improve their decision-making and problem-solving abilities. Most importantly, information technology is shown as a key enabler to help organizations operate successfully in highly competitive environments.

You, as a business student, must recognize the tight correlation between business and technology. You must first understand information technology's role in daily business activities, and then understand information technology's role in supporting and implementing enterprisewide initiatives and global business strategies. After reading this unit, you should have acquired a solid grasp of business driven information systems, technology fundamentals, and business strategies. You should also have gained an appreciation of the various kinds of information systems employed by organizations and how you can use them to help make strategically informed decisions. All leaders must appreciate the numerous ethical and security concerns voiced by customers today. These concerns directly influence a customer's likelihood to embrace electronic technologies and conduct business over the web. In this sense, these concerns affect a company's bottom line. You can find evidence in recent news reports about how the stock price of organizations dramatically falls when information privacy and security breaches are publicized. Further, organizations face potential litigation if they fail to meet their ethical, privacy, and security obligations concerning the handling of information in their companies.

Apple—Merging Technology, Business, and Entertainment

This might sound hard to believe, but a bit more than a decade ago, Apple was on the brink of bankruptcy. Apple Inc., now back from near oblivion, is blazing a trail through the digital world with innovation and creativity that has been missing from the company for the past 20 years. The unique feature of Apple's competitive advantages is that they come from customers and users, not Apple employees. That's right; the company welcomes products created by consumers to sell to consumers, a trend new to business.

Capitalizing on the iPod

With millions of iPods in the hands of consumers, many people are finding ways to capitalize on the product. John Lin created a prototype of a remote control for the iPod and took his prototype to *Macworld,* where he found success. A few months later, Lin's company had Apple's blessing and a commitment for shelf space in its retail stores. "This is how Apple supports the iPod economy," Lin said.

In the iPod-dominated market, hundreds of companies have been inspired to develop more than 500 accessories—everything from rechargers for the car to $1,500 Fendi bags. Eric Tong, vice president at Belkin, a cable and peripheral manufacturer, believes that 75 percent of all iPod owners purchase at least one accessory—selling over 30 million accessories to date. With most of the products priced between $10 and $200, that puts the iPod economy well over $300 million and perhaps as high as $6 billion. Popular iPod accessories include:

- Altec Lansing Technologies—iPod speakers and recharger dock ($150).
- Belkin—TuneCast mobile FM transmitter ($40).
- Etymotic Research—high-end earphones ($150).
- Griffin Technology—iTrip FM transmitter ($35).

- Kate Spade—Geneva faux-croc mini iPod holder ($55).
- Apple—socks set in six colors: green, purple, blue, orange, pink, and gray ($29).
- Apple—digital camera connector ($29).

Capitalizing on the iPhone

Looking at someone using an iPhone is an interesting experience because there is a good chance they are not making a phone call. They could be doing a number of things from playing a game to trading stocks, watching a TV show, or even conducting business with a mobile version of salesforce.com's customer-management software. In a brilliant strategic move, Apple let outsiders offer software for the iPhone and in less than six months, more than 10,000 applications had been created. In fact, more than 15,000 applications are available at its app store section of iTunes, and they have been downloaded a total of 500 million times. Now, many of the iPhone apps are available for the iPad.

The iPhone and iPad app store market is getting so huge relative to other smartphone markets that some developers argue there is little point adapting applications for Google's Android or any other iPhone competitor. According to Jeff Holden, CEO of Pelago Inc., when he created his social networking company he fully intended to follow the conventional wisdom for how to build a sizable, fast-growing software company: Get your programs on as many platforms and devices as possible. But when he crunched the numbers he came to an interesting business conclusion: The 13 million iPhone owners had already downloaded more applications than the 1.1 billion other cell phone owners! To entrepreneurs, developing a program for the iPhone automatically provides a significantly larger market—almost 94 times larger than its competitors. "Why would I ever build for anything but the iPhone?" Holden asked.

Capitalizing on the iPad

Apple's latest release, the iPad, is a lightweight, portable, tablet computer, similar to the iPhone, that allows customers to download applications, check email, and play music all at the touch of a button. Both the iPhone and the iPad can multitask, allowing customers to read a web page while downloading email in the background over wireless networks. The arrival of the iPad brought a simultaneous expansion of the network of accessories. Because the iPad was designed with an exposed screen and without a camera, separate keyboard, memory card slots, or expansion ports, one might say it was specifically built for accessories. Many owners will modify it in some way, whether for mere decoration or hard-core protection. A few of the new accessories include:

- iPad Clear Armor screen protector—$35.
- iPad Antique book case cover—$40.
- iPad wireless keyboard—$99.

- iPad overcoat sleeve—$35.
- iPad Joule luxury stand—$130.

Apple has consistently outperformed its key rivals through the development of its MP3 player, the iPod, and continues to make its products smaller and less expensive, while providing complementary features such as games and applications. For the iPhone, Apple developed a unique application called Siri, a voice-activation system that is capable of recognizing voice commands. Siri can perform all kinds of functions from dialing a contact and creating an email to location services such as "Find my Phone," ensuring lost phones are found quickly.

Apple's latest offering is a new service called the iCloud. The iCloud has the ability to collect all of the content, including videos, photos, songs, books, etc., from customer devices such as iPods, iPads, and iPhones in one secure location in "the cloud." Apple customers no longer have to worry about backing up their applications or data because everything is automatically uploaded and stored in the iCloud when using an Apple device. In a fast-paced, technology-driven sector, with competitors quickly following suit, Apple is constantly pressured to develop new products and product extensions. Luckily Apple stays ahead of the pack by focusing on the following key competitive advantages:

- **Customer focus:** Apple is driven by customer satisfaction and ensures customers are deeply involved in product development and application development.
- **Resources and capabilities:** Apple continues to invest heavily in research and development to take advantage of new technologies, improved facilities, and cloud infrastructures.
- **Strategic vision:** Apple has a clear alignment of its vision, mission, and business leadership and goals.
- **Branding:** Apple is the leader in brand loyalty as it has achieved cult status with its authentic product image.
- **Quality focus:** Apple has an outstanding commitment to quality.[1]

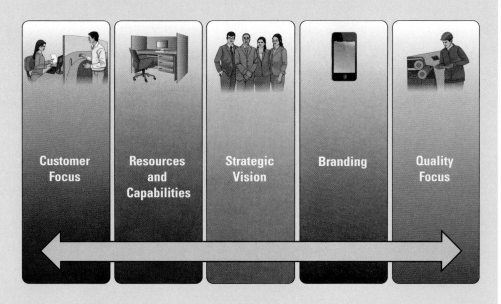

| Customer Focus | Resources and Capabilities | Strategic Vision | Branding | Quality Focus |

Introduction

Information is everywhere. Most organizations value information as a strategic asset. Consider Apple and its iPod, iPod accessories, and iTunes Music Store. Apple's success depends heavily on information about its customers, suppliers, markets, and operations for each of these product lines. For example, Apple must be able to predict the number of people who will purchase an iPod to help estimate iPod accessory and iTunes sales within the next year. Estimating too many buyers will lead Apple to produce an excess of inventory; estimating too few buyers will potentially mean lost sales due to lack of product (resulting in even more lost revenues).

Understanding the direct impact information has on an organization's bottom line is crucial to running a successful business. This text focuses on information, business, technology, and the integrated set of activities used to run most organizations. Many of these activities are the hallmarks of business today—supply chain management, customer relationship management, enterprise resource planning, outsourcing, integration, ebusiness, and others. The five core units of this text cover these important activities in detail. Each unit is divided into chapters that provide individual learning outcomes and case studies. In addition to the five core units, there are technology and business "plug-ins" (see Figure Unit 1.1) that further explore topics presented in the five core units.

The chapters in Unit 1 are:

- **Chapter One**—Business Driven Technology.
- **Chapter Two**—Identifying Competitive Advantages.
- **Chapter Three**—Strategic Initiatives for Implementing Competitive Advantages.
- **Chapter Four**—Measuring the Success of Strategic Initiatives.
- **Chapter Five**—Organizational Structures That Support Strategic Initiatives.

FIGURE UNIT 1.1

The Format and Approach
of This Text

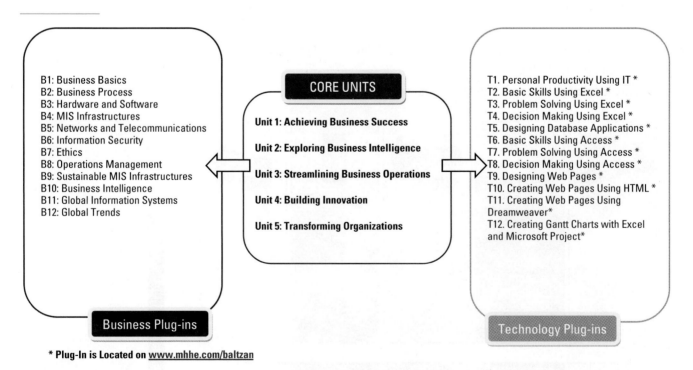

B1: Business Basics
B2: Business Process
B3: Hardware and Software
B4: MIS Infrastructures
B5: Networks and Telecommunications
B6: Information Security
B7: Ethics
B8: Operations Management
B9: Sustainable MIS Infrastructures
B10: Business Intelligence
B11: Global Information Systems
B12: Global Trends

CORE UNITS

Unit 1: Achieving Business Success

Unit 2: Exploring Business Intelligence

Unit 3: Streamlining Business Operations

Unit 4: Building Innovation

Unit 5: Transforming Organizations

T1. Personal Productivity Using IT *
T2. Basic Skills Using Excel *
T3. Problem Solving Using Excel *
T4. Decision Making Using Excel *
T5. Designing Database Applications *
T6. Basic Skills Using Access *
T7. Problem Solving Using Access *
T8. Decision Making Using Access *
T9. Designing Web Pages *
T10. Creating Web Pages Using HTML *
T11. Creating Web Pages Using Dreamweaver*
T12. Creating Gantt Charts with Excel and Microsoft Project*

Business Plug-ins

Technology Plug-ins

* Plug-In is Located on **www.mhhe.com/baltzan**

Business Driven Technology

1.1. Describe the information age and the differences among data, information, business intelligence, and knowledge.

1.2. Identify the different departments in a company and why they must work together to achieve success.

1.3. Explain systems thinking and how management information systems enable business communications.

Competing in the Information Age

Did you know that . . .

LO 1.1 Describe the information age and the differences among data, information, business intelligence, and knowledge.

- The movie *Avatar* took more than four years to create and cost $450 million.
- Lady Gaga's real name is Stefani Joanne Angelina Germanotta.
- Customers pay $2.6 million for a 30-second advertising time slot during the Super Bowl.[2]

A *fact* is the confirmation or validation of an event or object. In the past, people primarily learned facts from books. Today, by simply pushing a button people can find out anything, from anywhere, at any time. We live in the *information age,* when infinite quantities of facts are widely available to anyone who can use a computer. The impact of information technology on the global business environment is equivalent to the printing press's impact on publishing and electricity's impact on productivity. College student startups were mostly unheard of before the information age. Now, it's not at all unusual to read about a business student starting a multimillion-dollar company from his or her dorm room. Think of Mark Zuckerberg, who started Facebook from his dorm, or Michael Dell (Dell Computers) and Bill Gates (Microsoft), who both founded their legendary companies as college students.

You may think only students well versed in advanced technology can compete in the information age. This is simply not true. Many business leaders have created exceptional opportunities by coupling the power of the information age with traditional business methods. Here are just a few examples:

- Amazon is not a technology company; its original business focus was to sell books, and it now sells nearly everything.
- Netflix is not a technology company; its primary business focus is to rent videos.
- Zappos is not a technology company; its primary business focus is to sell shoes, bags, clothing, and accessories.

Amazon's founder, Jeff Bezos, at first saw an opportunity to change the way people purchase books. Using the power of the information age to tailor offerings to each customer and speed the payment process, he in effect opened millions of tiny virtual bookstores, each with a vastly larger selection and far cheaper product than traditional bookstores. The success of his original business model led him to expand Amazon to carry many other types of products. The founders of Netflix and Zappos have done the same thing for videos and shoes. All these entrepreneurs were business professionals, not technology experts. However, they understood enough about the information age to apply it to a particular business, creating innovative companies that now lead entire industries.

Students who understand business along with the power associated with the information age will create their own opportunities and perhaps even new industries, as co-founders Chris DeWolfe and Tom Anderson did with Myspace and Mark Zuckerberg did with Facebook. Our primary goal in this course is to arm you with the knowledge you need to compete in the information age. The core drivers of the information age are:

- Data
- Information
- Business intelligence
- Knowledge (see Figure 1.1)

DATA

Data are raw facts that describe the characteristics of an event or object. Before the information age, managers manually collected and analyzed data, a time-consuming and complicated task without which they would have little insight into how to run their business. Lacking data, managers often found themselves making business decisions about how many products to make, how much material to order, or how many employees to hire based on intuition or gut feelings. In the information age, successful managers compile, analyze, and comprehend massive amounts of data daily, which helps them make more successful business decisions.

FIGURE 1.1

The Differences among Data, Information, Business Intelligence, and Knowledge

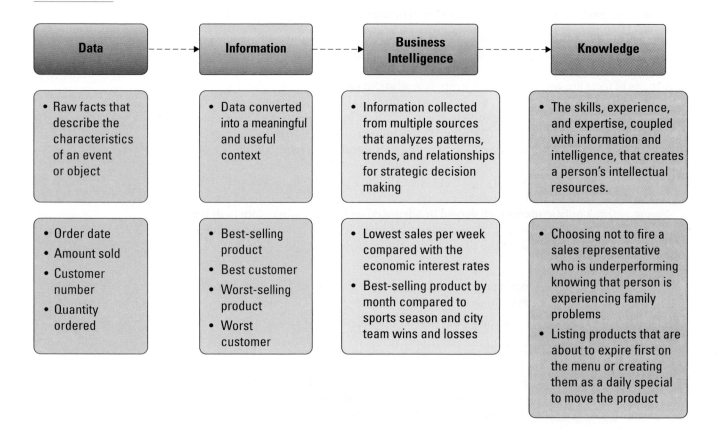

Data	Information	Business Intelligence	Knowledge
• Raw facts that describe the characteristics of an event or object	• Data converted into a meaningful and useful context	• Information collected from multiple sources that analyzes patterns, trends, and relationships for strategic decision making	• The skills, experience, and expertise, coupled with information and intelligence, that creates a person's intellectual resources.
• Order date • Amount sold • Customer number • Quantity ordered	• Best-selling product • Best customer • Worst-selling product • Worst customer	• Lowest sales per week compared with the economic interest rates • Best-selling product by month compared to sports season and city team wins and losses	• Choosing not to fire a sales representative who is underperforming knowing that person is experiencing family problems • Listing products that are about to expire first on the menu or creating them as a daily special to move the product

Figure 1.2 shows sales data for Tony's Wholesale Company, a fictitious business that supplies snacks to stores. The data highlight characteristics such as order date, customer, sales representative, product, quantity, and profit. The second line in Figure 1.2, for instance, shows that Roberta Cross sold 90 boxes of Ruffles to Walmart for $1,350, resulting in a profit of $450 (note that Profit = Sales − Costs). These data are useful for understanding individual sales; however, they do not provide us much insight into how Tony's business is performing as a whole. Tony needs to answer questions that will help him manage his day-to-day operations such as:

- Who are my best customers?
- Who are my least-profitable customers?
- What is my best-selling product?
- What is my slowest-selling product?
- Who is my strongest sales representative?
- Who is my weakest sales representative?

What Tony needs, in other words, is not data but *information.*

INFORMATION

Information is data converted into a meaningful and useful context. Having the right information at the right moment in time can be worth a fortune. Having the wrong information at the right moment; or the right information at the wrong moment can be disastrous. The truth about information is that its value is only as good as the people who use it. People using the same information can make different decisions depending on how they interpret or analyze the information. Thus information has value only insofar as the people using it do as well.

Tony can analyze his sales data and turn them into information to answer all the above questions and understand how his business is operating. Figures 1.3 and 1.4, for instance, show us that Walmart is Roberta Cross's best customer, and that Ruffles is Tony's best product measured in terms of total sales. Armed with this information, Tony can identify and then address such issues as weak products and underperforming sales representatives.

A *variable* is a data characteristic that stands for a value that changes or varies over time. For example, in Tony's data, price and quantity ordered can vary. Changing variables allows managers to create hypothetical scenarios to study future possibilities.

Order Date	Customer	Sales Representative	Product	Qty	Unit Price	Total Sales	Unit Cost	Total Cost	Profit
4-Jan	Walmart	PJ Helgoth	Doritos	41	$24	$ 984	$18	$738	$246
4-Jan	Walmart	Roberta Cross	Ruffles	90	$15	$1,350	$10	$900	$450
5-Jan	Safeway	Craig Schultz	Ruffles	27	$15	$ 405	$10	$270	$135
6-Jan	Walmart	Roberta Cross	Ruffles	67	$15	$1,005	$10	$670	$335
7-Jan	7-Eleven	Craig Schultz	Pringles	79	$12	$ 948	$ 6	$474	$474
7-Jan	Walmart	Roberta Cross	Ruffles	52	$15	$ 780	$10	$520	$260
8-Jan	Kroger	Craig Schultz	Ruffles	39	$15	$ 585	$10	$390	$195
9-Jan	Walmart	Craig Schultz	Ruffles	66	$15	$ 990	$10	$660	$330
10-Jan	Target	Craig Schultz	Ruffles	40	$15	$ 600	$10	$400	$200
11-Jan	Walmart	Craig Schultz	Ruffles	71	$15	$1,065	$10	$710	$355

FIGURE 1.2

Tony's Snack Company Data

Order Date	Customer	Sales Representative	Product	Quantity	Unit Price	Total Sales	Unit Cost	Total Cost	Profit
26-Apr	Walmart	Roberta Cross	Fritos	86	$ 19	$ 1,634	$ 17	$ 1,462	$ 172
29-Aug	Walmart	Roberta Cross	Fritos	76	$ 19	$ 1,444	$ 17	$ 1,292	$ 152
7-Sep	Walmart	Roberta Cross	Fritos	20	$ 19	$ 380	$ 17	$ 340	$ 40
22-Nov	Walmart	Roberta Cross	Fritos	39	$ 19	$ 741	$ 17	$ 663	$ 78
30-Dec	Walmart	Roberta Cross	Fritos	68	$ 19	$ 1,292	$ 17	$ 1,156	$ 136
7-Jul	Walmart	Roberta Cross	Pringles	79	$ 18	$ 1,422	$ 8	$ 632	$ 790
6-Aug	Walmart	Roberta Cross	Pringles	21	$ 12	$ 252	$ 6	$ 126	$ 126
2-Oct	Walmart	Roberta Cross	Pringles	60	$ 18	$ 1,080	$ 8	$ 480	$ 600
15-Nov	Walmart	Roberta Cross	Pringles	32	$ 12	$ 384	$ 6	$ 192	$ 192
21-Dec	Walmart	Roberta Cross	Pringles	92	$ 12	$ 1,104	$ 6	$ 552	$ 552
28-Feb	Walmart	Roberta Cross	Ruffles	67	$ 15	$ 1,005	$ 10	$ 670	$ 335
6-Mar	Walmart	Roberta Cross	Ruffles	8	$ 15	$ 120	$ 10	$ 80	$ 40
16-Mar	Walmart	Roberta Cross	Ruffles	68	$ 15	$ 1,020	$ 10	$ 680	$ 340
23-Apr	Walmart	Roberta Cross	Ruffles	34	$ 15	$ 510	$ 10	$ 340	$ 170
4-Aug	Walmart	Roberta Cross	Ruffles	40	$ 15	$ 600	$ 10	$ 400	$ 200
18-Aug	Walmart	Roberta Cross	Ruffles	93	$ 15	$ 1,395	$ 10	$ 930	$ 465
5-Sep	Walmart	Roberta Cross	Ruffles	41	$ 15	$ 615	$ 10	$ 410	$ 205
12-Sep	Walmart	Roberta Cross	Ruffles	8	$ 15	$ 120	$ 10	$ 80	$ 40
28-Oct	Walmart	Roberta Cross	Ruffles	50	$ 15	$ 750	$ 10	$ 500	$ 250
21-Nov	Walmart	Roberta Cross	Ruffles	79	$ 15	$ 1,185	$ 10	$ 790	$ 395
29-Jan	Walmart	Roberta Cross	Sun Chips	5	$ 22	$ 110	$ 18	$ 90	$ 20
12-Apr	Walmart	Roberta Cross	Sun Chips	85	$ 22	$ 1,870	$ 18	$ 1,530	$ 340
16-Jun	Walmart	Roberta Cross	Sun Chips	55	$ 22	$ 1,210	$ 18	$ 990	$ 220
				1,206	$383	$20,243	$273	$14,385	$5,858

Sorting the data reveals the information that Roberta Cross's total sales to Walmart were $20,243 resulting in a profit of $5,858. (Profit $5,858 = Sales $20,243 − Costs $14,385)

FIGURE 1.3

Tony's Data Sorted by Customer "Walmart" and Sales Representative "Roberta Cross"

Tony may find it valuable to anticipate how sales or cost increases affect profitability. To estimate how a 20 percent increase in prices might improve profits, Tony simply changes the price variable for all orders, which automatically calculates the amount of new profits. To estimate how a 10 percent increase in costs hurts profits, Tony changes the cost variable for all orders, which automatically calculates the amount of lost profits. Manipulating variables is an important tool for any business.

BUSINESS INTELLIGENCE

Business intelligence (BI) is information collected from multiple sources such as suppliers, customers, competitors, partners, and industries that analyzes patterns, trends, and relationships for strategic decision making. BI manipulates multiple variables and in some cases even hundreds of variables including such items as interest rates, weather conditions, and even gas prices. Tony could use BI to analyze internal data such as company sales, along with external data about the environment such as competitors, finances, weather, holidays, and

FIGURE 1.4

Information Gained after
Analyzing Tony's Data

Tony's Business Information	Name	Total Profit
Who is Tony's best customer by total sales?	Walmart	$ 560,789
Who is Tony's least-valuable customer by total sales?	Walgreens	$ 45,673
Who is Tony's best customer by profit?	7-Eleven	$ 324,550
Who is Tony's least-valuable customer by profit?	King Soopers	$ 23,908
What is Tony's best-selling product by total sales?	Ruffles	$ 232,500
What is Tony's weakest-selling product by total sales?	Pringles	$ 54,890
What is Tony's best-selling product by profit?	Tostitos	$ 13,050
What is Tony's weakest-selling product by profit?	Pringles	$ 23,000
Who is Tony's best sales representative by profit?	R. Cross	$1,230,980
Who is Tony's weakest sales representative by profit?	Craig Schultz	$ 98,980
What is the best sales representative's best-selling product by total profit?	Ruffles	$ 98,780
Who is the best sales representative's best customer by total profit?	Walmart	$ 345,900
What is the best sales representative's weakest-selling product by total profit?	Sun Chips	$ 45,600
Who is the best sales representative's weakest customer by total profit?	Krogers	$ 56,050

even sporting events. Both internal and external variables affect snack sales, and analyzing these variables will help Tony determine ordering levels and sales forecasts. For instance, BI can predict inventory requirements for Tony's business for the week before the Super Bowl if, say, the home team is playing, average temperature is above 80 degrees, and the stock market is performing well. This is BI at its finest, incorporating all types of internal and external variables to anticipate business performance.

Top managers use BI to define the future of the business, analyzing markets, industries, and economies to determine the strategic direction the company must follow to remain profitable. Tony will set the strategic direction for his firm, which might include introducing new flavors of potato chips or sport drinks as new product lines or schools and hospitals as new market segments.

KNOWLEDGE

Knowledge includes the skills, experience, and expertise, coupled with information and intelligence, that creates a person's intellectual resources. *Knowledge workers* are individuals valued for their ability to interpret and analyze information. Today's workers are commonly referred to as knowledge workers and they use BI along with personal experience to make decisions based on both information and intuition, a valuable resource for any company.

Imagine that Tony analyzes his data and finds his weakest sales representative for this period is Craig Schultz. If Tony considered only this information, he might conclude that firing Craig was a good business decision. However, because Tony has knowledge about how the company operates, he knows Craig has been out on medical leave for several weeks; hence, his sales numbers are low. Without this additional knowledge, Tony might have executed a bad business decision, delivered a negative message to the other employees, and sent his best sales representatives out to look for other jobs.

The key point in this scenario is that it is simply impossible to collect all the information about every situation, and yet without that, it can be easy to misunderstand the problem. Using data, information, business intelligence, and knowledge to make decisions and solve problems is the key to finding success in business. These core drivers of the information age are the building blocks of business systems.

LO 1.2 Identify the different departments in a company and why they must work together to achieve success.

The Challenge: Departmental Companies

Companies are typically organized by department or functional area such as:

- **Accounting:** Records, measures, and reports monetary transactions.
- **Finance:** Deals with strategic financial issues including money, banking, credit, investments, and assets.
- **Human resources:** Maintains policies, plans, and procedures for the effective management of employees.
- **Marketing:** Supports sales by planning, pricing, and promoting goods or services.
- **Operations management:** Manages the process of converting or transforming or resources into goods or services.
- **Sales:** Performs the function of selling goods or services (see Figure 1.5).

Each department performs its own activities. Sales and marketing focus on moving goods or services into the hands of consumers; they maintain transactional data. Finance and accounting focus on managing the company's resources and maintain monetary data. Operations management focuses on manufacturing and maintains production data, while human resources focuses on hiring and training people and

FIGURE 1.5

Departments Working Independently

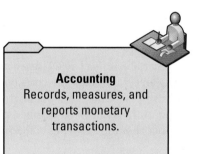

Accounting
Records, measures, and reports monetary transactions.

Sales
Performs the function of selling goods or services.

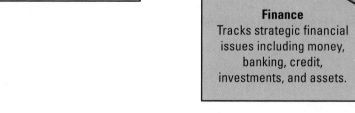

Finance
Tracks strategic financial issues including money, banking, credit, investments, and assets.

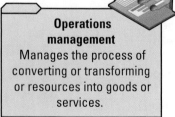

Operations management
Manages the process of converting or transforming or resources into goods or services.

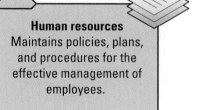

Human resources
Maintains policies, plans, and procedures for the effective management of employees.

Marketing
Supports sales by planning, pricing, and promoting goods or services.

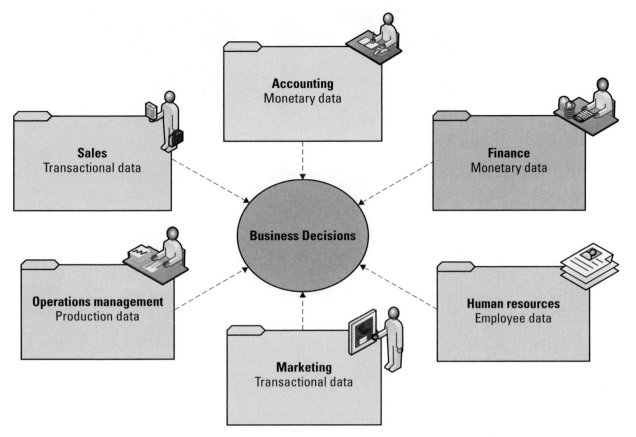

FIGURE 1.6

Departments Working
Together

maintains employee data. Although each department has its own focus and data, none can work independently if the company is to operate as a whole. It is easy to see how a business decision made by one department can affect other departments. Marketing needs to analyze production and sales data to come up with product promotions and advertising strategies. Production needs to understand sales forecasts to determine the company's manufacturing needs. Sales needs to rely on information from operations to understand inventory, place orders, and forecast consumer demand. All departments need to understand the accounting and finance departments' information for budgeting. For the firm to be successful, all departments must work together as a single unit sharing common information and not operate independently or in a silo (see Figure 1.6).

The Solution: Management Information Systems

LO 1.3 Explain systems thinking and how management information systems enable business communications.

You probably recall the old story of three blind men attempting to describe an elephant. The first man, feeling the elephant's girth, said the elephant seemed very much like a wall. The second, feeling the elephant's trunk, declared the elephant was like a snake. The third man felt the elephant's tusks and said the elephant was like a tree or a cane. Companies that operate departmentally are seeing only one part of the elephant, a critical mistake that hinders successful operation.

Successful companies operate cross-functionally, integrating the operations of all departments. Systems are the primary enabler of cross-functional operations. A *system* is a collection of parts that link to achieve a common purpose. A car is a good example of a system, since removing a part, such as the steering wheel or accelerator, causes the entire system to stop working.

Before jumping into how systems work, it is important to have a solid understanding of the basic production process for goods and services. *Goods* are material items or products that customers will buy to satisfy a want or need. Clothing, groceries, cell

FIGURE 1.7

Different Types of Goods
and Services

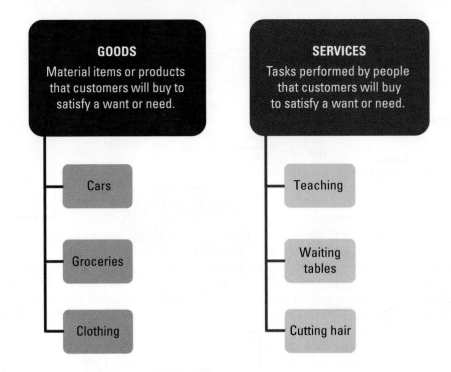

phones, and cars are all examples of goods that people buy to fulfill their needs. **Services** are tasks performed by people that customers will buy to satisfy a want or need. Waiting tables, teaching, and cutting hair are all examples of services that people pay for to fulfill their needs (see Figure 1.7).

Production is the process where a business takes raw materials and processes them or converts them into a finished product for its goods or services. Just think about making a hamburger (see Figure 1.8). First, you must gather all of the *inputs* or raw materials such as the bun, patty, lettuce, tomato, and ketchup. Second, you *process* the raw materials, so in this example you would need to cook the patty, wash and chop the lettuce and tomato, and place all of the items in the bun. Finally, you would have your *output* or finished product—your hamburger! **Productivity** is the rate at which goods and services are produced based upon total output given total inputs. Given our previous example, if a business could produce the same hamburger with less expensive inputs or more hamburgers with the same inputs it would see a rise in productivity and possibly an increase in profits. Ensuring the input, process, and output of goods and services work across all of the departments of a company is where systems add tremendous value to overall business productivity.

FIGURE 1.8

Input, Process, Output
Example

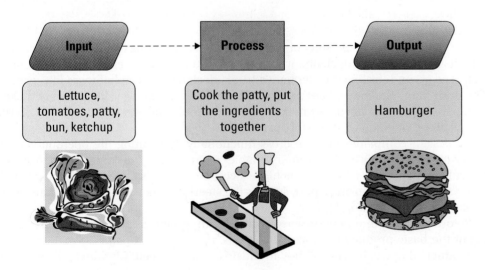

FIGURE 1.9

Overview of Systems Thinking

Systems thinking is a way of monitoring the entire system by viewing multiple inputs being processed or transformed to produce outputs while continuously gathering feedback on each part (see Figure 1.9). *Feedback* is information that returns to its original transmitter (input, transform, or output) and modifies the transmitter's actions. Feedback helps the system maintain stability. For example, a car's system continuously monitors the fuel level and turns on a warning light if the gas level is too low. Systems thinking provides an end-to-end view of how operations work together to create a product or service. Business students who understand systems thinking are valuable resources because they can implement solutions that consider the entire process, not just a single component.

Management information systems (MIS) is a business function, like accounting and human resources, which moves information about people, products, and processes across the company to facilitate decision making and problem solving. MIS incorporates systems thinking to help companies operate cross-functionally. For example, to fulfill product orders, an MIS for sales moves a single customer order across all functional areas including sales, order fulfillment, shipping, billing, and finally customer service. Although different functional areas handle different parts of the sale, thanks to MIS, to the customer the sale is one continuous process. If one part of the company is experiencing problems, however, then, like the car without a steering wheel, the entire system fails. If order fulfillment packages the wrong product, it will not matter that shipping, billing, and customer service did their jobs right, since the customer will not be satisfied when he or she opens the package.

MIS can be an important enabler of business success and innovation. This is not to say that MIS *equals* business success and innovation, or that MIS *represents* business success and innovation. MIS is a tool that is most valuable when it leverages the talents of people who know how to use and manage it effectively. To perform the MIS function effectively, almost all companies, particularly large and medium-sized ones, have an internal MIS department, often called information technology (IT), information systems (IS), or management information systems (MIS). For the purpose of this text, we will refer to it as MIS.

OPENING CASE STUDY QUESTIONS

1. Explain how Apple achieved business success through the use of information, information technology, and people.

2. Describe the types of information employees at an Apple store require and compare it to the types of information the executives at Apple's corporate headquarters require. Are there any links between these two types of information?

Chapter One Case: The World Is Flat—Thomas Friedman

In his book *The World Is Flat,* Thomas Friedman describes the unplanned cascade of technological and social shifts that effectively leveled the economic world and "accidentally made Beijing, Bangalore, and Bethesda next-door neighbors." Chances are good that Bhavya in Bangalore will read your next X-ray, or as Friedman learned firsthand, "Grandma Betty in her bathrobe" will make your JetBlue plane reservation from her Salt Lake City home.

Friedman believes this is Globalization 3.0. "In Globalization 1.0, which began around 1492, the world went from size large to size medium. In Globalization 2.0, the era that introduced us to multinational companies, it went from size medium to size small. And then around 2000 came Globalization 3.0, in which the world went from being small to tiny. There is a difference between being able to make long-distance phone calls cheaper on the Internet and walking around Riyadh with a PDA where you can have all of Google in your pocket. It is a difference in degree that's so enormous it becomes a difference in kind," Friedman states. Figure 1.10 displays Friedman's list of "flatteners."

FIGURE 1.10

Thomas Friedman's 10 Forces That Flattened the World

1. Fall of the Berlin Wall	The events of November 9, 1989, tilted the worldwide balance of power toward democracies and free markets.
2. Netscape IPO	The August 9, 1995, offering sparked massive investment in fiber-optic cables.
3. Work flow software	The rise of applications from PayPal to VPNs enabled faster, closer coordination among far-flung employees.
4. Open-sourcing	Self-organizing communities, such as Linux, launched a collaborative revolution.
5. Outsourcing	Migrating business functions to India saved money *and* a Third World economy.
6. Offshoring	Contract manufacturing elevated China to economic prominence.
7. Supply-chaining	Robust networks of suppliers, retailers, and customers increased business efficiency.
8. Insourcing	Logistics giants took control of customer supply chains, helping mom-and-pop shops go global.
9. Informing	Power searching allowed everyone to use the Internet as a "personal supply chain of knowledge."
10. Wireless	Wireless technologies pumped up collaboration, making it mobile and personal.

Friedman says these flatteners converged around the year 2000 and "created a flat world: a global, Web-enabled platform for multiple forms of sharing knowledge and work, irrespective of time, distance, geography, and increasingly, language." At the very moment this platform emerged, three huge economies materialized—those of India, China, and the former Soviet Union—"and 3 billion people who were out of the game, walked onto the playing field." A final convergence may determine the fate of the United States in this chapter of globalization. A "political perfect storm," as Friedman describes it—the dot-com bust, the attacks of 9/11, and the Enron scandal—"distract us completely as a country." Just when we need to face the fact of globalization and the need to compete in a new world, "we're looking totally elsewhere."

Friedman believes that the next great breakthrough in bioscience could come from a 5-year-old who downloads the human genome in Egypt. Bill Gates's view is similar: "Twenty years ago, would you rather have been a B-student in Poughkeepsie or a genius in Shanghai? Twenty years ago you'd rather be a B-student in Poughkeepsie. Today, it is not even close. You'd much prefer to be the genius in Shanghai because you can now export your talents anywhere in the world."[3]

Questions

1. Do you agree or disagree with Friedman's assessment that the world is flat? Be sure to justify your answer.

2. What are the potential impacts of a flat world for a student performing a job search?

3. What can students do to prepare themselves for competing in a flat world?

4. Identify a current flattener not mentioned on Friedman's list.

Identifying Competitive Advantages

2.1. Explain why competitive advantages are temporary.

2.2. Describe Porter's Five Forces Model and explain each of the five forces.

2.3. Compare Porter's three generic strategies.

2.4. Demonstrate how a company can add value by using Porter's value chain analysis.

LO 2.1 Explain why competitive advantages are temporary.

Identifying Competitive Advantages

Running a company today is similar to leading an army; the top manager or leader ensures all participants are heading in the right direction and completing their goals and objectives. Companies lacking leadership quickly implode as employees head in different directions attempting to achieve conflicting goals. To combat these challenges, leaders communicate and execute business strategies (from the Greek word *stratus* for army and *ago* for leading). A **business strategy** is a leadership plan that achieves a specific set of goals or objectives as displayed in Figure 2.1.

FIGURE 2.1

Examples of Business Strategies

Business strategies
Leadership plans that achieve a specific set of goals or objectives

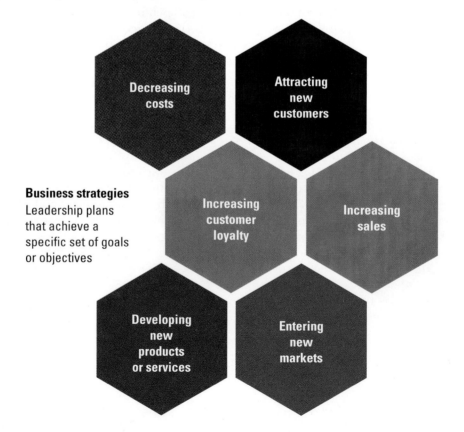

Good leaders also anticipate unexpected misfortunes, from strikes and economic recessions to natural disasters. Their business strategies build in buffers or slack, allowing the company the ability to ride out any storm and defend against competitive or environmental threats. Of course, updating business strategies is a continuous undertaking as internal and external environments rapidly change. Business strategies that match core company competencies to opportunities result in competitive advantages, a key to success!

A **competitive advantage** is a feature of a product or service on which customers place a greater value than they do on similar offerings from competitors. Competitive advantages provide the same product or service either at a lower price or with additional value that can fetch premium prices. Unfortunately, competitive advantages are typically temporary, because competitors often quickly seek ways to duplicate them. In turn, organizations must develop a strategy based on a new competitive advantage. Ways that companies duplicate competitive advantages include acquiring the new technology, copying the business operations, and hiring away key employees. The introduction of Apple's iPod and iTunes, a brilliant merger of technology, business, and entertainment, offers an excellent example.

In early 2000, Steve Jobs was fixated on developing video editing software when he suddenly realized that millions of people were using computers to listen to music, a new trend in the industry catapulted by illegal online services such as Napster. Jobs was worried that he was looking in the wrong direction and had missed the opportunity to jump on the online music bandwagon. He moved fast, however, and within four months he had developed the first version of iTunes for the Mac. Jobs' next challenge was to make a portable iTunes player that could hold thousands of songs and be completely transportable. Within nine months the iPod was born. With the combination of iTunes and iPod, Apple created a significant competitive advantage in the marketplace. Many firms began following Apple's lead by creating portable music players to compete with the iPod. In addition, Apple continues to create new and exciting products to gain competitive advantages, such as its iPad, a larger version of the iPod that functions more as a computer than a music player.[1]

When a company is the first to market with a competitive advantage, it gains a particular benefit, such as Apple did with its iPod. This **first-mover advantage** occurs when a company can significantly increase its market share by being first with a new competitive advantage. FedEx created a first-mover advantage by developing its customer self-service software, which allows people to request parcel pickups, print mailing slips, and track parcels online. Other parcel delivery companies quickly began creating their own online services. Today, customer self-service on the Internet is a standard feature of the parcel delivery business.

Competitive intelligence is the process of gathering information about the competitive environment, including competitors' plans, activities, and products, to improve a company's ability to succeed. It means understanding and learning as much as possible as soon as possible about what is occurring outside the company to remain competitive. Frito-Lay, a premier provider of snack foods such as Cracker Jacks and Cheetos, does not send its sales representatives into grocery stores just to stock shelves; they carry handheld computers and record the product offerings, inventory, and even product locations of competitors. Frito-Lay uses this information to gain competitive intelligence on everything from how well competing products are selling to the strategic placement of its own products.[2]

Managers use three common tools to analyze competitive intelligence and develop competitive advantages including:

1. The Five Forces Model (for evaluating industry attractiveness).
2. The three generic strategies (for choosing a business focus).
3. Value chain analysis (for executing business strategies).

The Five Forces Model— Evaluating Industry Attractiveness

Michael Porter, a university professor at Harvard Business School, identified the following pressures that can hurt potential sales:

- Knowledgeable customers can force down prices by pitting rivals against each other.
- Influential suppliers can drive down profits by charging higher prices for supplies.
- Competition can steal customers.
- New market entrants can steal potential investment capital.
- Substitute products can steal customers.

Formally defined, **Porter's Five Forces Model** analyzes the competitive forces within the environment in which a company operates to assess the potential for profitability in an industry. Its purpose is to combat these competitive forces by identifying opportunities, competitive advantages, and competitive intelligence. If the forces are strong, they increase competition; if the forces are weak, they decrease competition. This section details each of the forces and its associated MIS business strategy (see Figure 2.2).[3]

BUYER POWER

Buyer power is the ability of buyers to affect the price they must pay for an item. Factors used to assess buyer power include number of customers, their sensitivity to price, size of orders, differences between competitors, and availability of substitute products. If buyer power is high, customers can force a company and its competitors to compete on price, which typically drives prices down.

One way to reduce buyer power is by manipulating **switching costs,** costs that make customers reluctant to switch to another product or service. Switching costs include financial as well as intangible values. The cost of switching doctors, for instance, includes the powerful intangible components of having to build relationships with the new doctor and nurses, as well as transferring all your medical history. With MIS, however, patients can store their medical records on DVDs or thumb drives, allowing easy transferability. The Internet also lets patients review websites for physician referrals, which takes some of the fear out of trying someone new.[4]

FIGURE 2.2

Porter's Five Forces Model

Threat of Substitute Products or Services
The power of customers to purchase alternatives

Supplier Power
The power of suppliers to drive up prices of materials

Rivalry among Existing Competitors
The power of competitors

Buyer Power
The power of customers to drive down prices

Threat of New Entrants
The power of competitors to enter a market

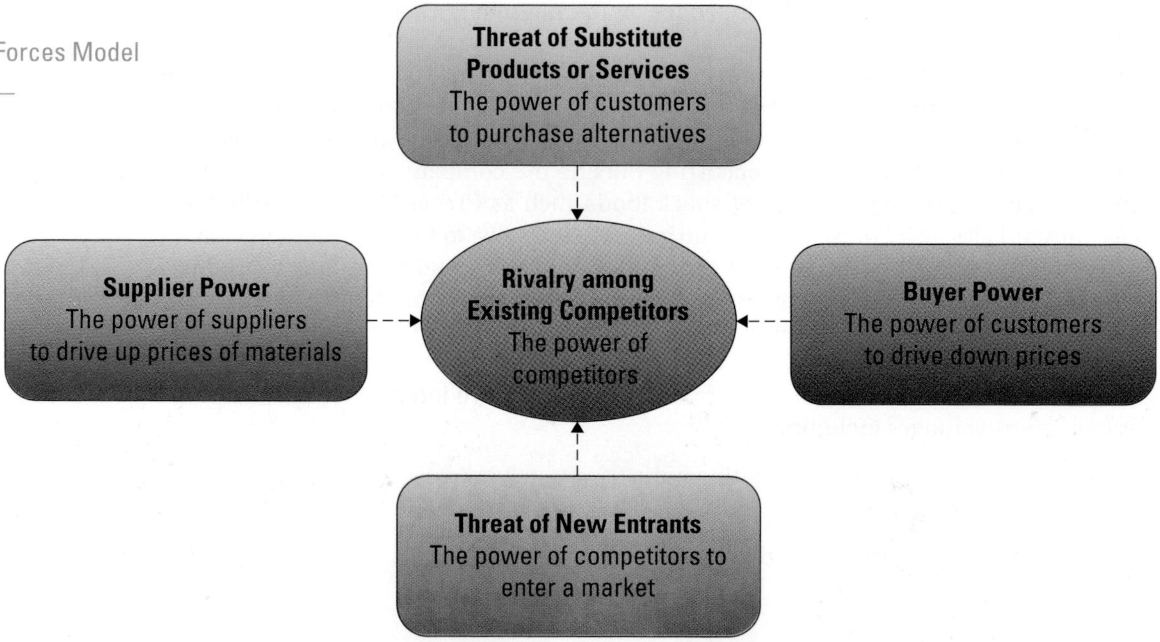

Companies can also reduce buyer power with **loyalty programs,** which reward customers based on their spending. The airline industry is famous for its frequent-flyer programs, for instance. Because of the rewards travelers receive (free airline tickets, upgrades, or hotel stays), they are more likely to be loyal to or give most of their business to a single company. Keeping track of the activities and accounts of many thousands or millions of customers covered by loyalty programs is not practical without large-scale business systems, however. Loyalty programs are thus a good example of using MIS to reduce buyer power.[5]

SUPPLIER POWER

A **supply chain** consists of all parties involved, directly or indirectly, in obtaining raw materials or a product. In a typical supply chain, a company will be both a supplier (to customers) and a customer (of other suppliers), as illustrated in Figure 2.3. **Supplier power** is the suppliers' ability to influence the prices they charge for supplies (including materials, labor, and services). Factors used to appraise supplier power include number of suppliers, size of suppliers, uniqueness of services, and availability of substitute products. If supplier power is high, the supplier can influence the industry by:

- Charging higher prices.
- Limiting quality or services.
- Shifting costs to industry participants.[6]

Typically, when a supplier raises prices, the buyers will pass on the increase to their customers by raising prices on the end product. When supplier power is high, buyers lose revenue because they cannot pass on the raw material price increase to their customers. Some powerful suppliers, such as pharmaceutical companies, can exert a threat over an entire industry when substitutes are limited and the product is critical to the buyers. Patient who need to purchase cancer-fighting drugs have no power over price and must pay whatever the drug company asks because there are few available alternatives.

Using MIS to find alternative products is one way of decreasing supplier power. Cancer patients can now use the Internet to research alternative medications and practices, something that was next to impossible just a few decades ago. Buyers can also use MIS to form groups or collaborate with other buyers, increasing the size of the buyer group and reducing supplier power. For a hypothetical example, the collective group of 30,000 students from a university has far more power over price when purchasing laptops than a single student.[7]

THREAT OF SUBSTITUTE PRODUCTS OR SERVICES

The **threat of substitute products or services** is high when there are many alternatives to a product or service and low when there are few alternatives from which to choose. For example, travelers have numerous substitutes for airline transportation including automobiles, trains, and boats. Technology even makes videoconferencing and virtual meetings possible, eliminating the need for some business travel. Ideally, a company would like to be in a market in which there are few substitutes for the products or services it offers.

Polaroid had this unique competitive advantage for many years until it forgot to observe competitive intelligence. Then the firm went bankrupt when people began taking digital pictures with everything from video cameras to cell phones.

A company can reduce the threat of substitutes by offering additional value through wider product distribution. Soft-drink manufacturers distribute their products through vending machines, gas stations, and convenience stores, increasing the availability of

FIGURE 2.3

Traditional Supply Chain

soft drinks relative to other beverages. Companies can also offer various add-on services, making the substitute product less of a threat. For example, iPhones include capabilities for games, videos, and music, making a traditional cell phone less of a substitute.[8]

THREAT OF NEW ENTRANTS

The *threat of new entrants* is high when it is easy for new competitors to enter a market and low when there are significant entry barriers to joining a market. An *entry barrier* is a feature of a product or service that customers have come to expect and entering competitors must offer the same for survival. For example, a new bank must offer its customers an array of MIS-enabled services, including ATMs, online bill paying, and online account monitoring. These are significant barriers to new firms entering the banking market. At one time, the first bank to offer such services gained a valuable first-mover advantage, but only temporarily, as other banking competitors developed their own MIS services.[9]

RIVALRY AMONG EXISTING COMPETITORS

Rivalry among existing competitors is high when competition is fierce in a market and low when competitors are more complacent. Although competition is always more intense in some industries than in others, the overall trend is toward increased competition in almost every industry. The retail grocery industry is intensively competitive. Kroger, Safeway, and Albertsons in the United States compete in many different ways, essentially trying to beat or match each other on price. Most supermarket chains have implemented loyalty programs to provide customers special discounts while gathering valuable information about their purchasing habits. In the future, expect to see grocery stores using wireless technologies that track customer movements throughout the store to determine purchasing sequences.

Product differentiation occurs when a company develops unique differences in its products or services with the intent to influence demand. Companies can use differentiation to reduce rivalry. For example, while many companies sell books and videos on the Internet, Amazon differentiates itself by using customer profiling. When a customer visits Amazon.com repeatedly, Amazon begins to offer products tailored to that particular customer based on his or her profile. In this way, Amazon has reduced its rivals' power by offering its customers a differentiated service.

To review, the Five Forces Model helps managers set business strategy by identifying the competitive structure and economic environment of an industry. If the forces are strong, they increase competition; if the forces are weak, they decrease it (see Figure 2.4).[10]

ANALYZING THE AIRLINE INDUSTRY

Let us bring Porter's five forces together to look at the competitive forces shaping an industry and highlight business strategies to help it remain competitive. Assume a shipping

FIGURE 2.4

Strong and Weak Examples of Porter's Five Forces

	Weak Force: Decreases Competition or Few Competitors	Strong Force: Increases Competition or Lots of Competitors
Buyer Power	An international hotel chain purchasing milk	A single consumer purchasing milk
Supplier Power	A company that makes airline engines	A company that makes pencils
Threat of Substitute Products or Services	Cancer drugs from a pharmaceutical company	Coffee from McDonald's
Threat of New Entrants	A professional hockey team	A dog walking business
Rivalry among Existing Competitors	Department of Motor Vehicles	A coffee shop

FIGURE 2.5

Five Forces Model in the
Airline Industry

	Strong (High) Force: Increases Competition or Lots of Competitors
Buyer Power	Many airlines for buyers to choose from forcing competition based on price
Supplier Power	Limited number of plane and engine manufacturers to choose from along with unionized workers
Threat of Substitute Products or Services	Many substitutes including cars, trains, and busses. Even substitutes to travel such as video conferencing and virtual meetings.
Threat of New Entrants	Many new airlines entering the market all the time including the latest sky taxis.
Rivalry among Existing Competitors	Intense competition—many rivals.

company is deciding whether to enter the commercial airline industry. If performed correctly, an analysis of the five forces should determine that this is a highly risky business strategy because all five forces are strong. It will thus be difficult to generate a profit.

- **Buyer power:** Buyer power is high because customers have many airlines to choose from and typically make purchases based on price, not carrier.

- **Supplier power:** Supplier power is high since there are limited plane and engine manufacturers to choose from, and unionized workforces (suppliers of labor) restrict airline profits.

- **Threat of substitute products or services:** The threat of substitute products is high from many transportation alternatives including automobiles, trains, and boats, and from transportation substitutes such as videoconferencing and virtual meetings.

- **Threat of new entrants:** The threat of new entrants is high because new airlines are continuously entering the market, including sky taxies offering low-cost on-demand air taxi service.

- **Rivalry among existing competitors:** Rivalry in the airline industry is high, and websites such as Travelocity.com force them to compete on price (see Figure 2.5).[11]

The Three Generic Strategies—Choosing a Business Focus

LO 2.3 Compare Porter's three generic strategies.

Once top management has determined the relative attractiveness of an industry and decided to enter it, the firm must formulate a strategy for doing so. If our sample company decided to join the airline industry, it could compete as a low-cost, no-frills airline or as a luxury airline providing outstanding service and first-class comfort. Both options offer different ways of achieving competitive advantages in a crowded marketplace. The low-cost operator saves on expenses and passes the savings along to customers in the form of low prices. The luxury airline spends on high-end service and first-class comforts and passes the costs on to the customer in the form of high prices.

Porter has identified three generic business strategies for entering a new market: (1) broad cost leadership, (2) broad differentiation, and (3) focused strategy. Broad strategies reach a large market segment, while focused strategies target a niche or unique market with either cost leadership or differentiation. Trying to be all things to all people is a recipe for disaster, since doing so makes it difficult to project a consistent image to the entire marketplace. For this reason, Porter suggests adopting only one of the three generic strategies illustrated in Figure 2.6.[12]

FIGURE 2.6

Porter's Three Generic
Strategies

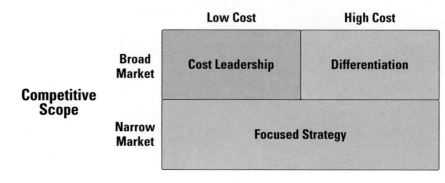

FIGURE 2.7

Examples of Porter's Three
Generic Strategies

Figure 2.7 applies the three strategies to real companies, demonstrating the relation-ships among strategies (cost leadership versus differentiation) and market segmenta-tion (broad versus focused).

- **Broad market and low cost:** Walmart competes by offering a broad range of products at low prices. Its business strategy is to be the low-cost provider of goods for the cost-conscious consumer.

- **Broad market and high cost:** Neiman Marcus competes by offering a broad range of differentiated products at high prices. Its business strategy offers a variety of specialty and upscale products to affluent consumers.

- **Narrow market and low cost:** Payless competes by offering a specific product, shoes, at low prices. Its business strategy is to be the low-cost provider of shoes. Payless competes with Walmart, which also sells low-cost shoes, by offering a far bigger selec-tion of sizes and styles.

- **Narrow market and high cost:** Tiffany & Co. competes by offering a differentiated product, jewelry, at high prices. Its business strategy allows it to be a high-cost pro-vider of premier designer jewelry to affluent consumers.

**LO 2.4 Demonstrate how a
company can add value by using
Porter's value chain analysis.**

Value Chain Analysis—
Executing Business Strategies

Firms make profits by taking raw inputs and applying a business process to turn them into a product or service that customers find valuable. A ***business process*** is a standard-ized set of activities that accomplish a specific task, such as processing a customer's order. Once a firm identifies the industry it wants to enter and the generic strategy it will focus on, it must then choose the business processes required to create its products or services. Of course, the firm will want to ensure the processes add value and create competitive advantages. To identify these competitive advantages, Michael Porter created **value chain analysis**, which views a firm as a series of business processes that each add value to the product or service.

Value chain analysis is a useful tool for determining how to create the greatest possible value for customers (see Figure 2.8). The goal of value chain analysis is to identify processes in which the firm can add value for the customer and create a competitive advantage for itself, with a cost advantage or product differentiation.

The *value chain* groups a firm's activities into two categories, primary value activities, and support value activities. **Primary value activities**, shown at the bottom of the value chain in Figure 2.8, acquire raw materials and manufacture, deliver, market, sell, and provide after-sales services.

1. **Inbound logistics:** acquires raw materials and resources and distributes to manufacturing as required.

2. **Operations:** transforms raw materials or inputs into goods and services.

3. **Outbound logistics:** distributes goods and services to customers.

4. **Marketing and sales:** promotes, prices, and sells products to customers.

5. **Service:** Provides customer support after the sale of goods and services.[13]

Support value activities, along the top of the value chain in Figure 2.8, include firm infrastructure, human resource management, technology development, and procurement. Not surprisingly, these support the primary value activities.

■ **Firm infrastructure:** includes the company format or departmental structures, environment, and systems.

■ **Human resource management:** provides employee training, hiring, and compensation.

■ **Technology development:** applies MIS to processes to add value.

■ **Procurement:** purchases inputs such as raw materials, resources, equipment, and supplies.

It is easy to understand how a typical manufacturing firm takes raw materials such as wood pulp and transforms it into paper. Adding value in this example might include using high-quality raw materials or offering next-day free shipping on any order. How, though, might a typical service firm take raw inputs such as time, knowledge, and MIS and transform them into valuable customer service knowledge? A hotel might use MIS to track customer reservations and then inform front-desk employees when a loyal customer is checking in so the employee can call the guest by name and offer additional

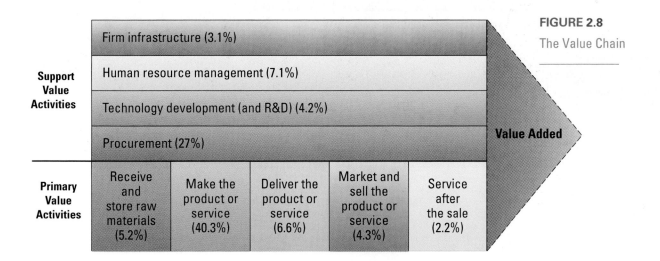

FIGURE 2.8

The Value Chain

services, gift baskets, or upgraded rooms. Examining the firm as a value chain allows managers to identify the important business processes that add value for customers and then find MIS solutions that support them.

When performing a value chain analysis, a firm could survey customers about the extent to which they believe each activity adds value to the product or service. This step generates responses the firm can measure, shown as percentages in Figure 2.9, to describe how each activity adds (or reduces) value. Then the competitive advantage decision for the firm is whether to (1) target high value-adding activities to further enhance their value, (2) target low value-adding activities to increase their value, or (3) perform some combination of the two.

MIS adds value to both primary and support value activities. One example of a primary value activity facilitated by MIS is the development of a marketing campaign management system that could target marketing campaigns more efficiently, thereby reducing marketing costs. The system would also help the firm better pinpoint target market needs, thereby increasing sales. One example of a support value activity facilitated by MIS is the development of a human resources system that could more efficiently reward employees based on performance. The system could also identify employees who are at risk of quitting, allowing manager's time to find additional challenges or opportunities that would help retain these employees and thus reduce turnover costs.

Value chain analysis is a highly useful tool that provides hard and fast numbers for evaluating the activities that add value to products and services. Managers can find additional value by analyzing and constructing the value chain in terms of Porter's Five Forces Model (see Figure 2.9). For example, if the goal is to decrease buyer power, a company can construct its value chain activity of "service after the sale" by offering high levels of customer service. This will increase customers' switching costs and reduce their power. Analyzing and constructing support value activities can help decrease the threat of new entrants. Analyzing and constructing primary value activities can help decrease the threat of substitute products or services. Revising Porter's three business strategies is critical. Firms must continually adapt to their competitive environments, which can cause business strategy to shift.[14]

FIGURE 2.9

The Value Chain and Porter's Five Forces Model

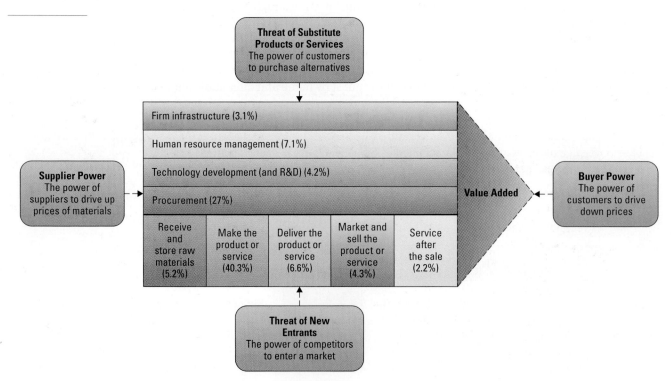

1. How can Apple use competitive intelligence to gain business intelligence?

2. Using Porter's Five Forces Model, analyze Apple's buyer power and supplier power.

3. Which of the three generic strategies is Apple following?

4. Which of Porter's Five Forces did Apple address through the introduction of the iPhone and customer-developed iPhone applications?

Chapter Two Case: *BusinessWeek* Interview with Michael Porter

The Harvard professor and popular author explains the "location paradox" and talks about the competitive challenges facing the United States. Ever since his 1990 book *The Competitive Advantage of Nations,* Harvard Business School professor Michael Porter has been regarded as a leading authority on the economic development of nations, regions, and cities. Both as an academic and consultant, Porter is best known for his work on the importance of developing a specialty in industrial clusters—high concentrations of companies in a sector such as semi-conductors, cars, or textiles. In an interview with Senior Writer Pete Engardio, Porter explains why he believes globalization has actually made industry clusters and local advantages even more important, rather than weakened them.

If globalization means that work, technology, and money can now move anywhere over the Internet, does the physical location of an industry still really matter?
"I call it the location paradox. If you think of globalization, your first reaction is to think that location doesn't matter anymore. There are no barriers to investment. But the paradox is that location still matters. The U.S. is still the most important space in the world, for example, and regions have tremendous specialization. Anything that can be easily accessed from a distance no longer is a competitive advantage. But the more there are no barriers, the more things are mobile, the more decisive location becomes. This point has tripped up a lot of really smart people.

"As a result, the bottom half of U.S. locations are facing more stress. Many cities used to have a natural advantage just because they were in the U.S. But that is not such an advantage anymore. We are finding a tendency for the rich regions to get richer."

How has globalization affected the idea of regional clusters?
"Now that globalization continues to power forward, what has happened is that clusters must become more specialized in individual locations. The global economy is speeding up the process by which clusters get more focused. There is a footwear cluster in Italy, for example, where they still produce very advanced products. The design, marketing, and technology still are in Italy. But much of the production has shifted to Romania, where the Italians have developed another cluster. All of the production companies actually are Italian-owned. Taiwan has done the same by shifting production to China. The innovation is in Taiwan, but its companies are moving aspects of their cluster that don't need to be in Taiwan."

What are the big differences in the way communities approach development today compared to 1990, when you wrote *The Competitive Advantage of Nations?*
"There has been tremendous change in the last 15 or 20 years. Before *Competitive Advantage* was published, the dominant view was that you need to get costs down, offer incentives, and have a development department that hunts for investment. I think the level of sophistication has risen at the state and local level. They now understand that competitiveness does not just mean low costs.

"Another big change from 20 years ago is that the notion of industry clusters is now pretty much ubiquitous. Many regions now look at development in these terms, and have identified hundreds and hundreds of different clusters. I think that the fact that productivity growth has risen dramatically shows that economic development has been a big success over the past few years."

If every community is developing the same industry clusters, how do they stand out?
"I think it's very important to understand that the bar has risen substantially. Everything matters now. The schools matter. The roads matter. You have to understand this is a marathon. Also, you can't try to build clusters across the board and be into everything. You have to build on your strengths."

Many local officials in the U.S. talk a lot about collaboration among universities, companies, and governments across an entire region. Is this new?
"There is a growing recognition that the interaction between one region or metropolitan area and its neighbors is important. The overlap between clusters is very important in stimulating growth. Isolated clusters are less powerful than integrated clusters. That's because new clusters often grow out of old clusters. I also think there is more recognition that you need a lot of cross-company collaboration in a region. Companies realize they have a lot of shared issues. Meanwhile, universities used to be seen as standalone institutions. Now, more regional economies see universities as players and are integrating them into industrial clusters."

Does the U.S. have a competitiveness problem?
"I think the U.S. is facing some very serious challenges. But the most important drivers of competitiveness are not national. They are regional and local. National policies and circumstances explain about 20 percent to 25 percent of why a regional economy is doing well. What really matters is where the skills and highly competitive institutions are based. Some of these assets take a very long time to build. But competitiveness essentially is in the hands of regions."[15]

Questions

1. In today's global business environment, does the physical location of a business matter?

2. Why is collaboration among universities important?

3. Is there a competitiveness problem in the United States?

4. What are the big differences in the way communities approach development today compared to 1990, when Porter wrote *The Competitive Advantage of Nations?*

Strategic Initiatives for Implementing Competitive Advantages

3.1. Identify how an organization can use business process reengineering to improve its business.

3.2. Explain supply chain management and its role in business.

3.3. Explain customer relationship management systems and how they can help organizations understand their customers.

3.4. Summarize the importance of enterprise resource planning systems.

Business Process Reegineering

This chapter introduces high-profile strategic initiatives that an organization can undertake to help it gain competitive advantages and business efficiencies—business process reengineering, supply chain management, customer relationship management, and enterprise resource planning (see Figure 3.1). Each of these strategic initiatives is covered in detail throughout this text. This chapter provides a brief introduction only.

A ***business process*** is a standardized set of activities that accomplish a specific task, such as processing a customer's order. Business processes transform a set of inputs into

LO 3.1 Identify how an organization can use business process reengineering to improve its business.

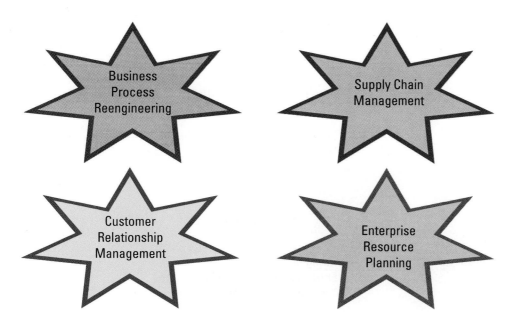

FIGURE 3.1

Strategic Initiatives for Competitive Advantages

a set of outputs—goods or services—for another person or process by using people and tools. Understanding business processes helps a manager envision how the entire company operates. *Workflow* includes the tasks, activities, and responsibilities required to execute each step in a business process. Understanding business processes, workflow, customers' expectations, and the competitive environment provides managers with the necessary ingredients to design and evaluate alternative business processes in order to maintain competitive advantages when internal or external circumstances change.

Business process reengineering (BPR) is the analysis and redesign of workflow within and between enterprises. Most companies pride themselves on providing breakthrough products and services for customers. But if customers do not receive what they want quickly, accurately, and hassle-free, even fantastic offerings will not prevent a company from annoying customers and ultimately eroding its own financial performance. To avoid this pitfall and protect its competitive advantage, a company must continually evaluate all the business processes in its value chain. Improving the efficiency and effectiveness of its business processes will improve the firm's value chain.

The common business processes outlined in Figure 3.2 reflect functional thinking. Some processes, such as a programming process, may be contained wholly within a single department. However, most, such as ordering a product, are cross-functional or cross-departmental processes and span the entire organization. The process of "order

FIGURE 3.2

Sample Business Processes

Accounting and Finance
- Creating financial statements
- Paying of Accounts Payable
- Collecting of Accounts Receivable

Marketing and Sales
- Promoting of discounts
- Communicating marketing campaigns
- Attracting customers
- Processing sales

Operations Management
- Ordering inventory
- Creating production schedules
- Manufacturing goods

Human Resources
- Hiring employees
- Enrolling employees in health care
- Tracking vacation and sick time

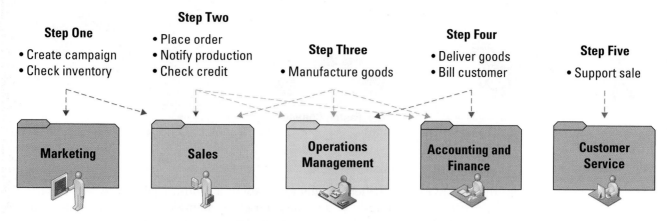

Step One
- Create campaign
- Check inventory

Step Two
- Place order
- Notify production
- Check credit

Step Three
- Manufacture goods

Step Four
- Deliver goods
- Bill customer

Step Five
- Support sale

Marketing   Sales   Operations Management   Accounting and Finance   Customer Service

FIGURE 3.3

Five Steps in the Order-to-Delivery Business Process

to delivery" focuses on the entire customer order process across functional departments (see Figure 3.3). Another example is "product realization," which includes not only the way a product is developed, but also the way it is marketed and serviced. Some other cross-functional business processes are taking a product from concept to market, acquiring customers, loan processing, providing post-sales service, claim processing, and reservation handling.

Customer-facing processes, also called front-office processes, result in a product or service received by an organization's external customer. They include fulfilling orders, communicating with customers, and sending out bills and marketing information. *Business-facing processes*, also called back-office processes, are invisible to the external customer but essential to the effective management of the business; they include goal setting, day-to-day planning, giving performance feedback and rewards, and allocating resources. Figure 3.4 displays the different categories of customer-facing and business-facing processes along with an example of each. A company's strategic vision should provide guidance on which business processes are core, that is, which are directly linked to the firm's critical success factors. Mapping these core business processes to the value chain reveals where the processes touch the customers and affect their perceptions of value.

Figure 3.5 highlights an analogy to business process reengineering by explaining the different means of traveling along the same route. A company could improve the way it travels by changing from foot to horse and then from horse to car. With a BPR mind-set, however, it would look beyond automating and streamlining to find a completely different approach. It would ignore the road and travel by air to get from point A to point B. Companies often follow the same indirect path for doing business, not realizing there might be a different, faster, and more direct way.

Creating value for the customer is the leading reason for instituting BPR, and MIS often plays an important enabling role. Fundamentally new business processes enabled Progressive Insurance to slash its claims settlement time from 31 days to four hours, for instance. Typically, car insurance companies follow this standard claims resolution process: The customer gets into an accident, has the car towed, and finds a ride home. The customer then calls the insurance company to begin the claims process, which includes an evaluation of the damage, assignment of fault, and an estimate

FIGURE 3.4

Customer-Facing, Industry-Specific, and Business-Facing Processes

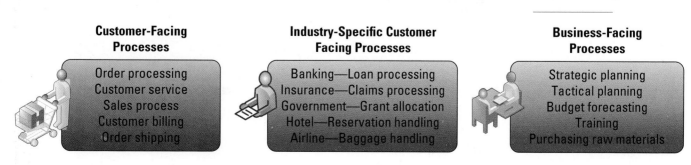

Customer-Facing Processes
- Order processing
- Customer service
- Sales process
- Customer billing
- Order shipping

Industry-Specific Customer Facing Processes
- Banking—Loan processing
- Insurance—Claims processing
- Government—Grant allocation
- Hotel—Reservation handling
- Airline—Baggage handling

Business-Facing Processes
- Strategic planning
- Tactical planning
- Budget forecasting
- Training
- Purchasing raw materials

Better, Faster, Cheaper

FIGURE 3.5

Different Ways to Travel the Same Route

of the cost of repairs, which usually takes about a month (see Figure 3.6). Progressive Insurance's innovation was to offer a mobile claims process. When a customer has a car accident, he or she calls in the claim on the spot. The Progressive claims adjuster comes to the accident site, surveys the scene and takes digital photographs. The adjuster then offers the customer on-site payment, towing services, and a ride home. A true BPR effort does more for a company than simply improve a process by performing it better, faster, and cheaper. Progressive Insurance's BPR effort redefined best practices for an entire industry.

When selecting a business process to reengineer, wise managers focus on those core processes that are critical to performance, rather than marginal processes that have little impact. The effort to reengineer a business process as a strategic activity requires a different mind-set than that required in continuous business process improvement programs. Because companies have tended to overlook the powerful contribution that processes can make to strategy, they often undertake process improvement efforts using their current processes as the starting point. Managers focusing on reengineering can instead use several criteria to identify opportunities:

- Is the process broken?
- Is it feasible that reengineering of this process will succeed?
- Does it have a high impact on the agency's strategic direction?
- Does it significantly impact customer satisfaction?
- Is it antiquated?
- Does it fall far below best-in-class?
- Is it crucial for productivity improvement?
- Will savings from automation be clearly visible?
- Is the return on investment from implementation high and preferably immediate?

FIGURE 3.6

Auto Insurance Claims Processes Reengineering

Company A: Claims Resolution Process

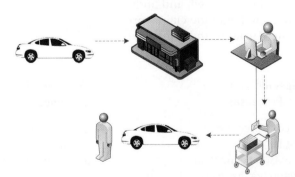

Resolution Cycle Time: 3–8 weeks

Progressive Insurance: Claims Resolution Process

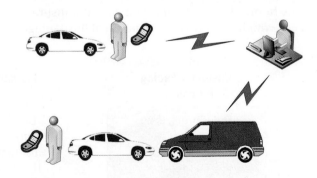

Resolution Cycle Time: 30 minutes–3 hours

Supply Chain Management

Trek, a leader in bicycle products and accessories, gained more than 30 percent of the worldwide market by streamlining operations through the implementation of several IT systems. According to Jeff Stang, director of IT and operational accounting, the most significant improvement realized from the new systems was the ability to obtain key management information to drive business decisions in line with the company's strategic goals. Other system results included a highly successful website developed for the 1,400 Trek dealers where they could enter orders directly, check stock availability, and view accounts receivable and credit summaries. Tonja Green, Trek channel manager for North America, stated, "We wanted to give our dealers an easier and quicker way to enter their orders and get information. Every week the number of web orders increases by 25 to 30 percent due to the new system."

A **supply chain** includes all parties involved, directly or indirectly, in obtaining raw materials or a product. To understand a supply chain, consider a customer purchasing a Trek bike from a dealer. On one end, the supply chain has the customer placing an order for the bike with the dealer. The dealer purchases the bike from the manufacturer, Trek. Trek purchases raw materials such as packaging material, metal, and accessories from many different suppliers to make the bike. The supply chain for Trek encompasses every activity and party involved in the process of fulfilling the order from the customer for the new bike. Figure 3.7 displays a typical supply chain for a bike manufacturer including all processes and people required to fulfill the customer's order. Figure 3.8 highlights the five basic supply chain activities a company undertakes to manufacture and distribute products. To automate and enable sophisticated decision making in these critical areas, companies are turning to systems that provide demand forecasting, inventory control, and information flows between suppliers and customers.

Supply chain management (SCM) is the management of information flows between and among activities in a supply chain to maximize total supply chain effectiveness and corporate profitability. In the past, manufacturing efforts focused primarily on quality improvement efforts within the company; today these efforts reach across the entire supply chain, including customers, customers' customers, suppliers, and suppliers' suppliers. Today's supply chain is an intricate network of business partners linked through communication channels and relationships. Supply chain management systems manage and enhance these relationships with the primary goal of creating a fast, efficient, and low-cost network of business relationships that take products from concept to market. SCM systems create the integrations or tight process and information linkages between all participants in the supply chain.

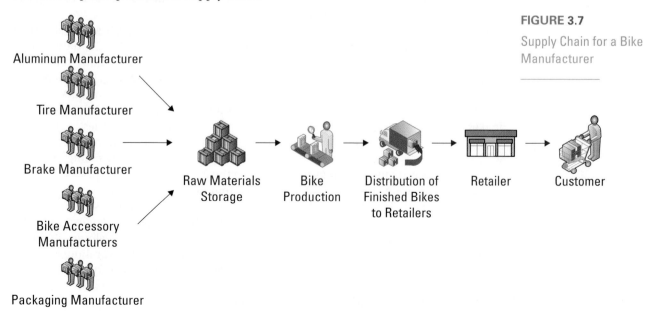

FIGURE 3.7

Supply Chain for a Bike Manufacturer

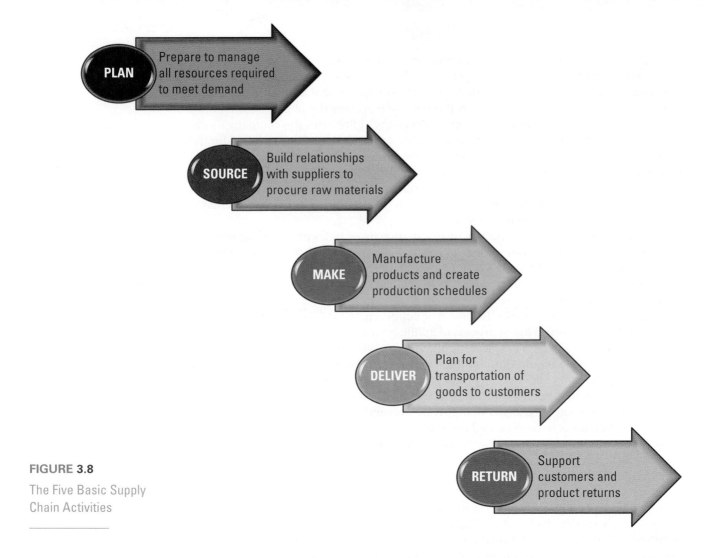

FIGURE 3.8

The Five Basic Supply
Chain Activities

Dozens of steps are required to achieve and carry out each of the preceding components. SCM software can enable an organization to generate efficiencies within these steps by automating and improving the information flows throughout and among the different supply chain components.

Walmart and Procter & Gamble (P&G) implemented a tremendously successful SCM system. The system linked Walmart distribution centers directly to P&G's manufacturing centers. Every time a Walmart customer purchases a P&G product, the system sends a message directly to the factory alerting P&G to restock the product. The system also sends an automatic alert to P&G whenever a product is running low at one of Walmart's distribution centers. This real-time information allows P&G to efficiently make and deliver products to Walmart without having to maintain large inventories in its warehouses. The system also generates invoices and receives payments automatically. The SCM system saves time, reduces inventory, and decreases order-processing costs for P&G. P&G passes on these savings to Walmart in the form of discounted prices.[1]

Figure 3.9 diagrams the stages of the SCM system for a customer purchasing a product from Walmart. The diagram demonstrates how the supply chain is dynamic and involves the constant flow of information between the different parties. For example, the customer generates order information by purchasing a product from Walmart. Walmart supplies the order information to its warehouse or distributor. The warehouse or distributor transfers the order information to the manufacturer, who provides pricing and availability information to the store and replenishes the product to the store. Payment funds among the various partners are transferred electronically.

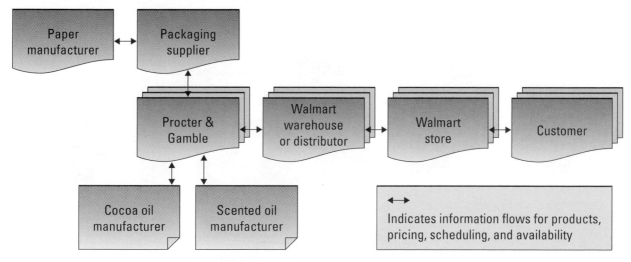

FIGURE **3.9**

Supply Chain for a Product
Purchased from Walmart

Effective and efficient supply chain management systems can enable an organization to:

- Decrease the power of its buyers.
- Increase its own supplier power.
- Increase switching costs to reduce the threat of substitute products or services.
- Create entry barriers thereby reducing the threat of new entrants.
- Increase efficiencies while seeking a competitive advantage through cost leadership (see Figure 3.10).

Customer Relationship Management

LO 3.3 Explain customer relationship management systems and how they can help organizations understand their customers.

Today, most competitors are simply a mouse-click away. This intense marketplace has forced organizations to switch from being sales focused to being customer focused.

Charles Schwab recouped the cost of a multimillion-dollar customer relationship management system in less than two years. The system, developed by Siebel, allows the brokerage firm to trace each interaction with a customer or prospective customer and then provide services (retirement planning, for instance) to each customer's needs and interests. The system gives Schwab a better and more complete view of its customers, which it can use to determine which customers are serious investors and which ones are not. Automated deposits from paychecks, for example, are a sign of a serious investor, while stagnant balances signal a nonserious investor. Once Schwab is able to make this determination, the firm allocates its resources accordingly, saving money by not investing time or resources in subsidizing nonserious investors.[2]

Customer relationship management (CRM) involves managing all aspects of a customer's relationship with an organization to increase customer loyalty and retention and an organization's profitability. CRM allows an organization to gain insights into customers' shopping and buying behaviors in order to develop and implement enterprisewide

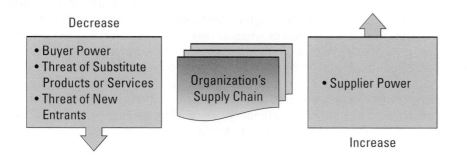

FIGURE **3.10**

Effective and Efficient Supply Chain Management's Effect on Porter's Five Forces

FIGURE 3.11

CRM Overview

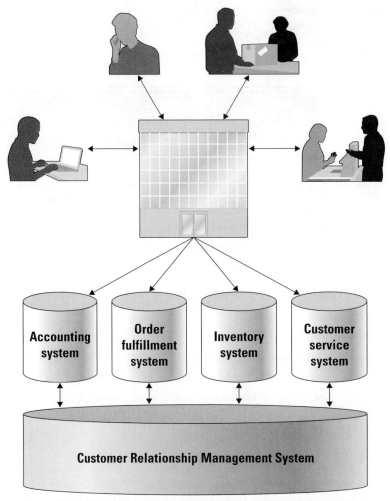

Customer information flows
are represented by arrows.

strategies. Kaiser Permanente undertook a CRM strategy to improve and prolong the lives of diabetics. After compiling CRM information on 84,000 of its diabetic patients among its 2.4 million northern California members, Kaiser determined that only 15 to 20 percent of its diabetic patients were getting their eyes checked routinely. (Diabetes is the leading cause of blindness.) As a result, Kaiser is now enforcing more rigorous eye-screening programs for diabetics and creating support groups for obesity and stress (two more factors that make diabetes even worse). This CRM-based "preventive medicine" approach is saving Kaiser considerable sums of money and saving the eyesight of diabetic patients.[3]

Figure 3.11 provides an overview of a typical CRM system. Customers contact an organization through various means including call centers, web access, email, faxes, and direct sales. A single customer may access an organization multiple times through many different channels. The CRM system tracks every communication between the customer and the organization and provides access to CRM information within different systems from accounting to order fulfillment. Understanding all customer communications allows the organization to communicate effectively with each customer. It gives the organization a detailed understanding of each customer's products and services record regardless of the customer's preferred communication channel. For example, a customer service representative can easily view detailed account information and history through a CRM system when providing information to a customer such as expected delivery dates, complementary product information, and customer payment and billing information.

Companies that understand individual customer needs are best positioned to achieve success. Of course, building successful customer relationships is not a new business practice; however, implementing CRM systems allows a company to operate more efficiently and effectively in the area of supporting customer needs. CRM moves far beyond technology by identifying customer needs and designing specific marketing campaigns tailored to each. This enables a firm to treat customers as individuals, gaining important insights into their buying preferences and shopping behaviors. Firms that treat their customers well reap the rewards and generally see higher profits and highly loyal customers. Identifying the most valuable customers allows a firm to ensure that these customers receive the highest levels of customer service and are offered the first opportunity to purchase new products. Firms can find their most valuable customers by using the RFM formula—recency, frequency, and monetary value. In other words, an organization must track:

- How *recently* a customer purchased items.
- How *frequently* a customer purchases items.
- The *monetary* value of each customer purchase.

After gathering this initial CRM information, the firm can analyze it to identify patterns and create marketing campaigns and sales promotions for different customer segments. For example, if a customer buys only at the height of the season, the firm should send a special offer during the off-season. If a certain customer segment purchases shoes but never accessories, the firm can offer discounted accessories with the purchase of a new pair of shoes. If the firm determines that its top 20 percent of customers are responsible for 80 percent of the revenue, it can focus on ensuring these customers are always satisfied and receive the highest levels of customer service.

There are three phases of CRM: (1) reporting, (2) analyzing, and (3) predicting. **CRM reporting technologies** help organizations identify their customers across other applications. **CRM analysis technologies** help organizations segment their customers into categories such as best and worst customers. **CRM predicting technologies** help organizations predict customer behavior, such as which customers are at risk of leaving. Figure 3.12 highlights a few of the important questions an organization can answer in these areas by using CRM technologies.

REPORTING Customer Identification: Asking What Happened	ANALYZING Customer Segmentation: Asking Why It Happened	PREDICTING Customer Prediction: Asking What Will Happen
• What is the total revenue by customer? • How many units did we make? • What were total sales by product? • How many customers do we have? • What are the current inventory levels?	• Why did sales not meet forecasts? • Why was production so low? • Why did we not sell as many units as previous years? • Who are our customers? • Why was revenue so high? • Why are inventory levels low?	• What customers are at risk of leaving? • Which products will our customers buy? • Who are the best customers for a marketing campaign? • How do we reach our customers? • What will sales be this year? • How much inventory do we need to preorder?

FIGURE 3.12

Three Phases of CRM

Enterprise Resource Planning

Today's business leaders need significant amounts of information to be readily accessible with real-time views into their businesses so that decisions can be made when they need to be, without the added time of tracking data and generating reports. ***Enterprise resource planning (ERP)*** integrates all departments and functions throughout an organization into a single IT system (or integrated set of IT systems) so that employees can make decisions by viewing enterprisewide information on all business operations.

Many organizations fail to maintain consistency across business operations. If a single department, such as sales, decides to implement a new system without considering the other departments, inconsistencies can occur throughout the company. Not all systems are built to talk to each other and share data, and if sales suddenly implements a new system that marketing and accounting cannot use or is inconsistent in the way it handles information, the company's operations become siloed. Figure 3.13 displays sample data from a sales database, and Figure 3.14 displays samples from an accounting database. Notice the differences in data formats, numbers, and identifiers. Correlating this data would be difficult, and the inconsistencies would cause numerous reporting errors from an enterprisewide perspective.

Los Angeles is a city of 3.5 million, with 44,000 city employees, and a budget of $4 billion. Yet a few years ago each department conducted its own purchasing. That meant 2,000 people in 600 city buildings and 60 warehouses were ordering material. Some 120,000 purchase orders (POs) and 50,000 checks per year went to more than 7,000 vendors. Inefficiency was rampant.

"There was a lack of financial responsibility in the old system, and people could run up unauthorized expenditures," said Bob Jensen, the city's ERP project manager. Each department maintained its own inventories on different systems. Expense-item mismatches piled up. One department purchased one way, others preferred a different approach. Mainframe-based systems were isolated. The city chose an ERP system as part of a $22 million project to integrate purchasing and financial reporting across the entire city. The project resulted in cutting the check processing staff in half, processing

FIGURE 3.13

Sales Information Sample

OrderDate	ProductName	Quantity	Unit Price	Unit Cost	Customer ID	SalesRep ID
Monday, January 04, 2015	Mozzarella cheese	41.5	$ 24.15	$ 15.35	AC45	EX-107
Monday, January 04, 2015	Romaine lettuce	90.65	$ 15.06	$ 14.04	AC45	EX-109
Tuesday, January 05, 2015	Red onions	27.15	$ 12.08	$ 10.32	AC67	EX-104
Wednesday, January 06, 2015	Romaine lettuce	67.25	$ 15.16	$ 10.54	AC96	EX-109
Thursday, January 07, 2015	Black olives	79.26	$ 12.18	$ 9.56	AC44	EX-104
Thursday, January 07, 2015	Romaine lettuce	46.52	$ 15.24	$ 11.54	AC32	EX-104
Thursday, January 07, 2015	Romaine lettuce	52.5	$ 15.26	$ 11.12	AC84	EX-109
Friday, January 08, 2015	Red onions	39.5	$ 12.55	$ 9.54	AC103	EX-104
Saturday, January 09, 2015	Romaine lettuce	66.5	$ 15.98	$ 9.56	AC4	EX-104
Sunday, January 10, 2015	Romaine lettuce	58.26	$ 15.87	$ 9.50	AC174	EX-104
Sunday, January 10, 2015	Pineapple	40.15	$ 33.54	$ 22.12	AC45	EX-104
Monday, January 11, 2015	Pineapple	71.56	$ 33.56	$ 22.05	AC4	EX-104
Thursday, January 14, 2015	Romaine lettuce	18.25	$ 15.00	$ 10.25	AC174	EX-104
Thursday, January 14, 2015	Romaine lettuce	28.15	$ 15.26	$ 10.54	AC44	EX-107
Friday, January 15, 2015	Pepperoni	33.5	$ 15.24	$ 10.25	AC96	EX-109
Friday, January 15, 2015	Parmesan cheese	14.26	$ 8.05	$ 4.00	AC96	EX-104
Saturday, January 16, 2015	Parmesan cheese	72.15	$ 8.50	$ 4.00	AC103	EX-109
Monday, January 18, 2015	Parmesan cheese	41.5	$ 24.15	$ 15.35	AC45	EX-107
Monday, January 18, 2015	Romaine lettuce	90.65	$ 15.06	$ 14.04	AC45	EX-109
Wednesday, January 20, 2015	Tomatoes	27.15	$ 12.08	$ 10.32	AC67	EX-104
Thursday, January 21, 2015	Peppers	67.25	$ 15.16	$ 10.54	AC96	EX-109
Thursday, January 21, 2015	Mozzarella cheese	79.26	$ 12.18	$ 9.56	AC44	EX-104
Saturday, January 23, 2015	Black olives	46.52	$ 15.24	$ 11.54	AC32	EX-104
Sunday, January 24, 2015	Mozzarella cheese	52.5	$ 15.26	$ 11.12	AC84	EX-109
Tuesday, January 26, 2015	Romaine lettuce	39.5	$ 12.55	$ 9.54	AC103	EX-104
Wednesday, January 27, 2015	Parmesan cheese	66.5	$ 15.98	$ 9.56	AC4	EX-104
Thursday, January 28, 2015	Peppers	58.26	$ 15.87	$ 9.50	AC174	EX-104
Thursday, January 28, 2015	Mozzarella cheese	40.15	$ 33.54	$ 22.12	AC45	EX-104
Friday, January 29, 2015	Tomatoes	71.56	$ 33.56	$ 22.05	AC4	EX-104
Friday, January 29, 2015	Peppers	18.25	$ 15.00	$ 10.25	AC174	EX-104

	OrderDate	ProductName	Quantity	Unit Price	Total Sales	Unit Cost	Total Cost	Profit	Customer	SalesRep
2	04-Jan-15	Mozzarella cheese	41	24	984	18	738	246	The Station	Debbie Fernandez
3	04-Jan-15	Romaine lettuce	90	15	1,350	14	1,260	90	The Station	Roberta Cross
4	05-Jan-15	Red onions	27	12	324	8	216	108	Bert's Bistro	Loraine Schultz
5	06-Jan-15	Romaine lettuce	67	15	1,005	14	938	67	Smoke House	Roberta Cross
6	07-Jan-15	Black olives	79	12	948	6	474	474	Flagstaff House	Loraine Schultz
7	07-Jan-15	Romaine lettuce	46	15	690	14	644	46	Two Bitts	Loraine Schultz
8	07-Jan-15	Romaine lettuce	52	15	780	14	728	52	Pierce Arrow	Roberta Cross
9	08-Jan-15	Red onions	39	12	468	8	312	156	Mamm'a Pasta Palace	Loraine Schultz
10	09-Jan-15	Romaine lettuce	66	15	990	14	924	66	The Dandelion	Loraine Schultz
11	10-Jan-15	Romaine lettuce	58	15	870	14	812	58	Carmens	Loraine Schultz
12	10-Jan-15	Pineapple	40	33	1,320	28	1,120	200	The Station	Loraine Schultz
13	11-Jan-15	Pineapple	71	33	2,343	28	1,988	355	The Dandelion	Loraine Schultz
14	14-Jan-15	Romaine lettuce	18	15	270	14	252	18	Carmens	Loraine Schultz
15	14-Jan-15	Romaine lettuce	28	15	420	14	392	28	Flagstaff House	Debbie Fernandez
16	15-Jan-15	Pepperoni	33	53	1,749	35	1,155	594	Smoke House	Roberta Cross
17	15-Jan-15	Parmesan cheese	14	8	112	4	56	56	Smoke House	Loraine Schultz
18	16-Jan-15	Parmesan cheese	72	8	576	4	288	288	Mamm'a Pasta Palace	Roberta Cross
19	18-Jan-15	Parmesan cheese	10	8	80	4	40	40	Mamm'a Pasta Palace	Loraine Schultz
20	18-Jan-15	Romaine lettuce	42	15	630	14	588	42	Smoke House	Roberta Cross
21	20-Jan-15	Tomatoes	48	9	432	7	336	96	Two Bitts	Loraine Schultz
22	21-Jan-15	Peppers	29	21	609	12	348	261	The Dandelion	Roberta Cross
23	21-Jan-15	Mozzarella cheese	10	24	240	18	180	60	Mamm'a Pasta Palace	Debbie Fernandez
24	23-Jan-15	Black olives	98	12	1,176	6	588	588	Two Bitts	Roberta Cross
25	24-Jan-15	Mozzarella cheese	45	24	1,080	18	810	270	Carmens	Loraine Schultz
26	26-Jan-15	Romaine lettuce	58	15	870	14	812	58	Two Bitts	Loraine Schultz
27	27-Jan-15	Parmesan cheese	66	8	528	4	264	264	Flagstaff House	Loraine Schultz
28	28-Jan-15	Peppers	85	21	1,785	12	1,020	765	Pierce Arrow	Loraine Schultz
29	28-Jan-15	Mozzarella cheese	12	24	288	18	216	72	The Dandelion	Debbie Fernandez
30	29-Jan-15	Tomatoes	40	9	360	7	280	80	Pierce Arrow	Roberta Cross

POs faster than ever, reducing the number of workers in warehousing by 40 positions, decreasing inventories from $50 million to $15 million, and providing a single point of contact for each vendor. In addition, $5 million a year has been saved in contract consolidation.[4]

Figure 3.15 shows how an ERP system takes data from across the enterprise, consolidates and correlates the data, and generates enterprisewide organizational reports. Original ERP implementations promised to capture all information onto one true "enterprise" system, with the ability to touch all the business processes within the organization. Unfortunately, ERP solutions have fallen short of these promises, and typical implementations have penetrated only 15 to 20 percent of the organization. The issue ERP intends to solve is that knowledge within a majority of organizations currently resides in silos that are maintained by a select few, without the ability to be shared across the organization, causing inconsistency across business operations.

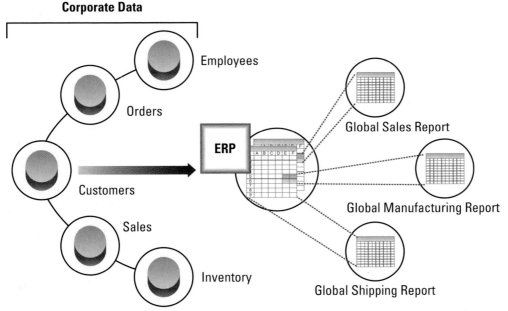

Corporate Data

Employees
Orders
Customers
Sales
Inventory

ERP

Global Sales Report
Global Manufacturing Report
Global Shipping Report

1. Evaluate how Apple can gain business intelligence through the implementation of a customer relationship management system.

2. Create an argument against the following statement: "Apple should not invest any resources to build a supply chain management system."

3. Why would a company like Apple invest in BPR?

Chapter Three Case: Got Milk? It's Good for You—Unless It Is Contaminated!

Dong Lizhong, a farmer and migrant worker dairy farmer in China, bet that being a dairy farmer was his golden ticket out of a factory job. Unfortunately, a contamination crisis shattered his dairy business when babies mysteriously started developing kidney stones from contaminated baby formula. A chemical called melamine—an additive used to make plastic—was discovered in the milk supply of China's third-largest dairy producer. Tragically, four infants died from the contamination and at least 53,000 fell ill. According to the official Xinhua news agency, officials knew about problems with the milk for months before informing the public.

China's four largest dairy organizations, accounting for nearly half the country's milk market, pulled their goods off shelves. More than 20 countries, including France, India, and South Korea, banned not only dairy products from China, but also candies, cookies, and chocolates. "This is a disastrous setback. I estimate that it will take one or two years to rebuild confidence in dairy products," says Luo Yunbo, dean of the College of Food Science and Nutritional Engineering at China Agricultural University.

The local milk-collection station in Dong Lizhong's village has discontinued purchasing milk. Farmers are continuing to milk their cows, but they now drink the milk themselves or "feed the cabbages"—pour the milk in their cabbage fields. Dong estimates that he has already lost $1,461, or a quarter of his annual income last year, in expenses to feed corn and fresh grass to his 20 dairy cows. "Unless someone starts buying milk, we're going to see a lot of cows being slaughtered very soon," states Dong.

Cutting Corners

Chinese do not traditionally drink milk. However, as the country has grown more affluent over the past few decades, the domestic dairy industry has skyrocketed. China's two largest dairy companies have greatly benefited from this new trend: China Mengniu Dairy and Inner Mongolia Yili Industrial Group. Simultaneously, numerous entrepreneurs—from dairy farmers to milk-collection station owners to milk distributors—have jumped into the supply chain of dairy products to make their fortunes. Due to the fierce competition within China's dairy industry a few companies decided to cut corners to reduce costs, regardless of the consequences.

As Mengniu and Yili expanded at breathtaking speed, they found themselves in the unique position where supply could not keep up with demand. According to KPMG, China consumes 25 million tons of milk yearly, putting its dairy market ahead of France and Germany. In their quest for more raw milk, Mengniu and Yili have expanded outside their base in the northern province of Inner Mongolia and set up milk production facilities in other parts of China. Not surprisingly, most of the quality problems in milk have been found in dairy farms in Hebei and Inner Mongolia provinces, where the competition for raw milk supplies has been the fiercest.

Most dairy farmers in Hebei province traditionally sold their milk to milk-collection stations established by local heavyweight Sanlu. In recent years, new privately owned milk-collection stations to buy raw milk for Mengniu and Yili started popping up next to existing stations. These new entrants captured raw milk supplies by offering dairy farmers slightly higher prices. "This competition broke the rules. As milk buyers fought over milk supplies, their standards for quality fell," says Roger Liu, vice-chairman of American Dairy (ADY), a Heilongjiang province-based powdered milk company.

Additives to Boost Protein

Many of the milking stations do not have the equipment to test milk for additives. At the Nanxincheng station, 16 households bring their dairy cows in the area to be milked in the red brick farmhouse. The farmers hook up the cows up to a milking machine, which pumps the milk directly into a big vat. "They didn't test the milk here. They sent it to Sanlu for testing," says Du Yanjun, a government inspector posted to monitor the Nanxincheng station after the contamination crisis broke.

The milk is collected from the stations and shipped by middlemen to big dairy companies like Sanlu, which do their own testing and grading. It now appears that unscrupulous middlemen commonly add melamine into the raw milk to increase protein levels in their milk samples, so their milk will be graded higher. Ingesting melamine can cause kidney stones or kidney failure, especially in infants.

Matthew Estes, president and CEO of BabyCare, had looked into switching from Australian and New Zealand sources of milk for the company's infant-formula business in China. BabyCare did extensive testing of possible suppliers and realized it could not locate a suitable supplier in China. "We couldn't the find quality that met our standards. We chose to not sell rather than take the risk," he says.

Going to Jail

A Chinese court sentenced two of the primary middlemen to death and a dairy boss to life in prison for their roles in the milk contamination scandal. The swift trial and harsh sentences show Beijing's resolve in tackling the country's stubborn food safety problems and an eagerness by the communist leadership to move past the embarrassing scandal.

Going to Starbucks

Starbucks Corp. has launched a new brand of coffee grown by farmers in China and says it hopes to bring the blend to stores all over the world. The Seattle-based company, which has been closing stores in the U.S. to cut costs, says its new blend is made in China's southwestern province of Yunnan, bordering Vietnam, Laos, and Myanmar. "Our intention is to work with the officials and the farmers in Yunnan province to bring Chinese coffee not (only) to China, but Chinese coffee to the world," Martin Coles, president of Starbucks Coffee International, told the Associated Press. "Ultimately I'd love to see our coffees from China featured on the shelves of every one of our stores in 49 countries around the world," he said. A launch date for foreign distribution hasn't been announced and will depend on how soon farmers can grow enough beans to ensure local and overseas supply.

The company has been working for three years with farmers and officials in the province before the launch, and the coffee will initially combine Arabica beans from Latin America and the Asia-Pacific with local Yunnan beans. But Coles said they hope to develop a source of superpremium Arabica coffee from the province, expanding it to new brand offerings in China, and then internationally. The new blend will be called "South of the Clouds," the meaning of Yunnan in Chinese.[5]

Questions

1. Explain why the supply chain can dramatically impact a company's base performance.

2. List all of the products that could possibly be affected by a problem in the U.S. milk supply chain.

3. How can a CRM system help communicate issues in the supply chain?

4. How could BPR help uncover issues in a company's supply chain?

5. What are the pros and cons for Starbucks of outsourcing the growing of its coffee beans to Chinese farmers?

Measuring the Success of Strategic Initiatives

4.1. Define critical success factors (CSFs) and key performance indicators (KPIs), and explain how managers use them to measure the success of MIS projects.

4.2. Explain why a business would use metrics to measure the success of strategic initiatives.

Metrics: Measuring Success

A *project* is a temporary activity a company undertakes to create a unique product, service, or result. For example, the construction of a new subway station is a project, as is a movie theater chain's adoption of a software program to allow online ticketing. Peter Drucker, a famous management writer, once said that if you cannot measure something, you cannot manage it. How do managers measure the progress of a complex business project?

Metrics are measurements that evaluate results to determine whether a project is meeting its goals. Two core metrics are critical success factors and key performance indicators. *Critical success factors (CSFs)* are the crucial steps companies perform to achieve their goals and objectives and implement their strategies (see Figure 4.1). *Key performance indicators (KPIs)* are the quantifiable metrics a company uses to evaluate progress toward critical success factors. KPIs are far more specific than CSFs.

It is important to understand the relationship between critical success factors and key performance indicators. CSFs are elements crucial for a business strategy's success. KPIs measure the progress of CSFs with quantifiable measurements, and one CSF can have several KPIs. Of course, both categories will vary by company and industry. Imagine *improve graduation rates* as a CSF for a college. The KPIs to measure this CSF can include:

- Average grades by course and gender.
- Student dropout rates by gender and major.
- Average graduation rate by gender and major.
- Time spent in tutoring by gender and major.

KPIs can focus on external and internal measurements. A common external KPI is *market share*, or the proportion of the market that a firm captures. We calculate it by dividing the firm's sales by the total market sales for the entire industry. Market share measures a firm's external performance relative to that of its competitors. For example, if a firm's total sales (revenues) are $2 million and sales for the entire industry are $10 million, the firm has captured 20 percent of the total market (2/10 = 20%) or a 20 percent market share.

A common internal KPI is *return on investment (ROI)*, which indicates the earning power of a project. We measure it by dividing the profitability of a project by the costs. This sounds easy, and for many departments where the projects are tangible and

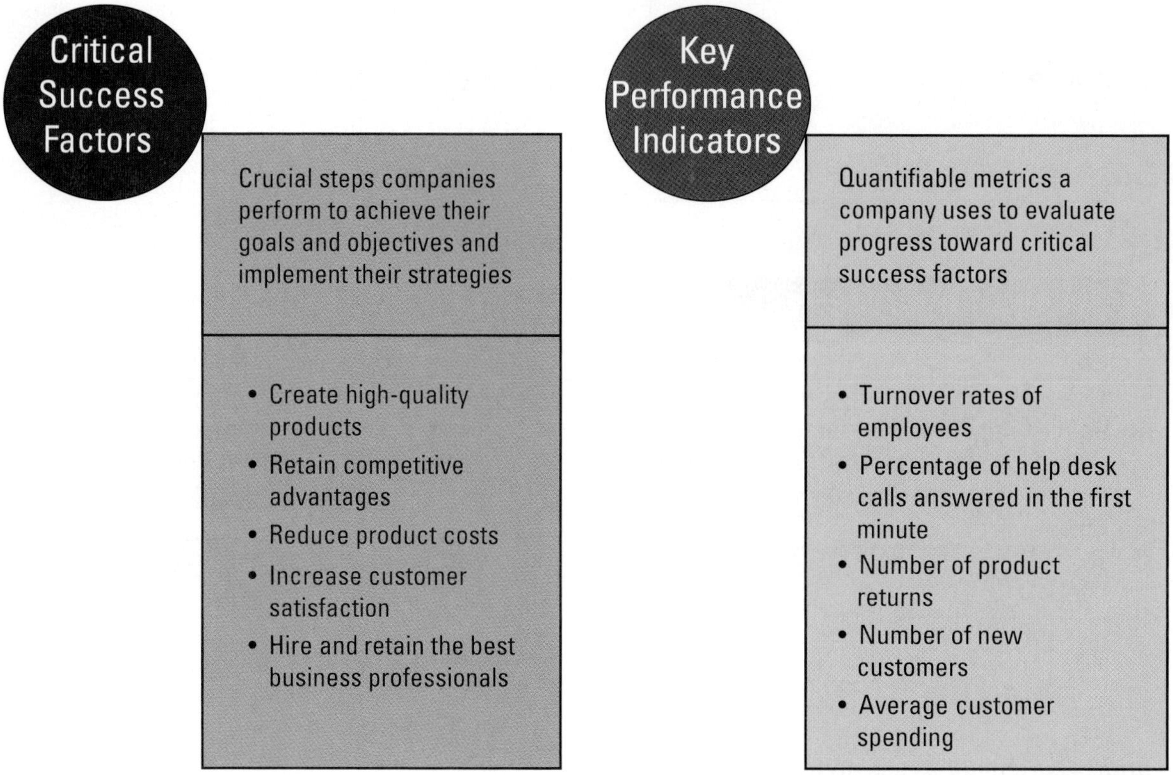

Critical Success Factors

Crucial steps companies perform to achieve their goals and objectives and implement their strategies

- Create high-quality products
- Retain competitive advantages
- Reduce product costs
- Increase customer satisfaction
- Hire and retain the best business professionals

Key Performance Indicators

Quantifiable metrics a company uses to evaluate progress toward critical success factors

- Turnover rates of employees
- Percentage of help desk calls answered in the first minute
- Number of product returns
- Number of new customers
- Average customer spending

FIGURE 4.1

CSF and KPI Metrics

self-contained it is; however, for projects that are intangible and cross departmental lines (such as MIS projects), ROI is challenging to measure. Imagine attempting to calculate the ROI of a fire extinguisher. If the fire extinguisher is never used, its ROI is low. If the fire extinguisher puts out a fire that could have destroyed the entire building, its ROI is astronomically high.

Creating KPIs to measure the success of an MIS project offers similar challenges. Think about a firm's email system. How could managers track departmental costs and profits associated with company email? Measuring by volume does not account for profitability, because one sales email could land a million-dollar deal while 300 others might not generate any revenue. Non-revenue-generating departments such as human resources and legal require email but will not be using it to generate profits. For this reason, many managers turn to higher-level metrics, such as efficiency and effectiveness, to measure MIS projects. *Best practices* are the most successful solutions or problem-solving methods that have been developed by a specific organization or industry. Measuring MIS projects helps determine the best practices for an industry.

EFFICIENCY AND EFFECTIVENESS METRICS

Efficiency MIS metrics measure the performance of MIS itself, such as throughput, transaction speed, and system availability. *Effectiveness MIS metrics* measure the impact MIS has on business processes and activities, including customer satisfaction and customer conversion rates. Efficiency focuses on the extent to which a firm is using its resources in an optimal way, while effectiveness focuses on how well a firm is achieving its goals and objectives. Peter Drucker offers a helpful distinction between efficiency and effectiveness: Doing things right addresses efficiency—getting the most from each resource. Doing the right things addresses effectiveness—setting the right goals and objectives and ensuring they are accomplished. Figure 4.2 describes a few of the common types of efficiency and effectiveness MIS metrics. KPIs that measure MIS

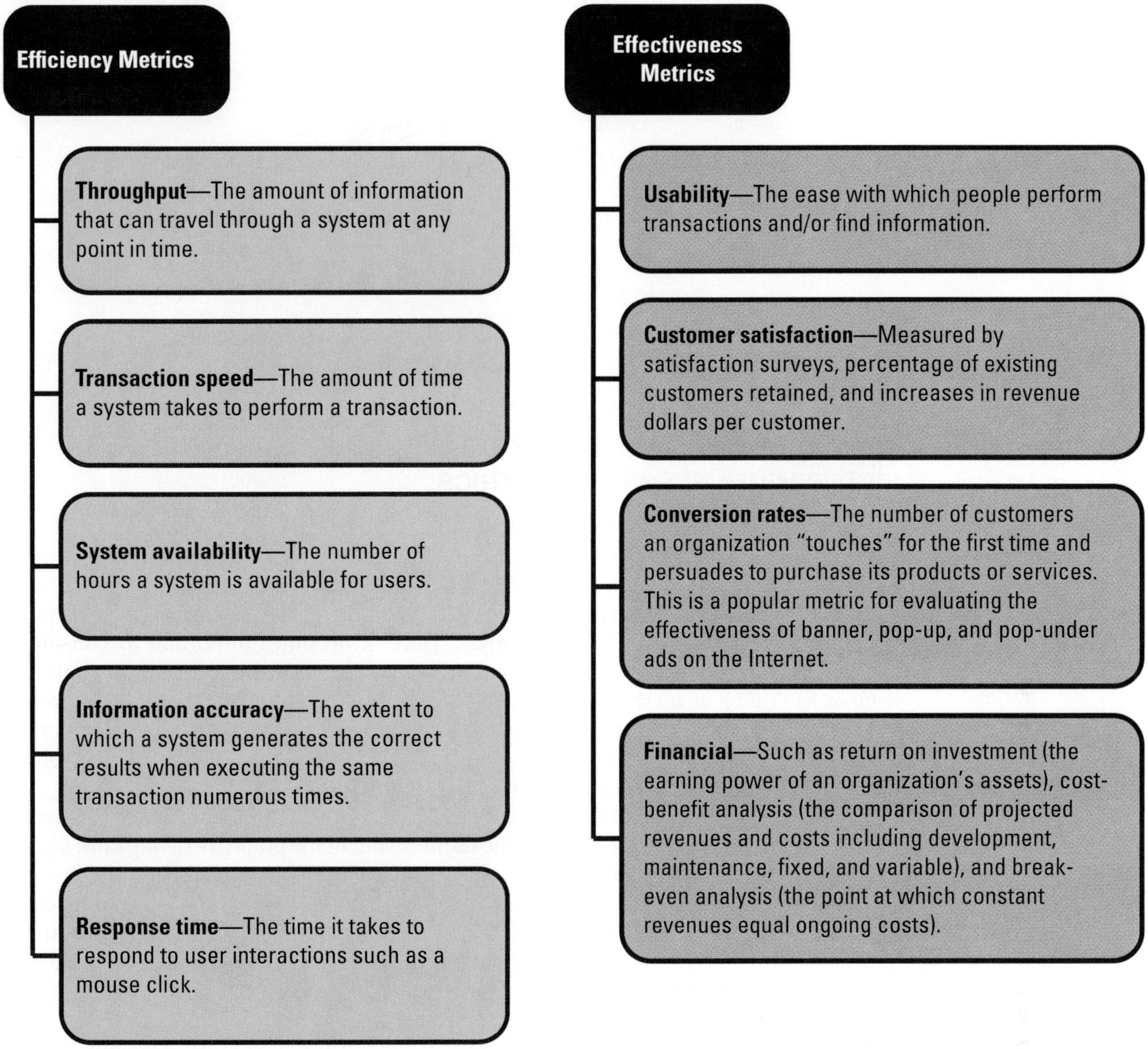

Efficiency Metrics

Throughput—The amount of information that can travel through a system at any point in time.

Transaction speed—The amount of time a system takes to perform a transaction.

System availability—The number of hours a system is available for users.

Information accuracy—The extent to which a system generates the correct results when executing the same transaction numerous times.

Response time—The time it takes to respond to user interactions such as a mouse click.

Effectiveness Metrics

Usability—The ease with which people perform transactions and/or find information.

Customer satisfaction—Measured by satisfaction surveys, percentage of existing customers retained, and increases in revenue dollars per customer.

Conversion rates—The number of customers an organization "touches" for the first time and persuades to purchase its products or services. This is a popular metric for evaluating the effectiveness of banner, pop-up, and pop-under ads on the Internet.

Financial—Such as return on investment (the earning power of an organization's assets), cost-benefit analysis (the comparison of projected revenues and costs including development, maintenance, fixed, and variable), and break-even analysis (the point at which constant revenues equal ongoing costs).

FIGURE 4.2

Common Types of Efficiency and Effectiveness Metrics

projects include both efficiency and effectiveness metrics. Of course, these metrics are not as concrete as market share or ROI, but they do offer valuable insight into project performance.[1]

Large increases in productivity typically result from increases in effectiveness, which focus on CSFs. Efficiency MIS metrics are far easier to measure, however, so most managers tend to focus on them, often incorrectly, to measure the success of MIS projects. Consider measuring the success of automated teller machines (ATMs). Thinking in terms of MIS efficiency metrics, a manager would measure the number of daily transactions, the average amount per transaction, and the average speed per transaction to determine the success of the ATM. Although these offer solid metrics on how well the system is performing, they miss many of the intangible or value-added benefits associated with ATM effectiveness. Effectiveness MIS metrics might measure how many new customers joined the bank due to its ATM locations or the ATMs' ease of use. They can also measure increases in customer satisfaction due to reduced ATM fees or additional ATM services such as the sale of stamps and movie tickets, significant time savers and value-added features for customers. Being a great manager means taking the added viewpoint offered by effectiveness MIS metrics to analyze all benefits associated with an MIS project.

FIGURE 4.3

The Interrelationships
between Efficiency and
Effectiveness

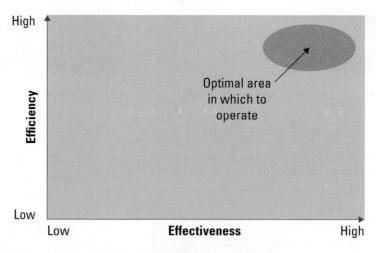

THE INTERRELATIONSHIP BETWEEN EFFICIENCY AND EFFECTIVENESS MIS METRICS

Efficiency and effectiveness are definitely related. However, success in one area does not necessarily imply success in the other. Efficiency MIS metrics focus on the technology itself. While these efficiency MIS metrics are important to monitor, they do not always guarantee effectiveness. Effectiveness MIS metrics are determined according to an organization's goals, strategies, and objectives. Here, it becomes important to consider a company's CSFs, such as a broad cost leadership strategy (Walmart, for example), as well as KPIs such as increasing new customers by 10 percent or reducing new-product development cycle times to six months. In the private sector, eBay continuously benchmarks its MIS projects for efficiency and effectiveness. Maintaining constant website availability and optimal throughput performance are CSFs for eBay.

Figure 4.3 depicts the interrelationships between efficiency and effectiveness. Ideally, a firm wants to operate in the upper right-hand corner of the graph, realizing both significant increases in efficiency and effectiveness. However, operating in the upper left-hand corner (minimal effectiveness with increased efficiency) or the lower right-hand corner (significant effectiveness with minimal efficiency) may be in line with an organization's particular strategies. In general, operating in the lower left-hand corner (minimal efficiency and minimal effectiveness) is not ideal for the operation of any organization.

Benchmarks

Regardless of what process is measured, how it is measured, and whether it is performed for the sake of efficiency or effectiveness, managers must set **benchmarks**, or baseline values the system seeks to attain. **Benchmarking** is a process of continuously measuring system results, comparing those results to optimal system performance (benchmark values), and identifying steps and procedures to improve system performance. Benchmarks help assess how an MIS project performs over time. For instance, if a system held a benchmark for response time of 15 seconds, the manager would want to ensure response time continued to decrease until it reached that point. If response time suddenly increased to 1 minute, the manager would know the system was not functioning correctly and could start looking into potential problems. Continuously measuring MIS projects against benchmarks provides feedback so managers can control the system.

LO 4.2 Explain why a business would use metrics to measure the success of strategic initiatives.

Metrics for Strategic Initiatives

What is a metric? A metric is nothing more than a standard measure to assess performance in a particular area. Metrics are at the heart of a good, customer-focused management system and any program directed at continuous improvement. A focus on customers and performance standards shows up in the form of metrics that assess the ability to meet customers' needs and business objectives.

Business leaders want to monitor key metrics in real time to actively track the health of their business. Most business professionals are familiar with financial metrics. Different financial ratios are used to evaluate a company's performance. Companies can gain additional insight into their performance by comparing financial ratios against other companies in their industry. A few of the more common financial ratios include:

- Internal rate of return (IRR)—the rate at which the net present value of an investment equals zero.

- Return on investment (ROI)—indicates the earning power of a project and is measured by dividing the benefits of a project by the investment.

- Payback method—number of years to recoup the cost of an initiative based on projected annual net cash flow.

- Break-even analysis—determines the volume of business required to make a profit at the current prices charged for the products or services. For example, if a promotional mailing costs $1,000 and each item generates $50 in revenue, the company must generate 20 sales to break even and cover the cost of the mailing. The break-even point is the point at which revenues equal costs. The point is located by performing a break-even analysis. All sales over the break-even point produce profits; any drop in sales below that point will produce losses (see Figure 4.4).

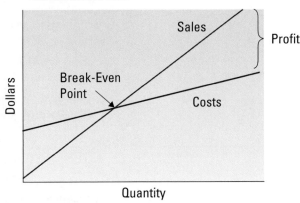

FIGURE 4.4

Break-Even Analysis

Most managers are familiar with financial metrics but unfamiliar with information system metrics. The following metrics will help managers measure and manage their strategic initiatives:

- Website metrics.
- Supply chain management (SCM) metrics.
- Customer relationship management (CRM) metrics.
- Business process reengineering (BPR) metrics.
- Enterprise resource planning (ERP) metrics.

WEBSITE METRICS

Most companies measure the traffic on a website as the primary determinant of the website's success. However, heavy website traffic does not necessarily indicate large sales. Many organizations with lots of website traffic have minimal sales. A company can use web traffic analysis or web analytics to determine the revenue generated, the number of new customers acquired, any reductions in customer service calls, and so on. The Yankee Group reports that 66 percent of companies determine website success solely by measuring the amount of traffic. New customer acquisition ranked second on the list at 34 percent, and revenue generation ranked third at 23 percent. Figure 4.5 displays a few metrics managers should be familiar with to help measure website success along with an organization's strategic initiatives. A web-centric metric is a measure of the success of web and ebusiness initiatives. Of the hundreds of web-centric metrics available, some are general to almost any web or ebusiness initiative and others are dependent on the particular initiative.[2]

SUPPLY CHAIN MANAGEMENT (SCM) METRICS

Supply chain management metrics can help an organization understand how it's operating over a given time period. Supply chain measurements can cover many areas including procurement, production, distribution, warehousing, inventory, transportation, and customer service. However, a good performance in one part of the supply

FIGURE 4.5

Website Metrics

Website Metrics

- **Abandoned registrations:** Number of visitors who start the process of completing a registration page and then abandon the activity.

- **Abandoned shopping carts:** Number of visitors who create a shopping cart and start shopping and then abandon the activity before paying for the merchandise.

- **Click-through:** Count of the number of people who visit a site, click on an ad, and are taken to the site of the advertiser.

- **Conversion rate:** Percentage of potential customers who visit a site and actually buy something.

- **Cost-per-thousand (CPM):** Sales dollars generated per dollar of advertising. This is commonly used to make the case for spending money to appear on a search engine.

- **Page exposures:** Average number of page exposures to an individual visitor.

- **Total hits:** Number of visits to a website, many of which may be by the same visitor.

- **Unique visitors:** Number of unique visitors to a site in a given time. This is commonly used by Nielsen/Net ratings to rank the most popular websites.

chain is not sufficient. A supply chain is only as strong as its weakest link. The solution is to measure all key areas of the supply chain. Figure 4.6 displays common supply chain management metrics.[3]

CUSTOMER RELATIONSHIP MANAGEMENT (CRM) METRICS

Wondering what CRM metrics to track and monitor using reporting and real-time performance dashboards? Best practice is no more than seven (plus or minus two) metrics out of the hundreds possible should be used at any given management level. Figure 4.7 displays common CRM metrics tracked by organizations.[4]

BUSINESS PROCESS REENGINEERING (BPR) AND ENTERPRISE RESOURCE PLANNING (ERP) METRICS

Business process reengineering and enterprise resource planning are large, organizationwide initiatives. Measuring these types of strategic initiatives is extremely difficult. One of the best methods is the balanced scorecard. This approach to strategic management was developed in the early 1990s by Drs. Robert Kaplan of the Harvard Business School and David Norton. Addressing some of the weaknesses and vagueness of previous measurement techniques, the balanced scorecard approach provides a clear prescription as to what companies should measure in order to balance the financial perspective.

FIGURE 4.6

Supply Chain Management Metrics

Supply Chain Management Metrics

- **Back order:** An unfilled customer order. A back order is demand (immediate or past due) against an item whose current stock level is insufficient to satisfy demand.

- **Customer order promised cycle time:** The anticipated or agreed upon cycle time of a purchase order. It is a gap between the purchase order creation date and the requested delivery date.

- **Customer order actual cycle time:** The average time it takes to actually fill a customer's purchase order. This measure can be viewed on an order or an order line level.

- **Inventory replenishment cycle time:** Measure of the manufacturing cycle time plus the time included to deploy the product to the appropriate distribution center.

- **Inventory turns (inventory turnover):** The number of times that a company's inventory cycles or turns over per year. It is one of the most commonly used supply chain metrics.

FIGURE 4.7

CRM Metrics

Sales Metrics	Service Metrics	Marketing Metrics
■ Number of prospective customers	■ Cases closed same day	■ Number of marketing campaigns
■ Number of new customers	■ Number of cases handled by agent	■ New customer retention rates
■ Number of retained customers	■ Number of service calls	■ Number of responses by marketing campaign
■ Number of open leads	■ Average number of service requests by type	■ Number of purchases by marketing campaign
■ Number of sales calls	■ Average time to resolution	■ Revenue generated by marketing campaign
■ Number of sales calls per lead	■ Average number of service calls per day	■ Cost per interaction by marketing campaign
■ Amount of new revenue	■ Percentage compliance with service-level agreement	■ Number of new customers acquired by marketing campaign
■ Amount of recurring revenue	■ Percentage of service renewals	■ Customer retention rate
■ Number of proposals given	■ Customer satisfaction level	■ Number of new leads by product

The ***balanced scorecard*** is a management system, in addition to a measurement system, that enables organizations to clarify their vision and strategy and translate them into action. It provides feedback around both the internal business processes and external outcomes in order to continuously improve strategic performance and results. When fully deployed, the balanced scorecard transforms strategic planning from an academic exercise into the nerve center of an enterprise. Kaplan and Norton describe the innovation of the balanced scorecard as follows:

> The balanced scorecard retains traditional financial measures. But financial measures tell the story of past events, an adequate story for industrial age companies for which investments in long-term capabilities and customer relationships were not critical for success. These financial measures are inadequate, however, for guiding and evaluating the journey that information age companies must make to create future value through investment in customers, suppliers, employees, processes, technology, and innovation.[5]

The balanced scorecard views the organization from four perspectives, and users should develop metrics, collect data, and analyze their business relative to each of these perspectives:

■ The learning and growth perspective.
■ The internal business process perspective.
■ The customer perspective.
■ The financial perspective (see Figure 4.8).

Recall that companies cannot manage what they cannot measure. Therefore, metrics must be developed based on the priorities of the strategic plan, which provides the key business drivers and criteria for metrics that managers most desire to watch.

One warning regarding metrics—do not go crazy. The trick is to find a few key metrics to track that provide significant insight. Remember to tie metrics to other financial and business objectives in the firm. The key is to get good insight without becoming a slave to metrics. The rule of thumb is to develop seven key metrics, plus or minus two.

FIGURE 4.8

The Four Primary
Perspectives of the
Balanced Scorecard

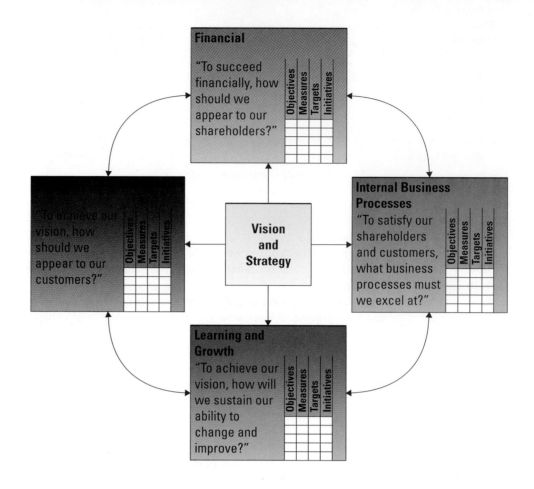

OPENING CASE STUDY QUESTIONS

1. Formulate a strategy describing how Apple can use efficiency MIS metrics to improve its business.

2. Formulate a strategy describing how Apple can use effectiveness MIS metrics to improve its business.

3. List three CRM metrics Apple should track, along with the reasons these metrics will add value to Apple's business strategy.

4. List three SCM metrics Apple should track, along with the reasons these metrics will add value to Apple's business strategy.

5. How can Apple use the balanced scorecard to make its business more efficient?

Chapter Four Case: Manipulating the Data to Find Your Version of the Truth

How can global warming be real when there is so much snow and cold weather? That's what some people wondered after a couple of massive snowstorms buried Washington, DC, in the winter of 2009–2010. Politicians across the capital made jokes and built igloos as they disputed the existence of climate change. Some concluded the planet simply could not be warming with all the snow on the ground.

These comments frustrated Joseph Romm, a physicist and climate expert with the Center for American Progress. He spent weeks turning data into information and graphs to educate anyone who would listen as to why this reasoning was incorrect. Climate change is all about analyzing data, turning it into information to detect trends. You cannot observe climate change by looking out the window; you have to review decades of weather data with advanced tools to really understand the trends.

Increasingly we see politicians, economists, and newscasters taking tough issues and boiling them down to simplistic arguments over what the data mean, each interpreting the data and spinning the data to support their views and agendas. You need to understand the data and turn them into useful information or else you will not understand when someone is telling the truth and when you are being lied to.

Brainstorm two or three types of data economists use to measure the economy.[6]

Questions

1. How do they turn the data into information?

2. What issues do they encounter when attempting to measure the economy?

3. As a manager, what do you need to understand when reading or listening to economic and business reports?

Organizational Structures That Support Strategic Initiatives

5.1. Define the primary IT roles along with their associated responsibilities.

5.2. Explain the gap between IT and business professionals.

5.3. Explain why ethics and security are fundamental building blocks of business today.

LO 5.1 Define the primary IT roles along with their associated responsibilities.

Structures

Employees across the organization must work closely together to develop strategic initiatives that create competitive advantages. Understanding the basic structure of a typical IT department including titles, roles, and responsibilities will help an organization build a cohesive enterprisewide team.

IT Roles and Responsibilities

Information technology is a relatively new functional area, having been around formally in most organizations only for about 40 years. Job titles, roles, and responsibilities often differ dramatically from organization to organization. Nonetheless, clear trends are developing toward elevating some IT positions within an organization to the strategic level.

Most organizations maintain positions such as chief executive officer (CEO), chief financial officer (CFO), and chief operations officer (COO) at the strategic level. Recently there are more IT-related strategic positions such as chief information officer (CIO), chief technology officer (CTO), chief security officer (CSO), chief privacy officer (CPO), and chief knowledge officer (CKO). See Figure 5.1.

J. Greg Hanson is proud to be the first CIO of the U.S. Senate. Contrary to some perceptions, the technology found in the Senate is quite good, according to Hanson. Hanson's responsibilities include creating the Senate's technology vision, leading the IT department, and deploying the IT infrastructure. Hanson must work with everyone from the 137 network administrators to the senators themselves to ensure that everything is operating smoothly. Hanson is excited to be the first CIO of the U.S. Senate and proud of the honor and responsibility that come with the job.[1]

The ***chief information officer (CIO)*** is responsible for (1) overseeing all uses of information technology and (2) ensuring the strategic alignment of IT with business goals and objectives. The CIO often reports directly to the CEO. (See Figure 5.2 for the average CIO compensation.) CIOs must possess a solid and detailed understanding of every aspect of an organization coupled with tremendous insight into the capability of IT. Broad functions of a CIO include:

1. *Manager*—ensure the delivery of all IT projects, on time and within budget.

2. *Leader*—ensure the strategic vision of IT is in line with the strategic vision of the organization.

Chief security officer (CSO)

Responsible for ensuring the security of business systems and developing strategies and safeguards against attacks by hackers and viruses.

Chief knowledge officer (CKO)

Responsible for collecting, maintaining, and distributing company knowledge.

MIS Department Roles and Responsibilities

Chief technology officer (CTO)

Responsible for ensuring the speed, accuracy, availability, and reliability of the MIS.

Chief information officer (CIO)

Responsible for (1) overseeing all uses of MIS and (2) ensuring that MIS strategically aligns with business goals and objectives.

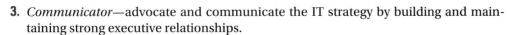

Chief privacy officer (CPO)

Responsible for ensuring the ethical and legal use of information within a company.

FIGURE 5.1

The Roles and Responsibilities of MIS

3. *Communicator*—advocate and communicate the IT strategy by building and maintaining strong executive relationships.

Although CIO is considered a position within IT, CIOs must be concerned with more than just IT. According to a recent survey (see Figure 5.3), most CIOs ranked "enhancing customer satisfaction" ahead of their concerns for any specific aspect of IT. CIOs with the broad business view that customer satisfaction is more crucial and critical than specific aspects of IT should be applauded.

The *chief technology officer (CTO)* is responsible for ensuring the throughput, speed, accuracy, availability, and reliability of an organization's information technology. CTOs are similar to CIOs, except that CIOs take on the additional responsibility for effectiveness of ensuring that IT is aligned with the organization's strategic initiatives. CTOs have direct responsibility for ensuring the *efficiency* of IT systems throughout the organization. Most CTOs possess well-rounded knowledge of all aspects of IT, including hardware, software, and telecommunications.

The *chief security officer (CSO)* is responsible for ensuring the security of IT systems and developing strategies and IT safeguards against attacks from hackers and viruses. The role of a CSO has been elevated in recent years because of the number of attacks from hackers and viruses. Most CSOs possess detailed knowledge of networks and telecommunications because hackers and viruses usually find their way into IT systems through networked computers.

FIGURE 5.2

Average CIO Compensation by Industry

Industry	Average CIO Compensation
Wholesale/Retail/Distribution	$243,304
Finance	$210,547
Insurance	$197,697
Manufacturing	$190,250
Medical/Dental/Health Care	$171,032
Government	$118,359
Education	$ 93,750

Percentage	CIOs' Concerns
94%	Enhancing customer satisfaction
92	Security
89	Technology evaluation
87	Budgeting
83	Staffing
66	ROI analysis
64	Building new applications
45	Outsourcing hosting

FIGURE 5.3

What Concerns CIOs the Most?

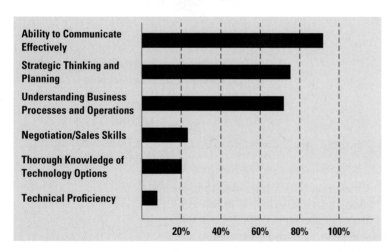

FIGURE 5.4

Skills Pivotal for Success in Executive IT Roles

The ***chief privacy officer (CPO)*** is responsible for ensuring the ethical and legal use of information within an organization. CPOs are the newest senior executive position in IT. Recently, 150 of the *Fortune* 500 companies added the CPO position to their list of senior executives. Many CPOs are lawyers by training, enabling them to understand the often complex legal issues surrounding the use of information.[2]

The ***chief knowledge officer (CKO)*** is responsible for collecting, maintaining, and distributing the organization's knowledge. The CKO designs programs and systems that make it easy for people to reuse knowledge. These systems create repositories of organizational documents, methodologies, tools, and practices, and they establish methods for filtering the information. The CKO must continuously encourage employee contributions to keep the systems up-to-date. The CKO can contribute directly to the organization's bottom line by reducing the learning curve for new employees or employees taking on new roles.

Danny Shaw was the first CKO at Children's Hospital in Boston. His initial task was to unite information from disparate systems to enable analysis of both the efficiency and effectiveness of the hospital's care. Shaw started by building a series of small, integrated information systems that quickly demonstrated value. He then gradually built on those successes, creating a knowledge-enabled organization one layer at a time. Shaw's information systems have enabled administrative and clinical operational analyses.[3]

With the election of President Barack Obama comes the appointment of the first-ever national chief technology officer (CTO). The job description, as listed on Change.gov, states that the first CTO must "ensure the safety of our networks and lead an interagency effort, working with chief technology and chief information officers of each of the federal agencies, to ensure that they use best-in-class technologies and share best practices." A federal level CTO demonstrates the ongoing growth of technology positions outside corporate America. In the future expect to see many more technology positions in government and nonprofit organizations.

All the above IT positions and responsibilities are critical to an organization's success. While many organizations may not have a different individual for each of these positions, they must have leaders taking responsibility for all these areas of concern. The individuals responsible for enterprisewide IT and IT-related issues must provide guidance and support to the organization's employees. Figure 5.4 displays the personal skills pivotal for success in an executive IT role.[4]

The Gap between Business Personnel and IT Personnel

LO 5.2 Explain the gap between IT and business professionals.

One of the greatest challenges today is effective communication between business personnel and IT personnel. Business personnel possess expertise in functional areas such as marketing, accounting, sales, and so forth. IT personnel have the technological expertise. Unfortunately, a communications gap often exists between the two. Business personnel have their own vocabularies based on their experience and expertise. IT personnel have their own vocabularies consisting of acronyms and technical terms. Effective communication between business and IT personnel should be a two-way street with each side making the effort to better understand the other (including through written and oral communication).

IMPROVING COMMUNICATIONS

Business personnel must seek to increase their understanding of IT. Although they do not need to know every technical detail, it will benefit their careers to understand what they can and cannot accomplish using IT. Business managers and leaders should read business-oriented IT magazines, such as *InformationWeek* and *CIO,* to increase their IT knowledge.

At the same time, an organization must develop strategies for integrating its IT personnel into the various business functions. Too often, IT personnel are left out of strategy meetings because of the belief they do not understand the business so they will not add any value. That is a dangerous position to take. IT personnel must understand the business if the organization is going to determine which technologies can benefit (or hurt) the business. With a little effort to communicate, IT personnel, by providing information on the functionality available in CRM systems, might add tremendous value to a meeting about how to improve customer service. Working together, business and IT personnel have the potential to create customer-service competitive advantages.

It is the responsibility of the CIO to ensure effective communications between business and IT personnel. While the CIO assumes the responsibility on an enterprisewide level, it is also each employee's responsibility to communicate effectively on a personal level.

Organizational Fundamentals— Ethics and Security

LO 5.3 Explain why ethics and security are fundamental building blocks of business today.

Ethics and security are two fundamental building blocks that organizations must base their businesses on. Such events as the Enron and Bernie Madoff scandals along with 9/11 have shed new light on the meaning of ethics and security. When the behavior of a few individuals can destroy billion-dollar organizations because of a lapse in ethics or security, the value of highly ethical and highly secure organizations should be evident. Review the Ethics and Security plug-ins to gain a detailed understanding of these topics. Due to the importance of these topics, they will be readdressed throughout this text.

Ethics

Ian Clarke, the inventor of a file-swapping service called Freenet, decided to leave the United States for the United Kingdom, where copyright laws are more lenient. Wayne Rosso, the inventor of a file-sharing service called Grokster, left the United States for Spain, again saying goodbye to tough U.S. copyright protections. File sharing encourages a legal network of shared thinking that can improve drug research, software development, and flow of information. The United States copyright laws, designed decades before the Internet was invented, make file sharing and many other Internet technologies illegal.[5]

The ethical issues surrounding copyright infringement and intellectual property rights are consuming the ebusiness world. Advances in technology make it easier and easier for people to copy everything from music to pictures. Technology poses new challenges for our *ethics*—the principles and standards that guide our behavior toward other people. Review Figure 5.5 for an overview of concepts, terms, and ethical issues stemming from advances in technology.

In today's electronic world, privacy has become a major ethical issue. *Privacy* is the right to be left alone when you want to be, to have control over your own personal possessions, and to not be observed without your consent. Some of the most problematic decisions organizations face lie in the murky and turbulent waters of privacy. The burden comes from the knowledge that each time employees make a decision regarding issues of privacy, the outcome could sink the company some day.

Privacy is one of the biggest ethical issues facing organizations today. Trust between companies, customers, partners, and suppliers is the support structure of the ebusiness world. One of the main ingredients in trust is privacy. Widespread fear about privacy continues to be one of the biggest barriers to the growth of ebusiness. People are concerned

FIGURE 5.5

Issues Affected by
Technology Advances

Intellectual property	Intangible creative work that is embodied in physical form.
Copyright	The legal protection afforded an expression of an idea, such as a song, video game, and some types of proprietary documents.
Fair use doctrine	In certain situations, it is legal to use copyrighted material.
Pirated software	The unauthorized use, duplication, distribution, or sale of copyrighted software.
Counterfeit software	Software that is manufactured to look like the real thing and sold as such.

FIGURE 5.6

Primary Reasons Privacy
Issues Reduce Trust for
Business

1.	Loss of personal privacy is a top concern for Americans in the 21st century.
2.	Among Internet users, 37 percent would be "a lot" more inclined to purchase a product on a website that had a privacy policy.
3.	Privacy/security is the number one factor that would convert Internet researchers into Internet buyers.

their privacy will be violated as a consequence of interactions on the web. Unless an organization can effectively address this issue of privacy, its customers, partners, and suppliers may lose trust in the organization, which hurts its business. Figure 5.6 displays the results from a *CIO* survey as to how privacy issues reduce trust for business.[6]

Security—How Much Will Downtime Cost Your Business?

The old business axiom "time is money" needs to be updated to more accurately reflect the crucial interdependence between IT and business processes. To reflect the times, the phrase should be "uptime is money." The leading cause of downtime is a software failure followed by human error, according to Infonetics research. Unplanned downtime can strike at any time from any number of causes, ranging from tornadoes to sink overflows to network failures to power outages. Although natural disasters may appear to be the most devastating causes of IT outages, they are hardly the most frequent or biggest threats to uptime. Figure 5.7 highlights sources of unplanned downtime.[7]

According to Gartner Group, on average, enterprises lose $108,000 of revenue every hour their IT infrastructure is down. Figure 5.8 displays the four categories of costs associated with downtime, according to the Gartner Group. A few questions companies should ask when determining the cost of downtime include:

- How many transactions can the company afford to lose without significantly impacting business?
- Does the company depend upon one or more mission-critical applications to conduct business?
- How much revenue will the company lose for every hour a critical application is unavailable?
- What is the productivity cost associated with each hour of downtime?
- How will collaborative business processes with partners, suppliers, and customers be affected by an unexpected IT outage?
- What is the total cost of lost productivity and lost revenue during unplanned downtime?[8]

Sources of Unplanned Downtime		
Bomb threat	Hacker	Snowstorm
Burst pipe	Hail	Sprinkler malfunction
Chemical spill	Hurricane	Static electricity
Construction	Ice storm	Strike
Corrupted data	Insects	Terrorism
Earthquake	Lightning	Theft
Electrical short	Network failure	Tornado
Epidemic	Plane crash	Train derailment
Equipment failure	Frozen pipe	Smoke damage
Evacuation	Power outage	Vandalism
Explosion	Power surge	Vehicle crash
Fire	Rodents	Virus
Flood	Sabotage	Water damage (various)
Fraud	Shredded data	Wind

FIGURE 5.7

Sources of Unplanned Downtime

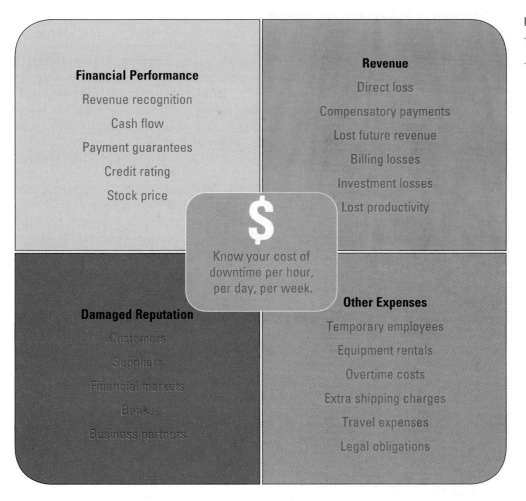

FIGURE 5.8

The Cost of Downtime

Financial Performance

Revenue recognition
Cash flow
Payment guarantees
Credit rating
Stock price

Revenue

Direct loss
Compensatory payments
Lost future revenue
Billing losses
Investment losses
Lost productivity

$
Know your cost of downtime per hour, per day, per week.

Damaged Reputation

Customers
Suppliers
Financial markets
Banks
Business partners

Other Expenses

Temporary employees
Equipment rentals
Overtime costs
Extra shipping charges
Travel expenses
Legal obligations

The reliability and resilience of IT systems have never been more essential for success as businesses cope with the forces of globalization, 24/7 operations, government and trade regulations, and overextended IT budgets and resources. Any unexpected IT downtime in today's business environment has the potential to cause both short- and long-term costs with far-reaching consequences. Understanding information security's role in a business is critical to keeping downtime to a minimum and uptime to a maximum.

PROTECTING INTELLECTUAL ASSETS

Smoking is not just bad for a person's health; it seems that it is also bad for company security, according to a new study. With companies banning smoking inside their offices, smokers are forced outside—usually to specific smoking areas in the back of the building. The doors leading out to them are a major security hole, according to a study undertaken by NTA Monitor Ltd., a U.K.-based Internet security tester.

NTA's tester was able to easily get inside a corporate building through a back door that was left open so smokers could easily and quickly get out and then back in, according to the company. Once inside, the tester asked an employee to take him to a meeting room, claiming that the IT department had sent him. Even without a pass, he reportedly gained access unchallenged and was then able to connect his laptop to the company's network.[9]

Organizational information is intellectual capital. Just as organizations protect their assets—keeping their money in an insured bank or providing a safe working environment for employees—they must also protect their intellectual capital. An organization's intellectual capital includes everything from its patents to its transactional and analytical information. With security breaches on the rise and computer hackers everywhere, an organization must put in place strong security measures to survive.

The Health Insurance Portability and Accountability Act (HIPAA) protects the privacy and security of personal health records and has the potential to impact every business in the United States. HIPAA affects all companies that use electronic data interchange (EDI) to communicate personal health records. HIPAA requires health care organizations to develop, implement, and maintain appropriate security measures when sending electronic health information. Most important, these organizations must document and keep current records detailing how they are performing security measures for all transmissions of health information. On April 21, 2005, security rules for HIPAA became enforceable by law.

Beyond the health care industry, all businesses must understand the importance of information security, even if it is not enforceable by law. *Information security* is a broad term encompassing the protection of information from accidental or intentional misuse by persons inside or outside an organization. With current advances in technologies and business strategies such as CRM, organizations are able to determine valuable information—such as who are the top 20 percent of their customers who produce 80 percent of their revenues. Most organizations view this type of information as valuable intellectual capital, and they are implementing security measures to prevent the information from walking out the door or falling into the wrong hands.

Adding to the complexity of information security is the fact that organizations must enable employees, customers, and partners to access all sorts of information electronically to be successful. Doing business electronically automatically creates tremendous information security risks for organizations. There are many technical aspects of security, but the biggest information security issue is not technical, but human. Most information security breaches result from people misusing an organization's information either intentionally or inadvertently. For example, many individuals freely give up their passwords or leave them on sticky notes next to their computers, leaving the door wide open to intruders.

Figure 5.9 displays the typical size of an organization's information security budget relative to the organization's overall IT budget from the CSI/FBI Computer Crime and Security Survey. Forty-six percent of respondents indicated that their organization spent

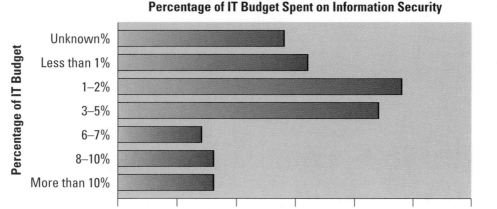

Percentage of IT Budget Spent on Information Security

(Vertical axis — Percentage of IT Budget)
- Unknown%
- Less than 1%
- 1–2%
- 3–5%
- 6–7%
- 8–10%
- More than 10%

(Horizontal axis — Percentage of Respondents: 0%, 5%, 10%, 15%, 20%, 25%, 30%)

FIGURE 5.9

Organizational Spending on Information Security

between 1 and 5 percent of the total IT budget on security. Only 16 percent indicated that their organization spent less than 1 percent of the IT budget on security.[10]

Figure 5.10 displays the spending per employee on computer security broken down by both public and private industries. The highest average computer security investment per employee was found in the transportation industry.[11]

Security is perhaps the most fundamental and critical of all the technologies/disciplines an organization must have squarely in place to execute its business strategy. Without solid security processes and procedures, none of the other technologies can develop business advantages.

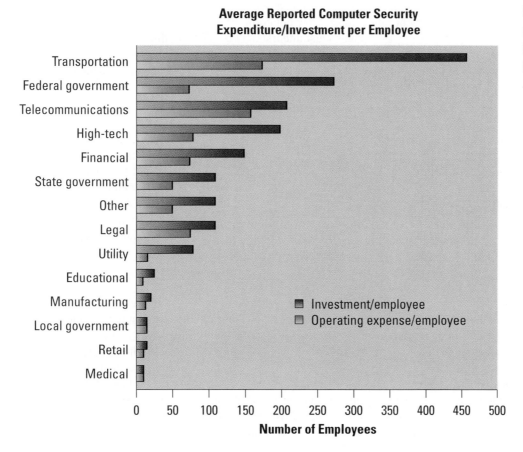

Average Reported Computer Security Expenditure/Investment per Employee

(Vertical axis — Industry)
- Transportation
- Federal government
- Telecommunications
- High-tech
- Financial
- State government
- Other
- Legal
- Utility
- Educational
- Manufacturing
- Local government
- Retail
- Medical

Legend:
- ■ Investment/employee
- ■ Operating expense/employee

(Horizontal axis — Number of Employees: 0, 50, 100, 150, 200, 250, 300, 350, 400, 450, 500)

FIGURE 5.10

Computer Security Expenditures/Investments by Industry

1. Predict what might have happened to Apple if its top executives had not supported investments in IT.

2. Explain why it would be unethical for Apple to allow its customers to download free music from iTunes.

3. Evaluate the effects on Apple's business if it failed to secure its customer information and all of it was accidentally posted to an anonymous website.

4. Explain why Apple should have a CIO, CTO, CPO, CSO, and CKO.

Chapter Five Case: Executive Dilemmas in the Information Age

The vast array of business initiatives from supply chain management to customer relationship management, business process reengineering, and enterprise resource planning makes it clear that information technology has evolved beyond the role of mere infrastructure to the support of business strategy. Today, in more and more industries, IT is a business strategy, and is quickly becoming a survival issue.

Board and executive team agendas are increasingly peppered with, or even hijacked by, a growing range of IT issues from compliance to ethics and security. In most companies today, computers are key business tools. They generate, process, and store the majority of critical business information. Executives must understand how IT can affect a business by successfully addressing a wide range of needs—from large electronic discovery projects to the online review of document collections by geographically dispersed teams. A few examples of executive IT issues follow.

Stolen Proprietary Information

A computer company investigated to determine if an executive who accepted a job with a competitor stole proprietary information. The hard drive from the executive's laptop and desktop machine were forensically imaged. The analysis established that the night before the executive left, he downloaded all of the company's process specifications and distributor agreements, which he then zipped and emailed to the competitor. Additionally, reconstruction of deleted files located emails between the executive and the competitor discussing his intent to provide the proprietary information if he was offered additional options in the new company.

Sexual Harassment

A woman employed by a large defense contractor accused her supervisor of sexual harassment. The woman was fired from her job for poor performance and subsequently sued her ex-boss and the former employer.

A computer company was retained by the plaintiff's attorneys to investigate allegations of the former supervisor's harassing behavior. After making a forensic image backup of the ex-boss's hard drive, the forensic company was able to recover deleted electronic messages that showed the ex-boss had a history of propositioning women under his supervision for "special favors." A situation that might have been mired in a "he said/she said" controversy was quickly resolved; the woman got her job back, and the real culprit was terminated.

Stolen Trade Secrets

The board of directors of a technical research company demoted the company's founder and CEO. The executive, disgruntled because of his demotion, was later terminated. It was subsequently determined that the executive had planned to quit about the same time he was fired and establish a competitive company. Upon his termination, the executive took home two computers; he returned them to the company four days later, along with another company computer that he had previously used at home. Suspicious that critical information had been taken, the company's attorneys sent the computers to a computer forensic company for examination.

After making a forensic image backup of the hard drives, the forensic analysis identified a file directory that had been deleted during the aforementioned four-day period that had the same name as the competing company the executive had established. A specific search of the deleted files in this directory identified the executive's "to do list" file. This file indicated the executive planned to copy the company's database (valued at $100 million) for his personal use. Another item specified the executive was to "learn how to destroy evidence on a computer."

The computer forensic company's examination also proved that the executive had been communicating with other competing companies to establish alliances, in violation of the executive's nondisclosure agreement with the company. It was also shown that numerous key company files were located on removable computer storage media that had not been turned over by the executive to the company.[12]

Questions

1. Explain why understanding technology, especially in the areas of security and ethics, is important for a CEO. How do a CEO's actions affect the organizational culture?

2. Identify why executives in nontechnological industries need to worry about technology and its potential business ramifications.

3. Describe why continuously learning about technology allows an executive to better analyze threats and opportunities.

4. Identify three things that a CTO, CPO, or CSO could do to prevent these issues.

U nderstanding and working with technology have become an integral part of life in the 21st century. Most students take courses in various disciplines in their educational careers, such as in marketing, operations management, management, finance, accounting, and information technology, each of which is designed to provide insight into the tasks of each functional area. In the business world, these are all intertwined and inextricably linked.

Information technology can be an important enabler of business success and innovation and is most useful when it leverages the talents of people. Technology in and of itself is not useful unless the right people know how to use and manage it effectively.

Organizations use information technology to capture, process, organize, distribute, and massage information. Information technology enables an organization to:

- Integrate all functional areas and the tasks they perform.
- Gain an enterprisewide view of its operations.
- Efficiently and effectively utilize resources.
- Realize tremendous market and industry growth by gaining insight into the market at large (through environmental scanning) and insight into internal operations.

✱ **KEY TERMS**

Balanced scorecard, 49
Benchmark, 46
Benchmarking, 46
Best practices, 44
Business-facing
  processes, 31
Business intelligence (BI), 10
Business process, 24, 29
Business process
  reengineering (BPR), 30
Business strategy, 18
Buyer power, 20
Chief information officer
  (CIO), 52
Chief knowledge officer
  (CKO), 54
Chief privacy officer
  (CPO), 54
Chief security officer
  (CSO), 53
Chief technology officer
  (CTO), 53
Competitive advantage, 19
Competitive intelligence, 19
Copyright, 56
Counterfeit software, 56
Critical success factors
  (CSFs), 43
CRM reporting
  technologies, 37

CRM analysis technologies, 37
CRM predicting
  technologies, 37
Customer-facing
  processes, 31
Customer relationship
  management (CRM), 35
Data, 8
Efficiency MIS metrics, 44
Effectiveness MIS metrics, 44
Enterprise resource planning
  (ERP), 38
Entry barrier, 22
Ethics, 55
Fact, 7
Fair use doctrine, 56
Feedback, 15
First-mover advantage, 19
Goods, 13
Information, 9
Information age, 7
Information security, 58
Intellectual property, 56
Key performance indicator
  (KPI), 43
Knowledge, 11
Knowledge workers, 11
Loyalty program, 21
Management information
  systems (MIS), 15

Market share, 43
Metrics, 43
Pirated software, 56
Porter's Five Forces
  Model, 20
Primary value activities, 25
Privacy, 55
Production, 14
Productivity, 14
Project, 43
Product differentiation, 22
Return on investment
  (ROI), 43
Rivalry among existing
  competitors, 22
Services, 14
Supplier power, 21
Supply chain, 21, 33
Supply chain management
  (SCM), 33
Support value activities, 25
System, 13
Systems thinking, 15
Switching cost, 20
Threat of new entrants, 22
Threat of substitute products
  or services, 21
Value chain analysis, 25
Variable, 9
Workflow, 30

Best of the Best of the Best—Under 25

Bloomberg Businessweek runs a yearly article featuring the top five American entrepreneurs under 25 years old. With between 200 and 300 applications each year, choosing 5 is difficult. To help ensure fair competition, the magazine narrows it down to 25 and then asks its readers to decide which 5 have the greatest potential. Below are the top five winners from 2011.

1: SCOREASCORE

Founder: Jordan Passman, 24
Revenue: $250,000

Growing up in Los Angeles, Jordan Passman knew the ins and outs of the music business where his father worked as a high-profile music attorney. Passman, wanting to follow in his father's footsteps, was working for the American Society of Composers when he noticed an unmet need in the marketplace—music buyers in the film, commercial, and television market looking for music composers. An idea was born and Passman began working on a website that connected music buyers with music composers. "People were still scrounging Craigslist for composers, and I knew there were so many composers out there that didn't have representation," says Passman. ScoreAscore links music buyers who are looking for scores for film, commercials, video games, or other productions with 100 select professional music composers represented by Passman, who charges 20 to 40 percent as a fee for each transaction. Passman aspires to be the go-to for YouTube filmmakers!

2: THINKLITE

Founders: Dinesh Wadhwani, 21; Enrico Palmerino, 22
Revenue: $3,500,000

In 2009, Babson College students Dinesh Wadhwani and Enrico Palmerino were reading an article about energy-efficient lightbulbs when their own lightbulbs went off! The roommates began collaborating on how they could build a business with the primary competitive advantage of saving money with energy-efficient lights, instead of focusing solely on saving the environment as most of the current manufacturers in the market were focusing on as their product niche. ThinkLite's mission is to help companies reduce electric bills through energy-efficient lighting. The pair began ThinkLite by licensing technologies from private companies in Germany, coupled with parts from Korea, and designs from Boston, with final production occurring in China. Clients, such as AT&T and Kodak, boast lighting bill reductions ranging from 50 percent to 80 percent, a significant savings for big business! ThinkLite now has over 100 clients and is looking to expand into smaller markets such as restaurants and stores.

3: DELTA PRODUCE

Founders: Kosta Dionisopoulos, 24; Christos Marafatsos, 24
Revenue: $2,600,000

The supply chain of food distribution is a tough business, and getting the right perishable goods to the correct location at the perfect time is more an art form than analytics and logistics. Kosta Dionisopoulos was driving a van delivering produce while attending the University of Maryland when Christos Marafatsos saw an opportunity to start a unique produce delivery business. Delta Produce not only delivers food, but also provides online marketing, allowing customers to reduce costs by buying in bulk or in groups. Delta Produce now has 18 employees and its customers include restaurants, grocery stores, and wholesalers. "Both my partner and I are young, so interacting online is something we're accustomed to doing," says Marafatsos.

4: APPLETON LEARNING

Founder: Glenn Clayton, 25
Revenue: $4,200,000

Glenn Clayton found himself looking for ways to earn extra money while attending the University of Alabama, so he began tutoring local high school students. Clayton soon recognized a need in the market and launched Appleton Learning, which matches college tutors with high school students. Clayton began hiring friends to help meet the tutoring needs, and by the end of his sophomore year he was spending over 60 hours each week managing Appleton Learning. "I realized if people were leaving big name tutoring companies to come to some college kid working out of a broom closet, there was a need in the market not being met," Clayton says. Appleton Learning has found sales doubling yearly, and Clayton has built a unique website that matches students with tutors based on their individual learning needs and styles. Appleton Learning has over 1,000 tutors, including college students, professionals, and retirees, serving over 6,000 high school students. Appleton Learning is looking to expand opening 20 new branches across the Southeast over the next few years.

5: DESMOS

Founder: Eli Luberoff, 24
Revenue: $200,000

While taking a year off from Yale, Eli Luberoff noticed a problem in the education arena—software compatibility issues. Luberoff decided to create software that would overcome these issues and allow teachers and students to collaborate regardless of the systems they were using or their location. Luberoff launched his company, Desmos, by testing software from several large publishers, including McGraw-Hill, Houghton Mifflin Harcourt, and Pearson just to name a few. Luberoff's strategy for making money is to provide the software for free while charging licensing fees to publishers.[13]

Questions

1. If you had $1 million to invest in one of the five above-mentioned start-ups, which one would you choose and why? Be sure to justify your answer using Porter's Five Forces Model and three generic strategies analysis.

2. Choose one of the above businesses and explain why data, information, business intelligence, and knowledge are important to successfully running the business over the next few years. Be sure to list examples of the different types of data, information, business intelligence, and knowledge you might find in this company.

3. Review *Bloomberg Businessweek's* most current top five under 25. Choose one of the companies and perform a detailed analysis of the company using the strategies discussed in this chapter. Determine a few ways the company can improve its business by creating competitive advantages using the ideas and methods discussed throughout this chapter.

Business 2.0: Bad Business Decisions

Business 2.0 magazine looked at the top 100 bad business decisions of all time including bungled layoffs, customer-service snafus, executive follies, and other madness. Five of the top 10 bad business decisions of all time were made because business personnel did not understand information technology; these five are highlighted below. Perhaps one good reason to pay attention in this course is so that you will not end up on *Business 2.0*'s bad business decisions!

Bad Business Decision 3 of 10: Starbucks

Winner: Dumbest Moment—Marketing

Starbucks directs baristas in the southeastern United States to email a coupon for a free iced coffee to friends and family members. But email knows no geographic boundaries and, worse, can be printed repeatedly.

After the email spreads to every corner of the country and is reproduced en masse, Starbucks yanks the offer, leading disgruntled customer Kelly Coakley to file a $114 million class-action lawsuit.

Bad Business Decision 4 of 10: Radioshack

Winner: Dumbest Moment—Human Resources

From: RadioShack
To: RadioShack employees
Subject: Your former job
RadioShack fires 400 staffers via email. Affected employees receive a message that reads, "The work force reduction notification is currently in progress. Unfortunately your position is one that has been eliminated."

Bad Business Decision 7 of 10: AOL

Winner: Dumbest Moment—Data Security

In an "attempt to reach out to the academic community with new research tools," AOL releases the search queries of 657,000 users.

Though AOL insists that the information contains no personally identifiable data, *The New York Times* and other news outlets promptly identify a number of specific users, including searcher No. 4417749, soon-to-be-ex-AOL-subscriber Thelma Arnold of Lilburn, Georgia, whose queries include "women's underwear" and "dog that urinates on everything."

The gaffe leads to the resignation of AOL's chief technology officer and a half-billion-dollar class-action lawsuit.

Winner: Dumbest Moment—Ecommerce

On the morning of April 3, 2006, Amazon.com sends an email headed "UCLA Wins!" to virtually everyone to whom it has ever sold a sports-related item, attempting to hawk a cap celebrating the Bruins' stirring victory in college basketball's championship game.

Just one problem: The game isn't scheduled to be played until later that night. When it is, UCLA is trounced by Florida, 73–57.

Bad Business Decision 9 of 10: Bank of America

Winner: Dumbest Moment—Outsourcing

After Bank of America announces plans to outsource 100 tech support jobs from the San Francisco Bay Area to India, the American workers are told that they must train their own replacements in order to receive their severance payments.

Here are a few other bad ones that did not make the top 10, but are worth mentioning.

Bad Business Decision: McDonald's

Guess the translator took the phrase "viral marketing" a bit too literally. McDonald's runs a promotional contest in Japan in which it gives away 10,000 Mickey D's-branded MP3 players.

The gadgets come preloaded with 10 songs—and, in some cases, a version of the QQPass family of Trojan horse viruses, which, when uploaded to a PC, seek to capture passwords, user names, and other data and then forward them to hackers.

Bad Business Decision: General Motors

Then again, viral marketing can be messed up in English too. As part of a cross promotion with the NBCTV show *The Apprentice,* GM launches a contest to promote its Chevy Tahoe SUV. At Chevyapprentice.com, viewers are given video and music clips with which to create their own 30-second commercials.

Among the new Tahoe ads that soon proliferate across the web are ones with taglines like "Yesterday's technology today" and "Global warming isn't a pretty SUV ad—it's a frightening reality."

Bad Business Decision: New York Times Company

We were wondering how Billy the paperboy could afford that gold-plated Huffy. News carriers and retailers in Worcester, Massachusetts, get an unexpected bonus with their usual shipment of the *Telegram & Gazette:* the credit and debit card numbers of 240,000 subscribers to the paper and its sister publication, the *Boston Globe,* both owned by the New York Times Co.

The security breach is the result of a recycling program in which paper from the *Telegram & Gazette*'s business office is reused to wrap bundles of newspapers.

Bad Business Decision: Sony

PC-B-Q. Defects in batteries made by Sony for portable computing cause a handful of notebooks to burst into spectacularly photogenic flames.

The end result is the biggest computer-related recall ever, as Dell replaces the batteries in more than 4 million laptops. In short order, Apple (1.8 million), Lenovo/IBM (500,000), and others do the same.[14]

QUESTION

1. Explain why understanding information technology and management information systems can help you achieve business success—or more importantly, help you avoid business disasters—regardless of your major.

1. Competitive Analysis

Cheryl O'Connell is the owner of a small, high-end retailer of women's clothing called Excelus. Excelus's business has been successful for many years, largely because of Cheryl's ability to anticipate the needs and wants of her loyal customer base and provide them with personalized service. Cheryl does not see any value in IT and does not want to invest any capital in something that will not directly affect her bottom line. Develop a proposal describing the potential IT-enabled competitive opportunities or threats Cheryl might be missing by not embracing IT. Be sure to include a Porter's Five Forces analysis and discuss which one of the three generic strategies Cheryl should pursue.

2. Using Efficiency and Effectiveness Metrics

You are the CEO of a 500-bed acute care general hospital. Your internal IT department is responsible for running applications that support both administrative functions (e.g., patient accounting) as well as medical applications (e.g., medical records). You need assurance that your IT department is a high quality operation in comparison to similar hospitals. What metrics should you ask your CIO to provide you to give the assurance you seek? Provide the reasoning behind each suggested metric. Also, determine how the interrelationship between efficiency metrics and effectiveness metrics can drive your business's success.

3. Building Business Relationships

Synergistics Inc. is a start-up company that specializes in helping businesses build successful internal relationships. You have recently been promoted to senior manager of the Business and IT Relationship area. Sales for your new department have dwindled over the last two years for a variety of reasons including the burst of the technological stock bubble, recent economic conditions, and a poorly communicated business strategy. Your first task on the job is to prepare a report detailing the following:

■ Fundamental reasons for the gap between the IT and business sides.

■ Strategies you can take to convince your customers that this is an area that is critical to the success of their business.

■ Strategies your customers can follow to ensure that synergies exist between the two sides.

4. Acting Ethically

Assume you are an IT manager and one of your projects is failing. You were against the project from the start; however, the project had powerful sponsorship from all of the top executives. You know that you are doomed and that the project is doomed. The reasons for the failure are numerous including the initial budget was drastically understated, the technology is evolving and not stable, the architecture was never scaled for growth, and your resources do not have the necessary development skills for the new technology. One of your team leads has come to you with a plan to sabotage the project that would put the project out of its misery without assigning any blame to the individuals on the project. Create a document detailing how you would handle this situation.

5. Determining IT Organizational Structures

You are the chief executive officer for a start-up telecommunications company. The company currently has 50 employees and plans to ramp up to 3,000 by the end of the year.

Your first task is to determine how you are going to model your organization. You decide to address the IT department's organizational structure first. You need to consider if you want to have a CIO, CPO, CSO, CTO, and CKO, and if so, what their reporting structure will look like and why. You also need to determine the different roles and responsibilities for each executive position. Once you have compiled this information, put together a presentation describing your IT department's organizational structure.

6. Applying the Three Generic Strategies

The unit discussed examples of companies that pursue differentiated strategies so that they are not forced into positions where they must compete solely on the basis of price. Pick an industry and have your team members find and compare two companies, one that is competing on the basis of price and another that has chosen to pursue a differentiated strategy enabled by the creative use of IT. Some industries you may want to consider are clothing retailers, grocery stores, airlines, and personal computers. Prepare a presentation for the class on the ways that IT is being used to help the differentiating company compete against the low-cost provider. Before you begin, spend some class time to make sure each team selects a different industry if at all possible.

7. The Five Forces Model

Your team is working for a small investment company that specializes in technology investments. A new company, Geyser, has just released an operating system that plans to compete with Microsoft's operating systems. Your company has a significant amount of capital invested in Microsoft. Your boss, Jan Savage, has asked you to compile a Porter's Five Forces analysis for Microsoft to ensure that your company's Microsoft investment is not at risk.

8. Focusing on Friedman

Thomas Friedman's newest book is titled *Hot, Flat, and Crowded: Why We Need a Green Revolution—And How It Can Renew America.* Research the Internet to find out as much information as you can about this text. Why would a business manager be interested in reading this text? How will this text impact global business? Do you think *Hot, Flat, and Crowded* will have as great an impact on society as *The World Is Flat* had on business? Why or why not?[15]

9. Pursuing Porter

There is no doubt that Michael Porter is one of the more influential business strategists of the 21st century. Research Michael Porter on the Internet for interviews, additional articles, and new or updated business strategies. Create a summary of your findings to share with your class. How can learning about people such as Thomas Friedman and Michael Porter help prepare you for a career in business? Name three additional business professionals you should follow to help prepare for your career in business.

10. Renting Movies

The video rental industry is fiercely competitive. Customers have their choice of renting a movie by driving to a store (Blockbuster), ordering through the mail (Netflix), or watching directly from their television (pay-per-view or Netflix). Using Porter's Five Forces Model (buyer power, supplier power, threat of new entrants, threat of substitute products, and competition), evaluate the attractiveness of entering the movie rental business. Be sure to include product differentiation, switching costs, and loyalty programs in your analysis.

11. Working for the Best

Each year, *Fortune* magazine creates a list of the top 100 companies to work for. Find the most recent list. What types of data do you think *Fortune* analyzed to determine the company ranking? What issues could occur if the analysis of the data was inaccurate? What types of information can you gain by analyzing the list? Create five questions a student performing a job search could answer by analyzing this list.

12. Salary Surveys

Salary surveys offer great tools for highlighting the opportunities associated with an MIS major. The starting annual salaries in the MIS field range from $50,000 to $85,000 and many are rising. Figure MBD.1 displays a *Computerworld* salary survey. Research the Internet for a current MIS salary survey. Which types of jobs are on the rise? If there are any jobs you are unfamiliar with, research the Internet to determine the job characteristics. List the top three jobs you would want if you were to pursue a career in MIS. What do you find interesting about these jobs? What skills can you build to help you prepare for these jobs?[16]

13. Starting Your Own Business

Josh James recently sold his web analytics company, Omniture, to Adobe for $1.8 billion. Yes, James started Omniture from his dorm room! Have you begun to recognize the unbelievable opportunities available to those students who understand the power of MIS, regardless of their major? Answer the following questions.[17]

a. Why is it so easy today for students to create start-ups while still in college?
b. What would it take for you to start a business from your dorm room?
c. How will this course help you prepare to start your own business?
d. Research the Internet and find three examples of college student start-ups.
e. What's stopping you from starting your own business today? You are living in the information age and with the power of MIS, it is easier than ever to jump into the business game with very little capital investment. Why not start your own business today?

FIGURE MBD.1

Computerworld Salary Survey

Job Description	Compensation
Business intelligence analyst	$ 81,866
Communications specialist	$ 85,938
Database architect	$ 98,995
Ebusiness specialist	$ 71,717
Information security specialist	$ 83,693
IT / IS technology / business systems analyst	$ 78,305
Network architect	$ 96,302
Programmer / analyst	$ 75,995
Project leader	$ 87,922
Senior systems analyst	$ 89,987
Software developer	$ 85,684
Software engineer	$ 93,726
Storage architect / engineer	$111,077
Systems programmer	$ 89,472
Web developer	$ 66,347

14. Ten Best Things You Will Say to Your Grandchildren

Wired magazine recently posted the top 10 things you will say to your grandchildren. For each expression below try to identify what it is referring to and why it will be considered outdated.[18]

- Back in my day, we only needed 140 characters.
- There used to be so much snow up here, you could strap a board to your feet and slide all the way down.
- Televised contests gave cash prizes to whoever could store the most data in their head.
- Well, the screens were bigger, but they only showed the movies at certain times of day.
- We all had one, but nobody actually used it. Come to think of it, I bet my LinkedIn profile is still out there on the web somewhere.
- Translation: "English used to be the dominant language. Crazy, huh?"
- Our bodies were made of meat and supported by little sticks of calcium.
- You used to keep files right on your computer, and you had to go back to that same computer to access them!
- Is that the new iPhone 27G? Got multitasking yet?
- I just can't get used to this darn vat-grown steak. Texture ain't right.

✱ APPLY YOUR KNOWLEDGE

1. Capitalizing on Your Career

Business leaders need to be involved in information technology—any computer-based tool that people use to work with information and support the information and information-processing needs of an organization—for the following (primary) reasons:

- The sheer magnitude of the dollars spent on IT must be managed to ensure business value.
- Research has consistently shown that when business leaders are involved in information technology, it enables a number of business initiatives, such as gaining a competitive advantage, streamlining business processes, and even transforming entire organizations.
- Research has consistently shown that when business leaders are not involved in IT, systems fail, revenue is lost, and even entire companies can fail as a result of poorly managed IT.

One of the biggest challenges facing organizations is, "How do we get general business leaders involved in IT?" Research has shown that involvement is highly correlated with personal experience with IT and IT education, including university classes and IT executive seminars. Once general business leaders understand IT through experience and education, they are more likely to be involved in IT, and more likely to lead their organizations in achieving business success through IT.

Project Focus

1. Search the Internet to find examples of the types of technologies that are currently used in the field or industry that you plan to pursue. For example, if you are planning on a career in

accounting or finance, you should become familiar with financial systems such as Oracle Financials. If you are planning a career in logistics or distribution, you should research supply chain management systems. If you are planning a career in marketing, you should research customer relationship management systems, blogs, and emarketing.

2. IT is described as an enabler/facilitator of competitive advantage, organizational effectiveness, and organizational efficiency. As a competitive tool, IT can differentiate an organization's products, services, and prices from its competitors by improving product quality, shortening product development or delivery time, creating new IT-based products and services, and improving customer service before, during, and after a transaction. Search the Internet and find several examples of companies in the industry where you plan to work that have achieved a competitive advantage through IT.

3. Create a simple report of your findings; include a brief overview of the type of technologies you found and how organizations are using them to achieve a competitive advantage.

2. Achieving Alignment

Most companies would like to be in the market-leading position of JetBlue, Dell, or Walmart, all of which have used information technology to secure their respective spots in the marketplace. These companies have a relentless goal of keeping the cost of technology down by combining the best of IT and business leadership.

It takes more than a simple handshake between groups to start on the journey toward financial gains; it requires operational discipline and a linkage between business and technology units. Only recently have companies not on the "path for profits" followed the lead of their successful counterparts, requiring more operational discipline from their IT groups as well as more IT participation from their business units. Bridging this gap is one of the greatest breakthroughs a company can make.

Companies that master the art of finely tuned, cost-effective IT management will have a major advantage. Their success will force their competitors to also master the art or fail miserably. This phenomenon has already occurred in the retail and wholesale distribution markets, which have had to react to Walmart's IT mastery, as one example. Other industries will follow. This trend will change not only the face of IT, but also the future of corporate America.

As world markets continue to grow, the potential gains are greater than ever. However, so are the potential losses. The future belongs to those who are perceptive enough to grasp the significance of IT and resourceful enough to synchronize business management and information technology.

Project Focus

1. Use any resource to answer the question, "Why is business-IT alignment so difficult?" Use the following questions to begin your analysis:
   a. How do companies prioritize the demands of various business units as they relate to IT?
   b. What are some of the greatest IT challenges for the coming year?
   c. What drives IT decisions?
   d. Who or what is the moving force behind IT decisions?
   e. What types of efficiency metrics and effectiveness metrics might these companies use to measure the impact of IT?
   f. How can a company use financial metrics to monitor and measure IT investments?
   g. What are some of the issues with using financial metrics to evaluate IT?

3. Market Dissection

To illustrate the use of the three generic strategies, consider Figure AYK.1. The matrix shown demonstrates the relationships among strategies (cost leadership versus differentiation) and market segmentation (broad versus focused).

- Hyundai is following a broad cost leadership strategy. Hyundai offers low-cost vehicles, in each particular model stratification, that appeal to a large audience.

- Audi is pursuing a broad differentiation strategy with its Quattro models available at several price points. Audi's differentiation is safety and it prices its various Quattro models (higher than Hyundai) to reach a large, stratified audience.

- Kia has a more focused cost leadership strategy. Kia mainly offers low-cost vehicles in the lower levels of model stratification.

- Hummer offers the most focused differentiation strategy of any in the industry (including Mercedes-Benz).

Project Focus

Create a similar graph displaying each strategy for a product of your choice. The strategy must include an example of the product in each of the following markets: (1) cost leadership, broad market, (2) differentiation, broad market, (3) cost leadership, focused market, and (4) differentiation, focused market. Potential products include:

- Cereal
- Dog food
- Soft drinks
- Computers
- Shampoo
- Snack foods
- Jeans
- Sneakers

FIGURE AYK.1

Porter's Three
Generic Strategies

Cost Leadership strategy   Differentiation strategy

Broad market

Focused market

- Sandals
- Mountain bikes
- TV shows
- Movies

4. Grading Security

Making The Grade is a nonprofit organization that helps students learn how to achieve better grades in school. The organization has 40 offices in 25 states and more than 2,000 employees. The company wants to build a website to offer its services online. Making The Grade's online services will provide parents seven key pieces of advice for communicating with their children to help them achieve academic success. The website will offer information on how to maintain open lines of communication, set goals, organize academics, regularly track progress, identify trouble spots, get to know their child's teacher, and celebrate their children's successes.

Project Focus

You and your team work for the director of information security. Your team's assignment is to develop a document discussing the importance of creating information security polices and an information security plan. Be sure to include the following:

- The importance of educating employees on information security.

- A few samples of employee information security policies specifically for Making The Grade.

- Other major areas the information security plan should address.

- Signs the company should look for to determine if the website is being hacked.

- The major types of attacks the company should expect to experience.

5. Eyes Everywhere

The movie *Minority Report* chronicled a futuristic world where people are uniquely identifiable by their eyes. A scan of each person's eyes gives or denies them access to rooms, computers, and anything else with restrictions. The movie portrayed a black market in new eyeballs to help people hide from the authorities. (Why did they not just change the database entry instead? That would have been much easier, but a lot less dramatic.)

The idea of using a biological signature is entirely plausible since biometrics is currently being widely used and is expected to gain wider acceptance in the near future because forging documents has become much easier with the advances in computer graphics programs and color printers. The next time you get a new passport, it may incorporate a chip that has your biometric information encoded on it. Office of Special Investigations agents with fake documents found that it was relatively easy to enter the United States from Canada, Mexico, and Jamaica, by land, sea, and air.

The task of policing the borders is daunting. Some 500 million foreigners enter the country every year and go through identity checkpoints. More than 13 million permanent-resident and border-crossing cards have been issued by the U.S. government. Also, citizens of 27 countries do not need visas to enter this country. They are expected to have passports that comply with U.S. specifications that will also be readable at the border.

In the post–9/11 atmosphere of tightened security, unrestricted border crossing is not acceptable. The Department of Homeland Security is charged with securing the nation's borders, and as part of this plan, new entry/exit procedures were instituted at the beginning of 2003. An integrated system, using biometrics, will be used to identify foreign visitors to the United States and reduce the likelihood of terrorists entering the country.

Early in 2003, after 6 million biometric border-crossing cards had been issued, a pilot test conducted at the Canadian border detected more than 250 imposters. The testing started with two biometric identifiers: photographs for facial recognition and fingerprint scans. As people enter and leave the country, their actual fingerprints and facial features are compared to the data on the biometric chip in the passport.

Project Focus

In a group, discuss the following:

1. How do you feel about having your fingerprints, facial features, and perhaps more of your biometric features encoded in documents like your passport? Explain your answer.
2. Would you feel the same way about having biometric information on your driver's license as on your passport? Why or why not?
3. Is it reasonable to have different biometric identification requirements for visitors from different nations? Explain your answer. What would you recommend as criteria for deciding which countries fall into what categories?
4. The checkpoints U.S. citizens pass through upon returning to the country vary greatly in the depth of the checks and the time spent. The simplest involves simply walking past the border guards who may or may not ask you your citizenship. The other end of the spectrum requires that you put up with long waits in airports where you have to line up with hundreds of other passengers while each person is questioned and must produce a passport to be scanned. Would you welcome biometric information on passports if it would speed the process, or do you think that the disadvantages of the reduction in privacy, caused by biometric information, outweigh the advantages of better security and faster border processing? Explain your answer.

6. Setting Boundaries

Even the most ethical people sometimes face difficult choices. Acting ethically means behaving in a principled fashion and treating other people with respect and dignity. It is simple to say, but not so simple to do since some situations are complex or ambiguous. The important role of ethics in our lives has long been recognized. As far back as 44 B.C., Cicero said that ethics are indispensable to anyone who wants to have a good career. Having said that, Cicero, along with some of the greatest minds over the centuries, struggled with what the rules of ethics should be.

Our ethics are rooted in our history, culture, and religion, and our sense of ethics may shift over time. The electronic age brings with it a new dimension in the ethics debate—the amount of personal information that we can collect and store, and the speed with which we can access and process that information.

Project Focus

In a group, discuss how you would react to the following situations:

1. A senior marketing manager informs you that one of her employees is looking for another job and she wants you to give her access to look through her email.
2. A vice president of sales informs you that he has made a deal to provide customer information to a strategic partner, and he wants you to burn all of the customer information onto a DVD.
3. You are asked to monitor your employee's email to discover if he is sexually harassing another employee.
4. You are asked to install a video surveillance system in your office to watch if employees are taking office supplies home with them.

5. You are looking on the shared network drive and discover that your boss's entire hard drive has been copied to the network for everyone to view. What do you do?

6. You have been accidentally copied on an email from the CEO, which details who will be the targets of the next round of layoffs. What would you do?

7. Porter's Five Forces

Porter's Five Forces Model is an easy framework with which to understand market forces. Break into groups and choose two products from the list below on which to perform a Porter's Five Forces analysis.

- Laptop computer and desktop computer.
- PDA and laptop computer.
- iPod and Walkman.
- DVD player and VCR player.
- Digital camera and Polaroid camera.
- Cell phone and BlackBerry PDA.
- Coca-Cola plastic bottle and Coca-Cola glass bottle.
- GPS device and a road atlas.
- Roller skates and Rollerblades.
- Digital books and printed books.
- Digital paper and paper.

8. Measuring Efficiency and Effectiveness

In a group, create a plan to measure the efficiency and effectiveness of this course and recommendations on how you could improve the course to make it more efficient and more effective. You must determine ways to benchmark current efficiency and effectiveness and ways to continuously monitor and measure against the benchmarks to determine if the course is becoming more or less efficient and effective (class quizzes and exams are the most obvious benchmarks). Be sure your plan addresses the following:

- Design of the classroom.
- Room temperature.
- Lighting and electronic capabilities of the classroom.
- Technology available in the classroom.
- Length of class.
- Email and instant messaging.
- Students' attendance.
- Students' preparation.
- Students' arrival time.
- Quizzes and exams (frequency, length, grades).

9. Adding Value

To identify these competitive advantages, Michael Porter created value chain analysis, which views a firm as a series of business processes that each add value to the product or service. Value chain analysis is a useful tool for determining how to create the greatest possible value for customers. The goal of value chain analysis is to identify processes in which the firm can add value for the customer and create a competitive advantage for itself, with a cost advantage or product differentiation.

Project Focus

Starbucks has hired you after your graduation for a temporary position that could turn into a full-time opportunity. With new cafés and juice shops popping up on every corner, coupled with the global recession, Starbucks is worried about losing market share to competitors. Your boss, Heather Sweitzer, is out of ideas for ways to improve the company's profitability. You decide that one of the most useful tools for identifying competitive advantages is Porter's value chain analysis. Of course, you do not yet have the detailed knowledge to complete all of the elements required, but you know enough to get started and plan to take your draft to Sweitzer next week. Using your knowledge of Starbucks, create a value chain analysis. Feel free to make assumptions about operations; just be sure to list any that you make. Also, be sure to write an overview of the tool and its potential value so Sweitzer can understand how it works.

10. Flat Competition

"When I was growing up in Minneapolis, my parents always said, 'Tom, finish your dinner. There are people starving in China and India.' Today I tell my girls, 'Finish your homework, because people in China and India are starving for your jobs.' And in a flat world, they can have them, because there's no such thing as an American job anymore." Thomas Friedman.

Project Focus

In his book, *The World Is Flat,* Thomas Friedman describes the unplanned cascade of technological and social shifts that effectively leveled the economic world, and "accidentally made Beijing, Bangalore, and Bethesda next-door neighbors." The video of Thomas Friedman's lecture at MIT discussing the flat world is available at http://mitworld.mit.edu/video/266. If you want to be prepared to compete in a flat world you must watch this video and answer the following questions:

- Do you agree or disagree with Friedman's assessment that the world is flat?
- What are the potential impacts of a flat world for a student performing a job search?
- What can students do to prepare themselves for competing in a flat world?[19]

11. Wikiblunders

According to *PC World* these false facts all appeared on Wikipedia:

- Robbie Williams eats domestic pets in pubs for money.
- David Beckham was a Chinese goalkeeper in the 18th century.
- Paul Reiser's dead. (Reiser is an actor.)
- Sinbad's dead. (Sinbad is an actor.)
- Sergey Brin's sexy, dating Jimmy Wales, and dead. (Brin founded Google and Wales founded Wikipedia.)
- Tony Blair worships Hitler. (Blair was the former Prime Minister of the United Kingdom.)
- The Duchess of Cornwall's Christian name is Cow-miller.
- Robert Byrd's dead. (Byrd is a U.S. Senator from West Virginia.)
- John Seigenthaler helped assassinate John and Robert Kennedy. (Seigenthaler is a journalist.)
- Conan O'Brien assaults sea turtles while canoeing.[20]

Project Focus

We know that people use information technology to work with information. Knowing this, how could these types of errors occur? What could happen if you decided to use

Wikipedia to collect business intelligence for a research paper? What could Wikipedia do to help prevent these types of errors?

12. What's Wrong with This Bathroom?

If you were the CEO of a global financial company that was experiencing a financial crisis, would you invest $1 million to renovate your office? Probably not and you are possibly wondering if this is a fabricated story from *The Onion*. Guess what, this is a true story! John Thain, the former CEO of Merrill Lynch, decided to spend $1.2 million refurbishing his office—well after Merrill Lynch posted huge financial losses. Thain personally signed-off all of the following:

- Area Rug: $87,784
- Mahogany Pedestal Table: $25,713
- 19th Century Credenza: $68,179
- Pendant Light Furniture: $19,751
- 4 Pairs of Curtains: $28,091
- Pair of Guest Chairs: $87,784
- George IV Chair: $18,468
- 6 Wall Sconces: $2,741
- Parchment Waste Can: $1,405 (yes, for a trash can!!)
- Roman Shade Fabric: $10,967
- Roman Shades: $7,315
- Coffee Table: $5,852
- Commode on Legs: $35,115[21]

Project Focus

It takes years of education and work experience for people to build the skills necessary to take on the role of CEO. Obviously, a company like Merrill Lynch would only hire a highly qualified person for the job. What do you think happened to John Thain? Why would he spend an obscene amount of money redecorating his office when his company was having financial trouble? What happens to a company whose executives are not aligned with company goals? How can you ensure that your company's executives are not making monumental mistakes, such as million dollar bathroom renovations?

13. I Love TED!

A small nonprofit started in 1984, TED (Technology, Entertainment, Design) hosts conferences for Ideas Worth Spreading. TED brings people from all over the globe to share award-winning talks covering the most innovative, informative, and exciting speeches ever given in 20 minutes. You can find TED talks by Al Gore, Bill Gates, Steve Jobs, Douglas Adams, Steven Levitt, Seth Godin, Malcolm Gladwell, and so on.[22]

Project Focus

Visit www.ted.com and peruse the thousands of videos that are available, then answer the following:

- Review the TED website and find three talks you would want to watch. Why did you pick these three and will you make time outside of class to watch them?
- How can you gain a competitive advantage by watching TED?
- How can you find innovative ideas for a start-up by watching TED?
- How can you find competitive intelligence by watching TED?

If you are looking for Excel projects to incorporate into your class, try any of the following after reading this chapter.

Project Number	Project Name	Project Type	Plug-In Focus Area	Project Level	Skill Set	Page Number
1	Financial Destiny	Excel	T2	Personal Budget	Introductory Formulas	AYK.4
2	Cash Flow	Excel	T2	Cash Flow	Introductory Formulas	AYK.4
3	Technology Budget	Excel	T1, T2	Hardware and Software	Introductory Formulas	AYK.4
4	Tracking Donations	Excel	T2	Employee Relationships	Introductory Formulas	AYK.4
5	Convert Currency	Excel	T2	Global Commerce	Introductory Formulas	AYK.5
6	Cost Comparison	Excel	T2	Total Cost of Ownership	Introductory Formulas	AYK.5
7	Time Management	Excel or Project	T12 Project Management	Introductory	Gantt Charts	AYK.6

Build Your Own Business

You have recently inherited your grandfather's business, which is conveniently located in your city's downtown. The business offers many different kinds of specialized products and services and was first opened in 1952 and was a local hot spot for many years. Unfortunately, business has been steadily declining over the past few years. The business runs without any computers and all ordering takes place manually. Your grandfather had a terrific memory and knew all of his customers and suppliers by name, but unfortunately, none of this information is located anywhere in the store. The operational information required to run the business, such as sales trends, vendor information, promotional information, and so on, is all located in your grandfather's memory. Inventory is tracked in a note pad, along with employee payroll, and marketing coupons. The business does not have a website, uses very little marketing except word of mouth, and essentially still operates the same as it did in 1952.

Throughout this course you will own and operate your grandfather's business, and by taking advantage of business practices discussed in this text, you will attempt to increase profits, decrease expenses, and bring the business into the 21st century. For the purpose of this case, please choose the business you wish to operate and create a name for the business. For example, the business could be a coffee shop called The Broadway Café, an extreme sports store called Cutting Edge Sports, or even a movie store called *The Silver Screen*. Try to pick a business you are genuinely interested in running and that aligns with your overall career goals.

Project Focus: Competitive Advantage

1. Identify the business you are going to build throughout this course and choose a name for your business.

2. Write an analysis of buyer power and supplier power for your business using Porter's Five Forces Model. Be sure to discuss how you could combat the competition with strategies such as switching costs and loyalty programs.

3. Write an analysis of rivalry, entry barriers, and the threat of substitute products for your business using Porter's Five Forces Model. Be sure to discuss how you could combat the competition with strategies such as product differentiation.

4. Describe which of Porter's three generic strategies you would use for your business. Be sure to describe the details of how you will implement this strategy and how it will help you create a competitive advantage in your industry.

2

Exploring Business Intelligence

What's in IT for Me?

This unit introduces the concept of information and its relative importance to organizations. It distinguishes between data stored in transactional databases and information housed in enterprise data warehouses. This unit also provides an overview of database fundamentals and the steps required to integrate various bits of data stored across multiple, operational data stores into a comprehensive and centralized repository of summarized information, which can be turned into powerful business intelligence.

You, as a business student, must understand the difference between transactional data and summarized information and the different types of questions you would use a transactional database or enterprise data warehouse to answer. You need to be aware of the complexity of storing data in databases and the level of effort required to transform operational data into meaningful, summarized information. You need to realize the power of information and the competitive advantage a data warehouse brings an organization in terms of facilitating business intelligence. Understanding the power of information will help you prepare to compete in a global marketplace. Armed with the power of information, you will make smart, informed, and data-supported managerial decisions.

Informing Information

Since the beginning of time, man has been using pictures and images to communicate, moving from caveman drawings to hieroglyphics to the Internet. Today, it is easier than ever to paint a picture worth 100,000 words, thanks to technological advances. The primary advantages are databases and data warehouses that capture enormous amounts of data. Informing means accessing large amounts of data from different management information systems. According to a recent analysis of press releases by *PR Newswire*, an article or advertisement that uses visual images can significantly improve the number of views a message generates. This can be a true competitive advantage in the digital age.

An infographic (or information graphic) displays information graphically so it can be more easily understood. Infographics cut straight to the point by taking complex information and presenting it in a simple visual format. Infographics can present the results of large data analysis, looking for patterns and relationships that monitor changes in variables over time. Because infographics can easily become overwhelming, users need to be careful to not display too much data or the resulting infographics can result in information overload. Effective infographics can achieve outstanding results for marketing, advertising, and public relations. According to *PR Newswire*, infographics gain the greatest competitive advantage when they have the following:

- Survey results that are too hard to understand in text format.
- Statistical data that are not interesting for readers.
- Comparison research where the impact can be far more dramatic when presented visually.
- Messages for multilingual audiences.
- Any information that can use a visual element to make it more interesting (see Figure Unit 6.1 through Figure Unit 6.3 for examples).[1]

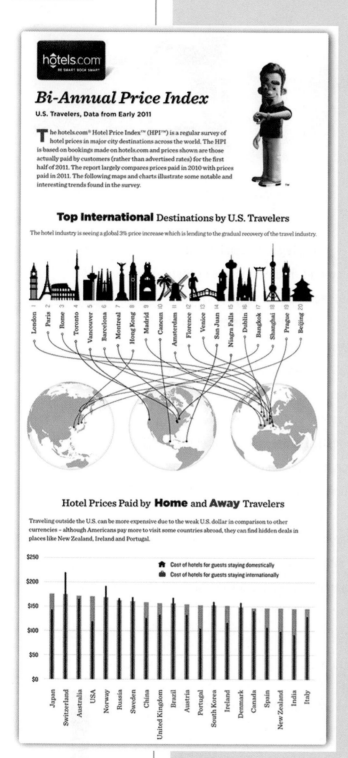

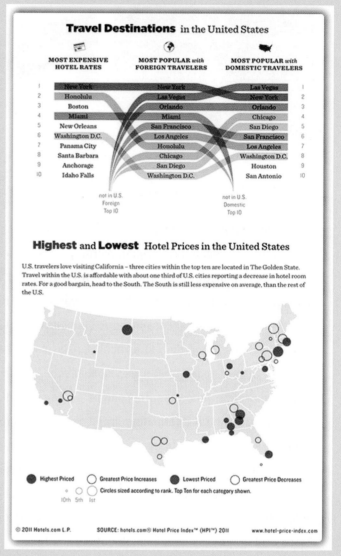

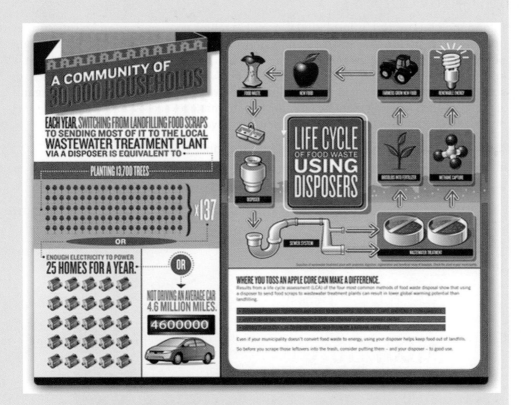

Introduction

Information is powerful. Information is useful in telling an organization how its current operations are performing and estimating and strategizing how future operations might perform. New perspectives open up when people have the right information and know how to use it. The ability to understand, digest, analyze, and filter information is a key to success for any professional in any industry. Unit Two demonstrates the value an organization can uncover and create by learning how to manage, access, analyze, and protect organizational information. The chapters in Unit Two are:

- **Chapter Six**—Valuing Organizational Information.
- **Chapter Seven**—Storing Organizational Information—Databases.
- **Chapter Eight**—Accessing Organizational Information—Data Warehouse.

Valuing Organizational Information

6.1. Explain the four primary traits that determine the value of information.

The Business Benefits of High-Quality Information

LO 6.1 Explain the four primary traits that determine the value of information.

Information is powerful. Information can tell an organization how its current operations are performing and help it estimate and strategize about how future operations might perform. The ability to understand, digest, analyze, and filter information is key to growth and success for any professional in any industry. Remember that new perspectives and opportunities can open up when you have the right data that you can turn into information and ultimately business intelligence.

Information is everywhere in an organization. Managers in sales, marketing, human resources, and management need information to run their departments and make daily decisions. When addressing a significant business issue, employees must be able to obtain and analyze all the relevant information so they can make the best decision possible. Information comes at different levels, formats, and granularities. ***Information granularity*** refers to the extent of detail within the information (fine and detailed or coarse and abstract). Employees must be able to correlate the different levels, formats, and granularities of information when making decisions. For example, a company might be collecting information from various suppliers to make needed decisions, only to find that the information is in different levels, formats, and granularities. One supplier might send detailed information in a spreadsheet, while another supplier might send summary information in a Word document, and still another might send a collection of information from emails. Employees will need to compare these different types of information for what they commonly reveal to make strategic decisions. Figure 6.1 displays the various levels, formats, and granularities of organizational information.

Successfully collecting, compiling, sorting, and finally analyzing information from multiple levels, in varied formats, and exhibiting different granularities can provide tremendous insight into how an organization is performing. Exciting and unexpected results can include potential new markets, new ways of reaching customers, and even new methods of doing business. After understanding the different levels, formats, and granularities of information, managers next want to look at the four primary traits that help determine the value of information (see Figure 6.2).

INFORMATION TYPE: TRANSACTIONAL AND ANALYTICAL

Transactional information encompasses all of the information contained within a single business process or unit of work, and its primary purpose is to support daily operational tasks. Organizations need to capture and store transactional information to perform operational tasks and repetitive decisions such as analyzing daily sales reports and production

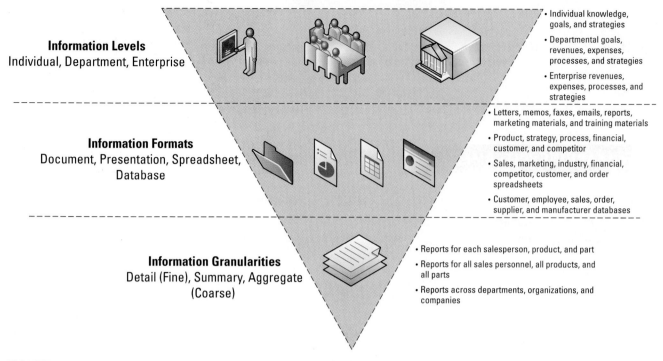

Information Levels
Individual, Department, Enterprise

- Individual knowledge, goals, and strategies
- Departmental goals, revenues, expenses, processes, and strategies
- Enterprise revenues, expenses, processes, and strategies

Information Formats
Document, Presentation, Spreadsheet, Database

- Letters, memos, faxes, emails, reports, marketing materials, and training materials
- Product, strategy, process, financial, customer, and competitor
- Sales, marketing, industry, financial, competitor, customer, and order spreadsheets
- Customer, employee, sales, order, supplier, and manufacturer databases

Information Granularities
Detail (Fine), Summary, Aggregate (Coarse)

- Reports for each salesperson, product, and part
- Reports for all sales personnel, all products, and all parts
- Reports across departments, organizations, and companies

FIGURE 6.1

Levels, Formats, and Granularities of Organizational Information

schedules to determine how much inventory to carry. Consider Walmart, which handles more than 1 million customer transactions every hour, and Facebook, which keeps track of 400 million active users (along with their photos, friends, and web links). In addition, every time a cash register rings up a sale, a deposit or withdrawal is made from an ATM, or a receipt is given at the gas pump, capturing and storing of the transactional information are required.

Analytical information encompasses all organizational information, and its primary purpose is to support the performing of managerial analysis tasks. Analytical information is useful when making important decisions such as whether the organization should build a new manufacturing plant or hire additional sales personnel. Analytical information makes it possible to do many things that previously were difficult to accomplish, such as spot business trends, prevent diseases, and fight crime. For example, credit card companies crunch through billions of transactional purchase records to identify fraudulent activity. Indicators such as charges in a foreign country or consecutive purchases of gasoline send a red flag highlighting potential fraudulent activity.

Walmart was able to use its massive amount of analytical information to identify many unusual trends, such as a correlation between storms and Pop-Tarts. Yes, Walmart discovered an increase in the demand for Pop-Tarts during the storm season.

FIGURE 6.2

The Four Primary Traits of the Value of Information

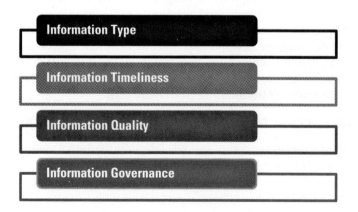

- Information Type
- Information Timeliness
- Information Quality
- Information Governance

Armed with the valuable information the retail chain was able to stock up on Pop-Tarts that were ready for purchase when customers arrived. Figure 6.3 displays different types of transactional and analytical information.

INFORMATION TIMELINESS

Timeliness is an aspect of information that depends on the situation. In some firms or industries, information that is a few days or weeks old can be relevant, while in others information that is a few minutes old can be almost worthless. Some organizations, such as 911 response centers, stock traders, and banks, require up-to-the-second information. Other organizations, such as insurance and construction companies, require only daily or even weekly information.

Real-time information means immediate, up-to-date information. *Real-time systems* provide real-time information in response to requests. Many organizations use real-time systems to uncover key corporate transactional information. The growing demand for real-time information stems from organizations' need to make faster and more effective decisions, keep smaller inventories, operate more efficiently, and track performance more carefully. Information also needs to be timely in the sense that it meets employees' needs, but no more. If employees can absorb information only on an hourly or daily basis, there is no need to gather real-time information in smaller increments.

Most people request real-time information without understanding one of the biggest pitfalls associated with real-time information—continual change. Imagine the following scenario: Three managers meet at the end of the day to discuss a business problem. Each manager has gathered information at different times during the day to create a picture of the situation. Each manager's picture may be different because of the time differences. Their views on the business problem may not match because the information they are basing their analysis on is continually changing. This approach may not speed up decision making, and it may actually slow it down. Business decision makers must evaluate the timeliness for the information for every decision. Organizations do not want to find themselves using real-time information to make a bad decision faster.

INFORMATION QUALITY

Business decisions are only as good as the quality of the information used to make them. *Information inconsistency* occurs when the same data element has different values. Take for example the amount of work that needs to occur to update a customer who had changed her last name due to marriage. Changing this information in only a few organizational systems will lead to data inconsistencies causing customer 123456 to be associated with two last names. *Information integrity issues* occur when a system produces incorrect, inconsistent, or duplicate data. Data integrity issues can cause managers to consider the system reports invalid and will make decisions based on other sources.

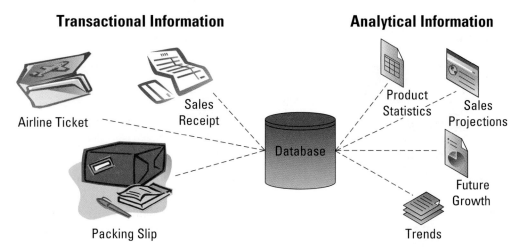

Transactional Information   **Analytical Information**

Airline Ticket   Sales Receipt   Database   Product Statistics   Sales Projections   Future Growth   Trends   Packing Slip

FIGURE 6.3

Transactional versus Analytical Information

FIGURE 6.4

Five Common
Characteristics of
High-Quality Information

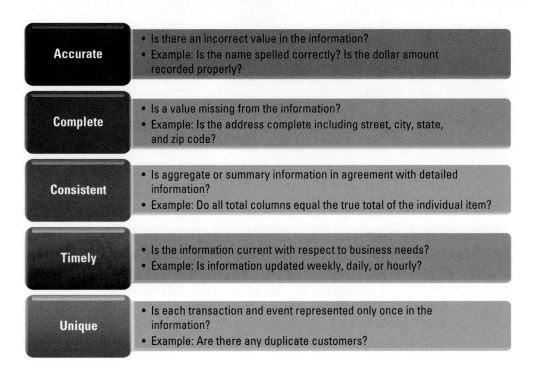

Accurate	• Is there an incorrect value in the information? • Example: Is the name spelled correctly? Is the dollar amount recorded properly?
Complete	• Is a value missing from the information? • Example: Is the address complete including street, city, state, and zip code?
Consistent	• Is aggregate or summary information in agreement with detailed information? • Example: Do all total columns equal the true total of the individual item?
Timely	• Is the information current with respect to business needs? • Example: Is information updated weekly, daily, or hourly?
Unique	• Is each transaction and event represented only once in the information? • Example: Are there any duplicate customers?

To ensure your systems do not suffer from data integrity issues, review Figure 6.4 for the five characteristics common to high-quality information: accuracy, completeness, consistency, timeliness, and uniqueness. Figure 6.5 provides an example of several problems associated with using low-quality information including:

1. *Completeness.* The customer's first name is missing.

2. Another issue with *completeness.* The street address contains only a number and not a street name.

3. *Consistency.* There may be a duplication of information since there is a slight difference between the two customers in the spelling of the last name. Similar street addresses and phone numbers make this likely.

4. *Accuracy.* This may be inaccurate information because the customer's phone and fax numbers are the same. Some customers might have the same number for phone and fax, but the fact that the customer also has this number in the email address field is suspicious.

FIGURE 6.5

Example of Low-Quality
Information

1. Missing information (no first name)
2. Incomplete information (no street)
5. Inaccurate information (invalid email)

ID	Last Name	First Name	Street	City	State	Zip	Phone	Fax	Email
113	Smith		123 S. Main	Denver	CO	80210	(303) 777-1258	(303) 777-5544	ssmith@aol.com
114	Jones	Jeff	12A	Denver	CO	80224	(303) 666-6868	(303) 666-6868	(303) 666-6868
115	Roberts	Jenny	1244 Colfax	Denver	CO	85231	759-5654	853-6584	jr@msn.com
116	Robert	Jenny	1244 Colfax	Denver	CO	85231	759-5654	853-6584	jr@msn.com

3. Probable duplicate information (similar names, same address, phone number)
4. Potential wrong information (are the phone and fax numbers the same or is this an error?)
6. Incomplete information (missing area codes)

5. Another issue with *accuracy.* There is inaccurate information because a phone number is located in the email address field.

6. Another issue with *completeness.* The information is incomplete because there is not a valid area code for the phone and fax numbers.

Nestlé uses 550,000 suppliers to sell more than 100,000 products in 200 countries. However, due to poor information, the company was unable to evaluate its business effectively. After some analysis, it found that it had 9 million records of vendors, customers, and materials, half of which were duplicated, obsolete, inaccurate, or incomplete. The analysis discovered that some records abbreviated vendor names while other records spelled out the vendor names. This created multiple accounts for the same customer, making it impossible to determine the true value of Nestlé's customers. Without being able to identify customer profitability, a company runs the risk of alienating its best customers.[2]

Knowing how low-quality information issues typically occur can help a company correct them. Addressing these errors will significantly improve the quality of company information and the value to be extracted from it. The four primary reasons for low-quality information are:

1. Online customers intentionally enter inaccurate information to protect their privacy.

2. Different systems have different information entry standards and formats.

3. Data-entry personnel enter abbreviated information to save time or erroneous information by accident.

4. Third-party and external information contains inconsistencies, inaccuracies, and errors.

Understanding the Costs of Using Low-Quality Information

Using the wrong information can lead managers to make erroneous decisions. Erroneous decisions in turn can cost time, money, reputations, and even jobs. Some of the serious business consequences that occur due to using low-quality information to make decisions are:

- Inability to accurately track customers.
- Difficulty identifying the organization's most valuable customers.
- Inability to identify selling opportunities.
- Lost revenue opportunities from marketing to nonexistent customers.
- The cost of sending nondeliverable mail.
- Difficulty tracking revenue because of inaccurate invoices.
- Inability to build strong relationships with customers.

Understanding the Benefits of Using High-Quality Information

High-quality information can significantly improve the chances of making a good decision and directly increase an organization's bottom line. One company discovered that even with its large number of golf courses, Phoenix, Arizona, is not a good place to sell golf clubs. An analysis revealed that typical golfers in Phoenix are tourists and conventioneers who usually bring their clubs with them. The analysis further revealed that two of the best places to sell golf clubs in the United States are Rochester, New York, and Detroit, Michigan. Equipped with this valuable information, the company was able to strategically place its stores and launch its marketing campaigns.

High-quality information does not automatically guarantee that every decision made is going to be a good one, because people ultimately make decisions and no one is perfect. However, such information ensures that the basis of the decisions is accurate. The success of the organization depends on appreciating and leveraging the true value of timely and high-quality information.

INFORMATION GOVERNANCE

Information is a vital resource and users need to be educated on what they can and cannot do with it. To ensure a firm manages its information correctly, it will need special policies and procedures establishing rules on how the information is organized, updated, maintained, and accessed. Every firm, large and small, should create an information policy concerning data governance. **Data governance** refers to the overall management of the availability, usability, integrity, and security of company data. A company that supports a data governance program has a defined a policy that specifies who is accountable for various portions or aspects of the data, including its accuracy, accessibility, consistency, timeliness, and completeness. The policy should clearly define the processes concerning how to store, archive, back up, and secure the data. In addition, the company should create a set of procedures identifying accessibility levels for employees. Then, the firm should deploy controls and procedures that enforce government regulations and compliance with mandates such as Sarbanes-Oxley.

OPENING CASE STUDY QUESTIONS

1. List the reasons a business would want to display information in a graphic or visual format.

2. Categorize the five common characteristics of high-quality information and rank them in order of importance for Hotels.com.

3. Explain how Hotels.com is preventing any issues associated with low-quality information.

Chapter Six Case: Political Microtargeting: What Data Crunchers Did for Obama

In his presidential inauguration speech, President Barack Obama spoke a word rarely expressed—*data*—referencing indicators of economic and other crises. It is not surprising that the word *data* was spoken in his inauguration speech because capturing and analyzing data has been crucial to Obama's rise to power. Throughout Obama's historic campaign he used the Internet not only for social networking and fund raising, but also to identify potential swing voters. Obama's team carefully monitored contested states and congressional districts, because 1,000 to 2,000 voters could prove decisive—meaning the focus was on only a tiny fraction of the voting public. Both political parties hired technology wizards to help sift through the mountains of consumer and demographic details to recognize these important voters.

Ten "Tribes"

Spotlight Analysis, a Democratic consultancy, used political microtargeting to analyze neighborhood details, family sizes, and spending patterns to categorize every American of voting age—175 million of us—into 10 "values tribes." Individual tribe members do not necessarily share the same race, religion, or income bracket, but they have common mind-sets about political issues: God, community, responsibility, opportunity. Spotlight identified a particular morally guided (but not necessarily religious) tribe of some 14 million voters that it dubbed "Barn Raisers." Barn Raisers comprise many races, religions, and ethnic groups and around 40 percent of Barn Raisers favor Democrats and 27 percent favor Republicans. Barn Raisers are slightly less likely to have a college education than Spotlight's other swing groups. They are active in community organizations, are ambivalent about government, and care deeply about "playing by the rules" and "keeping promises," to use Spotlight's definitions. Spotlight believed that the Barn Raisers held the key to the race between Obama and his Republican challenger, Arizona Senator John McCain.

Not typically seen outside of such corporate American icons as Google, Amazon, and eBay, political microtargeting, which depends on data, databases, and data analysis techniques, is turning political parties into sophisticated, intelligent, methodical machines. In nanoseconds, computers sort 175 million voters into segments and quickly calculate the potential that each individual voter has to swing from red or purple to blue or vice versa.

For some, political microtargeting signals the dehumanization of politics. For others, this type of sophisticated analysis is a highly efficient way of pinpointing potential voters. For example, analyzing a voter in Richmond, Virginia, traditionally simply identifies the number of school-age children, type of car, zip code, magazine subscriptions, and mortgage balance. But data crunching could even indicate if the voter has dogs or cats. (Cat owners lean slightly for Democrats, dog owners trend Republican.) After the analysis, the voter is placed into a political tribe, and analyzers can draw conclusions about the issues that matter to this particular voter. Is that so horrible?

Behavioral Grouping

For generations, governments lacked the means to study individual behaviors and simply placed all citizens into enormous groupings such as Hispanics, Jews, union members, hunters, soccer moms, etc. With the use of sophisticated databases and data analysis techniques, companies such as Spotlight can group individuals based more on specific behavior and choices and less on the names, colors, and clans that mark us from birth.

When Spotlight first embarked on its research, the company interviewed thousands of voters the old-fashioned way. At first, the Barn Raisers did not seem significant and the tribe represented about 9 percent of the electorate. However, when Spotlight's analysts dug deeper, they discovered that Barn Raisers stood at the epicenter of America's political swing. In 2004, 90 percent of them voted for President Bush, but then the group's political leanings shifted, with 64 percent of them saying they voted for Democrats in the 2006 election. Spotlight surveys showed that political scandals, tax-funded boondoggles like Alaska's Bridge to Nowhere, and the botched job on Hurricane Katrina sent them packing.

Suddenly, Spotlight identified millions of potential swing voters. The challenge then became locating the swing voters by states. For this, the company analyzed the demographics and buying patterns of the Barn Raisers they surveyed personally. Then it began correlating data from the numerous commercially available databases with matching profiles. By Spotlight's count, this approach nailed Barn Raisers three times out of four. So Democrats could bet that at least three-quarters of them would be likely to welcome an appeal stressing honesty and fair play.

Still Swing Voters

It is still undetermined to what extent Spotlight's strategy worked, and the company has not correlated the Barn Raisers to their actual votes. However, it is reasonable to presume that amid that sea of humanity stretched out before Obama on Washington's Mall on January 20, 2008, at least some were moved by microtargeted appeals. And if Obama and his team fail to honor their mathematically honed vows, the Barn Raisers may abandon them in droves. They are swing voters, after all.[3]

Questions

1. Describe the difference between transactional and analytical information, and determine which of these types Spotlight used to identify its 10 tribes.

2. Explain the importance of high-quality information for political microtargeting.

3. Review the five common characteristics of high-quality information, and rank them in order of importance for political microtargeting.

4. In terms of political microtargeting, explain the following sentence: It is never possible to have all of the information required to make a 100 percent accurate prediction.

5. Do you agree that political microtargeting signals the dehumanization of politics?

Storing Organizational Information—Databases

7.1. Describe a database, a database management system, and the relational database model.

7.2. Identify the business advantages of a relational database.

7.3. Explain the business benefits of a data-driven website.

7.4. Explain why an organization would want to integrate its databases.

LO 7.1 Describe a database, a database management system, and the relational database model.

Storing Information Using a Relational Database Management System

The core component of any system, regardless of size, is a database and a database management system. Broadly defined, a ***database*** maintains information about various types of objects (inventory), events (transactions), people (employees), and places (warehouses). A ***database management system (DBMS)*** creates, reads, updates, and deletes data in a database while controlling access and security. Managers send requests to the DBMS, and the DBMS performs the actual manipulation of the data in the database. Companies store their information in databases, and managers access these systems to answer operational questions such as how many customers purchased Product A in December or what were the average sales by region. There are two primary tools available for retrieving information from a DBMS. First is a ***query-by-example (QBE) tool*** that helps users graphically design the answer to a question against a database. Second is a ***structured query language (SQL)*** that asks users to write lines of code to answer questions against a database. Managers typically interact with QBE tools, and MIS professionals have the skills required to code SQL. Figure 7.1 displays the relationship between a database, a DBMS, and a user. Some of the more popular examples of DBMS include MySQL, Microsoft Access, SQL Server, FileMaker, Oracle, and FoxPro.

A ***data element*** (or ***data field***) is the smallest or basic unit of information. Data elements can include a customer's name, address, email, discount rate, preferred shipping method, product name, quantity ordered, and so on. ***Data models*** are logical data structures that detail the relationships among data elements using graphics or pictures.

FIGURE 7.1

Relationship of Database, DBMS, and User

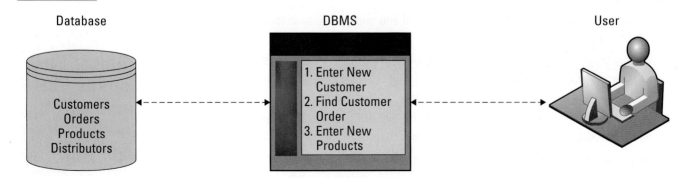

Database	DBMS	User
Customers Orders Products Distributors	1. Enter New Customer 2. Find Customer Order 3. Enter New Products	

Metadata provides details about data. For example, metadata for an image could include its size, resolution, and date created. Metadata about a text document could contain document length, data created, author's name, and summary. Each data element is given a description, such as Customer Name; metadata is provided for the type of data (text, numeric, alphanumeric, date, image, binary value) and descriptions of potential predefined values such as a certain area code; and finally the relationship is defined. A **data dictionary** compiles all of the metadata about the data elements in the data model. Looking at a data model along with reviewing the data dictionary provides tremendous insight into the database's functions, purpose, and business rules.

DBMS use three primary data models for organizing information—hierarchical, network, and the relational database, the most prevalent. A **relational database model** stores information in the form of logically related two-dimensional tables. A **relational database management system** allows users to create, read, update, and delete data in a relational database. Although the hierarchical and network models are important, this text focuses only on the relational database model.

STORING DATA ELEMENTS IN ENTITIES AND ATTRIBUTES

For flexibility in supporting business operations, managers need to query or search for the answers to business questions such as which artist sold the most albums during a certain month. The relationships in the relational database model help managers extract this information. Figure 7.2 illustrates the primary concepts of the relational database model—entities, attributes, keys, and relationships. An **entity** (also referred to as a table) stores information about a person, place, thing, transaction, or event. The entities, or tables, of interest in Figure 7.2 are *TRACKS, RECORDINGS, MUSICIANS,* and *CATEGORIES.* Notice that each entity is stored in a different two-dimensional table (with rows and columns).

Attributes (also called columns or fields) are the data elements associated with an entity. In Figure 7.2 the attributes for the entity *TRACKS* are *TrackNumber, TrackTitle, TrackLength,* and *RecordingID.* Attributes for the entity *MUSICIANS* are *MusicianID,*

FIGURE 7.2

Primary Concepts of the Relational Database Model

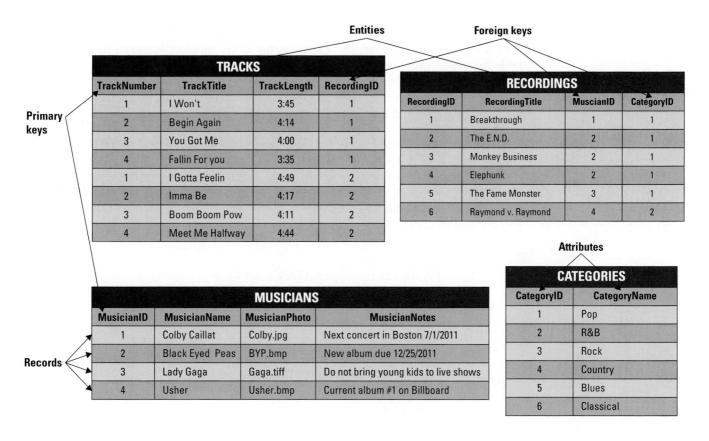

MusicianName, MusicianPhoto, and *MusicianNotes.* A **record** is a collection of related data elements (in the *MUSICIANS* table these include "3, Lady Gaga, gag.tiff, Do not bring young kids to live shows"). Each record in an entity occupies one row in its respective table.

CREATING RELATIONSHIPS THROUGH KEYS

To manage and organize various entities within the relational database model, you use primary keys and foreign keys to create logical relationships. A **primary key** is a field (or group of fields) that uniquely identifies a given record in a table. In the table *RECORDINGS,* the primary key is the field *RecordingID* that uniquely identifies each record in the table. Primary keys are a critical piece of a relational database because they provide a way of distinguishing each record in a table; for instance, imagine you need to find information on a customer named Steve Smith. Simply searching the customer name would not be an ideal way to find the information because there might be 20 customers with the name Steve Smith. This is the reason the relational database model uses primary keys to uniquely identify each record. Using Steve Smith's unique ID allows a manager to search the database to identify all information associated with this customer.

A **foreign key** is a primary key of one table that appears as an attribute in another table and acts to provide a logical relationship between the two tables. For instance, Black Eyed Peas in Figure 7.2 is one of the musicians appearing in the *MUSICIANS* table. Its primary key, *MusicianID,* is "2." Notice that *MusicianID* also appears as an attribute in the *RECORDINGS* table. By matching these attributes, you create a relationship between the *MUSICIANS* and *RECORDINGS* tables that states the Black Eyed Peas *(MusicianID 2)* have several recordings including The E.N.D., Monkey Business, and Elepunk. In essence, *MusicianID* in the *RECORDINGS* table creates a logical relationship (who was the musician that made the recording) to the *MUSICIANS* table. Creating the logical relationship between the tables allows managers to search the data and turn it into useful information.

COCA-COLA RELATIONAL DATABASE EXAMPLE

Figure 7.3 illustrates the primary concepts of the relational database model for a sample order of soda from Coca-Cola. Figure 7.3 offers an excellent example of how data is stored in a database. For example, the order number is stored in the *ORDER* table and each line item is stored in the *ORDER LINE* table. Entities include *CUSTOMER, ORDER, ORDER LINE, PRODUCT,* and *DISTRIBUTOR.* Attributes for *CUSTOMER* include *Customer ID, Customer Name, Contact Name,* and *Phone.* Attributes for *PRODUCT* include *Product ID, Description,* and *Price.* The columns in the table contain the attributes. Consider Hawkins Shipping, one of the distributors appearing in the *DISTRIBUTOR* table. Its primary key, *Distributor ID,* is DEN8001. Notice that *Distributor ID* also appears as an attribute in the *ORDER* table. This establishes the fact that Hawkins Shipping (*Distributor ID* DEN8001) was responsible for delivering orders 34561 and 34562 to the appropriate customer(s). Therefore, *Distributor ID* in the *ORDER* table creates a logical relationship (who shipped what order) between *ORDER* and *DISTRIBUTOR.*

LO 7.2 Identify the business advantages of a relational database.

Using a Relational Database for Business Advantages

Many business managers are familiar with Excel and other spreadsheet programs they can use to store business data. Although spreadsheets are excellent for supporting some data analysis, they offer limited functionality in terms of security, accessibility, and flexibility and can rarely scale to support business growth. From a business perspective, relational databases offer many advantages over using a text document or a spreadsheet, as displayed in Figure 7.4.

Order Number: 34562

Coca-Cola Bottling Company of Egypt
Sample Sales Order

Customer: Dave's Sub Shop	Date: 8/6/2008

Quantity	Product	Price	Amount
100	Vanilla Coke	$0.55	$55

	Distributor Fee	$12.95
	Order Total	$67.95

CUSTOMER

Customer ID	Customer Name	Contact Name	Phone
23	Dave's Sub Shop	David Logan	(555)333-4545
43	Pizza Palace	Debbie Fernandez	(555)345-5432
765	T's Fun Zone	Tom Repicci	(555)565-6655

ORDER

Order ID	Order Date	Customer ID	Distributor ID	Distributor Fee	Total Due
34561	7/4/2008	23	DEN8001	$22.00	$145.75
34562	8/6/2008	23	DEN8001	$12.95	$67.95
34563	6/5/2008	765	NY9001	$29.50	$249.50

ORDER LINE

Order ID	Line Item	Product ID	Quantity
34561	1	12345AA	75
34561	2	12346BB	50
34561	3	12347CC	100
34562	1	12349EE	100
34563	1	12345AA	100
34563	2	12346BB	100
34563	3	12347CC	50
34563	4	12348DD	50
34563	5	12349EE	100

DISTRIBUTOR

Distributor ID	Distributor Name
DEN8001	Hawkins Shipping
CHI3001	ABC Trucking
NY9001	Van Distributors

PRODUCT

Product ID	Product Description	Price
12345AA	Coca-Cola	$0.55
12346BB	Diet Coke	$0.55
12347CC	Sprite	$0.55
12348DD	Diet Sprite	$0.55
12349EE	Vanilla Coke	$0.55

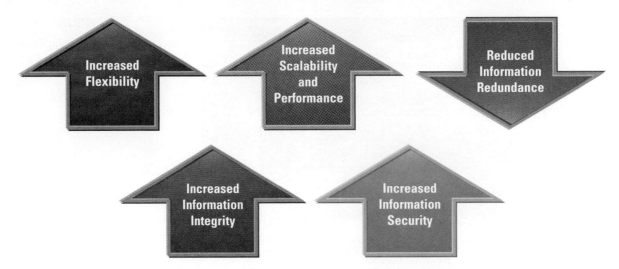

FIGURE 7.4

Business Advantages of
a Relational Database

INCREASED FLEXIBILITY

Databases tend to mirror business structures, and a database needs to handle changes quickly and easily, just as any business needs to be able to do. Equally important, databases need to provide flexibility in allowing each user to access the information in whatever way best suits his or her needs. The distinction between logical and physical views is important in understanding flexible database user views. The ***physical view of information*** deals with the physical storage of information on a storage device. The ***logical view of information*** focuses on how individual users logically access information to meet their own particular business needs.

In the database illustration from Figure 7.2, for example, one user could perform a query to determine which recordings had a track length of four minutes or more. At the same time, another user could perform an analysis to determine the distribution of recordings as they relate to the different categories. For example, are there more R&B recordings than rock, or are they evenly distributed? This example demonstrates that while a database has only one physical view, it can easily support multiple logical views that provides for flexibility.

Consider another example—a mail-order business. One user might want a report presented in alphabetical format, in which case last name should appear before first name. Another user, working with a catalog mailing system, would want customer names appearing as first name and then last name. Both are easily achievable, but different logical views of the same physical information.

INCREASED SCALABILITY AND PERFORMANCE

In its first year of operation, the official website of the American Family Immigration History Center, www.ellisisland.org, generated more than 2.5 billion hits. The site offers immigration information about people who entered America through the Port of New York and Ellis Island between 1892 and 1924. The database contains more than 25 million passenger names that are correlated to 3.5 million images of ships' manifests.[1]

The database had to be scalable to handle the massive volumes of information and the large numbers of users expected for the launch of the website. In addition, the database needed to perform quickly under heavy use. Some organizations must be able to support hundreds or thousands of users including employees, partners, customers, and suppliers, who all want to access and share the same information. Databases today scale to exceptional levels, allowing all types of users and programs to perform information-processing and information-searching tasks.

REDUCED INFORMATION REDUNDANCY

Information redundancy is the duplication of data, or the storage of the same data in multiple places. Redundant data can cause storage issues along with data integrity issues, making it difficult to determine which values are the most current or most accurate. Employees become confused and frustrated when faced with incorrect information causing disruptions to business processes and procedures. One primary goal of a database is to eliminate information redundancy by recording each piece of information in only one place in the database. This saves disk space, makes performing information updates easier, and improves information quality.

INCREASED INFORMATION INTEGRITY (QUALITY)

Information integrity is a measure of the quality of information. *Integrity constraints* are rules that help ensure the quality of information. The database design needs to consider integrity constraints. The database and the DBMS ensures that users can never violate these constraints. There are two types of integrity constraints: (1) relational and (2) business critical.

Relational integrity constraints are rules that enforce basic and fundamental information-based constraints. For example, a relational integrity constraint would not allow someone to create an order for a nonexistent customer, provide a markup percentage that was negative, or order zero pounds of raw materials from a supplier. A *business rule* defines how a company performs certain aspects of its business and typically results in either a yes/no or true/false answer. Stating that merchandise returns are allowed within 10 days of purchase is an example of a business rule. *Business-critical integrity constraints* enforce business rules vital to an organization's success and often require more insight and knowledge than relational integrity constraints. Consider a supplier of fresh produce to large grocery chains such as Kroger. The supplier might implement a business-critical integrity constraint stating that no product returns are accepted after 15 days past delivery. That would make sense because of the chance of spoilage of the produce. Business-critical integrity constraints tend to mirror the very rules by which an organization achieves success.

The specification and enforcement of integrity constraints produce higher-quality information that will provide better support for business decisions. Organizations that establish specific procedures for developing integrity constraints typically see an increase in accuracy that then increases the use of organizational information by business professionals.

INCREASED INFORMATION SECURITY

Managers must protect information, like any asset, from unauthorized users or misuse. As systems become increasingly complex and highly available over the Internet on many different devices, security becomes an even bigger issue. Databases offer many security features including passwords to provide authentication, access levels to determine who can access the data, and access controls to determine what type of access they have to the information.

For example, customer service representatives might need read-only access to customer order information so they can answer customer order inquiries; they might not have or need the authority to change or delete order information. Managers might require access to employee files, but they should have access only to their own employees' files, not the employee files for the entire company. Various security features of databases can ensure that individuals have only certain types of access to certain types of information.

Security risks are increasing as more and more databases and DBMS systems are moving to data centers run in the cloud. The biggest risks when using cloud computing are ensuring the security and privacy of the information in the database. Implementing data governance policies and procedures that outline the data management requirements can ensure safe and secure cloud computing.

Driving Websites with Data

A *content creator* is the person responsible for creating the original website content. A *content editor* is the person responsible for updating and maintaining website content. *Static information* includes fixed data incapable of change in the event of a user action. *Dynamic information* includes data that change based on user actions. For example, static websites supply only information that will not change until the content editor changes the information. Dynamic information changes when a user requests information. A dynamic website changes information based on user requests such as movie ticket availability, airline prices, or restaurant reservations. Dynamic website information is stored in a *dynamic catalog,* or an area of a website that stores information about products in a database.

Websites change for site visitors depending on the type of information they request. Consider, for example, an automobile dealer. The dealer would create a database containing data elements for each car it has available for sale including make, model, color, year, miles per gallon, a photograph, and so on. Website visitors might click on Porsche and then enter their specific requests such as price range or year made. Once the user hits "go" the website automatically provides a custom view of the requested information. The dealer must create, update, and delete automobile information as the inventory changes.

A *data-driven website* is an interactive website kept constantly updated and relevant to the needs of its customers using a database. Data-driven capabilities are especially useful when a firm needs to offer large amounts of information, products, or services. Visitors can become quickly annoyed if they find themselves buried under an avalanche of information when searching a website. A data-driven website can help limit the amount of information displayed to customers based on unique search requirements. Companies even use data-driven websites to make information in their internal databases available to customers and business partners.

There are a number of advantages to using the web to access company databases. First, web browsers are much easier to use than directly accessing the database using a custom-query tool. Second, the web interface requires few or no changes to the database model. Finally, it costs less to add a web interface in front of a DBMS than to redesign and rebuild the system to support changes. Additional data-driven website advantages include:

- **Easy to manage content:** Website owners can make changes without relying on MIS professionals; users can update a data-driven website with little or no training.

- **Easy to store large amounts of data:** Data-driven websites can keep large volumes of information organized. Website owners can use templates to implement changes for layouts, navigation, or website structure. This improves website reliability, scalability, and performance.

- **Easy to eliminate human errors:** Data-driven websites trap data-entry errors, eliminating inconsistencies while ensuring all information is entered correctly.

Zappos credits its success as an online shoe retailer to its vast inventory of nearly 3 million products available through its dynamic data-driven website. The company built its data-driven website catering to a specific niche market: consumers who were tired of finding that their most-desired items were always out of stock at traditional retailers. Zappos' highly flexible, scalable, and secure database helped it rank as the most-available Internet retailer. Figure 7.5 displays Zappos data-driven website illustrating a user querying the database and receiving information that satisfies the user's request.[2]

Companies can gain valuable business knowledge by viewing the data accessed and analyzed from their website. Figure 7.6 displays how running queries or using analytical tools, such as a PivotTable, on the database that is attached to the website can offer insight into the business, such as items browsed, frequent requests, items bought together, and so on.

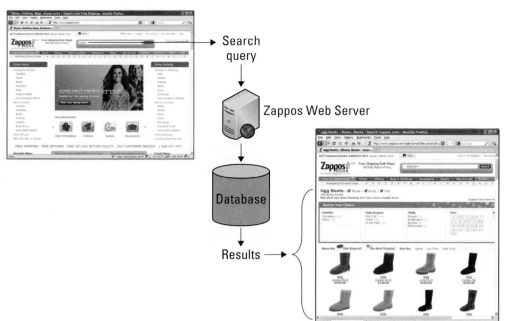

FIGURE 7.5

Zappos.com—
A Data-Driven Website

Search
query

Zappos Web Server

Database

Results

Integrating Information among Multiple Databases

LO 7.4 Explain why an organization would want to integrate its databases.

Until the 1990s, each department in the United Kingdom's Ministry of Defense (MOD) and Army headquarters had its own systems, each system had its own database, and sharing information among the departments was difficult. Manually inputting the same information multiple times into the different systems was also time consuming and inefficient. In many cases, management could not even compile the information it required to answer questions and make decisions.

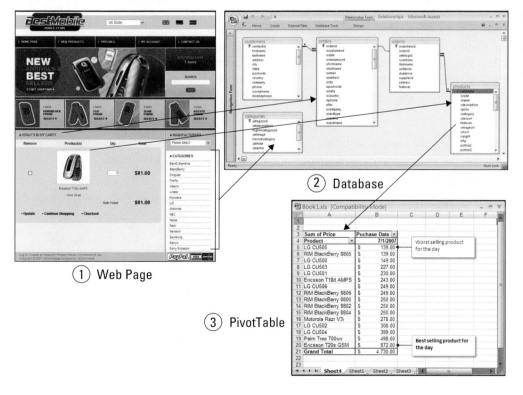

① Web Page

② Database

③ PivotTable

FIGURE 7.6

BI in a Data-Driven Website

The Army solved the problem by integrating its systems, or building connections between its many databases. These integrations allow the Army's multiple systems to automatically communicate by passing information between the databases, eliminating the need for manual information entry into multiple systems because after entering the information once, the integrations send the information immediately to all other databases. The integrations not only enable the different departments to share information, but have also dramatically increased the quality of the information. The Army can now generate reports detailing its state of readiness and other vital issues, nearly impossible tasks before building the integrations among the separate systems.[3]

An *integration* allows separate systems to communicate directly with each other. Similar to the UK's Army, an organization will probably maintain multiple systems, with each system having its own database. Without integrations, an organization will (1) spend considerable time entering the same information in multiple systems and (2) suffer from the low quality and inconsistency typically embedded in redundant information. While most integrations do not completely eliminate redundant information, they can ensure the consistency of it across multiple systems.

An organization can choose from two integration methods. The first is to create forward and backward integrations that link processes (and their underlying databases) in the value chain. A *forward integration* takes information entered into a given system and sends it automatically to all downstream systems and processes. A *backward integration* takes information entered into a given system and sends it automatically to all upstream systems and processes.

Figure 7.7 demonstrates how this method works across the systems or processes of sales, order entry, order fulfillment, and billing. In the order entry system, for example, an employee can update the information for a customer. That information, via the integrations, would be sent upstream to the sales system and downstream to the order fulfillment and billing systems.

Ideally, an organization wants to build both forward and backward integrations, which provide the flexibility to create, update, and delete information in any of the systems. However, integrations are expensive and difficult to build and maintain and most organizations build only forward integrations (sales through billing in Figure 7.7). Building only forward integrations implies that a change in the initial system (sales) will result in changes occurring in all the other systems. Integration of information is not possible for any changes occurring outside the initial system, which again can result in inconsistent organizational information. To address this issue, organizations can enforce business rules that all systems, other than the initial system, have read-only access to the integrated information. This will require users to change information in the initial system only, which will always trigger the integration and ensure that organizational information does not get out of sync.

FIGURE 7.7

A Forward and Backward Customer Information Integration Example

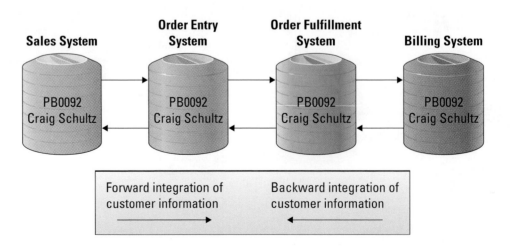

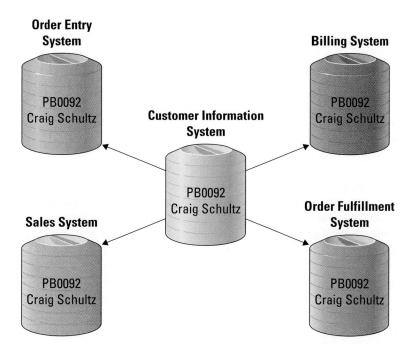

FIGURE 7.8

Integrating Customer
Information among
Databases

The second integration method builds a central repository for a particular type of information. Figure 7.8 provides an example of customer information integrated using this method across four different systems in an organization. Users can create, update, and delete customer information only in the central customer information database. As users perform these tasks on the central customer information database, integrations automatically send the new and/or updated customer information to the other systems. The other systems limit users to read-only access of the customer information stored in them. Again, this method does not eliminate redundancy—but it does ensure consistency of the information among multiple systems.

OPENING CASE STUDY QUESTIONS

1. Explain why database technology is important to a business.

2. Develop a list of some possible entities located in the Hotels.com database.

3. Develop a list of some possible attributes located in the Hotels.com database.

Chapter Seven Case: Keeper of the Keys

More than 145,000 consumers nationwide were placed at risk by a data theft at database giant ChoicePoint. Criminals tricked the company by posing as legitimate businesses to gain access to the various ChoicePoint databases, which contain a treasure trove of consumer data, including names, addresses, Social Security numbers, credit reports, and other information. At least 50 suspicious accounts had been opened in the name of nonexistent debt collectors, insurance agencies, and other companies, according to the company.

Without a doubt, databases are one of the most important IT tools that organizations use today. Databases contain large repositories of detailed data. When a transaction occurs, a sale, for example, a database stores every detail of the transaction including customer name, customer address, credit card number, products purchased, discounts received, and so on.

Organizations must carefully manage their databases. This management function includes properly organizing the information in these repositories in the most efficient way, ensuring that no erroneous information ever enters the databases, and—most important—protecting the information from thieves and hackers.

Information is a valuable commodity, and, sadly, this makes it a target for theft. Organizations store large amounts of customer information including Social Security numbers, credit card numbers, and bank account numbers—just think of the information stored at eBay, Amazon, or the IRS. When someone steals personal information (not necessarily by taking it from the person, but rather stealing it from a company), that person becomes a victim of identity theft. Consider this short list of organizations that have lost information and the huge numbers of customers affected.

- Bank of America: 1.2 million customers.
- CardSystems: 40 million customers.
- Citigroup: 3.9 million customers.
- DSW Shoe Warehouse: 1.4 million customers.
- TJX Companies: 45.6 million customers.
- Wachovia: 676,000 customers.

Adding up the numbers, more than 90 million people had their personal information either stolen or lost through organizations.

Business Accountability in Data Security

Companies may soon face stiff penalties for wayward data security practices. Massachusetts is considering legislation that would require companies to pay for any costs associated with a data breach of their IT systems. This move to protect customer data in Massachusetts comes at a fitting time, as two prominent retailers in the area, TJX Companies and Stop & Shop, wrestle with the aftermath of significant breaches that have exposed some of their customers to fraud.

Much of the expense associated with stopping fraudulent activity, such as canceling or reissuing credit or debit cards, stopping payment, and refunding customers, has been absorbed by the banks issuing credit or debit cards to the victims. The merchant banks that allow businesses such as TJX and Stop & Shop stores to accept credit and debit card transactions are penalized with fines from Visa, MasterCard, and other credit card organizations if the merchants they work with are found to violate the payment card industry's data security standards.

But the businesses that have had customer data stolen have largely suffered only from the costs to offer customers free credit-monitoring services and to repair a tarnished public image. In the case of popular retailers, this tarnish is easily polished away when juicy sales incentives are offered to get customers back.

Massachusetts House Bill 213, sponsored by Rep. Michael Costello, proposes to amend the Commonwealth's general laws to include a section that would require any corporation or other commercial entity whose sensitive customer information is stolen to notify customers about the data breach and also make companies liable to card-issuing banks for the costs those banks incur because of the breach and any subsequent fraudulent activity. This would include making businesses cover the costs to cancel or reissue cards, stop payments or block transactions with respect to any such account, open or reopen an account, and issue any refund or credit made to any customer of the bank as a result of unauthorized transactions.

The Massachusetts legislation is a key step in compelling companies to invest in better data security. Passage of this bill would put Massachusetts ahead of other states in terms of protecting customer data and spreading out the penalties so that both financial institutions and retailers have incentives to improve security. Security vendors are likely to be watching Massachusetts very closely, because the bill also would create an urgent need for companies doing business in that state to invest in ways to improve their ability to protect customer data. If the companies will not do this on their own, then holding them accountable for their customers' financial losses may be just what is needed to stop the next data breach from occurring.[4]

Questions

1. How many organizations have your personal information, including your Social Security number, bank account numbers, and credit card numbers?

2. What information is stored at your college? Is there a chance your information could be hacked and stolen from your college?

3. What can you do to protect yourself from identity theft?

4. Do you agree or disagree with changing laws to hold the company where the data theft occurred accountable? Why or why not?

5. What impact would holding the company liable where the data theft occurred have on large organizations?

6. What impact would holding the company liable where the data theft occurred have on small businesses?

Accessing Organizational Information—Data Warehouse

8.1. Describe the roles and purposes of data warehouses and data marts in an organization.

8.2. Identify the advantages of using business intelligence to support managerial decision making.

LO 8.1 Describe the roles and purposes of data warehouses and data marts in an organization.

Accessing Organizational Information

Applebee's Neighborhood Grill & Bar posts annual sales in excess of $3.2 billion and is actively using information from its data warehouse to increase sales and cut costs. The company gathers daily information for the previous day's sales into its data warehouse from 1,500 restaurants located in 49 states and seven countries. Understanding regional preferences, such as patrons in Texas preferring steaks more than patrons in New England, allows the company to meet its corporate strategy of being a neighborhood grill appealing to local tastes. The company has found tremendous value in its data warehouse by being able to make business decisions about customers' regional needs. The company also uses data warehouse information to perform the following:

- Base labor budgets on actual number of guests served per hour.
- Develop promotional sale item analysis to help avoid losses from overstocking or understocking inventory.
- Determine theoretical and actual costs of food and the use of ingredients.[1]

History of Data Warehousing

In the 1990s as organizations began to need more timely information about their business, they found that traditional operational information systems were too cumbersome to provide relevant data efficiently and quickly. Operational systems typically include accounting, order entry, customer service, and sales and are not appropriate for business analysis for the following reasons:

- Information from other operational applications is not included.
- Operational systems are not integrated, or not available in one place.
- Operational information is mainly current—does not include the history that is required to make good decisions.
- Operational information frequently has quality issues (errors)—the information needs to be cleansed.
- Without information history, it is difficult to tell how and why things change over time.
- Operational systems are not designed for analysis and decision support.

During the latter half of the 20th century, the numbers and types of databases increased. Many large businesses found themselves with information scattered across multiple platforms and variations of technology, making it almost impossible for any one individual to use information from multiple sources. Completing reporting requests across operational systems could take days or weeks using antiquated reporting tools that were designed to execute the business rather than run the business. From this idea, the data warehouse was born as a place where relevant information could be held for completing strategic reports for management. The key here is the word *strategic* as most executives were less concerned with the day-to-day operations than they were with a more overall look at the model and business functions.

A key idea within data warehousing is to take data from multiple platforms/ technologies (as varied as spreadsheets, databases, and word files) and place them in a common location that uses a common querying tool. In this way operational databases could be held on whatever system was most efficient for the operational business, while the reporting/strategic information could be held in a common location using a common language. Data warehouses take this a step further by giving the information itself commonality by defining what each term means and keeping it standard. An example of this would be gender, which can be referred to in many ways (Male, Female; M/F; 1/0), but should be standardized on a data warehouse with one common way of referring to each sex (M/F).

This design makes decision support more readily available without affecting day-to-day operations. One aspect of a data warehouse that should be stressed is that it is *not* a location for *all* of a business's information, but rather a location for information that is interesting, or information that will assist decision makers in making strategic decisions relative to the organization's overall mission.

Data warehousing is about extending the transformation of data into information. Data warehouses offer strategic level, external, integrated, and historical information so businesses can make projections, identify trends, and decide key business issues. The data warehouse collects and stores integrated sets of historical information from multiple operational systems and feeds them to one or more data marts. It may also provide end-user access to support enterprisewide views of information.

Data Warehouse Fundamentals

A ***data warehouse*** is a logical collection of information—gathered from many different operational databases—that supports business analysis activities and decision-making tasks. The primary purpose of a data warehouse is to aggregate information throughout an organization into a single repository in such a way that employees can make decisions and undertake business analysis activities. Therefore, while databases store the details of all transactions (for instance, the sale of a product) and events (hiring a new employee), data warehouses store that same information but in an aggregated form more suited to supporting decision-making tasks. Aggregation, in this instance, can include totals, counts, averages, and the like. Because of this sort of aggregation, data warehouses support only analytical processing.

The data warehouse modeled in Figure 8.1 compiles information from internal databases or transactional/operational databases and external databases through ***extraction, transformation, and loading (ETL),*** which is a process that extracts information from internal and external databases, transforms the information using a common set of enterprise definitions, and loads the information into a data warehouse. The data warehouse then sends subsets of the information to data marts. A ***data mart*** contains a subset of data warehouse information. To distinguish between data warehouses and data marts, think of data warehouses as having a more organizational focus and data marts as having focused information subsets particular to the needs of a given business unit such as finance or production and operations.

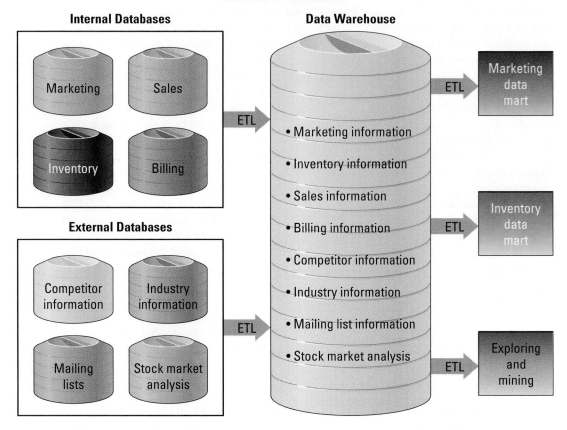

Data Warehouse Model

FIGURE 8.1

Model of a Typical Data Warehouse

Lands' End created an organizationwide data warehouse so all its employees could access organizational information. Lands' End soon found out that there could be "too much of a good thing." Many of its employees would not use the data warehouse because it was simply too big, too complicated, and had too much irrelevant information. Lands' End knew there was valuable information in its data warehouse, and it had to find a way for its employees to easily access the information. Data marts were the perfect solution to the company's information overload problem. Once the employees began using the data marts, they were ecstatic at the wealth of information. Data marts were a huge success for Lands' End.[2]

MULTIDIMENSIONAL ANALYSIS AND DATA MINING

A relational database contains information in a series of two-dimensional tables. In a data warehouse and data mart, information is multidimensional, meaning it contains layers of columns and rows. For this reason, most data warehouses and data marts are *multidimensional databases*. A *dimension* is a particular attribute of information. Each layer in a data warehouse or data mart represents information according to an additional dimension. A **cube** is the common term for the representation of multidimensional information. Figure 8.2 displays a cube (cube *a*) that represents store information (the layers), product information (the rows), and promotion information (the columns).

Once a cube of information is created, users can begin to slice and dice the cube to drill down into the information. The second cube (cube *b*) in Figure 8.2 displays a slice representing promotion II information for all products, at all stores. The third cube (cube *c*) in Figure 8.2 displays only information for promotion III, product B, at store 2. By using multidimensional analysis, users can analyze information in a number of different ways and with any number of different dimensions. For example, users might

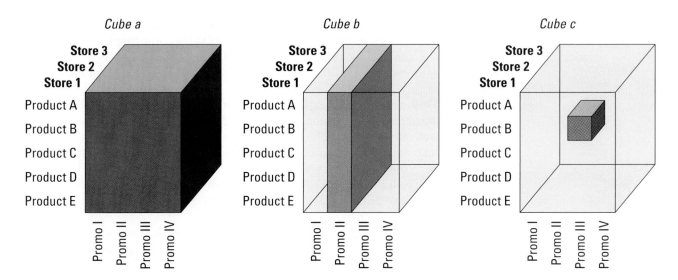

FIGURE 8.2

A Cube of Information for Performing a Multidimensional Analysis on Three Different Stores, for Five Different Products, and Four Different Promotions.

want to add dimensions of information to a current analysis including product category, region, and even forecasted versus actual weather. The true value of a data warehouse is its ability to provide multidimensional analysis that allows users to gain insights into their information.

Data warehouses and data marts are ideal for off-loading some of the querying against a database. For example, querying a database to obtain an average of sales for product B at store 2 while promotion III is under way might create a considerable processing burden for a database, essentially slowing down the time it takes another person to enter a new sale into the same database. If an organization performs numerous queries against a database (or multiple databases), aggregating that information into a data warehouse could be beneficial.

Data mining is the process of analyzing data to extract information not offered by the raw data alone. For example, Ruf Strategic Solutions helps organizations employ statistical approaches within a large data warehouse to identify customer segments that display common traits. Marketers can then target these segments with specially designed products and promotions.

Data mining can also begin at a summary information level (coarse granularity) and progress through increasing levels of detail (drilling down), or the reverse (drilling up). To perform data mining, users need data-mining tools. **Data-mining tools** use a variety of techniques to find patterns and relationships in large volumes of information and infer rules from them that predict future behavior and guide decision making. Data-mining tools for data warehouses and data marts include query tools, reporting tools, multidimensional analysis tools, statistical tools, and intelligent agents.

Sega of America, one of the largest publishers of video games, uses a data warehouse and statistical tools to distribute its annual advertising budget of more than $50 million. With its data warehouse, product line specialists and marketing strategists "drill" into trends of each retail store chain. Their goal is to find buying trends that help them determine which advertising strategies are working best and how to reallocate advertising resources by media, territory, and time.[3]

INFORMATION CLEANSING OR SCRUBBING

Maintaining quality information in a data warehouse or data mart is extremely important. The Data Warehousing Institute estimates that low-quality information costs U.S. businesses $600 billion annually. That number may seem high, but it is not. If an organization is using a data warehouse or data mart to allocate dollars across advertising strategies (such as in the case of Sega of America), low-quality information will definitely have a negative impact on its ability to make the right decision.[4]

To increase the quality of organizational information and thus the effectiveness of decision making, businesses must formulate a strategy to keep information clean. This is the concept of information cleansing or scrubbing. ***Information cleansing or scrubbing*** is a process that weeds out and fixes or discards inconsistent, incorrect, or incomplete information.

Specialized software tools use sophisticated algorithms to parse, standardize, correct, match, and consolidate data warehouse information. This is vitally important because data warehouses often contain information from several different databases, some of which can be external to the organization. In a data warehouse, information cleansing occurs first during the ETL process and second on the information once it is in the data warehouse. Companies can choose information cleansing software from several different vendors including Oracle, SAS, Ascential Software, and Group 1 Software. Ideally, scrubbed information is error free and consistent.

Dr Pepper/Seven Up, Inc., was able to integrate its myriad databases in a data warehouse (and subsequently data marts) in less than two months, giving the company access to consolidated, clean information. Approximately 600 people in the company regularly use the data marts to analyze and track beverage sales across multiple dimensions, including various distribution routes such as bottle/can sales, fountain foodservice sales, premier distributor sales, and chain and national accounts. The company is now performing in-depth analysis of up-to-date sales information that is clean and error free.[5]

Looking at customer information highlights why information cleansing is necessary. Customer information exists in several operational systems. In each system all details of this customer information could change from the customer ID to contact information (see Figure 8.3). Determining which contact information is accurate and correct for this customer depends on the business process that is being executed.

Figure 8.4 displays a customer name entered differently in multiple operational systems. Information cleansing allows an organization to fix these types of inconsistencies and cleans the information in the data warehouse. Figure 8.5 displays the typical events that occur during information cleansing.

Achieving perfect information is almost impossible. The more complete and accurate an organization wants its information to be, the more it costs (see Figure 8.6). The trade-off for perfect information lies in accuracy versus completeness. Accurate information means it is correct, while complete information means there are no blanks. A birth date of 2/31/10 is an example of complete but inaccurate information (February 31 does not exist). An address containing Denver, Colorado, without a ZIP code is an example of incomplete information that is accurate. For their information, most organizations determine a percentage high enough to make good decisions at a reasonable cost, such as 85 percent accurate and 65 percent complete.

FIGURE 8.3

Contact Information in Operational Systems

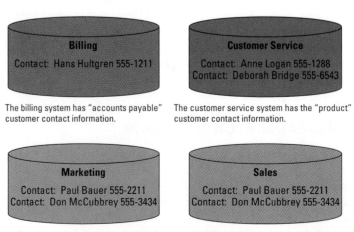

Billing
Contact: Hans Hultgren 555-1211

The billing system has "accounts payable" customer contact information.

Customer Service
Contact: Anne Logan 555-1288
Contact: Deborah Bridge 555-6543

The customer service system has the "product" customer contact information.

Marketing
Contact: Paul Bauer 555-2211
Contact: Don McCubbrey 555-3434

Sales
Contact: Paul Bauer 555-2211
Contact: Don McCubbrey 555-3434

The marketing and sales system has "decision maker" customer contact information.

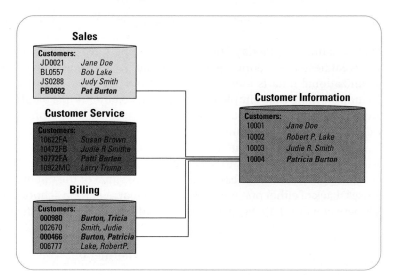

FIGURE 8.4

Standardizing Customer
Name from Operational
Systems

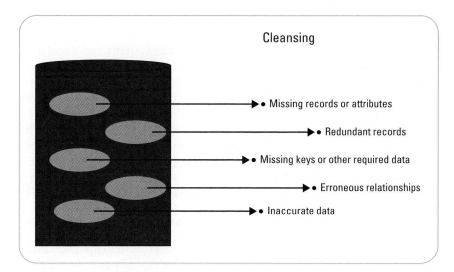

FIGURE 8.5

Information Cleansing
Activities

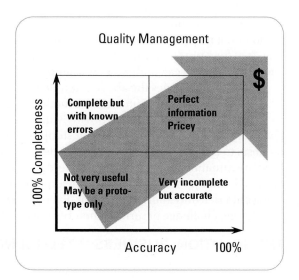

FIGURE 8.6

Accurate and Complete
Information

Supporting Decisions with Business Intelligence

Many organizations today find it next to impossible to understand their own strengths and weaknesses, let alone their biggest competitors, because the enormous volume of organizational data is inaccessible to all but the MIS department. Organization data include far more than simple structured data elements in a database; the set of data also includes unstructured data such as voice mail, customer phone calls, text messages, video clips, along with numerous new forms of data, such as tweets from Twitter.

An early reference to business intelligence occurs in Sun Tzu's book titled *The Art of War*. Sun Tzu claims that to succeed in war, one should have full knowledge of one's own strengths and weaknesses and full knowledge of the enemy's strengths and weaknesses. Lack of either one might result in defeat. A certain school of thought draws parallels between the challenges in business and those of war, specifically:

- Collecting information.
- Discerning patterns and meaning in the information.
- Responding to the resultant information.

Before the start of the information age in the late 20th century, businesses sometimes collected information from nonautomated sources. Businesses then lacked the computing resources to properly analyze the information and often made commercial decisions based primarily on intuition.

As businesses started automating more and more systems, more and more information became available. However, collection remained a challenge due to a lack of infrastructure for information exchange or to incompatibilities between systems. Reports sometimes took months to generate. Such reports allowed informed long-term strategic decision making. However, short-term tactical decision making continued to rely on intuition. In modern businesses, increasing standards, automation, and technologies have led to vast amounts of available information. Data warehouse technologies have set up repositories to store this information. Improved ETL has increased the speedy collecting of information. Business intelligence has now become the art of sifting through large amounts of data, extracting information, and turning that information into actionable knowledge.

THE PROBLEM: DATA RICH, INFORMATION POOR

An ideal business scenario would be as follows: As a business manager on his way to meet with a client reviews historical customer data, he realizes that the client's ordering volume has substantially decreased. As he drills down into the data, he notices the client had a support issue with a particular product. He quickly calls the support team to find out all of the information and learns that a replacement for the defective part can be shipped in 24 hours. In addition, he learns that the client has visited the website and requested information on a new product line. Armed with all this information, the business manager is prepared for a productive meeting with his client. He now understands the client's needs and issues, and he can address new sales opportunities with confidence.

For many companies the above example is simply a pipe dream. Attempting to gather all of the client information would actually take hours or even days to compile. With so much data available, it is surprisingly hard for managers to get information, such as inventory levels, past order history, or shipping details. Managers send their information requests to the MIS department where a dedicated person compiles the various reports. In some situations, responses can take days, by which time the information may be outdated and opportunities lost. Many organizations find themselves in the position of being data rich and information poor. Even in today's electronic world, managers struggle with the challenge of turning their business data into business intelligence.

THE SOLUTION: BUSINESS INTELLIGENCE

Employee decisions are numerous and they include providing service information, offering new products, and supporting frustrated customers. Employees can base their decisions on data, experience, or knowledge and preferably a combination of all three. Business intelligence can provide managers with the ability to make better decisions. A few examples of how different industries use business intelligence include:

- **Airlines:** Analyze popular vacation locations with current flight listings.
- **Banking:** Understand customer credit card usage and nonpayment rates.
- **Health care:** Compare the demographics of patients with critical illnesses.
- **Insurance:** Predict claim amounts and medical coverage costs.
- **Law enforcement:** Track crime patterns, locations, and criminal behavior.
- **Marketing:** Analyze customer demographics.
- **Retail:** Predict sales, inventory levels, and distribution.
- **Technology:** Predict hardware failures.

Figure 8.7 displays how organizations using BI can find the cause to many issues and problems simply by asking "Why?" The process starts by analyzing a report such as sales amounts by quarter. Managers will drill down into the report looking for why sales are up or why sales are down. Once they understand why a certain location or product is experiencing an increase in sales, they can share the information in an effort to raise enterprisewide sales. Once they understand the cause for a decrease in sales, they can take effective action to resolve the issue. Here are a few examples of how managers can use BI to answer tough business questions:

- **Where has the business been?** Historical perspective offers important variables for determining trends and patterns.
- **Where is the business now?** Looking at the current business situation allows managers to take effective action to solve issues before they grow out of control.
- **Where is the business going?** Setting strategic direction is critical for planning and creating solid business strategies.

Ask a simple question—such as who is my best customer or what is my worst-selling product—and you might get as many answers as you have employees. Databases, data warehouses, and data marts can provide a single source of "trusted" data that can answer questions about customers, products, suppliers, production, finances, fraud, and even employees. They can also alert managers to inconsistencies or help determine the cause and effects of enterprisewide business decisions. All business aspects can benefit from the added insights provided by business intelligence, and you, as a business student, will benefit from understanding how MIS can help you make intelligent decisions.[6]

VISUAL BUSINESS INTELLIGENCE

Informing is accessing large amounts of data from different management information systems. **Infographics (information graphics)** displays information graphically so it can

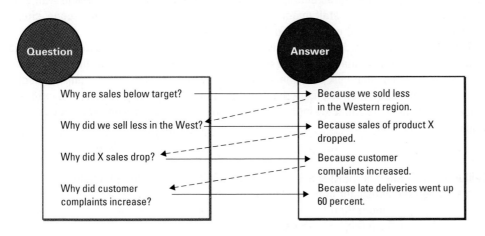

FIGURE 8.7

How BI Can Answer Tough Customer Questions

be easily understood. Infographics can present the results of large data analysis looking for patterns and relationships that monitor changes in variables over time. *Data visualization* describes technologies that allow users to "see" or visualize data to transform information into a business perspective. *Data visualization tools* move beyond Excel graphs and charts into sophisticated analysis techniques such as pie charts, controls, instruments, maps, time-series graphs, and more. Data visualization tools can help uncover correlations and trends in data that would otherwise go unrecognized. *Business intelligence dashboards* track corporate metrics such as critical success factors and key performance indicators and include advanced capabilities such as interactive controls allowing users to manipulate data for analysis. The majority of business intelligence software vendors offer a number of different data visualization tools and business intelligence dashboards.

OPENING CASE STUDY QUESTIONS

1. List the reasons a business would want to display information in a graphic or visual format.

2. Describe how a business could use a business intelligence digital dashboard to gain an understanding of how the business is operating.

3. Explain how a marketing department could use data visualization tools to help with the release of a new product.

4. Assess how Hotels.com is using BI to identify trends and change associated business processes.

Chapter Eight Case: Mining the Data Warehouse

According to a Merrill Lynch survey in 2006, business intelligence software and data-mining tools were at the top of CIOs' technology spending list. Following are a few examples of how companies are using data warehousing and data-mining tools to gain valuable business intelligence.

Ben & Jerry's

These days, when we all scream for ice cream, Ben & Jerry's cuts through the din by using integrated query, reporting, and online analytical processing technology from BI software vendor Business Objects. Through an Oracle database and with BI from Business Objects, Ben & Jerry's tracks the ingredients and life of each pint. If a consumer calls in with a complaint, the consumer affairs staff matches the pint with which supplier's milk, eggs, cherries, or whatever did not meet the organization's near-obsession with quality.

The BI tools let Ben & Jerry's officials access, analyze, and act on customer information collected by the sales, finance, purchasing, and quality-assurance departments. The company can determine what milk customers prefer in the making of the ice cream. The technology helped Ben & Jerry's track more than 12,500 consumer contacts in 2005. The information ranged from comments about the ingredients used in ice cream to queries about social causes supported by the company.

California Pizza Kitchen

California Pizza Kitchen (CPK) is a leading casual dining chain in the premium pizza segment with a recognized consumer brand and an established, loyal customer base. Founded in 1985, there are currently more than 130 full-service restaurants in more than 26 states, the District of Columbia, and five foreign countries.

Before implementing its BI tool, Cognos, CPK used spreadsheets to plan and track its financial statements and line items. The finance team had difficulty managing the volumes of data, complex calculations, and constant changes to the spreadsheets. It took several weeks of two people working full-time to obtain one version of the financial statements and future forecast. In addition, the team was limited by the software's inability to link cells and calculations across multiple spreadsheets, so updating other areas of corporate records became a time-consuming task. With Cognos, quarterly forecasting cycles have been reduced from eight days to two days. The finance team can now spend more time reviewing the results rather than collecting and entering the data.

Noodles & Company

Noodles & Company has more than 70 restaurants throughout Colorado, Illinois, Maryland, Michigan, Minnesota, Texas, Utah, Virginia, and Wisconsin. The company recently purchased Cognos BI tools to help implement reporting standards and communicate real-time operational information to field management throughout the United States.

Before implementing the first phase of the Cognos solution, IT and finance professionals spent days compiling report requests from numerous departments including sales and marketing, human resources, and real estate. Since completing phase one, operational Cognos reports are being accessed on a daily basis through the Noodles & Company website. This provides users with a single, 360-degree view of the business and consistent reporting throughout the enterprise.

Noodles & Company users benefit from the flexible query and reporting capabilities, allowing them to see patterns in the data to leverage new business opportunities. Cognos tools can pull information directly from a broad array of relational, operational, and other systems.[7]

Questions

1. Explain how Ben & Jerry's is using business intelligence tools to remain successful and competitive in a saturated market.

2. Identify why information cleansing is critical to California Pizza Kitchen's business intelligence tool's success.

3. Illustrate why 100 percent accurate and complete information is impossible for Noodles & Company to obtain.

4. Describe how each of the companies above is using BI to gain a competitive advantage.

The five common characteristics of quality information are accuracy, completeness, consistency, uniqueness, and timeliness. The costs to an organization of having low quality information can be enormous and could result in revenue losses and ultimately business failure. Databases maintain information about various types of objects, events, people, and places and help to alleviate many of the problems associated with low quality information such as redundancy, integrity, and security.

A data warehouse is a logical collection of information—gathered from many different operational databases—that supports business analysis activities and decision-making tasks. Data marts contain a subset of data warehouse information. Organizations gain tremendous insight into their business by mining the information contained in data warehouses and data marts.

Understanding the value of information is key to business success. Employees must be able to optimally access and analyze organizational information. The more knowledge employees have concerning how the organization stores, maintains, provides access to, and protects information the better prepared they will be when they need to use that information to make critical business decisions.

✳ **KEY TERMS**

Analytical information, 86
Attribute, 93
Backward integration, 100
Business intelligence
    dashboard, 112
Business-critical integrity
    constraint, 97
Business rule, 97
Content creator, 98
Cube, 106
Content editor, 98
Database, 92
Database management system
    (DBMS), 92
Data dictionary, 93
Data-driven website, 98
Data element (or data field), 92
Data governance, 90
Data model, 92
Data mart, 105
Data mining, 107

Data-mining tools, 107
Data visualization, 112
Data visualization tools, 112
Data warehouse, 105
Dynamic catalog, 98
Dynamic information, 98
Entity, 93
Extraction, transformation, and
    loading (ETL), 105
Foreign key, 94
Forward integration, 100
Informing, 111
Information cleansing or
    scrubbing, 108
Information granularity, 85
Information inconsistency, 87
Information integrity, 97
Information integrity issues, 87
Information redundancy, 97
Infographics (information
    graphics), 111

Integration, 100
Integrity constraint, 97
Logical view of information, 96
Metadata, 93
Physical view of information, 96
Primary key, 94
Query-by-example (QBE)
    tool, 92
Real-time information, 87
Real-time system, 87
Record, 94
Relational database
    management sytem, 93
Relational database model, 93
Relational integrity
    constraints, 97
Transactional information, 85
Static information, 98
Structured query language
    (SQL), 92

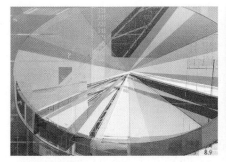 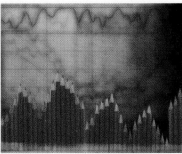 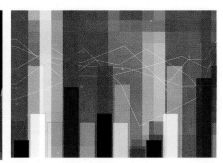

Data Visualization: Stories for the Information Age

At the intersection of art and algorithm, data visualization schematically abstracts information to bring about a deeper understanding of the data, wrapping it in an element of awe. While the practice of visually representing information is arguably the foundation of all design, a newfound fascination with data visualization has been emerging. After *The New York Times* and *The Guardian* recently opened their online archives to the public, artists rushed to dissect nearly two centuries worth of information, elevating this art form to new prominence.

For artists and designers, data visualization is a new frontier of self-expression, powered by the proliferation of information and the evolution of available tools. For enterprise, it is a platform for displaying products and services in the context of the cultural interaction that surrounds them, reflecting consumers' increasing demand for corporate transparency.

"Looking at something ordinary in a new way makes it extraordinary," says Aaron Koblin, one of the more recent pioneers of the discipline. As technology lead of Google's Creative Labs in San Francisco, he spearheaded the search giant's Chrome Experiments series designed to show off the speed and reliability of the Chrome browser.

Forget Pie Charts and Bar Graphs

Data visualization has nothing to do with pie charts and bar graphs. And it's only marginally related to "infographics," information design that tends to be about objectivity and clarification. Such representations simply offer another iteration of the data—restating it visually and making it easier to digest. Data visualization, on the other hand, is an interpretation, a different way to look at and think about data that often exposes complex patterns or correlations.

Data visualization is a way to make sense of the ever-increasing stream of information with which we're bombarded and provides a creative antidote to the analysis paralysis that can result from the burden of processing such a large volume of information. "It's not about clarifying data," says Koblin. "It's about contextualizing it."

Today algorithmically inspired artists are reimagining the art-science continuum through work that frames the left-brain analysis of data in a right-brain creative story. Some use data visualization as a bridge between alienating information and its emotional impact—see Chris Jordan's portraits of global mass culture. Others take a more technological angle and focus on cultural utility—the Zoetrope project offers a temporal and historical visualization of the ephemeral web. Still others are pure artistic indulgence—like Koblin's own Flight Patterns project, a visualization of air traffic over North America.

How Business Can Benefit

There are real implications for business here. Most cell phone providers, for instance, offer a statement of a user's monthly activity. Most often it's an overwhelming table of various numerical measures of how much you talked, when, with whom, and how much it cost. A visual representation of these data might help certain patterns emerge, revealing calling habits and perhaps helping users save money.

Companies can also use data visualization to gain new insight into consumer behavior. By observing and understanding what people do with the data—what they find useful and what they dismiss as worthless—executives can make the valuable distinction between what consumers say versus what they do. Even now, this can be a tricky call to make from behind the two-way mirror of a traditional qualitative research setting.

It's essential to understand the importance of creative vision along with the technical mastery of software. Data visualization isn't about using all the data available, but about deciding which patterns and elements to focus on, building a narrative, and telling the story of the raw data in a different, compelling way.

Ultimately, data visualization is more than complex software or the prettying up of spreadsheets. It's not innovation for the sake of innovation. It's about the most ancient of social rituals: storytelling. It's about telling the story locked in the data differently, more engagingly, in a way that draws us in, makes our eyes open a little wider and our jaw drop ever so slightly. And as we process it, it can sometimes change our perspective altogether.[8]

Questions

1. Identify the effects poor information might have on a data visualization project.
2. How does data visualization use database technologies?
3. How could a business use data visualization to identify new trends?
4. What is the correlation between data mining and data visualization?
5. Is data visualization a form of business intelligence? Why or why not?
6. What security issues are associated with data visualization?
7. What might happen to a data visualization project if it failed to cleanse or scrub its data?

✱ UNIT CLOSING CASE TWO

Zillow

Zillow.com is an online web-based real estate site helping homeowners, buyers, sellers, renters, real estate agents, mortgage professionals, property owners, and property managers find and share information about real estate and mortgages. Zillow allows users to access, anonymously and free of charge, the kinds of tools and information previously reserved for real estate professionals. Zillow's databases cover more than 90 million homes, which represents 95 percent of the homes in the United States. Adding to the sheer size of its databases, Zillow recalculates home valuations for each property every day, so they can provide historical graphs on home valuations over time. In some areas, Zillow is able to display 10 years of valuation history, a value-added benefit for many of its customers. This collection of data represents an operational data warehouse for anyone visiting the website.

As soon as Zillow launched its website, it immediately generated a massive amount of traffic. As the company expanded its services, the founders knew the key to its success would be the site's ability to quickly process and manage massive amounts of data, in real time. The company identified a need for accessible, scalable, reliable, secure databases that would enable it to continue to increase the capacity of its infrastructure indefinitely without sacrificing performance. Zillow's traffic continues to grow despite the weakening real estate market; the company is experiencing annual traffic growth of 30 percent and about a third of all U.S. mortgage professionals visit the site in a given month.

Data Mining and Business Intelligence

Zestimate® values on Zillow use data-mining features for spotting trends across property valuations. Data mining also allows the company to see how accurate Zestimate values are over time. Zillow has also built the industry's first search by monthly payment, allowing users to find homes that are for sale and rent based on a monthly payment they can afford. Along with the monthly payment search, users can also enter search criteria such as the number of bedrooms or bathrooms.

Zillow also launched a new service aimed at changing the way Americans shop for mortgages. Borrowers can use Zillow's new Mortgage Marketplace to get custom loan quotes from lenders without having to give their names, addresses, phone numbers, or Social Security numbers, or field unwanted telephone calls from brokers competing for their business. Borrowers reveal their identities only after contacting the lender of their choice. The company is entering a field of established mortgage sites such as LendingTree.com and Experian Group's Lowermybills.com, which charge mortgage companies for borrower information. Zillow, which has an advertising model, says it does not plan to charge for leads.

For mortgage companies, the anonymous leads come free; they can make a bid based on information provided by the borrower, such as salary, assets, credit score, and the type of loan. Lenders can browse borrower requests and see competing quotes from other brokers before making a bid.[9]

Questions

1. List the reasons Zillow would need to use a database to run its business.
2. Describe how Zillow uses business intelligence to create a unique product for its customers.
3. How could the marketing department at Zillow use a data mart to help with the release of a new product launch?
4. Categorize the five common characteristics of high-quality information and rank them in order of importance to Zillow.
5. Develop a list of some possible entities and attributes of Zillow's mortgage database.
6. Assess how Zillow uses a data-driven website to run its business.

1. Improving Information Quality

HangUps Corporation designs and distributes closet organization structures. The company operates five different systems: order entry, sales, inventory management, shipping, and billing. The company has severe information quality issues including missing, inaccurate, redundant, and incomplete information. The company wants to implement a data warehouse containing information from the five different systems to help maintain a single customer view, drive business decisions, and perform multidimensional analysis. Identify how the organization can improve its information quality when it begins designing and building its data warehouse.

2. Information Timeliness

Information timeliness is a major consideration for all organizations. Organizations need to decide the frequency of backups and the frequency of updates to a data warehouse. In a team, describe the timeliness requirements for backups and updates to a data warehouse for

- Weather tracking systems.
- Car dealership inventories.
- Vehicle tire sales forecasts.
- Interest rates.
- Restaurant inventories.
- Grocery store inventories.

3. Entities and Attributes

Martex Inc. is a manufacturer of athletic equipment and its primary lines of business include running, tennis, golf, swimming, basketball, and aerobics equipment. Martex currently supplies four primary vendors including Sam's Sports, Total Effort, The Underline, and Maximum Workout. Martex wants to build a database to help it organize its products. In a group, identify the different types of entity classes and the related attributes that Martex will want to consider when designing the database.

4. Integrating Information

You are currently working for the Public Transportation Department of Chatfield. The department controls all forms of public transportation including buses, subways, and trains. Each department has about 300 employees and maintains its own accounting, inventory, purchasing, and human resource systems. Generating reports across departments is a difficult task and usually involves gathering and correlating the information from the many different systems. It typically takes about two weeks to generate the quarterly balance sheets and profit and loss statements. Your team has been asked to compile a report recommending what the Public Transportation Department of Chatfield can do to alleviate its information and system issues. Be sure that your report addresses the various reasons departmental reports are presently difficult to obtain as well as how you plan to solve this problem.

5. Information—Business Intelligence or a Diversion from the Truth?

President Obama used part of his commencement address at Virginia's Hampton University to criticize the flood of incomplete information or downright incorrect information that flows in the 24-hour news cycle. The president said, "You're coming of age in a 24/7 media environment that bombards us with all kinds of content and exposes us to all kinds of arguments, some of which don't always rank all that high on the truth meter. With iPods and iPads and Xboxes and PlayStations—none of which I know how to work—information becomes a distraction, a diversion, a form of entertainment, rather than a tool of empowerment, rather than the means of emancipation."[10]

Do you agree or disagree with President Obama's statement? Who is responsible for verifying the accuracy of online information? What should happen to companies that post inaccurate information? What should happen to individuals who post inaccurate information? What should you remember when reading or citing sources for online information?

6. Illegal Database Access

Goldman Sachs has been hit with a $3 million lawsuit by a company that alleges the brokerage firm stole intellectual property from its database that had market intelligence facts. The U.S. District Court for the Southern District of New York filed the lawsuit in 2010 claiming Goldman Sachs employees used other people's access credentials to log into Ipreo's proprietary database, dubbed Bigdough. Offered on a subscription basis, Bigdough provides detailed information on more than 80,000 contacts within the financial industry. Ipreo complained to the court that Goldman Sachs employees illegally accessed Bigdough at least 264 times in 2008 and 2009.[11]

Do you agree or disagree with the lawsuit? Should Goldman Sachs be held responsible for rogue employees' behavior? What types of policies should Goldman Sachs implement to ensure this does not occur again?

7. Data Storage

Information is one of the most important assets of any business. Businesses must ensure information accuracy, completeness, consistency, timeliness, and uniqueness. In addition, business must have a reliable backup service. In part thanks to cloud computing, there are many data hosting services on the Internet. These sites offer storage of information that can be accessed from anywhere in the world.

These data hosting services include Hosting (www.hosting.com), Mozy (www.mozy.com), My Docs Online (www.mydocsonline.com), and Box (www.box.net). Visit a few of these sites along with a several others you find through research. Which sites are free? Are there limits to how much you can store? If so, what is the limit? What type of information can you store (video, text, photos, etc.)? Can you allow multiple users with different passwords to access your storage area? Are you contractually bound for a certain duration (annual, etc.)? Are different levels of services provided such as personal, enterprise, work group? Does it make good business sense to store business data on the Internet? What about personal data?

8. Gathering Business Intelligence

When considering new business opportunities, you need knowledge about the competition. One of the things many new business owners fail to do is to gather business intelligence on their competitors, such as how many there are and what differentiates each of them. You may find there are too many and that they would be tough competition for you. Or, you may find that there are few competitors and the ones who are out there offer very little value.

Generate a new business idea you could launch on the Internet. Research the Internet to find similar businesses in the area you have chosen. How many sites did you find that are offering the same products or services you are planning to offer? Did you come across any sites from another country that have a unique approach that you did not see on any of the sites in your own country? How would you use this information in pursuing your business idea?

9. Free Data!

The U.S. Bureau of Labor Statistics states that its role is as the "principal fact-finding agency for the federal government in the broad field of labor economics and statistics." And the data that the bureau provides via its website are available to anyone, free. This can represent a treasure trove of business intelligence and data mining for those who take advantage of this resource. Visit the website www.bls.gov. What type of information does the site provide? What information do you find most useful? What sort of information concerning employment and wages is available? How is this information categorized? How would this type of information be helpful to a business manager? What type of demographic information is available? How could this benefit a new start-up business?[12]

10. Explaining Relational Databases

You have been hired by Vision, a start-up clothing company. Your manager, Holly Henningson, is unfamiliar with databases and their associated business value. Henningson has asked you to create a report detailing the basics of databases. She would also like you to provide a detailed explanation of relational databases along with their associated business advantages.

1. Determining Information Quality Issues

Real People is a magazine geared toward working individuals that provides articles and advice on everything from car maintenance to family planning. *Real People* is currently experiencing problems with its magazine distribution list. More than 30 percent of the magazines mailed are returned because of incorrect address information, and each month it receives numerous calls from angry customers complaining that they have not yet received their magazines. Figure AYK.1 provides a sample of *Real People*'s customer information. Create a report detailing all of the issues with the information, potential causes of the information issues, and solutions the company can follow to correct the situation.

2. Mining the Data Warehouse

Alana Smith is a senior buyer for a large wholesaler that sells different types of arts and crafts to greeting card stores such as Hallmark. Alana's latest marketing strategy is to send all of her customers a new line of hand-made picture frames from Russia. Alana's data support her decision for the new line. Her analysis predicts that the frames should sell an average of 10 to 15 per store, per day. Alana is excited about the new line and is positive it will be a success.

One month later Alana learns that the frames are selling 50 percent below expectations and averaging between five and eight frames sold daily in each store. Alana decides to access the company's data warehouse to determine why sales are below expectations. Identify several different dimensions of data that Alana will want to analyze to help her decide what is causing the problems with the picture frame sales.

3. Cleansing Information

You are working for BI, a start-up business intelligence consulting company. You have a new client that is interested in hiring BI to clean up its information. To determine how good your work is, the client would like your analysis of the spreadsheet in Figure AYK.2.

4. Different Dimensions

The focus of data warehousing is to extend the transformation of data into information. Data warehouses offer strategic level, external, integrated, and historical information so businesses can make projections, identify trends, and make key business decisions. The data warehouse collects and stores integrated sets of historical information from multiple operational systems and feeds them to one or more data marts. It may also provide end-user access to support enterprisewide views of information.

FIGURE AYK.1

Sample Data

ID	First Name	Middle Name	Last Name	Street	City	State	ZIP Code
433	M	J	Jones	13 Denver	Denver	CO	87654
434	Margaret	J	Jones	13 First Ave.	Denver	CO	87654
434	Brian	F	Hoover	Lake Ave.	Columbus	OH	87654
435	Nick	H	Schweitzer	65 Apple Lane	San Francisco	OH	65664
436	Richard	A		567 55th St.	New York	CA	98763
437	Alana	B	Smith	121 Tenny Dr.	Buffalo	NY	142234
438	Trevor	D	Darrian	90 Fresrdestil	Dallas	TX	74532

CUST ID	First Name	Last Name	Address	City	State	ZIP	Phone	Last Order Date
233620	Christopher	Lee	12421 W Olympic Blvd	Los Angeles	CA	75080-1100	(972)680-7848	4/18/2002
233621	Bruce	Brandwen	268 W 44th St	New York	PA	10036-3906	(212)471-6077	5/3/2002
233622	Glr	Johnson	4100 E Dry Creek Rd	Littleton	CO	80122-3729	(303)712-5461	5/6/2002
233623	Dave	Owens	466 Commerce Rd	Staunton	VA	24401-4432	(540)851-0362	3/19/2002
233624	John	Coulbourn	124 Action St	Maynard	MA	1754	(978)987-0100	4/24/2002
233629	Dan	Gagliardo	2875 Union Rd	Cheektowaga	NY	14227-1461	(716)558-8191	5/4/2002
23362	Damanceee	Allen	1633 Broadway	New York	NY	10019-6708	(212)708-1576	
233630	Michael	Peretz	235 E 45th St	New York	NY	10017-3305	(212)210-1340	4/30/2002
							(608)238-9690	
233631	Jody	Veeder	440 Science Dr	Madison	WI	53711-1064	X227	3/27/2002
233632	Michael	Kehrer	3015 SSE Loop 323	Tyler	TX	75701	(903)579-3229	4/28/
233633	Erin	Yoon	3500 Carillon Pt	Kirkland	WA	98033-7354	(425)897-7221	3/25/2002
233634	Madeline	Shefferly	4100 E Dry Creek Rd	Littleton	CO	80122-3729	(303)486-3949	3/33/2002
233635	Steven	Conduit	1332 Enterprise Dr	West Chester	PA	19380-5970	(610)692-5900	4/27/2002
233636	Joseph	Kovach	1332 Enterprise Dr	West Chester	PA	19380-5970	(610)692-5900	4/28/2002
233637	Richard	Jordan	1700 N	Philadelphia	PA	19131-4728	(215)581-6770	3/19/2002
233638	Scott	Mikolajczyk	1655 Crofton Blvd	Crofton	MD	21114-1387	(410)729-8155	4/28/2002
233639	Susan	Shragg	1875 Century Park E	Los Angeles	CA	90067-2501	(310)785-0511	4/29/2002
233640	Rob	Ponto	29777 Telegraph Rd	Southfield	MI	48034-1303	(810)204-4724	5/5/2002
233642	Lauren	Butler	1211 Avenue Of The Americas	New York	NY	10036-8701	(212)852-7494	4/22/2002
233643	Christopher	Lee	12421 W Olympic Blvd	Los Angeles	CA	90064-1022	(310)689-2577	3/25/2002
233644	Michelle	Decker	6922 Hollywood Blvd	Hollywood	CA	90028-6117	(323)817-4655	5/8/2002
233647	Natalia	Galeano	1211 Avenue Of The Americas	New York	NY	10036-8701	(646)728-6911	4/23/2002
233648	Bobbie	Orchard	4201 Congress St	Charlotte	NC	28209-4617	(704)557-2444	5/11/2002
233650	Ben	Konfino	1111 Stewart Ave	Bethpage	NY	11714-3533	(516)803-1406	3/19/2002
233651	Lenee	Santana	1050 Techwood Dr NW	Atlanta	GA	30318-KKRR	(404)885-2000	3/22/2002
233652	Lauren	Monks	7700 Wisconsin Ave	Bethesda	MD	20814-3578	(301)771-4772	3/19/2005
233653	Mark	Woolley	10950 Washington Blvd	Culver City	CA	90232-4026	(310)202-2900	4/20/2002
233654	Stan	Matthews	1235 W St NE	Washington	DC	20018-1107	(202)608-2000	3/25/2002

Dimension	Value (1–5)	Dimension	Value (1–5)
Product number		Season	
Store location		Promotion	
Customer net worth		Payment method	
Number of sales personnel		Commission policy	
Customer eating habits		Manufacturer	
Store hours		Traffic report	
Salesperson ID		Customer language	
Product style		Weather	
Order date		Customer gender	
Product quantity		Local tax information	
Ship date		Local cultural demographics	
Current interest rate		Stock market closing	
Product cost		Customer religious affiliation	
Customer's political affiliation		Reason for purchase	
Local market analysis		Employee dress code policy	
Order time		Customer age	
Customer spending habits		Employee vacation policy	
Product price		Employee benefits	
Exchange rates		Current tariff information	
Product gross margin			

FIGURE AYK.3

Data Warehouse Data

Project Focus

You are currently working on a marketing team for a large corporation that sells jewelry around the world. Your boss has asked you to look at the following dimensions of data to determine which ones you want in your data mart for performing sales and market analysis (see Figure AYK.3). As a team, categorize the different dimensions ranking them from 1 to 5, with 1 indicating that the dimension offers the highest value and must be in your data mart and 5 indicating that the dimension offers the lowest value and does not need to be in your data mart.

5. Understanding Search

Pretend that you are a search engine. Choose a topic to query. It can be anything such as your favorite book, movie, band, or sports team. Search your topic on Google, pick three or four pages from the results, and print them out. On each printout, find the individual words from your query (such as "Boston Red Sox" or "The Godfather") and use a highlighter to mark each word with color. Do that for each of the documents that you print out. Now tape those documents on a wall, step back a few feet, and review your documents. If you did not know what the rest of a page said and could only judge by the colored words, which document do you think would be most relevant? Is there anything that would make a document look more relevant? Is it better to have the words be in a large heading or to occur several times in a smaller font? Do you prefer it if the words are at the top or the bottom of the page? How often do the words need to appear? Come up with two or three things you would look for to see if a document matched a query well. This exercise mimics search engine processes and should help you understand why a search engine returns certain results over others.

6. Predicting Netflix

Netflix Inc., the largest online movie rental service, provides more than 12 million subscribers access to more than 100,000 unique DVD titles along with a growing on-demand library in excess of 10,000 choices. Data and information are so important to Netflix that it created The Netflix Prize, an open competition for anyone who could improve the data used in prediction ratings for films (an increase of 10 percent), based on previous ratings. The winner would receive a $1 million prize.

Project Focus

The ability to search, analyze, and comprehend information is vital for any organization's success. It certainly was for Netflix, as it was happy to pay anyone $1 million to improve the quality of its information. In a group explain how Netflix might use databases, data warehouses, and data marts to predict customer movie recommendations. Here are a few characteristics you might want to analyze to get you started:

- Customer demographics.
- Movie genre, rating, year, producer, type.
- Actor information.
- Internet access.
- Location for mail pickup.

7. The Crunch Factory

The Crunch Factory is one of the fourth-largest gyms operating in Australia, and each gym operates its own system with its own database. Unfortunately, the company failed to develop any data-capturing standards and now faces the challenges associated with low-quality enterprisewide information. For example, one system has a field to capture email addresses while another system does not. Duplicate customer information among the different systems is another major issue, and the company continually finds itself sending conflicting or competing messages to customers from different gyms. A customer could also have multiple accounts within the company, one representing a membership, another representing additional classes, and yet another for a personal trainer. The Crunch Factory has no way to identify that the different customer accounts are actually for the same customer.

Project Focus

To remain competitive and be able to generate business intelligence The Crunch Factory has to resolve these challenges. The Crunch Factory has just hired you as its data quality expert. Your first task is to determine how the company can turn its low-quality information into high-quality business intelligence. Create a plan that The Crunch Factory can implement that details the following:

- Challenges associated with low-quality information.
- Benefits associated with high-quality information.
- Recommendations on how the company can clean up its data.

8. Too Much of a Good Thing

The Castle, a premium retailer of clothes and accessories, created an enterprisewide data warehouse so all its employees could access information for decision making. The Castle soon discovered that it is possible to have too much of a good thing. The Castle employees found themselves inundated with data and unable to make any decisions, a common occurrence called analysis paralysis. When sales representatives queried the data warehouse to determine if a certain product in the size, color, and category was available, they would get hundreds of results showing everything from production orders to supplier contracts. It became easier for the sales representatives to look in the warehouse themselves than to check the system. Employees found the data warehouse was simply too big, too complicated, and contained too much irrelevant information.

Project Focus

The Castle is committed to making its data warehouse system a success and has come to you for help. Create a plan that details the value of the data warehouse to the business, how it can be easier for all employees to use, along with the potential business benefits the company can derive from its data warehouse.

9. Twitter Buzz

Technology tools that can predict sales for the coming week, decide when to increase inventory, and determine when additional staff is required are extremely valuable. Twitter is not just for tweeting your whereabouts anymore. Twitter and other social-media sites have become great tools for gathering business intelligence on customers, including what they like, dislike, need, and want. Twitter is easy to use, and businesses can track every single time a customer makes a statement about a particular product or service. Good businesses turn this valuable information into intelligence spotting trends and patterns in customer opinion.

Project Focus

Do you agree that a business can use Twitter to gain business intelligence? How many companies do you think are aware of Twitter and exactly how they can use it to gain BI? How do you think Twitter uses a data warehouse? How do you think companies store Twitter information? How would a company use Twitter in a data mart? How would a company use cubes to analyze Twitter data?

If you are looking for Access projects to incorporate into your class, try any of the following after reading this chapter.

Project Number	Project Name	Project Type	Plug-In	Focus Area	Project Level	Skill Set	Page Number
28	Daily Invoice	Access	T5, T6, T7, T8	Business Analysis	Introductory	Entities, Relationships, and Databases	AYK.17
29	Billing Data	Access	T5, T6, T7, T8	Business Intelligence	Introductory	Entities, Relationships, and Databases	AYK.19
30	Inventory Data	Access	T5, T6, T7, T8	SCM	Intermediate	Entities, Relationships, and Databases	AYK.20
31	Call Center	Access	T5, T6, T7, T8	CRM	Intermediate	Entities, Relationships, and Databases	AYK.21
32	Sales Pipeline	Access	T5, T6, T7, T8	Business Intelligence	Advanced	Entities, Relationships, and Databases	AYK.23
33	Online Classified Ads	Access	T5, T6, T7, T8	Ecommerce	Advanced	Entities, Relationships, and Databases	AYK.23

✳ ENTREPRENEURIAL CHALLENGE

Build Your Own Business

Project Focus

1. Provide an example of your business data that fits each of the five common characteristics of high-quality information. Explain why each characteristic is important to your business data and what might happen if your business data were of low quality. (Be sure to identify your business and the name of your company.)
2. Identify the different entities and their associated attributes that would be found in your potential relational database model for your sales database.
3. Identify the benefits of having a data warehouse for your business. What types of data marts would you want to extract from you data warehouse to help you run your business and make strategic decisions?

3

Streamlining Business Operations

What's in IT for Me?

Information is a powerful asset. It is a key organizational asset that enables companies to carry out business initiatives and strategic plans. Companies that manage information are primed for competitive advantage and success. Information systems provide the key tools allowing access to and flow of information across enterprises. This unit emphasizes the important role strategic decision-making information systems play in increasing efficiency and effectiveness across global enterprises and providing the infrastructure required for supply chain management, customer relationship management, and enterprise resource planning. These systems facilitate interactions among customers, suppliers, partners, and employees providing new communication channels beyond those traditionally used by organizations such as face-to-face or paper-based methods.

A supply chain consists of all direct and indirect parties involved in the procurement of products and raw material. These parties can be internal groups or departments within an organization or external partner companies and end customers. You, as a business student, need to know the significance of a supply chain to organizational success and the critical role information technology plays in ensuring smooth operations of a supply chain.

You, as a business student, must understand the critical relationship your business will have with its customers. You must understand how to analyze your organizational data to ensure you are not just meeting, but exceeding your customers' expectations. Business intelligence is the best way to understand your customers' current and—more importantly—future needs. Like never before, enterprises are technologically empowered to reach their goals of integrating, analyzing, and making intelligent business decisions based on their data.

You, as a business student, must understand how to give employees, customers, and business partners access to information by means of newer technologies such as enterprise resource planning systems and enterprise portals. Creating access to information with the help of information systems facilitates completion of current tasks while encouraging the sharing and generation of new ideas that lead to the development of innovations, improved work habits, and best practices.

Action Finally—Actionly

Data are all over the Internet! Tons and tons and tons of data! For example, over 152 million blogs are created each year, along with 100 million Twitter accounts resulting in 25 billion Tweets, 107 trillion emails are sent, and 730 billion hours of YouTube videos are watched. Known as the social media sector, this arena is by far one of the fastest growing and most influential sectors in business. Companies are struggling to understand how the social media sector impacts it both financially and strategically.

Data are valuable to any company and the data on the Internet are unique because the information comes directly from customers, suppliers, competitors, and even employees. As the social media sector takes off, companies are finding themselves at a disadvantage when attempting to keep up with all of the "online chatter" about their goods and services on the many different social media websites, including Facebook, Twitter, Myspace, Flickr, LinkedIn, Yelp, Google, blogs, etc.

Any time there is a problem there is a potential business solution, and Actionly.com chooses to capitalize on the data glut problem. Actionly monitors multiple social media channels through one tracking service looking for specific keywords for industries, brands, companies, and trends. Actionly customers choose a keyword to monitor—such as a brand, product names, industry terms, or competitors—and then Actionly constantly collects the data from these social channels and pulls that data into a cohesive digital dashboard. The digital dashboard tracks the desired information, such as marketplace trends, specific companies, competitive brands, entire industries (for example, clean technology), by simultaneously searching Twitter, Facebook, Google, YouTube, Flickr, and blogs. After completing a search, Actionly.com uses Google Analytics to create graphs and charts indicating how frequently each keyword was found throughout the various channels. Additionally, it links each respective channel to the dashboard and filters them with "positive" and "negative" connections, allowing users to respond to any comments.

Actionly.com's business model sets it up for success in this emerging industry. Actionly has a first-mover advantage because it was the first online brand management company offering this service to customers. And the company benefits by using its own services to ensure its brand stays number one on all social media websites. Actionly uses Google Analytics to help transform the data it collects from the various social media websites into valuable business intelligence. Its digital dashboard monitors several key metrics, including:

- **Reputation Management:** Actionly's easy to use digital dashboard allows customers to observe and analyze trends and track mentions about brands based on historical data as well as continuously updated data. For example, a customer can view graphs that highlight key trends across 30 days for specific brands, products, or companies.

- **Social ROI:** By connecting to Google Analytics from Actionly, a customer can analyze its campaign performance for individual tweets or Facebook posts to determine which are successful and which are failing. Actionly analyzes every post and click to track page views, visitor information, goal completions, and so on, through its digital dashboard, allowing users to customize reports tracking the performance of daily posts.

- **Twitter Analytics:** After adding Twitter accounts to the dashboard, a user can drill down into the data to view graphs of followers, mentions, and retweets. This eliminates the need to manually track a number of Twitter accounts, and a user can view the data in graphs or export the data in Excel for further analysis.

- **Marketing Campaign Tracking:** If a company is launching a big promotion or contest, it can post messages across multiple Facebook or Twitter accounts; all the user has to do is select which Twitter or Facebook accounts it wants to use and when. Actionly's Campaign Tracking helps a user view which posts are resonating well with customers and measure metrics such as page views, signups, conversions, and revenue by post. Actionly even segments the data by post, account, campaign, or channel, allowing users to measure performance over time.

- **Click Performance:** Actionly tracks performance by hour and day of week, allowing customers to view which clicks are getting the most attention. Actionly's algorithm automatically assigns a sentiment to tweets, allowing the customer to immediately filter positive or negative or neutral posts to react to information quickly.

- **Sentiment Analysis:** Reviewing positive and negative feedback helps gauge how a brand is doing over time, allowing the client to try to increase the positive sentiment. However, no sentiment scoring is 100 percent accurate due to the complexities of interpretation, culture, sarcasm, and other language nuances. For example, if Actionly is incorrectly tracking a metric, it can change it, allowing users to assign their unique sentiments directly to their tweets. A user can also select to have positive or negative alerts for keywords emailed as soon as the keyword is posted to help manage online brand and company reputations.

- **Competitive Analysis:** Actionly tracks competitor intelligence by watching new-product releases, acquisitions, or customer feedback, allowing a company to stay on top of market entrants, market-related blogs, news, or industry-related seminars/webinars.

- **Find Influencers:** Actionly's digital dashboard allows a user to engage directly with key influencers or people who are driving the online chatter about goods and services. Actionly identifies influencers and determines their relevance to the company, brand, or product. It then compiles a list of influencers based on users with the most followers and who have been most active for the specific searches in the past 30 days.[1]

Introduction

Decision making and problem solving in today's electronic world encompass large-scale, opportunity-oriented, strategically focused solutions. The traditional "cookbook" approach to decisions simply will not work in the ebusiness world. Decision-making and problem-solving abilities are now the most sought-after traits in up-and-coming executives. To put it mildly, decision makers and problem solvers have limitless career potential.

Ebusiness is the conducting of business on the Internet, not only buying and selling, but also serving customers and collaborating with business partners. (Unit Four discusses ebusiness in detail.) With the fast growth of information technology and the accelerated use of the Internet, ebusiness is quickly becoming standard. This unit focuses on technology to help make decisions, solve problems, and find new innovative opportunities. The unit highlights how to bring people together with the best IT processes and tools in complete, flexible solutions that can seize business opportunities (see Figure Unit 3.1). The chapters in Unit 3 are:

- **Chapter Nine**—Enabling the Organization—Decision Making.
- **Chapter Ten**—Extending the Organization—Supply Chain Management.
- **Chapter Eleven**—Building a Customer-centric Organization—Customer Relationship Management.
- **Chapter Twelve**—Integrating the Organization from End to End—Enterprise Resource Planning.

FIGURE UNIT 3.1

Decision-Enabling, Problem-Solving, and Opportunity-Seizing Systems

Artificial Intelligence (AI)

Executive Information Systems (EIS)

Data Mining

Employees | Customers

Suppliers | Partners

Decision Support Systems (DSS)

Enterprise Resource Planning (ERP)

Customer Relationship Management (CRM)

Supply Chain Management (SCM)

Enabling the Organization—Decision Making

LEARNING OUTCOMES

9.1. Explain the importance of decision making for managers at each of the three primary organization levels along with the associated decision characteristics.

9.2. Classify the different operational support systems, managerial support systems, and strategic support systems, and explain how managers can use these systems to make decisions and gain competitive advantages.

9.3. Describe artificial intelligence, and identify its five main types.

Making Business Decisions

Porter's strategies outlined in Unit 1 suggest entering markets with a competitive advantage in either overall cost leadership, differentiation, or focus. To achieve these results, managers must be able to make decisions and forecast future business needs and requirements. The most important and most challenging question confronting managers today is how to lay the foundation for tomorrow's success while competing to win in today's business environment. A company will not have a future if it is not cultivating strategies for tomorrow. The goal of this section is to expand on Porter's Five Forces Model, three generic strategies, and value chain analysis to demonstrate how managers can learn the concepts and practices of business decision making to add value. It will also highlight how companies heading into the 21st century are taking advantage of advanced MIS capable of generating significant competitive advantages across the value chain.

LO 9.1 Explain the importance of decision making for managers at each of the three primary organization levels along with the associated decision characteristics.

As we discussed in Unit 1, decision making is one of the most important and challenging aspects of management. Decisions range from routine choices, such as how many items to order or how many people to hire, to unexpected ones such as what to do if a key employee suddenly quits or needed materials do not arrive. Today, with massive volumes of information available, managers are challenged to make highly complex decisions—some involving far more information than the human brain can comprehend—in increasingly shorter time frames. Figure 9.1 displays the three primary challenges managers face when making decisions.

THE DECISION-MAKING PROCESS

The process of making decisions plays a crucial role in communication and leadership for operational, managerial, and strategic projects. **Analytics** is the science of fact-based decision making. There are numerous academic decision-making models; Figure 9.2 presents just one example.[2]

DECISION-MAKING ESSENTIALS

A few key concepts about organizational structure will help our discussion of MIS decision-making tools. The structure of a typical organization is similar to a pyramid,

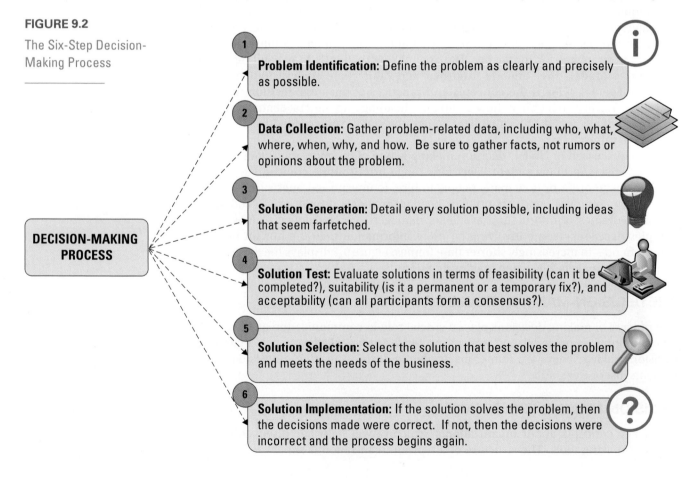

1. Managers need to analyze large amounts of information: Innovations in communication and globalization have resulted in a dramatic increase in the variables and dimensions people need to consider when making a decision, solving a problem, or appraising an opportunity.

2. Managers must make decisions quickly: Time is of the essence and people simply do not have time to sift through all the information manually.

3. Managers must apply sophisticated analysis techniques, such as Porter's strategies or forecasting, to make strategic decisions: Due to the intensely competitive global business environment, companies must offer far more than just a great product to succeed.

MANAGERIAL DECISION-MAKING CHALLENGES

FIGURE 9.1

Managerial Decision-Making Challenges

and the different levels require different types of information to assist in decision making, problem solving, and opportunity capturing (see Figure 9.3).

Operational

At the **operational level,** employees develop, control, and maintain core business activities required to run the day-to-day operations. Operational decisions are considered **structured decisions,** which arise in situations where established processes offer potential solutions. Structured decisions are made frequently and are almost repetitive in nature; they affect short-term business strategies. Reordering inventory and creating the

FIGURE 9.2

The Six-Step Decision-Making Process

DECISION-MAKING PROCESS

1. **Problem Identification:** Define the problem as clearly and precisely as possible.

2. **Data Collection:** Gather problem-related data, including who, what, where, when, why, and how. Be sure to gather facts, not rumors or opinions about the problem.

3. **Solution Generation:** Detail every solution possible, including ideas that seem farfetched.

4. **Solution Test:** Evaluate solutions in terms of feasibility (can it be completed?), suitability (is it a permanent or a temporary fix?), and acceptability (can all participants form a consensus?).

5. **Solution Selection:** Select the solution that best solves the problem and meets the needs of the business.

6. **Solution Implementation:** If the solution solves the problem, then the decisions made were correct. If not, then the decisions were incorrect and the process begins again.

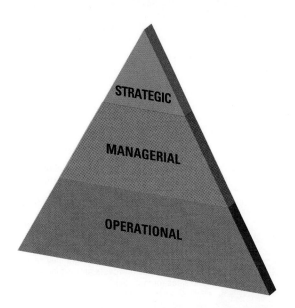

FIGURE 9.3

Common Company
Structure

employee staffing and weekly production schedules are examples of routine structured decisions. Figure 9.4 highlights the essential elements required for operational decision making. All the elements in the figure should be familiar, except metrics which are discussed in detail below.

Managerial

At the *managerial level,* employees are continuously evaluating company operations to hone the firm's abilities to identify, adapt to, and leverage change. A company that has a

FIGURE 9.4

Overview of Operational
Decision Making

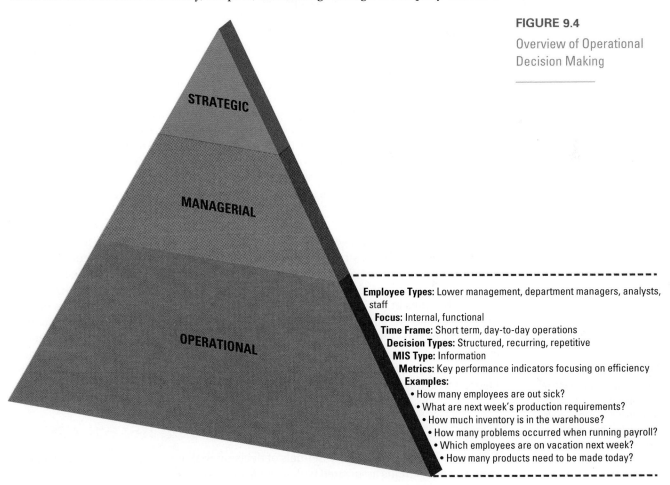

Employee Types: Lower management, department managers, analysts, staff
Focus: Internal, functional
Time Frame: Short term, day-to-day operations
Decision Types: Structured, recurring, repetitive
MIS Type: Information
Metrics: Key performance indicators focusing on efficiency
Examples:
  • How many employees are out sick?
  • What are next week's production requirements?
  • How much inventory is in the warehouse?
  • How many problems occurred when running payroll?
  • Which employees are on vacation next week?
  • How many products need to be made today?

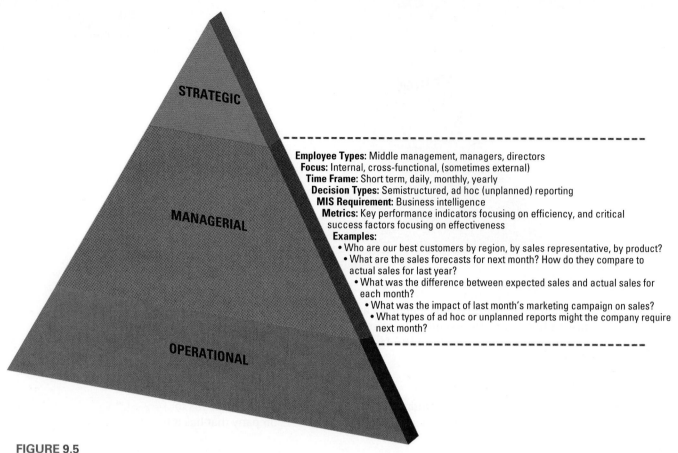

FIGURE 9.5

Overview of Managerial
Decision Making

competitive advantage needs to constantly adjust and revise its strategy to remain ahead of fast-following competitors. Managerial decisions cover short- and medium-range plans, schedules, and budgets along with policies, procedures, and business objectives for the firm. They also allocate resources and monitor the performance of organizational subunits, including departments, divisions, process teams, project teams, and other work groups. These types of decisions are considered **semistructured decisions;** they occur in situations in which a few established processes help to evaluate potential solutions, but not enough to lead to a definite recommended decision. For example, decisions about producing new products or changing employee benefits range from unstructured to semistructured. Figure 9.5 highlights the essential elements required for managerial decision making.

Strategic

At the **strategic level,** managers develop overall business strategies, goals, and objectives as part of the company's strategic plan. They also monitor the strategic performance of the organization and its overall direction in the political, economic, and competitive business environment. Strategic decisions are highly **unstructured decisions,** occurring in situations in which no procedures or rules exist to guide decision makers toward the correct choice. They are infrequent, extremely important, and typically related to long-term business strategy. Examples include the decision to enter a new market or even a new industry over, say, the next three years. In these types of decisions, managers rely on many sources of information, along with personal knowledge, to find solutions. Figure 9.6 highlights the essential elements required for strategic decision making.

LO 9.2 Classify the different operational support systems, managerial support systems, and strategic support systems, and explain how managers can use these systems to make decisions and gain competitive advantages.

Support: Enhancing Decision Making with MIS

Now that we've reviewed the essentials of decision making, we are ready to understand the powerful benefits associated with using MIS to support managers making decisions.

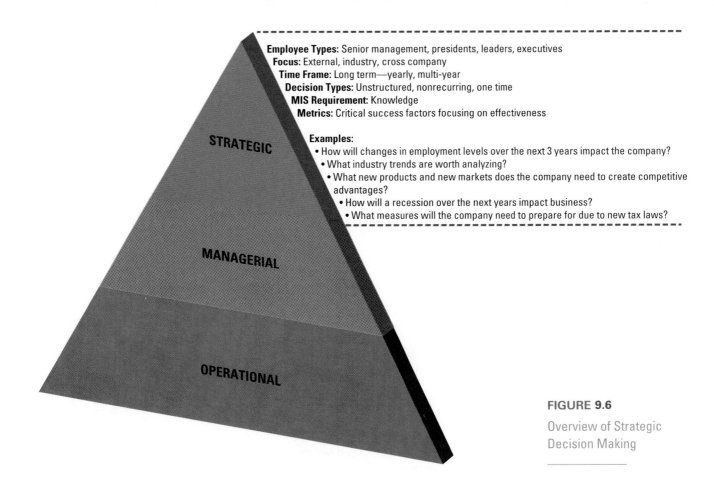

Employee Types: Senior management, presidents, leaders, executives
Focus: External, industry, cross company
Time Frame: Long term—yearly, multi-year
Decision Types: Unstructured, nonrecurring, one time
MIS Requirement: Knowledge
Metrics: Critical success factors focusing on effectiveness

Examples:
- How will changes in employment levels over the next 3 years impact the company?
- What industry trends are worth analyzing?
- What new products and new markets does the company need to create competitive advantages?
- How will a recession over the next years impact business?
- What measures will the company need to prepare for due to new tax laws?

STRATEGIC

MANAGERIAL

OPERATIONAL

FIGURE 9.6

Overview of Strategic Decision Making

A ***model*** is a simplified representation or abstraction of reality. Models help managers calculate risks, understand uncertainty, change variables, and manipulate time to make decisions. MIS support systems rely on models for computational and analytical routines that mathematically express relationships among variables. For example, a spreadsheet program, such as Microsoft Office Excel, might contain models that calculate market share or ROI. MIS have the capability and functionality to express far more complex modeling relationships that provide information, business intelligence, and knowledge. Figure 9.7 highlights the three primary types of management information systems available to support decision making across the company levels.

OPERATIONAL SUPPORT SYSTEMS

Transactional information encompasses all the information contained within a single business process or unit of work, and its primary purpose is to support the performance of daily operational or structured decisions. Transactional information is created, for example, when customers are purchasing stocks, making an airline reservation, or withdrawing cash from an ATM. Managers use transactional information when making structured decisions at the operational level, such as when analyzing daily sales reports to determine how much inventory to carry.

Online transaction processing (OLTP) is the capture of transaction and event information using technology to (1) process the information according to defined business rules, (2) store the information, and (3) update existing information to reflect the new information. During OLTP, the organization must capture every detail of transactions and events. A ***transaction processing system (TPS)*** is the basic business system that serves the operational level (analysts) and assists in making structured decisions. The most common example of a TPS is an operational accounting system such as a payroll system or an order-entry system.

FIGURE 9.7

Primary Types of MIS
Systems for Decision
Making

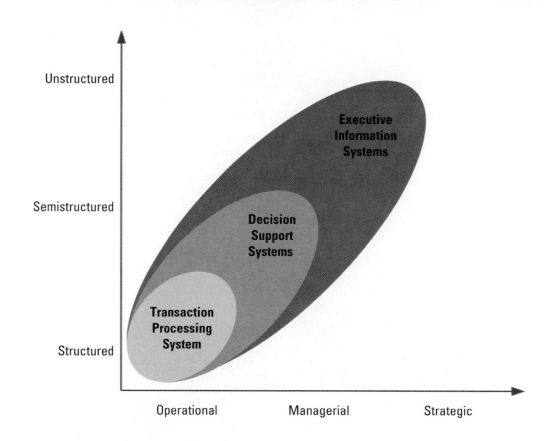

Using systems thinking, we can see that the inputs for a TPS are *source documents,* the original transaction record. Source documents for a payroll system can include time sheets, wage rates, and employee benefit reports. Transformation includes common procedures such as creating, reading, updating, and deleting (commonly referred to as CRUD) employee records, along with calculating the payroll and summarizing benefits. The output includes cutting the paychecks and generating payroll reports. Figure 9.8 demonstrates the systems thinking view of a TPS.[3]

MANAGERIAL SUPPORT SYSTEMS

FIGURE 9.8

Systems Thinking Example
of a TPS

Analytical information encompasses all organizational information, and its primary purpose is to support the performance of managerial analysis or semistructured decisions.

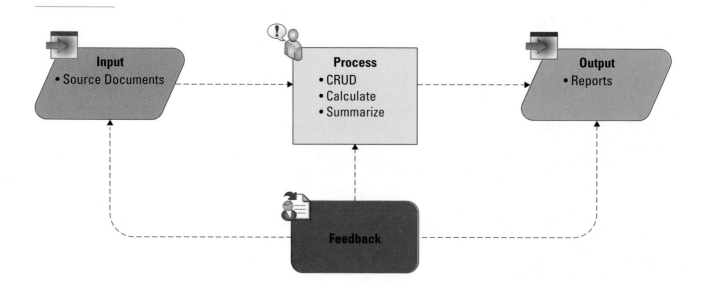

Analytical information includes transactional information along with other information such as market and industry information. Examples of analytical information are trends, sales, product statistics, and future growth projections. Managers use analytical information when making important semistructured decisions, such as whether the organization should build a new manufacturing plant or hire additional sales reps.

Online analytical processing (OLAP) is the manipulation of information to create business intelligence in support of strategic decision making. *Decision support systems (DSSs)* model information using OLAP, which provides assistance in evaluating and choosing among different courses of action. DSSs enable high-level managers to examine and manipulate large amounts of detailed data from different internal and external sources. Analyzing complex relationships among thousands or even millions of data items to discover patterns, trends, and exception conditions is one of the key uses associated with a DSS. For example, doctors may enter symptoms into a decision support system so it can help diagnose and treat patients. Insurance companies also use a DSS to gauge the risk of providing insurance to drivers who have imperfect driving records. One company found that married women who are homeowners with one speeding ticket are rarely cited for speeding again. Armed with this business intelligence, the company achieved a cost advantage by lowering insurance rates to this specific group of customers. The following are common DSS analysis techniques.

What-If Analysis

What-if analysis checks the impact of a change in a variable or assumption on the model. For example, "What will happen to the supply chain if a hurricane in South Carolina reduces holding inventory from 30 percent to 10 percent?" A user would be able to observe and evaluate any changes that occurred to the values in the model, especially to a variable such as profits. Users repeat this analysis with different variables until they understand all the effects of various situations.

Sensitivity Analysis

Sensitivity analysis, a special case of what-if analysis, is the study of the impact on other variables when one variable is changed repeatedly. Sensitivity analysis is useful when users are uncertain about the assumptions made in estimating the value of certain key variables. For example, repeatedly changing revenue in small increments to determine its effects on other variables would help a manager understand the impact of various revenue levels on other decision factors.

Goal-Seeking Analysis

Goal-seeking analysis finds the inputs necessary to achieve a goal such as a desired level of output. It is the reverse of what-if and sensitivity analysis. Instead of observing how changes in a variable affect other variables, goal-seeking analysis sets a target value (a goal) for a variable and then repeatedly changes other variables until the target value is achieved. For example, goal-seeking analysis could determine how many customers must purchase a new product to increase gross profits to $5 million.

Optimization Analysis

Optimization analysis, an extension of goal-seeking analysis, finds the optimum value for a target variable by repeatedly changing other variables, subject to specified constraints. By changing revenue and cost variables in an optimization analysis, managers can calculate the highest potential profits. Constraints on revenue and cost variables can be taken into consideration, such as limits on the amount of raw materials the company can afford to purchase and limits on employees available to meet production needs.

Figure 9.9 shows the common systems view of a DSS. Figure 9.10 shows how TPSs supply transactional data to a DSS. The DSS then summarizes and aggregates the information from the different TPSs, which assist managers in making semistructured decision.

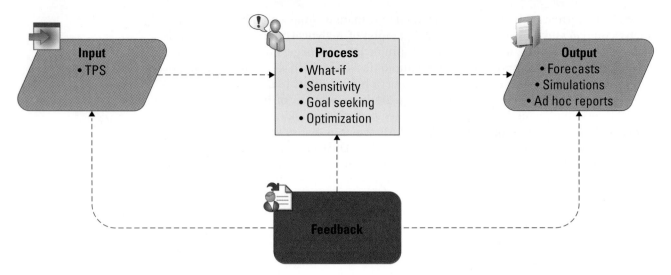

FIGURE 9.9

Systems Thinking Example
of a DSS

STRATEGIC SUPPORT SYSTEMS

Decision making at the strategic level requires both business intelligence and knowledge to support the uncertainty and complexity associated with business strategies. An *executive information system (EIS)* is a specialized DSS that supports senior-level executives and unstructured, long-term, nonroutine decisions requiring judgment, evaluation, and insight. These decisions do not have a right or wrong answer, only efficient and effective answers. Moving up through the organizational pyramid, managers deal less with the details ("finer" information) and more with meaningful aggregations of information ("coarser" information). *Granularity* refers to the level of detail in the model or the decision-making process. The greater the granularity, the deeper the level of detail or fineness of data (see Figure 9.11).

A DSS differs from an EIS in that an EIS requires data from external sources to support unstructured decisions (see Figure 9.12). This is not to say that DSSs never use data from external sources, but typically DSS semistructured decisions rely on internal data only.

Visualization produces graphical displays of patterns and complex relationships in large amounts of data. Executive information systems use visualization to deliver specific key information to top managers at a glance, with little or no interaction with

FIGURE 9.10

Interaction Between
TPS and DSS to Support
Semistructured Decisions

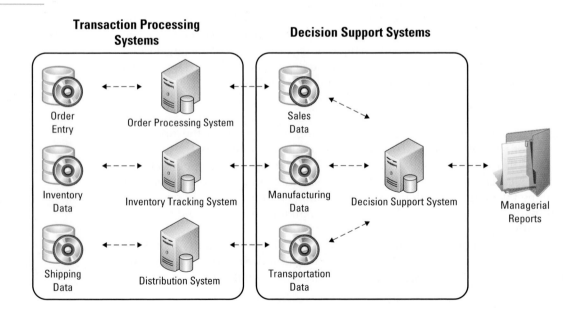

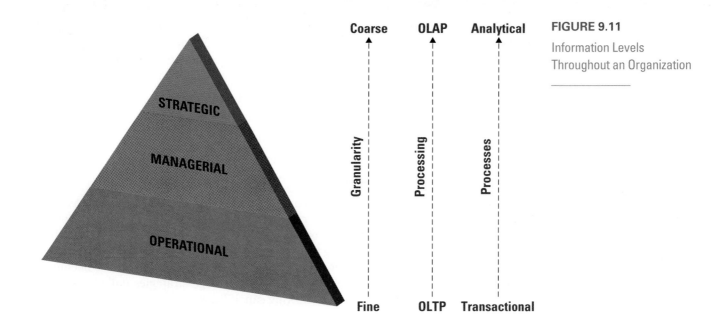

FIGURE 9.11

Information Levels
Throughout an Organization

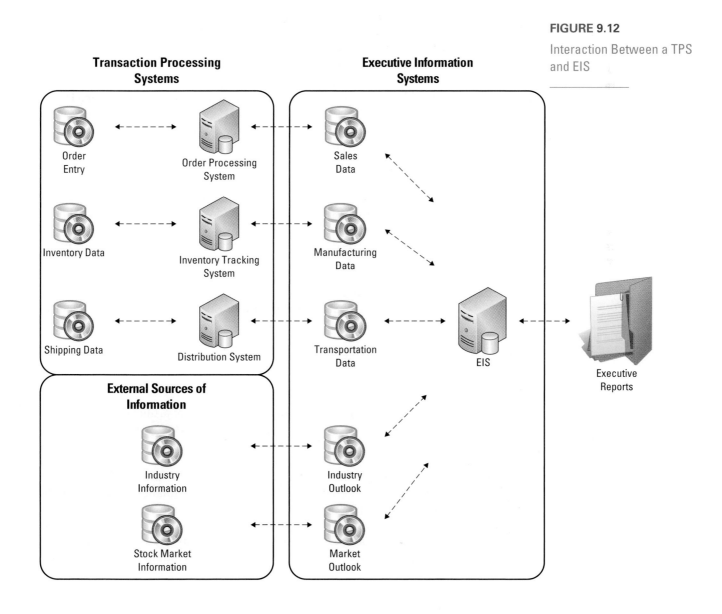

FIGURE 9.12

Interaction Between a TPS
and EIS

the system. A common tool that supports visualization is a ***digital dashboard,*** which tracks key performance indicators (KPIs) and critical success factors (CSFs) by compiling information from multiple sources and tailoring it to meet user needs. Following is a list of potential features included in a dashboard designed for a manufacturing team:

- A hot list of key performance indicators, refreshed every 15 minutes.
- A running line graph of planned versus actual production for the past 24 hours.
- A table showing actual versus forecasted product prices and inventories.
- A list of outstanding alerts and their resolution status.
- A graph of stock market prices.

Digital dashboards, whether basic or comprehensive, deliver results quickly. As they become easier to use, more employees can perform their own analyses without inundating MIS staff with questions and requests for reports. Digital dashboards enable employees to move beyond reporting to using information to directly increase business performance. With them, employees can react to information as soon as it becomes available and make decisions, solve problems, and change strategies daily instead of monthly. Digital dashboards offer the following capabilities:

Consolidation

Consolidation is the aggregation of data from simple roll-ups to complex groupings of interrelated information. For example, data for different sales representatives can then be rolled up to an office level, then a state level, then a regional sales level.

Drill-Down

Drill-down enables users to view details, and details of details, of information. This is the reverse of consolidation; a user can view regional sales data and then drill down all the way to each sales representative's data at each office. Drill-down capability lets managers view monthly, weekly, daily, or even hourly information.

Slice-and-Dice

Slice-and-dice is the ability to look at information from different perspectives. One slice of information could display all product sales during a given promotion. Another slice could display a single product's sales for all promotions. Slicing and dicing is often performed along a time axis to analyze trends and find time-based patterns in the information.

One thing to remember when making decisions is the old saying, "Garbage in, garbage out." If the transactional data used in the support system are wrong, then the managerial analysis will be wrong and the DSS will simply assist in making a wrong decision faster. Managers should also ask, "What is the DSS *not* telling me before I make my final decision?"

LO 9.3 Describe artificial intelligence, and identify its five main types.

The Future: Artificial Intelligence

Executive information systems are starting to take advantage of artificial intelligence to facilitate unstructured strategic decision making. ***Artificial intelligence (AI)*** simulates human thinking and behavior, such as the ability to reason and learn. Its ultimate goal is to build a system that can mimic human intelligence.

Intelligent systems are various commercial applications of artificial intelligence. They include sensors, software, and devices that emulate and enhance human capabilities, learn or understand from experience, make sense of ambiguous or contradictory information, and even use reasoning to solve problems and make decisions effectively. Intelligent systems perform such tasks as boosting productivity in factories by monitoring equipment and signaling when preventive maintenance is required. They are beginning to show up everywhere:

- At Manchester Airport in England, the Hefner AI Robot Cleaner alerts passengers to security and nonsmoking rules while it scrubs up to 65,600 square feet of floor per day. Laser scanners and ultrasonic detectors keep it from colliding with passengers.

- Shell Oil's SmartPump keeps drivers in their cars on cold, wet winter days. It can service any automobile built after 1987 that has been fitted with a special gas cap and a windshield-mounted transponder that tells the robot where to insert the pump.

- Matsushita's courier robot navigates hospital hallways, delivering patient files, X-ray films, and medical supplies.

- The FireFighter AI Robot can extinguish flames at chemical plants and nuclear reactors with water, foam, powder, or inert gas. The robot puts distance between human operators and the fire.[4]

AI systems increase the speed and consistency of decision making, solve problems with incomplete information, and resolve complicated issues that cannot be solved by conventional computing. There are many categories of AI systems; five of the most familiar are (1) expert systems, (2) neural networks, (3) genetic algorithms, (4) intelligent agents, and (5) virtual reality (see Figure 9.13).

EXPERT SYSTEMS

Expert systems are computerized advisory programs that imitate the reasoning processes of experts in solving difficult problems. Typically, they include a knowledge base containing various accumulated experience and a set of rules for applying the knowledge base to each particular situation. Expert systems are the most common form of AI in the business arena because they fill the gap when human experts are difficult to find or retain or are too expensive. The best-known systems play chess and assist in medical diagnosis.

NEURAL NETWORKS

A *neural network,* also called an artificial neural network, is a category of AI that attempts to emulate the way the human brain works. Neural networks analyze large quantities of information to establish patterns and characteristics in situations where the logic or rules are unknown. Neural networks' many features include:

- Learning and adjusting to new circumstances on their own.
- Lending themselves to massive parallel processing.

FIGURE 9.13

Examples of Artificial Intelligence

Artificial Intelligence

Expert Systems	Neural Networks	Genetic Algorithms	Intelligent Agents	Virtual Reality
Example: Playing chess.	Example: Credit card companies checking for fraud.	Example: Investment companies in trading decisions.	Example: Environmental scanning and competitive intelligence.	Example: Working virtually around the globe.

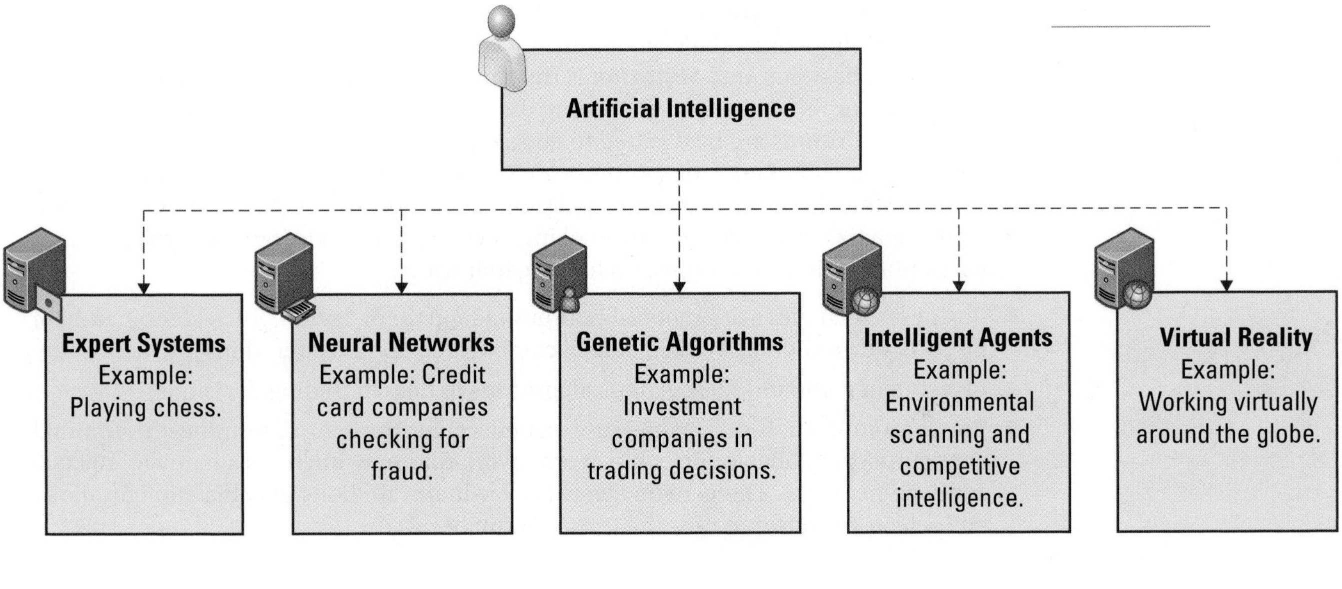

- Functioning without complete or well-structured information.
- Coping with huge volumes of information with many dependent variables.
- Analyzing nonlinear relationships in information (they have been called fancy regression analysis systems).

The finance industry is a veteran in the use of neural network technology and has been relying on various forms for over two decades. It uses neural networks to review loan applications and create patterns or profiles of applications that fall into two categories—approved or denied. Here are some examples of neural networks in finance:

- Citibank uses neural networks to find opportunities in financial markets. By carefully examining historical stock market data with neural network software, Citibank financial managers learn of interesting coincidences or small anomalies (called market inefficiencies). For example, it could be that whenever IBM stock goes up, so does Unisys stock, or that a U.S. Treasury note is selling for 1 cent less in Japan than in the United States. These snippets of information can make a big difference to Citibank's bottom line in a very competitive financial market.

- Visa, MasterCard, and many other credit card companies use a neural network to spot peculiarities in individual accounts and follow up by checking for fraud. MasterCard estimates neural networks save it $50 million annually.

- Insurance companies along with state compensation funds and other carriers use neural network software to identify fraud. The system searches for patterns in billing charges, laboratory tests, and frequency of office visits. A claim for which the diagnosis was a sprained ankle but treatment included an electrocardiogram would be flagged for the account manager.[5]

Fuzzy logic is a mathematical method of handling imprecise or subjective information. The basic approach is to assign values between 0 and 1 to vague or ambiguous information. Zero represents information not included, while 1 represents inclusion or membership. For example, fuzzy logic is used in washing machines that determine by themselves how much water to use or how long to wash (they continue washing until the water is clean). In accounting and finance, fuzzy logic allows people to analyze information with subjective financial values (intangibles such as goodwill) that are very important considerations in economic analysis. Fuzzy logic and neural networks are often combined to express complicated and subjective concepts in a form that makes it possible to simplify the problem and apply rules that are executed with a level of certainty.

GENETIC ALGORITHMS

A *genetic algorithm* is an artificial intelligence system that mimics the evolutionary, survival-of-the-fittest process to generate increasingly better solutions to a problem. A genetic algorithm is essentially an optimizing system: It finds the combination of inputs that gives the best outputs. *Mutation* is the process within a genetic algorithm of randomly trying combinations and evaluating the success (or failure) of the outcome.

Genetic algorithms are best suited to decision-making environments in which thousands, or perhaps millions, of solutions are possible. Genetic algorithms can find and evaluate solutions with many more possibilities, faster and more thoroughly than a human. Organizations face decision-making environments for all types of problems that require optimization techniques, such as the following:

- Business executives use genetic algorithms to help them decide which combination of projects a firm should invest in, taking complicated tax considerations into account.

- Investment companies use genetic algorithms to help in trading decisions.

- Telecommunication companies use genetic algorithms to determine the optimal configuration of fiber-optic cable in a network that may include as many as 100,000 connection points. The genetic algorithm evaluates millions of cable configurations and selects the one that uses the least amount of cable.

INTELLIGENT AGENTS

An *intelligent agent* is a special-purpose knowledge-based information system that accomplishes specific tasks on behalf of its users. Intelligent agents usually have a graphical representation, such as "Sherlock Holmes" for an information search agent.

One of the simplest examples of an intelligent agent is a shopping bot. A *shopping bot* is software that will search several retailer websites and provide a comparison of each retailer's offerings including price and availability. Increasingly, intelligent agents handle the majority of a company's Internet buying and selling and complete such processes as finding products, bargaining over prices, and executing transactions. Intelligent agents also have the capability to handle all supply chain buying and selling.

Another application for intelligent agents is in environmental scanning and competitive intelligence. For instance, an intelligent agent can learn the types of competitor information users want to track, continuously scan the web for it, and alert users when a significant event occurs.

Multiagent Systems and Agent-Based Modeling

What do cargo transport systems, book distribution centers, the video game market, and a flu epidemic have in common with an ant colony? They are all complex adaptive systems. By observing parts of Earth's ecosystem, like ant colonies, artificial intelligence scientists can use hardware and software models that incorporate insect characteristics and behavior to (1) learn how people-based systems behave, (2) predict how they will behave under a given set of circumstances, and (3) improve human systems to make them more efficient and effective. This process of learning from ecosystems and adapting their characteristics to human and organizational situations is called biomimicry.

In the past few years, AI research has made much progress in modeling complex organizations as a whole with the help of multiagent systems. In a multiagent system, groups of intelligent agents have the ability to work independently and to interact with each other. Agent-based modeling is a way of simulating human organizations using multiple intelligent agents, each of which follows a set of simple rules and can adapt to changing conditions.

Agent-based modeling systems are being used to model stock market fluctuations, predict the escape routes people seek in a burning building, estimate the effects of interest rates on consumers with different types of debt, and anticipate how changes in conditions will affect the supply chain, to name just a few.

VIRTUAL REALITY

Virtual reality is a computer-simulated environment that can be a simulation of the real world or an imaginary world. Virtual reality is a fast-growing area of artificial intelligence that had its origins in efforts to build more natural, realistic, multisensory human-computer interfaces. Virtual reality enables telepresence where users can be anywhere in the world and use virtual reality systems to work alone or together at a remote site. Typically, this involves using a virtual reality system to enhance the sight and touch of a human who is remotely manipulating equipment to accomplish a task. Examples range from virtual surgery, where surgeon and patient may be on opposite sides of the globe, to the remote use of equipment in hazardous environments such as chemical plants and nuclear reactors. *Augmented reality* is the viewing of the physical world with computer-generated layers of information added to it.

Virtual Workforce

At Microsoft's headquarters in Redmond, Washington, traffic congestion occurs daily for the 35,000 commuters. To alleviate the congestion Microsoft is offering its employees the ability to work virtually from home. Over 42 percent of IBM's 330,000 employees work virtually, saving over $100 million per year in real estate-related expenses. Working virtually offers several advantages such as fewer cars on the road, increases in worker productive, and decreased real estate expenses. Drawbacks include the fear among workers that they will jeopardize their careers by working from home, and some workers need a busy environment to stay productive. Virtual workers also tend to feel alone, secluded, and deprived of vital training and mentoring.

OPENING CASE STUDY QUESTIONS

1. Define the three primary types of decision-making systems, and explain how a customer of Actionly might use them to find business intelligence.

2. Describe the difference between transactional and analytical information, and determine which types Actionly uses to create a customer's digital dashboard.

3. Identify the five different types of artificial intelligence systems, and create an example of each for Actionly.

Chapter Nine Case: Defense Advanced Research Projects Agency (DARPA) Grand Challenge

The goal of the DARPA Grand Challenge is to save lives by making one-third of ground military forces autonomous or driverless vehicles by 2015. Created in response to a congressional and U.S. Department of Defense (DoD) mandate, the DARPA Grand Challenge brings together individuals and organizations from industry, the research and development (R&D) community, government, the armed services, and academia and includes students, backyard inventors, and automotive enthusiasts.

The DARPA Grand Challenge 2004

The DARPA Grand Challenge 2004 field test of autonomous ground vehicles ran from Barstow, California, to Primm, Nevada, and offered a $1 million prize. From the qualifying round at the California Speedway, 15 finalists emerged to attempt the Grand Challenge. However, the prize went unclaimed when no vehicles were able to complete the difficult desert route.

The DARPA Grand Challenge 2005

The DARPA Grand Challenge 2005 was held in the Mojave Desert and offered a $2 million prize to the team that completed the 132-mile course in the shortest time under 10 hours. The race, over desert terrain, included narrow tunnels, sharp turns, and a winding mountain pass with a sheer drop-off on one side and a rock face on the other. Five teams completed the course, and "Stanley," the Stanford Racing Team's car, won the $2 million prize with a time of 6 hours, 53 minutes.

The DARPA Grand Challenge 2007

The third DARPA Grand Challenge was an urban challenge on the site of the now-closed George Air Force Base in Victorville, California. It offered a $2 million prize to the autonomous vehicle that could cover the 60-mile course in less than 6 hours. The vehicles had to obey stop lights, navigate around other vehicles, and even merge into heavy traffic. Tartan Racing, a collaborative effort by Carnegie Mellon University and General Motors Corporation, won the prize with "Boss," a Chevy Tahoe. The Stanford Racing Team's "Junior," a 2006 Volkswagen Passat, won second prize of $1 million. "Victor Tango," a 2005 Ford Escape hybrid from Virginia Tech, won third place along with a $500,000 prize.[6]

Questions

1. How is the DoD using AI to improve its operations and save lives?

2. Why would the DoD use an event like the DARPA Grand Challenge to further technological innovation?

3. Describe how autonomous vehicles could be used by organizations around the world to improve business efficiency and effectiveness.

4. Research the Internet and determine if DARPA achieved its goal of creating one-third of ground military forces autonomous or driverless vehicles by 2015.

Extending the Organization—Supply Chain Management

10.1. Describe the four changes resulting from advances in IT that are driving supply chains.

10.2. Summarize the best practices for implementing a successful supply chain management system.

LO 10.1 Describe the four changes resulting from advances in IT that are driving supply chains.

Information Technology's Role in the Supply Chain

As companies evolve into extended organizations, the roles of supply chain participants are changing. It is now common for suppliers to be involved in product development and for distributors to act as consultants in brand marketing. The notion of virtually seamless information links within and between organizations is an essential element of integrated supply chains.

Information technology's primary role in SCM is creating the integrations or tight process and information linkages between functions within a firm—such as marketing, sales, finance, manufacturing, and distribution—and between firms, which allow the smooth, synchronized flow of both information and product between customers, suppliers, and transportation providers across the supply chain. Information technology integrates planning, decision-making processes, business operating processes, and information sharing for business performance management (see Figure 10.1). Considerable evidence shows that this type of supply chain integration results in superior supply chain capabilities and profits.

Adaptec Inc. of California manufactures semiconductors and markets them to the world's leading PC, server, and end-user markets through more than 115 distributors and thousands of value-added resellers worldwide. Adaptec designs and manufactures products at various third-party locations around the world. The company uses supply chain integration software over the Internet to synchronize planning. Adaptec personnel at the company's geographically dispersed locations communicate in real time and exchange designs, test results, and production and shipment information. Internet-based supply chain collaboration software helped the company reduce inventory levels and lead times.[1]

Although people have been talking about the integrated supply chain for a long time, it has only been recently that advances in information technology have made it possible to bring the idea to life and truly integrate the supply chain. Visibility, consumer behavior, competition, and speed are a few of the changes resulting from information technology advances that are driving supply chains (see Figure 10.2).

VISIBILITY

Supply chain visibility is the ability to view all areas up and down the supply chain. Changing supply chains requires a comprehensive strategy buoyed by information technology.

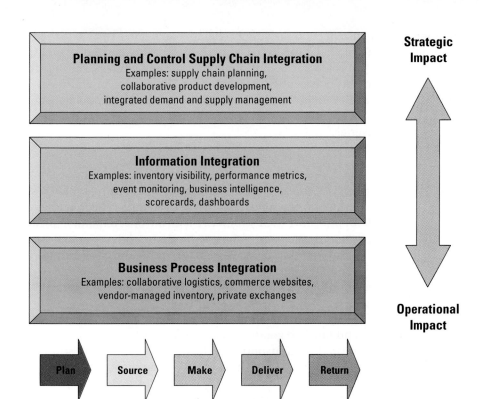

FIGURE 10.1

The Integrated Supply
Chain

Organizations can use technology tools that help them integrate upstream and downstream, with both customers and suppliers.

To make a supply chain work most effectively, organizations must create visibility in real time. Organizations must know about customer events triggered downstream, but so must their suppliers and their suppliers' suppliers. Without this information, partners throughout the supply chain can experience a bullwhip effect, in which disruptions intensify throughout the chain. The **bullwhip effect** occurs when distorted product demand information passes from one entity to the next throughout the supply chain. The misinformation regarding a slight rise in demand for a product could cause different members in the supply chain to stockpile inventory. These changes ripple throughout the supply chain, magnifying the issue and creating excess inventory and costs.

Today, information technology allows additional visibility in the supply chain. Electronic information flows allow managers to view their suppliers' and customers' supply chains. Some organizations have completely changed the dynamics of their industries because of the competitive advantage gained from high visibility in the supply chain. Dell is the obvious example. The company's ability to get product to the customer and the impact of the economics have clearly changed the nature of competition and caused others to emulate this model.

FIGURE 10.2

Factors Driving Supply
Chain Management

CONSUMER BEHAVIOR

The behavior of customers has changed the way businesses compete. Customers will leave if a company does not continually meet their expectations. They are more demanding because they have information readily available, they know exactly what they want, and they know when and how they want it. **Demand planning software** generates demand forecasts using statistical tools and forecasting techniques. Companies can respond faster and more effectively to consumer demands through supply chain enhancements such as demand planning software. Once an organization understands customer demand and its effect on the supply chain it can begin to estimate the impact that its supply chain will have on its customers and ultimately the organization's performance. The payoff for a successful demand planning strategy can be tremendous. A study by Peter J. Metz, executive director of the MIT Center for ebusiness, found that companies have achieved impressive bottom-line results from managing demand in their supply chains, averaging a 50 percent reduction in inventory and a 40 percent increase in timely deliveries.[2]

COMPETITION

Supply chain management software can be broken down into (1) supply chain planning software and (2) supply chain execution software—both increase a company's ability to compete. ***Supply chain planning (SCP) software*** uses advanced mathematical algorithms to improve the flow and efficiency of the supply chain while reducing inventory. SCP depends entirely on information for its accuracy. An organization cannot expect the SCP output to be accurate unless correct and up-to-date information regarding customer orders, sales information, manufacturing capacity, and delivery capability is entered into the system.

An organization's supply chain encompasses the facilities where raw materials, intermediate products, and finished goods are acquired, transformed, stored, and sold. These facilities are connected by transportation links, where materials and products flow. Ideally, the supply chain consists of multiple organizations that function as efficiently and effectively as a single organization, with full information visibility. ***Supply chain execution (SCE) software*** automates the different steps and stages of the supply chain. This could be as simple as electronically routing orders from a manufacturer to a supplier. Figure 10.3 details how SCP and SCE software correlate to the supply chain.

General Motors, Ford, and DaimlerChrysler made history when the three automotive giants began working together to create a unified supply chain planning/execution system that all three companies and their suppliers could leverage. The combined automotive giants' purchasing power is tremendous with GM spending $85 billion per year, Ford spending $80 billion per year, and DaimlerChrysler spending $73 billion per year. The ultimate goal is to process automotive production from ordering materials and forecasting demand to making cars directly to consumer specifications through the web. The automotive giants understand the impact strategic supply chain planning and execution can have on their competition.[3]

FIGURE 10.3

Supply Chain Planning and Supply Chain Execution: Software's Correlation to the Supply Chain

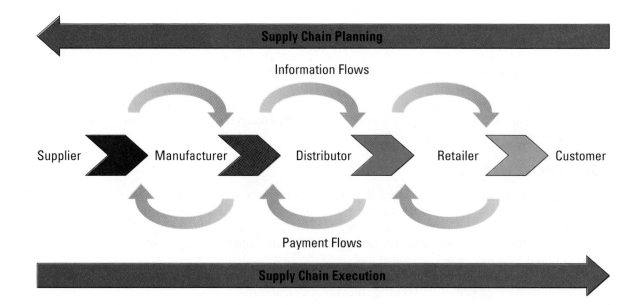

SPEED

During the past decade, competition has focused on speed. New forms of servers, telecommunications, wireless applications, and software are enabling companies to perform activities that were once never thought possible. These systems raise the accuracy, frequency, and speed of communication between suppliers and customers, as well as between internal users. Another aspect of speed is the company's ability to satisfy continually changing customer requirements efficiently, accurately, and quickly. Timely and accurate information is more critical to businesses than ever before. Figure 10.4 displays the three factors fostering this change.

Supply Chain Management Success Factors

To succeed in today's competitive markets, companies must align their supply chains with the demands of the markets they serve. Supply chain performance is now a distinct competitive advantage for companies proficient in the SCM area. Perdue Farms excels at decision making based on its supply chain management system. Perdue Farms moves roughly 1 million turkeys, each within 24 hours of processing, to reach holiday tables across the nation yearly. The task is no longer as complicated as it was before Perdue Farms invested $20 million in SCM technology. SCM makes Perdue more adept at delivering the right number of turkeys, to the right customers, at the right time.[4]

To achieve success such as reducing operating costs, improving asset productivity, and compressing order cycle time, an organization should follow the seven principles of supply chain management outlined in Figure 10.5.

These seven principles run counter to previous built-in functional thinking of how companies organize, operate, and serve customers. Old concepts of supply chains are typified by discrete manufacturing, linear structure, and a focus on buy-sell transactions ("I buy from my suppliers, I sell to my customers"). Because the traditional supply chain is spread out linearly, some suppliers are removed from the end customer. Collaboration adds the value of visibility for these companies. They benefit by knowing immediately what is being transacted at the customer end

LO 10.2 Summarize the best practices for implementing a successful supply chain management system.

FIGURE 10.4

Three Factors Fostering Speed

Factors Fostering Supply Chain Speed

1. Pleasing customers has become something of a corporate obsession. Serving the customer in the best, most efficient, and most effective manner has become critical, and information about issues such as order status, product availability, delivery schedules, and invoices has become a necessary part of the total customer service experience.

2. Information is crucial to managers' abilities to reduce inventory and human resource requirements to a competitive level.

3. Information flows are essential to strategic planning for and deployment of resources.

FIGURE 10.5

Seven Principles of Supply Chain Management

Seven Principles of Supply Chain Management

1. Segment customers by service needs, regardless of industry, and then tailor services to those particular segments.

2. Customize the logistics network and focus intensively on the service requirements and on the profitability of the preidentified customer segments.

3. Listen to signals of market demand and plan accordingly. Planning must span the entire chain to detect signals of changing demand.

4. Differentiate products closer to the customer, since companies can no longer afford to hold inventory to compensate for poor demand forecasting.

5. Strategically manage sources of supply, by working with key suppliers to reduce overall costs of owning materials and services.

6. Develop a supply chain information technology strategy that supports different levels of decision making and provides a clear view (visibility) of the flow of products, services, and information.

7. Adopt performance evaluation measures that apply to every link in the supply chain and measure true profitability at every stage.

of the supply chain (the end customer's activities are visible to them). Instead of waiting days or weeks (or months) for the information to flow upstream through the supply chain, with all the potential pitfalls of erroneous or missing information, suppliers can react in near real-time to fluctuations in end-customer demand.

Dell Inc. offers one of the best examples of an extremely successful SCM system. Dell's highly efficient build-to-order business model enables it to deliver customized computer systems quickly. As part of the company's continual effort to improve its supply chain processes, Dell deploys supply chain tools to provide global views of forecasted product demand and materials requirements, as well as improved factory scheduling and inventory management.

Organizations should study industry best practices to improve their chances of successful implementation of SCM systems. Figure 10.6 displays SCM success keys.

RFID AND THE SUPPLY CHAIN

A television commercial shows a man in a uniform quietly moving through a family home. The man replaces the empty cereal box with a full one just before a hungry child opens the cabinet; he then opens a new sack of dog food as the hungry bulldog eyes him warily, and finally hands a full bottle of shampoo to the man in the shower who had just run out. The next wave in supply chain management will be home-based supply chain fulfillment.

Walgreens is differentiating itself from other national chains by marketing itself as the family's just-in-time supplier. Consumers today are becoming incredibly comfortable with the idea of going online to purchase products when they want, how they want, and at the price they want. Walgreens is developing custom websites for each household that allow families to order electronically and then at their convenience go to the store to pick up their goods at a special self-service counter or the drive-through window. Walgreens is making a promise that goes beyond low prices and customer service and extends right into the home.

FIGURE 10.6

SCM Keys to Success

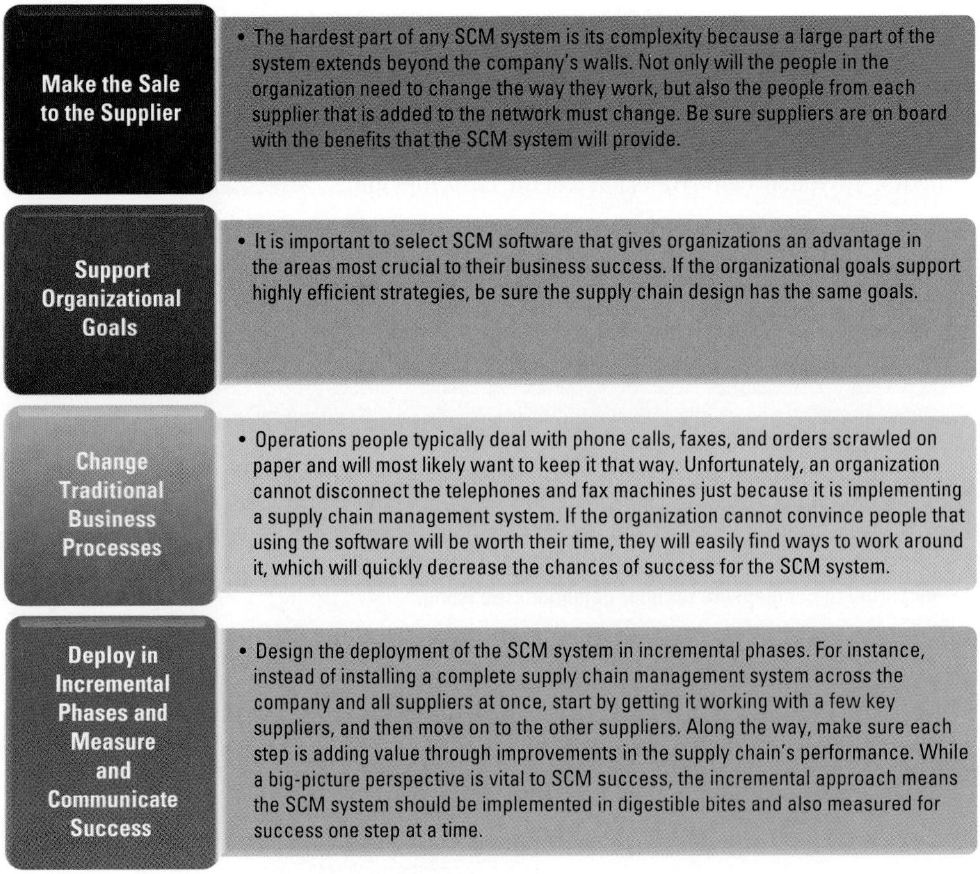

Make the Sale to the Supplier	• The hardest part of any SCM system is its complexity because a large part of the system extends beyond the company's walls. Not only will the people in the organization need to change the way they work, but also the people from each supplier that is added to the network must change. Be sure suppliers are on board with the benefits that the SCM system will provide.
Support Organizational Goals	• It is important to select SCM software that gives organizations an advantage in the areas most crucial to their business success. If the organizational goals support highly efficient strategies, be sure the supply chain design has the same goals.
Change Traditional Business Processes	• Operations people typically deal with phone calls, faxes, and orders scrawled on paper and will most likely want to keep it that way. Unfortunately, an organization cannot disconnect the telephones and fax machines just because it is implementing a supply chain management system. If the organization cannot convince people that using the software will be worth their time, they will easily find ways to work around it, which will quickly decrease the chances of success for the SCM system.
Deploy in Incremental Phases and Measure and Communicate Success	• Design the deployment of the SCM system in incremental phases. For instance, instead of installing a complete supply chain management system across the company and all suppliers at once, start by getting it working with a few key suppliers, and then move on to the other suppliers. Along the way, make sure each step is adding value through improvements in the supply chain's performance. While a big-picture perspective is vital to SCM success, the incremental approach means the SCM system should be implemented in digestible bites and also measured for success one step at a time.

The functionality in supply chain management systems is becoming more and more sophisticated as supply chain management matures. Now and in the future, the next stages of SCM will incorporate more functions such as marketing, customer service, and product development. This will be achieved through more advanced communication, adoption of more user-friendly decision support systems, and availability of shared information to all participants in the supply chain. SCM is an ongoing development as technology makes it possible to acquire information ever more accurately and frequently from all over the world, and introduces new tools to aid in the analytical processes that deal with the supply chain's growing complexity.

According to Forrester Research, Inc., U.S. firms will spend $35 billion over the next five years to improve business processes that monitor, manage, and optimize their extended supply chains. Figure 10.7 displays the fastest growing SCM components because they have the greatest potential impact on an organization's bottom line.

Radio frequency identification (RFID) technologies use active or passive tags in the form of chips or smart labels that can store unique identifiers and relay this information to electronic readers. At Starbucks, good service is nearly as important as good coffee to customer loyalty. But when a delivery person comes knocking on the back door to drop off muffins, it means employees may need to leave their countertop posts, jeopardizing customer service. To help solve the problem, Starbucks is considering using radio frequency identification technology as part of a proposed plan to let its 40,000 suppliers drop off pastries, milk, coffee beans, and other supplies at night, after stores have closed. This solution solves one problem while causing another: How does Starbucks ensure that delivery people do not walk out with as much stuff as they drop off?

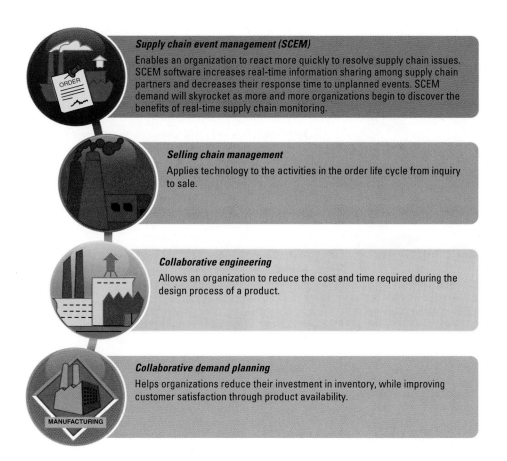

FIGURE 10.7

Growing SCM Components

Supply chain event management (SCEM)

Enables an organization to react more quickly to resolve supply chain issues. SCEM software increases real-time information sharing among supply chain partners and decreases their response time to unplanned events. SCEM demand will skyrocket as more and more organizations begin to discover the benefits of real-time supply chain monitoring.

Selling chain management

Applies technology to the activities in the order life cycle from inquiry to sale.

Collaborative engineering

Allows an organization to reduce the cost and time required during the design process of a product.

Collaborative demand planning

Helps organizations reduce their investment in inventory, while improving customer satisfaction through product availability.

To solve the problem, the company will distribute to its suppliers cards with RFID chips that give delivery people access to stores at night, while recording who is coming and going. RFID tags contain a microchip and an antenna and typically work by transmitting a serial number via radio waves to an electronic reader, which confirms the identity of a person or object bearing the tag.

As many as 10,000 radio frequency identification tags are taking to the skies, affixed to everything from airline seats to brakes, as part of the Airbus A380, a 550-seat jet. The tags contain serial numbers, codes, and maintenance history that should make it easier to track, fix, and replace parts. Not to be outdone, Boeing is using tags on many of the parts in its upcoming 7E7 Dreamliner. These initiatives are not the first use of RFID in the airline industry, but they represent aggressive plans to further leverage the real-time and detail capabilities of RFID. Boeing and Airbus are equipping all tools and toolboxes with RFID tags.

INTEGRATING RFID AND SOFTWARE

Integrating RFID with enterprise software is expected to change the way companies manage maintenance, combat theft, and even augment Sarbanes-Oxley Act IT initiatives. Oracle and SAP have begun adding RFID capability to their enterprise application suites. Oracle's RFID and Sensor-Based Services analyze and respond to data from RFID so the information can be integrated with Oracle's applications.

RFID tags are evolving, too, and the advances will provide more granular information to enterprise software. Today's tags can store an electronic product code. In time, tags could hold more information, making them portable mini-databases. The possibilities of RFID are endless. Delta Air Lines recently completed a pilot project that used baggage tags incorporating RFID chips instead of the standard bar codes. With RFID readers installed at counters and key sorting locations, not a single duffel was misplaced. Figures 10.8 and 10.9 display how an RFID system works in the supply chain.

FIGURE 10.8

Three RFID Components

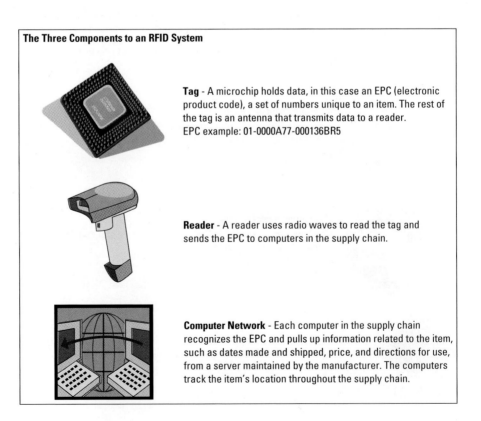

The Three Components to an RFID System

Tag - A microchip holds data, in this case an EPC (electronic product code), a set of numbers unique to an item. The rest of the tag is an antenna that transmits data to a reader. EPC example: 01-0000A77-000136BR5

Reader - A reader uses radio waves to read the tag and sends the EPC to computers in the supply chain.

Computer Network - Each computer in the supply chain recognizes the EPC and pulls up information related to the item, such as dates made and shipped, price, and directions for use, from a server maintained by the manufacturer. The computers track the item's location throughout the supply chain.

RFID in the Retail Supply Chain

RFID tags are added to every product and shipping box. At every step of an item's journey, a reader scans one of the tags and updates the information on the server.

The Manufacturer
A reader scans the tags as items leave the factory.

The Distribution Center
Readers in the unloading area scan the tags on arriving boxes and update inventory, avoiding the need to open packages.

The Store
Tags are scanned upon arrival to update inventory. At the racks, readers scan tags as shirts are stocked. At the checkout counter, a cashier can scan individual items with a handheld reader. As items leave the store, inventory is updated. Manufacturers and retailers can observe sales patterns in real time and make swift decisions about production, ordering, and pricing.

The Home
The consumer can have the tag disabled at the store for privacy or place readers in closets to keep track of clothes. With customers' approval, stores can follow purchasing patterns and notify them of sales.

FIGURE 10.9

RFID in the Supply Chain

OPENING CASE STUDY QUESTIONS

1. Explain why virtual companies such as Actionly would need to worry about supply chain management.

2. If you ran an apparel company, such as Nike or REI, how could you use RFID to improve the supply chain?

Chapter Ten Case: RFID—Future Tracking the Supply Chain

One of the hottest new technologies in the supply chain is a radio frequency identification (RFID) tag. These tags are tiny and can carry large amounts of data tracking everything from price to temperature. Supply chains around the globe are being revamped with RFID tags. However, some people might be taking the ability to track the supply chain with RFID tags a bit too far.

Tracking People

The elementary school that required students to wear RFID tags to track their movements ended the program because the company that developed the technology pulled out. "I'm disappointed; that's about all I can say at this point," stated Ernie Graham, the superintendent and principal of Brittan Elementary School. "I think I let my staff down."

Students were required to wear identification cards around their necks with their picture, name, and grade and a wireless transmitter that beamed ID numbers to a teacher's handheld computer when the children passed under an antenna posted above a classroom door. The school instituted the system, without parental input, to simplify attendance-taking and potentially reduce vandalism and improve student safety. "I'm happy for now that kids are not being tagged, but I'm still fighting to keep it out of our school system," said parent Dawn Cantrall, who filed a complaint with the American Civil Liberties Union. "It has to stop here."

While many parents criticized the tags for violating privacy and possibly endangering children's health, some parents supported the plan. "Technology scares some people; it's a fear of the unknown," parent Mary Brower said. "Any kind of new technology has the potential for misuse, but I feel confident the school is not going to misuse it."

Tracking Children

Children's sleepwear with radio frequency identification tags sewn into the seams hit stores in early 2006. Made by Lauren Scott California, the nightgowns and pajamas will be one of the first commercial RFID-tagged clothing lines sold in the United States. The PJs are designed to keep kids safe from abductions, says proprietor Lauren Scott, who licensed the RFID technology from SmartWear Technologies Inc., a maker of personal security systems. Readers positioned in doorways and windows throughout a house scan tags within a 30-foot radius and trigger an alarm when boundaries are breached.

A pamphlet attached to the garment informs customers that the sleepwear is designed to help prevent child abductions. It directs parents to a website that explains how to activate and encode the RFID tag with a unique digital identification number. The site also provides information on a $500 home-installed system that consists of RFID readers and a low-frequency encoder that connects through a USB port to a computer. Parents can sign up to include data about their children, including photos, in the SmartWear database. That information can be shared with law enforcement agencies or the Amber Alert system if a child disappears.

SmartWear has several other projects in the works including an extended-range RFID tag that can transmit signals up to 600 feet. The tag could be inserted into law enforcement and military uniforms or outerwear, such as ski jackets, and used to find a missing or lost person or to recover and identify a body.

Plastic RFID

A typical RFID tag costs 40 cents, making price a barrier for many potential applications. Start-up OrganicID is creating a plastic RFID tag that it expects will reduce the price to a penny or less.[5]

Questions

1. What are some advantages and disadvantages of tagging students with RFID tags?
2. What are some advantages and disadvantages of tagging children's pajamas with RFID tags?
3. Do you agree or disagree that tagging students with RFID tags is a violation of privacy rights? Explain why.
4. Do you agree or disagree that tagging children's pajamas with RFID tags is a violation of privacy rights? Explain why.
5. Describe the relationship between privacy rights and RFID.
6. Determine a way that schools could use RFID tags without violating privacy rights.

Building a Customer-centric Organization—Customer Relationship Management

11.1. Describe customer relationship management along with its importance to a business.

11.2. Identify the three current CRM trends.

Customer Relationship Management

LO 11.1 Describe customer relationship management along with its importance to a business.

Today, most competitors are simply a mouse-click away, and this intense competition is forcing firms to switch from sales-focused business strategies to customer-focused business strategies. Customers are one of a firm's most valuable assets, and building strong loyal customer relationships is a key competitive advantage. Harley-Davidson offers an excellent example of a company that knows the value of customer loyalty, and it finds itself in the coveted position of demand outweighing its supply. No other motorcycle in the world has the look, feel, and sound of a Harley-Davidson. Demand for Harley-Davidson motorcycles outweighs supply and some models have up to a two-year waiting list. Knowing the value of its customers, Harley-Davidson started the Harley's Owners Group (HOG), which is the largest motorcycle club in the world with more than 600,000 members. HOG offers a wide array of events, rides, and benefits to its members and is a key competitive advantage as it helps to build a strong sense of community among Harley-Davidson owners. Harley-Davidson has built a customer following that is extremely loyal, a difficult task to accomplish in any industry.

Customer relationship management (CRM) is a means of managing all aspects of a customer's relationship with an organization to increase customer loyalty and retention and an organization's profitability. CRM allows an organization to gain insights into customers' shopping and buying behaviors. Every time a customer communicates with a company, the firm has the chance to build a trusting relationship with that particular customer. Harley-Davidson realizes that it takes more than just building and selling motorcycles to fulfill the dreams of its loyal customers. For this reason, the company strives to deliver unforgettable experiences along with its top-quality products. When the company began selling products online it found itself facing a dilemma—its online strategy for selling accessories directly to consumers would bypass Harley-Davidson's dealers, who depend on the high-margin accessories for store revenues. The solution was to deploy Harley-Davidson.com, which prompts customers to select a participating Harley-Davidson dealership before placing any online orders. The selected dealership is then responsible for fulfilling the order. This strategy ensured that the dealers remained the focus point of each customer's buying experiences. To guarantee that every customer has a highly satisfying online buying experience, the company asks the dealers to agree to a number of standards including:

- Checking online orders twice daily.
- Shipping online orders within 24 hours.
- Responding to customer inquiries within 24 hours.

Harley-Davidson still monitors online customer metrics such as time taken to process orders, number of returned orders, and number of incorrect orders, guaranteeing that the company delivers on its critical success factor of providing prompt, excellent customer service consistently to all its loyal customers.

A primary component of managing a customer relationship is knowing when and why the customer is communicating with the company. Imagine an irate customer who has just spent an hour on the phone with your call center complaining about a defective product. While the customer is on the phone, your sales representative decides to drop by the customer's office in an attempt to sell additional products. Obviously, this is not the ideal time to try to up-sell or cross-sell products to this particular customer. A customer relationship management system would inform the sales representative that the customer was on the phone with customer service and even provide details of the call. Then your sales representative could stop by and offer assistance in resolving the product issue, which might help restore the relationship with the customer and provide opportunities for future sales.

The complicated piece of this puzzle is that customers have many communication channels they can use to contact a company including call centers, websites, email, faxes, and telephones (see Figure 11.1). To make matters even more complex, a single customer can communicate with a firm using all of the different communication channels multiple times. Keeping track of customer communications is important if the firm wants to continue to build and manage that relationship. A CRM system can track every form of customer communication providing this information to all employees. The firm can then implement strategies for the best ways to communicate effectively with each and every customer. With a CRM system, a firm can obtain an overview of the customer's products, preferences, account information, communications, and purchasing history, allowing it to send customized product offers, expedite shipping, ensure satisfaction, and use other marketing and sales techniques that can greatly add to sales and profits.

Using CRM metrics to track and monitor performance is a best practice for many companies. Figure 11.2 displays a few common CRM metrics a manager can use to track the success of the system. Just remember that you only want to track between five and seven of the hundreds of CRM metrics available.

The two primary components of a CRM strategy are operational CRM and analytical CRM. **Operational CRM** supports traditional transactional processing for day-to-day

FIGURE 11.1

Customer Contact Points

Sales Metrics	Customer Service Metrics	Marketing Metrics
Number of prospective customers	Cases closed same day	Number of marketing campaigns
Number of new customers	Number of cases handled by agent	New customer retention rates
Number of retained customers	Number of service calls	Number of responses by marketing campaign
Number of open leads	Average number of service requests by type	Number of purchases by marketing campaign
Number of sales calls	Average time to resolution	Revenue generated by marketing campaign
Number of sales calls per lead	Average number of service calls per day	Cost per interaction by marketing campaign
Amount of new revenue	Percentage compliance with service-level agreement	Number of new customers acquired by marketing campaign
Amount of recurring revenue	Percentage of service renewals	Customer retention rate
Number of proposals given	Customer satisfaction level	Number of new leads by product

FIGURE 11.2

Common CRM Metrics

front-office operations or systems that deal directly with the customers. ***Analytical CRM*** supports back-office operations and strategic analysis and includes all systems that do not deal directly with the customers. Figure 11.3 provides an overview of the two. Figure 11.4 shows the different technologies marketing, sales, and customer service departments can use to perform operational CRM.

THE UGLY SIDE OF CRM—ANGRY CUSTOMERS

Business 2.0 ranked "You—the customer" as number one in the top 50 people who matter most in business. It has long been said that the customer is always right, but for a long time companies never really meant it. Now, companies have no choice as the power of the customer grows exponentially as the Internet grows. You—or rather, the collaborative intelligence of tens of millions of people, the networked you—continually create and filter new forms of content, anointing the useful, the relevant, and the amusing and

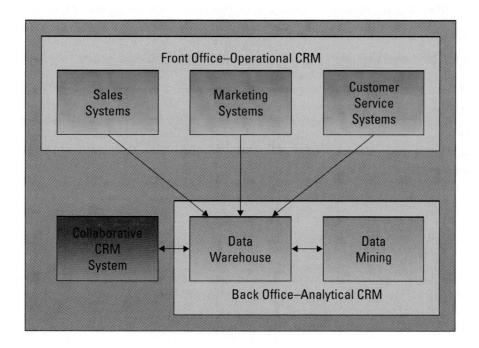

FIGURE 11.3

Operational CRM and Analytical CRM

FIGURE 11.4

Operational CRM
Technologies

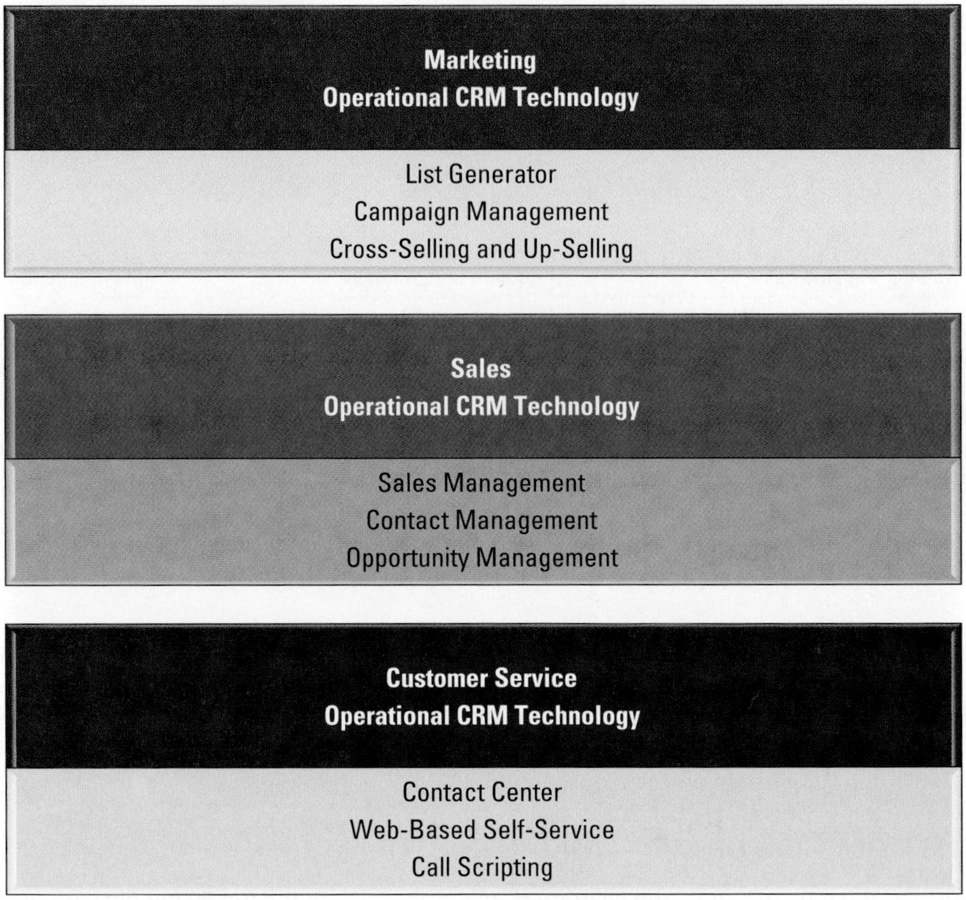

**Marketing
Operational CRM Technology**

List Generator
Campaign Management
Cross-Selling and Up-Selling

**Sales
Operational CRM Technology**

Sales Management
Contact Management
Opportunity Management

**Customer Service
Operational CRM Technology**

Contact Center
Web-Based Self-Service
Call Scripting

rejecting the rest. You do it on websites like Amazon, Flickr, and YouTube, via podcasts and SMS polling, and on millions of self-published blogs. In every case, you have become an integral part of the action as a member of the aggregated, interactive, self-organizing, auto-entertaining audience. But the "You Revolution" goes well beyond user-generated content. Companies as diverse as Delta Air Lines and T-Mobile are turning to you to create their ad slogans. Procter & Gamble and Lego are incorporating your ideas into new products. You constructed open-source software and are its customer and its caretaker.

None of this should be a surprise, since it was you—your crazy passions and hobbies and obsessions—that built out the web in the first place. And somewhere out there, you are building web 3.0. We do not yet know what that is, but one thing is for sure: It will matter. Figure 11.5 displays a few examples of the power of the people. CRM is critical to business success. It is the key competitive strategy to stay focused on customer needs and to integrate a customer-centric approach throughout an organization. CRM can acquire enterprisewide knowledge about customers and improve the business processes that deliver value to an organization's customers, suppliers, and employees. Using the analytical capabilities of CRM can help a company anticipate customer needs and proactively serve customers in ways that build relationships, create loyalty, and enhance bottom lines.

LO 11.2 Identify the three current CRM trends.

Current Trends: SRM, PRM, and ERM

Organizations are discovering a wave of other key business areas where it is beneficial to take advantage of building strong relationships. These emerging areas include supplier relationship management (SRM), partner relationship management (PRM), and employee relationship management (ERM).

SUPPLIER RELATIONSHIP MANAGEMENT

Supplier relationship management (SRM) focuses on keeping suppliers satisfied by evaluating and categorizing suppliers for different projects, which optimizes supplier selection. SRM applications help companies analyze vendors based on a number of key variables including strategy, business goals, prices, and markets. The company can then determine the best supplier to collaborate with and can work on developing strong relationships with that supplier. The partners can then work together to streamline processes, outsource services, and provide products that they could not provide individually.

With the merger of the Bank of Halifax and Bank of Scotland, the new company, HBOS, implemented an SRM system to supply consistent information to its suppliers. The system integrates procurement information from the separate Bank of Halifax and Bank of Scotland operational systems, generating a single repository of management information for consistent reporting and analysis. Other benefits HBOS derived from the SRM solution include:

- A single consolidated view of all suppliers.
- Consistent, detailed management information allowing multiple views for every executive.
- Elimination of duplicate suppliers.

PARTNER RELATIONSHIP MANAGEMENT

Organizations have begun to realize the importance of building relationships with partners, dealers, and resellers. ***Partner relationship management (PRM)*** focuses on keeping vendors satisfied by managing alliance partner and reseller relationships that provide customers with the optimal sales channel. PRM's business strategy is to select and manage partners to optimize their long-term value to an organization. In effect, it means picking the right partners, working with them to help them be successful in dealing with mutual customers, and ensuring that partners and the ultimate end customers are satisfied and successful. Many of the features of a PRM application include real-time product information on availability, marketing materials, contracts, order details, and pricing, inventory, and shipping information.

PRM is one of the smaller segments of CRM that has superb potential. PRM has grown to more than a $1 billion industry. This is a direct reflection of the growing interdependency of organizations in the new economy. The primary benefits of PRM include:

- Expanded market coverage.
- Offerings of specialized products and services.
- Broadened range of offerings and a more complete solution.

EMPLOYEE RELATIONSHIP MANAGEMENT

Jim Sinegal runs Costco, one of the largest wholesale club chains, but there are two things he does not discount: employee benefits and customer service. Average hourly wages trounce those of rival Sam's Club, and 86 percent of workers have health insurance (versus a reported 47 percent at Sam's). Sinegal is not just being nice. Happy employees, he believes, make for happier customers. Low prices (he caps per-item profits at 14 percent) and a generous return policy certainly help. Although Wall Street has long been arguing for smaller benefits, a stingier return policy, and bigger profits, Sinegal sides with customers and staff. "We're trying to run Costco in a fashion that is not just going to satisfy our shareholders this year or this month," he said, "but next year and on into the future."

Employee relationship management (ERM) provides employees with a subset of CRM applications available through a web browser. Many of the ERM applications assist the employee in dealing with customers by providing detailed information on company products, services, and customer orders.

At Rackspace, a San Antonio-based web-hosting company, customer focus borders on the obsessive. Joey Parsons, 24, won the Straightjacket Award, the most coveted employee distinction at Rackspace. The award recognizes the employee who best lives up to the Rackspace motto of delivering "fanatical support," a dedication to customers that is so intense it borders on the loony. Rackspace motivates its staff by treating each team as a separate business, which is responsible for its own profits and losses and has its own ERM website. Each month, employees can earn bonuses of up to 20 percent of their monthly base salaries depending on the performance of their units by both financial and customer-centric measurements such as customer turnover, customer expansion, and customer referrals. Daily reports are available through the team's ERM website.

CRM revenue forecast for 2018 is $21.5 billion. In the future, CRM applications will continue to change from employee-only tools to tools used by suppliers, partners, and even customers. Providing a consistent view of customers and delivering timely and accurate customer information to all departments across an organization will continue to be the major goal of CRM initiatives.

As technology advances (intranet, Internet, extranet, wireless), CRM will remain a major strategic focus for companies, particularly in industries whose product is difficult to differentiate. Some companies approach this problem by moving to a low-cost producer strategy. CRM will be an alternative way to pursue a differentiation strategy with a nondifferentiable product.

CRM applications will continue to adapt wireless capabilities supporting mobile sales and mobile customers. Sales professionals will be able to access email, order details, corporate information, inventory status, and opportunity information all from a PDA in their car or on a plane. Real-time interaction with human CSRs over the Internet will continue to increase.

CRM suites will also incorporate PRM and SRM modules as enterprises seek to take advantage of these initiatives. Automating interactions with distributors, resellers, and suppliers will enhance the corporation's ability to deliver a quality experience to its customers.

OPENING CASE STUDY QUESTIONS

1. Illustrate the business process used by a customer of Actionly following Twitter tweets.

2. Identify different metrics Actionly uses to measure the success of a customer marketing campaign.

3. Argue for or against the following statement: Actionly invades consumer privacy by taking data from different websites such as Twitter and Flickr without the consent of the customer who posted the information.

Chapter Eleven Case: Can You Find Your Customers?

Entrepreneurship is all about finding niche markets, which arise from an untapped potential in a corner of an existing market ignored by major companies. Finding customers for a specialized or niche business is no longer an arduous manual task. Somewhere there is a list of names that will allow a business, no matter how "niche," to locate its specific target customers.

Vinod Gupta was working for a recreational vehicle (RV) manufacturer in Omaha, Nebraska, in 1972. One day his boss requested a list of all the RV dealers in the country. Of course, at this time no such list existed. Gupta decided to create one. Gupta ordered every Yellow Pages phone book in the country, 4,500 total, took them home to his garage, and started manually sorting through each book one-by-one, compiling the RV list that his boss coveted. After providing the list Gupta told his boss he could have it for free if he could also sell it to other RV manufacturers. Gupta's boss agreed, and his company—infoUSA Inc.—was launched.

Today infoUSA no longer sells lists on yellow pieces of paper, but maintains one of the nation's largest databases, including 14 million businesses and 220 million consumers. More than 4 million customers access this resource. More than 90 percent are entrepreneurial companies and have only one or two employees. These small businesses account for 60 percent of infoUSA's annual revenue of $311 million.

The point is that entrepreneurial businesses that want to thrive in specialty markets can use databases for reaching customers. While this resource does not do the whole job, it can and should comprise the core of a marketing program which also includes publicity, word-of-mouth recommendations, or "buzz," savvy geographical placement of the company's physical outlets, such as retail stores and offices, and, if affordable, advertising.

Slicing and Dicing

Put another way, databases, which slice-and-dice lists to pinpoint just the right prospects for products or services, enable entrepreneurs to find the proverbial needle in the haystack. An entrepreneur might target a market of only 200 companies or a select universe of individuals who might have use for a specific product or service—such as feminist-oriented prayer books for Lutheran women ministers in their 20s, or seeds for gardeners who grow vegetables native to Sicily, or, like one of infoUSA's own customers, jelly beans for companies with employee coffee-break rooms.

Databases have the ability to take the legwork out of locating specialized customers and make the job as easy as one, two, three. According to infoUSA, to use databases effectively, company owners must take three distinct steps:

Step 1: Know Your Customers

"In any business, there is no substitute for retaining existing customers. Make these people happy, and they become the base from which you add others. As a niche marketer, you have at least an idea who might want what you have to sell, even if those prospects aren't yet actually buying. Get to know these people. Understand what they are looking for. Consider what they like and don't like about your product or service."

Step 2: Analyze Your Customers

"Your current customers or clients have all of the information you need to find other customers. Analyze them to find common characteristics. If you are selling to businesses, consider revenue and number of employees. If you are selling to consumers, focus on demographics, such as age, as well as income levels. Armed with this information about your customers, you are ready to make use of a database to look for new ones."

Step 3: Find New Customers Just Like Your Existing Customers

"In a niche business, you find new customers by cloning your existing customers. Once you know and understand your current customers, you can determine the types of businesses or customers to target.

"An online brokerage, for example, was seeking to build its business further and needed a list of names of people 'with a propensity to invest' just like its current clients. Our company used proprietary modeling to provide a set of names of individuals from throughout the U.S. with the required level of income.

"You should buy a database-generated list only if you have analyzed your current customers. In addition, you should wait to buy until you are ready to use the list, because lists do have a short shelf life—about 30 to 60 days if you are selling to consumers and six to nine months if you are selling to businesses. Indeed, about 70 percent of infoUSA's entire database changes over annually."

No Magic Bullet

The magic of databases is that there is no magic. Every entrepreneur has a product or service to sell. The trick is to match what you are selling with people who are buying. Used effectively, databases serve as the resource for making that happen. Do not make the mistake of expecting a database to perform the entire job of securing customers for products or services. An entrepreneur must be ever vigilant about prospecting—and not only when business is slow. Entrepreneurs must encourage sales representatives to call on customers even when business is booming and they do not require their revenues to keep the company afloat. Once customers are secured, make servicing them a top priority.[1]

Questions

1. Explain how technology has dramatically affected the efficiency and effectiveness of finding customers.

2. Explain the two different types of CRM systems, and explain how a company can use infoUSA's database for creating a CRM strategy.

3. Describe three ways a new small business can extend its customer reach by performing CRM functions from an infoUSA database.

4. infoUSA discussed three distinct steps company owners must take to use databases effectively. Rank these steps in order of importance to a CRM strategy.

Integrating the Organization from End to End—Enterprise Resource Planning

12.1. Describe the role information plays in enterprise resource planning systems.

12.2. Explain the business value of integrating supply chain management, customer relationship management, and enterprise resource planning systems.

LO 12.1 Describe the role information plays in enterprise resource planning systems.

Enterprise Resource Planning (ERP)

Enterprise resource planning systems serve as the organization's backbone in providing fundamental decision-making support. In the past, departments made decisions independent of each other. ERP systems provide a foundation for collaboration between departments, enabling people in different business areas to communicate. ERP systems have been widely adopted in large organizations to store critical knowledge used to make the decisions that drive performance.

To be competitive, organizations must always strive for excellence in every business process enterprisewide, a daunting challenge if the organization has multisite operations worldwide. To obtain operational efficiencies, lower costs, improve supplier and customer relations, and increase revenues and market share, all units of the organization must work together harmoniously toward congruent goals. An ERP system will help an organization achieve this.

The heart of an ERP system is a central database that collects information from and feeds information into all the ERP system's individual application components (called modules), supporting diverse business functions such as accounting, manufacturing, marketing, and human resources. When a user enters or updates information in one module, it is immediately and automatically updated throughout the entire system, as illustrated in Figure 12.1.

ERP automates business processes such as order fulfillment—taking an order from a customer, shipping the purchase, and then billing for it. With an ERP system, when a customer service representative takes an order from a customer, he or she has all the information necessary to complete the order (the customer's credit rating and order history, the company's inventory levels, and the delivery schedule). Everyone else in the company sees the same information and has access to the database that holds the customer's new order. When one department finishes with the order, it is automatically routed via the ERP system to the next department. To find out where the order is at any point, a user need only log in to the ERP system and track it down, as illustrated in Figure 12.2. The order process moves like a bolt of lightning through the organization, and customers get their orders faster and with fewer errors than ever before. ERP can apply that same magic to the other major business processes, such as employee benefits or financial reporting.

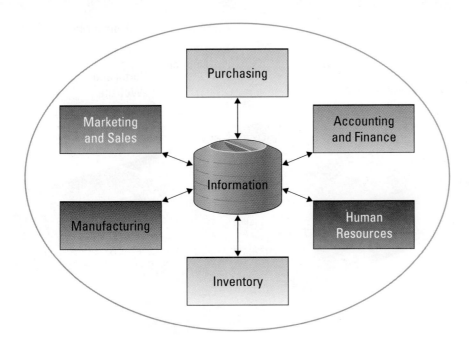

FIGURE 12.1

ERP Integration Data Flow

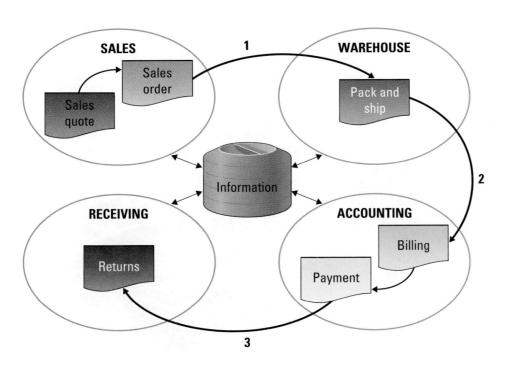

FIGURE 12.2

ERP Process Flow

BRINGING THE ORGANIZATION TOGETHER

In most organizations, information has traditionally been isolated within specific departments, whether on an individual database, in a file cabinet, or on an employee's PC. ERP
enables employees across the organization to share information across a single, centralized database. With extended portal capabilities, an organization can also involve
its suppliers and customers to participate in the workflow process, allowing ERP to
penetrate the entire value chain, and help the organization achieve greater operational
efficiency (see Figures 12.3 and 12.4).

FIGURE 12.3

The Organization before
ERP

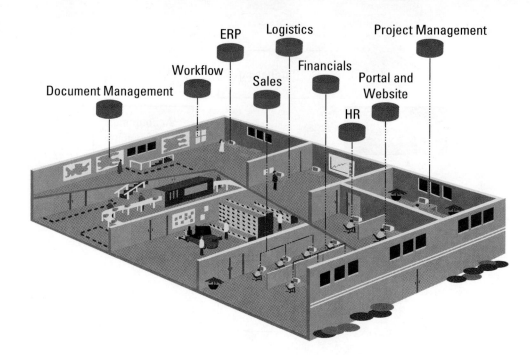

FIGURE 12.4

ERP—Bringing the
Organization Together

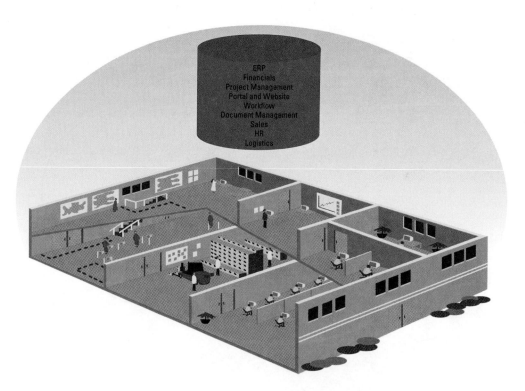

THE EVOLUTION OF ERP

Originally, ERP solutions were developed to deliver automation across multiple units of an organization, to help facilitate the manufacturing process and address issues such as raw materials, inventory, order entry, and distribution. However, ERP was unable to extend to other functional areas of the company such as sales, marketing, and shipping. It could not tie in any CRM capabilities that would allow organizations to capture customer-specific information, nor did it work with websites or portals used for customer service or order fulfillment. Call center or quality assurance staff could not tap into the ERP solution, nor could ERP handle document management, such as cataloging contracts and purchase orders.

ERP	Extended ERP	ERP-II
• Materials Planning	• Scheduling	• Project Management
• Order Entry	• Forecasting	• Knowledge Management
• Distribution	• Capacity Planning	• Workflow Management
• General Ledger	• Ecommerce	• Customer Relationship Management
• Accounting	• Warehousing	• Human Resource Management
• Shop Floor Control	• Logistics	• Portal Capability
		• Integrated Financials

FIGURE 12.5

The Evolution of ERP

| 1990 | 2000 | Present |

ERP has grown over the years to become part of the extended enterprise. From its beginning as a tool for materials planning, it has extended to warehousing, distribution, and order entry. With its next evolution, ERP expands to the front office including CRM. Now administrative, sales, marketing, and human resources staff can share a tool that is truly enterprisewide. To compete on a functional level today, companies must adopt an enterprisewide approach to ERP that utilizes the Internet and connects to every facet of the value chain. Figure 12.5 shows how ERP has grown since the 1990s to accommodate the needs of the entire organization.

INTEGRATING SCM, CRM, AND ERP

Applications such as SCM, CRM, and ERP are the backbone of ebusiness. Integration of these applications is the key to success for many companies. Integration allows the unlocking of information to make it available to any user, anywhere, anytime.

Most organizations today have no choice but to piece their SCM, CRM, and ERP applications together since no one vendor can respond to every organizational need; hence, customers purchase applications from multiple vendors. As a result, organizations face the challenge of integrating their systems. For example, a single organization might choose its CRM components from Siebel, SCM components from i2, and financial components and HR management components from Oracle. Figure 12.6 displays the general audience and purpose for each of these applications that have to be integrated.

INTEGRATION TOOLS

Effectively managing the transformation to an integrated enterprise will be critical to the success of the 21st century organization. The key is the integration of the disparate IT applications. An integrated enterprise infuses support areas, such as finance and human resources, with a strong customer orientation. Integrations are achieved using *middleware*—several different types of software that sit in the middle of and provide connectivity between two or more software applications. Middleware translates information between disparate systems. *Enterprise application integration (EAI) middleware* represents a new approach to middleware by packaging together commonly used functionality, such as providing prebuilt links to popular enterprise applications, which reduces the time necessary to develop solutions that integrate applications from multiple vendors. A few leading vendors of EAI middleware include

FIGURE 12.6

Primary Users and
Business Benefits of
Strategic Initiatives

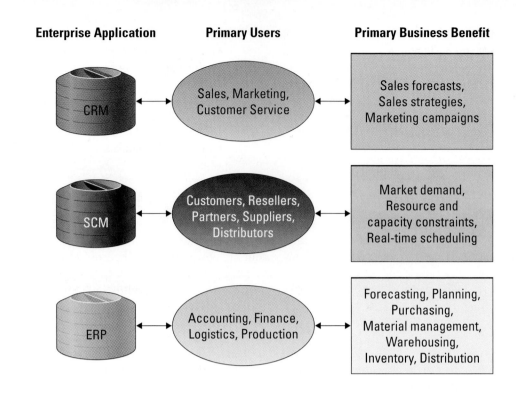

FIGURE 12.7

Integrations between
SCM, CRM, and ERP
Applications

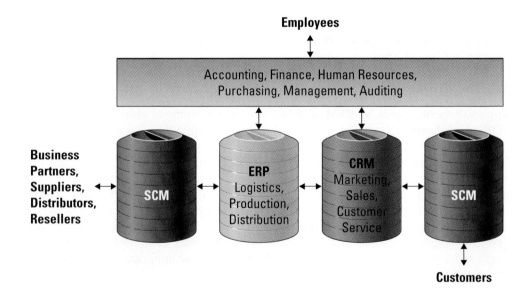

Active Software, Vitria Technology, and Extricity. Figure 12.7 displays the data points where these applications integrate and illustrates the underlying premise of architecture infrastructure design.

Companies run on interdependent applications, such as SCM, CRM, and ERP. If one application performs poorly, the entire customer value delivery system is affected. For example, no matter how great a company is at CRM, if its SCM system does not work and the customer never receives the finished product, the company will lose that customer. The world-class enterprises of tomorrow must be built on the foundation of world-class applications implemented today.

Core and Extended ERP Components

Turner Industries grew from $300 million in sales to $800 million in sales in less than 10 years thanks to the implementation of an ERP system. Ranked number 369 on the *Forbes* 500 list of privately held companies, Turner Industries is a leading industrial services firm. Turner Industries develops and deploys advanced software applications designed to maximize the productivity of its 25,000 employees and construction equipment valued at more than $100 million.

The company considers the biggest challenges in the industrial services industry to be completing projects on time, within budget, while fulfilling customers' expectations. To meet these challenges the company invested in an ERP system and named the project Interplan. Interplan won Constructech's Vision award for software innovation in the heavy construction industry. Interplan runs all of Turner's construction, turnaround, shutdown, and maintenance projects and is so adept at estimating and planning jobs that Turner Industries typically achieves higher profit margins on projects that use Interplan. As the ERP solution makes the company more profitable, the company can pass on the cost savings to its customers, giving the company an incredible competitive advantage.

Figure 12.8 provides an example of an ERP system with its core and extended components. ***Core ERP components*** are the traditional components included in most ERP systems and they primarily focus on internal operations. ***Extended ERP components*** are the extra components that meet the organizational needs not covered by the core components and primarily focus on external operations.

CORE ERP COMPONENTS

The three most common *core* ERP components focusing on internal operations are:

1. Accounting and finance.
2. Production and materials management.
3. Human resources.

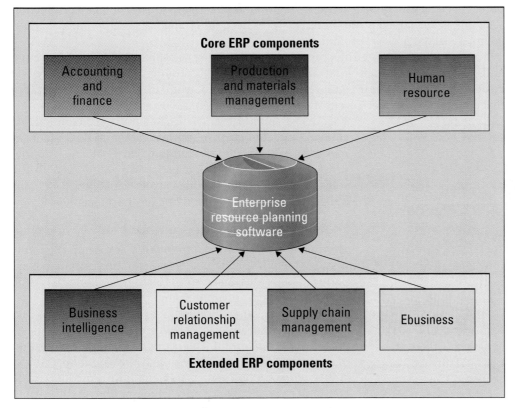

FIGURE 12.8

Core ERP Components and Extended ERP Components

Accounting and Finance ERP Components

Deeley Harley-Davidson Canada (DHDC), the exclusive Canadian distributor of Harley-Davidson motorcycles, has improved inventory, turnaround time, margins, and customer satisfaction—all with the implementation of a financial ERP system. The system has opened up the power of information to the company and is helping it make strategic decisions when it still has the time to change things. The ERP system provides the company with ways to manage inventory, turnaround time, and warehouse space more effectively.

Accounting and finance ERP components manage accounting data and financial processes within the enterprise with functions such as general ledger, accounts payable, accounts receivable, budgeting, and asset management. One of the most useful features included in an ERP accounting/finance component is its credit-management feature. Most organizations manage their relationships with customers by setting credit limits, or a limit on how much a customer can owe at any one time. The company then monitors the credit limit whenever the customer places a new order or sends in a payment. ERP financial systems help to correlate customer orders with customer account balances determining credit availability. Another great feature is the ability to perform product profitability analysis. ERP financial components are the backbone behind product profitability analysis and allow companies to perform all types of advanced profitability modeling techniques.

Production and Materials Management ERP Components

One of the main functions of an ERP system is streamlining the production planning process. *Production and materials management ERP components* handle the various aspects of production planning and execution such as demand forecasting, production scheduling, job cost accounting, and quality control. Companies typically produce multiple products, each of which has many different parts. Production lines, consisting of machines and employees, build the different types of products. The company must then define sales forecasting for each product to determine production schedules and materials purchasing. Figure 12.9 displays the typical ERP production planning process. The process begins with forecasting sales in order to plan operations. A detailed production schedule is developed if the product is produced and a materials requirement plan is completed if the product is purchased.

Grupo Farmanova Intermed, located in Costa Rica, is a pharmaceutical marketing and distribution company that markets nearly 2,500 products to approximately 500 customers in Central and South America. The company identified a need for software that could unify product logistics management in a single country. It decided to deploy PeopleSoft financial and distribution ERP components allowing the company to improve customer data management, increase confidence among internal and external users, and coordinate the logistics of inventory. With the software the company enhanced its capabilities for handling, distributing, and marketing its pharmaceuticals.

Human Resources ERP Components

Human resources ERP components track employee information including payroll, benefits, compensation, and performance assessment, and assure compliance with the legal requirements of multiple jurisdictions and tax authorities. Human resources components even offer features that allow the organization to perform detailed analysis on its employees to determine such things as the identification of individuals who are likely to leave the company unless additional compensation or benefits are provided. These components can also identify which employees are using which resources, such as online training and long-distance

FIGURE 12.9

The Production Planning Process

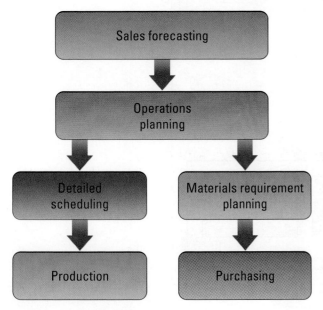

telephone services. They can also help determine whether the most talented people are working for those business units with the highest priority—or where they would have the greatest impact on profit.

EXTENDED ERP COMPONENTS

Extended ERP components are the extra components that meet the organizational needs not covered by the core components and primarily focus on external operations. Many of the numerous extended ERP components are Internet enabled and require interaction with customers, suppliers, and business partners outside the organization. The four most common extended ERP components are:

1. Business intelligence.
2. Customer relationship management.
3. Supply chain management.
4. Ebusiness.

Business Intelligence Components

ERP systems offer powerful tools that measure and control organizational operations. Many organizations have found that these valuable tools can be enhanced to provide even greater value through the addition of powerful business intelligence systems. The business intelligence components of ERP systems typically collect information used throughout the organization (including data used in many other ERP components), organize it, and apply analytical tools to assist managers with decisions. Data warehouses are one of the most popular extensions to ERP systems, with over two-thirds of U.S. manufacturers adopting or planning such systems.

Customer Relationship Management Components

ERP vendors are expanding their functionality to provide services formerly supplied by customer relationship management (CRM) vendors such as Siebel. CRM components provide an integrated view of customer data and interactions allowing organizations to work more effectively with customers and be more responsive to their needs. CRM components typically include contact centers, sales force automation, and marketing functions. These improve the customer experience while identifying a company's most (and least) valuable customers for better allocation of resources.

Supply Chain Management Components

ERP vendors are expanding their functionality to provide services formerly supplied by supply chain management vendors such as i2 Technologies and Manugistics. SCM components help an organization plan, schedule, control, and optimize the supply chain from its acquisition of raw materials to the receipt of finished goods by customers.

Ebusiness Components

The original focus of ERP systems was the internal organization. In other words, ERP systems are not fundamentally ready for the external world of ebusiness. The newest and most exciting extended ERP components are the ebusiness components. Two of the primary features of ebusiness components are elogistics and eprocurement. **Elogistics** manages the transportation and storage of goods. **Eprocurement** is the business-to-business (B2B) purchase and sale of supplies and services over the Internet.

Ebusiness and ERP complement each other by allowing companies to establish a web presence and fulfill orders expeditiously. A common mistake made by many businesses is deploying a web presence before the integration of back-office systems or an ERP system. For example, one large toy manufacturer announced less than a week before Christmas that it would be unable to fulfill any of its web orders. The company had all the toys in the warehouse, but it could not organize the basic order processing function to get the toys delivered to the consumers on time.

Customers and suppliers are now demanding access to ERP information including order status, inventory levels, and invoice reconciliation. Plus, the customers and partners want all this information in a simplified format available through a website. This is a difficult task to accomplish because most ERP systems are full of technical jargon, which is why employee training is one of the hidden costs associated with ERP implementations. Removing the jargon to accommodate untrained customers and partners is one of the more difficult tasks when web-enabling an ERP system. To accommodate the growing needs of the ebusiness world, ERP vendors need to build two new channels of access into the ERP system information—one channel for customers (B2C) and one channel for businesses, suppliers, and partners (B2B).

ERP IS EXPENSIVE

There is no guarantee of success for an ERP system. ERPs focus on how a corporation operates internally, and optimizing these operations takes significant time and energy. According to Meta Group, it takes the average company 8 to 18 months to see any benefits from an ERP system. The good news is that the average savings from new ERP systems are $1.6 million per year.

Along with understanding the benefits an organization can gain from an ERP system, it is just as important to understand the primary risk associated with an ERP implementation—cost. ERP systems do not come cheap. Meta Group studied the total cost of ownership (TCO) for an ERP system. The study included hardware, software, professional services, and internal staff costs. Sixty-three companies were surveyed ranging in size from small to large over a variety of industries. The average TCO was $15 million (highest $300 million and lowest $400,000). The price tag for an ERP system can easily start in the multiple millions of dollars and implementation can take an average of 23 months. Figure 12.10 displays a few of the costs associated with an ERP system.

FIGURE 12.10

Associated ERP Risks (Cost)

Associated ERP Risks (Cost)
Software cost: Purchasing the software.
Consulting fees: Hiring external experts to help implement the system correctly.
Process rework: Redefining processes in order to ensure the company is using the most efficient and effective processes.
Customization: If the software package does not meet all of the company's needs, customizing the software may be required.
Integration and testing: Ensuring all software products, including disparate systems not part of the ERP system, are working together or are integrated. Testing the ERP system includes testing all integrations.
Training: Training all new users.
Data warehouse integration and data conversion: Moving data from an old system into the new ERP system.

OPENING CASE STUDY QUESTION

1. How would a company like Actionly take advantage of an ERP system?

Chapter Twelve Case: Shell Canada Fuels Productivity with ERP

Shell Canada is one of the nation's largest integrated petroleum companies and is a leading manufacturer, distributor, and marketer of refined petroleum products. The company, headquartered in Calgary, produces natural gas, natural gas liquids, and bitumen. Shell Canada is also the country's largest producer of sulphur. There is a Canada-wide network of 1,809 Shell-branded retail gasoline stations and convenience food stores from coast-to-coast.

To run such a complex and vast business operation successfully, the company relies heavily on the use of a mission-critical enterprise resource planning (ERP) system. The use of such a system is a necessity in helping the company integrate and manage its daily operations—operations that span from wells and mines, to processing plants, to oil trucks and gas pumps.

For example, the ERP system has helped the company immensely in terms of reducing and streamlining the highly manual process of third-party contractors submitting repair information and invoices. On average, there are between 2,500 and 4,000 service orders handled by these contractors per month on a nationwide basis.

Before implementation of the ERP system, contractors had to send Shell Canada monthly summarized invoices that listed maintenance calls the contractors made at various Shell gasoline stations. Each one of these invoices would take a contractor between 8 and 20 hours to prepare. Collectively, the contractors would submit somewhere between 50 and 100 invoices every month to Shell Canada. This involved each invoice being reviewed by the appropriate territory manager and then forwarded to the head office for payment processing. This alone consumed another 16 to 30 hours of labor per month. At the head office, another 200 hours of work was performed by data entry clerks who had to manually enter batch invoice data into the payment system.

And this would be the amount of time needed if things went smoothly! More hours of labor were required to decipher and correct errors if any mistakes were introduced from all the manual invoice generation and data reentry involved. Often errors concerning one line item on an invoice would deter payment of the whole invoice. This irritated the contractors and did not help foster healthy contractor relationships.

To make matters worse, despite the hours involved and the amount of human data-handling required, detailed information about the service repairs that contractors did was often not entered into the payment system. And if it was entered, the information was not timely—it was often weeks or even months old by the time it made it into the payment processing system. As a result, Shell was not collecting sufficient information about what repairs were being done, what had caused the problem, and how it had been resolved.

Fortunately, the ERP solution solved these inadequacies by providing an integrated web-based service order, invoicing, and payment submission system. With this tool, third-party contractors can enter service orders directly into Shell's ERP system via the web. When this is done, the contractors can also enter detailed information about the work that was performed—sometimes even attaching photos and drawings to help describe the work that was done. With the ERP system, it takes only a few minutes for a contractor to enter details about a service order. Further, this information can be transmitted through a wireless PDA to the appropriate Shell manager for immediate approval—shaving off more time in unnecessary delays.

Another bonus of the ERP system is that the contractor's monthly summarized invoices can now be generated automatically and fed directly into the ERP system's account payables application for processing. No rekeying of data required! Even better, if there is an issue or concern with one invoice item, the other items on the invoice can still be processed for payment.

Shell Canada's ERP system also handles other operational tasks. For example, the system can help speed up maintenance and repair operations at the company's refineries. With the ERP system in place, rather than trying to utilize a variety of disparate internal systems to access blueprints, schematics, spare parts lists, and other tools and information, workers at the refineries can now use the ERP system to access these things directly from a centralized database.

An added benefit of the ERP system is its ease of use. Past systems used by refinery workers were complex and difficult to search for information. The ERP system in place now has a portal-like interface that allows refinery workers to access the functions and information they need to keep operations running. The web interface allows workers access to this information with one or two clicks of a mouse.

An important part of any successful ERP implementation is training end users to learn how to utilize the system and teaching them about the functions and abilities of the ERP system. Recognizing this, Shell Canada offered its personnel both formal and informal ERP training. These proved to be invaluable in teaching end users the mechanics of the system and raising awareness of the benefits of the system and the efficiencies that the ERP system could offer Shell Canada. This not only helped promote end-user acceptance of the ERP system, but also greatly increased employees' intentions to use the system in their daily work.

Shell Canada executives are pleased and optimistic about the advantages of the ERP system. With this new system, employees across the company have gained fast and easy access to the tools and information they need to conduct their daily operations.[1]

Questions

1. How did ERP help improve business operations at Shell?

2. How important was training in helping roll out the system to Shell personnel?

3. How could extended ERP components help improve business operations at Shell?

4. What advice would you give Shell if it decided to choose a different ERP software solution?

5. How can integrating SCM, CRM, and ERP help improve business operations at Shell?

Today, organizations of various sizes are proving that systems that support decision making and opportunity seizing are essential to thriving in the highly competitive electronic world. We are living in an era when information technology is a primary tool, knowledge is a strategic asset, and decision making and problem solving are paramount skills. The tougher, larger, and more demanding a problem or opportunity is, and the faster and more competitive the environment is, the more important decision-making and problem-solving skills become. This unit discussed numerous tools and strategic initiatives that an organization can take advantage of to assist in decision making:

- Supply chain management (SCM)—managing information flows within the supply chain to maximize total supply chain effectiveness and profitability.

- Customer relationship management (CRM)—managing all aspects of customers' relationships with an organization to increase customer loyalty and retention and an organization's profitability.

- Enterprise resource planning (ERP)—integrating all departments and functions throughout an organization into a single IT system (or integrated set of IT systems) so that managers and leaders can make enterprisewide decisions by viewing enterprisewide information on all business operations.

* KEY TERMS

Accounting and finance ERP
    component, 172
Analytical CRM, 159
Analytics, 133
Artificial intelligence (AI), 142
Augmented reality, 145
Bullwhip effect, 149
Collaborative demand
    planning, 153
Collaborative engineering, 153
Consolidation, 142
Core ERP component, 171
Customer relationship
    management (CRM), 157
Decision support system
    (DSS), 139
Demand planning
    software, 149
Digital dashboard, 142
Drill-down, 142
Ebusiness, 132
Elogistics, 173
Employee relationship
    management (ERM), 162
Enterprise application
    integration (EAI)
    middleware, 169
Eprocurement, 173
Extended ERP component, 171

Executive information system
    (EIS), 140
Expert system, 143
Fuzzy logic, 144
Genetic algorithm, 144
Goal-seeking analysis, 139
Granularity, 140
Human resources ERP
    component, 172
Intelligent agent, 145
Intelligent system, 142
Managerial level, 135
Middleware, 169
Mutation, 144
Model, 137
Neural network or artificial
    neural network, 143
Online analytical processing
    (OLAP), 139
Online transaction processing
    (OLTP), 137
Operational CRM, 158
Operational level, 134
Optimization analysis, 139
Partner relationship
    management (PRM), 162
Production and materials
    management ERP
    component, 172

Radio frequency identification
    (RFID), 153
Selling chain
    management, 153
Semistructured
    decisions, 136
Sensitivity analysis, 139
Shopping bot, 145
Slice-and-dice, 142
Source document, 138
Strategic level, 136
Structured decisions, 134
Supply chain execution (SCE)
    software, 150
Supply chain planning (SCP)
    software, 150
Supply chain visibility, 148
Supplier relationship
    management (SRM), 162
Supply chain event
    management (SCEM), 153
Transaction processing system
    (TPS), 137
Unstructured decisions, 136
Virtual reality, 145
What-if analysis, 139

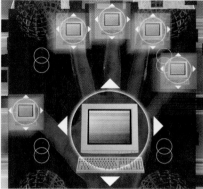

Can Customer Loyalty Be a Bad Thing?

What happens when you find out that your business's most faithful customers aren't necessarily the most profitable ones? The economic crisis has jolted companies into the need to redouble efforts to foster customer loyalty. Numerous articles now tout the increased importance of giving customers premium service in troubled times to ensure customer retention. The underlying reasoning is simple—through their continued patronage, loyal customers help a company to weather the storm.

Without question, there is some truth to this logic. No firm can survive for long without loyal customers. The problem, however, is that success through loyalty isn't nearly so simple. Like most big ideas, there are conditions where it is unarguably correct, and less popular but equally true conditions where it is wrong.

Loyalty is a big idea. At its most basic level, it is a feeling of attachment that causes someone to be willing to continue a relationship. And while exclusive loyalty has been replaced in customers' hearts and minds with multiple loyalties for many if not most product categories, often greater than 50 percent of a company's customers would classify themselves as holding some level of loyalty to a particular company. Even if we narrow our classification of loyalty to customers who feel loyal and give the majority of their purchases in a category to the firm, typically we find this to represent one-third of a firm's customers.

The fly in the ointment is that typically only 20 percent of a firm's customers are actually profitable. And many—often most—of a company's profitable customers are not loyal. This presents managers with a loyalty problem, although not one that they expect. If typically most loyal customers in a firm aren't profitable, how does a customer loyalty strategy ever generate a positive return on investment? Instead of asking whether you have enough loyal customers in your customer base, you need to ask yourself three more complex questions: (1) which loyal customers are good for the business, (2) how do we hang onto them, and (3) how do we get more customers like them?

In this slow economy, customers in both B2B and B2C settings are naturally much more sensitive to economic issues. Furthermore, companies in B2B relationships are often more reliant on their vendor partners to help them shoulder this burden. There is nothing inherently wrong with this, and managers need to recognize that their job is to meet customers' needs to deserve their loyalty.

But the simple solution to improving customer loyalty in a down market is to offer price deals. Firms that track their customer loyalty can be guaranteed that loyalty scores will increase with each substantial decrease in price.

But that's a bad loyalty strategy. This doesn't mean businesses shouldn't find ways to be more efficient so they can pass cost savings on to customers. But price-driven loyalty is always the lowest form of loyalty. It means the firm isn't offering differentiated value to its customers.

The place to begin any loyalty strategy is to determine which loyal customers are profitable and which are not. A closer examination of these two types of customers always reveals very different reasons for their loyalty. Unprofitable loyal customers tend to be loyal for one of two reasons: (1) they are driven by unprofitable pricing or exchange policies, or (2) they demand an excessive amount of service that they are not willing to pay fairly to receive.

Profitable loyal customers, on the other hand, are almost always driven by differentiating aspects of the product or service offering. The key to a successful loyalty strategy is to become clear as to what these differentiating aspects are, and to focus on tangibly improving these elements. It is also imperative to actively tell customers and prospective customers that these are the things the company stands for and that the firm is committed to being best at. By doing this, the best customers will have the necessary information to clearly articulate why an organization deserves their loyalty in good times and in bad.[2]

Questions

1. Why are customer relationships important to an organization? Do you agree that every business needs to focus on customers to survive in the information age?

2. How can a company find its most loyal customers?

3. Choose a business (maybe Starbucks, Disney, or Nissan). Answer each of the following questions based on your business choice.

   a. Which loyal customers are good for the business?

   b. How do we hang onto them?

   c. How do we get more customers like them?

4. Do you agree or disagree with the following statement: "The fly in the ointment is that typically only 20 percent of a firm's customers are actually profitable. And many—often most—of a company's profitable customers are not loyal."

 UNIT CLOSING CASE TWO

Revving Up Sales at Harley-Davidson

Harley-Davidson produces 290,000 motorcycles and generates over $4 billion in net revenues yearly. There is a mystique associated with a Harley-Davidson motorcycle. No other motorcycle in the world has the look, feel, and sound of a Harley-Davidson, and many people consider it a two-wheeled piece of art. Demand for Harley-Davidson motorcycles outweighs supply. Some models have up to a two-year wait list. Harley-Davidson has won a number of awards including:

- Rated second in *ComputerWorld*'s Top 100 Best Places to Work in IT.
- Rated 51st in *Fortune*'s 100 Best Companies to Work For.

- Rated first in *Fortune's* 5 Most Admired Companies in the motor vehicles industry.
- Rated first in the Top 10 Sincerest Corporations by the *Harris Interactive Report*.
- Rated second in the Top 10 Overall Corporations by the *Harris Interactive Report*.

Harley-Davidson's Focus on Technology

Harley-Davidson's commitment to technology is paying off: In 2003 it decreased production costs and inventories by $40 million as a direct result of using technology to increase production capacity. The company's technology budget of $50 million is more than 2 percent of its revenue, which is far above the manufacturing industry average. More than 50 percent of this budget is devoted to developing new technology strategies.

Harley-Davidson focuses on implementing ebusiness strategies to strengthen its market share and increase customer satisfaction. More than 80 projects were in development in 2003, and the majority of the new projects focused on sharing information, gaining business intelligence, and enhancing decision making.

Talon, Harley-Davidson's proprietary dealer management system, is one of its most successful technology initiatives. Talon handles inventory, vehicle registration, warranties, and point-of-sale transactions for all Harley-Davidson dealerships. The system performs numerous time-saving tasks such as checking dealer inventory, automatically generating parts orders, and allowing the company to review and analyze information across its global organization. Talon gives Harley-Davidson managers a 360-degree view into enterprisewide information that supports strategic goal setting and decision making throughout all levels of the organization.

Building Supplier Relationships

Harley-Davidson invests time, energy, and resources into continually improving its company-to-company strategic business initiatives such as supply chain management. The company understands and values the importance of building strong relationships with its suppliers. To develop these important relationships the company deployed Manugistics, an SCM system that allows it to do business with suppliers in a collaborative, web-based environment. The company plans to use the SCM software to better manage its flow of materials and improve collaboration activities with its key suppliers.

Building Customer Relationships

Each time a customer reaches out to the company, Harley-Davidson has an opportunity to build a trusting relationship with that particular customer. Harley-Davidson realizes that it takes more than just building and selling motorcycles to fulfill the dreams of its customers. For this reason, the company strives to deliver unforgettable experiences along with its top quality products.

Harley-Davidson sells more than $500 million worth of parts and accessories to its loyal followers. Ken Ostermann, Harley-Davidson's manager of electronic commerce and communications, decided that the company could increase these sales if it could offer the products online. The dilemma facing Ostermann's online strategy was that selling jackets, saddlebags, and T-shirts directly to consumers would bypass Harley-Davidson's 650 dealers, who depend on the high-margin accessories to fuel their businesses' profits. Ostermann's solution was to build an online store, Harley-Davidson.com, which prompts customers to select a participating Harley-Davidson dealership before placing any online orders. The selected dealership is then responsible for fulfilling the order. This strategy has helped ensure that the dealers remain the focal point of customers' buying experiences.

To guarantee that every customer has a highly satisfying online buying experience, the company asks the dealers to agree to a number of standards including:

- Checking online orders twice daily.
- Shipping online orders within 24 hours.
- Responding to customer inquiries within 24 hours.

The company still monitors online customer metrics such as time taken to process orders, number of returned orders, and number of incorrect orders, ensuring that Harley-Davidson delivers on its message of prompt, excellent service consistently to all its loyal customers. The company receives more than 1 million visitors a month to its online store. Customer satisfaction scores for the website moved from the extremely satisfied level to the exceptional level in a year.

Another of Harley-Davidson's customer-centric strategies is its Harley's Owners Group (HOG), established in 1983. HOG is the largest factory-sponsored motorcycle club in the world with more than 600,000 members. HOG offers a wide array of events, rides, and benefits to its members. HOG is one of the key drivers helping to build a strong sense of community among Harley-Davidson owners. Harley-Davidson has built a customer following that is extremely loyal, a difficult task to accomplish in any industry.

Harley-Davidson's Corporate Culture

Harley-Davidson employees are the engine behind its outstanding performance and the foundation of the company's overall success. Harley-Davidson believes in a strong sense of corporate ethics and values, and the company's top five core values serve as a framework for the entire corporation:

1. Tell the truth.
2. Be fair.
3. Keep your promises.
4. Respect the individual.
5. Encourage intellectual curiosity.

The company credits its core values as the primary reason it won the two prestigious awards from the *Harris Interactive Report,* one of the most respected consumer reviews for corporate sincerity, ethics, and standards. Sticking to strong ethics and values is and will continue to be a top priority for the company and its employees.

To enhance its enterprise further Harley-Davidson plans to keep taking advantage of new technologies and strategies including a web-based approach to accessing information and an enterprisewide system to consolidate procurement at its eight U.S. facilities.[3]

Questions

1. Explain how Talon helps Harley-Davidson employees improve their decision-making capabilities.
2. Identify a few key metrics a Harley-Davidson marketing executive might want to monitor on a digital dashboard.
3. How can Harley-Davidson benefit from using decision support systems and executive information systems in its business?
4. How would Harley-Davidson's business be affected if it decided to sell accessories directly to its online customers? Include a brief discussion of the ethics involved with this decision.
5. Evaluate the HOG CRM strategy and recommend an additional benefit Harley-Davidson could provide to its HOG members to increase customer satisfaction.

6. How could Harley-Davidson's SCM system, Manugistics, improve its business operations?

7. Provide a potential illustration of Harley-Davidson's SCM system including all upstream and downstream participants.

8. Explain how an ERP system could help Harley-Davidson gain business intelligence in its operations.

✳ MAKING BUSINESS DECISIONS

1. Implementing an ERP System

Blue Dog Inc. is a leading manufacturer in the high-end sunglasses industry. Blue Dog Inc. reached record revenue levels of over $250 million last year. The company is currently deciding on the possibility of implementing an ERP system to help decrease production costs and increase inventory control. Many of the executives are nervous about making such a large investment in an ERP system due to its low success rates. As a senior manager at Blue Dog Inc. you have been asked to compile a list of the potential benefits and risks associated with implementing an ERP system along with your recommendations for the steps the company can take to ensure a successful implementation.

2. DSS and EIS

Dr. Rosen runs a large dental conglomerate—Teeth Doctors—that staffs more than 700 dentists in six states. Dr. Rosen is interested in purchasing a competitor called Dentix that has 150 dentists in three additional states. Before deciding whether to purchase Dentix, Dr. Rosen must consider several issues:

- The cost of purchasing Dentix.
- The location of the Dentix offices.
- The current number of customers per dentist, per office, and per state.
- The merger between the two companies.
- The professional reputation of Dentix.
- Other competitors.

Explain how Dr. Rosen and Teeth Doctors can benefit from the use of information systems to make an accurate business decision in regard to the potential purchase of Dentix.

3. SCM, CRM, and ERP

Jamie Ash is interested in applying for a job at a large software vendor. One of the criteria for the job is a detailed understanding of strategic initiatives such as SCM, CRM, and ERP. Jamie has no knowledge of any of these initiatives and cannot even explain what the acronyms mean. Jamie has come to you for help. She would like you to compile a summary of the three initiatives including an analysis of how the three are similar and how they are different. Jamie would also like to perform some self-training via the web so be sure to provide her with several additional links to key websites that offer detailed overviews on SCM, CRM, and ERP.

4. Customer Relationship Management Strategies

On average, it costs an organization six times more to sell to a new customer than to sell to an existing customer. As the co-owner of a medium-sized luggage distributor, you have recently been notified by your EIS systems that sales for the past three months have decreased by an average of 17 percent. The reasons for the decline in sales are numerous, including a poor economy, people's aversion to travel because of the terrorist attacks, and some negative publicity your company received regarding a defective product line. In a group, explain how implementing a CRM system can help you understand and combat the decline in sales. Be sure to justify why a CRM system is important to your business and its future growth.

5. Finding Information on Decision Support Systems

You are working on the sales team for a small catering company that maintains 75 employees and generates $1 million in revenues per year. The owner, Pam Hetz, wants to understand how she can use decision support systems to help grow her business. Pam has an initial understanding of DSS systems and is interested in learning more about what types are available, how they can be used in a small business, and the cost associated with different DSS systems. In a group, research the website www.dssresources.com and compile a presentation that discusses DSS systems in detail. Be sure to answer all Pam's questions on DSS systems in the presentation.

6. Analyzing Dell's Supply Chain Management System

Dell's supply chain strategy is legendary. Essentially, if you want to build a successful SCM system your best bet is to model your SCM system after Dell's. In a team, research Dell's supply chain management strategy on the web and create a report discussing any new SCM updates and strategies the company is using that were not discussed in this text. Be sure to include a graphical presentation of Dell's current supply chain model.

7. Gaining Business Intelligence from Strategic Initiatives

You are a new employee in the customer service department at Premier One, a large pet food distributor. The company, founded by several veterinarians, has been in business for three years and focuses on providing nutritious pet food at a low cost. The company currently has 90 employees and operates in seven states. Sales over the past three years have tripled and the manual systems currently in place are no longer sufficient to run the business. Your first task is to meet with your new team and create a presentation for the president and chief executive officer describing supply chain management, customer relationship management, and enterprise resource planning systems. The presentation should highlight the main benefits Premier One can receive from these strategic initiatives along with any additional added business value that can be gained from the systems.

✳ APPLY YOUR KNOWLEDGE

1. Great Stories

With the advent of the Internet, when customers have an unpleasant customer experience, the company no longer has to worry about them telling a few friends and family; the company has to worry about them telling everyone. Internet service providers are giving consumers frustrated with how they were treated by a company another means of fighting back. Free or low-cost computer space for Internet websites is empowering consumers to tell not only their friends, but also the world about the way they have been treated. A few examples of disgruntled customer stories from the Internet include:

- **Bad Experience with Blue Marble Biking**—Tourist on biking tour is bitten by dog, requires stitches. Company is barred from hotel because of incident, and in turn it bars the tourist from any further tours.

- **Best Buy Receipt Check**—Shopper declines to show register receipt for purchase to door guard at Lakewood Best Buy, which is voluntary. Employees attempt to seize cart, stand in shopper's path, and park a truck behind shopper's car to prevent departure.
- **Enterprise Rent-A-Car Is a Failing Enterprise**—Enterprise Rent-A-Car did not honor reservations, did not have cars ready as stated, rented cars with nearly empty tanks, and charged higher prices to corporate account holders.

Project Focus

The Internet is raising the stakes for customer service. With the ability to create a website dedicated to a particular issue, a disgruntled customer can have nearly the same reach as a manufacturer. The Internet is making it more difficult for companies to ignore their customers' complaints. In a group, search the web for the most outrageous story of a disgruntled customer. A few places to start include:

- **Complain Complain (complaincomplain.net)**—provides professionally written, custom complaint letters to businesses.
- **The Complaint Department (www.thecomplaintdepartment.ca)**—a for-fee consumer complaint resolution and letter writing service.
- **The Complaint Station (www.thecomplaintstation.com)**—provides a central location to complain about issues related to companies' products, services, employment, and get rich quick scams.
- **Complaints.com Consumer Complaints (www.complaints.com)**—database of consumer complaints and consumer advocacy.
- **Baddealings.com (www.baddealings.com)**—forum and database on consumer complaints and scams on products and services.

2. Classic Car Problems

Classic Cars Inc. operates high-end automotive dealerships that offer luxury cars along with luxury service. The company is proud of its extensive inventory, top-of-the-line mechanics, and especially its exceptional service, which even includes a cappuccino bar at each dealership.

The company currently has 40 sales representatives at four locations. Each location maintains its own computer systems, and all sales representatives have their own contact management systems. This splintered approach to operations causes numerous problems including customer communication issues, pricing strategy issues, and inventory control issues. A few examples include:

- A customer shopping at one dealership can go to another dealership and receive a quote for a different price for the same car.
- Sales representatives are frequently stealing each other's customers and commissions.
- Sales representatives frequently send their customers to other dealerships to see specific cars and when the customer arrives, the car is not on the lot.
- Marketing campaigns are not designed to target specific customers; they are typically generic, such as 10 percent off a new car.
- If a sales representative quits, all of his or her customer information is lost.

Project Focus

You are working for Customer One, a small consulting company that specializes in CRM strategies. The owner of Classic Cars Inc., Tom Repicci, has hired you to help him formulate a strategy to put his company back on track. Develop a proposal for Tom detailing how a CRM system can alleviate the company's issues and create new opportunities.

3. Building Visibility

Visionary companies are building extended enterprises to best compete in the new Internet economy. An extended enterprise combines the Internet's power with new business structures and processes to eliminate old corporate boundaries and geographic restrictions. Networked supply chains create seamless paths of communication among partners, suppliers, manufacturers, retailers, and customers. Because of advances in manufacturing and distribution, the cost of developing new products and services is dropping, and time to market is speeding up. This has resulted in increasing customer demands, local and global competition, and increased pressure on the supply chain.

To stay competitive, companies must reinvent themselves so that the supply chain—sourcing and procurement, production scheduling, order fulfillment, inventory management, and customer care—is no longer a cost-based back-office exercise, but rather a flexible operation designed to effectively address today's challenges.

The Internet is proving an effective tool in transforming supply chains across all industries. Suppliers, distributors, manufacturers, and resellers now work together more closely and effectively than ever. Today's technology-driven supply chain enables customers to manage their own buying experiences, increases coordination and connectivity among supply partners, and helps reduce operating costs for every company in the chain.

Project Focus

In the past, assets were a crucial component of success in supply chain management. In today's market, however, a customer-centric orientation is key to retaining competitive advantage. Using the Internet and any other resources available, develop a strategic plan for implementing a networked, flexible supply chain management system for a start-up company of your choice. Research Netflix if you are unfamiliar with how start-up companies are changing the supply chain. Be sure that your supply chain integrates all partners—manufacturers, retailers, suppliers, carriers, and vendors—into a seamless unit and views customer relationship management as a key competitive advantage. There are several points to consider when creating your customer-centric supply chain strategy:

- Taking orders is only one part of serving customer needs.
- Businesses must fulfill the promise they make to customers by delivering products and information upon request—not when it is convenient for the company.
- Time to market is a key competitive advantage. Companies must ensure uninterrupted supply, and information about customer demands and activities is essential to this requirement.
- Cost is an important factor. Companies need to squeeze the costs from internal processes to make the final products less expensive.
- Reducing design-cycle times is critical, as this allows companies to get their products out more quickly to meet customer demand.

4. Netflix Your Business

Netflix reinvented the video rental business using supply chain technology. Netflix, established in 1998, is the largest online DVD rental service, offering flat-rate rental-by-mail to customers in the United States. Headquartered in Los Gatos, California, it has amassed a collection of 80,000 titles and more than 6.8 million subscribers. Netflix has more than 42 million DVDs and ships 1.6 million a day, on average, costing a reported $300 million a year in postage. On February 25, 2007, Netflix announced the delivery of its billionth DVD.

The company provides a monthly flat-fee service for the rental of DVD movies. A subscriber creates an ordered list, called a rental queue, of DVDs to rent. The DVDs are delivered individually via the United States Postal Service from an array of regional warehouses

(44 in 29 states). A subscriber keeps a rented DVD as long as desired but has a limit on the number of DVDs (determined by subscription level) that can be checked out at any one time. To rent a new DVD, the subscriber mails the previous one back to Netflix in a prepaid mailing envelope. Upon receipt of the disc, Netflix ships another disc in the subscriber's rental queue.

Project Focus

Netflix's business is video rental, but it used technology to revamp the supply chain to completely disrupt the entire video rental industry. Reinvent IT is a statewide contest where college students can propose a new business that they will reinvent by revamping the supply chain (such as Netflix has done). You want to enter and win the contest. Reinvent a traditional business, such as the video rental business, using supply chain technologies.

5. Finding Shelf Space at Walmart

Walmart's business strategy of being a low-cost provider by managing its supply chain down to the minutiae has paid off greatly. Each week, approximately 100 million customers, or one-third of the U.S. population, visit Walmart's U.S. stores. Walmart is currently the world's largest retailer and the second largest corporation behind ExxonMobil. It was founded by Sam Walton in 1962 and is the largest private employer in the United States and Mexico. Walmart is also the largest grocery retailer in the United States, with an estimated 20 percent of the retail grocery and consumables business, and the largest toy seller in the United States, with an estimated 45 percent of the retail toy business, having surpassed Toys "R" Us in the late 1990s.

Walmart's business model is based on selling a wide variety of general merchandise at "always low prices." The reason Walmart can offer such low prices is due to its innovative use of information technology tools to create its highly sophisticated supply chain. Over the past decade, Walmart has famously invited its major suppliers to jointly develop powerful supply chain partnerships. These are designed to increase product flow efficiency and, consequently, Walmart's profitability.

Many companies have stepped up to the challenge, starting with the well-known Walmart/Procter & Gamble alliance, which incorporated vendor-managed inventory, category management, and other intercompany innovations. Walmart's CFO became a key customer as P&G's objective became maximizing Walmart's internal profitability. Unlike many other retailers, Walmart does not charge a slotting fee to suppliers for their products to appear in the store. Alternatively, Walmart focuses on selling more popular products and often pressures store managers to drop unpopular products in favor of more popular ones, as well as pressuring manufacturers to supply more popular products.

Project Focus

You are the owner of a high-end collectible toy company. You create everything from authentic sports figure replicas to famous musicians and movie characters including Babe Ruth, Hulk Hogan, Mick Jagger, Ozzy Osbourne, Alien, and the Terminator. It would be a huge win for your company if you could get your collectibles into Walmart. Compile a strategic plan highlighting the steps required to approach Walmart as your supply chain partner. Be sure to address the pros and cons of partnering with Walmart, including the cost to revamp your current supply chain to meet Walmart's tough supply chain requirements.

6. Shipping Problems

Entrepreneurship is in Alyssa Stuart's blood. Alyssa has been starting businesses since she was 10 years old, and she finally has the perfect business of custom-made furniture. Customers who visit Alyssa's shop can choose from a number of different fabrics and 50 different styles of couch and chair designs to create their custom-made furniture. Once the customer decides on a fabric pattern and furniture design, the information is sent to

China where the furniture is built and shipped to the customer via the West Coast. Alyssa is excited about her business; all of her hard work has finally paid off as she has more than 17,000 customers and 875 orders currently in the pipe.

Project Focus

Alyssa's business is booming. Her high-quality products and outstanding customer service have created an excellent reputation for her business. But Alyssa's business is at risk of losing everything and she has come to you for help solving her supply chain issues.

Yesterday, a dockworkers' union strike began and shut down all of the West Coast shipping docks from San Francisco to Canada. Work will resume only when the union agrees to new labor contracts, which could take months. Alyssa has asked you to summarize the impact of the dock shutdown on her business and create a strategy to keep her business running, which is especially difficult because Alyssa guarantees 30-day delivery on all products or the product is free. What strategies do you recommend for Alyssa's business to continue working while her supply chain is disrupted by the dockworkers' strike?

7. Political Supply Chains

The U.S. government has crafted a deal with the United Arab Emirates (UAE) that would let a UAE-based firm, Dubai Ports World (DPW), run six major U.S. ports. If the approval is unchallenged, Dubai Ports World would run the ports of New York, New Jersey, Baltimore, New Orleans, Miami, and Philadelphia. Currently, London-based Peninsular and Oriental Steam Navigation Co. (P&O), the fourth largest port operator in the world, runs the six ports. But the $6.8 billion sale of P&O to DPW would effectively turn over North American operations to the government-owned company in Dubai.

Project Focus

Some citizens are worried that the federal government may be outsourcing U.S. port operations to a company prone to terrorist infiltration by allowing a firm from the United Arab Emirates to run port operations within the United States. You have been called in on an investigation to determine the potential effects on U.S. businesses' supply chains if these ports were shut down due to terrorist activities. The United Arab Emirates has had people involved in terrorism. In fact, some of its financial institutions laundered the money for the 9/11 terrorists. Create an argument for or against outsourcing these ports to the UAE. Be sure to detail the effect on U.S. businesses' supply chains if these ports are subjected to terrorist acts.

8. JetBlue on YouTube

JetBlue took an unusual and interesting CRM approach by using YouTube to apologize to its customers. JetBlue's founder and CEO, David Neeleman, apologized to customers via YouTube after a very, very bad week for the airline: 1,100 flights canceled due to snow storms and thousands of irate passengers. Neeleman's unpolished, earnest delivery makes this apology worth accepting. But then again, we were not stuck on a tarmac for eight hours. With all of the new advances in technology and the many ways to reach customers, do you think using YouTube is a smart approach? What else could JetBlue do to help gain back its customers' trust?

Project Focus

You are the founder and CEO of GoodDog, a large pet food manufacturing company. Recently, at least 16 pet deaths have been tied to tainted pet food, fortunately not manufactured by your company. A recall of potentially deadly pet food has dog and cat owners studying their animals for even the slightest hint of illness and swamping veterinarians nationwide with calls about symptoms both real and imagined. Create a strategy for using

YouTube as a vehicle to communicate with your customers as they fear for their pets' lives. Be sure to highlight the pros and cons of using YouTube as a customer communication vehicle. Are there any other new technologies you could use as a customer communication vehicle that would be more effective than YouTube?

9. Second Life CRM

The virtual world of Second Life could become the first point of contact between companies and customers and could transform the whole customer experience. Since it began hosting the likes of Adidas, Dell, Reuters, and Toyota, Second Life has become technology's equivalent of India or China—everyone needs an office and a strategy involving it to keep their shareholders happy. But beyond opening a shiny new building in the virtual world, what can such companies do with their virtual real estate?

Like many other big brands, PA Consulting has its own offices in Second Life and has learned that simply having an office to answer customer queries is not enough. Real people, albeit behind avatars, must be staffing the offices—in the same way having a website is not enough if there is not a call center to back it up when a would-be customer wants to speak to a human being. The consultants believe call centers could one day ask customers to follow up a phone call with them by moving the query into a virtual world.

Unlike many corporate areas in the virtual world, the National Basketball Association incorporates capabilities designed to keep fans coming back, including real-time 3-D diagrams of games as they are being played.

Project Focus

You are the executive director of CRM at StormPeak, an advanced AI company that develops robots. You are in charge of overseeing the first virtual site being built in Second Life. Create a CRM strategy for doing business in a virtual world. Here are a few questions to get you started:

- How will customer relationships be different in a virtual world?
- What is your strategy for managing customer relationships in this new virtual environment?
- How will supporting Second Life customers differ from supporting traditional customers?
- How will supporting Second Life customers differ from supporting website customers?
- What customer security issues might you encounter in Second Life?
- What customer ethical issues might you encounter in Second Life?

✱ ENTREPRENEURIAL CHALLENGE

Build Your Own Business

1. Netflix reinvented the video rental business using supply chain technology. Netflix is the largest online DVD rental service, offering flat-rate rental by mail and over the Internet to customers. Customers can create their own personal list of movie favorites and the DVDs are delivered by the US Post office from one of Netflix's warehouses. Customers can keep the DVDs for as long as they want and simply return them by mail to receive their next selection. Netflix's business is video rental, but it used technology to revamp its supply chain to completely disrupt the entire video rental industry. Define a way that you can revamp or reinvent your business using supply chain technologies.

2. Business is booming, and you have achieved your goal of driving operating costs down, which helps to drive revenues up. One of your best new products is from China, and it is accounting for a 20 percent increase in your profits. Yesterday, a dockworkers union strike began and shut down all of the West Coast shipping docks from San Francisco to Canada. Work will resume when the union agrees to new labor contracts, which could take months. You need to quickly assess the impact of the shutdown on your business. How will you keep business running if you cannot receive your shipments? What strategies do you recommend to help the business continue working while the supply chain is disrupted by the strike?

3. The web contains numerous examples of customer power. Examples include www .ihatedell.net and www.donotbuydodge.ca. Customers are using YouTube, Myspace, blogs, and a number of other web tools to slam or praise companies. Do you believe that the most influential person in your business is the customer? How could customers hurt or help your business? Will your employees agree that customers are the most important part of the business?

AYK APPLICATION PROJECTS

If you are looking for Excel projects to incorporate into your class, try any of the following after reading this chapter.

Project Number	Project Name	Project Type	Plug-In	Focus Area	Project Level	Skill Set	Page Number
9	Security Analysis	Excel	T3	Filtering Data	Intermediate	Conditional Formatting, Autofilter, Subtotal	AYK.7
10	Gathering Data	Excel	T3	Data Analysis	Intermediate	Conditional Formatting	AYK.8
11	Scanner System	Excel	T2	Strategic Analysis	Intermediate	Formulas	AYK.8
12	Competitive Pricing	Excel	T2	Profit Maximization	Intermediate	Formulas	AYK.9
13	Adequate Acquisitions	Excel	T2	Break Even Analysis	Intermediate	Formulas	AYK.9
15	Assessing the Value of Information	Excel	T3	Data Analysis	Intermediate	PivotTable	AYK.10
16	Growth, Trends, and Forecasts	Excel	T2, T3	Data Forecasting	Advanced	Average, Trend, Growth	AYK.11
18	Formatting Grades	Excel	T3	Data Analysis	Advanced	If, LookUp	AYK.12
22	Turnover Rates	Excel	T3	Data Mining	Advanced	PivotTable	AYK.15
23	Vital Information	Excel	T3	Data Mining	Advanced	PivotTable	AYK.15
24	Breaking Even	Excel	T4	Business Analysis	Advanced	Goal Seek	AYK.16
25	Profit Scenario	Excel	T4	Sales Analysis	Advanced	Scenario Manager	AYK.16

4 Building Innovation

The pace of technological change never ceases to amaze. What only a few years ago would have been considered Star Trek technology is becoming normal. What used to take hours to download over a dial-up modem connection can now transfer in a matter of seconds through an invisible, wireless network connection from a computer thousands of miles away. We are living in an increasingly wireless present and hurtling ever faster toward a wireless future. The tipping point of ubiquitous, wireless, handheld, mobile computing is not far away.

Managers must understand the importance of ebusiness and how it has revolutionized fundamental business processes. Ebusiness offers new opportunities for growth and new ways of performing business activities that were simply not possible before the Internet. As a business student, you should understand the fundamental impact of the Internet and the innovations in mobile technologies on business. As a future manager and organizational knowledge worker, you need to understand what benefits ebusiness and wireless business practices can offer an organization and your career. Furthermore, you need to understand the challenges that come along with the adoption of web technologies, how Web 2.0 is impacting communication and the limitations on the mobile worker. This unit will give you this knowledge and help prepare you for success in today's electronic wireless global marketplace.

Pinterest—Billboards for the Internet

Pinterest has been called the latest addiction for millions of people around the world. Pinterest, a visual social media network, allows users to create "interest boards" where they "pin" items of interests found on the web. Terms you need to understand to use Pinterest include:

- **Pin:** A link to an image from a computer or a website. Pins can include captions for other users. Users upload, or "pin," photos or videos to boards.
- **Board:** Pins live on boards and users can maintain separate boards, which can be categorized by activity or interests, such as cooking, do-it-yourself activities, fitness, music, movies, etc.
- **Repin:** After pinning an item, it can be repinned by other Pinterest users, spreading the content virally. Repinning allows users to share items they like with friends and family.

"Pinning" is simply done by clicking on a photo or video that captures the attention of a user, whether it be by uploading personal photos or repinning a photo or video from a fellow user. Started in 2010, Pinterest has already attracted over 10 million users with the majority being women between the ages of 25 and 54. Millions of people visit the website each day to find what new items will spark their interest as there are always more and more things to see.

Pinterest is considered a social network, but unlike other social networks, such as Twitter and Facebook, Pinterest is open to invited users only; meaning it is an invitation-only website and users must "ask" for an invitation before gaining access. Upon accepting the invitation, users can gain access to the website and begin inviting their own "friends" with whom they have connections on Facebook or Twitter. Pinterest's primary mission is to:

connect everyone in the world through the 'things' they find interesting. We think that a favorite book, toy, or recipe can reveal a common link between two people. With millions of new pins added every week, Pinterest is connecting people all over the world based on shared tastes and interests.

Just like on other social networks, Pinterest users can compile a list of people they want to follow. A user can link a Pinterest board to a Facebook account, allowing instant access to quickly see which of his or her Facebook friends are on the social network. Adding bookmarks allows the user to pin images to other websites such as a book at Barnes & Noble or a set of mugs at Pier 1 Imports. The image is automatically linked to the retailer's website, and if another users clicks on the image, that user receives additional information on the product or service. If users pin a specific image of a plate or sweater, they can add the item's price in the description, which will automatically place a banner ad on the image and show the listed price. If users are unsure of what they are looking for, they can search for a specific event or theme such as "twenty-first birthday party" for a whole array of ideas.

Essentially, Pinterest allows users to paint a visual picture. Just imagine a wedding planner talking to a bride about her upcoming event, and the bride mentions she would like a "classic modernism" wedding. If the wedding planner was confused on what exactly the bride meant by classic modernism, she could quickly visit Pinterest to find an entire suite of photos and videos to spark ideas of how to coordinate the event.

The Business Value of Pinterest

Visual Communication

Pinterest is by far one of the hottest social media spaces available today. Offering all kinds of valuable information from useful cleaning tips to fantastic recipes to beautiful photos and videos, the website is extremely valuable for sharing anything visual. Pinterest is in no way simply a passing fad as companies begin to use the website for social marketing.

One of the best business uses of Pinterest is allowing employees to visually communicate and brainstorm. Visual communication is a new experience for many employees and the phrase "A picture is worth a thousand words" can help a company perform many tasks from generating new products to transforming business processes. In fact, many companies are using Pinterest to solicit feedback directly from employees, customers, and suppliers to ensure the company is operating efficiently and effectively. Soliciting feedback directly from customers allows companies to have a customer service support team handle problems before they become mainstream issues. Providing customers with a new channel to post their thoughts and concerns about products or services can provide valuable feedback for any company. Companies typically state that they may not respond to every question or comment, but that they take each and every concern into account, demonstrating that they are devoted to creating a bond between themselves and their customers.

Driving Traffic

Pinterest drives traffic—it is that simple! Even though the website operates under an invitation-only model, it has attracted more than 10 million users in less than two years. That number might seem small compared to powerhouses such as Facebook, Twitter, or Google, but it demonstrates there is enough of an audience to send a decent amount of traffic to any business. The images a business pins up should be linked to the relevant page of its website. If users are attracted by it, they may click on it to find out more.

Pinterest also drives traffic by providing higher rankings on search engine optimization as companies appear higher and higher on search lists the more users are pinning to their boards. Linking is one of the key factors search engines consider, and with Pinterest gaining in popularity, it is also growing as a trustworthy domain. The number of Pinterest users combined with its ability to increase search rankings will play an important role when a company is looking to increase visibility and drive traffic to its website. Data from Shareholic found that Pinterest sent more referral traffic to bloggers than Google+, YouTube, and LinkedIn combined, falling just behind Twitter.

Product Branding

Pinterest is an extraordinary branding tool, offering a place where companies can create a presence and community around a product, idea, event, or company. Just like other social networking websites, Pinterest allows a company to reach out and engage its customers, vendors, suppliers, and even employees to communicate about its products and services. Recently the National Football League's Minnesota Vikings began using Pinterest to create a following of favorite photos, statistics, and even game-day recipes!

Pinterest recently deployed an iPhone application that allows users to pin photos and video from their cameras instantly on their boards. Pinterest's unique competitive advantage is its ability to host billions of images and redirect users to the appropriate sources in a user-friendly interface.

Pinterest's Dilemma

Since its inception, Pinterest has been under fire from sites such as Flikr, Photobucket, and Instagram over attributing credit to those who own the images that are pinned. Many users are concerned that they may one day be sued for the improper use of an image they pinned.

The Pinterest Terms of Use state, "If you are a copyright owner, or are authorized to act on behalf of one, or authorized to act under any exclusive right under copyright, please report alleged copyright infringements taking place on or through the Site by completing the following DMCA Notice of Alleged Infringement and delivering it to Pinterest's Designated Copyright Agent."

To protect Pinterest from third-party litigation claims (such as those from authors claiming copyright infringement), Pinterest has incorporated the following statement into its indemnity clause: "You agree to indemnify and hold harmless Pinterest and its officers, directors, employees and agents, from and against any claims, suits, proceedings, disputes, demands, liabilities, damages, losses, costs and expenses, including, without limitation, reasonable legal and accounting fees (including costs of defense of claims, suits or proceedings brought by third parties), arising out of or in any way related to (i) your access to or use of the Services or Pinterest Content, (ii) your User Content, or (iii) your breach of any of these Terms."

Pinterest is well-aware of the probability that many of the pinned images might be violating copyright infringement and is attempting to protect itself against any litigation claims resulting from users intentionally or unintentionally breaking the law through its site.[1]

Introduction

One of the biggest forces changing business is the Internet. Technology companies like Intel and Cisco were among the first to seize the Internet to overhaul their operations. Intel deployed web-based automation to liberate its 200 salesclerks from tedious order-entry positions. Instead, salesclerks concentrate on customer relationship management functions such as analyzing sales trends and pampering customers. Cisco handles 75 percent of its sales online, and 45 percent of online orders never touch employees' hands. This type of Internet-based ordering has helped Cisco hike productivity by 20 percent over the past few years.

Ebusiness is the conducting of business on the Internet, not only buying and selling, but also serving customers and collaborating with business partners. Organizations realize that putting up simple websites for customers, employees, and partners does not create an ebusiness. Ebusiness websites must create a buzz, much as Amazon has done in the book-selling industry. Ebusiness websites must be innovative, add value, and provide useful information. In short, the site must build a sense of community and collaboration, eventually becoming the port of entry for business. This unit focuses on the opportunities and advantages found with developing collaborative partnerships in ebusiness and includes:

- **Chapter Thirteen**—Creating Innovative Organizations.
- **Chapter Fourteen**—Ebusiness.
- **Chapter Fifteen**—Creating Collaborative Partnerships.
- **Chapter Sixteen**—Integrating Wireless Technology in Business.

13 Creating Innovative Organizations

13.1. Compare disruptive and sustaining technologies, and explain how the Internet and WWW caused business disruption.

13.2. Describe Web 1.0 along with ebusiness and its associated advantages.

LO 13.1 Compare disruptive and sustaining technologies, and explain how the Internet and WWW caused business disruption.

Disruptive Technologies and Web 1.0

Polaroid, founded in 1937, produced the first instant camera in the late 1940s. The Polaroid camera, whose pictures developed themselves, was one of the most exciting technological advances the photography industry had ever seen. The company eventually went public, becoming one of Wall Street's most prominent enterprises, with its stock trading above $60 per share in 1997. In 2002, the stock dropped to 8 cents and the company declared bankruptcy.[2]

How could a company such as Polaroid, which had innovative technology and a captive customer base, go bankrupt? Perhaps company executives failed to use Porter's Five Forces Model to analyze the threat of substitute products or services. If they had, would they have noticed the two threats—one-hour film processing and digital cameras—which eventually stole Polaroid's market share? Would they have understood that their customers, people who want instant access to their pictures, would be the first to try these alternatives? Could the company have found a way to compete with one-hour film processing and the digital camera to save Polaroid?

Many organizations face the same dilemma as Polaroid—what's best for the current business might not be what's best for it in the long term. Some observers of our business environment have an ominous vision of the future—digital Darwinism. **Digital Darwinism** implies that organizations that cannot adapt to the new demands placed on them for surviving in the information age are doomed to extinction.

DISRUPTIVE VERSUS SUSTAINING TECHNOLOGY

A **disruptive technology** is a new way of doing things that initially does not meet the needs of existing customers. Disruptive technologies tend to open new markets and destroy old ones. A **sustaining technology,** on the other hand, produces an improved product customers are eager to buy, such as a faster car or larger hard drive. Sustaining technologies tend to provide us with better, faster, and cheaper products in established markets. Incumbent companies most often lead sustaining technology to market, but they virtually never lead in markets opened by disruptive technologies. Figure 13.1 positions companies expecting future growth from new investments (disruptive technology) and companies expecting future growth from existing investments (sustaining technology).[3]

Disruptive technologies typically enter the low end of the marketplace and eventually evolve to displace high-end competitors and their reigning technologies. Sony is a

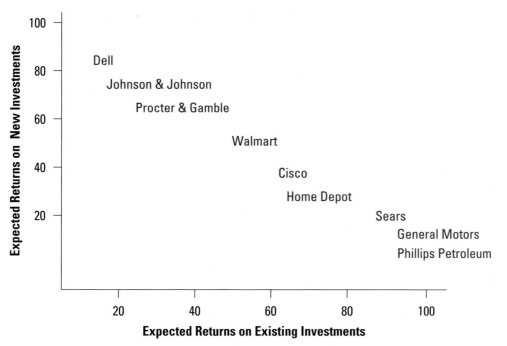

FIGURE 13.1

Disruptive and Sustaining Technologies

perfect example. Sony started as a tiny company that built portable, battery-powered transistor radios. The sound quality was poor, but customers were willing to overlook that for the convenience of portability. With the experience and revenue stream from the portables, Sony improved its technology to produce cheap, low-end transistor amplifiers that were suitable for home use and invested those revenues in improving the technology further, which produced still-better radios.[4]

The Innovator's Dilemma, a book by Clayton M. Christensen, discusses how established companies can take advantage of disruptive technologies without hindering existing relationships with customers, partners, and stakeholders. Xerox, IBM, Sears, and DEC all listened to existing customers, invested aggressively in technology, had their competitive antennae up, and still lost their market-dominant positions. They may have placed too much emphasis on satisfying customers' current needs, while neglecting new disruptive technology to meet customers' future needs and thus losing market share. Figure 13.2 highlights several companies that launched new businesses by capitalizing on disruptive technologies.[5]

Company	Disruptive Technology
Apple	iPod, iPhone, iPad
Charles Schwab	Online brokerage
Hewlett-Packard	Microprocessor-based computers, ink-jet printers
IBM	Minicomputers; personal computers
Intel	Low-end microprocessors
Intuit	QuickBooks software; TurboTax software; Quicken software
Microsoft	Internet-based computing; operating system software; SQL and Access database software
Oracle	Database software
Quantum	3.5-inch disks
Sony	Transistor-based consumer electronics

FIGURE 13.2

Companies That Capitalized on Disruptive Technologies

THE INTERNET AND WORLD WIDE WEB—THE ULTIMATE BUSINESS DISRUPTORS

The **Internet** is a massive network that connects computers all over the world and allows them to communicate with one another. Computers connected via the Internet can send and receive information including text, graphics, voice, video, and software. Originally the Internet was essentially an emergency military communications system operated by the U.S. Department of Defense Advanced Research Project Agency (DARPA), which called the network ARPANET. No one foresaw the dramatic impact it would have on both business and personal communications. In time, all U.S. universities that had defense-related funding installed ARPANET computers, forming the first official Internet network. As users began to notice the value of electronic communications, the purpose of the network started shifting from a military pipeline to a communications tool for scientists.

Millions of corporate, educational, and research networks now connect billions of computer systems and users in more than 200 countries. Internet users are expected to top the 2 billion mark, about one-third of the world's population.[6]

Although the Internet was an excellent communication tool for scientists and government officials, it was technically challenging for everyday people to operate. This changed with the inventions of the World Wide Web and web browsers. The **World Wide Web (WWW)** provides access to Internet information through documents including text, graphics, audio, and video files that use a special formatting language called HTML. **Hypertext markup language (HTML)** links documents, allowing users to move from one to another simply by clicking on a hot spot or link. **Web browsers,** such as Internet Explorer or Mozilla's Firefox, allow users to access the WWW. **Hypertext transport protocol (HTTP)** is the Internet protocol web browsers use to request and display web pages using universal resource locators. A **universal resource locator (URL)** is the address of a file or resource on the web such as www.apple.com. A domain name identifies a URL address and in the previous example apple.com is the domain name.

Notice that the Internet and the World Wide Web are not synonymous. The WWW is just one part of the Internet, and its primary use is to correlate and disseminate information. The Internet includes the WWW and also other forms of communication systems such as email. Figure 13.3 lists the reasons for the massive growth of the WWW.[7]

WEB 1.0: THE CATALYST FOR EBUSINESS

As people began learning about the WWW and the Internet, they understood that it enabled a company to communicate with anyone, anywhere, at anytime, creating a new way to participate in business. The competitive advantages for first movers would be enormous, thus spurring the beginning of the Web 1.0 Internet boom. **Web 1.0** is a term to refer to the World Wide Web during its first few years of operation between 1991 and 2003. **Ecommerce** is the buying and selling of goods and services over the Internet. Ecommerce refers only to online transactions. **Ebusiness** includes ecommerce along with all activities related to internal and external business operations such as servicing customer accounts, collaborating with partners, and exchanging real-time information. During Web 1.0, entrepreneurs began creating the first forms of ebusiness.

FIGURE 13.3

Reasons for Growth of the World Wide Web

The microcomputer revolution made it possible for an average person to own a computer.
Advancements in networking hardware, software, and media made it possible for business computers to be connected to larger networks at a minimal cost.
Browser software such as Microsoft's Internet Explorer and Netscape Navigator gave computer users an easy-to-use graphical interface to find, download, and display web pages.
The speed, convenience, and low cost of email have made it an incredibly popular tool for business and personal communications.
Basic web pages are easy to create and extremely flexible.

Industry	Business Changes Due to Technology
Auto	AutoTrader.com is the world's largest used-car marketplace, listing millions of cars from both private owners and dealers. AutoTrader.com actually helps to increase used-car dealers' business as it drives millions of qualified leads (potential used-car buyers) to participating automotive dealers and private sellers.
Publishing	With the Internet, anyone can publish online content. Traditionally, publishers screened many authors and manuscripts and selected those that had the best chances of succeeding. Lulu.com turned this model around by providing self-publishing along with print-on-demand capabilities.
Education and Training	Continuing medical education is costly, and just keeping up-to-date with advances often requires taking training courses and traveling to conferences. Now continuing education in many fields is moving online, and by 2016 more than 50 percent of doctors will be building their skills through online learning. Companies such as Cisco save millions by moving training to the Internet.
Entertainment	The music industry was hit hard by ebusiness, and online music traders such as iTunes average billions of annual downloads. Unable to compete with online music, the majority of record stores closed. The next big entertainment industry to feel the effects of ebusiness will be the multibillion-dollar movie business. Video rental stores are closing their doors as they fail to compete with online streaming and home rental delivery companies such as Netflix.
Financial Services	Nearly every public efinance company makes money, with online mortgage service Lending Tree leading the pack. Processing online mortgage applications is more than 50 percent cheaper for customers.
Retail	Forrester Research predicts ebusiness retail sales will grow at a 10 percent annual growth rate through 2014. It forecasts U.S. online retail sales will be nearly $250 billion, up from $155 billion in 2009. Online retail sales were recently up 11 percent, compared to 2.5 percent for all retail sales.
Travel	Travel site Expedia.com is now the biggest leisure-travel agency, with higher profit margins than even American Express. The majority of travel agencies closed as a direct result of ebusiness.

Ebusiness opened up a new marketplace for any company willing to move its business operations online. A ***paradigm shift*** occurs when a new radical form of business enters the market that reshapes the way companies and organizations behave. Ebusiness created a paradigm shift, transforming entire industries and changing enterprise-wide business processes that fundamentally rewrote traditional business rules. Deciding not to make the shift to ebusiness proved fatal for many companies (see Figure 13.4 for an overview of industries revamped by the disruption of ebusiness).[8]

FIGURE 13.4

Ebusiness Disruption of Traditional Industries

Advantages of Ebusiness

LO 13.2 Describe Web 1.0 along with ebusiness and its associated advantages.

Both individuals and organizations have embraced ebusiness to enhance productivity, maximize convenience, and improve communications. Companies today need to deploy a comprehensive ebusiness strategy, and business students need to understand its advantages, outlined in Figure 13.5. Let's look at each.

EXPANDING GLOBAL REACH

Easy access to real-time information is a primary benefit of ebusiness. ***Information richness*** refers to the depth and breadth of details contained in a piece of textual, graphic, audio, or video information. ***Information reach*** measures the number of people a firm can communicate with all over the world. Buyers need information richness to make informed purchases, and sellers need information reach to properly market and differentiate themselves from the competition.

Ebusinesses operate 24 hours a day, 7 days a week. This availability directly reduces transaction costs, since consumers no longer have to spend a lot of time researching

FIGURE 13.5

Ebusiness Advantages

Ebusiness Advantages

- Expanding global reach
- Opening new markets
- Reducing costs
- Improving operations
- Improving effectiveness

purchases or traveling great distances to make them. The faster delivery cycle for online sales helps strengthen customer relationships, improving customer satisfaction and ultimately sales.

A firm's website can be the focal point of a cost-effective communications and marketing strategy. Promoting products online allows the company to precisely target its customers whether they are local or around the globe. A physical location is restricted by size and limited to those customers who can get there, while an online store has a global marketplace with customers and information seekers already waiting in line.

OPENING NEW MARKETS

Ebusiness is perfect for increasing niche-product sales. *Mass customization* is the ability of an organization to tailor its products or services to the customers' specifications. For example, customers can order M&M's in special colors or with customized sayings such as "Marry Me." *Personalization* occurs when a company knows enough about a customer's likes and dislikes that it can fashion offers more likely to appeal to that person, say by tailoring its website to individuals or groups based on profile information, demographics, or prior transactions. Amazon uses personalization to create a unique portal for each of its customers.

Chris Anderson, editor-in-chief of *Wired* magazine, describes niche-market ebusiness strategies as capturing the *long tail*, referring to the tail of a typical sales curve. This strategy demonstrates how niche products can have viable and profitable business models when selling via ebusiness. In traditional sales models, a store is limited by shelf space when selecting products to sell. For this reason, store owners typically purchase products that will be wanted or needed by masses, and the store is stocked with broad products as there is not room on the shelf for niche products that only a few customers might purchase. Ebusinesses such as Amazon and eBay eliminated the shelf-space dilemma and were able to offer infinite products.

Netflix offers an excellent example of the long tail. Let's assume that an average Blockbuster store maintains 3,000 movies in its inventory, whereas Netflix, without physical shelf limitations, can maintain 100,000 movies in its inventory. Looking at sales data, the majority of Blockbuster's revenue comes from new releases that are rented daily, whereas older selections are rented only a few times a month and don't repay the cost of keeping them in stock. Thus Blockbuster's sales tail ends at title 3,000 (see Figure 13.6) However, Netflix, with no physical limitations, can extend its tail beyond 100,000 (and with streaming video perhaps 200,000). By extending its tail, Netflix increases sales, even if a title is rented only a few times.[9]

Intermediaries are agents, software, or businesses that provide a trading infrastructure to bring buyers and sellers together. The introduction of ebusiness brought about *disintermediation,* which occurs when a business sells directly to the customer online and cuts out the intermediary (see Figure 13.7). This business strategy lets the company shorten the order process and add value with reduced costs or a more responsive and efficient service. The disintermediation of the travel agent occurred as people began to book their own vacations online, often at a cheaper rate. At Lulu.com anyone can publish and sell print-on-demand books, online music, and custom calendars, making the publisher obsolete.[10]

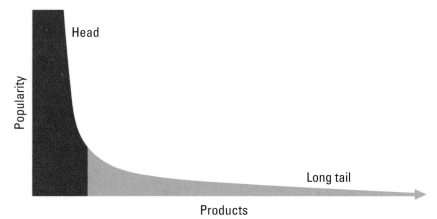

FIGURE 13.6

The Long Tail

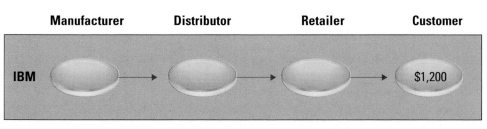
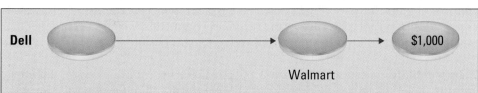
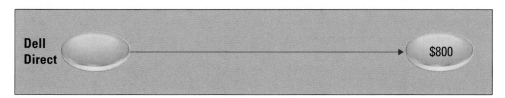

FIGURE 13.7

Business Value of Disintermediation

The more intermediaries that are cut from the distribution chain, the lower the product price. When Dell decided to sell its PCs through Walmart many were surprised, because Dell's direct-to-customer sales model was the competitive advantage that had kept Dell the market leader for years.

In *reintermediation,* steps are *added* to the value chain as new players find ways to add value to the business process. Levi Strauss originally thought it was a good business strategy to limit all online sales to its own website. A few years later, the company realized it could gain a far larger market share by allowing all retailers to sell its products directly to customers. As ebusiness matures it has become evident that to serve certain markets in volume, some reintermediation may be desirable. *Cybermediation* refers to the creation of new kinds of intermediaries that simply could not have existed before the advent of ebusiness, including comparison-shopping sites such as Kelkoo and bank account aggregation services such as Citibank.[11]

REDUCING COSTS

Operational benefits of ebusiness include business processes that require less time and human effort or can be eliminated. Compare the cost of sending out 100 direct mailings (paper, postage, labor) to the cost of a bulk email campaign. Think about the cost of renting a physical location and operating phone lines versus the cost of maintaining an online site. Switching to an ebusiness model can eliminate many traditional costs associated with communicating by substituting systems, such as Live Help, that let customers chat live with support or sales staff.

Online air travel reservations cost less than those booked over the telephone. Online ordering also offers the possibility of merging a sales order system with order fulfillment and delivery so customers can check the progress of their orders at all times. Ebusinesses can also inexpensively attract new customers with innovative marketing and retain present customers with improved service and support.[12]

One of the most exciting benefits of ebusiness is its low start-up costs. Today, anyone can start an ebusiness with just a website and a great product or service. Even a dog-walking operation can benefit from being an ebusiness.

IMPROVING OPERATIONS

Ebusiness has had some of its biggest impacts on customer service. Communication is often faster, more available, and more effective, encouraging customers to learn more about the product. Customers can often help themselves, using the content richness only a website can provide, and they can both shop and pay online without having to leave the house. Companies can also use email, special messages, and private password access to special areas for top customers.

IMPROVING EFFECTIVENESS

Just putting up a simple website does not create an ebusiness. Ebusiness websites must create buzz, be innovative, add value, and provide useful information. In short, they must build a sense of community and collaboration.

IT measures of efficiency, such as the amount of traffic on a site, don't tell the whole story. They do not necessarily indicate large sales volumes, for instance. Many websites with lots of traffic have minimal sales. The best way to measure ebusiness success is to use *effectiveness* IT metrics, such as the revenue generated by web traffic, number of new customers acquired by web traffic, and reductions in customer service calls resulting from web traffic.

Interactivity measures advertising effectiveness by counting visitor interactions with the target ad, including time spent viewing the ad, number of pages viewed, and number of repeat visits to the advertisement. Interactivity measures are a giant step forward for advertisers, since traditional advertising methods—newspapers, magazines, radio, and television—provide few ways to track effectiveness. Figure 13.8 displays the

FIGURE 13.8

Marketing Received Tremendous Benefits from Ebusiness

Marketing via Ebusiness

An **associate (affiliate) program** allows a business to generate commissions or referral fees when a customer visiting its website clicks on a link to another merchant's website. For example, if a customer to a company website clicks on a banner ad to another vendor's website, the company will receive a referral fee or commission when the customer performs the desired action, typically making a purchase or completing a form.

A **banner ad** is a box running across a website that advertises the products and services of another business, usually another ebusiness. The banner generally contains a link to the advertiser's website. Advertisers can track how often customers click on a banner ad resulting in a click-through to their website. Often the cost of the banner ad depends on the number of customers who click on the banner ad. Web-based advertising services can track the number of times users click the banner, generating statistics that enable advertisers to judge whether the advertising fees are worth paying. Banner ads are like living, breathing classified ads. Tracking the number of banner ad clicks is an excellent way to understand the effectiveness of the ad on the website.

A **click-through** is a count of the number of people who visit one site and click on an advertisement that takes them to the site of the advertiser. Tracking effectiveness based on click-throughs guarantees exposure to target ads; however, it does not guarantee that the visitor liked the ad, spent any substantial time viewing the ad, or was satisfied with the information contained in the ad.

A **cookie** is a small file deposited on a hard drive by a website containing information about customers and their browsing activities. Cookies allow websites to record the comings and goings of customers, usually without their knowledge or consent.

A **pop-up ad** is a small web page containing an advertisement that appears outside of the current website loaded in the browser. A pop-under ad is a form of a pop-up ad that users do not see until they close the current web browser screen.

Viral marketing is a technique that induces websites or users to pass on a marketing message to other websites or users, creating exponential growth in the message's visibility and effect. One example of successful viral marketing is Hotmail, which promotes its service and its own advertisers' messages in every user's email notes. Viral marketing encourages users of a product or service supplied by an ebusiness to encourage friends to join. Viral marketing is a word-of-mouth type advertising program.

---

ebusiness marketing initiatives allowing companies to expand their reach while measuring effectiveness.[13]

The ultimate outcome of any advertisement is a purchase. Organizations use metrics to tie revenue amounts and number of new customers created directly back to the websites or banner ads. Through ***clickstream data*** they can observe the exact pattern of a consumer's navigation through a site. Figure 13.9 displays different types of clickstream metrics, and Figure 3.10 provides definitions of common metrics based on clickstream data. To interpret such data properly, managers try to benchmark against other companies. For instance, consumers seem to visit their preferred websites regularly, even checking back multiple times during a given session.[14]

Types of Clickstream Data Metrics
The number of page views (i.e., the number of times a particular page has been presented to a visitor).
The pattern of websites visited, including most frequent exit page and most frequent prior website.
Length of stay on the website.
Dates and times of visits.
Number of registrations filled out per 100 visitors.
Number of abandoned registrations.
Demographics of registered visitors.
Number of customers with shopping carts.
Number of abandoned shopping carts.

FIGURE 13.9

Clickstream Data Metrics

METRICS MEASURING WEBSITE SUCCESS	
Website Visit Metrics	
Stickiness (visit duration time)	The length of time a visitor spends on a website.
Raw visit depth (total web pages exposure per session)	The total number of pages a visitor is exposed to during a single visit to a website.
Visit depth (total unique web pages exposure per session)	The total number of unique pages a visitor is exposed to during a single visit to a website.
Website Visitor Metrics	
Unidentified visitor	A visitor is an individual who visits a website. An "unidentified visitor" means that no information about that visitor is available.
Unique visitor	A unique visitor is one who can be recognized and counted only once within a given period of time.
Identified visitor	An ID is available that allows a user to be tracked across multiple visits to a website.
Website Hit Metrics	
Hits	When visitors reach a website, their computer sends a request to the site's computer server to begin displaying pages. Each element of a requested page is recorded by the website's server log file as a "hit."

FIGURE 13.10

Website Metrics

1. Do you consider Pinterest a form of disruptive or sustaining technology? Why or why not?

2. What types of security and ethical dilemmas are facing Pinterest?

Chapter Thirteen Case: Failing to Innovate

It is a sad but common tale—a dynamic company comes up with an innovative new product that utilizes cutting-edge technology in an exciting way that generates lots of hype and attention. But for some reason this new product fails to click with the masses and falls into oblivion, only to see other products gain massive success by following in its footsteps.

It's not always a case of right technology at the wrong time. Sometimes these first movers failed to build on their innovation, instead sitting on their initial achievements and letting more nimble competitors refine their idea into something more attractive and functional. And some just made too many mistakes to succeed.

Obtaining the first-mover advantage is critical to any business that wants to compete in the Internet economy. However, gaining a first-mover advantage is typically temporary, and without remaining innovative the company can soon fail. Here is a list of the top 10 first movers that flopped, according to Jim Rapoza of *eWeek*.

1. **Apple Newton PDA**—When it was launched in the early 90s, the Apple Newton was first lauded but later mocked because of its failings (it even had the honor of being spoofed on *The Simpsons*). But one can draw a straight line from the Newton to current products such as tablet PCs, smartphones, and the Apple iPhone.

2. **PointCast**—In 1997, one of the hottest products found on the desktop of nearly every IT worker was PointCast, which delivered selected news items directly to the desktop. It quickly launched the "push" craze, which just as quickly imploded spectacularly. But today's RSS and news feeds all owe a debt to PointCast.

3. **Gopher Protocol**—It was so close. Launched just before the web itself, Gopher quickly became popular in universities and business. Using search technology, it worked very much like a website, but it could not compete with the web itself.

4. **VisiCalc**—Often lauded as the first killer application for the PC, the VisiCalc spreadsheet was a must-have for early PC-enabled businesses but quickly fell behind more polished spreadsheets from Lotus and Microsoft.

5. **Atari**—For those of a certain age, the word *Atari* is synonymous with video games. The pioneer in home gaming consoles failed to innovate in the face of more nimble competitors.

6. **Diamond Rio**—For $200 and with 32MB of RAM (with a SmartMedia slot for memory expansion), the Rio helped launch the MP3 revolution. That is, until white earbuds and a thing called the iPod took over.

7. **Netscape Navigator**—Netscape Navigator was essentially the web for users in the early to mid-1990s. But Netscape could not withstand the Microsoft onslaught, along with plenty of mistakes the company made itself, and now only lives on as the original basis of the Mozilla browsers.

8. **AltaVista**—Not the first search engine, but the first to use many of the natural language technologies common today and the first to gain real web popularity, AltaVista failed to keep up with technological changes.

9. **Ricochet Networks**—Nothing created geek lust like sitting next to someone who had a Ricochet card plugged into the laptop. Look, she is in a cab and accessing the Internet at ISDN speeds! But Ricochet never expanded to enough cities to be a serious player.

10. **IBM Simon Phone**—The iPhone's $499 price is nothing compared with the $900 price tag the IBM Simon had when it finally became available in 1994. But it pioneered most of the features found in today's smartphones and even beat the iPhone when it came to a buttonless touch-screen interface.[15]

Questions

1. If these companies all had a first-mover advantage, then why did the products fail?

2. For each of the listed products, determine if the technology used was disruptive or sustaining.

3. Choose one of the products listed and determine what the company could have done to prevent the product from failing.

4. Can you name another technology product that failed? Why did it fail? What could the company have done differently for it to succeed?

14 Ebusiness

LEARNING OUTCOMES

14.1. Compare the four categories of ebusiness models.
14.2. Describe the six ebusiness tools for connecting and communicating.

14.3. Identify the four challenges associated with ebusiness.

LO 14.1 Compare the four categories of ebusiness models.

Ebusiness Models

A ***business model*** is a plan that details how a company creates, delivers, and generates revenues. Some models are quite simple: A company produces a good or service and sells it to customers. If the company is successful, sales exceed costs and the company generates a profit. Other models are less straightforward, and sometimes it's not immediately clear who makes money and how much. Radio and network television are broadcast free to anyone with a receiver, for instance; advertisers pay the costs of programming.

The majority of online business activities consist of the exchange of products and services either between businesses or between businesses and consumers. An ***ebusiness model*** is a plan that details how a company creates, delivers, and generates revenues on the Internet. Ebusiness models fall into one of the four categories: (1) business-to-business, (2) business-to-consumer, (3) consumer-to-business, and (4) consumer-to-consumer (see Figure 14.1).

BUSINESS-TO-BUSINESS (B2B)

Business-to-business (B2B) applies to businesses buying from and selling to each other over the Internet. Examples include medical billing service, software sales and licensing, and virtual assistant businesses. B2B relationships represent 80 percent of all online business and are more complex with greater security needs than the other types.

FIGURE 14.1

Ebusiness Models

Ebusiness Term	Definition
Business-to-business (B2B)	Applies to businesses buying from and selling to each other over the Internet.
Business-to-consumer (B2C)	Applies to any business that sells its products or services to consumers over the Internet.
Consumer-to-business (C2B)	Applies to any consumer that sells a product or service to a business over the Internet.
Consumer-to-consumer (C2C)	Applies to sites primarily offering goods and services to assist consumers interacting with each other over the Internet.

	Business	Consumer
Business	B2B	B2C
Consumer	C2B	C2C

Brick-and-Mortar Business
A business that operates in a physical store without an Internet presence.
Example: T.J. Maxx

Click-and-Mortar Business
A business that operates in a physical store and on the Internet.
Example: Barnes & Noble

Pure-Play (Virtual) Business
A business that operates on the Internet only without a physical store.
Example: Google

Electronic marketplaces, or emarketplaces, are interactive business communities providing a central market where multiple buyers and sellers can engage in ebusiness activities. By tightening and automating the relationship between the two parties, they create structures for conducting commercial exchange, consolidating supply chains, and creating new sales channels.

FIGURE 14.2

Forms of Business-to-Consumer Operations

BUSINESS-TO-CONSUMER (B2C)

Business-to-consumer (B2C) applies to any business that sells its products or services directly to consumers online. Carfax offers car buyers detailed histories of used vehicles for a fee. An *eshop,* sometimes referred to as an *estore* or *etailer,* is an online version of a retail store where customers can shop at any hour. It can be an extension of an existing store such as The Gap or operate only online such as Amazon.com. There are three ways to operate as a B2C: brick-and-mortar, click-and-mortar, and pure play (see Figure 14.2).

CONSUMER-TO-BUSINESS (C2B)

Consumer-to-business (C2B) applies to any consumer who sells a product or service to a business on the Internet. One example is customers of Priceline.com, who set their own prices for items such as airline tickets or hotel rooms and wait for a seller to decide whether to supply them. The demand for C2B ebusiness will increase over the next few years due to customers' desire for greater convenience and lower prices.

CONSUMER-TO-CONSUMER (C2C)

Consumer-to-consumer (C2C) applies to customers offering goods and services to each other on the Internet. A good example of C2C is an auction where buyers and sellers solicit consecutive bids from each other and prices are determined dynamically. EBay, the Internet's most successful C2C online auction website, links like-minded buyers and sellers for a small commission. Other types of online auctions include forward auctions, where sellers market to many buyers and the highest bid wins, and reverse auctions, where buyers select goods and services from the seller with the lowest bid.

EBUSINESS FORMS AND REVENUE-GENERATING STRATEGIES

As more and more companies began jumping on the ebusiness bandwagon, new forms of ebusiness began to emerge (see Figure 14.3). Many of the new forms of ebusiness went to market without clear strategies on how they were going to generate revenue.

FIGURE 14.3

Ebusiness Forms

Form	Description	Examples
Content providers	Generate revenues by providing digital content such as news, music, photos, or videos.	Netflix.com, iTunes.com, CNN.com
Infomediaries	Provide specialized information on behalf of producers of goods and services and their potential customers	Edmunds.com, BizRate.com, Bloomberg.com, Zillow.com
Online marketplaces	Bring together buyers and sellers of products and services.	Amazon.com, eBay.com, Priceline.com
Portals	Operate central website for users to access specialized content and other services.	Google.com, Yahoo.com, MSN.com
Service providers	Provide services such as photo sharing, video sharing, online backup and storage.	Flickr.com, Mapquest.com, YouTube.com
Transaction brokers	Process online sales transactions.	Etrade.com, Charlesschwab.com, Fidelity.com

Google is an excellent example of an ebusiness that did not figure out a way to generate profits until many years after its launch.[1]

Google's primary line of business is its search engine; however, the company does not generate revenue from people using its site to search the Internet. It generates revenue from the marketers and advertisers that pay to place their ads on the site. About 200 million times each day, people from all over the world access Google to perform searches.

AdWords, a part of the Google site, allows advertisers to bid on common search terms. The advertisers simply enter in the keywords they want to bid on and the maximum amounts they want to pay per click per day. Google then determines a price and a search ranking for those keywords based on how much other advertisers are willing to pay for the same terms. Pricing for keywords can range from 5 cents to $10 a click. Paid search is the ultimate in targeted advertising because consumers type in exactly what they want. A general search term such as *tropical vacation* costs less than a more specific term such as *Hawaiian vacation*. Whoever bids the most for a term appears in a sponsored advertisement link either at the top or along the side of the search-results page.[2]

A **search engine** is website software that finds other pages based on keyword matching similar to Google. **Search engine ranking** evaluates variables that search engines use to determine where a URL appears on the list of search results. **Search engine optimization (SEO)** combines art along with science to determine how to make URLs more attractive to search engines resulting in higher search engine ranking (see Figure 14.4). The better the SEO, the higher the ranking for a website in the list of search engine results. SEO is critical because most people view only the first few pages of a search result. After that a person is more inclined to begin a new search than review pages and pages of search results. Websites can generate revenue through:

FIGURE 14.4

Different Forms of Searching

- **Pay-per-click:** generates revenue each time a user clicks on a link to a retailer's website.
- **Pay-per-call:** generates revenue each time a user clicks on a link that takes the user directly to an online agent waiting for a call.
- **Pay-per-conversion:** generates revenue each time a website visitor is converted to a customer.

FIGURE 14.5

Ebusiness Revenue
Models

Ebusiness Revenue Model	Benefits	Challenges
Advertising fees	■ Well-targeted advertisements can be perceived as value-added content by trading participants. ■ Easy to implement	■ Limited revenue potential ■ Overdone or poorly targeted advertisements can be disturbing elements on the website.
License fees	■ Creates incentives to do many transactions ■ Customization and back-end integration lead to lock-in of participants.	■ Up-front fee is a barrier to entry for participants. ■ Price differentiation is complicated.
Subscription fees	■ Creates incentives to do transactions ■ Price can be differentiated. ■ Possibility to build additional revenue from new user groups	■ Fixed fee is a barrier to entry for participants.
Transaction fees	■ Can be directly tied to savings (both process and price savings) ■ Important revenue source when high level of liquidity (transaction volume) is reached	■ If process savings are not completely visible, use of the system is discouraged (incentive to move transactions offline). ■ Transaction fees likely to decrease with time
Value-added services fees	■ Service offering can be differentiated. ■ Price can be differentiated. ■ Possibility to build additional revenue from established and new user groups (third parties)	■ Cumbersome process for customers to continually evaluate new services

Ebusinesses must have a revenue model, or a model for making money. For instance, will they accept advertising, or sell subscriptions or licensing rights? Figure 14.5 lists the different benefits and challenges of various ebusiness revenue models.[3]

Ebusiness Tools for Connecting and Communicating

LO 14.2 Describe the six ebusiness tools for connecting and communicating.

As firms began to move online, more MIS tools were created to support ebusiness processes and requirements. The tools supporting and driving ebusiness are highlighted in Figure 14.6 and covered below in detail.

EMAIL

Email, short for electronic mail, is the exchange of digital messages over the Internet. No longer do business professionals have to wait for the mail to receive important documents as email single-handedly increased the speed of business by allowing the transfer of documents with the same speed as the telephone. Its chief business advantage is the ability to inform and communicate with many people simultaneously, immediately, and with ease. There are no time or place constraints, and users can check, send, and view emails whenever they require.

An *Internet service provider (ISP)* is a company that provides access to the Internet for a monthly fee. Major ISPs in the United States include AOL, AT&T, Comcast, Earthlink, and Netzero, as well as thousands of local ISPs including regional telephone companies.

FIGURE 14.6

Ebusiness Tools

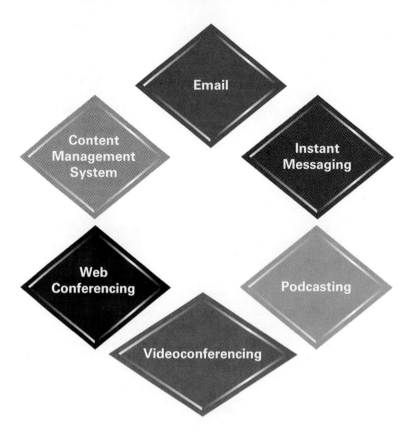

INSTANT MESSAGING

Real-time communication occurs when a system updates information at the same rate it receives it. Email was a great advancement over traditional communication methods such as the U.S. mail, but it did not operate in real time. *Instant messaging (IMing)* is a service that enables instant or real-time communication between people. Businesses immediately saw what they could do:

- Answer simple questions quickly and easily.
- Resolve questions or problems immediately.
- Transmit messages as fast as naturally flowing conversation.
- Easily hold simultaneous IM sessions with multiple people.
- Eliminate long-distance phone charges.
- Quickly identify which employees are at their computers.

PODCASTING

Podcasting converts an audio broadcast to a digital music player. Podcasts can increase marketing reach and build customer loyalty. Companies use podcasts as marketing communication channels discussing everything from corporate strategies to detailed product overviews. The senior executive team can share weekly or monthly podcasts featuring important issues or expert briefings on new technical or marketing developments.

VIDEOCONFERENCING

A videoconference allows people at two or more locations to interact via two-way video and audio transmissions simultaneously as well as share documents, data, computer displays, and whiteboards. Point-to-point videoconferences connect two people, and multipoint conferences connect more than two people at multiple locations.

Videoconferences can increase productivity because users participate without leaving their offices. They can improve communication and relationships, because participants see each other's facial expressions and body language, both important aspects of communication that are lost with a basic telephone call or email. They also reduce travel expenses, a big win for firms facing economic challenges. Of course, nothing can replace meeting someone face-to-face and shaking hands, but videoconferencing offers a viable and cost-effective alternative.

WEB CONFERENCING

Web conferencing, or a ***webinar,*** blends videoconferencing with document sharing and allows the user to deliver a presentation over the web to a group of geographically dispersed participants. Regardless of the type of hardware or software the attendees are running, every participant can see what is on anyone else's screen. Schools use web conferencing tools such as Illuminate Live to deliver lectures to students, and businesses use tools such as WebEx to demonstrate products. Web conferencing is not quite like being there, but professionals can accomplish more sitting at their desks than in an airport waiting to make travel connections.

CONTENT MANAGEMENT SYSTEMS

In the fourth century BC Aristotle catalogued the natural world according to a systematic organization, and the ancient library at Alexandria was reportedly organized by subject, connecting like information with like. Today ***content management systems (CMS)*** help companies manage the creation, storage, editing, and publication of their website content. CMSs are user-friendly; most include web-based publishing, search, navigation, and indexing to organize information; and they let users with little or no technical expertise make website changes.

A search is typically carried out by entering a keyword or phrase (query) into a text field and clicking a button or a hyperlink. Navigation facilitates movement from one web page to another. Content management systems play a crucial role in getting site visitors to view more than just the home page. If navigation choices are unclear, visitors may hit the "Back" button on their first (and final) visit to a website. One rule of thumb to remember is that each time a user has to click to find search information, there is a 50 percent chance the user will leave the website instead. A key principle of good website design, therefore, is to keep the number of clicks to a minimum.

Taxonomy is the scientific classification of organisms into groups based on similarities of structure or origin. Taxonomies are also used for indexing the content on the website into categories and subcategories of topics. For example, car is a subtype of vehicle. Every car is a vehicle, but not every vehicle is a car; some vehicles are vans, buses, and trucks. Taxonomy terms are arranged so that narrower/more specific/"child" terms fall under broader/more generic/"parent" terms. ***Information architecture*** is the set of ideas about how all information in a given context should be organized. Many companies hire information architects to create their website taxonomies. A well-planned taxonomy ensures search and navigation are easy and user-friendly. If the taxonomy is confusing, the site will soon fail.

The Challenges of Ebusiness

LO 14.3 Identify the four challenges associated with ebusiness.

Although the benefits of ebusiness are enticing, developing, deploying, and managing ebusiness systems is not always easy. Figure 14.7 lists the challenges facing ebusiness.

IDENTIFYING LIMITED MARKET SEGMENTS

The main challenge of ebusiness is the lack of growth in some sectors due to product or service limitations. The online food sector has not grown in sales, in part because food products are perishable and consumers prefer to buy them at the supermarket as needed. Other sectors with limited ebusiness appeal include fragile or consumable goods and highly sensitive or confidential businesses such as government agencies.

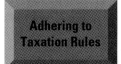

FIGURE 14.7

Challenges Facing Ebusiness

MANAGING CONSUMER TRUST

Trust in the ebusiness exchange deserves special attention. The physical separation of buyer and seller, the physical separation of buyer and merchandise, and customer perceptions about the risk of doing business online provide unique challenges. Internet marketers must develop a trustworthy relationship to make that initial sale and generate customer loyalty. A few ways to build trust when working online include being accessible and available to communicate in person with your customers; using customers' testimonials that link to your client website or to provide their contact information; accepting legitimate forms of payment such as credit cards.

ENSURING CONSUMER PROTECTION

An organization that wants to dominate with superior customer service as a competitive advantage must not only serve but also protect its customers, guarding them against unsolicited goods and communication, illegal or harmful goods, insufficient information about goods and suppliers, invasion of privacy and misuse of personal information, and online fraud. System security, however, must not make ebusiness websites inflexible or difficult to use.

ADHERING TO TAXATION RULES

Many believe that U.S. tax policy should provide a level playing field for traditional retail businesses, mail-order companies, and online merchants. Yet the Internet marketplace remains mostly free of traditional forms of sales tax, partly because ecommerce law is vaguely defined and differs from state to state. For now, companies that operate online must obey a patchwork of rules about which customers are subject to sales tax on their purchases and which are not.

OPENING CASE STUDY QUESTIONS

1. What is the ebusiness model implemented by Pinterest?

2. What is the revenue model implemented by Pinterest?

Chapter Fourteen Case: eBiz

Amazing things are happening on the Internet, things nobody would believe. Here are two stories that demonstrate how innovation, creativity, and a great idea can turn the Internet into a cash cow.

A Million Dollar Homepage

The Million Dollar Homepage is a website conceived by Alex Tew, a 21-year-old student from Cricklade, Wiltshire, England, to help raise money for his university education. Launched on August 26, 2005, the website is said to have generated a gross income of $1,037,100 and has a current Google PageRank of 7.

The index page of the site consists of a 1000 by 1000 pixel grid (1 million pixels), on which he sells image-based links for $1 per pixel, in minimum 10 by 10 blocks. A person who buys one or more of these pixel blocks can design a tiny image that will be displayed on the block, decide which URL the block will link to, and write a slogan that appears when the cursor hovers over the link. The aim of the site was to sell all of the pixels in the image, thus generating $1 million of income for the creator, which seems to have been accomplished. On January 1, 2006, the final 1,000 pixels left were put up for auction on eBay. The auction closed on January 11 with the winning bid of $38,100. This brought the final tally to $1,037,100 in gross income. The Million Dollar Homepage is shown above.

One Red Paperclip

The website One Red Paperclip was created by Kyle MacDonald, a Canadian blogger who bartered his way from a single paper clip to a house in a series of trades spanning almost one year. MacDonald began with one red paper clip on July 14, 2005. By July 5, 2006, a chain of bartering had ultimately led to trading a movie role for a two-story farmhouse in Kipling, Saskatchewan. On July 7, 2006—almost exactly one year after MacDonald began his experiment—the deed to the house was signed. In September, at the housewarming party where 12 of the 14 traders were present, he proposed to his girlfriend and she accepted. The wedding ring was made from the original red paper clip he got back from the first woman to have agreed to trade with him.

Following is the timeline, based on the website and as summarized by the BBC:

- On July 14, 2005, MacDonald went to Vancouver and traded the paper clip for a fish-shaped pen.
- MacDonald then traded the pen the same day for a hand-sculpted doorknob from Seattle, Washington, which he nicknamed Knob-T.
- On July 25, 2005, MacDonald traveled to Amherst, Massachusetts, with a friend to trade the Knob-T for a Coleman camp stove (with fuel).

- On September 24, 2005, he went to San Clemente, California, and traded the camp stove for a Honda generator, from a U.S. Marine.
- On November 16, 2005, MacDonald made a second (and successful) attempt (after having the generator confiscated by the New York City Fire Department) in Maspeth, Queens, to trade the generator for an "instant party": an empty keg, an IOU for filling the keg with the beer of the holder's choice, and a neon Budweiser sign.
- On December 8, 2005, he traded the "instant party" to Quebec comedian and radio personality Michel Barrette for a Ski-doo snowmobile.
- Within a week of that, MacDonald traded the snowmobile for a two-person trip to Yahk, British Columbia, in February 2006.
- On or about January 7, 2006, the second person on the trip to Yahk traded MacDonald a cube van for the privilege.
- On or about February 22, 2006, he traded the cube van for a recording contract with Metal Works in Toronto.
- On or about April 11, 2006, MacDonald traded the recording contract to Jody Gnant for a year's rent in Phoenix, Arizona.
- On or about April 26, 2006, he traded the one year's rent in Phoenix, Arizona, for one afternoon with Alice Cooper.
- On or about May 26, 2006, MacDonald traded the one afternoon with Alice Cooper for a KISS motorized snow globe.
- On or about June 2, 2006, he traded the KISS motorized snow globe to Corbin Bernsen for a role in the film *Donna on Demand.*
- On or about July 5, 2006, MacDonald traded the movie role for a two-story farmhouse in Kipling, Saskatchewan.[4]

Questions

1. How else can you use the Internet to raise money?
2. What types of businesses could benefit from trading on the Internet?
3. Can you think of any other disruptive or nontraditional ways that you could use the Internet?

15 Creating Collaborative Partnerships

15.1. Explain Web 2.0, and identify its four characteristics.

15.2. Explain how Business 2.0 is helping communities network and collaborate.

15.3. Describe the three Business 2.0 tools for collaborating.

15.4. Explain the three challenges associated with Business 2.0.

15.5. Describe Web 3.0 and the next generation of online business.

Web 2.0: Advantages of Business 2.0

LO 15.1 Explain Web 2.0, and identify its four characteristics.

In the mid-1990s the stock market reached an all-time high as companies took advantage of ebusiness and Web 1.0, and many believed the Internet was the wave of the future. When new online businesses began failing to meet earning expectations, however, the bubble burst. Some then believed the ebusiness boom was over, but they could not have been more wrong.

Web 2.0 (or *Business 2.0*) is the next generation of Internet use—a more mature, distinctive communications platform characterized by new qualities such as collaboration, sharing, and free. Business 2.0 encourages user participation and the formation of communities that contribute to the content. In Business 2.0, technical skills are no longer required to use and publish information to the World Wide Web, eliminating entry barriers for online business.

Traditional companies tended to view technology as a tool required to perform a process or activity, and employees picked up information by walking through the office or hanging out around the water cooler. Business 2.0 technologies provide a virtual environment that, for many new employees, is just as vibrant and important as the physical environment. Figure 15.1 highlights the common characteristics of Business 2.0.[1]

CONTENT SHARING THROUGH OPEN SOURCING

An *open system* consists of nonproprietary hardware and software based on publicly known standards that allow third parties to create add-on products to plug into or interoperate with the system. Thousands of hardware devices and software applications created and sold by third-party vendors interoperate with computers, such as iPods, drawing software, and mice.

Source code contains instructions written by a programmer specifying the actions to be performed by computer software. *Open source* refers to any software whose source code is made available free (not on a fee or licensing basis as in ebusiness) for any third party to review and modify. Business 2.0 is capitalizing on open source software. Mozilla, for example, offers its Firefox web browser and Thunderbird email software free. Mozilla believes the Internet is a public resource that must remain open and accessible to all; it continuously develops free products by bringing together thousands of dedicated volunteers from around the world. Mozilla's Firefox now holds more than 20 percent of the

FIGURE 15.1

Characteristics of
Business 2.0

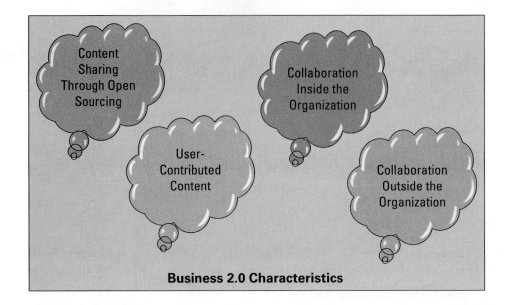

Business 2.0 Characteristics

browser market and is quickly becoming a threat to Microsoft's Internet Explorer. How do open source software companies generate revenues? Many people are still awaiting an answer to this very important question.[2]

USER-CONTRIBUTED CONTENT

Ebusiness was characterized by a few companies or users posting content for the masses. Business 2.0 is characterized by the masses posting content for the masses. **User-contributed content** (or **user-generated content**) is created and updated by many users for many users. Websites such as Flickr, Wikipedia, and YouTube, for example, move control of online media from the hands of leaders to the hands of users. Netflix and Amazon both use user-generated content to drive their recommendation tools, and websites such as Yelp use customer reviews to express opinions on products and services. Companies are embracing user-generated content to help with everything from marketing to product development and quality assurance.

One of the most popular forms of user-generated content is a **reputation system,** where buyers post feedback on sellers. eBay buyers voluntarily comment on the quality of service, their satisfaction with the item traded, and promptness of shipping. Sellers comment about prompt payment from buyers or respond to comments left by the buyer. Companies ranging from Amazon to restaurants are using reputation systems to improve quality and enhance customer satisfaction.

COLLABORATION INSIDE THE ORGANIZATION

A **collaboration system** is a set of tools that supports the work of teams or groups by facilitating the sharing and flow of information. Business 2.0's collaborative mind-set generates more information faster from a wider audience. **Collective intelligence** is collaborating and tapping into the core knowledge of all employees, partners, and customers. Knowledge can be a real competitive advantage for an organization. The most common form of collective intelligence found inside the organization is **knowledge management (KM),** which involves capturing, classifying, evaluating, retrieving, and sharing information assets in a way that provides context for effective decisions and actions. The primary objective of knowledge management is to be sure that a company's knowledge of facts, sources of information, and solutions are readily available to all employees whenever it is needed. A **knowledge management system (KMS)** supports the capturing, organization, and dissemination of knowledge (i.e., know-how) throughout an organization. KMS can distribute an organization's knowledge base by interconnecting people and digitally gathering their expertise.

A great example of a knowledge worker is a golf caddie. Golf caddies give advice such as, "The rain makes the third hole play 10 yards shorter." If a golf caddie is good and gives accurate advice it can lead to big tips. Collaborating with other golf caddies can provide bigger tips for all. How can knowledge management make this happen? Caddies could be rewarded for sharing course knowledge by receiving prizes for sharing knowledge. The course manager could compile all of the tips and publish a course notebook for distribution to all caddies. The goal of a knowledge management system is that everyone wins. Here the caddies make bigger tips and golfers improve their play by benefiting from the collaborative experiences of the caddies, and the course owners win as business increases.

KM has assumed greater urgency in American business over the past few years as millions of baby boomers prepare to retire. When they punch out for the last time, the knowledge they gleaned about their jobs, companies, and industries during their long careers will walk out with them—unless companies take measures to retain their insights.

Explicit and Tacit Knowledge

Not all information is valuable. Individuals must determine what information qualifies as intellectual and knowledge-based assets. In general, intellectual and knowledge-based assets fall into one of two categories: explicit or tacit. As a rule, *explicit knowledge* consists of anything that can be documented, archived, and codified, often with the help of IT. Examples of explicit knowledge are assets such as patents, trademarks, business plans, marketing research, and customer lists. *Tacit knowledge* is the knowledge contained in people's heads. The challenge inherent in tacit knowledge is figuring out how to recognize, generate, share, and manage knowledge that resides in people's heads. While information technology in the form of email, instant messaging, and related technologies can help facilitate the dissemination of tacit knowledge, identifying it in the first place can be a major obstacle.

COLLABORATION OUTSIDE THE ORGANIZATION

The most common form of collective intelligence found outside the organization is *crowdsourcing,* which refers to the wisdom of the crowd. The idea that collective intelligence is greater than the sum of its individual parts has been around for a long time (see Figure 15.2). With Business 2.0 the ability to efficiently tap into its power is emerging. For many years organizations believed that good ideas came from the top. CEOs collaborated only with the heads of sales and marketing, the quality assurance expert, or the road warrior salesman. The organization chart governed who should work with whom

FIGURE 15.2

Crowdsourcing: The Crowd Is Smarter than the Individual

and how far up the chain of command a suggestion or idea would travel. With Buisness 2.0 this belief is being challenged, as firms capitalize on crowdsourcing by opening up a task or problem to a wider group to find better or cheaper results from outside the box.

With Business 2.0, people can be continuously connected, a driving force behind collaboration. Traditional ebusiness communications were limited to face-to-face conversations and one-way technologies that used *asynchronous communications,* or communication such as email in which the message and the response do not occur at the same time. Business 2.0 brought *synchronous communication,* or communications that occur at the same time such as IM or chat. Ask a group of college students when they last spoke to their parents. For most the answer is less than hour ago, as opposed to the traditional response of a few days ago. In business too, continuous connections are now expected in today's collaborative world.

LO 15.2 Explain how Business 2.0 is helping communities network and collaborate.

Networking Communities with Business 2.0

Social media refers to websites that rely on user participation and user-contributed content, such as Facebook, YouTube, and Digg. A *social network* is an application that connects people by matching profile information. Providing individuals with the ability to network is by far one of the greatest advantages of Business 2.0. *Social networking* is the practice of expanding your business and/or social contacts by constructing a personal network (see Figure 15.3). Social networking sites provide two basic functions. The first is the ability to create and maintain a profile that serves as an online identity within the environment. The second is the ability to create connections between other people within the network. *Social networking analysis (SNA)* maps group contacts (personal and professional) identifying who knows each other and who works together. In a company it can provide a vision of how employees work together. It can also identify key experts with specific knowledge such as how to solve a complicated programming problem or launch a new product.

Business 2.0 simplifies access to information and improves the ability to share it. Instead of spending $1,000 and two days at a conference to meet professional peers, business people can now use social networks such as LinkedIn to meet new contacts for recruiting, prospecting, and identifying experts on a topic. With executive members from all the *Fortune* 500 companies, LinkedIn has become one of the more useful recruiting tools on the web.

Social networking sites can be especially useful to employers trying to find job candidates with unique or highly specialized skill sets that may be harder to locate in larger communities. Many employers also search social networking sites to find "dirt" and character references for potential employees. Keep in mind that what you post on the Internet stays on the Internet.[4]

FIGURE 15.3

Social Network Example[3]

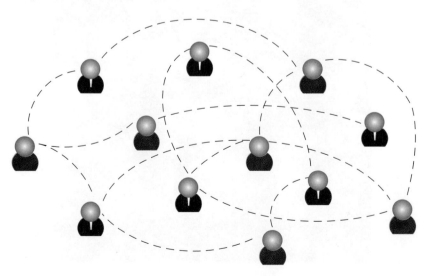

SOCIAL TAGGING

Tags are specific keywords or phrases incorporated into website content for means of classification or taxonomy. An item can have one or more tags associated with it, to allow for multiple browseable paths through the items, and tags can be changed with minimal effort (see Figure 15.4). *Social tagging* describes the collaborative activity of marking shared online content with keywords or tags as a way to organize it for future navigation, filtering, or search. The entire user community is invited to tag, and thus essentially defines, the content. Flickr allows users to upload images and tag them with appropriate keywords. After enough people have done so, the resulting tag collection will identify images correctly and without bias.

Folksonomy is similar to taxonomy except that crowdsourcing determines the tags or keyword-based classification system. Using the collective power of a community to identify and classify content significantly lowers content categorization costs, because there is no complicated nomenclature to learn. Users simply create and apply tags as they wish. For example, while cell phone manufacturers often refer to their products as mobile devices, the folksonomy could include mobile phone, wireless phone, smartphone, iPhone, BlackBerry, and so on. All these keywords, if searched, should take a user to the same site. Folksonomies reveal what people truly call things (see Figure 15.5). They have been a point of discussion on the web because the whole point of having a website is for your customers to find it. The majority of websites are found through search terms that match the content.[5]

A *website bookmark* is a locally stored URL or the address of a file or Internet page saved as a shortcut. *Social bookmarking* allows users to share, organize, search, and manage bookmarks. Del.icio.us, a website dedicated to social bookmarking, provides users with a place to store, categorize, annotate, and share favorites. StumbleUpon is another popular social bookmarking website that allows users to locate interesting websites based on their favorite subjects. The more you use the service, the more the system "learns" about your interests and the better it can show you websites that interest you. StumbleUpon represents a new social networking model in which content finds the users instead of the other way around. StumbleUpon is all about the users and the content they enjoy.[6]

FIGURE 15.4

Social Tagging Occurs When Many Individuals Categorize Content

FIGURE 15.5

Folksonomy Example: The User-Generated Names for Cellular Phones

Business 2.0 Tools for Collaborating

Social networking and collaborating are leading businesses in new directions, and Figure 15.6 provides an overview of the tools that harness the "power of the people," allowing users to share ideas, discuss business problems, and collaborate on solutions.

BLOGS

A **blog,** or **web log,** is an online journal that allows users to post their own comments, graphics, and video. Unlike traditional HTML web pages, blog websites let writers communicate—and readers respond—on a regular basis through a simple yet customizable interface that does not require any programming.

From a business perspective, blogs are no different from marketing channels such as video, print, audio, or presentations. They all deliver results of varying kinds. Consider Sun Microsystem's Jonathan Schwartz and GM's Bob Lutz, who use their blogs for marketing, sharing ideas, gathering feedback, press response, and image shaping. Starbucks has developed a blog called My Starbucks Idea, allowing customers to share ideas, tell Starbucks what they think of other people's ideas, and join discussions. Blogs are an ideal mechanism for many businesses because they can focus on topic areas more easily than traditional media, with no limits on page size, word count, or publication deadline.[7]

Microblogs

Microblogging is the practice of sending brief posts (140 to 200 characters) to a personal blog, either publicly or to a private group of subscribers who can read the posts as IMs or as text messages. The main advantage of microblogging is that posts can be submitted by a variety of means, such as instant messaging, email, or the web. By far the most popular microblogging tool is Twitter, which allows users to send microblog entries called tweets to anyone who has registered to "follow" them. Senders can restrict delivery to people they want to follow them or, by default, allow open access.

Real Simple Syndication (RSS)

Real Simple Syndication (RSS) is a web format used to publish frequently updated works, such as blogs, news headlines, audio, and video, in a standardized format. An RSS document or feed includes full or summarized text, plus other information such as publication date and authorship. News websites, blogs, and podcasts use RSS, constantly feeding news to consumers instead of having them search for it. In addition to facilitating syndication, RSS allows a website's frequent readers to track updates on the site.

FIGURE 15.6

Business 2.0 Communication and Collaboration Tools

BLOG	WIKI	MASHUP
• An online journal that allows users to post their own comments, graphics, and videos	• Collaborative website that allows users to add, remove, and change content	• Content from more than one source to create a new product or service
• Popular business examples include Sweet Leaf Tea, Stoneyfield Farm, Nuts about Southwest, Disney Parks	• Popular business examples include Wikipedia, National Institute of Health, Intelopedia, LexisNexis, Wiki for Higher Education	• Examples include Zillow, Infopedia, Trendsmap, SongDNA, ThisWeKnow

WIKIS

A *wiki* (the word is Hawaiian for quick) is a type of collaborative web page that allows users to add, remove, and change content, which can be easily organized and reorganized as required. While blogs have largely drawn on the creative and personal goals of individual authors, wikis are based on open collaboration with any and everybody. Wikipedia, the open encyclopedia that launched in 2001, has become one of the 10 most popular web destinations, reaching an estimated 217 million unique visitors a month.[8]

A wiki user can generally alter the original content of any article, while the blog user can only add information in the form of comments. Large wikis, such as Wikipedia, protect the quality and accuracy of their information by assigning users roles such as reader, editor, administrator, patroller, policy maker, subject matter expert, content maintainer, software developer, and system operator. Access to some important or sensitive Wikipedia material is limited to users in these authorized roles.[9]

The *network effect* describes how products in a network increase in value to users as the number of users increases. The more users and content managers on a wiki, the greater the network effect because more users attract more contributors, whose work attracts more users, and so on. For example, Wikipedia becomes more valuable to users as the number of its contributors increases.

Wikis internal to firms can be vital tools for collecting and disseminating knowledge throughout an organization, across geographic distances, and between functional business areas. For example, what U.S. employees call a "sale" may be called "an order booked" in the United Kingdom, an "order scheduled" in Germany, and an "order produced" in France. The corporate wiki can answer any questions about a business process or definition. Companies are also using wikis for documentation, reporting, project management, online dictionaries, and discussion groups. Of course, the more employees who use the corporate wiki, the greater the network effect and valued added for the company.

MASHUPS

A *mashup* is a website or web application that uses content from more than one source to create a completely new product or service. The term is typically used in the context of music; putting Jay-Z lyrics over a Radiohead song makes something old new. The web version of a mashup allows users to mix map data, photos, video, news feeds, blog entries, and so on to create content with a new purpose. Content used in mashups is typically sourced from an *application programming interface (API),* which is a set of routines, protocols, and tools for building software applications. A programmer then puts these building blocks together.

Most operating environments, such as Microsoft Windows, provide an API so that programmers can write applications consistent with them. Many people experimenting with mashups are using Microsoft, Google, eBay, Amazon, Flickr, and Yahoo! APIs, leading to the creation of mashup editors. *Mashup editors* are WYSIWYG, or What You See Is What You Get, tools. They provide a visual interface to build a mashup, often allowing the user to drag and drop data points into a web application.

Whoever thought technology could help sell bananas? Dole Organic now places three-digit farm codes on each banana and creates a mashup using Google Earth and its banana database. Socially and environmentally conscious buyers can plug the numbers into Dole's website and look at a bio of the farm where the bananas were raised. The site tells the story of the farm and its surrounding community, lists its organic certifications, posts some photos, and offers a link to satellite images of the farm in Google Earth. Customers can personally monitor the production and treatment of their fruit from the tree to the grocer. The process assures customers that their bananas have been raised to proper organic standards on an environmentally friendly, holistically minded plantation.[10]

The Challenges of Business 2.0

As much as Business 2.0 has positively changed the global landscape of business, a few challenges remain in open source software, user-contributed content systems, and collaboration systems, all highlighted in Figure 15.7. We'll briefly describe each one.

FIGURE 15.7

Challenges of Business 2.0

TECHNOLOGY DEPENDENCE

Many people today expect to be continuously connected, and their dependence on technology glues them to their web connections for everything from web conferencing for a university class or work project to making plans with friends for dinner. If a connection is down, how will they function? How long can people go without checking email, text messaging, or listening to free music on Pandora or watching on-demand television? As society becomes more technology-dependent, outages hold the potential to cause ever-greater havoc for people, businesses, and educational institutions.

INFORMATION VANDALISM

Open source and sharing are both major advantages of Business 2.0, and ironically they are major challenges as well. Allowing anyone to edit anything opens the door for individuals to purposely damage, destroy, or vandalize website content. One of the most famous examples of wiki vandalism occurred when a false biography entry read that John Seigenthaler Sr. was assistant to Attorney General Robert F. Kennedy in the early 1960s and was thought to have been directly involved in the assassinations of both Kennedy and his brother, President John F. Kennedy. Seigenthaler did work as an assistant to Robert Kennedy, but he was never involved in the assassinations. Wiki vandalism is a hot issue and for this reason wiki software can now store all versions of a web page, tracking updates and changes and ensuring the site can be restored to its original form if the site is vandalized. It can also color-code the background ensuring the user understands which areas have been validated and which areas have not. The real trick to wiki software is to determine which statements are true and which are false, a huge issue when considering how easy and frequently wiki software is updated and changed.[11]

VIOLATIONS OF COPYRIGHT AND PLAGIARISM

Online collaboration makes plagiarism as easy as clicking a mouse. Unfortunately a great deal of copyrighted material tends to find its ways to blogs and wikis where many times blame cannot be traced to a single person. Clearly stated copyright and plagiarism policies are a must for all corporate blogs and wikis.

Web 3.0: Defining the Next Generation of Online Business Opportunities

While Web 1.0 refers to static text-based information websites and Web 2.0 is about user-contributed content, Web 3.0 is based on "intelligent" web applications using natural language processing, machine-based learning and reasoning, and intelligent applications. Web 3.0 is the next step in the evolution of the Internet and web applications. Business leaders who explore its opportunities will be the first to market with competitive advantages.

Web 3.0 offers a way for people to describe information such that computers can start to understand the relationships among concepts and topics. To demonstrate the power of Web 3.0, let's look at a few sample relationships, such as Adam Sandler is a comedian, Lady Gaga is a singer, and Hannah is friends with Sophie. These are all examples of descriptions that can be added to web pages allowing computers to learn about relationships while displaying the information to humans. With this kind of information in place, there will be a far richer interaction between people and machines with Web 3.0.

Applying this type of advanced relationship knowledge to a company can create new opportunities. After all, businesses run on information. Where Web 2.0 brings people closer together with information using machines, Web 3.0 brings *machines* closer together using *information.* These new relationships unite people, machines, and information so a business can be smarter, quicker, more agile, and more successful.

One goal of Web 3.0 is to tailor online searches and requests specifically to users' preferences and needs. For example, instead of making multiple searches, the user might type a complex sentence or two in a Web 3.0 browser, such as "I want to see a funny movie and then eat at a good Mexican restaurant. What are my options?" The Web 3.0 browser will analyze the request, search the web for all possible answers, organize the results, and present them to the user.

Tim Berners-Lee, one of the founders of the WWW, has described the ***semantic web*** as a component of Web 3.0 that describes things in a way that computers can understand. The semantic web is not about links between web pages; rather it describes the relationships between *things* (such as A is a part of B and Y is a member of Z) and the properties of things (size, weight, age, price). If information about music, cars, concert tickets, and so on is stored in a way that describes the information and associated resource files, semantic web applications can collect information from many different sources, combine it, and present it to users in a meaningful way. Although Web 3.0 is still a bit speculative, some topics and features are certain to be included in it, such as:[12]

- Integration of legacy devices: the ability to use current devices such as iPhones, laptops, and so on, as credit cards, tickets, and reservations tools.
- Intelligent applications: the use of agents, machine learning, and semantic web concepts to complete intelligent tasks for users.
- Open ID: the provision of an online identity that can be easily carried to a variety of devices (cell phones, PCs) allowing for easy authentication across different websites.
- Open technologies: the design of websites and other software so they can be easily integrated and work together.
- A worldwide database: the ability for databases to be distributed and accessed from anywhere.

EGOVERNMENT: THE GOVERNMENT MOVES ONLINE

Recent business models that have arisen to enable organizations to take advantage of the Internet and create value are within egovernment. ***Egovernment*** involves the use of strategies and technologies to transform government(s) by improving the delivery of services and enhancing the quality of interaction between the citizen-consumer and all branches of government.

One example of an egovernment portal, FirstGov.gov, the official U.S. gateway to all government information, is the catalyst for a growing electronic government. Its powerful search engine and ever-growing collection of topical and customer-focused links connect users to millions of web pages, from the federal government, to local and tribal governments, to foreign nations around the world. Figure 15.8 highlights and adds to our discussion specific egovernment models.

MBUSINESS: SUPPORTING ANYWHERE BUSINESS

Internet-enabled mobile devices are quickly outnumbering personal computers. ***Mobile business*** (or ***mbusiness, mcommerce***) is the ability to purchase goods and services through a wireless Internet-enabled device. The emerging technology behind mbusiness is a mobile device equipped with a web-ready micro-browser that can perform the following services:

- Mobile entertainment—downloads for music, videos, games, voting, ring tones, as well as text-based messaging services.
- Mobile sales/marketing—advertising, campaigns, discounts, promotions, and coupons.

FIGURE 15.8

Extended Ebusiness
Models

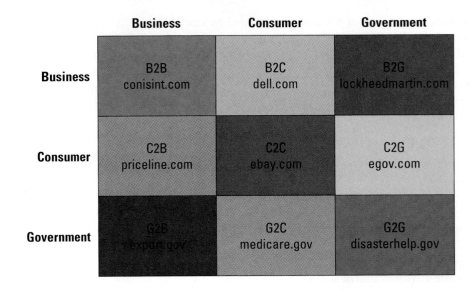

	Business	Consumer	Government
Business	B2B conisint.com	B2C dell.com	B2G lockheedmartin.com
Consumer	C2B priceline.com	C2C ebay.com	C2G egov.com
Government	G2B export.gov	G2C medicare.gov	G2G disasterhelp.gov

- Mobile banking—manage accounts, pay bills, receive alerts, and transfer funds.
- Mobile ticketing—purchase tickets for entertainment, transportation, and parking including the ability to automatically feed parking meters.
- Mobile payments—pay for goods and services including in-store purchases, home delivery, vending machines, taxis, gas, and so on.

Organizations face changes more extensive and far reaching in their implications than anything since the modern industrial revolution occurred in the early 1900s. Technology is a primary force driving these changes. Organizations that want to survive must recognize the immense power of technology, carry out required organizational changes in the face of it, and learn to operate in an entirely different way.

OPENING CASE STUDY QUESTIONS

1. Categorize Pinterest as an example of Web 1.0 (ebusiness) or Web 2.0 (Business 2.0).

2. What is open source software, and how could Pinterest take advantage of it?

Chapter Fifteen Case: Social Media and Ashton Kutcher

Where celebrities go, fans follow. The truism applies as much in social media as in the real world, David Karp noticed after famous artists began using his blogging service Tumblr. As a result, encouraging celebrities to set up accounts on the site has become "absolutely part of our road map and our business plan," Karp says. In fact, he recently hired a full-time employee to help high-profile users design and manage their blogs.

It's no secret that well-recognized players in a host of fields—from acting to athletics, music to politics—are using social media sites to connect with fans and promote their brands. Celebrities used to seek out promotion "in *People* magazine or *Vogue*," says

Robert Passikoff, president of Brand Keys, a researcher that tracks the value of celebrity brands. "It's now become a necessity to have a Facebook page."

But the benefits go both ways. Sites benefit greatly from the online cavalcade of stars. Oprah Winfrey's recent debut on microblogging service Twitter sent visits to the site sky-rocketing 43 percent over the previous week, according to analytics firm Hitwise. Facebook, Google's YouTube, Ning, and other Web 2.0 destinations have also seen swarms of activity around the profile pages of their famous members. And like Tumblr, social sites are going out of their way to keep the celebrities happy and coming back.

Obama on Myspace, Facebook, and Twitter

The Obama administration created profile pages on Myspace, Facebook, and Twitter. To accommodate 1600 Pennsylvania Avenue, News Corp.'s Myspace agreed to build ad-free pages and equipped the profile to get automatic updates from the White House's official blog. In some cases social networks give VIPs a heads-up on changes. Recently, Facebook worked with the handlers of select celebrity members, including CBS news anchor Katie Couric and French President Nicolas Sarkozy, to get feedback on the new design of the site before it was opened to the public. "We don't have a formalized support program for public figures, but we do offer some support," says Facebook spokeswoman Brandee Barker.

Some privileged members of Facebook have also been assigned "vanity URLs," or short, simple, personalized web addresses such as www.facebook.com/KatieCouric. Elsewhere the perks of fame are offered up more casually. Twitter co-founder Biz Stone credits high-profile users like actor Ashton Kutcher and basketball professional Shaquille O'Neal for bringing attention to the site of 140-character messages but says the company doesn't reserve any "special resources" for them. "Sometimes celebrities who love Twitter stop by and say hello," Stone says. "It's usually just a quiet tour and a lunchtime chat but it's really fun for us."

John Legend Taps Tumblr

In addition to their promotional value, social networking celebrities represent a potential revenue source for these young start-ups. Tumblr recently helped musician John Legend design a professional-looking blog that matches the look of his promotional site, created by Sony Music Entertainment. Tumblr's Karp says he took that project on at no charge—in part to bring in Legend's fans but also to explore whether it makes sense to offer similar services at a cost. "For people who want the reach on our network, who want to be able to take advantage of our platform, at some point this does turn into a premium service," he says.

Ning already collects monthly fees from some of its users, many of whom are celebrities. The site is free for anyone who wants to build their own social network but charges as much as $55 a month to users who prefer to keep their pages clear of ads or who want to collect revenue generated by ads on their pages. Although the service is not exclusive to stars, many of the most successful networks on Ning draw on the fame of their operators, including hip-hop artists 50 Cent and Q-Tip, rock band Good Charlotte, and Ultimate Fighting Championship titleholder BJ Penn. "The next generation of celebrities and social networks is in much richer and deeper collaborations [with fans] than what you see today on the more general social networks out there," says Ning CEO Gina Bianchini.

Many big names in business, including Dell CEO Michael Dell, use professional networking site LinkedIn more as a business tool than to amass legions of followers. Whatever their reasons for being on the site, LinkedIn uses the fact that executives from all of the 500 biggest companies are among its members to encourage other businesspeople to join the site, too.[13]

Questions

1. What is open source software, and can a business use it for a social networking platform?

2. Create a plan for how a start-up company could take advantage of Web 3.0, and generate ideas for the next website.

3. Evaluate the challenges facing social networking websites, and identify ways companies can prepare to face these issues.

Integrating Wireless Technology in Business

16.1. Describe the different wireless network categories.
16.2. Explain the different wireless network business applications.

16.3. Identify the benefits and challenges of business mobility.

Wireless Network Categories

As far back as 1896, Italian inventor Guglielmo Marconi demonstrated a wireless telegraph, and in 1927, the first radiotelephone system began operating between the United States and Great Britain. Automobile-based mobile telephones were offered in 1947. In 1964, the first communications satellite, Telstar, was launched, and soon after, satellite-relayed telephone service and television broadcasts became available. Wireless networks have exploded since then, and newer technologies are now maturing that allow companies and home users alike to take advantage of both wired and wireless networks.[1]

Before delving into a discussion of wireless networks, we should distinguish between mobile and wireless, terms that are often used synonymously but actually have different meanings. *Mobile* means the technology can travel with the user, for instance, users can download software, email messages, and web pages onto a laptop or other mobile device for portable reading or reference. Information collected while on the road can be synchronized with a PC or company server. *Wireless,* on the other hand, refers to any type of operation accomplished without the use of a hard-wired connection. There are many environments in which the network devices are wireless but not mobile, such as wireless home or office networks with stationary PCs and printers. Some forms of mobility do not require a wireless connection; for instance, a worker can use a wired laptop at home, shut down the laptop, drive to work, and attach the laptop to the company's wired network.

In many networked environments today, users are both wireless and mobile; for example, a mobile user commuting to work on a train can maintain a VoIP call and multiple TCP/IP connections at the same time. Figure 16.1 categorizes wireless networks by type.

PERSONAL AREA NETWORKS

A *personal area network (PAN)* provides communication for devices owned by a single user that work over a short distance. PANs are used to transfer files, including email, calendar appointments, digital photos, and music. A PAN can provide communication between a wireless headset and a cell phone or between a computer and a wireless mouse or keyboard. Personal area networks generally cover a range of less than 10 meters (about 30 feet). *Bluetooth* is a wireless PAN technology that transmits signals over short distances among cell phones, computers, and other devices. The name is borrowed from

LO 16.1 Describe the different wireless network categories.

FIGURE 16.1

Wireless Communication
Network Categories

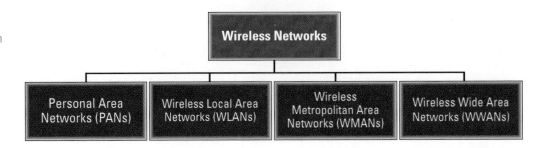

Harald Bluetooth, a king in Denmark more than 1,000 years ago. Bluetooth eliminates the need for wires, docking stations, or cradles, as well as all the special attachments that typically accompany personal computing devices. Bluetooth operates at speeds up to 1 Mbps within a range of 33 feet or less. Devices that are Bluetooth-enabled communicate directly with each other in pairs, like a handshake. Up to eight can be paired simultaneously. And Bluetooth is not just for technology devices. An array of Bluetooth-equipped appliances, such as a television set, a stove, and a thermostat, can be controlled from a cell phone—all from a remote location.[2]

WIRELESS LANs

A *wireless LAN (WLAN)* is a local area network that uses radio signals to transmit and receive data over distances of a few hundred feet. An *access point (AP)* is the computer or network device that serves as an interface between devices and the network. Each computer initially connects to the access point and then to other computers on the network. A *wireless access point (WAP)* enables devices to connect to a wireless network to communicate with each other. WAPs with *multiple-in/multiple-out (MIMO) technology* have multiple transmitters and receivers, allowing them to send and receive greater amounts of data than traditional networking devices. *Wireless fidelity (Wi-Fi)* is a means by which portable devices can connect wirelessly to a local area network, using access points that send and receive data via radio waves. Wi-Fi has a maximum range of about 1,000 feet in open areas such as a city park and 250 to 400 feet in closed areas such as an office building. *Wi-Fi infrastructure* includes the inner workings of a Wi-Fi service or utility, including the signal transmitters, towers, or poles, along with additional equipment required to send out a Wi-Fi signal. Most WLANs use a Wi-Fi infrastructure in which a wireless device, often a laptop, communicates through an access point or base station by means of, for instance, wireless fidelity.

Areas around access points where users can connect to the Internet are often called hotspots. *Hotspots* are designated locations where Wi-Fi access points are publically available. Hotspots are found in places such as restaurants, airports, and hotels—places where business professionals tend to gather. Hotspots are extremely valuable for those business professionals who travel extensively and need access to business applications. By positioning hotspots at strategic locations throughout a building, campus, or city, network administrators can keep Wi-Fi users continuously connected to a network or the Internet, no matter where they roam.[3]

In a Wi-Fi network, the user's laptop or other Wi-Fi-enabled device has a wireless adapter that translates data into a radio signal and transmits it to the wireless access point. The wireless access point, which consists of a transmitter with an antenna that is often built into the hardware, receives the signal and decodes it. The access point then sends the information to the Internet over a wired broadband connection, as illustrated in Figure 16.2. When receiving data, the wireless access point takes the information from the Internet, translates it into a radio signal, and sends it to the computer's wireless adapter. If too many people try to use the Wi-Fi network at one time, they can experience interference or dropped connections. Most laptop computers come with built-in wireless transmitters and software to enable computers to automatically discover the existence of a Wi-Fi network.

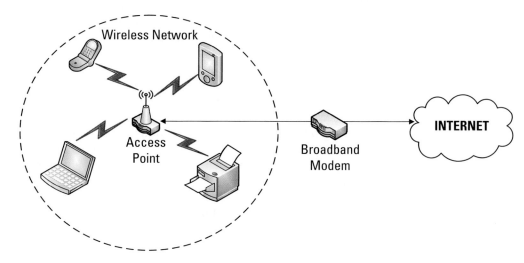

FIGURE 16.2

Wi-Fi Networks

Wi-Fi operates at considerably higher frequencies than cell phones use, which allows greater bandwidth. The bandwidths associated with Wi-Fi are separated according to several wireless networking standards, known as 802.11, for carrying out wireless local area network communication. The ***Institute of Electrical and Electronics Engineers (IEEE)*** researches and institutes electrical standards for communication and other technologies. ***IEEE 802.11n (or Wireless-N)*** is the newest standard for wireless networking. Compared with earlier standards such as 802.11b, Wireless-N offers faster speeds, more flexibility, and greater range. The organization denotes different versions of the standard—for example, Wireless-G and Wireless-N—by a lowercase letter at the end of this number. Figure 16.3 outlines the bandwidths associated with a few of these standards.[4]

An increasing number of digital devices, including most laptops, netbooks, tablets such as the iPad, and even printers are incorporating Wi-Fi technology into their design. Cell phones are incorporating Wi-Fi so they can automatically switch from the cell network to a faster Wi-Fi network where available for data communications. BlackBerrys and iPhones can connect to an access point for data communications such as email and web browsing, but not for voice unless they use the services of Skype or another VoIP.

WIRELESS MANs

A ***wireless MAN (WMAN)*** is a metropolitan area network that uses radio signals to transmit and receive data. WMAN technologies have not been highly successful to date, mainly because they are not widely available, at least in the United States. One with the potential for success is ***Worldwide Interoperability for Microwave Access (WiMAX),*** a communications technology aimed at providing high-speed wireless data over metropolitan area networks. In many respects, WiMAX operates like Wi-Fi, only over greater distances and with higher bandwidths. A WiMAX tower serves as an access point and can connect to the Internet or another tower. A single tower can provide up to 3,000 square miles of coverage, so only a few are needed to cover an entire city. WiMAX can support data communications at a rate of 70 Mbps. In New York City, for example, one or two WiMAX access points around the city might meet the heavy demand more cheaply than

Wi-Fi Standard	Bandwidth
802.11a	54 Mbps
802.11b	11 Mbps
802.11g	54 Mbps
802.11n	140 Mbps

FIGURE 16.3

Wi-Fi Standards and Bandwidths

hundreds of Wi-Fi access points. WiMAX can also cover remote or rural areas where cabling is limited or nonexistent, and where it is too expensive or physically difficult to install wires for the relatively few users.[5]

WiMAX can provide both line-of-sight and non-line-of-sight service. A non-line-of-sight service uses a small antenna on a mobile device that connects to a WiMAX tower less than six miles away where transmissions are disrupted by physical obstructions. This form of service is similar to Wi-Fi but has much broader coverage area and higher bandwidths. A line-of-sight option offers a fixed antenna that points at the WiMAX tower from a rooftop or pole. This option is much faster than non-line-of-sight service, and the distance between the WiMAX tower and antenna can be as great as 30 miles. Figure 16.4 illustrates the WiMAX infrastructure.[6]

Some cellular companies are evaluating WiMAX as a means of increasing bandwidth for a variety of data-intensive applications such as those used by smartphones. Sprint Nextel and Clearwire are building a nationwide WiMAX network in the United States. WiMAX-capable gaming devices, laptops, cameras, and even cell phones are being manufactured by companies including Intel, Motorola, Nokia, and Samsung.[7]

WIRELESS WAN—CELLULAR COMMUNICATION SYSTEM

A *wireless WAN (WWAN)* is a wide area network that uses radio signals to transmit and receive data. WWAN technologies can be divided into two categories: cellular communication systems and satellite communication systems.

Although mobile communications have been around for generations, including the walkie-talkies of the 1940s and mobile radiophones of the 1950s, it was not until 1983 that cellular telephony became available commercially. A cell phone is a device for voice and data, communicating wirelessly through a collection of stationary ground-based sites

FIGURE 16.4

WiMAX Infrastructure

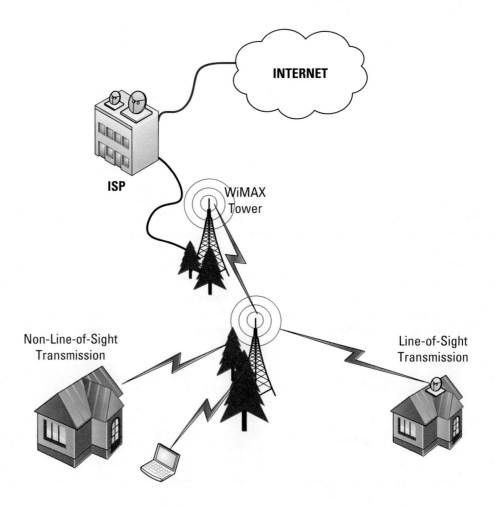

FIGURE 16.5

Cell Phone Communication
System Overview

Cell

Each cell is typically sized
at about 10 square miles

Each cell has a base
station that
consists of an
antennae or tower
to relay signals

called base stations, each of which is linked to its nearest neighbor stations. Base station coverage areas are about 10 square miles and are called cells, as Figure 16.5 illustrates.

The first cell phone was demonstrated in 1973 by Motorola (it weighed almost 2 pounds), but it took 10 years for the technology to become commercially available. The Motorola DynaTAC, marketed in 1983, weighed one pound and cost about $4,000. Cellular technology has come a long way since then.[8]

Cellular systems were originally designed to provide voice services to mobile customers and thus were designed to interconnect cells to the public telephone network. Increasingly, they provide data services and Internet connectivity. There are more cell phones than landline phones in many countries today, and it is no longer uncommon for cell phones to be the only phones people have.

Cell phones have morphed into **smartphones** that offer more advanced computing ability and connectivity than basic cell phones. They allow for web browsing, emailing, listening to music, watching video, computing, keeping track of contacts, sending text messages, and taking and sending photos. The Apple iPhone and RIM BlackBerry are examples of smartphones.

Cell phones and smartphones, or mobile phones as they are collectively called, need a provider to offer services, much as computer users need an ISP to connect to the Internet. The most popular mobile phone providers in the United States are AT&T, Sprint, T-Mobile, and Verizon. They offer different cell phones, features, coverage areas, and services. One of the newer services is third-generation, or **3G,** services that bring wireless broadband to mobile phones. Figure 16.6 lists the cell phone generations. The 3G networks let users surf web pages, enjoy streaming music, watch video-on-demand programming, download and play 3-D games, and participate in social media and teleconferencing. **Streaming** is a method of sending audio and video files over the Internet in such a way that the user can view the file while it is being transferred. Streaming is not limited to cellular usage; all wireless and even wired networks can take advantage of this method. The most obvious advantage is speed, a direct benefit for mobile and wireless devices since they are still not as fast as their wired counterparts.

WIRELESS WAN—SATELLITE COMMUNICATION SYSTEM

The other wireless WAN technology is a satellite communication system. A **satellite** is a space station that orbits the Earth receiving and transmitting signals from Earth-based stations over a wide area. When satellite systems first came into consideration in the 1990s, the goal was to provide wireless voice and data coverage for the entire planet, without the need for mobile phones to roam between many different provider networks.

FIGURE 16.6

Cell Phone Generations

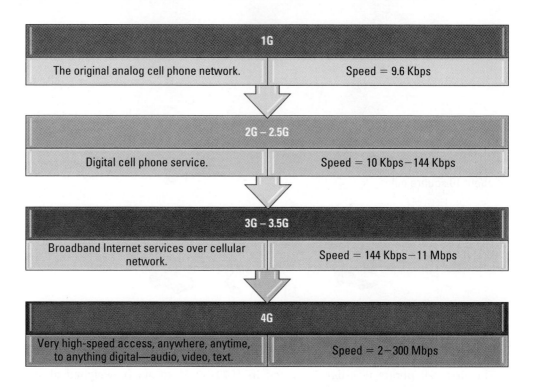

1G	
The original analog cell phone network.	Speed = 9.6 Kbps

2G – 2.5G	
Digital cell phone service.	Speed = 10 Kbps – 144 Kbps

3G – 3.5G	
Broadband Internet services over cellular network.	Speed = 144 Kbps – 11 Mbps

4G	
Very high-speed access, anywhere, anytime, to anything digital—audio, video, text.	Speed = 2 – 300 Mbps

But by the time satellite networks were ready for commercial use, they had already been overtaken by cellular systems.

The devices used for satellite communication range from handheld units to mobile base stations to fixed satellite dish receivers. The peak data transmission speeds range from 2.4 Kbps to 2 Mbps. For the everyday mobile professional, satellite communication may not provide a compelling benefit, but for people requiring voice and data access from remote locations or guaranteed coverage in nonremote locations, satellite technology is a viable solution.

Conventional communication satellites move in stationary orbits approximately 22,000 miles above Earth. A newer satellite medium, the low-orbit satellite, travels much closer to Earth and is able to pick up signals from weak transmitters. Low-orbit satellites also consume less power and cost less to launch than conventional satellites. With satellite networks, businesspeople almost anywhere in the world have access to full communication capabilities, including voice, videoconferencing, and Internet access. Figure 16.7 briefly illustrates the satellite communication system.[9]

Business Applications of Wireless Networks

Companies of all types and sizes have relied on wireless technology for years. Shipping and trucking companies developed some of the earliest wireless applications to help

FIGURE 16.7

Satellite Communication System

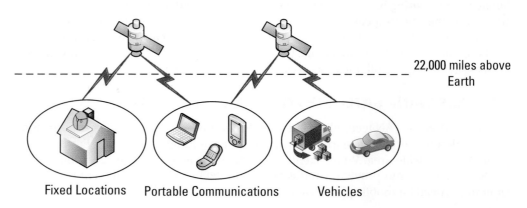

22,000 miles above Earth

Fixed Locations   Portable Communications   Vehicles

track vehicles and valuable cargo, optimize the logistics of their global operations, perfect their delivery capabilities, and reduce theft and damage. Government agencies such as the National Aeronautics and Space Administration and the Department of Defense have relied on satellite technologies for decades to track the movement of troops, weaponry, and military assets; to receive and broadcast data; and to communicate over great distances.

Wireless technologies have also aided the creation of new applications. Some build upon and improve existing capabilities. UPS, for example, is combining several types of wireless network technologies from Bluetooth to WWANs and deploying scanners and wearable data-collection terminals to automate and standardize package management and tracking across all its delivery centers. Figure 16.8 displays the three business applications taking advantage of wireless technologies.

Radio-Frequency Identification (RFID)

Global Positioning Systems (GPS)

Geographic Information Systems (GIS)

FIGURE 16.8

Wireless Business Applications

RADIO-FREQUENCY IDENTIFICATION (RFID)

Radio-frequency identification (RFID) uses electronic tags and labels to identify objects wirelessly over short distances. It holds the promise of replacing existing identification technologies such as the bar code. RFID wirelessly exchanges information between a tagged object and a reader/writer. An ***RFID tag*** is an electronic identification device that is made up of a chip and antenna. An ***RFID reader (RFID interrogator)*** is a transmitter/receiver that reads the contents of RFID tags in the area. A RFID system is comprised of one or more RFID tags, one or more RFID readers, two or more antennas (one on the tag and one on each reader), RFID application software, and a computer system or server, as Figure 16.9 illustrates. Tags, often smaller than a grain of rice, can be applied to books or clothing items as part of an adhesive bar-code label, or included in items such as ID cards or packing labels. Readers can be stand-alone devices, such as for self-checkout in a grocery store, integrated with a mobile device for portable use, or built in as in printers. The reader sends a wireless request that is received by all tags in the area that have been programmed to listen to wireless signals. Tags receive the signal via their antennas and respond by transmitting their stored data. The tag can hold many types of data, including a product number, installation instructions, and history of activity (such as the date the item was shipped). The reader receives a signal from the tag using its antenna, interprets the information sent, and transfers the data to the associated computer system or server.

Passive RFID tags do not have a power source, whereas ***active RFID tags*** have their own transmitter and a power source (typically a battery). The power source runs the microchip's circuitry and broadcasts a signal to the reader (similar to the way a cell phone transmits signals to a base station). Passive RFID tags draw power from the RFID reader, which sends out electromagnetic waves that induce a current in the tag's antenna. ***Semi-passive RFID tags*** use a battery to run the microchip's circuitry, but communicate by drawing power from the RFID reader. ***Asset tracking*** occurs when

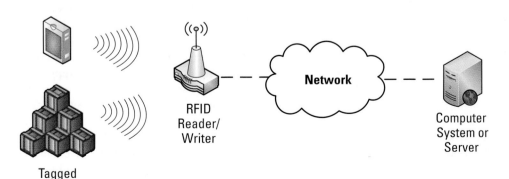

FIGURE 16.9

Elements of an RFID system

a company places active or semi-passive RFID tags on expensive products or assets to gather data on the items' location with little or no manual intervention. Asset tracking allows a company to focus on its supply chain, reduce theft, identify the last known user of assets, and automate maintenance routines. Active and semi-passive tags are useful for tracking high-value goods that need to be scanned over long ranges, such as railway cars on a track. The cost of active and semi-passive RFID tags is significant; hence, low-cost items typically use passive RFID tags.

The ***RFID accelerometer*** is a device that measures the acceleration (the rate of change of velocity) of an item and is used to track truck speeds or taxi cab speeds. ***Chipless RFID tags*** use plastic or conductive polymers instead of silicon-based microchips, allowing them to be washed or exposed to water without damaging the chip. Examples of the innovative uses of RFID include:

- RFID chips injected under the skin of animals using a syringe can help ranchers meet regulations, track wild animals for ecological studies, and return lost pets to their owners.

- Retail stores use RFID to track and monitor inventory. Hospitals and pharmaceutical companies meet government regulations and standards with RFID. Even local libraries are using RFID to control theft and speed up the checkout process.

- Car manufacturers install RFID antitheft systems. Toll roads use RFID to collect payments from passing cars.

- Hospitals track patients', doctors', and nurses' locations to facilitate emergency situations and ensure safety. RFID also tracks equipment location to ensure quick response times during an emergency.

- American Express and MasterCard use RFID for automatic payments.

- Walmart and other large retailers use RFID to maintain inventory, stop shoplifting, and speed customer checkout processes.[10]

GLOBAL POSITIONING SYSTEM (GPS)

A ***global positioning system (GPS)*** is a satellite-based navigation system providing extremely accurate position, time, and speed information. The U.S. Department of Defense developed the technology in the early 1970s and later made it available to the public. GPS uses 24 global satellites that orbit Earth, sending signals to a receiver that can communicate with three or four satellites at a time. A GPS receiver can be a separate unit connected to a mobile device using cable or wireless technology such as Bluetooth, or it can be included in devices such as mobile phones or vehicle navigation systems. ***Automatic vehicle location (AVL)*** uses GPS tracking to track vehicles. AVL systems use a GPS receiver in the vehicle that links to a control center. Garmin is one of the more popular manufacturers of GPS tracking systems, offering vehicle tracking, phone and laptop integration, and hiker navigation for water and air.

The satellites broadcast signals constantly, while the receiver measures the time it takes for the signals to reach it. This measurement, which uses the speed of the signal to determine the distance, is taken from three distinct satellites to provide precise location information. The time measurements depend on high-powered clocks on each satellite and must be precise, because an error of one-thousandth of a second can result in a location variation of more than 200 miles. GPS can produce very accurate results, typically within 5 to 50 feet of the actual location (military versions have higher accuracy). GPS also provides latitude, longitude, and elevation information. ***Latitude*** represents a north/south measurement of position. ***Longitude*** represents an east/west measurement of position. ***Geocache*** is a GPS technology adventure game that posts the longitude and latitude location for an item on the Internet for users to find. GPS users find the geocache and typically sign a guest book or take an item and leave an item for the next adventure players to find. Caches are often placed in locations that are interesting or challenging for people to discover. A ***geocoin,*** a round coin-sized object, is uniquely numbered and hidden in geocache. Geocoins can also be shaped to match a theme such as the state of Colorado or a birthday party hat. Geocoins are often decorative or commemorative, making them collectible and highly valuable for technology adventures.

GPS applications are in every kind of company vehicle these days—from police cars to bulldozers, from dump trucks to mayoral limousines. Emergency response systems use GPS to track each of their vehicles and so dispatch those closest to the scene of an accident. If a vehicle is missing, its GPS locator can help locate it. *Estimated time of arrival (ETA)* is the time of day of an expected arrival at a certain destination and is typically used for navigation applications. *Estimated time enroute (ETE)* is the time remaining before reaching a destination using the present speed and is typically used for navigation applications.

GEOGRAPHIC INFORMATION SYSTEMS (GIS)

GPS provides the foundation for geographic information systems. A *geographic information system (GIS)* stores, views, and analyzes geographic data creating, multidimensional charts or maps. For example, GIs are monitoring global warming by measuring the speed of glaciers melting in Canada, Greenland, and Antarctica. *Cartography* is the science and art of making an illustrated map or chart. GIS allows users to interpret, analyze, and visualize data in different ways that reveal patterns and trends in the form of reports, charts, and maps. *Edge matching (warping, rubber sheeting)* occurs when paper maps are laid edge to edge and items that run across maps but do not match are reconfigured to match. Edge matching is a critical component of creating a GIS database because map misalignments occur frequently for many reasons, including survey error and cartographic errors. *GIS map automation* links business assets to a centralized system where they can be tracked and monitored over time.

Spatial data (geospatial data or geographic information) identifies the geographic location of features and boundaries on Earth, such as natural or constructed features, oceans, and more. Spatial data can be mapped and is stored as coordinates and topology. A GIS accesses, manipulates, and analyzes spatial data. *Geocoding* in spatial databases is a coding process that assigns a digital map feature to an attribute that serves as a unique ID (tract number, node number) or classification (soil type, zoning category). GIS professionals are certified in geocoding practices to ensure industry standards are met when classifying spatial data.

Companies that deal in transportation combine GISs with database and GPS technology. Airlines and shipping companies can plot routes with up-to-the-second information about the location of all their transport vehicles. Hospitals can locate their medical staff with GIS and sensors that pick up transmissions from ID badges. Automobiles have GPSs linked to GIS maps that display the car's location and driving directions on a dashboard screen. GM offers the OnStar system, which sends a continuous stream of information to the OnStar center about the car's exact location.

Some mobile phone providers combine GPS and GIS capabilities so they can locate users within a geographical area about the size of a tennis court to assist emergency services such as 911. Farmers can use GIS to map and analyze fields, telling them where to apply the proper amounts of seed, fertilizer, and herbicides.

A GIS can find the closest gas station or bank or determine the best way to get to a particular location. But it is also good at finding patterns, such as finding the most feasible location to hold a conference according to where the majority of a company's customers live and work. GIS can present this information in a visually effective way.

Some common GIS uses include:

- **Finding what is nearby.** Given a specific location, the GIS finds sources within a defined radius. These might be entertainment venues, medical facilities, restaurants, or gas stations. Users can also use GIS to locate vendors that sell a specific item they want and get the results as a map of the surrounding area or an address.

- **Routing information.** Once users have an idea where they want to go, GIS can provide directions to get there using either a map or step-by-step instructions. Routing information can be especially helpful when combined with search services.

- **Sending information alerts.** Users may want to be notified when information relevant to them becomes available near their location. A commuter might want to know that a section of the highway has traffic congestion, or a shopper might want to be notified when a favorite store is having a sale on a certain item.

- **Mapping densities.** GIS can map population and event densities based on a standard area unit, such as square miles, making it easy to see distributions and concentrations. Police can map crime incidents to determine where additional patrolling is required, and stores can map customer orders to identify ideal delivery routes.

- **Mapping quantities.** Users can map quantities to find out where the most or least of a feature may be. For example, someone interested in opening a specialty coffee shop can determine how many others are already in the area, and city planners can determine where to build more parks.[11]

A GIS can provide information and insight to both mobile users and people at fixed locations. Google Earth combines satellite imagery, geographic data, and Google's search capabilities to create a virtual globe that users can download to a computer or mobile device. Not only does this provide useful business benefits, but it also allows for many educational opportunities. Instead of just talking about the Grand Canyon, an instructor can use Google Earth to view that region.

GPS and GIS both utilize **location-based services (LBS),** applications that use location information to provide a service. LBS is designed to give mobile users instant access to personalized local content and range from 911 applications to buddy finders ("Let me know when my friend is within 1,000 feet") to games (treasure hunts) to location-based advertising ("Visit the Starbucks on the corner and get $1.00 off a latte"). Many LBS applications complement GPS and GIS, such as:

- Emergency services
- Field service management
- Find-it services
- Mapping
- Navigation
- Tracking assets
- Traffic information
- Vehicle location
- Weather information
- Wireless advertising[12]

Just as Facebook and Twitter helped fuel the Web 2.0 revolution, applications such as Foursquare, Gowalla, and Loopt are bringing attention to LBS. Each application is a mobile phone service that helps social media users find their friends' location. Facebook and Twitter have added location-based services to complement their applications.

LO 16.3 Identify the benefits and challenges of business mobility.

Benefits of Business Mobility

Mobile and wireless development has come a long way. Consider Dr Pepper/Seven-Up Inc., of Plano, Texas, which monitors the operation of its antenna-equipped vending machines via wireless technology. The company collects inventory, sales, and "machine-health" data and polls the machines daily; managers and salespeople can access the stored information via its intranet. Dr Pepper/Seven-Up Inc. understands the business value of the data, both for daily operations and for data-mining purposes. The information collected is helpful for deciding where to place new vending machines, such as in front of a Target store or a high-traffic supermarket. Figure 16.10 lists many of the advantages of wireless networks.[13]

FIGURE 16.10

Advantages of Wireless
Networks

ENHANCES MOBILITY

Enhancing mobility is one of the greatest advantages provided by wireless networks. It allows activities that were formerly tied to physical locations to be performed almost anywhere. Companies can bring employees, information, and computing resources to a job location instead of forcing the job to be located at the company's site. Consider how mobile phones alone have changed the way most companies operate. Executives and sales professionals can conduct business wherever they are, eliminating downtime during travel and speeding their response to customers. Mobility means more face-to-face contact with customers and business partners. Even people with internal jobs, such as custodians, floor salespeople, production supervisors, and emergency room doctors, keep moving throughout the day. Instead of returning periodically to their offices or other fixed location for information access or doing without, they can rely on wireless technology to bring that access to them, where and when they need it.

Mobility gives a company the power to place the right resources in the right place at the right time. It allows for the redistribution of operations to gain efficiencies or react to changing conditions. For example, a mobile checkout stand allows additional checkouts to be set up during holiday rushes and store sales events.

PROVIDES IMMEDIATE DATA ACCESS

Mobility allows activities to be performed where needed; however, providing immediate data access offers the value. Wireless networks can support a wide variety of immediate data access options, from collecting usage data using Wi-Fi or RFID technologies when driving past a water meter to having full Internet access on a laptop or other mobile device. A mobile worker can submit a status report or credit card scan or be notified about a new assignment. When up-to-the-second data are required, such as for stock transactions and credit card authorizations, wireless technology is the only mobile option. Employees can "pull" data by linking to the source and requesting the desired information, or "push" it by sending an alert to a user's device or automatically refreshing data.

Whether through voice, email, or text messaging, the quality and frequency of information exchange increases with wireless access. An emergency room doctor can be notified of lab test results immediately upon completion. A service worker and appropriate information can be rerouted to a higher-priority assignment. A salesperson can submit updates right after a sales call.

Instant access to customer profiles, account history, and current order status significantly improves the quality of interactions with customers, suppliers, and business partners. A salesperson can check inventories, generate quotes, take orders, and resolve problems all at the customer's site. Field workers can identify problems with online manuals and diagnostic tools. Decision making is always improved by access to accurate and current information.

INCREASES LOCATION AND MONITORING CAPABILITY

The ability to locate and monitor assets reduces losses from theft and damage, gathers information from remote or difficult-to-reach locations, enhances safety, and makes possible a new wave of personalized services. RFID tags permit the tracking of assets from cattle to container shipments. LBS devices send storm data from buoys far at sea. LBS in cars provide driving directions and enable rescuers to locate the vehicle in case of an accident.

Through a combination of LBS devices and applications, companies can trace shipments from point of origin to final destination. More advanced applications can monitor their condition (e.g., ensuring that refrigeration equipment is operating) and notify users of tampering or attempted theft. Wireless applications can collect billing data, monitor operating conditions, gather scientific measurements, and relay requests for service from locations that are too dangerous, difficult, or costly to access by other means. Oil companies use wireless technology to monitor offshore oil rig equipment. We have seen that other wireless applications can tailor information to the needs of the user, such as listing resources near a given location or offering local traffic reports and driving directions.

IMPROVES WORK FLOW

Many work flows and job responsibilities are constrained by paper or wired processes. Wireless technology offers the opportunity to redesign and simplify those processes to be faster, cheaper, and more responsive, and to eliminate redundant activities, integrate activities and services, and redistribute tasks. For example, when mobile workers capture data on paper forms and clerical workers enter it into computer systems, the process is costly, time-consuming, and error-prone. Using a wireless device for the original data capture eliminates the need to reenter the data, increases data accuracy, and provides immediate access to results. Rental car staff members now use wireless devices to quickly and easily check and enter mileage, fuel levels, and damage for returning cars. Drivers receive faster service and staff can focus on providing value-added services.

PROVIDES MOBILE BUSINESS OPPORTUNITIES

Unlike ebusiness, which normally requires desktop or laptop computers to connect to the Internet, mbusiness offers the advantages of making a purchase via the Internet an anywhere, anytime experience. It provides consumers with the ability to obtain information and order goods and services quickly and easily using a mobile device. The growing popularity of iPhones along with iPhone apps have helped fuel the growth of mbusiness.

A few mbusiness offerings include:

■ **Digital purchases.** The most suitable purchase for a mobile user is for products that can be downloaded and used immediately such as music and (electronic) books.

- **Location-based services.** The ability for merchants to capture and react to a user's current location and requirements can be a powerful tool for selling products and services.

- **Mobile banking and payments.** Using a mobile device can provide access to personal bank accounts to view account history and execute transactions. In addition, a mobile device can be used for making payments, essentially acting as digital cash. For example, someone can order and pay for a Starbucks latte using a mobile device and app.

- **Mobile shopping.** Most forms of shopping may be impractical using mobile devices; however, some forms of purchases lend themselves to mbusiness. For example, having the ability to purchase movie tickets for a show playing the same evening can be quite valuable. Mobile devices can also be used for comparison shopping. Before making a purchase, a shopper in a retail store may want to first see what the current price of a product is from another vendor to ensure he is getting a good price.[14]

PROVIDES ALTERNATIVE TO WIRING

Wireless networks provide an attractive alternative where physical constraints or convenience make wired solutions costly or impractical. Many office buildings already have a maze of wires in their ceilings, floors, and walls representing many generations of network technologies. Tracing existing wires or adding new lines becomes increasingly cumbersome and difficult. In other cases, building design or aesthetic considerations make wired networks unattractive. In manufacturing facilities or production lines with moving equipment or complex setups, wireless connections are simpler to implement and safer for workers. The higher per unit cost of a wireless solution may be more than offset by its advantages over physical lines.

WLANs allow MIS employees to relocate equipment at will, attractive for trade shows, temporary offices, and seasonal selling areas. In conference rooms, WLANs enable attendees to bring laptops or other Wi-Fi-enabled devices for Internet access.

Finally, wireless technology allows voice and data connections with ships at sea, passengers in airliners, and travelers in remote locations. In developing countries, it is a means to bypass the effort and expense of installing and maintaining telephone lines across inhospitable terrain.

Challenges of Business Mobility

The mobile employee has become the norm rather than the exception, driven by lifestyle choices, productivity gains, and technology improvements. Although the advantages of using wireless networks are significant, added challenges exist such as protecting against theft, protecting wireless connections, preventing viruses on mobile devices, and addressing privacy concerns with RFID and LBS (see Figure 16.11).

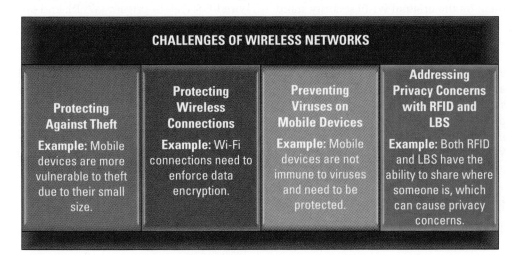

FIGURE 16.11

Challenges of Using Wireless Networks

CHALLENGES OF WIRELESS NETWORKS

Protecting Against Theft

Example: Mobile devices are more vulnerable to theft due to their small size.

Protecting Wireless Connections

Example: Wi-Fi connections need to enforce data encryption.

Preventing Viruses on Mobile Devices

Example: Mobile devices are not immune to viruses and need to be protected.

Addressing Privacy Concerns with RFID and LBS

Example: Both RFID and LBS have the ability to share where someone is, which can cause privacy concerns.

PROTECTING AGAINST THEFT

Any mobile device is vulnerable to loss no matter how big or small it is. The company may face significant exposure from stolen IDs, passwords, encryption keys, and confidential information if the device falls into the wrong hands, especially if the theft is not discovered or reported immediately and the company does not have time to revoke access.

Power-on passwords—passwords implemented at the hardware level that must be entered before gaining access to the computer—are the first line of defense against unauthorized use. Companies should activate these passwords before giving their workforce the devices. They should also prohibit storing passwords on devices and periodically monitor compliance with the policy. Companies need to consider encrypting and password-protecting data stored on the device, including any flash drives or other mobile storage devices. In addition, some device management tools can send messages to a device to lock it or destroy its contents, which can be an attractive security feature.

PROTECTING WIRELESS CONNECTIONS

Network intrusions can occur if access codes or passwords are stored on a device that is lost or stolen. However, any time a wireless network connects to a wired one, the wireless network can serve as a conduit for a hacker to gain entry into an otherwise secure wired network. This risk is especially high if the wireless network is not sufficiently secured in its own right.

Before the emergence of the Internet, hackers generally had to be physically present within the corporate complex to gain access to a wired network. The thousands, if not millions, of access points enabled by the Internet now allow hackers to work from a distance. This threat has spawned a variety of different security techniques from firewalls to VPNs to SSL and HTTPS.

Several techniques can secure wireless networks from unauthorized access whether used separately or in combination. One method is authenticating Wi-Fi access points. Because Wi-Fi communications are broadcast, anyone within listening distance can intercept communications. Every time someone uses an unsecured website via a public Wi-Fi access point, his or her log-on name and password are sent over the open airwaves, with a high risk that someone might "eavesdrop" or capture log-on names, passwords, credit card numbers, and other vital information. **Wired equivalent privacy (WEP)** is an encryption algorithm designed to protect wireless transmission data. If using a Wi-Fi connection, WEP encrypts the data using a key that converts the data into a non-human readable form. The purpose of WEP was to provide wireless networks with the equivalent level of security as wired networks. Unfortunately, the underlying technology behind WEP has been demonstrated to be relatively insecure compared to newer protocols such as WPA. WLANs that use Wi-Fi have a built-in security mechanism called **Wi-Fi Protected Access (WPA),** a wireless security protocol to protect Wi-Fi networks. It is an improvement on the original Wi-Fi security standard, Wired Equivalent Privacy (WEP), and provides more sophisticated data encryption and user authentication. Anyone who wants to use an access point must know the WPA encryption key to access the Wi-Fi connection.

War chalking is the practice of tagging pavement with codes displaying where Wi-Fi access is available. The codes for war chalking tell other users the kind of access available, the speed of the network, and if the network is secured. **War driving** is deliberately searching for Wi-Fi signals while driving by in a vehicle. Many individuals who participate in war driving simply map where Wi-Fi networks are available. Other individuals have a more malicious intent and use war driving to hack or break into these networks. War driving has been a controversial practice since its inception and has raised the awareness of the importance of wireless network security.

PREVENTING VIRUSES ON A MOBILE DEVICE

The potential for contracting viruses on mobile devices is becoming a reality. The need for virus protection at the device level is critical. Any device that can access the Internet or receive email is at risk of catching a virus and passing it on to other devices. Because of the memory limitations of most mobile devices, antivirus software has typically been hosted on a PC or laptop, with the mobile device physically connecting to a PC or laptop to perform virus scanning. The first known mobile phone virus, named Cabir, appeared several years ago and infected only a small number of Bluetooth-enabled phones that carried out no malicious action; the virus was created by a group of malware developers to prove it could be done. The developers sent Cabir to anti-virus researchers, so they could begin to develop a solution to a problem that promises to get a lot worse. At present, mobile phone viruses do not do much damage, but if protective measures are not taken, they could be as devastating as their computer counterparts.[15]

The best way to protect against mobile phone viruses is the same way users protect themselves from computer viruses—never open anything that seems suspicious. Another method is to turn Bluetooth discoverable mode off. By setting the Bluetooth option to "hidden," other devices cannot detect it and send it the virus. In addition, install some type of security software on the mobile device. Many of the mobile phone manufacturers, such as Nokia and Samsung, have developed security software for their mobile phones that detect and remove a virus as well as protect it from getting certain viruses in the first place.

ADDRESSING PRIVACY CONCERNS WITH RFID AND LBS

As technology advances, the potential for privacy infringement does as well. RFID already has the capability to determine the distance of a tag from the reader location. It is not difficult to imagine that retailers could determine the location of individuals within the store and target specific advertisements to them based upon past purchases and shopping and behavior patterns. Many consumers would consider gathering such information intrusive enough, but the possibility that it could be sold to other retailers might lead consumers to refuse to give retailers any information.

Several steps are being taken to address these privacy concerns. For example, one proposal would require all RFID-tagged products to be clearly labeled. This would act as an alert mechanism to which items are being tracked. Another measure being considered is "Kill Codes," which would turn off all RFID tags when someone comes into contact with them. Another measure is "RSA Blocker Tags," which try to address privacy concerns while maintaining the integrity of the product. Only that store's authorized reader can track items with these tags; customers cannot be tracked outside the store in which they made a purchase.[16]

LBS can track and monitor objects much like RFID. Tracking vulnerable individuals and company assets is beneficial. But the dark side of LBS risks the invasion of privacy and security caused by indiscreet location tracking. For example, if a company is using LBS to know where each employee is on duty, it must not observe their positions when they are off duty. Advertising at random to users in a specific area may violate privacy if mobile users in the area do not want to receive these advertisements. Criminals might also take advantage of illegal location tracking. And because LBS are based on message exchange in a wireless network, there are always security risks because location information could be stolen, lost, or modified.

Security mechanisms must eliminate or minimize the potential for attacks against LBS entities and reduce exposure of the user's identity and location. One way to solve the location privacy problem is to provide strong privacy practices that counterbalance the invisible nature of location collection in the wireless world. LBS policies should specify that:

- Direct marketing purposes are permitted only with the business or service a user has a contract with.
- Electronic messages cannot hide the identity of the sender.
- Solicitation is allowed only if the user has given prior consent.
- The location service must tell the user about the type, duration, and purpose of the data they are collecting.
- The user must be given the opportunity to reject any direct marketing opportunities.[17]

For mobile service providers, an unwelcome push can lead to increased customer care cost. When a user has issues with her PC, she tries to fix it herself. However, when a user's mobile phone is not working, she usually contacts the service provider. As a result, subscribers receiving unsolicited messages through LBS would contact their mobile service providers with complaints.

With the power of a network, business professionals can share data and resources around the globe. With the power of a wireless network, business professionals can take advantage of mobility allowing them to work from anywhere, at any time, using many different devices.

Watching people work in airports, restaurants, stores, trains, planes, and automobiles is common, and soon even remote villages in Africa, South America, and Asia will have access to the Internet along with all the power that comes with wireless networking.

OPENING CASE STUDY QUESTIONS

1. What are the three different wireless business applications? How is Pinterest using each one?

2. What are the mobility benefits and challenges facing Pinterest?

Chapter Sixteen Case: Wireless Electricity

Imagine a future in which wireless power transfer is feasible: cell phones, MP3 players, laptop computers and other portable electronics capable of charging themselves without ever being plugged in, finally freeing us from the power cord. Some of these devices might not even need their bulky batteries to operate.

Scientists have known for nearly two centuries how to transmit electricity without wires, and the phenomenon has been demonstrated several times before. But it was not until the rise of personal electronic devices that the demand for wireless power materialized. In the past few years, at least three companies have debuted prototypes of wireless power devices, though their distance range is relatively limited. Thanks to wireless technology, researchers at MIT extended the Wi-Fi concept to allow the beaming of power to anything that uses electricity. The MIT scientists successfully powered a 60-watt light bulb from a power source seven feet away. The team called their invention WiTricity, short for "wireless electricity."

The first wireless powering system to market is an inductive device that looks like a mouse pad and can send power through the air, over a distance of up to a few inches. A powered coil inside the pad creates a magnetic field, which induces current to flow through a small secondary coil that's built into any portable device, such as a flashlight, a phone, or a BlackBerry. The electrical current that then flows in that secondary coil charges the device's onboard rechargeable battery. Although many portable devices, such as the iPhone, have yet to be outfitted with this tiny coil, a number of companies are about to introduce products that are.

The practical benefit of this approach is huge. You can drop any number of devices on the charging pad, and they will recharge—wirelessly. No more tangle of power cables or jumble of charging stations. What's more, because you are invisible to the magnetic fields created by the system, no electricity will flow into you if you stray between device and pad. Nor are there any exposed "hot" metal connections. And the pads are smart with built-in coils which know if the device sitting on them is authorized to receive power, or if it needs power at all. So car keys won't be charged or the flashlight overcharged.

One of the dominant players in this technology is Michigan-based Fulton Innovation. Fulton's new pad-based system, called eCoupled, will be available to police, fire-and-rescue, and contractor fleets—an initial market of as many as 700,000 vehicles annually. The system is being integrated into a truck console to allow users to charge anything from a compatible rechargeable flashlight to a PDA. The tools and other devices now in the pipeline at companies such as Bosch, Energizer, and others will look just like their conventional ancestors. Companies such as Philips Electronics, Olympus, and Logitech will create a standard for products, from flashlights to drills to cell phones to TV remotes.

Applications

- Wireless power transfer technology can be applied in a wide variety of applications and environments. The ability of the technology to transfer power safely, efficiently, and over distance can improve products by making them more convenient, reliable, and environmentally friendly. Wireless power transfer technology can be used to provide:

  - Direct wireless power—when all the power a device needs is provided wirelessly, and no batteries are required. This mode is for a device that is always used within range of its power source.

  - Automatic wireless charging—when a device with rechargeable batteries charges itself while still in use or at rest, without requiring a power cord or battery replacement. This mode is for a mobile device that may be used both in and out of range of its power source.

Consumer Electronics

- Automatic wireless charging of mobile electronics (phones, laptops, game controllers, etc.) in home, car, office, Wi-Fi hotspots while devices are in use and mobile.

- Direct wireless powering of stationary devices (flat-screen TVs, digital picture frames, home theater accessories, wireless loud speakers, etc.) eliminating expensive custom wiring, unsightly cables and power supplies.

- Direct wireless powering of desktop PC peripherals: wireless mouse, keyboard, printer, speakers, display, and the like, eliminating disposable batteries and awkward cabling.

Industrial

- Direct wireless power and communication interconnections across rotating and moving "joints" (robots, packaging machinery, assembly machinery, machine tools) eliminating costly and failure-prone wiring.

- Direct wireless power and communication interconnections at points of use in harsh environments (drilling, mining, underwater, etc.) where it is impractical or impossible to run wires.

- Direct wireless power for wireless sensors, eliminating the need for expensive power wiring or battery replacement and disposal.

- Automatic wireless charging for mobile robots, automatic guided vehicles, cordless tools and instruments eliminating complex docking mechanisms and labor intensive manual recharging and battery replacement.

Transportation

- Automatic wireless charging for existing electric vehicle classes: golf carts, industrial vehicles.

- Automatic wireless charging for future hybrid and all-electric passenger and commercial vehicles, at home, in parking garages, at fleet depots, and at remote kiosks.

- Direct wireless power interconnections to replace costly vehicle wiring harnesses.

Other Applications

- Direct wireless power interconnections and automatic wireless charging for implantable medical devices (pacemaker, defibrillator, etc.).
- Automatic wireless charging for high-tech military systems (battery-powered mobile devices, covert sensors, unmanned mobile robots and aircraft, etc.).
- Direct wireless powering and automatic wireless charging of smart cards.
- Direct wireless powering and automatic wireless charging of consumer appliances, mobile robots, and more.[18]

Questions

1. Explain the fundamentals of wireless power transfer technology.
2. Describe the business benefits of using wireless electricity.
3. Identify two types of business opportunities companies could use to gain a competitive advantage using wireless electricity.
4. What are some other creative uses of wireless electricity not mentioned in the case?
5. How would a wireless power distribution network operate similar to cell networks?

In a remarkably short time, the Internet has grown from a virtual playground into a vital, sophisticated medium for business, more specifically, ebusiness. Online consumers are flooding to the Internet, and they come with very high expectations and a degree of control that they did not have with traditional bricks-and-mortar companies. The enticement of doing business online must be strengthened by the understanding that, to succeed online, businesses will have to be able to deliver a satisfying and consistent customer experience, building brand loyalty and guaranteeing high rates of customer retention.

Strategic alliances enable businesses to gain competitive advantage(s) through access to a partner's resources, including markets, technologies, and people. Teaming up with another business adds complementary resources and capabilities, enabling participants to grow and expand more quickly and efficiently.

★ KEY TERMS

3G, 231
Access point (AP), 228
Active RFID tags, 233
Application programming
    interface (API), 221
Asset tracking, 233
Asynchronous
    communication, 218
Automatic vehicle location
    (AVL), 234
Bluetooth, 227
Blog, or web log, 220
Business model, 206
Business-to-business
    (B2B), 206
Business-to-consumer
    (B2C), 207
Cartography, 235
Chipless RFID tags, 234
Clickstream data, 203
Collaboration system, 216
Collective intelligence, 216
Consumer-to-business (C2B), 207
Consumer-to-consumer
    (C2C), 207
Content management system
    (CMS), 211
Crowdsourcing, 217
Cybermediation, 201
Digital Darwinism, 196
Disintermediation, 200
Disruptive technology, 196
Ebusiness, 198
Ebusiness model, 206
Edge matching (warping, rubber
    sheeting), 235
Ecommerce, 198

Egovernment, 223
Eshop (estore or etailer), 207
Estimated time enroute (ETE), 235
Estimated time of arrival
    (ETA), 235
Explicit knowledge, 217
Folksonomy, 219
Geocache, 234
Geocoding, 235
Geocoin, 234
Geographic information system
    (GIS), 235
GIS map automation, 235
Global positioning system
    (GPS), 234
Hotspots, 228
Hypertext markup language
    (HTML), 198
Hypertext transport protocol
    (HTTP), 198
IEEE 802.11n (or Wireless-N), 229
Information architecture, 211
Information reach, 199
Information richness, 199
Instant messaging (sometimes
    called IM or IMing), 210
Institute of Electrical and
    Electronics Engineers
    (IEEE), 229
Interactivity, 202
Intermediaries, 200
Internet, 198
Internet service provider (ISP), 209
Knowledge management
    (KM), 216
Knowledge management
    system (KMS), 216

Latitude, 234
Location-based services
    (LBS), 236
Longitude, 234
Long tail, 200
Mashup, 221
Mashup editor, 221
Mass customization, 200
Microblogging, 220
Mobile business (mcommerce,
    mbusiness), 223
Multiple-in/multiple-out (MIMO)
    technology, 228
Network effect, 221
Open source, 215
Open system, 215
Paradigm shift, 199
Passive RFID tags, 233
Pay-per-call, 208
Pay-per-click, 208
Pay-per-conversion, 208
Personalization, 200
Personal area network
    (PAN), 227
Podcasting, 210
Real Simple Syndication
    (RSS), 220
Real-time communication, 210
Reintermediation, 201
Reputation system, 216
RFID accelerometer, 234
RFID tag, 233
RFID reader (RFID
    interrogator), 233
Satellite, 231
Search engine, 208
Search engine ranking, 208

✳ UNIT CLOSING CASE ONE

BBC Taps Web 3.0 for New Music Site

The BBC's recently launched semantic web music project could indicate the future direction of the corporation's online presence. The public beta of the BBC Music website has been recently relaunched incorporating semantic web technology in its artist pages resource. The BBC artist pages, a repository of information on singers and bands played on several BBC radio stations, has been running as a closed beta project since June 2008, but with the launch of the new BBC Music website, its semantic web technology has now been exposed to the wider public.

For the BBC, the site represents a new way of thinking about online content—where the priority is publishing data rather than simply publishing web pages. Such thinking is likely to filter through to other parts of the BBC, with discussions taking place between editorial departments on how to aggregate and meaningfully link data. Matthew Shorter, interactive editor for music at the BBC, told silicon.com: "We're kind of on a journey of moving from what's effectively a magazine/print publication-based metaphor around web publishing . . . to a world where we recognize that that's not the way that people use the web. We're working towards a scenario where we really don't want to see any dead ends between bits of the BBC online offering."

The semantic technology is not the only improvement on the BBC Music site. The way in which the BBC's online music resource is constructed now makes it easier to search for content due to the way it's been tagged and linked to other content, according to Shorter. "From an SEO point of view, once we start generating a lot of meaningful links among our pages, then we're going to improve the find-ability of our content via web search which is a part of our strategy of doing this."

The BBC is also making its music-related application programming interfaces (APIs) available for third-party developers so they can reuse the content—in a similar way as YouTube and

Flickr. The open platform could see individuals use the artist play-count data as shown on the BBC Music homepage and display it in a different way, for example. By having an open system, the BBC hopes that people will create unique content that will benefit from incoming links.[19]

Questions

1. Do you consider the BBC's use of semantic technology a disruptive or sustaining technology?
2. Do you consider the BBC's new music site a form of Web 1.0 or Web 2.0?
3. What benefits will the BBC receive from using an open system?
4. Why would collaboration, collective intelligence, and crowdsourcing be important to the BBC's radio station?
5. Brainstorm a few of the security issues a company should prepare for when using Halo.

Social Networking

Not long ago, it seemed that four companies would forever dominate the web in traffic and ad dollars. Each of the Big Four—Google, Yahoo!, Microsoft's MSN, and Time Warner's AOL—attracts more than 100 million unique visitors a month. Collectively the group accounts for roughly 90 percent of gross ad dollars online. But now those companies are facing a threat to their dominance. Today's massive social networking systems are rapidly becoming webs within the web—one-stop shops for a wide range of services (from content to communications to commerce) that were once the unique province of the Big Four.

Facebook, Myspace, LinkedIn, and other social-networking sites have been the rage of the tech industry lately. Following investments by Microsoft, News Corp. and Goldman Sachs, the companies are valued in the billions of dollars and are considered blueprints for how to build a website. Facebook has become the web's largest social network as measured by active users, which offers bread-and-butter portal services like email and instant messaging as well as photo posting and video sharing. In addition, Facebook has partnered with Amazon.com to produce a shopping application that lets users buy items at Amazon without leaving Facebook's site, while using opt-in "news feeds" that broadcast activities on Amazon, such as product reviews and wish list updates, to Facebook friends. Additionally, Facebook now uses a chat feature that automatically populates itself with a user's Facebook "friends," that may render older instant messaging services, such as AOL's AIM, defunct.

Jumping on the wireless apps mega-trend, Facebook uses mobile alerts to deliver mobile services for traditional styled cell phones and more intelligent smartphones. Applications for popular devices, such as the iPhone or BlackBerry, deliver even richer social experiences. Video has taken off, too, with 45 million clips uploaded on Facebook including higher-resolution video formats allowing Facebook users to send video messages from the site and from mobiles devices.

Launched in 2003, Myspace became one of the most visited websites in the world within a few years. With almost a billion visits per month, Myspace is considered the most popular social network (by traffic volume). The site was originally started by musicians as a tool to help users discover new music and engage with bands. Today, Myspace members leverage the service to discover people with similar tastes or experiences. Utilizing a system of adding friends to your network, the ability to customize your profile, write blog entries, play favorite MP3 tracks, join groups and enter discussions, Myspace allows users to interact in a way unparalleled before its emergence. However, the most compelling reason to join Myspace is for fun. There are many avenues toward entertainment on the social network including browsing through musician profiles and exploring areas dedicated to television shows or movies. But Myspace isn't just for fun, as many businesses maintain Myspace profiles in order to use the social media site as a form of marketing. For musicians, actors, authors, entrepreneurs, and others that maintain a public image, a Myspace profile can be a very important connection to fans.

Since it scored a $900 million, three-year deal with Google in 2006, Myspace has been profitable. And it has given News Corp. a nice turn on its $650 million acquisition in 2005. Myspace has recently formed partnerships with major record labels Sony BMG Music Entertainment, Warner Music Group, and Vivendi's Universal Music Group to offer its 117 million members tickets, ring tones, and artist merchandise. Driving a good chunk of sales is a project launched last summer called HyperTargeting, software that mines the profiles of Myspace users to deliver ads tailored to their interests. Hundreds of advertisers are part of the program, including Toyota and Taco Bell. Another income source is the sale of mobile ring tones and ads.

When it comes to enterprise collaboration and social software, LinkedIn rules the roost. LinkedIn is more effective at meeting the requirements of social computing the enterprise environment demands. With more than 30 million users representing 150 industries around the world, LinkedIn is a fast-growing professional networking site that allows members to create business contacts, search for jobs, and find potential clients. Individuals have the ability to create their own professional profile that can be viewed by others in their network, and also view the profiles of their own contacts. While Myspace and Facebook are tailored to keeping members in touch with friends and family, LinkedIn is perceived as being "more professional" for business users.

Social networking sites are also growing at exponential rates and attracting users of all ages. Facebook's fastest-growing segment is users over 25 years of age. LinkedIn, the business-oriented social networking site, claims more than 30 million active members with an average age of 41. The social networking websites are typically divided into three categories: general interest, niche sites with a specific theme, and international sites. The following are the top sites in these three categories:

General Interest

- **Myspace:** Started in 2003, Myspace was a driving force in popularizing social networking and still maintains the largest userbase.
- **Facebook:** Founded by Mark Zuckerberg, Facebook was designed as a social networking site for Harvard students. After spreading from Harvard through the university ranks and down into high school, Facebook was opened to the public in 2006.
- **Hi5:** A fast-growing social network with a strong base in Central America, Hi5 has more than 50 million users worldwide.
- **Ning:** A social network for creating social networks, Ning takes the idea of groups to a whole new level.

Niche Sites

- **Flixster:** With a tagline of "stop watching bad movies," Flixster combines social networking with movie reviews.

- **Last.fm:** Billing itself as a social music site, Last.fm allows members to create their own radio station that learns what the person likes and suggests new music based on those interests. In addition to this, you can listen to the radio stations of friends and other Last.fm members.

- **LinkedIn:** A business-oriented social network, members invite people to be "connections" instead of "friends." LinkedIn is a contact management system as well as a social network, and has a question-and-answer section similar to Yahoo! Answers.

- **Xanga:** A social blogging site that combines social networking elements with blogging. Members earn credits for participating in the site and can spend credits on various things such as buying mini-pictures to post in the comments of a friend's blog.

International Sites

- **Badoo:** Based in London, Badoo is one of the top social networking sites in Europe.
- **Migente:** A social networking site targeted at Latin America.
- **Orkut:** Originally created by Google to compete with Myspace and Facebook, it has mainly caught hold in Brazil.
- **Studivz:** A German version of Facebook with a strong audience in students.

Corporate Use of Social Networking

Corporations and smaller businesses haven't embraced online business networks with nearly the same abandon as teens and college students who have flocked to social sites. Yet companies are steadily overcoming reservations and using the sites and related technology to craft potentially powerful business tools. Recruiters at Microsoft and Starbucks, for instance, troll online networks such as LinkedIn for potential job candidates. Goldman Sachs and Deloitte run their own online alumni networks for hiring back former workers (called boomerangs) and strengthening bonds with former alums. Maintaining such networks will be critical in industries like IT and health care that are likely to be plagued by worker shortages for years to come. Social networking can also be important for organizations like IBM, where some 42 percent of employees regularly work from home or client locations. IBM's social network makes it easier to locate employee expertise within the firm, organize virtual work groups, and communicate across large distances. As another example of corporate social networks, Reuters has rolled out Reuters Space, a private online community for financial professionals. Profile pages can also contain a personal blog and news feeds (from Reuters or external services). Every profile page is accessible to the entire Reuters Space community, but members can choose which personal details are available to whom. While IBM and Reuters have developed their own social network platforms, firms are increasingly turning to third-party vendors like SelectMinds (adopted by Deloitte, Dow Chemical, and Goldman Sachs) and LiveWorld (adopted by Intuit, eBay, the NBA, and Scientific American).[20]

Questions

1. Are Facebook, Myspace, and LinkedIn using disruptive or sustaining technology to run their businesses?
2. What are some of the business challenges facing social networking sites?
3. What are the characteristics of a social network?
4. What security issues do social networking sites create?
5. What are some current social networking trends?
6. How can social networking sites generate revenue beyond selling banner and text ads?

1. Everybody Needs an Internet Strategy

An Internet strategy addresses the reasons businesses want to "go online." "Going online" because it seems like the right thing to do now or because everyone else is doing it is not a good enough reason. A business must decide how it will best utilize the Internet for its particular needs. It must plan for where it wants to go and how best the Internet can help shape that vision. Before developing a strategy, a business should spend time on the Internet, see what similar businesses have, and what is most feasible, given a particular set of resources. Think of a new online business opportunity and answer the following questions:

a. Why do you want to put your business online?
b. What benefits will going online bring?
c. What effects will Internet connectivity have on your staff, suppliers, and customers?

2. Searching for Disruption

Scheduler.com is a large corporation that develops software that automates scheduling and record keeping for medical and dental practices. Scheduler.com currently holds 48 percent of its market share, has more than 8,700 employees, and operates in six countries. You are the vice president of product development at Scheduler.com. You have just finished reading *The Innovator's Dilemma* by Clayton Christensen and you are interested in determining what types of disruptive technologies you can take advantage of, or should watch out for, in your industry. Use the Internet to develop a presentation highlighting the types of disruptive technologies you have found that have the potential to give the company a competitive advantage or could cause the company to fail.

3. Leveraging the Competitive Value of the Internet

Physical inventories have always been a major cost component of business. Linking to suppliers in real time dramatically enhances the classic goal of inventory "turn." The Internet provides a multitude of opportunities for radically reducing the costs of designing, manufacturing, and selling goods and services. E-mango.com, a fruit emarketplace, must take advantage of these opportunities or find itself at a significant competitive disadvantage. Identify the disadvantages that confront E-mango.com if it does not leverage the competitive value of the Internet.

4. Assessing Internet Capabilities

Hoover's Rentals is a small privately owned business that rents sports equipment in Denver, Colorado. The company specializes in winter rentals including ski equipment, snowboarding equipment, and snowmobile equipment. Hoover's has been in business for 20 years and, for the first time, it is experiencing a decline in rentals. Brian Hoover, the company's owner, is puzzled by the recent decreases. The snowfall for the last two years has been outstanding, and the ski resorts have opened earlier and closed later than most previous years. Reports say tourism in the Colorado area is up, and the invention of loyalty programs has significantly increased the number of local skiers. Overall, business should be booming. The only reason for the decrease in sales might be the fact that big retailers such as Walmart and Gart Sports are now renting winter sports equipment. Brian would like your team's help in determining how he can use the Internet to help his company increase sales and decrease costs to compete with these big retailers.

5. Gaining Efficiency with Collaboration

During the past year, you have been working for a manufacturing firm to help improve its supply chain management by implementing enterprise resource planning and supply chain management systems. For efficiency gains, you are recommending that the manufacturing firm should be turning toward collaborative systems. The firm has a need to share intelligent plans and forecasts with supply chain partners, reduce inventory levels, improve working capital, and reduce manufacturing changeovers. Given the technologies presented to you in this unit, what type of system(s) would you recommend to facilitate your firm's future needs?

6. Collaboration on Intranets

MyIntranet.com is a worldwide leader in providing online intranet solutions. The MyIntranet .com online collaboration tool is a solution for small businesses and groups inside larger organizations that need to organize information, share files and documents, coordinate calendars, and enable efficient collaboration, all in a secure, browser-based environment. MyIntranet.com has just added conferencing and group scheduling features to its suite of hosted collaboration software. Explain why infrastructure integration is critical to the suite of applications to function within this environment.

7. Finding Innovation

Along with disruptive technologies, there are also disruptive strategies. The following are a few examples of companies that use disruptive strategies to gain competitive advantages:

- Best Buy—This company disrupted the consumer electronics departments of full-service and discount department stores, which has sent it up-market into higher margin goods.

- Ford—Henry Ford's Model T was so inexpensive that he enabled a much larger population of people, who historically could not afford cars, to own one.

- JetBlue—Whereas Southwest Airlines initially followed a strategy of new-market disruption, JetBlue's approach is low-end disruption. Its long-range viability depends on the major airlines' motivation to run away from the attack, as integrated steel mills and full-service department stores did.

- McDonald's—The fast-food industry has been a hybrid disrupter, making it so inexpensive and convenient to eat out that it created a massive wave of growth in the "eating out" industry. McDonald's earliest victims were mom-and-pop diners.

There are numerous other examples of corporations that have used disruptive strategies to create competitive advantages. In a team, prepare a presentation highlighting three additional companies that used disruptive strategies to gain a competitive advantage.

8. Communicating with Instant Messages

You are working for a new start-up magazine, *Jabber Inc.,* developed for information professionals that provides articles, product reviews, case studies, evaluation, and informed opinions. You need to collaborate on news items and projects, and exchange data with a variety of colleagues inside and outside the *Jabber Inc.* walls. You know that many companies are now embracing the instant messaging technology. Prepare a brief report for the CIO that will explain the reasons IM is not just a teenage fad, but also a valuable communications tool that is central to everyday business.

9. The Future of Wikipedia

Wikipedia is a multilingual, web-based, free-content encyclopedia project written collaboratively by volunteers around the world. Since its creation in 2001, it has grown rapidly into one of the largest reference websites. Some people believe Wikipedia will eventually fail under an assault by marketers and self-promoting users. Eric Goldman, a professor at the Santa Clara University School of Law, argues that Wikipedia will see increasingly vigorous efforts to subvert its editorial process, including the use of automated marketing tools to alter Wikipedia entries to generate online traffic. The site's editors will burn out trying to maintain it, he projects, or Wikipedia will change its open-access architecture and its mission. Do you agree or disagree with Professor Goldman's argument? What can Wikipedia do to combat the challenges of information vandalism and copyright/plagiarism issues?

10. Is Facebook Becoming the Whole World's Social Network?

Facebook's growth, which we already know is massive, is truly a global phenomenon. Nations with the fastest membership growth rate are in South America and Asia. Is Facebook becoming the global phone book? If you review InsideFacebook.com, you'll find a detailed analysis of the numerical growth rate of members per nation and the penetration Facebook is achieving among each nation's population. Particularly interesting was the monthly growth rate for Indonesia, the Philippines, Mexico, Argentina, and Malaysia—each of which showed about a 10 percent jump in Facebook membership in a single month. In a group answer the following:

- What potential business opportunities could be created by a worldwide social media network or phone book?
- Facebook, which contains personal data on each member, is becoming the world's phone book. What are the implications of a world phone book for social change?
- What do you think would be the benefits and challenges of global social networking?

11. The Toughest College Test You'll Ever Take

If your professor asked you today to kick your social networking habits, do you think you could do it? Can you go without Facebook, cell phones, or the Internet for a week? For a day? Recently, a University of Minnesota professor challenged her public relations class to go five days without media or gadgets that didn't exist before 1984. Out of the 43 students in the class, just a handful made it even three days without new technology. Among those who didn't, one student said, "My mother thought I died." How long could you go without any social media? What types of issues might you encounter without constant connections to your friends? How has social media affected society? How has social media impacted businesses?

12. Book'em

You are the CIO of Book'em, a company that creates and sells custom book bags. Book'em currently holds 28 percent of market share with more than 3,000 employees operating in six countries. You have just finished reading *The Long Tail* by Chris Anderson and *The Innovator's Dilemma* by Clayton Christensen, and you are interested in determining how you can grow your business while reducing costs. Summarize each book, and explain how Book'em could implement the strategies explained in each book to create competitive advantages and increase sales.

13. Five Ways Google Docs Speeds Up Collaboration

Google Docs wants you to skip Microsoft Office and collaborate with your group in your browser for free, especially when you're not in the same physical space. Visit Google Docs and answer the following questions.

- What are five ways the new Google Docs can help your team accomplish work more efficiently, even when you're not in the same room together?

- Is Google Docs open source software? What revenue model is Google Docs following?

- Why would putting Google Docs and Microsoft Office on your résumé help differentiate your skills?

- What other applications does Google create that you are interested in learning to help collaborate and communicate with peers and co-workers?

14. Secure Collaboration

As the methods and modes of communication continue to evolve, challenges will mount for businesses trying to secure their data and for law enforcement agencies looking to monitor communications as part of their investigations. That was the theme of the keynote that Sun Microsystems chief security officer and renowned cryptographer Whitfield Diffie delivered at the AT&T Cyber Security Conference.

Diffie believes that with millions of people joining Second Life and companies building facilities there, it may be that virtual communities will become the preferred communication method for humans as virtual communities become a growing source of collective intelligence that can be easily watched and monitored.

Who would be interested in monitoring and spying on the collective intelligence of virtual communities? What is your answer to the following question: As we create new and better ways to collaborate, what happens to information security?

15. City Council Member Fired for Playing Farmville Game at Work

More than 80 million Facebook users are obsessed with Farmville, and one of the more devoted players is Bulgaria's Plovidv City Council member Dimitar Kerin. During council meetings, Kerin would take advantage of the city hall's laptops and wireless connection to tend to his farm. This caught the attention of the council chair, who many times scolded Kerin for his virtual farming, warning him that the game was not allowed during meetings. Kerin kept on, arguing that he had to catch up with other council members, who achieved higher levels on the game. Kerin pointed out logically that many other members used city hall for their Farmville pleasures, and he cited the fact that one councilman had reached level 46, whereas Kerin was stuck at level 40. Shockingly, council members voted Kerin off the board in a split 20–19 decision, suggesting that perhaps half the council members in Bulgaria's second-largest city are committed to the Facebook application. Do you agree with the firing of Dimitar Kerin? Do you agree that it is inappropriate to use social networking applications at work? If Dimitar Kerin was fired for playing Farmville, should all other council members who use social networking applications at work be fired? Have you ever been reprimanded for playing a game while at school or at work? What could you do differently to ensure this situation does not happen to you?

16. 48 Hour Magazine

That sound you hear, of thousands of writers, designers, and photographers banging their heads against the wall to the beat of a ticking clock? That's the sound of *48 Hour Magazine,* an innovative publication that aims to go from inspiration to execution in 48 hours and begins . . . now. *48 Hour* is available to the eager public as a real, printed magazine and as a website too. What are the limitations of "old media"? How are the editors of the *48 Hour Magazine* using Web 2.0 to overcome these limitations? What are the advantages and disadvantages of *48 Hour Magazine's* model? What type of revenue model would you recommend *48 Hour Magazine* implement? If you had $50,000 would you invest in the *48 Hour Magazine?* Why or why not?

1. Working Together

Upon execution of a business process, a workflow system dictates the presentation of the information, tracks the information, and maintains the information's status. For example, the following highlights the common steps performed during a team project:

1. Find out what information and deliverables are required for the project and the due date.
2. Divide the work among the team members.
3. Determine due dates for the different pieces of work.
4. Compile all the completed work together into a single project.

One of the hardest parts of a team project is getting team members to complete their work on time. Often one team member cannot perform his or her work until another team member has finished. This situation causes work to sit idle waiting for a team member to pick it up to either approve it, continue working on it, or reformat it. Workflow systems help to automate the process of presenting and passing information around a team.

Project Focus

You have just received an assignment to work on a group project with 10 other students. The project requires you to develop a detailed business plan for a business of your choice. The types of activities you will need to perform include market analysis, industry analysis, growth opportunities, Porter's Five Forces analysis, financial forecasts, competitive advantage analysis, and so on. For your project, determine the following:

1. How could you use collaboration tools to facilitate the sharing of information and the completion of the project?
2. What advantages can your group gain from using groupware?
3. What advantages can your group gain from using IM?
4. How could you use a workflow system to manage the tasks for the group members?
5. Describe a few of the biggest issues you anticipate experiencing during the group project. Identify ways that you can resolve these issues using collaboration tools.

2. Internet Groceries

E-Grocery, founded in 2007, is an online grocery shopping and delivery service. The company caters to thousands of customers in the Phoenix, Seattle, and Denver areas. Established on the idea that people will buy groceries over the Internet, e-Grocery offers more than 25,000 items.

Ninety percent of e-Grocery's orders come in via computer; the rest are received by fax. Orders are received at the central office in Lakewood, Colorado, and then distributed by email to a local affiliate store. The store receives the order, the delivery address, and a map to the order location. A store employee designated to online orders will fill, deliver, and collect for the order. E-Grocery members are charged actual shelf prices, plus a per-order charge of $5.00 or 5 percent of the order amount, whichever is greater. Members also receive additional benefits such as electronic coupons, customer discounts, recipes, and tips.

Project Focus

The company is using interactive technology to change the shopping experience. The success of e-Grocery lies within many areas. Analyze the e-Grocery business model using the questions below. Feel free to think outside the box to develop your own analysis of online grocery shopping and ebusiness models.

1. What is e-Grocery's ebusiness model?
2. How does e-Grocery compete with traditional retailers?

3. What value can e-Grocery offer as a true competitive advantage in this marketplace?

4. What is the threat of new entrants in this market segment?

5. How is e-Grocery using technology to change the shopping experience?

6. What are the logistics for making e-Grocery profitable?

7. How does e-Grocery profit from online customer interaction?

8. What kinds of ebusiness strategies can e-Grocery's marketing department use to help grow its business?

9. What are some of the benefits and challenges facing e-Grocery?

3. Getting Personal

Consider Sally Albright, the reigning queen of customization in the movie *When Harry Met Sally*. Take, for example, the scene where she orders pie a la mode: "I'd like the pie heated. And I don't want the ice cream on top; I want it on the side. And I'd like strawberry instead of vanilla if you have it. If not, then no ice cream, just whipped cream, but only if it's real." Particular, yes, but Sally knew what she liked—and was not afraid to ask for it.

Project Focus

A growing number of online retailers are letting you have it your way, too. Choose a company highlighted in Figure AYK.1 and create your own product. Was the website easy to use? Would this service entice you as a customer to make a purchase over a generic product? If you could personalize a product what would it be and how would the website work?

4. Express Yourself

One of the most popular websites among students is Myspace, a site that allows students to express themselves by personalizing their home page. What is your favorite band? Who is your favorite author? What is your favorite movie? You can find out a lot about a person by finding out the answers to these questions.

Project Focus

Build a website dedicated to your favorite band, book, or movie. Your website must contain all of the following:

- An image.
- Two different size headings.
- Different sizes and colors of text.
- Two horizontal rules.
- Text that is bolded, underlined, and/or italicized.

FIGURE AYK.1

Customization Companies

Company	Product
Tommy Hilfiger, custom.tomm.com	Premium-cotton chinos and jeans ($98)
Lands' End, www.landsend.com	Utilitarian jeans and chinos made of luxurious twill in traditional silhouettes ($59)
JCPenney, www.custom.jcpenney.com	Substantial twill pants in classic cuts ($44)
Ralph Lauren Polo, www.polo.com	Everything from basic polos to oxford shirts ($80)
TIMBUK2; www.timbuk2.com	Hip nylon messenger bags ($105)
L.L.Bean, www.llbean.com	Sturdy and colorful books, totes, and messenger bags ($70)
Nike, www.nikeid.com	Full range of athletic shoes and accessories ($90)
VANS, www.vans.com	Classic "Old Skool" lace-up or slip-on sneakers ($50)
Converse, www.converseone.com	Custom Chuck Taylors, the company's most classic style ($60)

- A textured background.
- A link to a website.
- A link to your email.
- One numbered and one unnumbered list.

5. Creating a Presence

More than 1 billion people are on the Internet. Having an Internet presence is critical for any business that wants to remain competitive. Businesses need their websites to create a "buzz" to attract customers. Ebusiness websites must be innovative, stimulating, add value, and provide useful information. In short, the site must build a sense of community and collaboration, eventually becoming the "port of entry" for business.

Project Focus

You are applying for a job at BagEm, a start-up ebusiness devoted to selling custom book bags that does not have any physical stores and only sells bags over the Internet. You are up against several other candidates for the job. BagEm has asked you to use your business expertise and website development skills to design and build a potential website. The candidate with the best website will be awarded the job. Good luck!

6. GoGo Gadgets

Now that Wi-Fi and other types of high-speed wireless networks are becoming common, devices using that technology are multiplying rapidly. Wireless gadgets run the gamut from cell phones to kitchen appliances and digital cameras. Here are some of the hottest new wireless broadband gadgets.

- Samsung's $3,499 POPCON refrigerator will feature a Wi-Fi enabled, detachable screen that can function as a TV. The fridge also can be programmed to remember products' expiration dates and generate alerts when the milk is getting old.
- The Nokia 770 Internet Tablet is small enough to fit in a pocket. It comes with a 4.13-inch-wide touch screen that can be used to access the web over a Wi-Fi network. The $350 device can also access the web via a cell phone with a Bluetooth connection.
- Motorola's latest E815 mobile phone operates over Verizon Wireless's new EVDO (Evolution Data Optimized) wireless network, offering speeds comparable to digital subscriber line (DSL). The phone can even record and play back video clips. It also features a built-in MP3 digital music player.
- Hop-On's just-announced HOP 1515 may look like a typical cell phone, but it actually makes calls over Wi-Fi networks. Typically sold with a $20 to $30 monthly service plan, the phone allows for unlimited over-the-web international and long-distance calling. The $39 HOP 1515 is sold through Wi-Fi hotspot operators, wireless carriers, and retailers.
- Eastman Kodak's EasyShare-One is a digital camera with Wi-Fi capabilities, allowing users to share their snapshots wirelessly. You will be able to snap a photo and immediately show it to a friend on a Wi-Fi-enabled PC or TV.

Project Focus

A dizzying array of new wireless technologies now promises to make today's Wi-Fi networks seem like poky dial-up connections by comparison. These new technologies will extend the reach of wireless networks, not just geographically but also into new uses in the home and office.

1. Research the Internet and discover new wireless devices that entrepreneurs and established companies can use to improve their business.

2. Explain how businesses can use these devices to create competitive advantages, streamline production, and improve productivity.

7. WAP

Wireless Internet access is quickly gaining popularity among people seeking high-speed Internet connections when they are away from their home or office. The signal from a typical wireless access point (WAP) only extends for about 300 feet in any direction, so the user must find a "hotspot" to be able to access the Internet while on the road. Sometimes hotspots are available for free or for a small fee.

You work for a sales company, SalesTek, which has a salesforce of 25 representatives and customers concentrated in Denver, Colorado; Salt Lake City, Utah; and Santa Fe, New Mexico. Your sales representatives are constantly on the road and they require 24 / 7 Internet access.

Project Focus

You have been asked to find hotspots for your colleagues to connect to while they are on the road. It is critical that your salesforce can access the Internet 24 / 7 to connect with customers, suppliers, and the corporate office. Create a document detailing how your mobile workforce will be able to stay connected to the Internet while traveling. Here are a few tips to get you started:

1. Use websites such as www.wifinder.com and www.jiwire.com to determine which commercial hotspots would be the most appropriate for your salesforce and the commercial network service that these hotspots use.
2. Research the websites of two or three commercial networks that seem most appropriate to discover more about pricing and services. (Hint: T-Mobile is one example.)
3. Use www.wifinder.com and www.wififreespot.com to determine how many free public hotspots are available in these cities. Are there enough for your company to rely on them or should you use a commercial Wi-Fi system. If so, which one?
4. You might also research www.fon.com to see alternative methods of using home broadband connections to stay connected.

8. Securing Your Home Wireless Network

These days wireless networking products are so ubiquitous and inexpensive that anyone can easily build a wireless network with less than $100 worth of equipment. However, wireless networks are exactly that—wireless—they do not stop at walls. In fact, wireless networks often carry signals more than 300 feet from the wireless router. Living in an apartment, dorm, condominium, or house means that you might have dozens of neighbors who can access your wireless network.

It is one thing to let a neighbor borrow a lawn mower, but it is another thing to allow a neighbor to access a home wireless network. There are several good reasons for not sharing a home wireless network including:

- It may slow Internet performance.
- It allows others to view files on your computers and spread dangerous software such as viruses.
- It allows others to monitor the websites you visit, read your email and instant messages as they travel across the network, and copy your user names and passwords.
- It allows others to send spam or perform illegal activities with your Internet connection.

Project Focus

Securing a home wireless network is invaluable and allows you to enable security features that can make it difficult for uninvited guests to connect through your wireless network. Create a document detailing all of the features you can use to secure a home wireless network.

9. Weather Bots

Warren Jackson, an engineering graduate student at the University of Pennsylvania, was not interested in the weather until he started investigating how the National Weather

Service collected weather data. The weather service has collected most of its information using weather balloons that carry a device to measure items such as pressure, wind speed, and humidity. When the balloon reaches about 100,000 feet and pressure causes it to pop, the device falls and lands a substantial distance from its launch point. The National Weather Service and researchers sometimes look for the $200 device, but of the 80,000 sent up annually, they write off many as lost.

Convinced there had to be a better way, Warren began designing a GPS-equipped robot that launches a parachute after the balloon pops and brings the device back down to Earth, landing it at a predetermined location set by the researchers. The idea is so inventive that the Penn's Weiss Tech House, a university organization that encourages students to innovate and bring their ideas to market, awarded Warren and some fellow graduate engineering students first prize in its third annual PennVention Contest. Warren won $5,000 and access to expert advice on prototyping, legal matters, and branding.

Project Focus

GPS and GIS can be used in all sorts of devices, in many different industries, for multiple purposes. You want to compete, and win first prize, in the PennVention next year. Create a product, using a GPS or GIS, that is not currently in the market today that you will present at the fourth annual PennVention.

10. Wireless Networks and Streetlamps

Researchers at Harvard University and BBN Technologies have designed CitySense, a wireless network capable of reporting real-time sensor data across the entire city of Cambridge, Massachusetts. CitySense is unique because it solves a constraint on previous wireless networks—battery life. The network mounts each node on a municipal streetlamp, where it draws power from city electricity. Researchers plan to install 100 sensors on streetlamps throughout Cambridge by 2011, using a grant from the National Science Foundation. Each node will include an embedded PC running the Linux operating system, an 802.11 Wi-Fi interface, and weather sensors.

One of the challenges in the design was how the network would allow remote nodes to communicate with the central server at Harvard and BBN. CitySense will do that by letting each node form a mesh with its neighbors, exchanging data through multiple-hop links. This strategy allows a node to download software or upload sensor data to a distant server hub using a small radio with only a 1-kilometer range.

Project Focus

You are responsible for deploying a CitySense network around your city. What goals would you have for the system besides monitoring urban weather and pollution? What other benefits could a CitySense network provide? How could local businesses and citizens benefit from the network? What legal and ethical concerns should you understand before deploying the network? What can you do to protect your network and your city from these issues?

11. Sharptooth Incorporated

Stephen Kern is the founder and CEO of Sharptooth, a small business that buys and sells comic strips to magazines and newspapers around the country. Some of Sharptooth's artists have made it big and are syndicated in hundreds of magazines and newspapers, while others are new to the industry. Stephen started in the business as an artist and began contracting with other artists when he realized he had a knack for promoting and marketing comic materials. His artistic background is great for spotting talented young artists, but not so great for running the business.

Project Focus

Stephen recently began selling comics to new forms of media such as blog sites, websites, and other online tools. Stephen has hired you to build him a new system to track all online comic sales. You quickly notice that Stephen has a separate system for each of his different lines of business including newspaper sources, magazine sources, billboard sources, and now online sources. You notice that each system works independently to perform its job of creating, updating, and maintaining sales information, but you are wondering how Stephen operates his business as a whole. Create a list of issues Stephen will encounter if he continues to run his business with four separate systems performing the same operations. What could happen to Stephen's business if he cannot correlate the details of each? Be sure to highlight at least 10 issues where separate systems could cause Stephen problems.

12. Wiki Debate

Wikipedia is a multilingual, web-based, free content encyclopedia project. Wikipedia is written collaboratively by volunteers from all around the world. With rare exceptions, its articles can be edited by anyone with access to the Internet, simply by clicking a line to edit the page. The name Wikipedia is a portmanteau of the words *wiki* (a type of collaborative website) and *encyclopedia.* Since its creation in 2001, Wikipedia has grown rapidly into one of the largest reference websites.

In every article, links guide users to associated articles, often with additional information. Anyone is welcome to add information, cross-references, or citations, as long as they do so within Wikipedia's editing policies and to an appropriate standard. One need not fear accidentally damaging Wikipedia when adding or improving information, as other editors are always around to advise or correct obvious errors, and Wikipedia's software, known as MediaWiki, is carefully designed to allow easy reversal of editorial mistakes.

Project Focus

A group of people believe the end of Wikipedia is close as people use the tool to self-promote. Some believe that Wikipedia will fail in four years, crushed under the weight of an automated assault by marketers and others seeking online traffic. Eric Goldman, a professor at the Santa Clara University School of Law, argues that Wikipedia will see increasingly vigorous efforts to subvert its editorial process, much as Digg has seen. As marketers become more determined and turn to automated tools to alter Wikipedia entries to generate online traffic, Goldman predicts Wikipedians will burn out trying to keep entries clean. Goldman writes that Wikipedia will enter a death spiral where the rate of junkiness will increase rapidly until the site becomes a wasteland. Alternatively, to prevent this death spiral, Wikipedia will change its core open-access architecture, increasing the database's vitality by changing its mission somewhat. Create a paper discussing where you think the future of Wikipedia is headed.

13. Secure Collaboration

As the methods and modes of communication continue to evolve, challenges will mount for businesses trying to secure their data and for law enforcement looking to monitor communications as part of their investigations. That was the theme of the keynote speech that Sun Microsystems' chief security officer and renowned cryptographer Whitfield Diffie delivered at the AT&T Cyber Security Conference.

The growth of virtual communities across the web as a communications channel creates a double-edged sword in this respect. Second Life and other virtual communities offer a growing abundance of information, although this information will ultimately need to be protected if virtual communities are to grow as meaningful channels of business-to-business and business-to-customer communication.

Diffie believes that with millions of people joining Second Life and companies building facilities there, it may be that virtual communities become the preferred medium of human communication. This growing volume of information opens the opportunity to use virtual communities as a source of intelligence, and communications will always be spied on.

Of course, the volume of businesses present in virtual communities such as Second Life will have to grow before they become a meaningful source of information. Once this happens, though, watch out. Diffie believes that communication always outstrips the ability to protect it. Who would be interested in gathering intelligence floating through virtual communities? The answer is businesses, governments (domestic and foreign), and reporters—the same entities that have adapted every other form of communication preceding the web. Diffie feels the future will be a golden age for intelligence.

Project Focus

As we create new and better ways to collaborate, what happens to information security?

✱ ENTREPRENEURIAL CHALLENGE

Build Your Own Business

1. To build a sense of community, you have provided a mechanism on your business website where customers can communicate and post feedback. You review the communication daily to help understand customer issues and concerns. You log in and find the following anonymous posting: "I do not recommend visiting this business on Thursdays at 2:00 p.m. because the Children's Story Hour is taking place. I hate children, especially in a business. I'm not sure why this business encourages people to bring their children. In fact, I recommend that children should be banned from this business altogether." How would you respond to this post? Is the customer's viewpoint ethical? How do you encourage an open line of communication with your customers and still maintain an open forum on your website?

2. Your business needs to take advantage of ebusiness and Business 2.0 strategies if it wants to remain competitive. Detail how your business could use Web 1.0 and Web 2.0 to increase sales and decrease costs. Be sure to focus on the different areas of business such as marketing, finance, accounting, sales, customer service, and human resources. You would like to build a collaboration tool for all of your customers and events. Answer the questions below as they pertain to your business.

   ▣ What type of collaboration tool would you build?

   ▣ How could you use the tool to facilitate planning, product development, product testing, feedback, and so on.

   ▣ What additional benefits could a customer collaboration tool provide that could help you run your business?

3. The Yankee Group reports that 66 percent of companies determine website success solely by measuring the amount of traffic. Unfortunately, large amounts of website traffic do not necessarily indicate large sales. Many websites with lots of traffic have minimal sales. The best way to measure a website's success is to measure such things as the revenue generated by web traffic, the number of new customers acquired by web traffic, any reductions in customer service calls resulting from web traffic. As you deploy your Business 2.0 strategy, you want to build a website that creates stickiness and a sense of community for your customers. Explain why measuring web traffic is not a good indicator of web sales or website success. How would you implement Business 2.0 characteristics to create a sense of community for your customers? How could a wiki help grow your business? Could you use blogs to create a marketing buzz? What else can you do to ensure your website finds financial success?

If you are looking for Excel projects to incorporate into your class, try any of the following after reading this chapter.

Project Number	Project Name	Project Type	Plug-In Focus Area	Project Focus	Project Skill Set	Page Number
1	Financial Destiny	Excel	T2	Personal Budget	Introductory Formulas	AYK.4
2	Cash Flow	Excel	T2	Cash Flow	Introductory Formulas	AYK.4
3	Technology Budget	Excel	T1, T2	Hardware and Software	Introductory Formulas	AYK.4
4	Tracking Donations	Excel	T2	Employee Relationships	Introductory Formulas	AYK.4
5	Convert Currency	Excel	T2	Global Commerce	Introductory Formulas	AYK.5
6	Cost Comparison	Excel	T2	Total Cost of Ownership	Introductory Formulas	AYK.5
7	Time Management	Excel or Project	T2 or T12	Project Management	Introductory Gantt Charts	AYK.6
8	Maximize Profit	Excel	T2, T4	Strategic Analysis	Intermediate Formulas or Solver	AYK.6
9	Security Analysis	Excel	T3	Filtering Data	Intermediate Conditional Formatting, Autofilter, Subtotal	AYK.7
10	Gathering Data	Excel	T3	Data Analysis	Intermediate Conditional Formatting, PivotTable	AYK.8
11	Scanner System	Excel	T2	Strategic Analysis	Intermediate	AYK.8
12	Competitive Pricing	Excel	T2	Profit Maximization	Intermediate	AYK.9
13	Adequate Acquisitions	Excel	T2	Break-Even Analysis	Intermediate	AYK.9
24	Electronic Resumes	HTML	T9, T10, T11	Electronic Personal Marketing	Introductory Structural Tags	AYK.16
25	Gathering Feedback	Dreamweaver	T9, T10, T11	Data Collection	Intermediate Organization of Information	AYK.16

5 Transforming Organizations

What's in IT for Me?

This unit provides an overview of how organizations build information systems to prepare for competing in the 21st century. You as a business student need to know about this because information systems are the underlying foundation of how companies operate. A basic understanding of the principles of building information systems will make you a more valuable employee. You will be able to identify trouble spots early during the design process and make suggestions that will result in a better delivered information systems project—one that satisfies both you and your business.

Building an information system is analogous to constructing a house. You could sit back and let the developers do all the design work, construction, and testing with hopes that the house will satisfy your needs. However, participating in the house building process helps to guarantee that your needs are not only being heard, but also being met. It is good business practice to have direct user input steering the development of the finished product. The same is true for building information systems. Your knowledge of the systems development process will allow you to participate and ensure you are building flexible enterprise architectures that support not only current business needs, but also your future business needs.

Have you ever dreamed of traveling to exotic cities like Paris, Tokyo, Rio de Janeiro, or Cairo? In the past, the closest many people ever got to working in such cities was in their dreams. Today, the situation has changed. Most major companies cite global expansion as a link to future growth and a recent study noted that 91 percent of the companies doing business globally believe it is important to send employees on assignments in other countries.

If a career in global business has crossed your mind, this unit will help you understand the nature of competition in the global business world. The United States is a market of about 300 million people, but there are more than 6 billion potential customers in the 193 countries that make up the global market. Perhaps more interesting is that approximately 75 percent of the world's population lives in developing areas where technology, education, and per capita income still lag considerably behind developed (or industrialized) nations such as the United States. Developing countries are still a largely untapped market.

You, the business student, should be familiar with the potential of global business, including its many benefits and challenges. The demand for students with training in global business is almost certain to grow as the number of businesses competing in global markets increases.

To Share—Or Not to Share

People love social networks! Social networks are everywhere and a perfect way to share vacation photos, family events, and birthday parties with family, friends, and co-workers. About 40 percent of adults use at least one social media website, and 51 percent of those use more than one website. The majority of users are between the ages of 18 and 24. The Pew Research Center found that 89 percent of social network users primarily use the websites to update friends and family, while 57 percent use the websites to make plans with friends, and 49 percent use the websites to make new friends.

Facebook, Myspace, LinkedIn, Friendster, Urban Chat, and Black Planet are just a few of more than 100 websites connecting people around the world who are eager to share everything from photos to thoughts and feelings. But we need to remember that sometimes you can share too much; there can be too much information. Choosing who you share with and what you share is something you want to think about for your personal social networks and corporate social networks. According to Pew Research, more than 40 percent of users allow open access to their social networking profiles, which allows anyone from anywhere to view all of their personal information. The remaining 60 percent restrict access to friends, family, and co-workers. The following are the top 10 things you should consider before posting information to your social networks.

1: If You Don't Want to Share It – Don't Post It

You can select all the privacy settings you want on social networking sites, but the fact is, if you post it, it has the potential to be seen by someone you don't want seeing it. You know all those fun Facebook applications, quizzes, and polls you can't help but fill out? A study performed by the University of Virginia found that of the top 150 applications on Facebook, 90 percent were given access to information they didn't need in order for the application to function. So when you sign up to find out what sitcom star you most identify with, the makers of that poll now have access to your personal information. It's anybody's guess where it goes from there. Social networking is all about sharing, so something you think is in confidence can easily be shared and then shared again, and before you know it, someone you don't even know has access to something private. "When in doubt, leave it out" is a good motto to follow. And always remember that anything you share has the potential to be leaked in some way.

2: Never Give Out Your Password Hints

Most websites that contain secure personal information require a password and also have at least one password hint in case you forget. It typically goes like this: You sign up for something such as online banking and you get a log-in and password and then choose a security question for when you forget your password. What's the name of your first pet? What's your mother's maiden name? What was your high school mascot? What's the name of the first street you lived on? Including any of these details on a Facebook wall or status update may not seem like a big deal, but it could provide an identity thief with the last piece of the puzzle needed to hack into your bank account. Think before you post anything that could compromise this information.

3: Never Give Out Your Password

This one really seems like a no-brainer, but if it didn't happen, then Facebook probably wouldn't feel the need to list it in the No. 1 slot on its list of things you shouldn't share. Even sharing the password with a friend so he or she can log on and check something for you can be a risk. This is especially true with couples who feel like there's enough trust to share these kinds of things. Here's another scenario for you: You give your boyfriend your Facebook password because he wants to help you upload some vacation photos. A couple of months later, the relationship sours, he turns into a not-so-nice guy, and then there's a person out there who doesn't like you and has your log-in information. Time to cancel your account and get a new one. If you'd kept that information private, you could simply move on with your life. Now you have a compromised profile, and if you link to other sites or profiles, all that information is at risk as well. Keep your password to yourself, no matter what, and you never have to worry about it.

4: Never Provide Personal Financial Information

You would think that nobody would share things like where they do their banking or what their stock portfolio looks like, but it happens. It's easy for an innocent Facebook comment to reveal too much about your personal finances. Consider this scenario: You're posting to a long thread on a friend's wall about the bank crisis. You say something along the lines of, "We don't need to worry because we bank with a teacher's credit union," or even, "We put all our money into blue chip stocks and plan to ride it out." Again, if you're one of the 40 percent who allow open access to your profile, then suddenly identity thieves know where you bank and where you have the bulk of your investments. It's easy to forget that what may seem like a harmless comment on a Facebook wall could reveal a great deal about your personal finances. It's best to avoid that kind of talk.

5: Never Give Out Your Address or Phone Numbers

File this one under security risk. If you share your address and phone number on a social networking site, you open yourself up to threats of identity theft and other personal dangers such as burglaries. If you post that you're going on vacation and you have your address posted, then everyone knows you have an empty house. Identity thieves could pay a visit to your mailbox and open up a credit card in your name. Burglars could rid your home of anything of value. Even just posting your phone number gives people with Internet savvy easy access to your address. Reverse lookup services can supply anyone with your home address in possession of your phone number.

6: Never Share Photos of Your Children

Social networking sites are a common place for people to share pictures of their families, but if you're one of the 40 percent of users who don't restrict access to your profile, then those pictures are there for everyone to see. It's a sad fact, but a lot of predators use the Internet to stalk their prey. If you post pictures of your family and combine that with information like, "My husband is out of town this weekend" or "Little Johnny is old enough to stay at home by himself now," then your children's safety could be at risk. Nobody ever thinks it will happen to them until it does, so safety first is a good default mode when using social networking sites. Just like with other private matters, send family photos only to a select group of trusted friends and colleagues who you know won't share them.

7: Never Provide Company Information

You may be dying to tell the world about your new work promotion, but if it's news that could be advantageous to one of your company's competitors, then it's not something you should share. News of a planned expansion or a big project role and anything else about your workplace should be kept private. Sophos, a security software company, found that 63 percent of companies were afraid of what their employees were choosing to share on social networking sites. If you want to message it out, be selective and send private emails. Many companies are so serious about not being included in social networking sites that they forbid employees from using sites like Facebook at work. Some IT departments even filter the URLs and block access to these sites so employees aren't tempted to log on.

8: Never Give Links to Websites

With 51 percent of social network users taking advantage of more than one site, there's bound to be some crossover, especially if you have the sites linked. You may post something you find innocuous on Facebook, but then it's linked to your LinkedIn work profile and you've put your job at risk. If you link your various profiles, be aware that what you post in one world is available to the others. In 2009, a case of an employee caught lying on Facebook hit the news. The employee asked off for a weekend shift because he was ill and then posted pictures on his Facebook profile of himself at a party that same weekend. The news got back to his employer easily enough and he was fired. So if you choose to link your profiles, it's no longer a "personal life" and "work life" scenario.

9: Keep Your Social Plans to Yourself

Sharing your social plans for everybody to see isn't a good idea. Unless you're planning a big party and inviting all the users you're connected to, it will only make your other friends feel left out. There are also some security issues at stake here. Imagine a scenario where a jealous ex-boyfriend knows that you're meeting a new date out that night. What's to keep the ex from showing up and causing a scene or even potentially getting upset or violent? Nothing. If you're planning a party or an outing with a group of friends, send a personal "e-vite" for their eyes only and nobody is the wiser. If you're trying to cast a wide net by throwing out an idea for a social outing, just remember that anyone who has access to your profile sees it.

10: Do Not Share Personal Conversations

On Facebook, users can send personal messages or post notes, images, or videos to another user's wall. The wall is there for all to see, while messages are between the sender and the receiver, just like an email. Personal and private matters should never be shared on your wall. You wouldn't go around with a bullhorn announcing a private issue to the world, and the same thing goes on the Internet. This falls under the nebulous world of social networking etiquette. There is no official handbook for this sort of thing, but use your best judgment. If it's not something you'd feel comfortable sharing in person with extended family, acquaintances, work colleagues, or strangers, then you shouldn't share it on your Facebook wall.[1]

Introduction

In a competitive business climate, an organization's ability to efficiently align resources and business activities with strategic objectives can mean the difference between succeeding and just surviving. To achieve strategic alignment, organizations increasingly manage their systems development efforts and project planning activities to monitor performance and make better business decisions. Fast-growing companies outsource many areas of their business to extend their technical and operational resources. By outsourcing, they save time and boost productivity by not having to develop their own systems from scratch. They are then free to concentrate on innovation and their core business. The chapters in Unit 5 are:

- **Chapter Seventeen**—Developing Software to Streamline Operations.
- **Chapter Eighteen**—Methodologies for Supporting Agile Organizations.
- **Chapter Nineteen**—Managing Organizational Projects.
- **Chapter Twenty**—Developing a 21st-Century Organization.

Developing Software to Streamline Operations

17.1. Describe the seven phases of the systems development life cycle.

17.2. Explain why software problems are business problems.

LO 17.1 Describe the seven phases of the systems development life cycle.

The Systems Development Life Cycle (SDLC)

The multimillion-dollar Nike SCM system failure is legendary as Nike CEO Philip Knight famously stated, "This is what we get for our $400 million?" Nike partnered with i2 to implement an SCM system that never came to fruition. i2 blamed the failed implementation on the fact that Nike failed to use the vendor's implementation methodology and templates. Nike blamed the failure on faulty software.[2]

It is difficult to get an organization to work if its systems do not work. In the information age, software success, or failure, can lead directly to business success, or failure. Companies rely on software to drive business operations and ensure work flows throughout the company. As more and more companies rely on software to operate, so do the business-related consequences of software successes and failures.

The potential advantages of successful software implementations provide firms with significant incentives to manage software development risks. However, an alarmingly high number of software development projects come in late or over budget, and successful projects tend to maintain fewer features and functions than originally specified. Understanding the basics of software development, or the systems development life cycle, will help organizations avoid potential software development pitfalls and ensure that software development efforts are successful.

Before jumping into software development, it is important to understand a few key terms. A *legacy system* is an old system that is fast approaching or beyond the end of its useful life within an organization. *Conversion* is the process of transferring information from a legacy system to a new system. *Software customization* modifies software to meet specific user or business requirements. *Off-the-shelf application software* supports general business processes and does not require any specific software customization to meet the organization's needs.

The *systems development life cycle (SDLC)* is the overall process for developing information systems, from planning and analysis through implementation and maintenance. The SDLC is the foundation for all systems development methods, and hundreds of different activities are associated with each phase. These activities typically include determining budgets, gathering system requirements, and writing detailed user documentation.

The SDLC begins with a business need, proceeds to an assessment of the functions a system must have to satisfy the need, and ends when the benefits of the system no longer outweigh its maintenance costs. This is why it is referred to as a life cycle. The SDLC is comprised of seven distinct phases: planning, analysis, design, development, testing, implementation, and maintenance (see Figure 17.1).

FIGURE 17.1

The SDLC and Its
Associated Activities

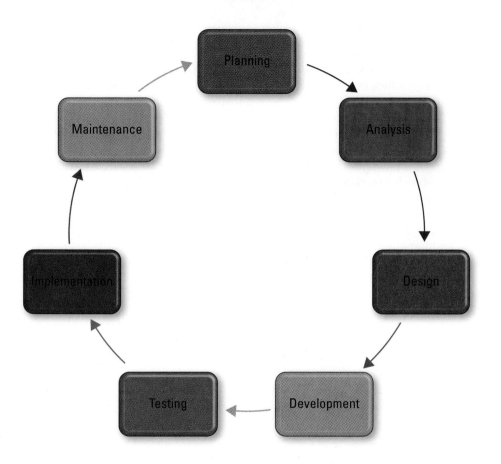

Phase	Associated Activity
Planning	■ Brainstorm issues and identify opportunities for the organization ■ Prioritize and choose projects for development ■ Set the project scope ■ Develop the project plan
Analysis	■ Gather the business requirement for the system ■ Define any constraints associated with the system
Design	■ Design the technical architecture required to support the system ■ Design the system models
Development	■ Build the technical architecture ■ Build the database ■ Build the applications
Testing	■ Write the test conditions ■ Perform system testing
Implementation	■ Write detailed user documentation ■ Provide training for the system users
Maintenance	■ Build a help desk to support the system users ■ Provide an environment to support system changes

PHASE 1: PLANNING

The **planning phase** establishes a high-level plan of the intended project and determines project goals. Planning is the first and most critical phase of any systems development effort, regardless of whether the effort is to develop a system that allows customers to order products online, determine the best logistical structure for warehouses around the world, or develop a strategic information alliance with another organization. Organizations must carefully plan the activities (and determine why they are necessary) to be successful. A **change agent** is a person or event that is the catalyst for implementing major changes for a system to meet business changes. **Brainstorming** is a technique for generating ideas by encouraging participants to offer as many ideas as possible in a short period without any analysis until all the ideas have been exhausted. Many times, new business opportunities are found as the result of a brainstorming session.

The Project Management Institute (PMI) develops procedures and concepts necessary to support the profession of project management (www.pmi.org). PMI defines a **project** as a temporary activity a company undertakes to create a unique product, service, or result. **Project management** is the application of knowledge, skills, tools, and techniques to project activities to meet project requirements. A **project manager** is an individual who is an expert in project planning and management, defines and develops the project plan, and tracks the plan to ensure the project is completed on time and on budget. The project manager is the person responsible for executing the entire project and defining the project scope that links the project to the organization's overall business goals. The **project scope** describes the business need (the problem the project will solve) and the justification, requirements, and current boundaries for the project. The **project plan** is a formal, approved document that manages and controls the entire project.

PHASE 2: ANALYSIS

In the **analysis phase** the firm analyzes its end-user business requirements and refines project goals into defined functions and operations of the intended system. **Business requirements** are the specific business requests the system must meet to be successful, so the analysis phase is critical because business requirements drive the entire systems development effort. A sample business requirement might state, "The CRM system must track all customer inquiries by product, region, and sales representative." The business requirement will state what the system must accomplish to be considered successful.

Gathering business requirements is basically conducting an investigation in which users identify all the organization's business needs and take measurements of these needs. Figure 17.2 displays a number of ways to gather business requirements. **Requirements management** is the process of managing changes to the business requirements throughout the project. Projects are typically dynamic in nature, and change should be expected and anticipated for successful project completion. A **requirements definition document** prioritizes all of the business requirements by order of importance to the company. **Sign-off** consists of the users' actual signatures indicating they approve all of the business requirements. If a system does not meet the business requirements, it will be deemed

FIGURE 17.2

Methods for Gathering Business Requirements

Methods for Gathering Business Requirements
Perform a *joint application development (JAD)* session where employees meet, sometimes for several days, to define or review the business requirements for the system.
Interview individuals to determine current operations and current issues.
Compile questionnaires to survey employees to discover issues.
Make observations to determine how current operations are performed.
Review business documents to discover reports, policies, and how information is used throughout the organization.

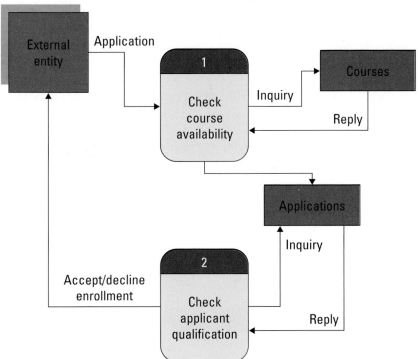

Automated Course Registration

FIGURE 17.3

Sample Data Flow Diagram

a failed project. For this reason, the organization must spend as much time, energy, and resources as necessary to gather accurate and detailed business requirements.

Once a business analyst takes a detailed look at how an organization performs its work and its processes, the analyst can recommend ways to improve these processes to make them more efficient and effective. ***Process modeling*** involves graphically representing the processes that capture, manipulate, store, and distribute information between a system and its environment. One of the most common diagrams used in process modeling is the data flow diagram. A ***data flow diagram (DFD)*** illustrates the movement of information between external entities and the processes and data stores within the system (see Figure 17.3). Process models and data flow diagrams establish the specifications of the system. ***Computer-aided software engineering (CASE)*** tools are software suites that automate systems analysis, design, and development. Process models and data flow diagrams can provide the basis for the automatic generation of the system if they are developed using a CASE tool.

PHASE 3: DESIGN

The ***design phase*** establishes descriptions of the desired features and operations of the system, including screen layouts, business rules, process diagrams, pseudo code, and other documentation. During the analysis phase, end users and MIS specialists work together to gather the detailed business requirements for the proposed project from a logical point of view. That is, during analysis, business requirements are documented without respect to technology or the technical infrastructure that will support the system. Moving into the design phase turns the project focus to the physical or technical point of view, defining the technical architecture that will support the system, including data models, screen designs, report layouts, and database models. (see Figure 17.4). The ***graphical user interface (GUI)*** is the interface to an information system. GUI screen design is the ability to model the information system screens for an entire system using icons, buttons, menus, and submenus. Data models represent a formal way to express data relationships to a database management system (DBMS). Entity relationship diagrams document the relationships between entities in a database environment (see Figure 17.5).

FIGURE 17.4

Sample Technical
Architecture

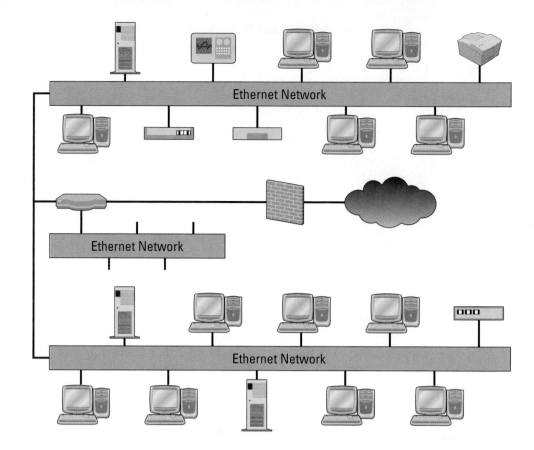

PHASE 4: DEVELOPMENT

The ***development phase*** takes all the detailed design documents from the design phase and transforms them into the actual system. In this phase, the project transitions from preliminary designs to actual physical implementation. During development, the company purchases and implements the equipment necessary to support the architecture. ***Software engineering*** is a disciplined approach for constructing information systems through the use of common methods, techniques, or tools. Software engineers use computer-aided software engineering (CASE) tools, which provide automated support for the development of the system. ***Control objects for information and related technology (COBIT)*** is a set of best practices that helps an organization to maximize the benefits of an information system, while at the same time establishing appropriate controls to ensure minimum errors.

During development, the team defines the programming language it will use to build the system. A ***scripting language*** is a programming method that provides for interactive modules to a website. ***Object-oriented languages*** group data and corresponding processes into objects. ***Fourth-generation languages (4GL)*** are programming languages that look similar to human languages. For example, a typical 4GL command might state, "FIND ALL RECORDS WHERE NAME IS "SMITH"." Programming languages are displayed in Figure 17.6.

PHASE 5: TESTING

The ***testing phase*** brings all the project pieces together into a special testing environment to eliminate errors and bugs and verify that the system meets all the business requirements defined in the analysis phase. ***Bugs*** are defects in the code of an information system. ***Test conditions*** detail the steps the system must perform along with the expected result of each step. Figure 17.7 displays several test conditions for testing user

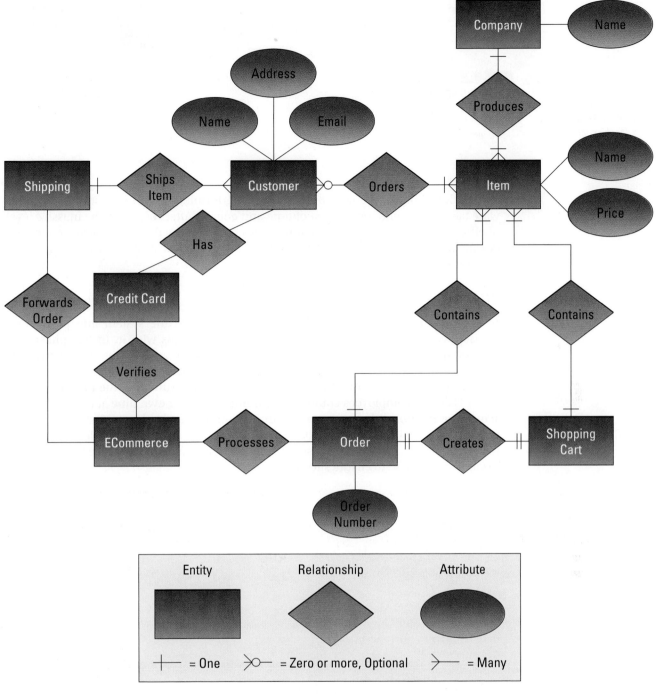

FIGURE 17.5

Sample Entity Relationship Diagram

log-on functionality in a system. The tester will execute each test condition and compare the expected results with the actual results in order to verify that the system functions correctly. Notice in Figure 17.7 how each test condition is extremely detailed and states the expected results that should occur when executing each test condition. Each time the actual result is different from the expected result, a "bug" is generated and the system goes back to development for a bug fix. Test condition 6 in Figure 17.7 displays a different actual result than the expected result because the system failed to allow the user to log on. After this test condition fails, it is obvious that the system is not functioning correctly, and it must be sent back to development for a bug fix.

A typical system development effort has hundreds or thousands of test conditions. Every single test condition must be executed to verify that the system performs as

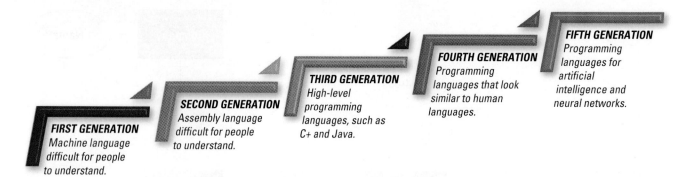

FIRST GENERATION
Machine language difficult for people to understand.

SECOND GENERATION
Assembly language difficult for people to understand.

THIRD GENERATION
High-level programming languages, such as C+ and Java.

FOURTH GENERATION
Programming languages that look similar to human languages.

FIFTH GENERATION
Programming languages for artificial intelligence and neural networks.

FIGURE 17.6

Overview of Programming Languages

expected. Writing all the test conditions and performing the actual testing of the software takes a tremendous amount of time and energy. After reviewing the massive level of effort required to test a system, it becomes obvious why this is a critical step in successful development. Figure 17.8 displays the different types of tests typically included in a systems development effort.

PHASE 6: IMPLEMENTATION

In the *implementation phase,* the organization places the system into production so users can begin to perform actual business operations with it. In this phase, the detailed *user documentation* is created that highlights how to use the system and how to troubleshoot issues or problems. Training is also provided for the system users and can take place online or in a classroom. *Online training* runs over the Internet or on a CD or DVD, and employees complete the training on their own time at their own pace. *Workshop training* is held in a classroom environment and led by an instructor. One of the best ways to support users is to create a *help desk* or a group of people who respond to users' questions. Figure 17.9 displays the different implementation methods an organization can choose to ensure success.

FIGURE 17.7

Sample Test Conditions

Test Condition Number	Date Tested	Tested	Test Condition	Expected Result	Actual Result	Pass/ Fail
1	1/1/17	Emily Hickman	Click on System Start Button	Main Menu appears	Same as expected result	Pass
2	1/1/17	Emily Hickman	Click on Log-on Button in Main Menu	Log-on Screen appears asking for User name and Password	Same as expected result	Pass
3	1/1/17	Emily Hickman	Type Emily Hickman in the User Name Field	Emily Hickman appears in the User Name Field	Same as expected result	Pass
4	1/1/17	Emily Hickman	Type Zahara123 in the password field	XXXXXXXXX appears in the password field	Same as expected result	Pass
5	1/1/17	Emily Hickman	Click on OK button	User log-on request is sent to database and user name and password are verified	Same as expected result	Pass
6	1/1/17	Emily Hickman	Click on Start	User name and password are accepted and the system main menu appears	Screen appeared stating log-on failed and user name and password were incorrect	Fail

Alpha Testing	Development Testing	Integration Testing
Assess if the entire system meets the design requirements of the users	Test the system to ensure it is bug-free	Verify that separate systems can work together, passing data back and forth correctly

System Testing	User Acceptance Testing (UAT)	Unit Testing
Verify that the units or pieces of code function correctly when integrated	Determine if the system satisfies the user and business requirements	Test individual units or pieces of code for a system

PHASE 7: MAINTENANCE

FIGURE 17.8

Different Forms of System Testing

Maintaining the system is the final sequential phase of any systems development effort. In the *maintenance phase,* the organization performs changes, corrections, additions, and upgrades to ensure the system continues to meet business goals. This phase continues for the life of the system because the system must change as the business evolves and its needs change, which means conducting constant monitoring, supporting the new system with frequent minor changes (for example, new reports or information capturing), and reviewing the system to be sure it is moving the organization toward its strategic goals. *Corrective maintenance* makes system changes to repair design flaws, coding errors, or implementation issues. *Preventive maintenance* makes system changes to reduce the chance of future system failure. During the maintenance phase, the system will generate reports to help users and MIS specialists ensure it is functioning correctly (see Figure 17.10).

Software Problems Are Business Problems

LO 17.2 Explain why software problems are business problems.

MIS project failures can cost companies financially and even ruin business reputations. The primary reasons for project failure are:

- Unclear or missing business requirements.
- Skipping SDLC phases.

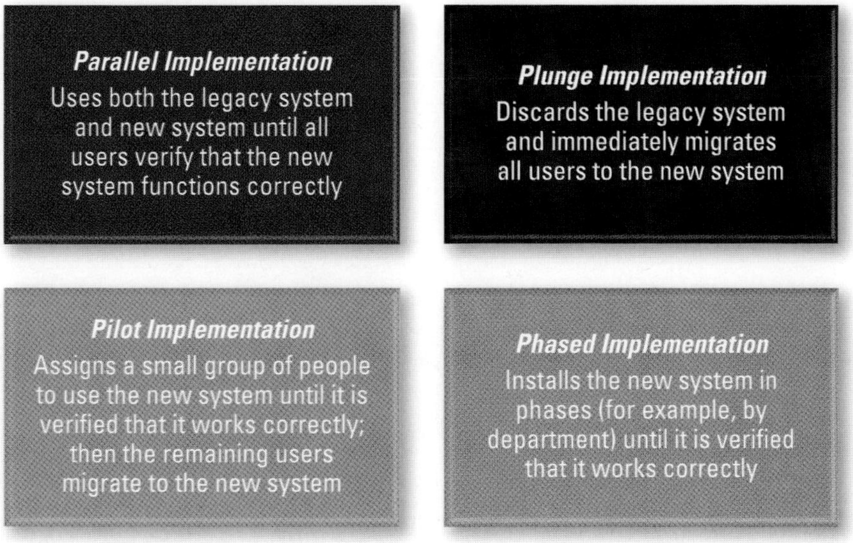

FIGURE 17.9

System Implementation Methods

Parallel Implementation	Plunge Implementation
Uses both the legacy system and new system until all users verify that the new system functions correctly	Discards the legacy system and immediately migrates all users to the new system

Pilot Implementation	Phased Implementation
Assigns a small group of people to use the new system until it is verified that it works correctly; then the remaining users migrate to the new system	Installs the new system in phases (for example, by department) until it is verified that it works correctly

Report	Examples
Internal report	Presents data that are distributed inside the organization and intended for employees within an organization. Internal reports typically support day-to-day operations monitoring that supports managerial decision making.
Detailed internal report	Presents information with little or no filtering or restrictions of the data.
Summary internal report	Organizes and categorizes data for managerial perusal. A report that summarizes total sales by product for each month is an example of a summary internal report. The data for a summary report are typically categorized and summarized to indicate trends and potential problems.
Exception reporting	Highlights situations occurring outside of the normal operating range for a condition or standard. These internal reports include only exceptions and might highlight accounts that are unpaid or delinquent or identify items that are low in stock.
Information system control report	Ensures the reliability of information, consisting of policies and their physical implementation, access restrictions, or record keeping of actions and transactions.
Information systems audit report	Assesses a company's information system to determine necessary changes and to help ensure the information systems' availability, confidentiality, and integrity.
Post-implementation report	Presents a formal report or audit of a project after it is up and running.

FIGURE 17.10

Examples of System Reports

- Failure to manage project scope.
- Failure to manage project plan.
- Changing technology.

UNCLEAR OR MISSING BUSINESS REQUIREMENTS

The most common reason systems fail is because the business requirements are either missing or incorrectly gathered during the analysis phase. The business requirements drive the entire system. If they are not accurate or complete, the system will not be successful.

It is important to discuss the relationship between the SDLC and the cost for the organization to fix errors. An error found during the analysis and design phase is relatively inexpensive to fix. All that is typically required is a change to a Word document. However, exactly the same error found during the testing or implementation phase is going to cost the organization an enormous amount to fix because it has to change the actual system. Figure 17.11 displays how the cost to fix an error grows exponentially the later the error is found in the SDLC.

FIGURE 17.11

The Cost of Finding Errors

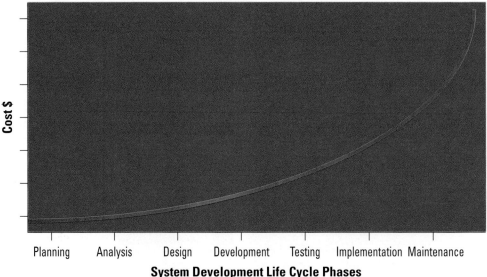

SKIPPING SDLC PHASES

The first thing individuals tend to do when a project falls behind schedule is to start skipping phases in the SDLC. For example, if a project is three weeks behind in the development phase, the project manager might decide to cut testing down from six weeks to three weeks. Obviously, it is impossible to perform all the testing in half the time. Failing to test the system will lead to unfound errors, and chances are high that the system will fail. It is critical that an organization perform all phases in the SDLC during every project. Skipping any of the phases is sure to lead to system failure.

FAILURE TO MANAGE PROJECT SCOPE

As the project progresses, the project manager must track the status of each activity and adjust the project plan if an activity is added or taking longer than expected. Scope creep and feature creep are difficult to manage and can easily cause a project to fall behind schedule.

FAILURE TO MANAGE PROJECT PLAN

Managing the project plan is one of the biggest challenges during systems development. The project plan is the road map the organization follows during the development of the system. Developing the initial project plan is the easiest part of the project manager's job. Managing and revising the project plan is the hard part. The project plan is a living document since it changes almost daily on any project. Failing to monitor, revise, and update the project plan can lead to project failure.

CHANGING TECHNOLOGY

Many real-world projects have hundreds of business requirements, take years to complete, and cost millions of dollars. Gordon Moore, co-founder of Intel Corporation, observed in 1965 that chip density doubles every 18 months. This observation, known as Moore's law, simply means that memory sizes, processor power, and so on, all follow the same pattern and roughly double in capacity every 18 months. As Moore's law states, technology changes at an incredibly fast pace; therefore, it is possible to have to revise an entire project plan in the middle of a project as a result of a change in technology. Technology changes so fast that it is almost impossible to deliver an information system without feeling the pain of changing technology.

OPENING CASE STUDY QUESTIONS

1. Which phase in the systems development life cycle is the most critical when building a social networking website?

2. Which phase in the systems development life cycle is the least critical when building a social networking website?

3. Why is the cost of finding errors important to a business when developing software?

Chapter Seventeen Case: Reducing Ambiguity in Business Requirements

The number one reason projects fail is bad business requirements. Business requirements are considered "bad" because of ambiguity or insufficient involvement of end users during analysis and design.

A requirement is unambiguous if it has the same interpretation for all parties. Different interpretations by different participants will usually result in unmet expectations. Here is an example of an ambiguous requirement and an example of an unambiguous requirement:

- **Ambiguous requirement:** The financial report must show profits in local and U.S. currencies.

- **Unambiguous requirement:** The financial report must show profits in local and U.S. currencies using the exchange rate printed in *The Wall Street Journal* for the last business day of the period being reported.

Ambiguity is impossible to prevent completely because it is introduced into requirements in natural ways. For example:

- Requirements can contain technical implications that are obvious to the IT developers but not to the customers.

- Requirements can contain business implications that are obvious to the customer but not to the IT developers.

- Requirements may contain everyday words whose meanings are "obvious" to everyone, yet different for everyone.

- Requirements are reflections of detailed explanations that may have included multiple events, multiple perspectives, verbal rephrasing, emotion, iterative refinement, selective emphasis, and body language—none of which are captured in the written statements.

Tips for Reviewing Business Requirements

When reviewing business requirements always look for the following words to help dramatically reduce ambiguity:

- **"And"** and **"or"** have well-defined meanings and ought to be completely unambiguous, yet they are often understood only informally and interpreted inconsistently. For example, consider the statement "The alarm must ring if button T is pressed and if button F is pressed." This statement may be intended to mean that to ring the alarm, both buttons must be pressed or it may be intended to mean that either one can be pressed. A statement like this should never appear in a requirement because the potential for misinterpretation is too great. A preferable approach is to be very explicit, for example, "The alarm must ring if both buttons T and F are pressed simultaneously. The alarm should not ring in any other circumstance."

- **"Always"** might really mean "most of the time," in which case it should be made more explicit. For example, the statement "We always run reports A and B together" could be challenged with "In other words, there is never any circumstance where you would run A without B and B without A?" If you build a system with an "always" requirement, then you are actually building the system to never run report A without report B. If a user suddenly wants report B without report A, you will need to make significant system changes.

- **"Never"** might mean "rarely," in which case it should be made more explicit. For example, the statement "We never run reports A and B in the same month" could be challenged with, "So that means that if I see that A has been run, I can be absolutely certain that no one will want to run B." Again, if you build a system that supports a "never" requirement then the system users can never perform that requirement. For example, the system would never allow a user to run reports A and B in the same month, no matter what the circumstances.

- **Boundary conditions** are statements about the line between true and false and do and do not. These statements may or may not be meant to include end points. For example, "We want to use method X when there are up to 10 pages, but method Y otherwise." If you were building this system, would you include page 10 in method X or in method Y? The answer to this question will vary causing an ambiguous business requirement.

Questions

1. Why are ambiguous business requirements the leading cause of system development failures?

2. Why do the words *and* and *or* tend to lead to ambiguous requirements?

3. Research the web and determine other reasons for "bad" business requirements.

4. What is wrong with the following business requirement: "The system must support employee birthdays since every employee always has a birthday every year."

18 Methodologies for Supporting Agile Organizations

18.1. Summarize the different software development methodologies.

LO 18.1 Summarize the different software development methodologies.

Software Development Methodologies

Today, systems are so large and complex that teams of architects, analysts, developers, testers, and users must work together to create the millions of lines of custom-written code that drive enterprises. For this reason, developers have created a number of different systems development life cycle methodologies. A ***methodology*** is a set of policies, procedures, standards, processes, practices, tools, techniques, and tasks that people apply to technical and management challenges. Firms use a methodology to manage the deployment of technology with work plans, requirements documents, and test plans, for instance. A formal methodology can include coding standards, code libraries, development practices, and much more.

The oldest and the best known is the ***waterfall methodology,*** a sequence of phases in which the output of each phase becomes the input for the next (see Figure 18.1). In the SDLC, this means the steps are performed one at a time, in order, from planning through implementation and maintenance. The traditional waterfall method no longer

FIGURE 18.1

The Traditional Waterfall Methodology

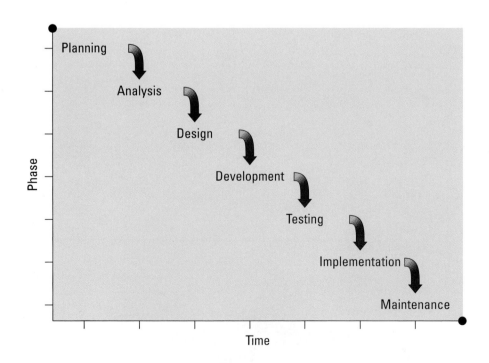

Planning

Analysis

Design

Development

Testing

Implementation

Maintenance

Phase

Time

FIGURE 18.2

Disadvantages of the
Waterfall Methodology

Issues Related to the Waterfall Methodology	
The business problem	Any flaws in accurately defining and articulating the business problem in terms of what the business users actually require flow onward to the next phase.
The plan	Managing costs, resources, and time constraints is difficult in the waterfall sequence. What happens to the schedule if a programmer quits? How will a schedule delay in a specific phase impact the total cost of the project? Unexpected contingencies may sabotage the plan.
The solution	The waterfall methodology is problematic in that it assumes users can specify all business requirements in advance. Defining the appropriate IT infrastructure that is flexible, scalable, and reliable is a challenge. The final IT infrastructure solution must meet not only current but also future needs in terms of time, cost, feasibility, and flexibility. Vision is inevitably limited at the head of the waterfall.

serves most of today's development efforts, however; it is inflexible and expensive, and it requires rigid adherence to the sequence of steps. Its success rate is only about 1 in 10. Figure 18.2 explains some issues related to the waterfall methodology.

Today's business environment is fierce. The desire and need to outsmart and outplay competitors remains intense. Given this drive for success, leaders push internal development teams and external vendors to deliver agreed-upon systems faster and cheaper so they can realize benefits as early as possible. Even so, systems remain large and complex. The traditional waterfall methodology no longer serves as an adequate systems development methodology in most cases. Because this development environment is the norm and not the exception anymore, development teams use a new breed of alternative development methods to achieve their business objectives.

Prototyping is a modern design approach where the designers and system users use an iterative approach to building the system. **Discovery prototyping** builds a small-scale representation or working model of the system to ensure it meets the user and business requirements. The advantages of prototyping include:

■ Prototyping encourages user participation.

■ Prototypes evolve through iteration, which better supports change.

■ Prototypes have a physical quality allowing users to see, touch, and experience the system as it is developed.

■ Prototypes tend to detect errors earlier.

■ Prototyping accelerates the phases of the SDLC, helping to ensure success.

It is common knowledge that the smaller the project, the greater the success rate. The iterative development style is the ultimate in small projects. Basically, **iterative development** consists of a series of tiny projects. It has become the foundation of multiple agile methodologies. Figure 18.3 displays an iterative approach.

An **agile methodology** aims for customer satisfaction through early and continuous delivery of useful software components developed by an iterative process using the bare minimum requirements. Agile methodology is what it sounds like: fast and efficient, with lower costs and fewer features. Using agile methods helps refine feasibility and supports the process for getting rapid feedback as functionality is introduced. Developers can adjust as they move along and better clarify unclear requirements.

One key to delivering a successful product or system is to deliver value to users as soon as possible—give them something they want and like early to create buy-in, generate enthusiasm, and, ultimately, reduce scope. Using agile methodologies helps maintain accountability and helps to establish a barometer for the satisfaction of end users. It

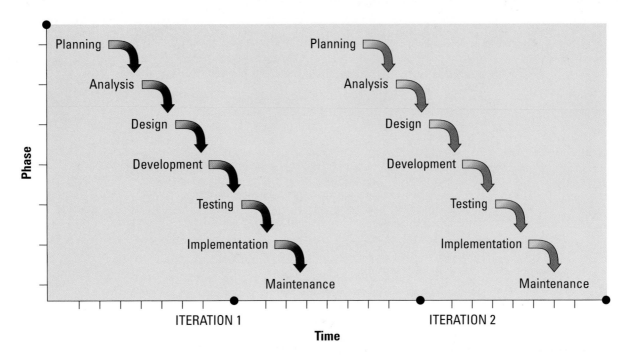

FIGURE 18.3

The Iterative Approach

does no good to accomplish something on time and on budget if it does not satisfy the end user. The primary forms of agile methodologies include:

- Rapid prototyping or rapid application development methodology.
- Extreme programming methodology.
- Rational unified process (RUP) methodology.
- Scrum methodology.

It is important not to get hung up on the names of the methodologies—some are proprietary brand names, others are generally accepted names. It is more important to know how these alternative methodologies are used in today's business environment and the benefits they can deliver.

RAPID APPLICATION DEVELOPMENT (RAD) METHODOLOGY

In response to the faster pace of business, rapid application development has become a popular route for accelerating systems development. **Rapid application development (RAD) methodology** (also called **rapid prototyping**) emphasizes extensive user involvement in the rapid and evolutionary construction of working prototypes of a system, to accelerate the systems development process. Figure 18.4 displays the fundamentals of RAD.

EXTREME PROGRAMMING METHODOLOGY

Extreme programming (XP) methodology, like other agile methods, breaks a project into four phases, and developers cannot continue to the next phase until the previous phase is complete. The delivery strategy supporting XP is that the quicker the feedback

FIGURE 18.4

Fundamentals of RAD

Fundamentals of RAD
Focus initially on creating a prototype that looks and acts like the desired system.
Actively involve system users in the analysis, design, and development phases.
Accelerate collecting the business requirements through an interactive and iterative construction approach.

the more improved the results. XP has four basic phases: planning, designing, coding, and testing. Planning can include user interviews, meetings, and small releases. During design, functionality is not added until it is required or needed. During coding, the developers work together soliciting continuous feedback from users, eliminating the communication gap that generally exists between developers and customers. During testing, the test requirements are generated before any code is developed. Extreme programming saves time and produces successful projects by continuously reviewing and revamping needed and unneeded requirements.

Customer satisfaction is the primary reason XP finds success as developers quickly respond to changing business requirements, even late in the life cycle. XP encourages managers, customers, and developers to work together as a team to ensure the delivery of high-quality systems. XP is similar to a puzzle; there are many small pieces and individually the pieces make no sense, but when they are pieced together they can create a new system.

RATIONAL UNIFIED PROCESS (RUP) METHODOLOGY

The *rational unified process (RUP) methodology,* owned by IBM, provides a framework for breaking down the development of software into four "gates." Each gate consists of executable iterations of the software in development. A project stays in a gate waiting for the stakeholder's analysis, and then it either moves to the next gate or is cancelled. The gates include:

- **Gate one: inception.** This phase ensures all stakeholders have a shared understanding of the proposed system and what it will do.
- **Gate two: elaboration.** This phase expands on the agreed-upon details of the system, including the ability to provide an architecture to support and build it.
- **Gate three: construction.** This phase includes building and developing the product.
- **Gate four: transition.** Primary questions answered in this phase address ownership of the system and training of key personnel.

Because RUP is an iterative methodology, the user can reject the product and force the developers to go back to gate one. RUP helps developers avoid reinventing the wheel and focuses on rapidly adding or removing reusable chunks of processes addressing common problems.

SCRUM METHODOLOGY

Another agile methodology, *scrum methodology,* uses small teams to produce small pieces of software using a series of "sprints," or 30-day intervals, to achieve an appointed goal. In rugby, a scrum is a team pack and everyone in the pack works together to move the ball down the field. In scrum methodology, each day ends or begins with a stand-up meeting to monitor and control the development effort.

OPENING CASE STUDY QUESTION

If you were consulting to a business that wanted to build a social networking website, which development methodology would you recommend and why?

June is the perfect time of year to reflect on the current state of all the key projects that were approved in January. At this stage, you and your management team should have enough data to know if each initiative will successfully meet its objectives. You may already know there are projects in your organization that are not positioned to succeed, yet they still receive funding and staff. When you assess the current state of your projects, do you see any of the following signs:

- Critical issues keep opening up, but they're not getting resolved.
- Project scope is constantly changing.
- The project is consistently behind its plan, despite efforts to get it back on schedule.
- Competing deliverables are distracting your attention.

If all of these signs appear, it may be time to cut your losses and cut the project—or at least radically restructure it. You know better than anyone that throwing good money after the bad will not save the project because it doesn't address the root cause of the project's woes. To determine a course of action, ask yourself the following questions about the project:

- What can be salvaged?
- What can be delivered with the time and budget that are left?
- Do you have the right leadership in place to complete the project successfully?
- Is the plan for the initiative sound and realistic?
- Am I and my management team doing everything we can to support the initiative?

If part of or the entire project can be salvaged and delivered on time and with the remaining budget, if the right leaders are present to steer the project, if the new plan is solid, and if management will continue to support the project, the following four steps will help you regain control and deliver the revised project successfully. These steps are basic blocking and tackling, but the detail behind the plan—and more importantly, the execution and focus the project team brings to the effort—will determine whether the project recovery effort will succeed.

Step One: Assess the Situation

Get as much information about the current state of the project as possible. Use that data to make informed decisions about what needs to happen next. Don't be afraid if, at this stage, there are more questions than answers; that is normal. The key is to ask the right question to obtain as accurate a picture of the project's status as possible. The following questions address key data points you need to collect:

- How critical is the delivery date?
- What functionality is exactly required by the delivery date?
- What has been completed and what is still outstanding?
- How willing will people be to change scope, dates, and budget?

The last question about change is critical because it touches on the people and political issues that are present in any project and any organization. Even when faced with sure failure, people find it hard to change unless there is a direct benefit to them and their team. For recovery to have a chance, expectations need to change, especially those of the key stakeholders.

When gathering data about the current state of the project, remember to ask the current team for their opinions on what went wrong. It can be easy to ignore their input since they're associated with the current failure. In fact, each individual can provide great insight into why the project arrived in its current state. Reach out to key team members and get their suggestions for correcting the situation.

Step Two: Prepare the Team for Recovery

Everyone involved in the project—from executive management to stakeholders to project team members—needs to accept that the current project is broken and needs to be fixed. They also need to accept that the existing project plan and approach to delivering the project is flawed and needs to be restructured. If they don't accept these facts, they will likely resist the steps needed for recovery.

Once everyone has accepted the need to change course, define realistic expectations for what can be delivered given the current state and time frame. Also establish metrics for success and control of the recovery. If you had metrics at the outset of the project, you may need to establish new ones, or you may simply need to hold yourself and others accountable to them.

Both management and the project manager in charge of the recovery need to develop a supportive environment for team members. Giving them realistic goals and providing them with the needed space, equipment, and training will position them for success.

Finally, take advantage of the new momentum associated with the recovery and involve all the key parties in the status of the project. This involvement will keep everyone focused and engaged. It will assure project team members and stakeholders that they're needed for more than just executing tasks.

Step Three: Develop a Game Plan for Recovery

Think of the recovery as a new project, separate from the old one. This new project requires its own scope of work to make the expectations around what is being delivered and the new criteria for judging success crystal clear. The new scope may require you to determine if you have the right resources on the project team or if you need to re-staff some team members.

Based on the new project scope, the project manager and project team should lay out a clear and realistic road map to achieve the objectives. The main difference in the plan this time is that it must not fail. It will also be under much greater scrutiny by management. Consequently, it will be critical to make sure the milestones are shorter in duration to demonstrate success and to allow for course correction if needed. The shorter milestones will provide valuable data points to determine the health of the project early.

Step Four: Execute the Game Plan

With the new plan in hand, it's time to get down to business. Remember that during execution, it is not just the project team members who are accountable. Everyone from management on down is on the hook. All facets of the project, from environment to support, need to be in sync at all times, and everyone needs to know they are accountable for the project recovery to succeed.

To make sure everyone is on the same page during the recovery, the project communication needs to be clear, informative, and frequent. Clearly define in your communication plan how information will be disseminated, how urgent items will be addressed, and how key decisions will be made.

Given the added level of scrutiny on the plan and the project, being able to provide the latest on the metrics to show the improved control over the project will be key. The data will also allow you to quickly make corrections when any sign of trouble surfaces.

Getting a flailing project back on track is not easy. It requires sustained effort, focus, commitment, and objectivity. During the project recovery there is no time for personal agendas. The ability to see and do what is best for the project is required from every team member.

It is also important to not lose sight of the pressure that everyone is under. Make sure there is a positive focus on people. The team needs to have the ability to bond, release a little steam, and be focused on the task at hand.

When the project has been successfully delivered, celebrate and recognize the effort of each and every team member. Finally, learn from this successful project recovery so that you and your organization can avoid having to recover a project again. Pay attention to the warning signs and act swiftly and decisively to make corrections early in the project's life cycle so that successful delivery is ensured the first time.[1]

Questions

1. What signs identify if a current project is experiencing issues?

2. Which software development methodology would you choose to build a new accounting system? Explain why.

3. Which software development methodology would you choose to build a personal website? Explain why.

CHAPTER **19**

Managing Organizational Projects

19.1. Explain project management and identify the primary reasons projects fail.

19.2. Identify the primary project planning diagrams.

19.3. Identify the three different types of outsourcing along with their benefits and challenges.

Using Project Management to Deliver Successful Projects

LO 19.1 Explain project management and identify the primary reasons projects fail.

No one would think of building an office complex by turning loose 100 different construction teams to build 100 different rooms with no single blueprint or agreed-upon vision of the completed structure. Yet this is precisely the situation in which many large organizations find themselves when managing information technology projects. Organizations routinely overschedule their resources (human and otherwise), develop redundant projects, and damage profitability by investing in nonstrategic efforts that do not contribute to the organization's bottom line. Business leaders face a rapidly moving and unforgiving global marketplace that will force them to use every possible tool to sustain competitiveness; project management is one of those tools. For this reason, business personnel must anticipate being involved in some form of project management during their career. Figure 19.1 displays a few examples of the different types of projects organizations encounter.

FIGURE 19.1

Types of Organizational Projects

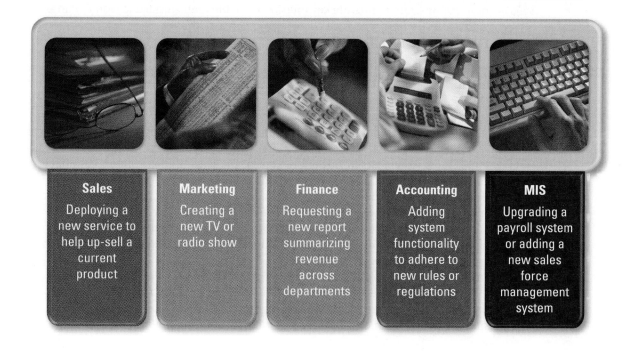

Sales	Marketing	Finance	Accounting	MIS
Deploying a new service to help up-sell a current product	Creating a new TV or radio show	Requesting a new report summarizing revenue across departments	Adding system functionality to adhere to new rules or regulations	Upgrading a payroll system or adding a new sales force management system

FIGURE 19.2

Examples of Tangible
and Intangible
Benefits

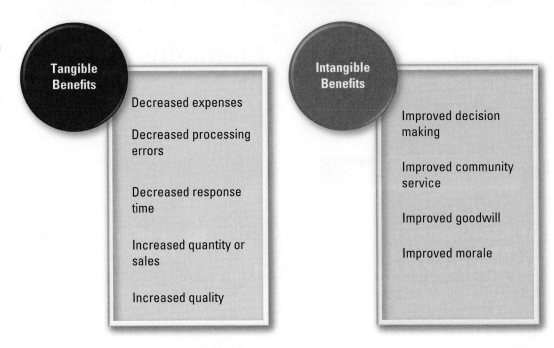

Tangible
Benefits

Decreased expenses

Decreased processing
errors

Decreased response
time

Increased quantity or
sales

Increased quality

Intangible
Benefits

Improved decision
making

Improved community
service

Improved goodwill

Improved morale

Tangible benefits are easy to quantify and typically measured to determine the success or failure of a project. *Intangible benefits* are difficult to quantify or measure (see Figure 19.2 for examples). One of the most difficult decisions managers make is identifying the projects in which to invest time, energy, and resources. An organization must choose what it wants to do—justifying it, defining it, and listing expected results—and how to do it, including project budget, schedule, and analysis of project risks. *Feasibility* is the measure of the tangible and intangible benefits of an information system. Figure 19.3 displays several types of feasibility studies business analysts can use to determine the projects that best fit business goals.

With today's volatile economic environment, many businesses are being forced to do more with less. Businesses today must respond quickly to a rapidly changing business environment by continually innovating goods and services. Effective project management provides a controlled way to respond to changing market conditions, to foster global communications, and to provide key metrics to enable managerial decision making.

BALANCE OF THE TRIPLE CONSTRAINT

Figure 19.4 displays the relationships among the three primary and interdependent variables in any project—time, cost, and scope. All projects are limited in some way by these three constraints. The Project Management Institute calls the framework for evaluating these competing demands *the triple constraint.*

The relationship among these variables is such that if any one changes, at least one other is likely to be affected. For example, moving up a project's finish date could mean either increasing costs to hire more staff or decreasing the scope to eliminate features or functions. Increasing a project's scope to include additional customer requests could extend the project's time to completion or increase the project's cost—or both—to accommodate the changes. Project quality is affected by the project manager's ability to balance these competing demands. High-quality projects deliver the agreed upon product or service on time and on budget. Project management is the science of making intelligent trade-offs between time, cost, and scope. Benjamin Franklin's timeless advice—*by failing to prepare, you prepare to fail*—applies to many of today's software development projects.

The Project Management Institute created the *Project Management Body of Knowledge (PMBOK)* for the education and certification of project managers. Figure 19.5 summarizes the key elements of project planning according to *PMBOK.*

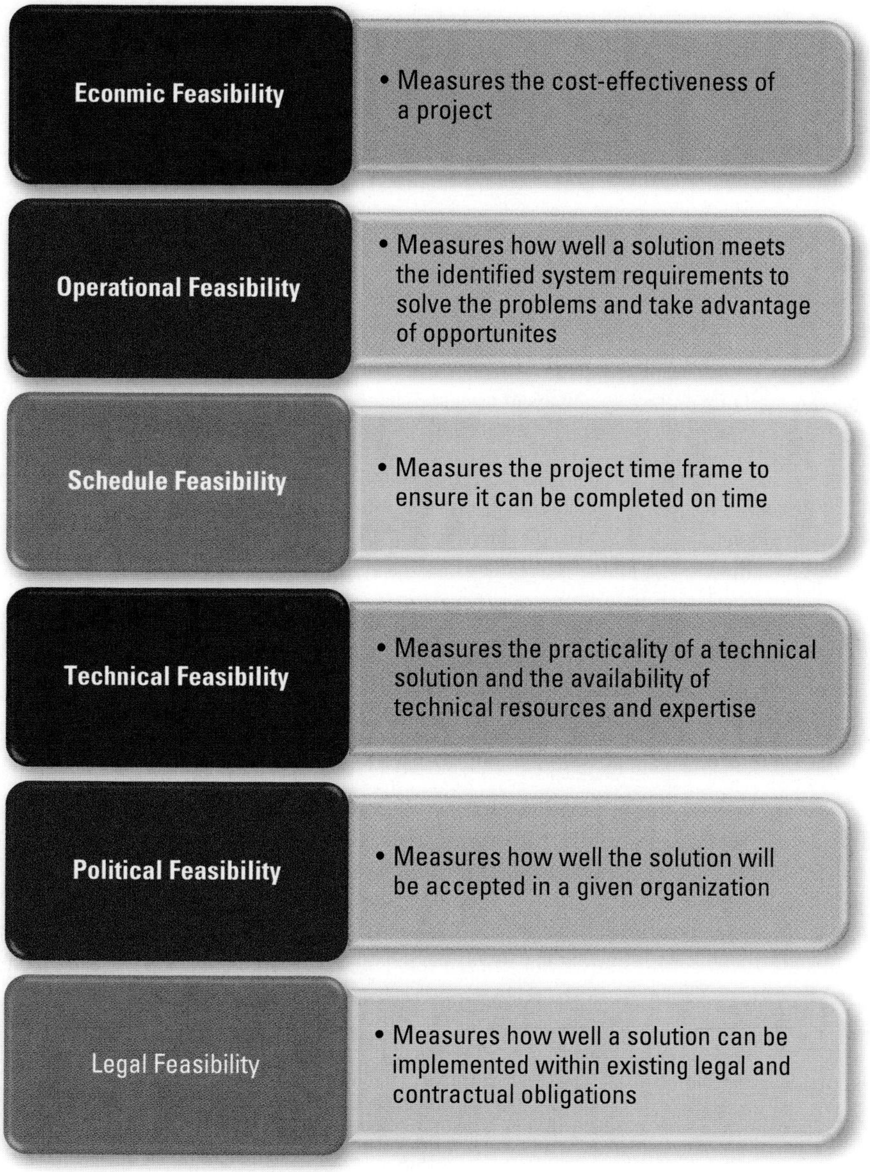

FIGURE 19.3

Types of Feasibility Studies

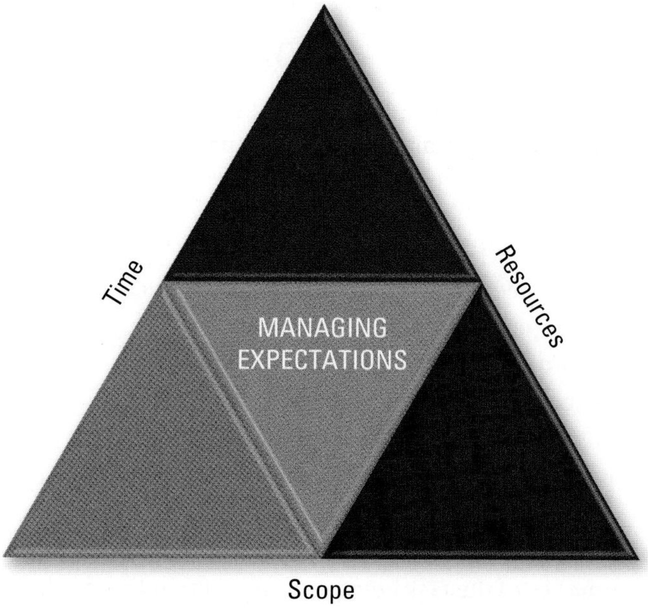

Econmic Feasibility
- Measures the cost-effectiveness of a project

Operational Feasibility
- Measures how well a solution meets the identified system requirements to solve the problems and take advantage of opportunites

Schedule Feasibility
- Measures the project time frame to ensure it can be completed on time

Technical Feasibility
- Measures the practicality of a technical solution and the availability of technical resources and expertise

Political Feasibility
- Measures how well the solution will be accepted in a given organization

Legal Feasibility
- Measures how well a solution can be implemented within existing legal and contractual obligations

FIGURE 19.4

The Triple Constraint:
Changing One Changes All

Time

Resources

MANAGING EXPECTATIONS

Scope

Tool	Description
Communication plan	Defines the how, what, when, and who regarding the flow of project information to stakeholders and is key for managing expectations.
Executive sponsor	The person or group who provides the financial resources for the project.
Project assumption	Factors considered to be true, real, or certain without proof or demonstration. Examples include hours in a workweek or time of year the work will be performed.
Project constraint	Specific factors that can limit options, including budget, delivery dates, available skilled resources, and organizational policies.
Project deliverable	Any measurable, tangible, verifiable outcome, result, or item that is produced to complete a project or part of a project. Examples of project deliverables include design documents, testing scripts, and requirements documents.
Project management office (PMO)	An internal department that oversees all organizational projects. This group must formalize and professionalize project management expertise and leadership. One of the primary initiatives of the PMO is to educate the organization on techniques and procedures necessary to run successful projects.
Project milestone	Represents key dates when a certain group of activities must be performed. For example, completing the planning phase might be a project milestone. If a project milestone is missed, then chances are the project is experiencing problems.
Project objectives	Quantifiable criteria that must be met for the project to be considered a success.
Project requirements document	Defines the specifications for product/output of the project and is key for managing expectations, controlling scope, and completing other planning efforts.
Project scope statement	Links the project to the organization's overall business goals. It describes the business need (the problem the project will solve) and the justification, requirements, and current boundaries for the project. It defines the work that must be completed to deliver the product with the specified features and functions, and it includes constraints, assumptions, and requirements—all components necessary for developing accurate cost estimates.
Project stakeholder	Individuals and organizations actively involved in the project or whose interests might be affected as a result of project execution or project completion.
Responsibility matrix	Defines all project roles and indicates what responsibilities are associated with each role.
Status report	Periodic reviews of actual performance versus expected performance.

FIGURE 19.5

PMBOK Elements of Project Management

LO 19.2 **Identify the primary project planning diagrams.**

Primary Project Planning Diagrams

Project planning is the process of detailed planning that generates answers to common operational questions such as why are we doing this project or what is the project going to accomplish for the business? Some of the key questions project planning can help answer include:

- How are deliverables being produced?
- What activities or tasks need to be accomplished to produce the deliverables?
- Who is responsible for performing the tasks?
- What resources are required to perform the tasks?
- When will the tasks be performed?
- How long will it take to perform each task?
- Are any tasks dependent upon other tasks being completed before they can begin?
- How much does each task cost?
- What skills and experience are required to perform each task?
- How is the performance of the task being measured including quality?
- How are issues being tracked?

- How is change being addressed?
- How is communication occurring and when?
- What risks are associated with each task?

The project objectives are among the most important areas to define because they are essentially the major elements of the project. When an organization achieves the project objectives, it has accomplished the major goals of the project and the project scope is satisfied. Project objectives must include metrics so that the project's success can be measured. The metrics can include cost, schedule, and quality metrics. Figure 19.6 lists the SMART criteria—useful reminders about how to ensure the project has created understandable and measurable objectives.

The project plan is a formal, approved document that manages and controls project execution. The project plan should include a description of the project scope, a list of activities, a schedule, time estimates, cost estimates, risk factors, resources, assignments, and responsibilities. In addition to these basic components, most project professionals also include contingency plans, review and communications strategies, and a **kill switch**—a trigger that enables a project manager to close the project before completion.

A good project plan should include estimates for revenue and strategic necessities. It also should include measurement and reporting methods and details as to how top leadership will engage in the project. It also informs stakeholders of the benefits of the project and justifies the investment, commitment, and risk of the project as it relates to the overall mission of the organization.

Managers need to continuously monitor projects to measure their success. If a project is failing, the manager must cancel the project and save the company any further project costs. Canceling a project is not necessarily a failure as much as it is successful resource management as it frees resources that can be used on other projects that are more valuable to the firm.

The most important part of the plan is communication. The project manager must communicate the plan to every member of the project team and to any key stakeholders and executives. The project plan must also include any project assumptions and be detailed enough to guide the execution of the project. A key to achieving project success is earning consensus and buy-in from all key stakeholders. By including key stakeholders in project plan development, the project manager allows them to have ownership of the plan. This often translates to greater commitment, which in turn results in enhanced motivation and productivity. The two primary diagrams most frequently used in project planning are PERT and Gantt charts.

A **PERT (Program Evaluation and Review Technique) chart** is a graphical network model that depicts a project's tasks and the relationships between them. A **dependency** is a logical relationship that exists between the project tasks, or between a project task and a milestone. PERT charts define dependency between project tasks before those tasks are scheduled (see Figure 19.7). The boxes in Figure 19.7 represent project tasks, and the project manager can adjust the contents of the boxes to display various project attributes such as schedule and actual start and finish times. The arrows indicate that a task depends on the start or the completion of a different task. The **critical path** estimates the shortest path through the project ensuring all critical tasks are completed from start to finish. The red line in Figure 19.7 displays the critical path for the project.

A **Gantt chart** is a simple bar chart that lists project tasks vertically against the project's time frame, listed horizontally. A Gantt chart works well for representing the project schedule. It also shows actual progress of tasks against the planned duration. Figure 19.8 displays a software development project using a Gantt chart.

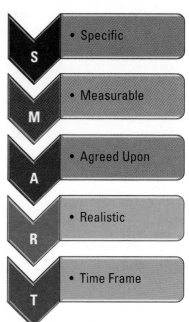

FIGURE 19.6

SMART Criteria for Successful Objective Creation

Outsourcing Projects

LO 19.3 Identify the three different types of outsourcing along with their benefits and challenges.

In the high-speed global business environment, an organization needs to increase profits, grow market share, and reduce costs. Two basic options are available to organizations wishing to develop and maintain their information systems—in-sourcing or outsourcing.

FIGURE 19.7

PERT Chart Expert, a PERT
Chart Example

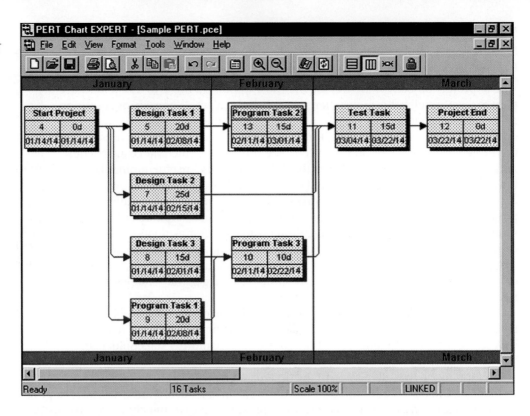

FIGURE 19.8

Microsoft Project, a Gantt
Chart Example

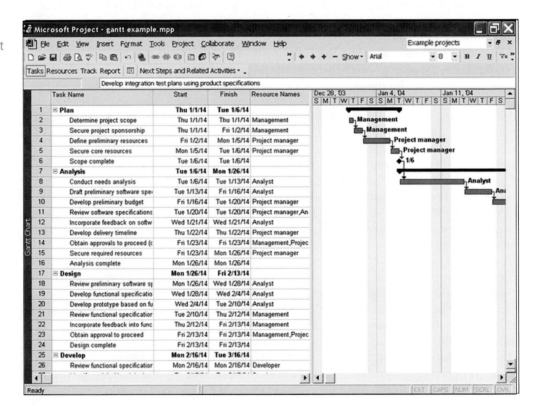

In-sourcing (in-house development) uses the professional expertise within an organization to develop and maintain its information technology systems. In-sourcing has been instrumental in creating a viable supply of IT professionals and in creating a better quality workforce combining both technical and business skills.

Outsourcing is an arrangement by which one organization provides a service or services for another organization that chooses not to perform them in-house. In some cases, the entire MIS department is outsourced, including planning and business analysis as well as the design, development, and maintenance of equipment and projects. Outsourcing can range from a large contract under which an organization such as IBM manages all MIS services for another company, to hiring contractors and temporary staff on an individual basis. Common reasons companies outsource include:

■ **Core competencies.** Many companies have recently begun to consider outsourcing as a way to acquire best-practices and the business process expertise of highly skilled technology resources for a low cost. Technology is advancing at such an accelerated rate that companies often lack the technical resources required to keep current.

■ **Financial savings.** It is far cheaper to hire people in China and India than pay the required salaries for similar labor in the United States.

■ **Rapid growth.** Firms must get their products to market quickly and still be able to react to market changes. By taking advantage of outsourcing, an organization can acquire the resources required to speed up operations or scale to new demand levels.

■ **The Internet and globalization.** The pervasive nature of the Internet has made more people comfortable with outsourcing abroad as India, China, and the United States become virtual neighbors.

Outsourcing MIS enables organizations to keep up with market and technology advances—with less strain on human and financial resources and more assurance that the IT infrastructure will keep pace with evolving business priorities (see Figure 19.9). The three forms of outsourcing options available for a project are:

1. ***Onshore outsourcing***—engaging another company within the same country for services.

2. ***Nearshore outsourcing***—contracting an outsourcing arrangement with a company in a nearby country. Often this country will share a border with the native country.

3. ***Offshore outsourcing***—using organizations from developing countries to write code and develop systems. In offshore outsourcing the country is geographically far away.

Since the mid-1990s, major U.S. companies have been sending significant portions of their software development work offshore—primarily to vendors in India, but also to vendors in China, eastern Europe (including Russia), Ireland, Israel, and the Philippines. The big selling point for offshore outsourcing is inexpensive but good work. The overseas counterpart to an American programmer who earns as much as $63,000 per year is paid as little as $5,000 per year (see Figure 19.10). Developing countries in Asia and South Africa offer some outsourcing services but are challenged by language difference, inadequate telecommunication equipment, and regulatory obstacles. India is the largest offshore marketplace because it promotes English along with a technologically advanced population. Infosys, NIIT, Mahindra Satyam, Tata Consultancy Services, and Wipro are among the biggest Indian outsourcing service providers, each of which has a large presence in the United States.[1]

OUTSOURCING BENEFITS

The many benefits associated with outsourcing include:

■ Increased quality and efficiency of business processes.

■ Reduced operating expenses for head count and exposure to risk for large capital investments.

■ Access to outsourcing service provider's expertise, economies of scale, best practices, and advanced technologies.

■ Increased flexibility for faster response to market changes and less time to market for new products or services.

FIGURE 19.9

Outsourcing Models

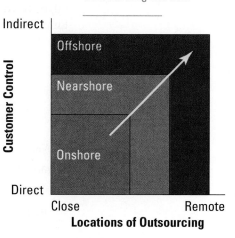

Locations of Outsourcing

FIGURE 19.10

Typical Salary Ranges for
Computer Programmers

Country	Salary Range Per Year
China	$5,000–$9,000
India	6,000–10,000
Philippines	6,500–11,000
Russia	7,000–13,000
Ireland	21,000–28,000
Canada	25,000–50,000
United States	60,000–90,000

OUTSOURCING CHALLENGES

Outsourcing comes with several challenges. These arguments are valid and should be considered when a company is thinking about outsourcing. Many challenges can be avoided with proper research. The challenges include:

- **Length of contract.** Most companies look at outsourcing as a long-term solution with a time period of several years. Training and transferring resources around the globe is difficult and expensive, hence most companies pursuing offshore outsourcing contract for multiple years of service. A few of the challenges facing the length of the contract include:

  1. It can be difficult to break the contract.

  2. Forecasting business needs for the next several years is challenging and the contract might not meet future business needs.

  3. Re-creating an internal MIS department if the outsource provider fails is costly and challenging.

- **Threat to competitive advantage.** Many businesses view MIS as a competitive advantage and view outsourcing as a threat because the outsourcer could share the company's trade secrets.

- **Loss of confidentiality.** Information on pricing, products, sales, and customers can be a competitive asset and often critical for business success. Outsourcing could place confidential information in the wrong hands. Although confidentiality clauses contained in the contracts are supposed to protect the company, the potential risk and costs of a breach must be analyzed.

Every type of organization in business today relies on software to operate and solve complex problems or create exciting opportunities. Software built correctly can support nimble organizations and transform with them as they and their businesses transform. Software that effectively meets employee needs will help an organization become more productive and enhance decision making. Software that does not meet employee needs might have a damaging effect on productivity and can even cause a business to fail. Employee involvement in software development, along with the right implementation, is critical to the success of an organization.

OPENING CASE STUDY QUESTIONS

1. What are the three interdependent variables shaping project management? Why are these variables important to a social media software development project?

2. What are the ethical and security issues associated with outsourcing the development of a social media system?

Chapter 19 Case: Death March

Edward Yourdon's book *Death March* describes the complete software developer's guide to surviving "mission impossible" projects. MIS projects are challenging, and project managers are expected to achieve the impossible by pulling off a successful project even when pitted against impossible challenges. In *Death March,* infamous software developer Edward Yourdon presents his project classification displayed here. Yourdon measures projects based on the level of pain and chances for success.

- **Mission Impossible Project:** This project has a great chance of success and your hard work will pay off as you find happiness and joy in the work. For example, this is the type of project where you work all day and night for a year and become the project hero as you complete the mission impossible and reap a giant promotion as your reward.

- **Ugly Project:** This project has a high chance of success but is very painful and offers little happiness. For example, you work day and night to install a new accounting system and although successful, you hate accounting and dislike the company and its products.

- **Kamikaze Project:** This is a project that has little chance of success but you are so passionate about the content that you find great happiness working on the project. For example, you are asked to build a website to support a cancer foundation, a cause near to your heart, but the company is nonprofit and doesn't have any funds to help buy the software you need to get everything working. You patch the system together and implement many manual work-arounds just to keep the system functioning.

- **Suicide Project:** This project has no chance of success and offers you nothing but pain. This is the equivalent of your worst nightmare project. Word of caution, avoid suicide projects![2]

Questions

1. Analyze your school and work projects and find a project that would fit in each box in the accompanying figure.

2. What could you have done differently on your suicide project to ensure its success?

3. What can you do to avoid being placed on a suicide project? Given the choice, which type of project would you choose to work on and why?

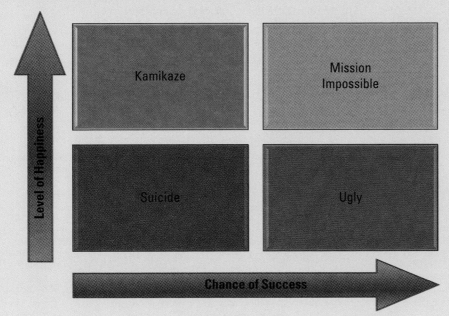

Developing a 21st-Century Organization

20.1. List and describe the four 21st-century trends that businesses are focusing on and rank them in order of business importance.

20.2. Explain how the integration of business and technology is shaping 21st-century organizations.

LO 20.1 List and describe the four 21st-century trends that businesses are focusing on and rank them in order of business importance.

Developing Organizations

Organizations face changes more extensive and far reaching in their implications than anything since the modern industrial revolution occurred in the early 1900s. Technology is one of the primary forces driving these changes. Organizations that want to survive in the 21st century must recognize the immense power of technology, carry out required organizational changes in the face of it, and learn to operate in an entirely different way. Figure 20.1 displays a few examples of the way technology is changing the business arena. On the business side, 21st-century organization trends are:

- Uncertainty in terms of future business scenarios and economic outlooks.
- Emphasis on strategic analysis for cost reduction and productivity enhancements.
- Focus on improved business resiliency via the application of enhanced security.

FIGURE 20.1

Examples of How Technology Is Changing Business

Industry	Business Changes Due to Technology
Travel	Travel site Expedia.com is now the biggest leisure-travel agency, with higher profit margins than even American Express.
Entertainment	The music industry has kept Napster and others from operating, but $35 billion annual online downloads are wrecking the traditional music business. The next big entertainment industry to feel the effects of ebusiness will be the $67 billion movie business.
Electronics	Using the Internet to link suppliers and customers, Dell dictates industry profits. Its operating margins have risen, even as it takes prices to levels where rivals cannot make money.
Financial services	Nearly every public efinance company remaining makes money, with online mortgage service Lending Tree growing 70 percent a year. Processing online mortgage applications is now 40 percent cheaper for customers.
Retail	eBay is on track to become one of the nation's top 15 retailers, and Amazon.com will join the top 40. Walmart's ebusiness strategy is forcing rivals to make heavy investments in technology.
Automobiles	The cost of producing vehicles is down because of SCM and web-based purchasing. Also, eBay has become the leading U.S. used-car dealer, and most major car sites are profitable.
Education and training	Cisco saved $133 million by moving training sessions to the Internet, and the University of Phoenix online college classes please investors.

On the technology side, there has been a focus on improved business management of IT in order to extract the most value from existing resources and create alignment between business and IT priorities. Today's organizations focus on defending and safeguarding their existing market positions in addition to targeting new market growth. The four primary information technology areas where organizations are focusing are:

- IT infrastructures
- Security
- Ebusiness
- Integration

INCREASED FOCUS ON IT INFRASTRUCTURE

A significant trend for the 21st century is to increase the focus on *IT infrastructure*—the hardware, software, and telecommunications equipment that, when combined, provide the underlying foundation to support the organization's goals. Organizations in the past underestimated the importance that IT infrastructures have for the many functional areas of an organization.

In the early days of the Internet, the basic infrastructure in terms of protocols and standards was unsophisticated (and still is), but software companies managed to enhance the Internet and offer compelling applications for functional business areas. The original design for the Internet and the web was for simple email, document exchange, and the display of static content, not for sophisticated and dynamic business applications that require access to back-end systems and databases.

Organizations today are looking to Internet-based cross-functional systems such as CRM, SCM, and ERP to help drive their business success. The days of implementing independent functional systems are gone. Creating an effective organization requires a 360-degree view of all operations. For this reason, ownership of the IT infrastructure now becomes the responsibility of the entire organization and not just the individual users or functional department. This is primarily because the IT infrastructure has a dramatic influence on the strategic capabilities of an organization (see Figure 20.2).

INCREASED FOCUS ON SECURITY

With war and terrorist attacks on many people's minds, security is a hot topic. For businesses, too, security concerns are widespread. Increasingly opening up their networks and applications to customers, partners, and suppliers using an ever more diverse set of computing devices and networks, businesses can benefit from deploying the latest advances in security technologies. These benefits include fewer disruptions to organizational systems, increased productivity of employees, and greater advances in administration, authorization, and authentication techniques. For businesses it is important to have the appropriate levels of authentication, access control, and encryption in place, which help to ensure (1) that only authorized individuals can gain access to the network, (2) that they have access to only those applications for which they are entitled, and (3) that they cannot understand or alter information while in transit.

Security breaches not only inconvenience business users and their customers and partners, but can also cost millions of dollars in lost revenues or lost market capitalization. The business cost of inadequate security does not stop at inconvenience and loss of revenues or market valuation. It can even force a business out of existence. For example, British Internet service provider CloudNine Communications was the victim of a

FIGURE 20.2

The Position of the Infrastructure within the Organization

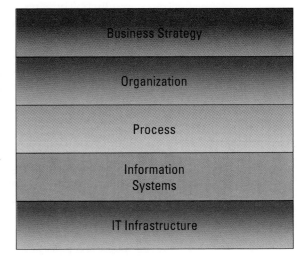

distributed denial-of-service (DDoS) attack that forced the company to close operations and to eventually transfer over 2,500 customers to a rival organization. While "disruptive technologies" can help a company to gain competitive advantage and market share (and avoid real business disruptions), lack of security can have the opposite effect, causing profitable companies to lose market share or even their entire business within hours or days of an attack.

It is now more important than ever for an organization to have well-rehearsed and frequently updated processes and procedures to insure against a variety of adverse scenarios—Internet email and denial-of-service attacks from worms and viruses, loss of communications, loss of documents, password and information theft, fire, flood, physical attacks on property, and even terrorist attacks.

INCREASED FOCUS ON EBUSINESS

Mobility and wireless are the new focus in ebusiness, and some upcoming trends are mobile commerce, telematics, electronic tagging, and RFID.

- Mobile commerce (m-commerce)—the ability to purchase goods and services through a wireless Internet-enabled device.

- Telematics—blending computers and wireless telecommunications technologies with the goal of efficiently conveying information over vast networks to improve business operations. The most notable example of telematics may be the Internet itself, since it depends on a number of computer networks connected globally through telecommunication devices.

- Electronic tagging—a technique for identifying and tracking assets and individuals via technologies such as radio frequency identification and smart cards.

- Radio frequency identification (RFID)—technologies use active or passive tags in the form of chips or smart labels that can store unique identifiers and relay this information to electronic readers. Within the supply chain, RFID can enable greater efficiencies in business processes such as inventory, logistics, distribution, and asset management. On the mobile commerce side, RFID can enable new forms of ebusiness through mobile phones and smart cards. This can increase loyalty by streamlining purchases for the consumer. For example, RFID readers are being embedded in store shelving to help retailers, including Marks & Spencer and The Gap, to better manage their assets and inventories and understand customer behavior.

These are all interesting subcategories within mobile business that open up new opportunities for mobility beyond simple employee applications. Electronic tagging and RFID are especially interesting because they extend wireless and mobile technologies not just to humans, but also to a wide range of objects such as consumer and industrial products. These products will gain intelligence via electronic product codes, which are a (potential) replacement for universal product code (UPC) bar codes, and via RFID tags with two-way communication capabilities.

Mobile employees will soon have the ability to leverage technology just as if they were in the office. Improvements in devices, applications, networks, and standards over the past few years have made this far more practical than it was when introduced. The drivers for adoption are finally starting to outweigh the barriers. For example, major vendors such as IBM, Microsoft, Oracle, and Sybase are all playing a larger role and taking a greater interest in mobile business than they had previously. These vendors all have mature, proven offerings for enterprise mobility.

Mobile technology will help extend an organization out to its edges in areas such as sales automation and enterprise operations. Benefits can include improved information accuracy, reduced costs, increased productivity, increased revenues, and improved customer service. Beyond being an additional channel for communications, mobile business will enable an organization to think about the powerful combination of business processes, ebusiness, and wireless communications.

INCREASED FOCUS ON INTEGRATION

Information technology has penetrated the heart of organizations and will stay there in the future. The IT industry is one of the most dynamic in the global economy. As a sector, it not only creates millions of high-level jobs, but also helps organizations to be more efficient and effective, which in turn stimulates innovation. The integration of business and technology has allowed organizations to increase their share of the global economy, transform the way they conduct business, and become more efficient and effective (see Figure 20.3).

The past few years have produced a confluence of events that has reshaped the global economy. Around the world, free-market competition has flourished and a new globally interdependent financial system has emerged. Reflecting these changes, core business relationships and models are dramatically changing, including shifts from:

■ Product-centricity to customer-centricity.

■ Mass production to mass customization.

■ The value in material things to the value of knowledge and intelligence.

In concert with these trends, a new series of business success factors and challenges has emerged that is helping to determine marketplace winners and losers:

■ Organization agility, often supported by a "plug and play" IT infrastructure (with a flexible and adaptable applications architecture).

■ A focus on core competencies and processes.

■ A redefinition of the value chain.

■ Instantaneous business response.

■ The ability to scale resources and infrastructure across geographic boundaries.

These developments add up to an environment that is vastly more complex than even five years ago. This in turn has resulted in organizations increasingly embracing new business models. The new environment requires organizations to focus externally on their business processes and integration architectures. The virtually integrated business model will cause a sharp increase in the number of business partners and the closeness of integration between them.

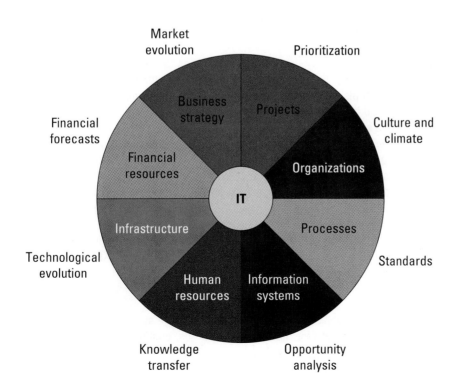

FIGURE 20.3

The Integration of Business and Technology

Never before have IT investments played such a critical role in business success. As business strategies continue to evolve, the distinction between "the business" and IT will virtually disappear.

OPENING CASE STUDY QUESTIONS

1. Why is it critical that a business develop its IT infrastructure using a 21st-century strategy?

2. How would a business define security when developing its 21st-century strategy?

3. How would a business define its ebusiness infrastructure when developing its 21st-century strategy?

4. Why is it important that a business control all integrations into its systems?

Chapter Twenty Case: Disaster at Denver International Airport

One good way to learn how to develop successful systems is to review past failures. One of the most infamous system failures is Denver International Airport's (DIA) baggage system. When the automated baggage system design for DIA was introduced, it was hailed as the savior of modern airport design. The design relied on a network of 300 computers to route bags and 4,000 cars to carry luggage across 21 miles of track. Laser scanners were to read bar-coded luggage tags, while advanced scanners tracked the movement of toboggan-like baggage carts.

When DIA finally opened its doors for reporters to witness its revolutionary baggage handling system, the scene was rather unpleasant. Bags were chewed up, lost, and misrouted in what has since become a legendary systems nightmare.

One of the biggest mistakes made in the baggage handling system fiasco was that not enough time was allowed to properly develop the system. In the beginning of the project, DIA assumed it was the responsibility of individual airlines to find their own way of moving the baggage from the plane to the baggage claim area. The automated baggage system was not involved in the initial planning of the DIA project. By the time the DIA developers decided to create an integrated baggage system, the time frame for designing and implementing such a complex and huge system was not possible.

Another common mistake that occurred during the project was that the airlines kept changing their business requirements. This caused numerous issues, including the implementation of power supplies that were not properly updated for the revised system design, which caused overloaded motors and mechanical failures. Besides the power supply design problem, the optical sensors did not read the bar codes correctly, causing issues with baggage routing.

Finally, BAE, the company that designed and implemented the automated baggage system for DIA, had never created a baggage system of this size before. BAE had created a similar system in an airport in Munich, Germany, where the scope was much smaller. Essentially, the baggage system had an inadequate IT infrastructure because it was designed for a much smaller system.

DIA simply could not open without a functional baggage system so the city had no choice but to delay the opening date for more than 16 months, costing taxpayers roughly $1 million per day, which totaled around $500 million.[1]

Questions

1. One problem with DIA's baggage system was inadequate testing. Why is testing important to a project's success? Why do so many projects decide to skip testing?

2. Evaluate the different systems development methodologies. Which one would have most significantly increased the chances of the project's success?

3. How could more time spent in the analysis and design phase have saved Colorado taxpayers hundreds of millions of dollars?

4. Why could BAE not take an existing IT infrastructure and simply increase its scale and expect it to work?

An organization must remain competitive in this quick-paced, constantly changing, global business environment. It must implement technology that is adaptive, disruptive, and transformable to meet new and unexpected customer needs. Focusing on the unexpected and understanding disruptive technologies can give an organization a competitive advantage.

Organizations need software that users can transform quickly to meet the requirements of the rapidly changing business environment. Software that effectively meets employee needs will help an organization become more productive and make better decisions. Software that does not meet employee needs may have a damaging effect on productivity. Employee involvement along with using the right implementation methodology in developing software is critical to the success of an organization.

Four areas of focus for organizations heading into the 21st century are IT infrastructure, security, ebusiness (mobility), and integration. Information technology has rapidly expanded from a backroom resource providing competitive advantage (e.g., cost, time, quality) to a front-office resource (e.g., marketing, sales) that is a competitive necessity. The dynamic business and technical environment of the 21st century is driving the need for technology infrastructures and applications architecture that are increasingly flexible, integrated, and maintainable (while always providing functionality, cost effectiveness, timeliness, and security).

✳ KEY TERMS

Agile methodology 281
Alpha testing 275
Analysis phase 270
Brainstorming 270
Bug 272
Business requirement 270
Change agent 270
Communication plan 290
Computer-aided software
   engineering (CASE) 271
Control objects for information
   and related technology
   (COBIT) 272
Conversion 268
Corrective maintenance 275
Critical path 291
Data flow diagram (DFD), 271
Dependency 291
Design phase 271
Development phase 272
Development testing 275
Discovery prototyping 281
Executive sponsor 290
Extreme programming (XP)
   methodology 282
Feasibility 288
Fourth-generation language
   (4GL), 272
Gantt chart 291
Graphical user interface
   (GUI), 271
Help desk 274
Implementation phase 274
In-sourcing (in-house
   development) 292

Intangible benefits 288
Integration testing 275
Iterative development 281
IT infrastructure, 297
Joint application development
   (JAD), 270
Kill switch 291
Legacy system 268
Maintenance phase 275
Methodology 280
Nearshore outsourcing 293
Object-oriented languages 272
Offshore outsourcing 293
Off-the-shelf application 268
Online training 274
Onshore outsourcing 293
Outsourcing 293
Parallel implementation 275
PERT (Program Evaluation and
   Review Technique) chart 291
Phased implementation 275
Pilot implementation 275
Planning phase 270
Plunge implementation 275
Preventive maintenance 275
Process modeling, 271
Project 270
Project assumption 290
Project constraint 290
Project deliverable 290
Project management 270
Project management office
   (PMO) 290
Project manager 270
Project milestones 290

Project objective 290
Project plan 270
Project requirements
   document 290
Project scope 270
Project scope statement 290
Project stakeholder 290
Prototyping 281
Rapid application development
   (RAD) methodology (rapid
   prototyping) 282
Rational unified process (RUP)
   methodology 283
Requirements definition
   document 270
Requirements management 270
Responsibility matrix 290
Scripting language 272
Scrum methodology 283
Sign-off 270
Software customization 268
Software engineering 272
Status report 290
Systems development life cycle
   (SDLC) 268
System testing 275
Tangible benefits 288
Test conditions 272
Testing phase 272
Unit testing 275
User acceptance testing
   (UAT) 275
User documentation 274
Waterfall methodology 280
Workshop training 274

Twitter

Twitter, a privately funded start-up, is a pioneer in the microblogging arena providing a service that allows users to send and receive updates to other users. Twitter customers can keep a network of friends informed of their current status by way of text messaging, instant messaging, email, or the web. Friends, family, and coworkers use Twitter's services to communicate and stay connected through a real-time short messaging service that works over multiple networks and devices. Twitter began as a small project in 2006 and has developed into one of the most popular sites on the Internet. People around the globe use Twitter for various reasons from breaking world news to streamlining business.

The Business of Twitter

Companies are using Twitter to follow customer dialogs about their brand. Comcast, Dell, General Motors, H&R Block, Kodak, and Whole Foods Market are using Twitter to do everything from building brand awareness to providing customer service. The attention to Twitter reflects the power of new social media tools in letting consumers shape public discussion over brands. "The real control of the brand has moved into the customer's hands, and technology has enabled that," says Lane Becker, president of Get Satisfaction, a website that draws together customers and companies to answer each other's questions and give feedback on products and services.

JetBlue, Comcast, and H&R Block are among the companies that recognize Twitter's potential in providing customer service. A single Twitter message—known informally as a *tweet*—sent in frustration over a product's or a service's performance can be read by hundreds or thousands of people. Similarly, positive interaction with a representative of the manufacturer or service provider can help change an influencer's perspective for the better. For companies, tools such as Tweetscan or Twitter's own search tool, formerly known as Summize, make it easy to unearth a company's name mentioned in tweets. Being able to address an issue the moment it appears is a great way to improve customer satisfaction

GM took notice the day a prospective buyer was at a Saturn dealership, ready to make a purchase, but could not find anyone to help him. "He was starting to get upset about it," says Adam Denison, who helps coordinate social media communications at GM. "When we saw it, we immediately let our Saturn colleagues know about it . . . and they could get the ball rolling a little bit better." The person bought a Saturn in the end—though at a different dealership, Denison says.

Monitoring Customers

Not all customers want Corporate America following their tweets. Jonathan Fields typed a quick tweet to his friends when he spotted William Shatner waiting to board a JetBlue flight at New York's JFK airport. Fields wrote: "JetBlue terminal, William Shatner waiting in pinstripe suit and shades to board flight to Burbank. Why's he flying JetBlue? Free, maybe?" To his surprise he received a reply within 10 seconds, but not from his friends; it was from JetBlue informing Fields that they were following him on Twitter. Fields was at first shocked by the reply, then the JetBlue employee Morgan Johnston quickly explained that the company was not spying on Fields, but uses Twitter as a scanning tool, to find customers who might need information, say, on flight delays or cancellations.

"It has potential for delivering business value, clearly, but at the same time there are some risks to it," says Ray Valdes, research director of web services at consulting firm Gartner. While it is a useful brand-monitoring tool, it "can come across as a little creepy." Christofer Hoff tweeted his displeasure with Southwest when his flight was delayed and his luggage disappeared. The next day he received the following message from Southwest: "Sorry to hear about your flight—weather was terrible in the NE. Hope you give us a 2nd chance to prove that Southwest = Awesomeness." In a blog post about the incident, Hoff wrote that it was "cool and frightening at the same time."

Twitter Ethics

Of course with all great good comes the potential of great evil and Twitter is no exception. A few individuals purchased unofficial accounts to send messages that were clearly not authorized by the company. For example, ExxonMobil discovered that a person named Janet was fooling many people by posing as an employee of ExxonMobil. "Our concern was that people reading the postings would think that this person was speaking on the company's behalf," says ExxonMobil spokesman Chris Welberry. "We didn't want to do anything heavy-handed about people expressing their views in a social networking environment. We just wanted to make sure that people who are doing that are open and transparent."

After Exxon discovered Janet, the company contacted Twitter. "Twitter does not allow impersonation or domain squatting, which is grabbing a user name and saying you want money," Twitter co-founder Biz Stone says. "But they really do have to be impersonating or infringing on copyright. If somebody's last name happens to be Mobil, the company does not have a strong case there." Janet's account was taken out of commission.

Twitter Growth

Large organizations are likely to begin integrating microblogging into their existing services to aggregate the various social media outposts. Facebook is already positioning itself to be an aggregator of microblogging sites. The social network's News Feed feature lets people pull in updates from Twitter, Blip.fm, and elsewhere. How valuable could a microblogging service be? Soon after Twitter raised $15 million in funding, it was speculated that the site may be worth as much as $1 billion. Twitter co-founder Biz Stone expects the site's user base to grow 10 times its current size yearly.[2]

Questions

1. Why do 21st-century organizations need to understand the power of micro-blogging?
2. How can a global organization use Twitter to improve operations?
3. How could a project manager use Twitter to help track project progress?
4. How could a global systems development effort use Twitter to improve the development process?

5. What types of strategic information systems could use Twitter to improve the system? Which development methodology would you recommend the company use when integrating Twitter into its current systems?

6. What types of ethical and security issues should a company using Twitter anticipate?

Women in Technology

Technology is a tough business. Tough for men and sometimes even tougher for women. Women who have succeeded in technology deserve recognition. They are an inspiration for everyone, demonstrating what can be achieved through creativity and hard work. *Fast Company* recently compiled a list of women in technology who are leading the wave of 21st-century business. *Fast Company*'s list includes:

▪ **Ning: Gina Bianchini, co-founder and CEO**

This custom social-network maker made a splash on the May 2008 cover, and not just because she knew what a viral expansion loop was. With 500,000-plus networks now running on Ning, the company has had its share of developer challenges but remains cashed up and growing.

▪ **Flickr: Caterina Fake, co-founder**

Fake not only cofounded photo-sharing behemoth Flickr but also sold it to Yahoo! for a reported $35 million. Now everyone is buzzing about her next project, something called Hunch, which is in stealth mode.

▪ **Blurb: Eileen Gittins, CEO**

Gittins's book self-publishing platform is lean and green and has unleashed the insta-author (and book retailer) in everyone from amateur photographers to big brands like Lexus. With 1 million-plus books created, Blurb is profitable.

▪ **Meebo: Sandy Jen and Elaine Wherry, co-founders**

Oft cited as the web's fastest growing IM tool, this third start-up for Jen and Wherry (and fellow co-founder Seth Sternberg) is on a cacophonous track. It lets some 40 million users yap over any IM network and in a variety of settings; new partnerships with Hearst and Universal Music point to an even chattier future.

▪ **Pixel Qi: Mary Lou Jepsen, founder and CEO**

As CTO of One Laptop Per Child (OLPC), Jepsen led the design and development of the least expensive and most energy efficient laptop ever made. She founded Pixel Qi in 2008 to commercialize the groundbreaking OLPC screen technology she invented.

▪ **Consorte Media: Alicia Morga, CEO**

Using science (not cultural hype) to match brand advertisers with Hispanic American consumers on the web, Morga's marketing firm had 100 percent growth last year.

- **SpikeSource: Kim Polese, CEO**

  Polese was part of the early Java team at Sun Microsystems and cofounded Marimba. Her new business, which boasts a partnership with Intel, helps companies test the security and quality of open-source software.

- **BabyCenter: Tina Sharkey, president**

  Sharkey's site reaches nearly 80 percent of new moms online in the United States and some 6 million visitors a month internationally. With the 2007 acquisition of MayasMom. com, a social-networking site, Sharkey's parental domination is nearly complete.

- **SlideShare: Rashmi Sinha, co-founder and CEO**

  The psychology PhD turned web designer and community expert has created a vibrant social hub around—of all things—the PowerPoint deck. Launched with less than $50,000, SlideShare now has a million registered users, plus a partnership with LinkedIn.

- **Six Apart: Mena Trott, co-founder and president**

  With cofounding husband, Ben, Trott created tools such as Movable Type and TypePad that enabled the blogosphere to bloom. Her firm recently snapped up social network Pownce, too, adding that site's co-founder Leah Culver, another woman we admire, to the team.

- **MyShape: Louise Wannier, CEO**

  Matching technology with fashion, MyShape has created an online bazaar with more than 400,000 members. What else would you expect from a serial entrepreneur with degrees in textile design and business administration?[3]

Questions

1. Which of the listed companies has the most disruptive technology that is capable of making the greatest impact on 21st-century business?

2. Choose one of the above companies and create a Porter's Five Forces analysis to highlight potential issues the company might face over the next decade.

3. Choose one of the above companies.

    a. List and describe the seven phases in the systems development life cycle and determine which phase is most important to the company.

    b. Review the primary principles of successful software development and prioritize them in order of importance to the company.

    c. Explain how the company can use project management to ensure success.

    d. Explain the pros and cons of outsourcing for the company.

4. Why is building agile software important for all of the companies?

5. What types of information security issues should the companies be aware of as they enter the 21st century?

6. What types of ethical dilemmas should the companies be aware of as they enter the 21st century?

✳ MAKING BUSINESS DECISIONS

1. Selecting a Systems Development Methodology

Exus Incorporated is an international billing outsourcing company. Exus currently has revenues of $5 billion, more than 3,500 employees, and operations on every continent. You have recently been hired as the CIO. Your first task is to increase the software development project success rate, which is currently at 20 percent. To ensure that future software development projects are successful, you want to standardize the systems development methodology across the entire enterprise. Currently, each project determines which methodology it uses to develop software.

Create a report detailing three additional system development methodologies that were not covered in this text. Compare each of these methodologies to the traditional waterfall approach. Finally, recommend which methodology you want to implement as your organizational standard. Be sure to highlight any potential roadblocks you might encounter when implementing the new standard methodology.

2. Transforming an Organization

Your college has asked you to help develop the curriculum for a new course titled "Building a 21st-Century Organization." Use the materials in this text, the Internet, and any other resources to outline the curriculum that you would suggest the course cover. Be sure to include your reasons why the material should be covered and the order in which it should be covered.

3. Approving a Project

You are working in the IT development team for Gear International, a privately held sports and recreational equipment manufacturer. To date, you have spent the majority of your career developing applications for your corporate intranet. Your team has an idea to add an application that allows employees to learn about corporate athletic teams, register online, determine team schedules, post team statistics, etc. Your supervisor likes your idea and would like your team to prepare a short presentation with 5 to 10 slides that she can use to convince senior management to approve the project. Be sure to list benefits of the project along with your suggested methodology to help guarantee the project's development success.

4. Patrolling by Remote

Today's gadgets offer all-weather, all-knowing, any time, any place. Whether you are trying to keep tabs on your children, your new home theater, or your streaming audio, here are a few wireless tools you can use around your house.

- **Wi-Fi camera**—A five-inch-high Wireless Observer lets you take pictures at regular intervals or in response to motion and you can access it anytime through a web browser (www.veo.com).

- **Security sensor**—This detector system alerts you to break-ins and errant pop flies. Its dual sensors record vibration and acoustic disturbances—signs of a shattered window—to help avoid false alarms. (www.getintellisense.com).

- **GPS tracking device**—Total Parental Information Awareness is here. Lock this GPS locator to your kids' wrists and whenever you want to check on them, just query Wherify's web page. It pinpoints their location on a street map and displays an aerial photo (www.wherify.com).

- **Wireless speakers**—Sony's versatile 900-MHz speakers connect the RF receiver to your stereo, TV, or PC, and get crystal-clear audio anywhere within 150 feet (www.sonystyle.com).

In a group, create a document discussing how these new wireless technologies could potentially change the business arena and list at least one company for each technology that should view these new products as potential threats.

5. Saving Failing Systems

Signatures Inc. specializes in producing personalized products for companies, such as coffee mugs and pens with company logos. The company generates more than $40 million in annual revenues and has more than 300 employees. The company is in the middle of a large multimillion-dollar SCM implementation and has just hired your Project Management Outsourcing firm to take over the project management efforts. On your first day, your team is told that the project is failing for the following reasons:

- The project is using the traditional waterfall methodology.
- The SDLC was not followed and the developers decided to skip the testing phase.
- A project plan was developed during the analysis phase, but the old project manager never updated or followed the plan.

In a group determine what your first steps would be to get this project back on track.

✳ APPLY YOUR KNOWLEDGE

1. Connecting Components

Components of a solid enterprise architecture include everything from documentation to business concepts to software and hardware. Deciding which components to implement and how to implement them can be a challenge. New IT components are released daily, and business needs continually change. An enterprise architecture that meets your organization's needs today may not meet those needs tomorrow. Building an enterprise architecture that is scalable, flexible, available, accessible, and reliable is key to your organization's success.

Project Focus

You are the enterprise architect for a large clothing company called Xedous. You are responsible for developing the initial enterprise architecture. Create a list of questions you will need answered to develop your architecture. Below are examples of a few questions you might ask.

- What are the company's growth expectations?
- Will systems be able to handle additional users?
- How long will information be stored in the systems?
- How much customer history must be stored?
- What are the organization's business hours?
- What are the organization's backup requirements?

2. Back on Your Feet

You are working for GetSmart, a document creation company for legal professionals. Due to the highly sensitive nature of the industry, employees must store all work on the network drive and are not allowed to back up the data to a CD, flash drive, or any other type of external storage including home computers. The company has been following this policy for the last three years without any issues. You return to work Monday morning after a long weekend to find that the building was struck by lightning destroying several servers. Unfortunately, the backup strategy failed and all of the data from your department have been lost.

When the head of the company demanded an explanation as to why there were no individual backups, he was shown the company policy he had signed not once but three times. The head of IT along with four of his cronies who had developed this ridiculous policy were fired.

Project Focus

You have been placed on a committee with several of your peers to revamp the backup and recovery policies and create a new disaster recovery plan. You must create policies and procedures that will preserve the sensitive nature of the documents, while ensuring the company is safe from disasters. Be sure to address a worst-case scenario where the entire building is lost.

3. Confusing Coffee

Business requirements are the detailed set of business requests that any new system must meet in order to be successful. A sample business requirement might state, "The system must track all customer sales by product, region, and sales representative." This requirement states what the system must do from the business perspective, giving no details or information on how the system is going to meet this requirement.

Project Focus

You have been hired to build an employee payroll system for a new coffee shop. Review the following business requirements and highlight any potential issues.

- All employees must have a unique employee ID.
- The system must track employee hours worked based on employee's last name.
- Employees must be scheduled to work a minimum of eight hours per day.
- Employee payroll is calculated by multiplying the employee's hours worked by $7.25.
- Managers must be scheduled to work morning shifts.
- Employees cannot be scheduled to work more than eight hours per day.
- Servers cannot be scheduled to work morning, afternoon, or evening shifts.
- The system must allow managers to change and delete employees from the system.

4. Picking Projects

You are a project management contractor attempting to contract work at a large telecommunications company, Hex Incorporated. Your interview with Debbie Fernandez, the senior vice president of IT, went smoothly. The last thing Debbie wants to see from you before she makes her final hiring decision is a prioritized list of the projects here. You are sure to land the job if Debbie is satisfied with your prioritization.

Project Focus

Create a report for Debbie prioritizing the following projects and be sure to include the business justifications for your prioritization.

- Upgrade accounting system.
- Develop employee vacation tracking system.
- Enhance employee intranet.
- Cleanse and scrub data warehouse information.
- Performance test all hardware to ensure 20 percent growth scalability.
- Implement changes to employee benefits system.

- Develop backup and recovery strategy.
- Implement supply chain management system.
- Upgrade customer relationship management system.
- Build executive information system for CEO.

5. Keeping Time

Time Keepers Inc. is a small firm that specializes in project management consulting. You are a senior project manager, and you have recently been assigned to the Tahiti Tanning Lotion account. The Tahiti Tanning Lotion company is currently experiencing a 10 percent success rate (90 percent failure rate) on all internal IT projects. Your first assignment is to analyze one of the current project plans being used to develop a new CRM system (see Figure AYK.1).

Project Focus

Review the project plan and create a document listing the numerous errors in the plan. Be sure to also provide suggestions on how to fix the errors.

6. Growing, Growing, Gone

FIGURE AYK.1

Sample Project Plan

You are the founder of Black Pearl, a small comic book start-up. The good news is Black Pearl has found tremendous success. You have 34 employees in a creative, yet functional, office in downtown Chicago. The comics you produce are of extremely high quality. The artwork is unmatched and the story lines are compelling, gripping, and addictive, according to your customers. Your comics are quickly becoming a cult classic and Black Pearl customers are extremely loyal. You produce all of the comics and sell them in your store and via the Internet to individuals all over the United States.

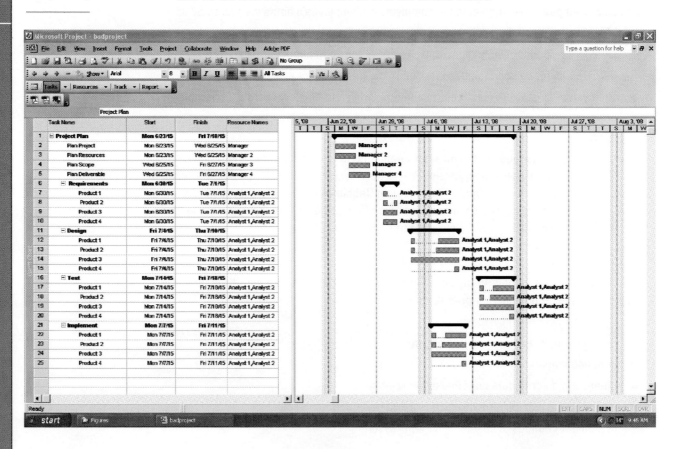

Project Focus

You had vision when you started Black Pearl. You knew the potential of your business model to revamp the comic industry. You purchased high-end computers and customizable software to support your operations. Now, you are faced with a new dilemma. You have a large international following and you have decided to pursue international opportunities. You would like to open stores in Japan, France, and Brazil during the next year. To determine if this is possible, you need to evaluate your current systems to see if they are flexible and scalable enough to perform business internationally. You know that you are going to run into many international business issues. Create a list of questions you need to answer to determine if your systems are capable of performing international business.

7. The Virtualization Opportunity

Virtualization makes good business sense. Organizations recognize the opportunity to use virtualization to break down the silos that keep applications from sharing infrastructure and that contribute to chronic underutilization of IT resources. Virtualization can help an organization simultaneously reduce costs, increase agility, and make IT more responsive to the needs of the business. So for many organizations, the question is not, "Should we virtualize?" Instead, the question is, "How can we transition to a virtualized environment in a predictable, cost-effective manner?"

Project Focus

You are the CFO for Martello's, a food distribution organization with locations in Chicago, New York, and San Francisco. Your CIO, Jeff Greenwald, has given you a proposal for a budget of $2 million to convert the organization to a virtualized environment. You are unfamiliar with virtualization, how it works, and the long-term goals it will satisfy for the company. You have a meeting with Jeff tomorrow and you want to be able to discuss his proposal. Use the Internet to research virtualization to prepare for your meeting. Once you have a solid understanding of virtualization, create a report detailing your decision to grant or deny Jeff's budget proposal.

★ ENTREPRENEURIAL CHALLENGE

Build Your Own Business

1. Your business is undertaking many new and exciting initiatives to boost growth, including employee blogs, customer wikis, and implementation of a new time and attendance system. Time and attendance software is critical to the business because it can ensure you have the right employees, at the right place, at the right time, which can increase sales. You never want to find yourself understaffed during busy times and overstaffed during slow times. Also, accurately accounting for employees' time is crucial to effectively analyzing labor expenses, which are the largest operating expense your business incurs. Conveniently, time and attendance solution providers, time clock manufacturers, and software development companies are developing high-quality affordable products. You have decided to replace the manual employee tracking system your grandfather implemented in the 1950s. You have a highly technical employee, Nick Zele, who has offered to build the system for you and ensures you it is a simple build. You could also purchase one of the many off-the-shelf applications and have an outsourcing firm customize the application for your business. What are the pros and cons of using an employee to build you a custom system? What are the pros and cons of purchasing an off-the-shelf time and attendance

application and outsourcing custom development? How will your older employees feel about the new system and what can you do to ensure a smooth transition?

2. You have decided to implement a new payroll system for your business. Review the following business requirements and highlight any potential issues.

   ■ All employees must have a unique employee ID.
   ■ The system must track employee hours worked based on employee's last name.
   ■ Employees must be scheduled to work a minimum of eight hours per day.
   ■ Employee payroll is calculated by multiplying the employee's hours worked by $7.25.
   ■ Managers must be scheduled to work morning shifts.
   ■ Employees cannot be scheduled to work more than eight hours per day.
   ■ Servers cannot be scheduled to work morning, afternoon, or evening shifts.
   ■ The system must allow managers to change and delete employees from the system.

3. You are in the middle of a implementing a new system at your business. Your project team is failing for the following three reasons: (1) The project is using the traditional waterfall methodology; (2) the SDLC was not followed and the developers decided to skip the testing phase; (3) a project plan was developed during the analysis phase, but the old project manager never updated or followed the plan and never updated the business requirements. Detail your strategy for getting your project back on track.

✱ AYK APPLICATION PROJECTS

If you are looking for Excel projects to incorporate into your class, try any of the following after reading this chapter.

Project Number	Project Name	Project Type	Plug-In	Focus Area	Project Level	Skill Set	Page Number
9	Security Analysis	Excel	T3	Filtering Data	Intermediate	Conditional Formatting, Autofilter, Subtotal	AYK.7
10	Gathering Data	Excel	T3	Data Analysis	Intermediate	Conditional Formatting	AYK.8
11	Scanner System	Excel	T2	Strategic Analysis	Intermediate	Formulas	AYK.8
12	Competitive Pricing	Excel	T2	Profit Maximization	Intermediate	Formulas	AYK.9
13	Adequate Acquisitions	Excel	T2	Break Even Analysis	Intermediate	Formulas	AYK.9
15	Assessing the Value of Information	Excel	T3	Data Analysis	Intermediate	PivotTable	AYK.10
16	Growth, Trends, and Forecasts	Excel	T2, T3	Data Forecasting	Advanced	Average, Trend, Growth	AYK.11
18	Formatting Grades	Excel	T3	Data Analysis	Advanced	If, LookUp	AYK.12
22	Turnover Rates	Excel	T3	Data Mining	Advanced	PivotTable	AYK.15
23	Vital Information	Excel	T3	Data Mining	Advanced	PivotTable	AYK.15
24	Breaking Even	Excel	T4	Business Analysis	Advanced	Goal Seek	AYK.16
25	Profit Scenario	Excel	T4	Sales Analysis	Advanced	Scenario Manager	AYK.16

PLUG-IN

B

Business Plug-Ins

The overall goal of the Business Plug-Ins is to enhance the coverage of text topics such as business processes, security, ethics, globalization, supply chain management, and so on. The flexibility of *Business Driven Technology* allows faculty to cover the additional material located in the Business Plug-Ins whenever they choose throughout the course. For example, if you want to cover security and ethics in the beginning of your course you can assign Unit 1, Business Plug-In B6 *Information Security* and Business Plug-In B7 *Ethics* during the first week of classes. If you choose to cover security and ethics during the end of your course you can assign Unit 5, Business Plug-In B6 *Information Security* and Business Plug-In B7 *Ethics* during your final week of classes. The flexibility of the Business Plug-Ins allows faculty to custom develop their course to meet their specific teaching needs.

PLUG-IN B1 >>

BUSINESS BASICS

B1 provides a comprehensive overview of business basics and should be assigned to any students who are new to the business environment. Plug-In B1 includes:

- Types of business: sole proprietorship, partnership, corporation
- Internal operations of a corporation: accounting, finance, human resources, sales, marketing, operations/production, and management information systems
- Business fundamentals: sales process, market share, marketing mix, customer segmentation, product life cycle, operations/production, business process reengineering

PLUG-IN B2 >>

BUSINESS PROCESS

B2 dives deeper into the world of business by reviewing business processes and their impacts on organizations. This is a great plug-in to cover early in the course if you plan on spending a significant amount of time covering enterprisewide processes. There are a number of sample business process models diagramming such processes as order entry, online bill payment, ebusiness processes, and process improvement. Plug-In B2 includes:

- Business processes
- Continuous process improvement
- Business process reengineering
- Business process modeling

HARDWARE AND SOFTWARE BASICS

<< PLUG-IN B3

B3 covers the two basic categories of information technology: (1) hardware and (2) software. Information technology can be composed of the Internet, a personal computer, a cell phone that can access the web, a personal digital assistant, or presentation software. All of these technologies help to perform specific information processing tasks. Plug-In B3 includes:

- Hardware basics: central processing unit, primary storage, secondary storage, input devices, output devices, communication devices, computer categories
- Software basics: system software, application software

MIS INFRASTRUCTURES

<< PLUG-IN B4

B4 discusses the essentials of how an organization will build, deploy, use, and share its data, processes, and IT assets. To support the volume and complexity of today's user and application requirements, information technology needs to take a fresh approach to enterprise architectures by constructing smarter, more flexible environments that protect it from system failures and crashes. A solid enterprise architecture can decrease costs, increase standardization, promote reuse of IT assets, and speed development of new systems. The end result is that the right enterprise architecture can make IT cheaper, strategic, and more responsive.

NETWORKS AND TELECOMMUNICATIONS

<< PLUG-IN B5

B5 offers a detailed look at telecommunication systems and networks. Businesses around the world are moving to network infrastructure solutions that allow greater choice in how they go to market; the solutions have a global reach. This plug-in takes a detailed look at key telecommunication and network technologies that are integrating businesses around the world. Plug-In B5 includes:

- Network basics: architecture, peer-to-peer networks, client/server networks
- Topology: bus, star, ring, hybrid, wireless
- Protocols: Ethernet, transmission control protocol/Internet protocol
- Media: wire media, wireless media
- Business advantages: voice over IP, networking businesses, increasing the speed of business, securing business networks

INFORMATION SECURITY

<< PLUG-IN B6

B6 explores the critical components of information security issues and features including information security policies and plans, hackers, viruses, public key encryption, digital certificates, digital signatures, firewalls, and authentication, authorization, and detection and response technologies. Plug-In B6 includes:

- The first line of defense—people: information security policies
- The second line of defense—technology: authentication and authorization, prevention and resistance, detection and response

PLUG-IN B7 >> ETHICS

B7 dives deep into ePolicies—policies and procedures that address the ethical use of computers and Internet usage in the business environment. Plug-In B7 includes:

- Information management policies: ethical computer use policy, information privacy policy, acceptable use policy, email privacy policy, Internet use policy, antispam policy
- Ethics in the workplace: monitoring technologies
- Future trends

PLUG-IN B8 >> OPERATIONS MANAGEMENT

B8 covers operations management, which is the management of systems or processes that convert or transform resources (including human resources) into goods and services. Operations management is responsible for managing the core processes used to manufacture goods and produce services. Plug-In B8 includes:

- Operations management's role in business
- Information technology's role in operations management
- Strategic business systems
- Competitive strategy: cost, quality, delivery, flexibility, service
- Operations management and the supply chain

PLUG-IN B9 >> SUSTAINABLE MIS INFRASTRUCTURES

B9 discusses new organizational architecture trends to help keep businesses up-and-running 24/7/365 while continuing to be flexible, scalable, reliable, available, and sustainable. Organizations today must continually watch new architecture trends to ensure they can keep up with new and disruptive technologies. This section discusses sustainability and the environmental impacts associated with MIS infrastructures alone with the three primary components of an MIS infrastructure including grid computing, virtualized computing, and cloud computing.

PLUG-IN B10 >> BUSINESS INTELLIGENCE

B10 uncovers why many organizations today find it next to impossible to understand their own strengths and weaknesses, let alone their enemies', because the enormous volume of organizational data is inaccessible to all but the IT department. Organization data includes far more than simple fields in a database; it also includes voice mail, customer phone calls, text messages, video clips, along with numerous new forms of data. Business intelligence (BI) refers to applications and technologies that are used to gather, provide access to, and analyze data and information to support decision-making efforts. Plug-In B10 includes:

- The problem: data rich, information poor
- The solution: business intelligence

- Operational, tactical, and strategic BI
- BI's operational value
- Data mining cluster analysis: association detection, statistical analysis
- Business benefits of BI: quantifiable benefits, indirectly quantifiable benefits, unpredictable benefits, intangible benefits

GLOBAL INFORMATION SYSTEMS

<< PLUG-IN B11

B11 covers globalization and working in an international global economy, which are integral parts of business today. Fortune 500 companies to mom-and-pop shops are now competing globally, and international developments affect all forms of business. Whether they are in Berlin or Bombay, Kuala Lumpur or Kansas City, San Francisco or Seoul, organizations around the globe are developing new business models to operate competitively in a digital economy. These models are structured, yet agile; global, yet local; and they concentrate on maximizing the risk-adjusted return from both knowledge and technology assets. Plug-In B11 includes:

- Globalization
- Global IT business strategies
- Global enterprise architectures
- Global information issues
- Global systems development

GLOBAL TRENDS

<< PLUG-IN B12

B12 explores the importance for an organization to anticipate and prepare for the future. Having a global view of emerging trends and new technologies as they relate to business can provide an organization with a valuable strategic advantage. Plug-In B12 includes:

- Reasons to watch trends
- Trends shaping our future
- Technologies shaping our future

Technology Plug-Ins

The overall goal of the Technology Plug-Ins is to provide additional information not covered in the text such as personal productivity using information technology, problem solving using Excel, and decision making using Access. These plug-ins also offer an all-in-one text to faculty, avoiding their having to purchase an extra book to support Microsoft Office. These plug-ins offer integration with the core chapters and provide critical knowledge using essential business applications, such as Microsoft Excel, Microsoft Access, and Microsoft Project with hands-on tutorials for comprehension and mastery.

PLUG-IN T1 >>

PERSONAL PRODUCTIVITY USING IT

This plug-in covers a number of things to do to keep a personal computer running effectively and efficiently. The 12 topics covered in this plug-in are:

- Creating strong passwords
- Performing good file management
- Implementing effective backup and recovery strategies
- Using Zip files
- Writing professional emails
- Stopping spam
- Preventing phishing
- Detecting spyware
- Threads to instant messaging
- Increasing PC performance
- Using antivirus software
- Installing a personal firewall

BASIC SKILLS USING EXCEL   www.mhhe.com/baltzan

<< PLUG-IN T2

This plug-in introduces the basics of using Microsoft Excel, a spreadsheet program for data analysis, along with a few fancy features. The six topics covered in this plug-in are:

- Workbooks and worksheets
- Working with cells and cell data
- Printing worksheets
- Formatting worksheets
- Formulas
- Working with charts and graphics

PROBLEM SOLVING USING EXCEL   www.mhhe.com/baltzan

<< PLUG-IN T3

This plug-in provides a comprehensive tutorial on how to use a variety of Microsoft Excel functions and features for problem solving. The five areas covered in this plug-in are:

- Lists
- Conditional Formatting
- AutoFilter
- Subtotals
- PivotTables

DECISION MAKING USING EXCEL   www.mhhe.com/baltzan

<< PLUG-IN T4

This plug-in examines a few of the advanced business analysis tools used in Microsoft Excel that have the capability to identify patterns, trends, and rules, and create "what-if" models. The four topics covered in this plug-in are:

- IF
- Goal Seek
- Solver
- Scenario Manager

DESIGNING DATABASE APPLICATIONS   www.mhhe.com/baltzan

<< PLUG-IN T5

This plug-in provides specific details on how to design relational database applications. One of the most efficient and powerful information management computer-based applications is the relational database. The four topics covered in this plug-in are:

- Entities and data relationships
- Documenting logical data relationships
- The relational data model
- Normalization

BASIC SKILLS USING ACCESS   www.mhhe.com/baltzan

<< PLUG-IN T6

This plug-in focuses on creating a Microsoft Access database file. One of the most efficient information management computer-based applications is Microsoft Access.

Access provides a powerful set of tools for creating and maintaining a relational database. The two topics covered in this plug-in are:

- ▨ Create a new database file
- ▨ Create and modify tables

PLUG-IN T7 >> **PROBLEM SOLVING USING ACCESS**   www.mhhe.com/baltzan

This plug-in provides a comprehensive tutorial on how to query a database in Microsoft Access. Queries are essential for problem solving, allowing a user to sort information, summarize data (display totals, averages, counts, and so on), display the results of calculations on data, and choose exactly which fields are shown. The three topics in this plug-in are:

- ▨ Create simple queries using the simple query wizard
- ▨ Create advanced queries using calculated fields
- ▨ Format results displayed in calculated fields

PLUG-IN T8 >> **DECISION MAKING USING ACCESS**   www.mhhe.com/baltzan

This plug-in provides a comprehensive tutorial on entering data in a well-designed form and creating functional reports using Microsoft Access. A form is essential to use for data entry and a report is an effective way to present data in a printed format. The two topics in this plug-in are:

- ▨ Creating, modifying, and running forms
- ▨ Creating, modifying, and running reports

PLUG-IN T9 >> **DESIGNING WEB PAGES**   www.mhhe.com/baltzan

This plug-in provides a comprehensive assessment into the functional aspects of web design. Websites are beginning to look more alike and to employ the same metaphors and conventions. The web has now become an everyday thing whose design should not make users think. The six topics in this plug-in are:

- ▨ The World Wide Web
- ▨ Designing for the unknown(s)
- ▨ The process of web design
- ▨ HTML basics
- ▨ Web fonts
- ▨ Web graphics

PLUG-IN T10 >> **CREATING WEB PAGES USING HTML**   www.mhhe.com/baltzan

This plug-in provides an overview of creating web pages using the HTML language. HTML is a system of codes that you use to create interactive web pages. It provides a means to describe the structure of text-based information in a document—by denoting certain text as headings, paragraphs, lists, and so on. The seven topics in this plug-in are:

- An introduction to HTML
- HTML tools
- Creating, saving, and viewing HTML documents
- Applying style tags and attributes
- Using fancy formatting
- Creating hyperlinks
- Displaying graphics

CREATING WEB PAGES USING DREAMWEAVER www.mhhe.com/baltzan

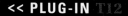

This plug-in provides a tour of using Dreamweaver to create web pages. Dreamweaver allows anyone with limited web page design experience to create, modify, and maintain pages without having to learn how to code all the functions and features from scratch. The five topics in this plug-in are:

- Navigation in Dreamweaver
- Adding content
- Formatting content
- Using cascading style sheets
- Creating tables

CREATING GANTT CHARTS WITH EXCEL AND MICROSOFT PROJECT www.mhhe.com/baltzan

This plug-in offers a quick and efficient way to manage projects. Excel and Microsoft Project are great for managing all phases of a project, creating templates, collaborating on planning processes, tracking project progress, and sharing information with all interested parties. The two topics in this plug-in are:

- Creating Gantt Charts with Excel
- Creating Gantt Charts with Microsoft Project

Business Basics

1. Define the three common business forms.
2. List and describe the seven departments commonly found in most organizations.

LO 1. Define the three common business forms.

Introduction

A sign posted beside a road in Colorado states, "Failing to plan is planning to fail." Playnix Toys posted the sign after successfully completing its 20th year in the toy business in Colorado. The company's mission is to provide a superior selection of high-end toys for children of all ages. When the company began, it generated interest by using unique marketing strategies and promotions. The toy business has a lot of tough competition. Large chain stores such as Walmart and Target offer toys at deep discount prices. Finding the right strategy to remain competitive is difficult in this industry, as FAO Schwarz discovered when it filed for bankruptcy after 143 years in the toy business.

This plug-in introduces basic business fundamentals beginning with the three most common business structures—sole proprietorship, partnership, and corporation. It then focuses on the internal operations of a corporation including accounting, finance, human resources, sales, marketing, operations/production, and management information systems.

Types of Business

Businesses come in all shapes and sizes and exist to sell products or perform services. Businesses make profits or incur losses. A *profit* occurs when businesses sell products or services for more than they cost to produce. A *loss* occurs when businesses sell products or services for less then they cost to produce. Businesses typically organize in one of the following types:

1. Sole proprietorship
2. Partnership
3. Corporation

SOLE PROPRIETORSHIP

The *sole proprietorship* is a business form in which a single person is the sole owner and is personally responsible for all the profits and losses of the business. The sole proprietorship is the quickest and easiest way to set up a business operation. No prerequisites or specific costs are associated with starting a sole proprietorship. A simple business license costing around $25 from the local county clerk is all that is required to start a sole proprietorship. The person who starts the sole proprietorship is the sole owner.

PARTNERSHIP

Partnerships are similar to sole proprietorships, except that this legal structure allows for more than one owner. Each partner is personally responsible for all the profits and losses of the business. Similar to the sole proprietorship, starting a partnership is a relatively easy process since there are no prerequisites or specific costs required. When starting a partnership, it is wise to have a lawyer draft a partnership agreement. A *partnership agreement* is a legal agreement between two or more business partners that outlines core business issues. Partnership agreements typically include:

- Amount of capital each partner expects to contribute. *Capital* represents money whose purpose is to make more money, for example, the money used to buy a rental property or a business.
- Duties and responsibilities expected from each partner.
- Expectations for sharing profits and losses.
- Partners' salary requirements.
- Methods for conflict resolution.
- Methods for dissolving the partnership.

Limited Partnership

A *limited partnership* is much like a general partnership except for one important fundamental difference; the law protects the limited partner from being responsible for all of the partnership's losses. The limited partner's legal liability in the business is limited to the amount of his or her investment. The limited partnership enables this special type of investor to share in the partnership profits without being exposed to its losses in the event the company goes out of business. However, this protection exists only as long as the limited partner does not play an active role in the operation of the business.

CORPORATION

The corporation is the most sophisticated form of business entity and the most common among large companies. The *corporation* (also called *organization, enterprise,* or *business*) is an artificially created legal entity that exists separate and apart from those individuals who created it and carry on its operations. In a corporation, the business entity is separate from the business owners. *Shareholder* is another term for business owners. An important advantage of using a corporation as a business form is that it offers the shareholders limited liability. *Limited liability* means that the shareholders are not personally liable for the losses incurred by the corporation. In most instances, financial losses incurred by a corporation are limited to the assets owned by the corporation. Shareholders' personal assets, such as their homes or investments, cannot be claimed to pay off debt or losses incurred by the corporation.

There are two general types of corporations—for profit and not for profit. *For profit corporations* primarily focus on making money and all profits and losses are shared by the business owners. *Not for profit* (or *nonprofit*) *corporations* usually exist to accomplish some charitable, humanitarian, or educational purpose, and the profits and losses are not shared by the business owners. Donations to nonprofit businesses may be tax deductible for the donor. Typical examples include hospitals, colleges, universities, and foundations.

Eleanor Josaitis is a tiny 72-year-old woman who cofounded the Detroit civil-rights group Focus: HOPE. Focus: HOPE, founded in 1968, began as a food program serving pregnant women, new mothers, and their children. Josaitis has built the nonprofit organization from a basement operation run by a handful of friends into a sprawling 40-acre campus in Detroit that now employs over 500 people, boasts more than 50,000 volunteers and donors, and has helped over 30,000 people become gainfully employed.

Josaitis and her team developed a technical school to help job seekers gain certifications in IT support. They operate a machinists' training program that funnels people into the employment pipeline at local automotive companies. The organization also teams up with local universities to help disadvantaged students receive college educations, and it runs a child care center to make sure all these opportunities are available to working and single parents. Josaitis states that the most courageous act she has performed in her life occurred 36 years ago when she turned off her television, got up off the couch, and decided to do something. "You have to have the guts to try something, because you won't change a thing by sitting in front of the TV with the clicker in your hand," Josaitis said.

Forming a corporation typically costs several hundred dollars in fees, and the owners must file a charter within the respective state. The charter typically includes:

- Purpose of the intended corporation.
- Names and addresses of the incorporators.
- Amount and types of stock the corporation will be authorized to issue.
- Rights and privileges of the shareholders.

The most common reason for incurring the cost of setting up a corporation is the recognition that the shareholder is not legally liable for the actions of the corporation. Figure B1.1 displays the primary reasons businesses choose to incorporate.

The Limited Liability Corporation (LLC)

The *limited liability corporation (LLC)* is a hybrid entity that has the legal protections of a corporation and the ability to be taxed (one time) as a partnership. A company can form an LLC for any lawful business as long as the nature of the business is not banking, insurance, and certain professional service operations. By simply filing articles of organization with the respective state agency, an LLC takes on a separate identity similar to a corporation, but without the tax problems of the corporation. Figure B1.2 summarizes the primary differences between the three most common business structures.

FIGURE B1.1

Reasons Businesses Choose to Incorporate

Reasons Businesses Choose to Incorporate	
Limited liability	In most instances, financial losses or judgments against the corporation are limited to the assets owned by the corporation.
Unlimited life	Unlike sole proprietorships and partnerships, the life of the corporation is not dependent on the life of a particular individual or individuals. It can continue indefinitely until it accomplishes its objective, merges with another business, or goes bankrupt. Unless stated otherwise, it could go on indefinitely.
Transferability of shares	It is easy to sell, transfer, or give the ownership interest in a corporation to another person. The process of divesting sole proprietorships or partnerships can be cumbersome and costly. Property has to be re-titled, new deeds drawn, and other administrative steps taken any time the slightest change of ownership occurs. With a corporation, all of the individual owners' rights and privileges are represented by the shares of stock they own. Corporations can quickly transfer ownership by simply having the shareholders endorse the back of each stock certificate to another party.
Ability to raise investment capital	It is easy to attract new investors into a corporate entity because of limited liability and the easy transferability of ownership.

	Sole Proprietorship	Partnership	Corporation
Licensing	Local license, $25–$100	Partnership agreement, legal fees	Articles of incorporation through the Secretary of State
Income	Business flows directly into personal income	Distributions taken by partners, as agreed by partners	Business and personal earnings separate, depending on corporate structure
Liability	Owner is liable	Owners are liable	Only business is liable

FIGURE B1.2

Comparison of Business Structures

Internal Operations of a Corporation

LO 2. List and describe the seven departments commonly found in most organizations.

The majority of corporations use different specialized departments to perform the unique operations required to run the business. These departments commonly include accounting, finance, human resources, sales, marketing, operations/production, and management information systems (see Figure B1.3).

Accounting

The **accounting department** provides quantitative information about the finances of the business including recording, measuring, and describing financial information. People tend to use the terms *accounting* and *bookkeeping* synonymously; however, the two are different. **Bookkeeping** is the actual recording of the business's transactions, without any analysis of the information. **Accounting** analyzes the transactional information of the business so the owners and investors can make sound economic decisions.

The two primary types of accounting are financial and managerial. **Financial accounting** involves preparing financial reports that provide information about the business's performance to external parties such as investors, creditors, and tax authorities. Financial accounting must follow strict guidelines known as Generally Accepted Accounting Principles (GAAP). **Managerial accounting** involves analyzing business operations for internal decision making and does not have to follow any rules issued by standard-setting bodies such as GAAP.

FINANCIAL STATEMENTS

All businesses operate using the same basic element, the transaction. A **transaction** is an exchange or transfer of goods, services, or funds involving two or more people. Each time a transaction occurs a source document captures all of the key data involved with

COMMON DEPARTMENTS FOUND IN A CORPORATION

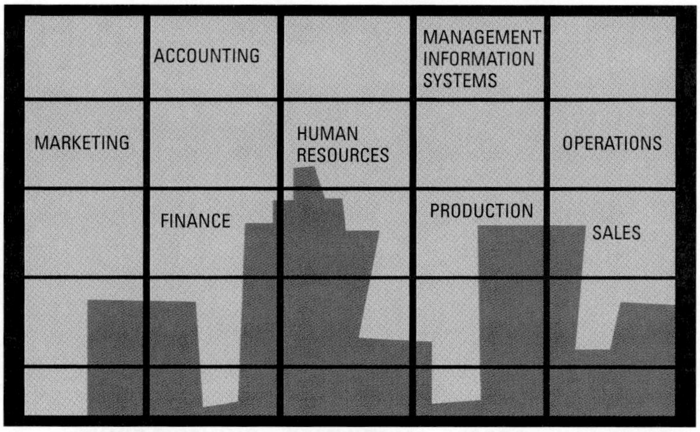

FIGURE B1.3

Departmental Structure of a Typical Organization

the transaction. The source document describes the basic transaction data such as its date, purpose, and amount and includes cash receipts, canceled checks, invoices, customer refunds, employee time sheet, etc. The source document is the beginning step in the accounting process and serves as evidence that the transaction occurred. *Financial statements* are the written records of the financial status of the business that allow interested parties to evaluate the profitability and solvency of the business. *Solvency* represents the ability of the business to pay its bills and service its debt. The financial statements are the final product of the accountant's analysis of the business transactions. Preparing the financial statements is a major undertaking and requires a significant amount of effort. Financial statements must be understandable, timely, relevant, fair, and objective in order to be useful. The four primary financial statements include:

- Balance sheet.
- Income statement.
- Statement of owner's equity.
- Statement of cash flows.

Balance Sheet

The *balance sheet* gives an accounting picture of property owned by a company and of claims against the property on a specific date. The balance sheet is based on the fundamental accounting principle that assets = liabilities + owner's equity. An *asset* is anything owned that has value or earning power. A *liability* is an obligation to make financial payments. *Owner's equity* is the portion of a company belonging to the owners. The left (debit) side of a balance sheet states assets. The right (credit) side shows liabilities and owners' equity. The two sides must be equal (balance). The balance sheet is like a snapshot of the position of an individual or business at one point in time (see Figure B1.4).

Income Statement

The *income statement* (also referred to as *earnings report, operating statement, and profit-and-loss (P&L) statement*) reports operating results (revenues minus expenses) for a given time period ending at a specified date. *Revenue* refers to the amount earned resulting from the delivery or manufacture of a product or from the rendering of a service. Revenue can include sales from a product or an amount received for performing a service. *Expenses* refer to the costs incurred in operating and maintaining a business. The income statement reports a company's *net income,* or the amount of money remaining after paying taxes (see Figure B1.5).

Statement of Owner's Equity

The *statement of owner's equity* (also called the *statement of retained earnings* or *equity statement*) tracks and communicates changes in the shareholder's earnings. Profitable

FIGURE B1.4

Balance Sheet Example

ASSETS			LIABILITIES	
Current Assets			**Current Liabilities**	
Cash		$ 250,000	Accounts Payable	$ 150,000
Securities		$ 30,000	Loans (due < 1 year)	$ 750,000
Accounts Receivable		$ 1,500,000	Taxes	$ 200,000
Inventory		$ 2,920,000		
			Long-term Liabilities	
Fixed Assets		$ 7,500,000	Loans (due > 1 year)	$ 2,500,000
			Total Liabilities	$ 3,600,000
			Owner's Equity	$ 8,600,000
Total Assets		$12,200,000	**Total Liabilities +** Owner's Equity	$12,200,000

ASSETS = LIABILITIES + OWNER'S EQUITY

organizations typically pay the shareholders dividends. *Dividends* are a distribution of earnings to shareholders.

Statement of Cash Flows

Cash flow represents the money an investment produces after subtracting cash expenses from income. The *statement of cash flows* summarizes sources and uses of cash, indicates whether enough cash is available to carry on routine operations, and offers an analysis of all business transactions, reporting where the firm obtained its cash and how it chose to allocate the cash. The cash flow statement shows where money comes from, how the company is going to spend it, and when the company will require additional cash. Companies typically project cash flow statements on a monthly basis for the current year and a quarterly basis for the next two to five years. A *financial quarter* indicates a three-month period (four quarters per year). Cash flow statements become less valid over time since numerous assumptions are required to project into the future.

When it comes to decreasing expenses and managing a company's cash flow, managers need to look at all costs. Ben Worthen, executive vice president and CIO of Manufacturers Bank in Los Angeles, states that everyone notices the million-dollar negotiation; however, a couple of thousand dollars here and there are just as important. When attempting to cut costs, Worthen listed every contract the bank had. He saved $5,000 by renegotiating a contract with the vendor who watered the plants, a vendor that most employees did not even know existed. He also saved $50,000 by renegotiating the contract with the bank's cleaning agency. "You need to think of everything when cutting costs," Worthen said. "$5,000 buys three or four laptops for salespersons."

Income Statement	
Revenue (Sales)	$60,000,000
Cost of Goods Sold	$30,000,000
Gross Profit	**$30,000,000**
(Sales – Cost of Goods Sold)	
Operating Expenses	$7,000,000
Profit Before Taxes	**$23,000,000**
(Gross Profit – Operating Expenses)	
Taxes	$18,000,000
Net Profit (or Loss)	**$5,000,000**

FIGURE B1.5

Income Statement Example

Finance

Finance deals with the strategic financial issues associated with increasing the value of the business while observing applicable laws and social responsibilities. Financial decisions include such things as:

- How the company should raise and spend its capital.
- Where the company should invest its money.
- What portion of profits will be paid to shareholders in the form of dividends.
- Whether the company should merge with or acquire another business.

Financial decisions are short term (usually up to one year), medium term (one to seven years), or long term (more than seven years). The typical forms of financing include loans (debt or equity) or grants. Financing may be required for immediate use in business operations or for an investment.

FINANCIAL ANALYSIS

Different financial ratios are used to evaluate a company's performance. Companies can gain additional insight into their performance by comparing financial ratios against other companies in their industry. A few of the more common financial ratios include:

- **Internal rate of return (IRR)**—the rate at which the net present value of an investment equals zero.
- **Return on investment (ROI)**—indicates the earning power of a project and is measured by dividing the benefits of a project by the investment.
- **Cash flow analysis**—a means to conduct a periodic check on the company's financial health. A projected cash flow statement estimates what the stream of

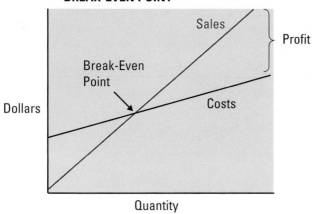

BREAK-EVEN POINT

Dollars

Break-Even Point

Sales

Profit

Costs

Quantity

FIGURE B1.6

Break-Even Analysis

money will be in coming months or years, based on a history of sales and expenses. A monthly cash flow statement reveals the current state of affairs. The ability to perform a cash flow analysis is an essential skill for every business owner; it can be the difference between being able to open a business and being able to stay in business.

■ **Break-even analysis**—a way to determine the volume of business required to make a profit at the current prices charged for the products or services. For example, if a promotional mailing costs $1,000 and each item generates $50 in revenue, the company must generate 20 sales to break even and cover the cost of the mailing. The **break-even point** is the point at which revenues equal costs. The point is located by performing a break-even analysis. All sales over the break-even point produce profits; any drop in sales below that point will produce losses (see Figure B1.6).

Human Resources

Human resources (HR) includes the policies, plans, and procedures for the effective management of employees (human resources). HR typically focuses on the following:

■ Employee recruitment.

■ Employee selection.

■ Employee training and development.

■ Employee appraisals, evaluations, and rewards.

■ Employee communications.

The primary goal of HR is to instill employee commitment by creating an environment of shared values, innovation, flexibility, and empowerment. Most organizations recognize that focusing on strong HR practices that foster employee growth and satisfaction can significantly contribute to achieving business success. The most obvious way HR practices create business success is through quality employee selection. Hiring the right employee who suits the company's culture is difficult. Organizations create employee value by implementing employment practices such as training, skill development, and rewards. An organization that focuses on HR creates valuable employees with strategic business competencies.

MANAGEMENT TECHNIQUES

There may be no such thing as a best practice for managing people. Numerous management techniques are used by all different types of managers in a variety of industries. For example, Sears and Nordstrom are legends in the retailing industry; however, their approaches to HR are completely different. Sears is one of the pioneering companies in the science of employee selection, relying on some of the most sophisticated selection tests in American industry. Sears employees receive extensive training in company practices; management tracks employee attitudes and morale through frequent and rigorous employee surveys. The company provides its sales representatives, who work on salary rather than commission, with intensive training in Sears products, the company's operating systems, and sales techniques.

Nordstrom operates with virtually no formal personnel practices. Its hiring is decentralized, using no formal selection tests. Managers look for applicants with experience in customer contact, but the main desirable quality appears to be pleasant personalities and motivation. The company has only one rule in its personnel handbook: "Use your best judgment at all times." Individual salesclerks virtually run their areas as private stores. Nordstrom maintains a continuous stream of programs to motivate employees to provide intensive service, but it offers very little training. Its commission-based payroll system makes it possible for salesclerks to earn sizable incomes. Nordstrom sales personnel are ranked within each department according to their monthly sales; the most successful are promoted (almost all managers are promoted from within the company) and the least successful are terminated.

Sears and Nordstrom are both highly successful retailers, yet they operate using widely different recruitment policies. One of the biggest success factors for any business is the company's management and personnel. Employees must possess certain critical skills for the company to succeed. The HR department takes on the important task of hiring, training, evaluating, rewarding, and terminating employees. Effective HR goes far beyond executing a standard set of policies and procedures; it requires questioning and understanding the relationships between choices in managing people, the strategies and goals of the organization, and the possibilities presented by the external environment. Today's competitive environment features rapid technological change, increasingly global markets, and a diverse workforce comprising not just men and women with different sorts of career objectives, but also potential workers from diverse cultural and ethnic backgrounds. HR must ensure that the choices made in managing people are made sensibly and with clear purposes in mind.

Sales

Sales is the function of selling a good or service and focuses on increasing customer sales, which increases company revenues. A salesperson has the main activity of selling a product or service. Many industries require a license before a salesperson can sell the products, such as real estate, insurance, and securities.

A common view of the sales department is to see the salespersons only concerned with making the sale now, without any regard to the cost of the sale to the business. This is called the hard sell, where the salesperson heavily pushes a product (even when the customer does not want the product) and where price cuts are given even if they cause financial losses for the company. A broader view of the sales department sees it as taking on the task of building strong customer relationships where the primary emphasis is on securing new customers and keeping current customers satisfied. Many sales departments are currently focusing on building strong customer relationships.

THE SALES PROCESS

Figure B1.7 depicts the typical sales process, which begins with an opportunity and ends with billing the customer for the sale. An opportunity is a name of a potential customer who might be interested in making a purchase (opportunities are also called *leads*). The company finds opportunities from a variety of sources such as mailing lists and customer inquiries. The name is sent to a salesperson who contacts the potential customer and sets up a meeting to discuss the products. During the meeting, all problems and issues are identified and resolved, and the salesperson generates a quote for the customer. If the customer decides to accept the quote, a sales order is placed. The company fulfills the order and delivers the product, and the process ends when the customer is billed.

MARKET SHARE

Sales figures offer a good indication of how well a company is performing. For example, high sales volumes typically indicate that a company is performing well. However, they do not always indicate how a firm is performing relative to its competitors. For example, changes in sales might simply reflect shifts in market size or in economic conditions. A sales increase might occur because the market increased in size, not because the company is performing better.

Measuring the proportion of the market that a firm captures is one way to measure a firm's performance relative to its competitors. This proportion is the firm's market

Sales Process

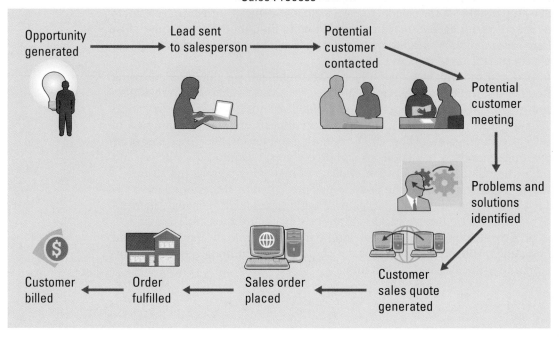

FIGURE B1.7

The Sales Process

share and is calculated by dividing the firm's sales by the total market sales for the entire industry. For example, if a firm's total sales (revenues) were $2 million and the sales for the entire industry were $10 million, the firm would have captured 20 percent of the total market, or have a 20 percent market share.

Many video game products launch with great enthusiasm and die a quick death such as Sega's GameGear and DreamCast, Atari's Lynx, and Nintendo's Virtual Boy. Video game consoles die quickly when only a limited number of game publishers sign up to supply games for the particular product. Producing video game products is a tough competitive business in a finicky market.

Reasons to Increase Market Share

Many organizations seek to increase their market share because many individuals associate market share with profitability. Figure B1.8 indicates the primary reasons organizations seek to increase their market share.

Ways to Increase Market Share

A primary way to increase market share is by changing one of the following variables: product, price, place, or promotion (see Figure B1.9). It is common to refer to these four variables as the marketing mix, discussed in detail below.

FIGURE B1.8

Reasons to Increase
Market Share

Reasons to Increase Market Share
Economies of scale—An organization can develop a cost advantage by selling additional products or higher volumes.
Sales growth in a stagnant industry—If an industry stops growing, an organization can increase its sales by increasing its market share.
Reputation—A successful organization with a solid reputation can use its clout to its advantage.
Increased bargaining power—Larger organizations have an advantage in negotiating with suppliers and distributors.

Ways to Increase Market Share
Product—An organization can change product attributes to provide more value to the customer. Improving product quality is one example.
Price—An organization can decrease a product's price to increase sales. This strategy will not work if competitors are willing to match discounts.
Place (Distribution)—An organization can add new distribution channels. This allows the organization to increase the size of its market, which should increase sales.
Promotion—An organization can increase spending on product advertising, which should increase sales. This strategy will not work if competitors also increase advertising.

Reasons Not to Increase Market Share
If an organization is near its production capacity and it experiences an increase in market share, it could cause the organization's supply to fall below its demand. Not being able to deliver products to meet demand could damage the organization's reputation.
Profits could decrease if an organization gains market share by offering deep discounts or by increasing the amount of money it spends on advertising.
If the organization is not prepared to handle the new growth, it could begin to offer shoddy products or less attentive customer service. This could result in the loss of its professional reputation and valuable customers.

Reasons Not to Increase Market Share

Surprisingly, it is not always a good idea to increase an organization's market share. Figure B1.10 offers a few reasons increasing an organization's market share can actually decrease an organization's revenues.

Marketing

Marketing is the process associated with promoting the sale of goods or services. The marketing department supports the sales department by creating promotions that help sell the company's products. **Marketing communications** seek to build product or service awareness and to educate potential consumers on the product or service.

Jenny Ming, president of Old Navy, a division of Gap Inc., believes that unique marketing ideas for Old Navy's original designs heavily contributed to the success of the $6.5 billion brand. Ideas come from anywhere, and Ming found one of the company's most successful products when she was dropping her daughter off at school. It was pajama day at school, and all of the girls were wearing pajama bottoms with a tank top. Ming began wondering why they even created and sold pajama tops; nobody seemed to wear them. The company, having problems selling pajama sets, quickly introduced "just bottoms," a line of pajama bottoms selling at $15. A full pajama set cost $25. Along with the bottoms, the company offered tank tops in different colors so the customer could mix and match the items. The company built a huge business from the "just bottoms" line. Ming encourages her staff to look for marketing and product opportunities everywhere, even in the most unlikely of places.

MARKETING MIX

The classic components of marketing include the four Ps in the marketing mix: product, price, place, and promotion. The **marketing mix** includes the variables that marketing managers can control in order to best satisfy customers in the target market (see

Figure B1.11). The organization attempts to generate a positive response in the target market by blending these four marketing mix variables in an optimal manner.

Figure B1.12 summarizes the primary attributes involved with each decision made in the marketing mix.

CUSTOMER SEGMENTATION

Market segmentation is the division of a market into similar groups of customers. It is not always optimal for an organization to offer the same marketing mix to vastly different customers. Market segmentation makes it possible for organizations to tailor the mar-

FIGURE B1.11

The Marketing Mix

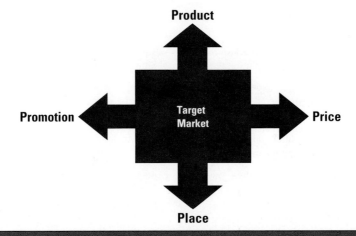

1. **Product** — the physical product or service offered to the consumer. Product decisions include function, appearance, packaging, service, warranty, etc.

2. **Price** — takes into account profit margins and competitor pricing. Pricing includes list price, discounts, financing, and other options such as leasing.

3. **Place** (distribution) — associated with channels of distribution that serve as the means for getting the product to the target customers. Attributes involved in place decisions include market coverage, channel member selection, logistics, and levels of service.

4. **Promotion** — related to communication to and selling to potential consumers. An organization can perform a break-even analysis when making promotion decisions. If an organization knows the value of each customer, it can determine whether additional customers are worth the coast of acquisition. Attributes involved in promotion decisions involve advertising, public relations, media types, etc.

FIGURE B1.12

Common Attributes Involved with Each P in the Marketing Mix

Product	Price	Place (Distribution)	Promotion
Quality	Discount	Channel	Advertising
Brand	Financing	Market	Sales
Appearance	Lease	Location	Public relations
Package		Logistics	Marketing message
Function		Service Level	Media type
Warranty			Budget
Service/Support			

keting mix for specific target markets, hence better satisfying its customer needs. Not all attributes of the marketing mix need to be changed for each market segment. For example, one market segment might require a discounted price, while another market segment might require better customer service. An organization uses marketing research, market trends, and managerial judgment when deciding the optimal way to segment a market. Market segmentation typically includes:

- **Geographic segmentation**—based on regional variables such as region, climate, population density, and population growth rate.

- **Demographic segmentation**—based on variables such as age, gender, ethnicity, education, occupation, income, and family status.

- **Psychographic segmentation**—based on variables such as values, attitudes, and lifestyles.

- **Behavioral segmentation**—based on variables such as usage rate, usage patterns, price sensitivity, and brand loyalty.

THE PRODUCT LIFE CYCLE

The *product life cycle* includes the four phases a product progresses through during its life cycle including introduction, growth, maturity, and decline. An organization's marketing of a product will change depending on its stage in the product life cycle. An organization can plot a product's profits as a function of the product life cycle (see Figure B1.13).

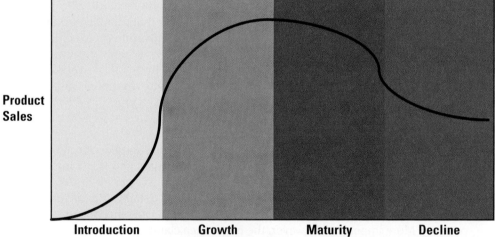

FIGURE B1.13

The Product Life Cycle

- **Introduction Stage**—The organization seeks to build product awareness and develop the product's market. The organization will use the marketing mix to help impact the target market. Product branding and quality level are established.

- **Growth Stage**—The organization seeks to build brand preference and increase market share. The organization maintains or increases the quality of the product and might add additional features or better customer service. The organization typically enjoys increases in demand with little competition allowing the price to remain constant.

- **Maturity Stage**—The strong growth in sales diminishes. Competition begins to appear with similar products. The primary objective at this point is to defend market share while maximizing profits. Some companies enhance product features to differentiate the product in the market.

- **Decline Stage**—Sales begin to decline. At this point, the organization has several options. It can maintain the product, possibly rejuvenating it by adding new features and finding new uses. It can reduce costs and continue to offer it, possibly to a loyal niche segment. It can discontinue the product, liquidating remaining inventory or selling it to another firm that is willing to continue the product.

Operations/Production

Operations management (also called *production management*) is the management of systems or processes that convert or transform resources (including human resources) into goods and services. The operations department oversees the transformation of input resources (i.e., labor, materials, and machines) into output resources (i.e., products and services). The operations department is critical because it manages the physical processes by which companies take in raw materials, convert them into products, and distribute them to customers. The operations department generally ranks high in the responsibilities of general management.

TRANSFORMING CORPORATIONS

Complete transformation of an organization, or an entire industry, is the ultimate goal of successful business process reengineering. Figure B1.14 displays a matrix that has project scope on one axis and project speed on the other. For a project with a relatively narrow scope where the speed is fast, reengineering occurs. Fast speed with broad scope may be a turnaround situation requiring downsizing and tough decision making. A project with a relatively slow speed and narrow scope results in continuous improvement. In the upper right-hand corner of Figure B1.14, where the project scope is broad and the time frame for achieving that change is longer, the term *transformation* is appropriate.

Progressive Insurance offers a great example of a corporation that transformed its entire industry by reengineering the insurance claims process. Progressive Insurance has seen phenomenal growth in an otherwise staid auto insurance market. Progressive's growth came not through acquisitions or mergers—the stuff that puts CEOs on the front page of *The Wall Street Journal*—but through substantial innovations in everyday operations. Progressive reengineered the insurance claim process. When a customer has an auto accident, Progressive representatives are on hand 24 hours a day to take the call and schedule a claims adjustor. The claims adjustor works out of a mobile van, enabling a nine-hour turnaround rather than the industry standard of 10 to 17 days. The Progressive adjustor prepares an estimate on the spot and will, in most cases, write the customer a check immediately and even offer a ride home.

What provoked this innovation? Progressive says it was the strong connection it has to its customers, its willingness to listen to customers' frustrations, and the common sense to act on those frustrations by changing the core of its business operations. As a result of customer feedback, the company did not merely tweak the details of the claims adjustment process. It dramatically rewrote the process, resulting in significant cost savings for the company. More important, however, the hassle-free claims process keeps customers happy and loyal, reducing the significant burden of constantly replacing lapsed customers with new ones.

FIGURE B1.14

Organizational Transformation through BPR

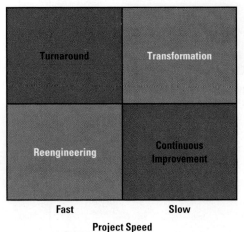

Broad
(Finding new ways to perform the process)

Project Scope

Narrow
(Finding better ways to perform the process)

Turnaround   Transformation

Reengineering   Continuous Improvement

Fast   Slow

Project Speed

Management Information Systems

Information technology (IT) is a field concerned with the use of technology in managing and processing information. Information technology is a broad subject concerned with technology and other aspects of managing and processing information, especially in large organizations. In particular, IT deals with the use of electronic computers and computer software to convert, store, protect, process, transmit, and retrieve information. For that reason, computer professionals are often called IT specialists, and the division that deals with software technology is often called the IT department.

Management information systems is a business function just as marketing, finance, operations, and human resources management are business functions. Formally defined, management information systems (MIS) is a general name for the business function and academic discipline covering the application of people, technologies, and procedures—collectively called information systems—to solve business problems. Other names for MIS include information services (IS), management information services (MIS), or managed service provider (MSP). In business, MIS supports business processes and operations, decision making, and competitive strategies. MIS involves collecting, recording, storing, and basic processing of information including:

- Accounting records such as sales, purchase, investment, and payroll information, processed into financial statements such as income statements, balance sheets, ledgers, management reports, and so on.

- Operations records such as inventory, work-in-process, equipment repair and maintenance, supply chain, and other production/operations information, processed into production schedules, production controllers, inventory systems, and production monitoring systems.

- Human resources records such as personnel, salary, and employment history information, processed into employee expense reports and performance-based reports.

- Marketing records such as customer profiles, customer purchase histories, marketing research, advertising, and other marketing information, processed into advertising reports, marketing plans, and sales activity reports.

- Strategic records such as business intelligence, competitor analysis, industry analysis, corporate objectives, and other strategic information, processed into industry trends reports, market share reports, mission statements, and portfolio models.

The bottom line is that management information systems use all of the above to implement, control, and monitor plans, strategies, tactics, new products, new business models, or new business ventures.

The study of business begins with understanding the different types of businesses including a sole proprietorship, partnership, or a corporation. Figure B1.15 highlights seven departments found in a typical business.

All of these departments must be able to execute activities specific to their business function and also be able to work with the other departments to create synergies throughout the entire business.

- **Accounting** provides quantitative information about the finances of the business including recording, measuring, and describing financial information.

- **Finance** deals with the strategic financial issues associated with increasing the value of the business, while observing applicable laws and social responsibilities.

- **Human resources (HR)** includes the policies, plans, and procedures for the effective management of employees (human resources).

- **Sales** is the function of selling a good or service and focuses on increasing customer sales, which increases company revenues.

- **Marketing** is the process associated with promoting the sale of goods or services. The marketing department supports the sales department by creating promotions that help sell the company's products.

- **Operations management** (also called **production management**) is the management of systems or processes that convert or transform resources (including human resources) into goods and services.

- **Management information systems (MIS)** is a general name for the business function and academic discipline covering the application of people, technologies, and procedures—collectively called information systems—to solve business problems.

FIGURE B1.15

Common Departments in a Business

✱ KEY TERMS

Battle of the Toys—FAO Schwarz Is Back!

German immigrant Frederick Schwarz established FAO Schwarz, a premier seller of fine toys, in 1862. After moving between several store locations in Manhattan, the growing company settled at 745 Fifth Avenue in 1931. FAO Schwarz soon became a toy institution, despite the impending Depression.

Unfortunately, the New York institution closed its doors in 2004 after its owner, FAO Inc., filed for bankruptcy twice in 2003. The company ran into trouble because it could not compete with the deep discounts offered on toys at chain stores like Walmart and Target. All the stores in the FAO chain were closed.

Some people believe that FAO Schwarz was its own worst enemy. The company sold Sesame Street figures for $9 while the same figure at a discount store went for less than $3.

In 2004, the New York investment firm D. E. Shaw & Co. bought the rights to the FAO Schwarz name and reopened the Manhattan and Las Vegas stores. The grand reopening of the New York store occurred on November 25, 2004, during the Macy's Thanksgiving Day parade. It appears that the company has learned from its previous mistakes and is moving forward with a new business strategy of offering high-end, hard-to-find toys and products along with outstanding customer service.

Jerry Welch, FAO chief executive officer, states the company based its new business strategy on offering customers—local, visitors, and Internet—a unique shopping experience in which they can spend thousands of dollars or just twenty, but still purchase an exclusive item. The store no longer carries any items from top toymakers Hasbro Inc. or Lego. The only toys it carries from Mattel Inc. are Hot Wheels and limited-edition Barbie dolls, starting at $130 for the Bridal Barbie dressed in a Badgley Mischka designer wedding gown and chandelier earrings. A few of the items the store is offering include:

- $20 made-to-order Hot Wheels car that a child can custom design via a computer.

- $50,000 miniature Ferrari with a full leather interior, fiberglass body, three-speed transmission, and working sound system that travels up to 24 kilometers an hour and is not recommended for children six and under.

- $15,000 stuffed elephant.

- $150,000 6.7-meter-long piano keyboard, which premiered in the Tom Hanks movie *Big*.

- Baby dolls that are arranged in incubators and sold by staff wearing nurses' uniforms.

Welch said, "FAO is a 142-year-old brand that, because of our location on Fifth Avenue, people all over the world know. So we start out with great recognition and what we've done here is pull together something that you just can't find anywhere else in the world. Everything here is made by small, unique manufacturers from all over the world." Welch is confident the stores will be richly profitable for its new owners because they have stopped offering mainstream products found in rival stores to generate sales volume. The new owners have returned to a business strategy focusing on quality and exclusivity that were the hallmark of the original store.

The Future of the Toy Store Playing Field

Toys 'R' Us began slashing prices during the 2004 holiday season in a last-ditch effort to fight off intense price competition from big discounters like Walmart and Target. Toys 'R' Us CEO John Eyler stated the company would not be outdone on pricing, during the holiday sales rush, though he cautioned he was not planning to engage in a price war. There have been several reports that the company might leave the toy business to focus on its more profitable Babies 'R' Us unit. Toys 'R' Us lost $25 million for the three months ended in October 2004. The company lost $46 million in the same period the year earlier. The decrease in losses can be attributed to a big cost-cutting effort.

Kurt Barnard of Barnard's *Retail Trend Report* stated that Toys 'R' Us is destined for oblivion—it cannot stand up to the discounters. Toymakers like Mattel and Hasbro, whose profits have also suffered from Walmart's market power, have given Toys 'R' Us a hand by offering it 21 exclusive items not available at other stores.

Toy manufacturers fear that greater monopoly power from Walmart will force them to slash their profit margins. Walmart carries fewer items than toy stores like Toys 'R' Us, which could lead to fewer choices for consumers.

FAO's new owners believe that Walmart cannot compare with the atmosphere now offered at FAO Schwarz, a true toy heaven. The company is hoping that its new business strategy will allow it to move beyond the battle of the toy stores. Toys 'R' Us will need to find new ways to compete with discounters like Walmart and Target.

Questions

1. Why did FAO Inc. have to declare bankruptcy?
2. Describe the issues with FAO's original business model.
3. Identify the toy retailer's new business model. Do you believe it will keep the new company in business? Why or why not?
4. What strategy can Toys 'R' Us follow that will help it compete with big discount chains like Walmart and Target?

✳ CLOSING CASE TWO

Innovative Managers	
Jeffrey Immelt, General Electric (GE)	■ Repositioned GE's portfolio with major acquisitions in health care, entertainment, and commercial finance ■ Created a more diverse, global, and customer-driven culture
Steven Reinemund, PepsiCo	■ Developed strong and diverse leadership that helped PepsiCo tap new markets ■ Attained consistent double-digit growth through product innovation and smart marketing
Steven Spielberg, Jeffrey Katzenberg, and David Geffen, DreamWorks SKG	■ Computer-animated *Shrek 2* set a record with a gross of $437 million ■ IPO pulled in $812 million
Robert Nardelli, Home Depot	■ Turned a $46 billion company focused on big stores into a $70 billion chain with urban, suburban, and international outlets ■ Drive for efficiency, such as centralizing purchasing and investing in technology, pushed margins above 30 percent
John Henry, Boston Red Sox	■ Broke the most fabled curse in sports, when the Boston Red Sox won the team's first World Championship since 1918 ■ Sold out all 81 home games for the first time in team history
Phil Knight, Nike	■ Transformed a volatile, fad-driven marketing and design icon into a more shareholder-friendly company

FIGURE B1.16

Innovative Business Managers

Innovative Business Managers

BusinessWeek magazine recognized several innovative managers who have demonstrated talent, vision, and the ability to identify excellent opportunities (see Figure B1.16).

Jeffrey Immelt, General Electric (GE)

When Jeffrey Immelt took over as CEO of General Electric, he had big shoes to fill. The former CEO, Jack Welch, had left an unprecedented record as one of the top CEOs of all time. Immelt proved his ability to run the company by creating a customer-driven global culture that spawns innovation and embraces technology.

Steven Reinemund, PepsiCo

Steven Reinemund has turned PepsiCo into a $27 billion food and beverage giant. "To be a leader in consumer products, it's critical to have leaders who represent the population we serve," states Reinemund, who created a diverse leadership group that defines the strategic vision for the company. Reinemund also takes a major role in mentoring and teaching his employees and demands that all senior executives do the same. The payoff: consistent double-digit earnings and solid sales at a time when many of the company's staple products— potato chips and soft drinks—are under attack for fears about childhood obesity and health concerns.

Steven Spielberg, Jeffrey Katzenberg, and David Geffen, DreamWorks

The DreamWorks studio, founded in 1994 by Steven Spielberg, Jeffrey Katzenberg, and David Geffen, suffered through its share of early bombs. Finally, the studio discovered a green ogre named Shrek and quickly became the hottest studio this side of Pixar Animation. DreamWorks Animation turned a $187 million loss in 2003 into a $196 million profit in 2004, with revenues of $1.1 billion. DreamWorks plans to release two animation films per year, each taking almost four years to produce.

Robert Nardelli, Home Depot

Robert Nardelli took several risks when he became CEO of Home Depot. First, he allocated $14 billion into upgrading merchandise, renovating outdated stores, and investing in new technology such as self-checkout lanes and cordless scan guns. Second, Nardelli expanded into Mexico, China, and other regions, tapping the growing homeowner market. Finally, Nardelli bet big on carrying products for aging baby boomers who wanted to spruce up their empty nests. The moves are paying off. The company sits on $3.4 billion in cash. With 2005 revenues headed to $80 billion, Home Depot is the number two U.S. retailer after Walmart.

John Henry, Boston Red Sox

John Henry earned his fortune in the global futures market by developing a proprietary futures-trading system that consistently produced double-digit returns. Henry's new system, Sabermetrics, helped him reverse the most fabled curse in sports history by leading the Boston Red Sox to the team's first World Championship since 1918. Sabermetrics mines baseball statistics to find undervalued players while avoiding long contracts for aging stars whose performance is likely to decline. With the help of Sabermetrics, Henry has built one of the most effective teams in baseball.

Philip Knight, Nike

Philip Knight, who got his start by selling Japanese sneakers from the trunk of his car, built the $12 billion sports behemoth Nike. Knight and his team transformed high-performance sports equipment into high-fashion gear and forever changed the rules of sports marketing with huge endorsement contracts and in-your-face advertising. Then, just as suddenly, Nike lost focus. In early 2000, kids stopped craving the latest sneaker, the company's image took a huge hit from its labor practices, sales slumped, and costs soared.

Thus began Knight's second act. He revamped management and brought in key outsiders to oversee finances and apparel lines. Knight devoted more energy to developing new information systems. Today, Nike's earnings are less volatile and less fad-driven. In 2004, Nike's earnings increased $1 billion.

Questions

1. Choose one of the companies listed here and explain how it has achieved business success.

2. Why is it important for all of DreamWorks' functional business areas to work together? Provide an example of what might happen if the DreamWorks marketing department failed to work with its sales department.

3. Why is marketing important to an organization like the Boston Red Sox? Explain where Major League Baseball is in the product life cycle.

4. Which types of financial statements are most important to Home Depot's business?

5. Identify the marketing mix and why customer segmentation is critical to PepsiCo's business strategy.

6. Explain business process reengineering and how a company like GE can use it to improve operations.

✱ MAKING BUSINESS DECISIONS

1. Setting Up a Business

Your friend, Lindsay Harvey, is going to start her own chocolate shop, called Chocolate-By-Design. Lindsay is an expert candy maker and one of the city's top pastry chefs. Lindsay has come to you for advice on what type of business Chocolate-By-Design should be—a sole proprietorship, partnership, or corporation. Create a report comparing the three different types of businesses, along with your recommendation for Chocolate-By-Design's business structure.

2. Guest Lecturing on Business

As a recent college graduate, your favorite professor, Dr. Henning, has asked you to come back and guest lecture at his introduction to business course. Create a presentation defining the different departments in a typical business, what roles each play, and why it is important that they all work together.

3. Expanding Markets

J. R. Cash created a small business selling handmade cowboy boots, and within a year his business is booming. J. R. currently builds all of the boots in his store and takes orders over the phone and from walk-in customers. There is currently a three-month waiting list for boots. J. R. is not sure how to grow his business and has come to you for advice. Describe the reasons and ways some businesses increase market share and why J. R. might choose not to increase his market share.

4. Segmenting Customers

Due to your vast marketing experience, you have been hired by a new company, Sugar, to perform a strategic analysis on chewing gum. The company wants to understand the many market segments for the different brands, flavors, sizes, and colors of gum. Create an analysis of the different market segments for chewing gum. What market segment would you recommend Sugar pursue?

5. Product Life Cycle

An associate, Carl Grotenhuis, has developed a new brand of laundry detergent called Clean. Carl wants your opinion on his potential to enter and dominate the laundry detergent market. Using the product life cycle create a recommendation for Carl's new product.

6. Redesigning a Business

Tom Walton is the new CEO for Lakeside, a large cereal manufacturing company. Tom's predecessor had run the company for 50 years and did little in terms of process improvement; in fact, his motto was "if it isn't broke, why fix it." Tom wants to take advantage of technology to create new processes for the entire company. He believes that improving operations will increase efficiency and lower costs.

Tom has a major hurdle to overcome before he can begin revamping the company—its employees. Many of the employees have worked at the company for decades and are comfortable with the motto "if it isn't broke, why fix it." Develop a plan Tom can use to communicate to his employees the potential value gained from business process reengineering.

Business Process

1. Describe business processes and their importance to an organization.
2. Compare the continuous process improvement model and business process reengineering.
3. Describe the importance of business process modeling (or mapping) and business process models.
4. Explain business process management along with the reason for its importance to an organization.

LO 1. Describe business processes and their importance to an organization.

Introduction

The benefits of business process improvement vary, but a rough rule of thumb is that it will, at a minimum, double the gains of a project by streamlining outdated practices, enhancing efficiency, promoting compliance and standardization, and making an organization more agile. Business process improvement involves three key steps:

1. Measure what matters to most customers.
2. Monitor the performance of key business processes.
3. Assign accountability for process improvement.

Comprehensive business process management systems help organizations model and define complete business processes, implement those processes integrated with existing systems, and provide business leaders with the ability to analyze, manage, and improve the execution of processes in real time.

Examining Business Processes

Waiting in line at a grocery store is a great example of the need for process improvement. In this case, the "process" is called checkout, and the purpose is to pay for and bag groceries. The process begins when a customer steps into line and ends when the customer receives the receipt and leaves the store. The *process* steps are the activities the customer and store personnel do to complete the transaction. A ***business process*** is a standardized set of activities that accomplish a specific task, such as processing a customer's order. Business processes transform a set of inputs into a set of outputs (goods or services) for another person or process by using people and tools. This simple example describes a customer checkout process. Imagine other business processes: developing new products, building a new home, ordering clothes from mail-order companies, requesting new telephone service from a telephone company, administering Social Security payments, and so on.

Examining business processes helps an organization determine bottlenecks and identify outdated, duplicate, and smooth running processes. To stay competitive, organizations must optimize and automate their business processes. To identify which business processes need to be optimized, the organization must clearly understand its business processes, which typically have the following important characteristics:

- The processes have internal and external users.
- A process is cross-departmental. Departments are functional towers of expertise, but processes cut across departments.
- The processes occur across organizations.
- The processes are based on how work is done in the organization.
- Every process should be documented and fully understood by everyone participating in the process.
- Processes should be modeled to promote complete understanding.

A business process can be viewed as a "value chain." By contributing to the creation or delivery of a product or service, each step in a process should add value to the preceding step. For example, one step in the product development process consists of conducting market acceptance tests. This step adds value by ensuring that the product meets the needs of the market before the product or service is finalized. A tremendous amount of learning and improvement can result from the documentation and examination of the input-output linkages. However, between every input and every output is a process. Knowledge and improvement can only be completed by peeling the layers of the onion and examining the processes through which inputs are converted into outputs. Figure B2.1 displays several sample business processes.

UNDERSTANDING THE IMPORTANCE OF BUSINESS PROCESSES

Organizations are only as effective as their business processes. Developing logical business processes can help an organization achieve its goals. For example, an automobile manufacturer might have a goal to reduce the time it takes to deliver a car to a customer. The automobile manufacturer cannot hope to meet this goal with an inefficient ordering process or a convoluted distribution process. Sales representatives might be making mistakes when completing order forms, data-entry clerks might not accurately code order information, and dock crews might be inefficiently loading cars onto trucks. All of these errors increase the time it will take to get the car to the customer. Improving any one of these business processes can have a significant effect on the total distribution process, made up of the order entry, production scheduling, and transportation processes.

IBM Business Consulting Services helped Bank of America's card services division identify $40 million of simplification and cost savings projects over two years by improving business processes to identify opportunities, eliminate redundancies, consolidate systems/applications, and remove duplicate processes. Within the card services and ecommerce division were several fragmented strategies and IT architectures. These were consolidated and simplified to streamline the business area and provide better and faster response to customer demand.

The scope of the IT strategy and architecture business process realignment project included all consumer card segments (including military, school, airlines, etc.), ATM cards and services, and ecommerce.

Sample Business Processes

ACCOUNTING BUSINESS PROCESSES

- Accounts payable
- Accounts receivable
- Bad/NSF checks
- Bank account reconciliation
- Cash receipts
- Check requests
- Check signing authority
- Depreciation
- Invoice billings
- Petty cash
- Month-end closing procedures

CUSTOMER SERVICE BUSINESS PROCESSES

- Customer satisfaction survey
- Customer service contact/complaint handling
- Guarantee customer service satisfaction
- Postsale customer follow-up
- Warranty and service policies

ENVIRONMENTAL BUSINESS PROCESSES

- Environmental protection
- Hazardous waste management
- Air/water/soil resource management

FINANCE BUSINESS PROCESSES

- Account collection
- Bank loan applications
- Banking policy and relations
- Business plans and forecasts
- Customer credit approval and credit terms
- Exercise of incentive stock options
- Property tax assessments
- Release of financial or confidential information
- Stock transactions
- Weekly financial and six-week cash flow reports

HUMAN RESOURCES BUSINESS PROCESSES

- Board of directors and shareholders meetings, minutes, and protocol
- Disabilities employment policies
- Drug-free workplace employment policies
- Employee hiring policies
- Employee orientation
- Family and medical leave act
- Files and records management
- Health care benefits
- Paid and unpaid time off
- Pay and payroll matters
- Performance appraisals and salary adjustments
- Resignations and terminations
- Sexual harassment policies
- Training/tuition reimbursement
- Travel and entertainment
- Workplace rules and guidelines
- Workplace safety

Sample Business Processes
MANAGEMENT INFORMATION SYSTEMS BUSINESS PROCESSES
■ Disaster recovery procedures
■ Backup/recovery procedures
■ Service agreements, emergency services, and community resources
■ Emergency notification procedures
■ Office and department recovery
■ User workstation standards
■ Use of personal software
■ Computer security incident reporting
■ Control of computer virus programs
■ Computer user/staff training plan
■ Internet use policy
■ Email policy
■ Computer support center
MANUFACTURING BUSINESS PROCESSES
■ Assembly manuals
■ Bill of materials
■ Calibration for testing and measuring equipment
■ FDA inspections
■ Manufacturing change orders
■ Master parts list and files
■ Serial number designation
■ Quality control for finished goods
■ Quality assurance audit procedure
SALES AND MARKETING BUSINESS PROCESSES
■ Collection of sales tax
■ Copyrights and trademarks
■ Marketing plans model number
■ Designation public relations
■ Return of goods from customers
■ Sales leads
■ Sales order entry
■ Sales training
■ Trade shows
SHIPPING, PURCHASING, AND INVENTORY CONTROL BUSINESS PROCESSES
■ Packing, storage, and distribution
■ Physical inventory procedures
■ Purchasing procedures
■ Receiving, inspection, and stocking of parts and materials
■ Shipping and freight claims
■ Vendor selection, files, and inspections

Business Process Improvement

LO 2. Compare the continuous process improvement model and business process reengineering.

Improving business processes is paramount for businesses to stay competitive in today's marketplace. Over the past 10 to 15 years, companies have been forced to improve their business processes because customers are demanding better products and services; if they do not receive what they want from one supplier, they have many others to choose from (hence the competitive issue for businesses). Figure B2.2 displays several opportunities for business process improvement.

Many organizations began business process improvement with a continuous improvement model. A ***continuous process improvement model*** attempts to understand and measure the current process, and make performance improvements accordingly. Figure B2.3

Business Process Improvement Examples
Eliminate duplicate activities
Combine related activities
Eliminate multiple reviews and approvals
Eliminate inspections
Simplify processes
Reduce batch sizes
Process in parallel
Implement demand pull
Outsource inefficient activities
Eliminate movement of work
Organize multifunctional teams
Design cellular workplaces
Centralize/decentralize

FIGURE B2.2

Opportunities for Business Process Improvement

illustrates the basic steps for continuous process improvement. Organizations begin by documenting what they do today, establish some way to measure the process based on what customers want, perform the process, measure the results, and then identify improvement opportunities based on the collected information. The next step is to implement process improvements, and then measure the performance of the new process. This loop repeats over and over again and is called continuous process improvement. It might also be called business process improvement or functional process improvement.

This method for improving business processes is effective to obtain gradual, incremental improvement. However, several factors have accelerated the need to improve business processes. The most obvious is technology. New technologies (like the Internet and wireless) rapidly bring new capabilities to businesses, thereby raising the competitive bar and the need to improve business processes dramatically.

Another apparent trend is the opening of world markets and increased free trade. Such changes bring more companies into the marketplace, adding to the competition. In today's marketplace, major changes are required just to stay in the game. As a result, companies have requested methods for faster business process improvement. Also, companies want breakthrough performance changes, not just incremental changes, and they want this now. Because the rate of change has increased for everyone, few businesses can afford a slow change process. One approach for rapid change and dramatic improvement is business process reengineering (BPR).

BUSINESS PROCESS REENGINEERING (BPR)

An organization must continuously revise and reexamine its decisions, goals, and targets to improve its performance. A bank may have many activities, such as investing, credit cards, loans, and so on, and it may be involved in cross-selling (e.g., insurance) with other preferred vendors in the market. If the credit card department is not functioning in an efficient manner, the bank might reengineer the credit card business process. This activity, *business process reengineering (BPR),* is the analysis and redesign of workflow within and between enterprises. BPR relies on a different school of thought than continuous process improvement. *In the extreme,* BPR assumes the current process is irrelevant, does not work, or is broken and must be overhauled from scratch. Such a clean slate enables business process designers to disassociate themselves from today's process and focus on a new process. It is like the designers projecting themselves into the future and asking: What should the process look like? What do customers want it to look like? What do other employees want it to look like? How do best-in-class companies do it? How can new technology facilitate the process?

Figure B2.4 displays the basic steps in a business process reengineering effort. It begins with defining the scope and objectives of the reengineering project, then goes through a learning process (with customers, employees, competitors, noncompetitors, and new technology). Given this knowledge base, the designers can create a vision for the future and design new business processes by creating a plan of action based on the gap between current processes, technologies, and structures, and process vision. It is then a matter of implementing the chosen solution. The Department of Defense (DoD) is an expert at reengineering business processes. Figure B2.5 highlights the Department of Defense's best-in-class suggestions for a managerial approach to a reengineering effort.

FIGURE B2.3

Continuous Process Improvement Model

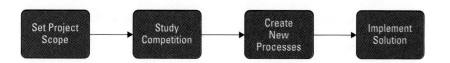

Managerial Approach to Reengineering Projects

1. **Define the scope.** Define functional objectives; determine the management strategy to be followed in streamlining and standardizing processes; and establish the process, data, and information systems baselines from which to begin process improvement.

2. **Analyze.** Analyze business processes to eliminate non-value-added processes; simplify and streamline processes of little value; and identify more effective and efficient alternatives to the process, data, and system baselines.

3. **Evaluate.** Conduct a preliminary, functional, economic analysis to evaluate alternatives to baseline processes and select a preferred course of action.

4. **Plan.** Develop detailed statements of requirements, baseline impacts, costs, benefits, and schedules to implement the planned course of action.

5. **Approve.** Finalize the functional economic analysis using information from the planning data, and present to senior management for approval to proceed with the proposed process improvements and any associated data or system changes.

6. **Execute.** Execute the approved process and data changes, and provide functional management oversight of any associated information system changes.

Business Process Design

After choosing the method of business process improvement that is appropriate for the organization, the process designers must determine the most efficient way to begin revamping the processes. To determine whether each process is appropriately structured, organizations should create a cross-functional team to build process models that display input-output relationships among process-dependent operations and departments. They should create business process models documenting a step-by-step process sequence for the activities that are required to convert inputs to outputs for the specific process.

Business process modeling (or *mapping*) is the activity of creating a detailed flow chart or process map of a work process showing its inputs, tasks, and activities, in a structured sequence. A *business process model* is a graphic description of a process, showing the sequence of process tasks, which is developed for a specific purpose and from a selected viewpoint. A set of one or more process models details the many functions of a system or subject area with graphics and text and its purpose is to:

- Expose process detail gradually and in a controlled manner.
- Encourage conciseness and accuracy in describing the process model.
- Focus attention on the process model interfaces.
- Provide a powerful process analysis and consistent design vocabulary.

A process model typically displays activities as boxes and uses arrows to represent data and interfaces. Process modeling usually begins with a functional process representation of *what* the process problem is or an As-Is process model. *As-Is process models* represent the current state of the operation that has been mapped, without any specific improvements or changes to existing processes. The next step is to build a To-Be process model that displays *how* the process problem will be solved or implemented. *To-Be process models* show the results of applying change improvement opportunities to the current (As-Is) process model. This approach ensures that the process is fully and clearly understood before the details of a process solution are decided. The To-Be process model shows *how* the *what* is to be realized. Figure B2.6 displays the As-Is and To-Be process models for ordering a hamburger.

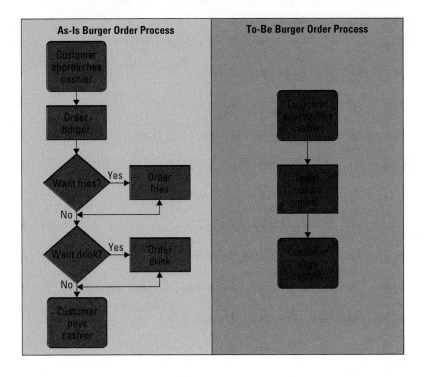

Analyzing As-Is business process models leads to success in business process reengineering since these diagrams are very powerful in visualizing the activities, processes, and data flow of an organization. As-Is and To-Be process models are integral in process reengineering projects. Figure B2.7 illustrates an As-Is process model of an order-filling process developed by a process modeling team representing all departments that contribute to the process. The process modeling team traces the process of converting the input (orders) through all the intervening steps until the final required output (payment) is produced. The map shows how all departments are involved as the order is processed.

It is easy to become bogged down in excessive detail when creating an As-Is process model. The objective is to aggressively eliminate, simplify, or improve the To-Be processes. Successful process improvement efforts result in positive answers to the key process design or improvement question: Is this the most efficient and effective process for accomplishing the process goals? This process modeling structure allows the team to identify all the critical interfaces, overlay the time to complete various processes, start to define the opportunities for process simulation, and identify disconnects (illogical, missing, or extraneous steps) in the processes. Figure B2.8 displays sample disconnects in the order filling process in Figure B2.7.

The team then creates a To-Be process model, which reflects a disconnect-free order fulfillment process (see Figure B2.9). Disconnects fixed by the new process include

■ Direct order entry by sales, eliminating sales administration.

■ Parallel order processing and credit checking.

■ Elimination of multiple order-entry and order-logging steps.

The consulting firm KPMG Peat Marwick uses process modeling as part of its business reengineering practice. Recently the firm helped a large financial services company slash costs and improve productivity in its Manufactured Housing Finance Division. Turnaround time for loan approval was reduced by half, using 40 percent fewer staff members.

Modeling helped the team analyze the complex aspects of the project. "In parts of the loan origination process, a lot of things happen in a short period of time," according to team leader Bob Karrick of KPMG. "During data capture, information is pulled from a number of different sources, and the person doing the risk assessment has to make judgment calls at different points throughout the process. There is often a need to stop, raise

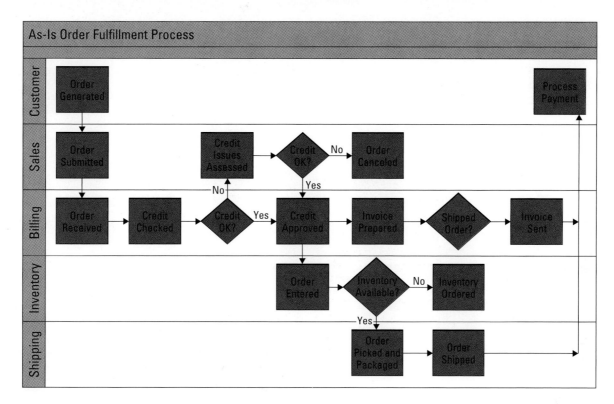

As-Is Order Fulfillment Process

questions, make follow-up calls, and so on and then continue with the process modeling effort. Modeling allows us to do a thorough analysis that takes into account all these decision points and variables."

Business Process Management (BPM)

A key advantage of technology is its ability to improve business processes. Working faster and smarter has become a necessity for companies. Initial emphasis was given to areas such as production, accounting, procurement, and logistics. The next big areas to discover technology's value in business process were sales and marketing automation, customer relationship management, and supplier relationship management. Some of these processes involve several departments of the company and some are the result of real-time interaction of the company with its suppliers, customers, and other business partners. The latest area to discover the power of technology in automating and reengineering business process is business process management. **Business process management (BPM)** integrates all of an organization's business process to make individual processes more efficient. BPM can be used to solve a single glitch or to create one unifying system to consolidate a myriad of processes.

Many organizations are unhappy with their current mix of software applications and dealing with business processes that are subject to constant change. These organizations

LO 4. Explain business process management along with the reason for its importance to an organization.

Issues in the As-Is Order Process Model
■ Sales representatives take too long to submit orders.
■ There are too many process steps.
■ Sales administration slows down the process by batch-processing orders.
■ Credit checking is performed for both old and new customers.
■ Credit checking holds up the process because it is done before (rather than concurrently with) order picking.

FIGURE B2.8

Issues in the As-Is
Process Model for
Order Entry

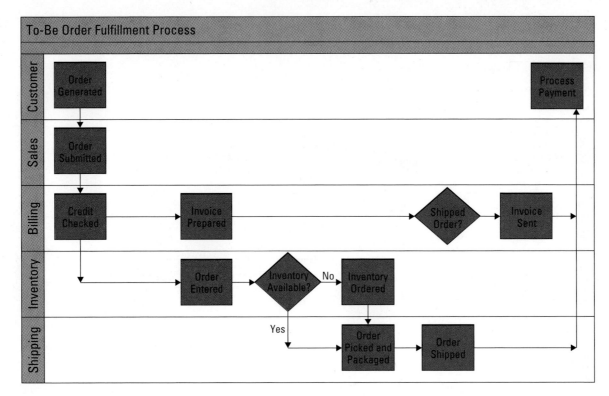

To-Be Order Fulfillment Process

FIGURE B2.9

To-Be Process Model for
Order Entry

are turning to BPM systems that can flexibly automate their processes and glue their enterprise applications together. Figure B2.10 displays the key reasons organizations are embracing BPM technologies.

BPM technologies effectively track and orchestrate the business process. BPM can automate tasks involving information from multiple systems, with rules to define the sequence in which the tasks are performed as well as responsibilities, conditions, and other aspects of the process (see Figure B2.11 for BPM benefits). BPM not only allows a business process to be executed more efficiently, but also provides the tools to measure performance and identify opportunities for improvement—as well as to easily make changes in processes to act upon those opportunities such as:

- Bringing processes, people, and information together.
- Identifying the business processes is relatively easy. Breaking down the barriers between business areas and finding owners for the processes are difficult.

FIGURE B2.10

Key Reasons for BPM

- Managing business processes within the enterprise and outside the enterprise with suppliers, business partners, and customers.
- Looking at automation horizontally instead of vertically.

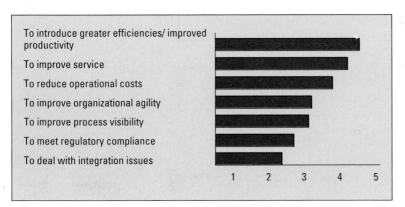

To introduce greater efficiencies/ improved productivity
To improve service
To reduce operational costs
To improve organizational agility
To improve process visibility
To meet regulatory compliance
To deal with integration issues

Scale 1 to 5 where 1 = not important and 5 = very important

IS BPM FOR BUSINESS OR IT?

A good BPM solution requires two great parts to work together as one. Since BPM solutions cross application and system boundaries, they often need to be sanctioned and implemented by the IT organization, while at the same time BPM products are business tools that business managers need to own. Therefore, confusion often arises in companies as to whether business or IT managers should be responsible for driving the selection of a new BPM solution.

The key requirement for BPM's success in an organization is the understanding that it is a collaboration of business and IT, and thus both parties need to be involved in evaluating, selecting, and implementing a BPM solution. IT managers need to understand the business drivers behind the processes, and business managers need to understand the impact the BPM solution may have on the infrastructure. Generally, companies that have successfully deployed BPM solutions are those whose business and IT groups have worked together as a cohesive team.

All companies can benefit from a better understanding of their key business processes, analyzing them for areas of improvement and implementing improvements. BPM applications have been successfully developed to improve complex business issues of some medium- to large-sized companies. Like many large-scale implementation projects, BPM solutions are most successful in companies with a good understanding of their technology landscape and management willing to approach business in a new way. BPM solutions are truly driven by the business process and the company's owners.

Effective BPM solutions allow business owners to manage many aspects of the technology through business rules they develop and maintain. Companies that cannot support or manage cultural and organizational changes may lack positive BPM results.

BPM Benefits
■ Update processes in real time
■ Reduce overhead expenses
■ Automate key decisions
■ Reduce process maintenance cost
■ Reduce operating cost
■ Improve productivity
■ Improve process cycle time
■ Improve forecasting
■ Improve customer service

FIGURE B2.11

Benefits of BPM

BPM TOOLS

Business process management tools are used to create an application that is helpful in designing business process models and also helpful in simulating, optimizing, monitoring, and maintaining various processes that occur within an organization. Many tasks are involved in achieving a goal, and these tasks are done either manually or with the help of software systems. For example, if an organization needs to buy a software application that costs $6 million, then a request has to be approved by several authorities and managers. The request approval may be done manually. However, when a person applies for a loan of $300,000, several internal and external business processes are triggered to find out details about that person before approving the loan. For these activities the BPM tool creates an application that coordinates the manual and automated tasks. Figure B2.12 displays several popular BPM tools.

BPM RISKS AND REWARDS

If an organization is considering BPM, it must be aware of the risks involved in implementing these systems. One factor that commonly derails a BPM project has nothing to do with technology and everything to do with people. BPM projects involve cultural and organizational changes that companies must make to support the new management approach required for success. Where 10 area leaders once controlled 10 pieces of an end-to-end process, now a new group is involved in implementing a BPM solution across all these areas. Suddenly the span of control is consolidated and all are accountable to the whole process, not just one piece of the puzzle.

The added benefit of BPM is not only a technology solution, but also a business solution. BPM is a new business architecture and approach to managing the process and enabling proactive, continuous improvement. The new organizational structure and roles created to support BPM help maximize the continuous benefits to ensure success.

An IT director from a large financial services company gave this feedback when asked about his experience in using a BPM solution to improve the company's application help desk process. "Before BPM, the company's

FIGURE B2.12

Popular BPM Tools

Tool Name	Company Name
BPM Suite	Ultimus
Process Suite	Stalfware
Business Manager	Savvion
Pega Rules Process Commander	PegaSystem
E Work Vision	MetaStorm
Team Works	Lombardi Software
Intalio	Intalio
Bizflow	Handysoft
FugeoBPM	Fugeo
Business Process Manager	Filenet

application help desk was a manual process, filled with inefficiencies, human error, and no personal accountability. In addition, the old process provided no visibility into the process. There was absolutely no way to track requests, since it was all manual. Business user satisfaction with the process was extremely low. A BPM solution provided a way for the company to automate, execute, manage, and monitor the process in real time. The biggest technical challenge in implementation was ensuring that the user group was self-sufficient. While the company recognized that the IT organization is needed, it wanted to be able to maintain and implement any necessary process changes with little reliance on IT. It views process management as empowering the business users to maintain, control, and monitor the process. BPM goes a long way to enable this process."

CRITICAL SUCCESS FACTORS

In a publication for the National Academy of Public Administration, Dr. Sharon L. Caudle identified six critical success factors that ensure government BPM initiatives achieve the desired results (see Figure B2.13).

FIGURE B2.13

Critical Success Factors for BPM Projects

Critical Success Factors for BPM Projects

1. **Understand reengineering.**
   - Understand business process fundamentals.
   - Know what reengineering is.
   - Differentiate and integrate process improvement approaches.

2. **Build a business and political case.**
   - Have necessary and sufficient business (mission delivery) reasons for reengineering.
   - Have the organizational commitment and capacity to initiate and sustain reengineering.
   - Secure and sustain political support for reengineering projects.

3. **Adopt a process management approach.**
   - Understand the organizational mandate and set mission strategic directions and goals cascading to process-specific goals and decision making across and down the organization.
   - Define, model, and prioritize business processes important for mission performance.
   - Practice hands-on senior management ownership of process improvement through personal involvement, responsibility, and decision making.
   - Adjust organizational structure to better support process management initiatives.
   - Create an assessment program to evaluate process management.

4. **Measure and track performance continuously.**
   - Create organizational understanding of the value of measurement and how it will be used.
   - Tie performance management to customer and stakeholder current and future expectations.

5. **Practice change management and provide central support.**
   - Develop human resource management strategies to support reengineering.
   - Build information resources management strategies and a technology framework to support process change.
   - Create a central support group to assist and integrate reengineering efforts and other improvement efforts across the organization.
   - Create an overarching and project-specific internal and external communication and education program.

6. **Manage reengineering projects for results.**
   - Have a clear criterion to select what should be reengineered.
   - Place the project at the right level with a defined reengineering team purpose and goals.
   - Use a well-trained, diversified, expert team to ensure optimum project performance.
   - Follow a structured, disciplined approach for reengineering.

Business Process Modeling Examples

A picture is worth a thousand words. Just ask Wayne Kendrick, a system analyst for Mobil Oil Corporation in Dallas, Texas. Kendrick, whose work involves planning and designing complex processes, was scheduled to make a presentation to familiarize top management with a number of projects his group was working on. "I was given 10 minutes for my presentation, and I had 20 to 30 pages of detailed documentation to present. Obviously, I could not get through it all in the time allocated." Kendrick turned to business process models to help communicate his projects. "I think people can relate to pictures better than words," Kendrick said. He applied his thinking to his presentation by using Microsoft's Visio to create business process models and graphs to represent the original 30 pages of text. "It was an effective way to get people interested in my projects and to quickly see the importance of each project," he stated. The process models worked and Kendrick received immediate approval to proceed with all of his projects. Figures B2.14 through B2.20 offer examples of business process models.

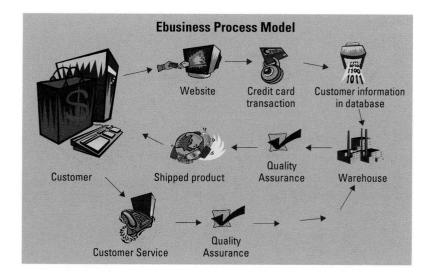

FIGURE B2.14

Ebusiness Process Model

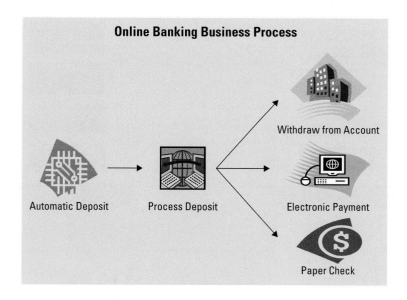

FIGURE B2.15

Online Banking Business Process Model

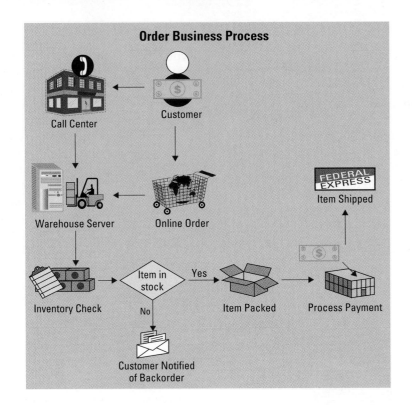

Order Business Process

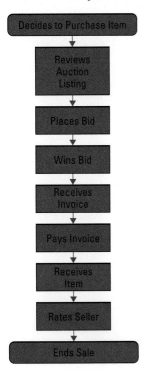

Purchase an Item on eBay Business Process

FIGURE B2.17

eBay Buyer Business
Process Model

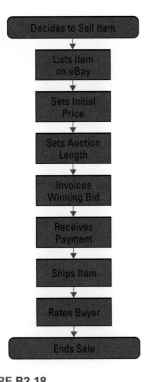

Sell an Item on eBay Business Process

FIGURE B2.18

eBay Seller Business
Process Model

Customer Service Business Process

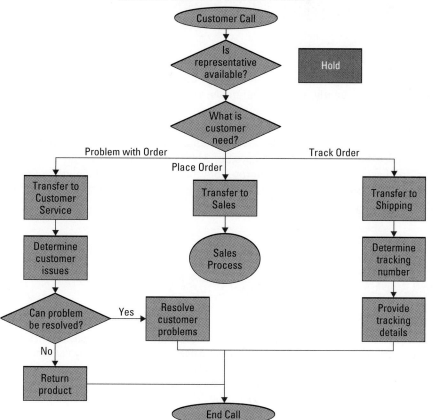

Process Improvement Model

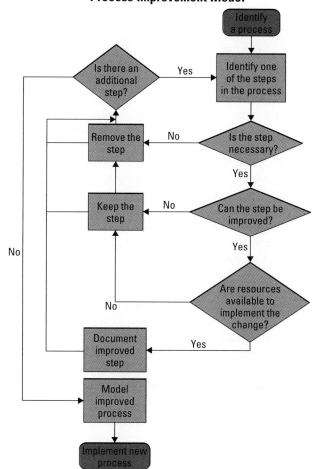

I nvestment in continuous process improvement, business process reengineering, or business process management is the same as any other technology-related investment. Planning the project properly, setting clear goals, educating those people who have to change their mind-set once the system is implemented, and retaining strong management support will help with a successful implementation generating a solid return on investment.

Organizations must go beyond the basics when implementing business process improvement and realize that it is not a one-time project. Management and improvement of end-to-end business processes is difficult and requires more than a simple, one-time effort. Continuously monitoring and improving core business processes will guarantee performance improvements across an organization.

✳ KEY TERMS

As-Is process model, 347
Business process, 342
Business process management
   (BPM), 349
Business process management
   tool, 351

Business process model, 347
Business process modeling
   (or mapping), 347
Business process
   reengineering (BPR), 346

Continuous process
   improvement model, 345
To-Be process model, 347

✳ CLOSING CASE ONE

Streamlining Processes at Adidas

The Adidas name resonates with athletes and retail consumers worldwide. Registered as a company in 1949, the company differentiated itself during the 1960s by supporting all athletes who were committed to raising performance levels, including athletes in what some considered fringe sports such as high jumping. During a banner year in 1996, the "three stripes company" equipped 6,000 Olympic athletes from 33 countries. Those athletes won 220 medals, including 70 gold, and helped increase immediate apparel sales by 50 percent.

In 1997, Adidas acquired the Salomon Group, which included the Salomon, Taylor Made, and Bonfire brands. Today, Adidas-Salomon strives to be the global leader in the sporting goods industry with a wide range of products that promote a passion for competition and a sports-oriented lifestyle. Its strategy is simple: continuously strengthen its brands and products to improve its competitive position and financial performance.

Adidas-Salomon competes in an environment as relentless as that of the Olympics. Staying in the forefront requires the support of world-class technology. Over the past 15 years, Adidas-Salomon transformed itself from a manufacturing organization to a global sports brand manager with 14,000 employees located around the world. Previously, Adidas-Salomon operated in a decentralized manner, and each operating unit chose software that suited its geography and internal preferences. The company believed that implementing and creating common processes, especially in its sales organization, would help it establish global direction. With common processes, the company could streamline and automate its business operations—improving flexibility, scalability, and visibility across the extended enterprise. Overall, system integration would translate into faster time to market, higher revenue, and lower costs.

Adidas-Salomon reviewed its IT systems and associated information. One finding was that the company needed to develop a better solution for business process integration and establish an easy way to automate new applications throughout the enterprise. Such an infrastructure required Adidas-Salomon to impose a common business process platform that would allow the company's operating units to remain flexible in meeting their own particular needs and goals.

Adidas-Salomon identified several major business requirements for the project. First, it wanted to automate business events and reduce the manual effort required to exchange data between internal and external parties. Second, Adidas-Salomon needed to develop a cost-effective solution that would be simple to use, maintain, and update in the future. Last, the company wanted to enable real-time data exchange among the key Adidas-Salomon business processes.

"We considered many metrics, and it was clear that TIBCO Software had the breadth and depth of product offering backed by a strong reputation," said Garry Semetka, head of development and integration services in global application development at Adidas-Salomon. With its desired infrastructure in place, Adidas-Salomon standardized on TIBCO products and moved toward real-time business process management of its internal supply chain. The company now publishes and makes the most of events when they occur on key systems, giving the most current, valuable information to business processes and decision makers.

Questions

1. Describe business processes and their importance for Adidas-Salomon.
2. How could Adidas-Salomon use continuous process improvement and business process reengineering to remain competitive?
3. How can a business process management tool help Adidas-Salomon remain at the top of its game?

✳ CLOSING CASE TWO

3Com Optimizes Product Promotion Processes

Product promotions, such as rebates or subsidized promotional items, can serve as excellent marketing and sales tools to drive increased revenues by providing incentives for customers to purchase select items. However, when you are a leading global networking provider like 3Com that serves thousands of channel partners and customers, such promotions must be easily managed and executed.

To gain better control over the creation and execution of its product promotions, 3Com used Savvion's business process automation and management platform to build a web-based system that streamlines the approval and management workflow of product promotions offered to distributors and resellers. "We needed to ensure that our product promotions were attractive to our channel partners while also being manageable in terms of execution," said Ari Bose, CIO at 3Com. "Using Savvion BusinessManager, we were able to quickly put a process in place that speeds approval and enhances awareness of product promotions to generate opportunities for increased revenue."

Promoting Effective Promotions

The Savvion BusinessManager-based promotions system provides significant time and cost savings by replacing former inefficient and uncontrollable email processes. Instead of informally sending promotion ideas around for approval, employees now use the automated system as a centralized location to manage the workflow involved in proposing new promotions and ensuring all needed approvals are in place before promotion details are shared on the 3Com partner and reseller website.

The promotions system automatically routes proposed promotions to each department that is required to sign off on the promotion, including marketing, promotions communications, and claims administration. The streamlined system also immediately notifies all key parties once new promotions are approved, increasing visibility and revenue opportunities through improved communication with 3Com sales representatives, distributors, and resellers.

Adding Muscle to Management

An important feature of the new system is the automatic auditing of each step taken. The company can easily establish an audit trail, increasing accountability as approvals are given. The structured process also ensures that approved promotions are manageable from an administrative perspective.

In addition, the system tracks promotion fulfillment, enforcing associated terms and conditions such as purchasing limits or available supplies—tracking that was previously almost impossible to do, creating numerous management headaches. The promotions system is also integrated with another BusinessManager-developed process that generates special price quotes (SPQs) for 3Com channel partners, creating built-in checks and balances to prevent the approval of an SPQ while a promotion is being offered for the same product.

The system also provides extensive reporting capabilities that 3Com now uses to gain a better understanding of all offered promotions, authorizations, and potential financial impacts. These online reports replace manually created Excel spreadsheets, enabling departments to generate reports on the fly for enhanced strategic planning.

Bottom-Line Benefits

Greater visibility of product promotions is yielding significant opportunities for increased revenue at 3Com. Sales representatives are immediately notified when promotions are approved, improving internal communications and enabling representatives to share promotion details with resellers and distributors more quickly to foster increased sales. Other business benefits delivered by the automated promotions system include the following:

- Real-time monitoring features enable 3Com employees to check the status of a promotion's approval at any time.
- Greater efficiency in the approval cycle and streamlined communications increase employee productivity, providing significant time and cost savings.
- Claims processing is also more effective because of the structured approval process, delivering additional savings.
- Increased visibility enables 3Com to reduce reserve spending by having a clearer idea of channel response to each promotion.
- Order and efficiency come to previously chaotic manual processes.

Questions

1. Describe business processes and their importance to 3Com's business model.
2. How can 3Com use continuous process improvement to become more efficient?
3. How can 3Com use business process reengineering to become more efficient?
4. Describe the importance of business process modeling (or mapping) and business process models for 3Com.
5. How did 3Com use business process management software to revamp its business?

1. Discovering Reengineering Opportunities

In an effort to increase efficiency, your college has hired you to analyze its current business processes for registering for classes. Analyze the current business processes from paying tuition to registering for classes and determine which steps in the process are:

- Broken
- Redundant
- Antiquated

Be sure to define how you would reengineer the processes for efficiency.

2. Modeling a Business Process

Do you hate waiting in line at the grocery store? Do you find it frustrating when you go to the movie store and cannot find the movie you wanted to rent? Do you get annoyed when the pizza delivery person brings you the wrong order? This is your chance to reengineer the annoying process that drives you crazy. Choose a problem you are currently experiencing and reengineer the process to make it more efficient. Be sure to provide an As-Is and To-Be process model.

3. Revamping Business Processes

The following is the sales order business process for MusicMan. Draw the As-Is process model based on the following narrative:

1. A customer submits an order for goods to MusicMan, a music retailer, through an online mechanism such as a browser-based order form. The customer supplies his or her name, the appropriate email address, the state to which the order will be shipped, the desired items (IDs and names), and the requested quantities.
2. The order is received by a processing system, which reads the data and appends an ID number to the order.
3. The order is forwarded to a customer service representative, who checks the customer's credit information.
4. If the credit check fails, the customer service representative is assigned the task of notifying the customer to obtain correct credit information, and the process becomes manual from this point on.
5. If the credit check passes, the system checks a database for the current inventory of the ordered item, according to the item ID, and it compares the quantity of items available with the quantity requested.
6. If the amount of stock is not sufficient to accommodate the order, the order is placed on hold until new inventory arrives. When the system receives notice of new incoming inventory, it repeats step 5 until it can verify that the inventory is sufficient to process the order.
7. If the inventory is sufficient, the order is forwarded simultaneously to a shipping agent who arranges shipment and an accounting agent who instructs the system to generate an invoice for the order.
8. If the system encounters an error in processing the input necessary to calculate the total price for the invoice, including state sales tax, the accounting agent who initiated the billing process is notified and prompted to provide the correct information.

9. The system calculates the total price of the order.
10. The system confirms that the order has been shipped and notifies the customer via email.
11. At any point in the transaction before shipping, the order can be canceled by notification from the customer.

4. Revamping Accounts

The accounting department at your company deals with the processing of critical documents. These documents must arrive at their intended destination in a secure and efficient manner. Such documents include invoices, purchase orders, statements, purchase requisitions, financial statements, sales orders, and quotes.

The current processing of documents is done manually, which causes a negative ripple effect. Documents tend to be misplaced or delayed through the mailing process. Unsecured documents are vulnerable to people making changes or seeing confidential documents. In addition, the accounting department incurs costs such as preprinted forms, inefficient distribution, and storage. Explain BPM and how it can be used to revamp the accounting department.

Hardware and Software Basics

1. Describe the six major categories of hardware, and provide an example of each.
2. Identify the different computer categories, and explain their potential business uses.
3. Identify the two main types of software.

LO 1. Describe the six major categories of hardware, and provide an example of each.

Introduction

Managers need to determine what types of hardware and software will satisfy their current and future business needs, the right time to buy the equipment, and how to protect their investments. This does not imply that managers need to be experts in all areas of technology; however, building a basic understanding of hardware and software can help them make the right investment choices.

Information technology can be an important enabler of business success and innovation. Information technology can be composed of the Internet, a personal computer, a cell phone that can access the web, a personal digital assistant, or presentation software. All of these technologies help to perform specific information processing tasks. There are two basic categories of information technology: hardware and software. **Hardware** consists of the physical devices associated with a computer system. **Software** is the set of instructions the hardware executes to carry out specific tasks. Software, such as Microsoft Excel, and various hardware devices, such as a keyboard and a monitor, interact to create a spreadsheet or a graph. This appendix covers the basics of computer hardware and software including terminology, characteristics, and the associated managerial responsibilities for building a solid enterprise architecture.

Hardware Basics

In many industries, exploiting computer hardware is key to gaining a competitive advantage. Frito-Lay gained a competitive advantage by using handheld devices to track the strategic placement and sale of items in convenience stores. Sales representatives could track sale price, competitor information, the number of items sold, and item location in the store all from their handheld device.[1]

A **computer** is an electronic device operating under the control of instructions stored in its own memory that can accept, manipulate, and store data. Figure B3.1 displays the two primary components of a computer—hardware and software. A computer system consists of six hardware components (see Figure B3.2). Figure B3.3 displays how these components work together to form a computer system.

CENTRAL PROCESSING UNIT

The dominant manufacturers of CPUs today include Intel (with its Celeron and Pentium lines for personal computers) and Advanced Micro Devices (AMD) (with its Athlon series).[2]

The **central processing unit (CPU)** (or **microprocessor**) is the actual hardware that interprets and executes the program (software) instructions and coordinates how all the other hardware devices work together. The CPU is built on a small flake of silicon and can contain the equivalent of several million transistors. CPUs are unquestionably one of the 20th century's greatest technological advances.

A CPU contains two primary parts: control unit and arithmetic/logic unit. The **control unit** interprets software instructions and literally tells the other hardware devices what to do, based on the software instructions. The **arithmetic-logic unit (ALU)** performs all arithmetic operations (for example, addition and subtraction) and all logic operations (such as sorting and comparing numbers). The control unit and ALU perform different functions. The control unit obtains instructions from the software. It then interprets the instructions, decides which tasks other devices perform, and finally tells each device to perform the task. The ALU responds to the control unit and does whatever it dictates, performing either arithmetic or logic operations.

The number of CPU cycles per second determines how fast a CPU carries out the software instructions; more cycles per second means faster processing, and faster CPUs cost more than their slower counterparts. CPU speed is usually quoted in megahertz

FIGURE B3.1

Hardware and Software Overview

HARDWARE

The physical devices associated with a computer system

CENTRAL PROCESSING UNIT
CPU: The computer's "brains"
RAM: Integrated circuits; works with the CPU

INPUT DEVICE
• Keyboard; mouse; scanner

OUTPUT DEVICE
• Monitor; printer; headphones

STORAGE DEVICE
• DVD; memory stick; hard drive

COMMUNICATION DEVICE
• Modem; wireless card

CONNECTING DEVICE
• Cables; USB port

SOFTWARE

The set of instructions the hardware executes to carry out specific tasks

SYSTEM SOFTWARE
Controls how the various tools work together along with application software

OPERATING SYSTEM SOFTWARE
• Windows; Mac OS; Linux

UTILITY SOFTWARE
• Antivirus; screen savers; data recovery

APPLICATION SOFTWARE
Performs specific information processing needs

WORD PROCESSING SOFTWARE
• Microsoft Word

SPREADSHEET SOFTWARE
• Microsoft Excel

CPU	• The actual hardware that interprets and executes the program (software) instructions and coordinates how all the other hardware devices work together
Primary Storage	• The computer's main memory, which consists of the random access memory (RAM), the cache memory, and the read-only memory (ROM) that is directly accessible to the central processing unit (CPU)
Secondary Storage	• Equipment designed to store large volumes of data for long-term storage (diskette, CD, DVD, memory stick)
Input Devices	• Equipment used to capture information and commands (mouse, keyboard, scanner)
Output Devices	• Equipment used to see, hear, or otherwise accept the results of information processing requests (monitor, printer, microphone)
Communication Device	• Equipment used to send information and receive it from one location to another (modem, wireless card)

and gigahertz. ***Megahertz (MHz)*** is the number of millions of CPU cycles per second. ***Gigahertz (GHz)*** is the number of billions of CPU cycles per second. Figure B3.4 displays the factors that determine CPU speed.

Advances in CPU Design

Chip makers are pressing more functionality into CPU technology. Most CPUs are ***complex instruction set computer (CISC) chips,*** which is a type of CPU that can recognize as many as 100 or more instructions, enough to carry out most computations directly. ***Reduced instruction set computer (RISC) chips*** limit the number of instructions the CPU can execute to increase processing speed. The idea of RISC is to reduce the instruction set to the bare minimum, emphasizing the instructions used most of the time and optimizing them for the fastest possible execution. An RISC processor runs faster than a CISC processor.

PRIMARY STORAGE

Primary storage is the computer's main memory, which consists of the random access memory (RAM), cache memory, and read-only memory (ROM) that is directly accessible to the CPU.

Random Access Memory

Random access memory (RAM) is the computer's primary working memory, in which program instructions and data are stored so that they can be accessed directly by the CPU via the processor's high-speed external data bus.

RAM is often called read/write memory. In RAM, the CPU can write and read data. Most programs set aside a portion of RAM as a temporary workspace for data so that one can modify (rewrite) as needed until the data are

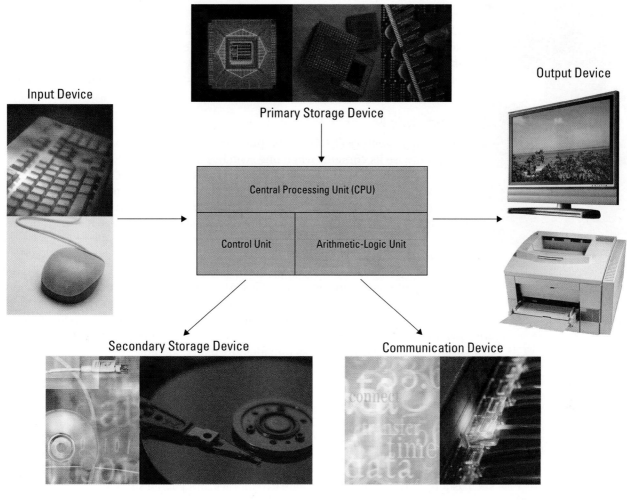

Input Device

Primary Storage Device

Output Device

Central Processing Unit (CPU)

Control Unit | Arithmetic-Logic Unit

Secondary Storage Device

Communication Device

FIGURE B3.3

How the Hardware Components Work Together

ready for printing or storage on secondary storage media, such as a hard drive or memory key. RAM does not retain its contents when the power to the computer is switched off, hence individuals should save their work frequently. When the computer is turned off, everything in RAM is wiped clean. *Volatility* refers to a device's ability to function with or without power. RAM is *volatile,* meaning it must have constant power to function; its contents are lost when the computer's electric supply fails.

FIGURE B3.4

Factors That Determine CPU Speed

CPU Speed Factors
Clock speed—the speed of the internal clock of a CPU that sets the pace at which operations proceed within the computer's internal processing circuitry.
Word length—number of bits (0s and 1s) that can be processed by the CPU at any one time. Computers work in terms of bits and bytes using electrical pulses that have two states: on and off.
Bus width—the size of the internal electrical pathway along which signals are sent from one part of the computer to another. A wider bus can move more data, hence faster processing.
Chip line width—the distance between transistors on a chip. The shorter the chip line width the faster the chip since more transistors can be placed on a chip and the data and instructions travel short distances during processing.

Cache Memory

Cache memory is a small unit of ultra-fast memory that is used to store recently accessed or frequently accessed data so that the CPU does not have to retrieve this data from slower memory circuits such as RAM. Cache memory that is built directly into the CPU's circuits is called primary cache. Cache memory contained on an external circuit is called secondary cache.

Read-Only Memory (ROM)

Read-only memory (ROM) is the portion of a computer's primary storage that does not lose its contents when one switches off the power. ROM is ***nonvolatile,*** meaning it does not require constant power to function. ROM contains essential system programs that neither the user nor the computer can erase. Since the computer's internal memory is blank during start-up, the computer cannot perform any functions unless given start-up instructions. These instructions are stored in ROM.

 Flash memory is a special type of rewritable read-only memory (ROM) that is compact and portable. ***Memory cards*** contain high-capacity storage that holds data such as captured images, music, or text files. Memory cards are removable; when one is full the user can insert an additional card. Subsequently, the data can be downloaded from the card to a computer. The card can then be erased and used again. Memory cards are typically used in digital devices such as cameras, cellular phones, and personal digital assistants (PDA). ***Memory sticks*** provide nonvolatile memory for a range of portable devices including computers, digital cameras, MP3 players, and PDAs.

SECONDARY STORAGE

Storage is a hot area in the business arena as organizations struggle to make sense of exploding volumes of data. ***Secondary storage*** consists of equipment designed to store large volumes of data for long-term storage. Secondary storage devices are nonvolatile and do not lose their contents when the computer is turned off. Some storage devices, such as a hard disk, offer easy update capabilities and a large storage capacity. Others, such as CD-ROMs, offer limited update capabilities but possess large storage capacities.

 Storage capacity is expressed in bytes, with megabytes being the most common. A ***megabyte (MB*** or ***M*** or ***Meg)*** is roughly 1 million bytes. Therefore, a computer with 256 MB of RAM translates into the RAM being able to hold roughly 256 million characters of data and software instructions. A ***gigabyte (GB)*** is roughly 1 billion bytes. A ***terabyte (TB)*** is roughly 1 trillion bytes (refer to Figure B3.5).[3]

 A typical double-spaced page of pure text is roughly 2,000 characters. Therefore, a 40 GB (40 gigabyte or 40 billion characters) hard drive can hold approximately 20 million pages of text.

 Common storage devices include:

- Magnetic medium
- Optical medium

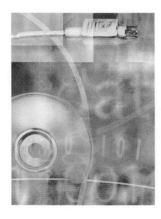

Magnetic Medium

Magnetic medium is a secondary storage medium that uses magnetic techniques to store and retrieve data on disks or tapes coated with magnetically sensitive materials. Like iron filings on a sheet of waxed paper, these materials are reoriented when a magnetic field passes over them. During write operations, the read/write heads emit a magnetic field that orients the magnetic materials on the disk or tape to represent encoded data. During read operations, the read/write heads sense the encoded data on the medium.

 One of the first forms of magnetic medium developed was magnetic tape. ***Magnetic tape*** is an older secondary storage medium that uses a strip of thin plastic coated with a magnetically sensitive recording medium. The most popular type of magnetic medium is a hard drive. A ***hard drive*** is a secondary storage medium that uses several rigid disks

Term	Size
Kilobyte (KB)	1,024 Bytes
Megabyte (MB)	1,024 KB 1,048,576 Bytes
Gigabyte (GB)	1,024 MB (10^9 bytes)
Terabyte (TB)	1,024 GB (10^{12} bytes) 1 TB = Printing of 1 TB would require 50,000 trees to be made into paper and printer
Petabyte (PB)	1,024 TB (10^{15} bytes) 200 PB = All production of digital magnetic tape in 1995
Exabyte (EB)	1,024 PB (10^{18} bytes) 2 EB = Total volume of information generated worldwide annually 5 EB = All words ever spoken by human beings

coated with a magnetically sensitive material and housed together with the recording heads in a hermetically sealed mechanism. Hard drive performance is measured in terms of access time, seek time, rotational speed, and data transfer rate.

Optical Medium

Optical medium is a secondary storage medium for computers on which information is stored at extremely high density in the form of tiny pits. The presence or absence of pits is read by a tightly focused laser beam. Optical medium types include:

- **Compact disk-read-only memory (CD-ROM) drive**—an optical drive designed to read the data encoded on CD-ROMs and to transfer this data to a computer.
- **Compact disk-read-write (CD-RW) drive**—an optical drive that enables users to erase existing data and to write new data repeatedly to a CD-RW.
- **Digital video disk (DVD)**—a CD-ROM format capable of storing up to a maximum of 17 GB of data; enough for a full-length feature movie.
- **DVD-ROM drive**—a read-only drive designed to read the data encoded on a DVD and transfer the data to a computer.
- **Digital video disk-read/write (DVD-RW)**—a standard for DVD discs and player/ recorder mechanisms that enables users to record in the DVD format.

CD-ROMs and DVDs offer an increasingly economical medium for storing data and programs. The overall trend in secondary storage is toward more direct-access methods, higher capacity with lower costs, and increased portability.

INPUT DEVICES

An **input device** is equipment used to capture information and commands. A keyboard is used to type in information, and a mouse is used to point and click on buttons and icons.

A **stylus** is used as a pen-like device that taps the screen to enter commands. Numerous input devices are available in many different environments, some of which have applications that are more suitable in a personal setting than a business setting. A keyboard, mouse, and scanner are the most common forms of input devices (see Figure B3.6).

New forms of input devices allow people to exercise and play video games at the same time. The Kilowatt Sport from Powergrid Fitness lets people combine strength training with their favorite video games. Players can choose any PlayStation

MANUAL INPUT DEVICES	
KEYBOARD	• Provides a set of alphabetic, numeric, punctuation, symbol, and control keys
MOUSE	• One or more control buttons housed in a palm-sized case and designed so that one can move it about on the table next to the keyboard
TOUCH PAD	• Form of a stationary mouse on which the movement of a finger causes the pointer on the screen to move; typically found below the space bar on laptops
TOUCH SCREEN	• Allows the use of a finger to point at and touch a monitor to execute commands
POINTING DEVICE	• Devices used to navigate and select objects on a display screen
GAME CONTROLLER	• Devices used for games to obtain better control screen action

AUTOMATED INPUT DEVICES	
IMAGE SCANNER	• Captures images, photos, graphics, and text that already exist on paper
BAR CODE SCANNER	• Captures information that exists in the form of vertical bars whose width and distance apart determine a number
BIOMETRIC SCANNER	• Captures human physical attributes such as a fingerprint or iris for security purposes
OPTICAL MARK READER	• Detects the presence or absence of a mark in a predetermined place (popular for multiple-choice exams)
OPTICAL CHARACTER READER	• Converts text into digital format for computer input
DIGITAL STILL CAMERA	• Digitally captures still images in varying resolutions
DIGITAL VIDEO CAMERA	• Digitally captures video
WEBCAM	• Digitally captures video and uploads it directly to the Internet
MICROPHONE	• Captures sounds such as a voice for voice-recognition software
POINT-OF-SALE (POS)	• Captures information at the point of a transaction, typically in a retail environment

FIGURE B3.6

Input Devices

or Xbox game that uses a joystick to run the elliptical trainer. After loading the game, participants stand on a platform while pushing and pulling a resistance rod in all directions to control what happens in the game. The varied movement targets muscle groups on the chest, arms, shoulders, abdomen, and back. The machine's display shows information such as pounds lifted and current resistance level, and players can use one-touch adjustment to vary the degree of difficulty.[4] ***Adaptive computer devices*** are input devices designed for special applications for use by people with different types of special needs. An example is a keyboard with tactile surfaces, which can be used by the visually impaired.

Another new input device is a stationary bicycle. A computer design team of graduate and undergraduate students at MIT built the Cyclescore, an integrated video game and bicycle. The MIT students tested current games on the market but found users would stop pedaling to concentrate on the game. To engage users, the team is designing games that interact with the experience of exercise itself, for example, monitoring heart rate and adjusting the difficulty of the game according to the user's bicycling capabilities. In one game, the player must pedal to make a hot-air balloon float over mountains, while collecting coins and shooting at random targets.[5]

OUTPUT DEVICES

An ***output device*** is equipment used to see, hear, or otherwise accept the results of information processing requests. Among output devices, printers and monitors are the most common; however, speakers and plotters (special printers that draw output on a page)

are widely used (see Figure B3.7). In addition, output devices are responsible for converting computer-stored information into a form that can be understood.

A new output device based on sensor technology aims to translate American Sign Language (ASL) into speech, enabling the millions of people who use ASL to better communicate with those who do not know the rapid gesturing system. The AcceleGlove is a glove lined on the inside with sensors embedded in rings. The sensors, called accelerometers, measure acceleration and can categorize and translate finger and hand movements. Additional, interconnected attachments for the elbow and shoulder capture ASL signs that are made with full arm motion. When users wear the glove while signing ASL, algorithms in the glove's software translate the hand gestures into words. The translations can be relayed through speech synthesizers or read on a PDA-size computer screen. Inventor Jose L. Hernandez-Rebollar started with a single glove that could translate only the ASL alphabet. Now, the device employs two gloves that contain a 1,000-word vocabulary.[6]

Other new output devices are being developed every day. Needapresent.com, a British company, has developed a vibrating USB massage ball, which plugs into a computer's USB port to generate a warm massage for sore body parts during those long evenings spent coding software or writing papers. Needapresent.com also makes a coffee cup warmer that plugs into the USB port.[7]

COMMUNICATION DEVICES

A **communication device** is equipment used to send information and receive it from one location to another. A telephone modem connects a computer to a phone line in order to access another computer. The computer works in terms of digital signals, while a standard telephone line works with analog signals. Each digital signal represents a bit

FIGURE B3.7

Output Devices

MONITORS	
CATHODE-RAY TUBE (CRT)	• A vacuum tube that uses an electron gun (cathode) to emit a beam of electrons that illuminates phosphors on a screen as the beam sweeps across the display repeatedly
LIQUID CRYSTAL DISPLAY (LCD)	• Low-powered displays used in laptop computers where rod-shaped crystal molecules change their orientation when an electrical current flows through them
LIGHT-EMITTING DIODE (LED)	• Tiny bulb used for backlight to improve the image on the screen
ORGANIC LIGHT-EMITTING DIODE (OLED)	• Displays use many layers of organic material emitting a visible light and therefore eliminating the need for backlighting

PRINTERS	
INK-JET PRINTER	• Printer that makes images by forcing ink droplets through nozzles
LASER PRINTER	• Printer that forms images using an electrostatic process, the same way a photocopier works
MULTIFUNCTION PRINTER	• Printer that can scan, copy, fax, and print all in one device
PLOTTER	• Printer that uses computer-directed pens for creating high-quality images, blueprints, schematics, etc.
3-D PRINTER	• Printer that can produce solid, three-dimensional objects

Carrier Technology	Description	Speed	Comments
Dial-up access	On demand access using a modem and regular telephone line (POT).	2400 bps to 56 Kbps	■ Cheap but slow.
Cable	Special cable modem and cable line required.	512 Kbps to 20 Mbps	■ Must have existing cable access in area. ■ Bandwidth is shared.
DSL Digital Subscriber Line	This technology uses the unused digital portion of a regular copper telephone line to transmit and receive information. A special modem and adapter card are required.	128 Kbps to 8 Mbps	■ Doesn't interfere with normal telephone use. ■ Bandwidth is dedicated. ■ Must be within 5 km (3.1 miles) of telephone company switch.
Wireless (LMCS)	Access is gained by connection to a high-speed cellular like local multipoint communications system (LMCS) network via wireless transmitter/receiver.	30 Mbps or more	■ Can be used for high-speed data, broadcast TV, and wireless telephone service.
Satellite	Newer versions have two-way satellite access, removing need for phone line.	6 Mbps or more	■ Bandwidth is not shared. ■ Some connections require an existing Internet service account. ■ Setup fees can range from $500–$1,000.

FIGURE B3.8

Comparing Modems

(either 0 or 1). The modem must convert the digital signals of a computer into analog signals so they can be sent across the telephone line. At the other end, another modem translates the analog signals into digital signals, which can then be used by the other computer. Figure B3.8 displays the different types of modems.

LO 2. Identify the different computer categories, and explain their potential business uses.

Computer Categories

Supercomputers today can hit processing capabilities of well over 200 teraflops—the equivalent of everyone on Earth performing 35,000 calculations per second (see Figure B3.9). For the past 20 years, federally funded supercomputing research has given birth to some of the computer industry's most significant technology breakthroughs including:

■ Clustering, which allows companies to chain together thousands of PCs to build mass-market systems.

■ Parallel processing, which provides the ability to run two or more tasks simultaneously and is viewed as the chip industry's future.

FIGURE B3.9

Supercomputer

■ Mosaic browser, which morphed into Netscape and made the web a household name.

Federally funded supercomputers have also advanced some of the country's most dynamic industries, including advanced manufacturing, gene research in the life sciences, and real-time financial-market modeling.[8]

Computers come in different shapes, sizes, and colors. And they meet a variety of needs. An *appliance* is a computer dedicated to a single function, such as a calculator or computer game. An *ebook* is an electronic book that can be read on a computer or special reading device. Some are small enough to carry around, while others are the size of a telephone booth. Size does not always correlate to power, speed, and price (see Figure B3.10).

Smartphone/Personal Digital Assistant (PDA)

Handheld/Ultra Portable/Pocket Computer

Laptop/Notebook/Portable Computer/Netbook

Tablet Computer

Personal/Desktop Computer

Mainframe Computer

Supercomputer

Computer Category	Description
Smartphone	A cellular telephone with a keypad that runs programs, music, photos, and email and includes many features of a PDA.
Personal digital assistant (PDA)	A small handheld computer that performs simple tasks such as taking notes, scheduling appointments, and maintaining an address book and a calendar. The PDA screen is touch-sensitive, allowing a user to write directly on the screen, capturing what is written.
Handheld (ultra portable, pocket) computer	Computer portable enough to fit in a purse or pocket and has its own power source or battery.
Laptop (portable, notebook) computer	Computer portable enough to fit on a lap or in a bag and has its own power source or battery. Laptops come equipped with all of the technology that a personal desktop computer has, yet weigh as little as two pounds.
Tablet computer	Computer with a flat screen that uses a mouse or fingertip for input instead of a keyboard. Similar to PDAs, tablet PCs use a writing pen or stylus to write notes on the screen and touch the screen to perform functions such as clicking on a link while visiting a website.
Personal computer (microcomputer)	Computer that is operated by a single user who can customize the functions to match personal preferences.
Desktop computer	Computer that sits on, next to, or under a user's desk and is too large to carry around. The computer box is where the CPU, RAM, and storage devices are held with a monitor on top, or a vertical system box (called a tower) usually placed on the floor within a work area.
Workstation computer	Similar to a desktop but has more powerful mathematical and graphics processing capabilities and can perform more complicated tasks in less time. Typically used for software development, web development, engineering, and ebusiness tools.
Minicomputer (server)	Designed to meet the computing needs of several people simultaneously in a small to medium-size business environment. A common type of minicomputer is a server and is used for managing internal company applications, networks, and websites.
Mainframe computer	Designed to meet the computing needs of hundreds of people in a large business environment. Mainframe computers are a step up in size, power, capability, and cost from minicomputers.
Supercomputer	The fastest, most powerful, and most expensive type of computer. Organizations such as NASA that are heavily involved in research and number crunching employ supercomputers because of the speed with which they can process information. Other large, customer-oriented businesses such as General Motors and AT&T employ supercomputers just to handle customer information and transaction processing.

MIT's Media Lab is developing a laptop that it will sell for $100 each to government agencies around the world for distribution to millions of underprivileged schoolchildren. Using a simplified sales model and reengineering the device helped MIT reach the $100 price point. Almost half the price of a current laptop comprises marketing, sales, distribution, and profit. Of the remaining costs, the display panel and backlight account for roughly half while the rest covers the operating system. The low-cost laptop will use a display system that costs less than $25, a 500 MHz processor from AMD, a wireless LAN connection, 1 GB of storage, and the Linux operating system. The machine will automatically connect with others. China and Brazil have already ordered 3 million and 1 million laptops, respectively. MIT's goal is to produce around 150 million laptops per year.[9]

Software Basics

LO 3. Identify the two main types of software.

Hardware is only as good as the software that runs it. Over the years, the cost of hardware has decreased while the complexity and cost of software have increased. Some large software applications, such as customer relationship management systems, contain millions of lines of code, take years to develop, and cost millions of dollars. The two main types of software are system software and application software.

SYSTEM SOFTWARE

System software controls how the various technology tools work together along with the application software. System software includes both operating system software and utility software.

Operating System Software

Linus Torvalds, a Finnish programmer, may seem an unlikely choice to be one of the world's top managers. However, Linux, the software project he created while a university student, is now one of the most powerful influences on the computer world. Linux is an operating system built by volunteers and distributed for free and has become one of the primary competitors to Microsoft. Torvalds coordinates Linux development with a few dozen volunteer assistants and more than 1,000 programmers scattered around the globe. They contribute code for the kernel—or core piece—of Linux. He also sets the rules for dozens of technology companies that have lined up behind Linux, including IBM, Dell, Hewlett-Packard, and Intel.

While basic versions of Linux are available for free, Linux is having a considerable financial impact.[10]

Operating system software controls the application software and manages how the hardware devices work together. When using Excel to create and print a graph, the operating system software controls the process, ensures that a printer is attached and has paper, and sends the graph to the printer along with instructions on how to print it. Some computers are configured with two operating systems so they can *dual boot*— provide the user with the option of choosing the operating system when the computer is turned on. An *embedded operating system* is used in computer appliances and special-purpose applications, such as an automobile, ATM, or media player and are used for a single purpose. An iPod has a single-purpose embedded operating system.

Operating system software also supports a variety of useful features, one of which is multitasking. *Multitasking* allows more than one piece of software to be used at a time. Multitasking is used when creating a graph in Excel and simultaneously printing a word processing document. With multitasking, both pieces of application software are operating at the same time. There are different types of operating system software for personal environments and for organizational environments (see Figure B.11).

Utility Software

Utility software provides additional functionality to the operating system. Utility software includes antivirus software, screen savers, and anti-spam software. Operating

Operating System Software	
Linux	An open source operating system that provides a rich environment for high-end workstations and network servers. Open source refers to any program whose source code is made available for use or modification as users or other developers see fit.
Mac OS X	The operating system of Macintosh computers.
Microsoft Windows	Generic name for the various operating systems in the Microsoft Windows family, including Microsoft Windows CE, Microsoft Windows, Microsoft Windows ME, Microsoft Windows, Microsoft Windows XP, Microsoft Windows NT, and Microsoft Windows Server.
MS-DOS	The standard, single-user operating system of IBM and IBM-compatible computers, introduced in 1981. MS-DOS is a command-line operating system that requires the user to enter commands, arguments, and syntax.
UNIX	A 32-bit multitasking and multiuser operating system that originated at AT&T's Bell Laboratories and is now used on a wide variety of computers, from mainframes to PDAs.

systems are customized by using the *control panel,* which is a Windows feature that provides options that set default values for the Windows operating system. For example, the *system clock* works like a wristwatch and uses a battery mounted on the motherboard to provide power when the computer is turned off. If the user moves to a different time zone, the system clock can be adjusted in the control panel. *Safe mode* occurs if the system is failing and will load only the most essential parts of the operating system and will not run many of the background operating utilities. *System restore* enables a user to return to the previous operating system. Figure B3.12 displays a few types of available utility software.

APPLICATION SOFTWARE

Application software is used for specific information processing needs, including payroll, customer relationship management, project management, training, and many others. Application software is used to solve specific problems or perform specific tasks.

Types of Utility Software	
Crash-proof	Helps save information if a computer crashes.
Disk image for data recovery	Relieves the burden of reinstalling applications if a hard drive crashes or becomes irretrievably corrupted.
Disk optimization	Organizes information on a hard disk in the most efficient way.
Encrypt data	Protects confidential information from unauthorized eyes.
File and data recovery	Retrieves accidental deletion of photos or documents.
Text protect	In Microsoft Word, prevents users from typing over existing text after accidentally hitting the Insert key. Launch the Insert Toggle Key program, and the PC will beep whenever a user presses the Insert key.
Preventive security	Through programs such as Window Washer, erases file histories, browser cookies, cache contents, and other crumbs that applications and Windows leave on a hard drive.
Spyware	Removes any software that employs a user's Internet connection in the background without the user's knowledge or explicit permission.
Uninstaller	Can remove software that is no longer needed.

From an organizational perspective, payroll software, collaborative software such as videoconferencing (within groupware), and inventory management software are all examples of application software (see Figure B3.13). ***Personal information management (PIM) software*** handles contact information, appointments, task lists, and email. ***Course management software*** contains course information such as a syllabus and assignments and offers drop boxes for quizzes and homework along with a grade book.

DISTRIBUTING APPLICATION SOFTWARE

After software has been deployed to its users, it is not uncommon to find bugs or additional errors that require fixing. ***Software updates (software patch)*** occur when the software vendor releases updates to software to fix problems or enhance features. ***Software upgrade*** occurs when the software vendor releases a new version of the software, making significant changes to the program. Application software can be distributed using one of the following methods:

- ***Single user license***—restricts the use of the software to one user at a time.
- ***Network user license***—enables anyone on the network to install and use the software.
- ***Site license***—enables any qualified users within the organization to install the software, regardless of whether the computer is on a network. Some employees might install the software on a home computer for working remotely.
- ***Application service provider license***—specialty software paid for on a license basis or per-use basis or usage-based licensing.

FIGURE B3.13

Application Software

Types of Application Software	
Browser	Enables the user to navigate the World Wide Web. The two leading browsers are Netscape Navigator and Microsoft Internet Explorer.
Communication	Turns a computer into a terminal for transmitting data to and receiving data from distant computers through the telephone system.
Data management	Provides the tools for data retrieval, modification, deletion, and insertion; for example, Access, MySQL, and Oracle.
Desktop publishing	Transforms a computer into a desktop publishing workstation. Leading packages include Adobe FrameMaker, Adobe PageMaker, and QuarkXpress.
Email	Provides email services for computer users, including receiving mail, sending mail, and storing messages. Leading email software includes Microsoft Outlook, Microsoft Outlook Express, and Eudora.
Groupware	Increases the cooperation and joint productivity of small groups of co-workers.
Presentation graphics	Creates and enhances charts and graphs so that they are visually appealing and easily understood by an audience. A full-features presentation graphics package such as Lotus Freelance Graphics or Microsoft PowerPoint includes facilities for making a wide variety of charts and graphs and for adding titles, legends, and explanatory text anywhere in the chart or graph.
Programming	Possesses an artificial language consisting of a fixed vocabulary and a set of rules (called syntax) that programmers use to write computer programs. Leading programming languages include Java, C++, C#, and .NET.
Spreadsheet	Simulates an accountant's worksheet onscreen and lets users embed hidden formulas that perform calculations on the visible data. Many spreadsheet programs also include powerful graphics and presentation capabilities to create attractive products. The leading spreadsheet application is Microsoft Excel.
Word processing	Transforms a computer into a tool for creating, editing, proofreading, formatting, and printing documents. Leading word processing applications include Microsoft Word and WordPerfect.

Information technology (IT) is a field concerned with the use of technology in managing and processing information. IT includes cell phones, PDAs, software such as spreadsheet software, and printers. There are two categories of IT: hardware and software. The six hardware components include CPU, primary storage, secondary storage, input devices, output devices, and communication devices. Computer categories include PDAs, laptops, tablets, desktops, workstations, minicomputers, mainframe computers, and supercomputers.

Software includes system software and application software. Operating system software and utility software are the two primary types of system software. There are many forms of application software from word processing to databases.

KEY TERMS

CLOSING CASE ONE

Changing Circuits at Circuit City

When Circuit City expanded the big-box warehouse format to consumer electronics retailing in the 1980s, the company was on its way to becoming the place to go for TVs and stereos. By the late 1980s, it had sidestepped its then top competitor, Silo, and it soon put the squeeze on the likes of Tweeter and RadioShack. Circuit City was doing so well in the 1990s that business consultant Jim Collins, in his best seller *Good to Great,* wrote: "From 1982 to 1999, Circuit City generated cumulative stock returns 22 times better than the market, handily beating Intel, Wal-Mart, GE, Hewlett-Packard and Coca-Cola."

Today, Circuit City is in a markedly different position. By 2001, Best Buy had raced past the Richmond, Virginia-based chain, usurping its position as the number one consumer electronics retailer. Best Buy now has 608 stores compared with Circuit City's 599 and nearly $25 billion in revenue to Circuit City's $9.7 billion. Circuit City is ranked by consultancy Retail Forward as the number three seller of consumer electronics, behind Best Buy and Walmart. "Circuit City was the 800-pound gorilla," said Joseph Feldman, a research analyst with the investment bank SG Cowen & Co. However, "they woke up one morning and Best Buy had doubled its size with the same number of stores."

Catching Best Buy

Circuit City has been trying to catch up to Best Buy, or at least cement its position as a serious contender in consumer electronics retailing. Its top executives announced plans to turn the company into a customer-focused business that delivers a personalized experience to all customers across all its channels (stores, web, and call centers). Michael Jones, who took over as Circuit City's CIO in January 2004, speaks passionately about the high-profile role technology will play in delivering personalized customer experiences. However, before he can achieve his vision of store associates recognizing customers through their loyalty cards as soon as they enter the store, he has a lot of unglamorous groundwork to lay. Circuit City's strategy hinges on a robust IT infrastructure that makes information readily accessible to decision makers. Everything the company is doing to improve its business—from developing more effective promotions to deciding which products should be displayed at the ends of aisles in stores—hinges on data. "This is heavy analytical work. It's fact-based, data-driven," said Philip Schoonover, Circuit City's new president who was hired in October 2004 from Best Buy.

Circuit City is just starting to invest heavily in the technology needed to act on this strategy. It is upgrading its mostly proprietary point-of-sale (POS) system and building an enterprise data warehouse to replace siloed databases. However, some analysts say Circuit City's turnaround effort has been hampered by a stodgy, overly complacent leadership that lacks vision. Top executives saw the Best Buy locomotive coming but failed to react as it steamed past them. Indeed, some analysts say they doubt Circuit City will ever catch up.

Bottom-Up Changes

As part of its turnaround effort over the past few years, Circuit City has sold all of its non-core businesses to focus on its core: consumer electronics. It also has changed the pay structure for in-store employees, begun relocating stores (it closed 19), and hired new management. In addition, the company is finally starting to hone its customer-centric strategy. Circuit City is already improving the customer experience in its stores by, among other things, locating accessories and services close to big-ticket items so that customers can see more quickly what they might need to furnish their home office or outfit a home theater. For example, when a customer is looking at a high-definition television, nearby is a selection of furniture to hold the TV, the cables needed to hook it up, and DirectTV or digital cable service products. Circuit City is also making merchandising decisions based on what is important to the customer. For example, its stores are beginning to feature products deemed most important to customers on the displays at the ends of aisles. The company is trying to nail the basics of customer service by making sure that items are not out of stock.

Questions

1. How would anticipating Best Buy's growth have helped Circuit City remain as an industry leader?
2. Why is keeping up with technology critical to a global company such as Circuit City?
3. Highlight some of the potential risks facing Circuit City's new business model.
4. Why is Circuit City benefiting from implementing strategic product placement techniques?

Electronic Breaking Points

What happens when someone accidentally spills a cup of hot coffee on a laptop, puts a USB memory key in a washing machine, or drops an iPod in the sand? How much abuse can electronic products take and keep on working? *PC World* tested several products to determine their breaking points.

Laptop

A Gateway laptop was placed in a shoulder bag and smashed into several doors and walls. It was also dropped off a six-foot-high bookcase to simulate a drop from an airplane's overhead bin. Finally, it was knocked off a desk onto a carpeted floor without the bag. After all the abuse, the Gateway consistently rebooted and recognized the wireless network; however, the battery did become slightly dislodged and the optical drive opened.

Severe physical damage was caused when the laptop was dropped onto a hardwood floor. The laptop's screen cracked, and the black plastic molding above the keyboard cracked. Plastic splinters littered the floor, and the optical drive refused to open.

Spilling coffee in a travel-size mug onto the keyboard caused a slight sizzle, after which the Gateway's blue light winked out. The machine was quickly turned off, the battery removed, the liquid drained, the keys mopped, and the unit set aside. Unfortunately, the laptop never recovered.

Smartphone

The PalmOne Treo 600 smartphone was stepped on, buried in the sand, bounced around in a car, and dropped off a desk onto carpeted and hardwood floors. Even though the Treo 600 was not protected by a shock-absorbent case or plastic screen cover, there were no signs of failure. Repeatedly knocking it off the desk onto a carpeted floor also left it undamaged, although the unit did turn off on several occasions.

The desk-to-hardwood-floor test produced scratches but nothing else. If dropped when in phone mode, the Treo automatically turned off. If an application was running—the calculator, for example—the device stayed on and the data remained on the screen, though a mysterious extra numeral nine appeared every time it was dropped.

MP3 Player

A 6 GB silver iPod Mini went for a bouncy car ride, was dropped on wet grass and dry pavement, was knocked off a desk onto carpeted and hardwood floors, and was finally dropped in dry sand. Bouncing inside the car caused a couple of skips. Drops on soft wet grass and carpet had no ill effect. Dropping it from the car seat to the curb and off a desk onto a hardwood floor produced a few nicks and caused songs to skip and the device to shut down repeatedly. Still, all the unit's features continued to work after the abuse, and songs played.

However, the Mini did not like the beach. Without the benefit of a protective case or plastic display covering on the unit, sand wedged under the scroll wheel, affecting all controls. Feature settings could be seen and highlighted, but the crunching sand prevented the Mini from launching them. The unit turned on but could not turn off until the iPod's automatic shutdown feature took over.

Memory Stick

Lexar claims that its JumpDrive Sport 256 MB USB 2.0 Flash Drive is "built for the rugged life." A rubber cap protects the device, absorbing shock from any drops. For these experiments, the device was used without its cap. It was dropped, stepped on, buried in the sand, and knocked off a desk onto a hardwood floor. It also took a spin through the washing machine and dryer and was even run over by a car.

Protecting Electronic Products

Bag it. Place your product in a cushioned case or shock-absorbent travel bag. The secret is to make sure it has plenty of padding.

Get protection. Almost every technology manufacturer offers some type of warranty and equipment-replacement program. For example, Sprint provides the PCS Total Equipment Protection service, which costs $5 per month and covers loss, theft, and accidental damage to a cell phone.

Clean up spills. Try these tips to bring a laptop and data back from the dead after a spill.

1. **Disconnect the battery.** The faster the battery is disconnected the less likely components will burn out.

2. **Empty it.** Turn over the device and pour out as much liquid as possible.

3. **Open it up.** Remove the optical drive and keyboard. This can be tricky, so check the user manual for instructions. Once open, use a towel to soak up as much liquid as possible. According to Herman De Hoop, HP's technical marketing manager, you can even use a hair dryer set on cool (not hot) to dry the liquid.

4. **Leave it alone.** Let the device sit for at least 12 to 24 hours. Robert Enochs, IBM's worldwide product manager for the ThinkPad Series, warns that you should not turn the device on until all the liquid is gone and it is completely dry.

5. **Plug and pray.** Reassemble the device, and if it powers up, copy off important data, and then call the manufacturer. Even if the unit works, a professional cleaning is recommended.

6. **Enter a recovery program.** For an average price of $900, enlist the help of data recovery services like DriveSavers to rescue data from drowned hard disks.

There is truth in advertising. Neither water, heat, sand, nor car could keep the memory stick from its appointed storage rounds. The car did squeeze the metal USB connector tip a tad tighter, but the device was still able to make contact with the USB port, and it worked perfectly.

Memory Card

The SanDisk SD 64 MB memory card is easy to misplace, but not easy to break. It was swatted off a desk onto a hardwood floor, dropped, stepped on, and buried in the sand. It also underwent a two-rinse cycle in the wash in a jeans pocket and then tumbled in the dryer for an hour on a high-heat setting. The SanDisk memory card aced every torture test.

For tips on how to protect electronic products, review Figure B3.14.

Questions

1. Identify the six hardware categories and place each product listed in the case in its appropriate category.
2. Describe the CPU and identify which products would use a CPU.
3. Describe the relationship between memory sticks and laptops. How can a user employ one to help protect information loss from the other?
4. Identify the different types of software each of the products listed in the case might use.

1. Purchasing a Computer

Dell is considered the fastest company on earth and specializes in computer customization. Connect to Dell's website at www.dell.com. Go to the portion of Dell's site that allows you to customize either a laptop or a desktop computer. First, choose an already prepared system and note its price and capability in terms of CPU speed, RAM size, monitor quality, and storage capacity. Now, customize that system to increase CPU speed, add more RAM, increase monitor size and quality, and add more storage capacity. What is the difference in price between the two? Which system is more in your price range? Which system has the speed and capacity you need?

2. Web-Enabled Cell Phones

When categorizing computers by size for personal needs, we focused on PDAs, laptops, and desktop computers. Other variations include web-enabled cell phones that provide instant text messaging and web computers. For this project, you will need a group of four people, which you will then split into two groups of two. Have the first group research web-enabled cell phones, their capabilities and costs. Have that group make a purchase recommendation based on price and capability. Have the second group do the same for web computers. What is your vision of the future? Will we ever get rid of clunky laptops and desktops in favor of more portable and cheaper devices such as web-enabled cell phones and web computers? Why or why not?

3. Small Business Computers

Many different types of computers are available for small businesses. Use the Internet to find three different vendors of laptops or notebooks that are good for small businesses. Find the most expensive and the least expensive that the vendor offers and create a table comparing the different computers based on the following:

- CPU
- Memory
- Hard drive
- Optical drive
- Operating system
- Utility software
- Application software
- Support plan

Determine which computer you would recommend for a small business looking for an inexpensive laptop. Determine which computer you would recommend for a small business looking for an expensive laptop.

MIS Infrastructures

1. Explain MIS infrastructure and its three primary types.
2. Identify the three primary areas associated with an information MIS infrastructure.
3. Describe the characteristics of an agile MIS infrastructure.

LO 1. Explain MIS infrastructure and its three primary types.

The Business Benefits of a Solid MIS Infrastructure

Management information systems have played a significant role in business strategies, affected business decisions and processes, and even changed the way companies operate. What is the foundation supporting all of these systems that enable business growth, operations, and profits? What supports the volume and complexity of today's user and application requirements? What protects systems from failures and crashes? It is the *MIS infrastructure*, which includes the plans for how a firm will build, deploy, use, and share its data, processes, and MIS assets. A solid MIS infrastructure can reduce costs, improve productivity, optimize business operations, generate growth, and increase profitability.

Briefly defined, *hardware* consists of the physical devices associated with a computer system, and *software* is the set of instructions the hardware executes to carry out specific tasks. In today's business environment, most hardware and software is run via a network. A *network* is a communications system created by linking two or more devices and establishing a standard methodology in which they can communicate. As more companies need to share more information, the network takes on greater importance in the infrastructure. Most companies use a specific form of network infrastructure called a client and server network. A *client* is a computer designed to request information from a server. A *server* is a computer dedicated to providing information in response to requests. A good way to understand this is when someone uses a web browser (this would be the client) to access a website (this would be a server that would respond with the web page being requested by the client).

In the physical world, a detailed blueprint would show how public utilities, such as water, electricity, and gas support the foundation of a building. MIS infrastructure is similar as it shows in detail how the hardware, software, and network connectivity support the firm's

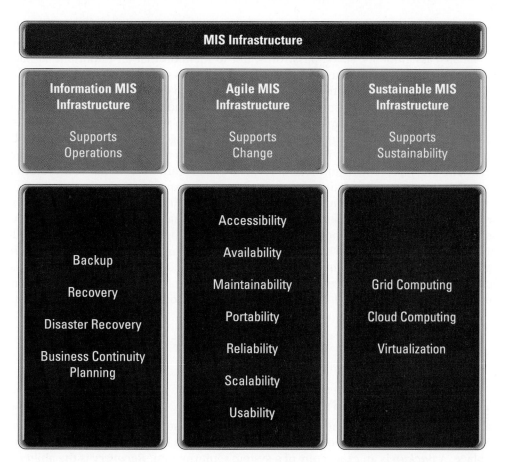

processes. Every company, regardless of size, relies on some form of MIS infrastructure, whether it is a few personal computers networked together sharing an Excel file or a large multinational company with thousands of employees interconnected around the world.

An MIS infrastructure is dynamic; it continually changes as the business needs change. Each time a new form of Internet-enabled device, such as an iPhone or BlackBerry, is created and made available to the public, a firm's MIS infrastructure must be revised to support the device. This moves beyond just innovations in hardware to include new types of software and network connectivity. An **enterprise architect** is a person grounded in technology, fluent in business, and able to provide the important bridge between MIS and the business. Firms employ enterprise architects to help manage change and dynamically update MIS infrastructure. Figure B4.1 displays the three primary areas where enterprise architects focus when maintaining a firm's MIS infrastructure.

- **Supporting operations:** *Information MIS infrastructure* identifies where and how important information, such as customer records, is maintained and secured.

- **Supporting change:** *Agile MIS Infrastructure* includes the hardware, software, and telecommunications equipment that, when combined, provides the underlying foundation to support the organization's goals.

- **Supporting the environment:** *Sustainable MIS infrastructure* identifies ways that a company can grow in terms of computing resources while simultaneously becoming less dependent on hardware and energy consumption.

Supporting Operations: Information MIS Infrastructure

LO 2. Identify the three primary areas associated with an information MIS infrastructure.

Imagine taking a quick trip to the printer on the other side of the room, and when you turn around you find that your laptop has been stolen. How painful would you find this experience? What types of information would you lose? How much time would it take you to recover all of that information? A few things you might lose include music, movies, emails, assignments, saved passwords, not to mention that all-important 40-page paper that took you more than a month to complete. If this sounds painful then you want to pay particular attention to this section and learn how to eliminate this pain.

An information MIS infrastructure identifies where and how important information is maintained and secured. An information infrastructure supports day-to-day business operations and plans for emergencies such as power outages, floods, earthquakes, malicious attacks via the Internet, theft, and security breaches to name just a few. Managers must take every precaution to make sure their systems are operational and protected around the clock every day of the year. Losing a laptop or experiencing bad weather in one part of the country simply cannot take down systems required to operate core business processes. In the past, someone stealing company information would have to carry out boxes upon boxes of paper. Today, as data storage technologies grow in capabilities while shrinking in size, a person can simply walk out the front door of the building with the company's data files stored on a thumb drive or external hard drive. Today's managers must act responsibly to protect one of their most valued assets, information. To support continuous business operations, an information infrastructure provides three primary elements:

- Backup and recovery plan.
- Disaster recovery plan.
- Business continuity plan (see Figure B4.2).

BACKUP AND RECOVERY PLAN

Each year businesses lose time and money because of system crashes and failures. One way to minimize the damage of a system crash is to have a backup and recovery strategy in place. A *backup* is an exact copy of a system's information. *Recovery* is the ability to get a system up and running in the event of a system crash or failure that includes restoring the information backup. Many different types of backup and recovery media are available, including maintaining an identical replica or redundant of the storage server, external hard drives, thumb drives, and even DVDs. The primary differences between them are speed and cost.

Fault tolerance is the ability for a system to respond to unexpected failures or system crashes as the backup system immediately and automatically takes over with no loss of

FIGURE B4.2

Areas of Support Provided by Information Infrastructure

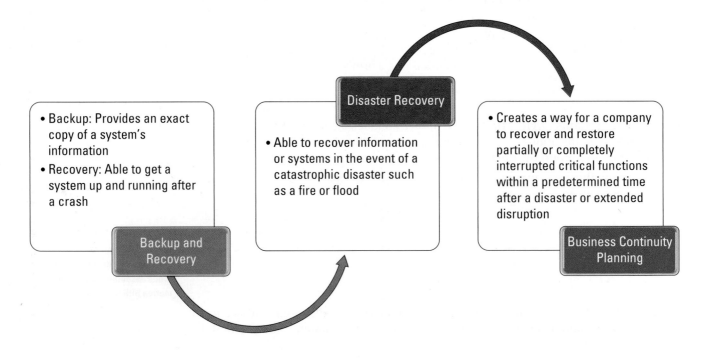

service. For example, fault tolerance enables a business to support continuous business operations if there is a power failure or flood. Fault tolerance is an expensive form of backup, and only mission-critical applications and operations use it. *Failover,* a specific type of fault tolerance, occurs when a redundant storage server offers an exact replica of the real-time data, and if the primary server crashes, the users are automatically directed to the secondary server or backup server. This is a high-speed and high-cost method of backup and recovery. *Failback* occurs when the primary machine recovers and resumes operations, taking over from the secondary server.

Using DVDs or thumb drives to store your data offers a low-speed and low-cost backup method. It is a good business practice to back up data at least once a week using a low-cost method. This will alleviate the pain of having your laptop stolen or your system crash as you will still have access to your data, and it will only be a few days old.

Deciding how often to back up information and what media to use is a critical decision. Companies should choose a backup and recovery strategy in line with their goals and operational needs. If the company deals with large volumes of critical information, it will require daily, perhaps hourly, backups to storage servers. If it relies on small amounts of noncritical information, then it might require only weekly backups to external hard drives or thumb drives. A company that backs up on a weekly basis is taking the risk that, if a system crash occurs, it could lose a week's worth of work. If this risk is acceptable, a weekly backup strategy will work. If it is unacceptable, the company needs more frequent backup.

DISASTER RECOVERY PLAN

Disasters such as power outages, fires, floods, hurricanes, and even malicious activities such as hackers and viruses strike companies every day. Disasters can have the following effects on companies and their business operations.

- **Disrupting communications:** Most companies depend on voice and data communications for daily operational needs. Widespread communications outages, from either direct damage to the infrastructure or sudden spikes in usage related to an outside disaster, can be as devastating to some firms as shutting down the whole business.

- **Damaging physical infrastructures:** Fire and flood can directly damage buildings, equipment, and systems, making structures unsafe and systems unusable. Law enforcement officers and firefighters may prohibit business professionals from entering a building, thereby restricting access to retrieve documents or equipment.

- **Halting transportation:** Disasters such as floods and hurricanes can have a deep effect on transportation. Disruption to major highways, roads, bridges, railroads, and airports can prevent business professionals from reporting to work or going home, slow the delivery of supplies, and stop the shipment of products.

- **Blocking utilities:** Public utilities, such as the supply of electric power, water, and natural gas, can be interrupted for hours or days even in incidents that cause no direct damage to the physical infrastructure. Buildings are often uninhabitable and systems unable to function without public utilities.

These effects can devastate companies by causing them to cease operations for hours, days, or longer and risk losing customers whom they cannot then supply. Therefore, to combat these disasters a company can create a *disaster recovery plan*, which is a detailed process for recovering information or a system in the event of a catastrophic disaster. This plan includes such factors as which files and systems need to have backups and their corresponding frequency and methods along with the strategic location of the storage in a separate physical site that is geographically dispersed. A company might strategically maintain operations in New York and San Francisco, ensuring that a natural disaster would not impact both locations. A disaster recovery plan also foresees the possibility that not only the computer equipment but also the building where employees work may be destroyed. A *hot site* is a separate and fully equipped facility where the company can move immediately after a disaster and resume business.

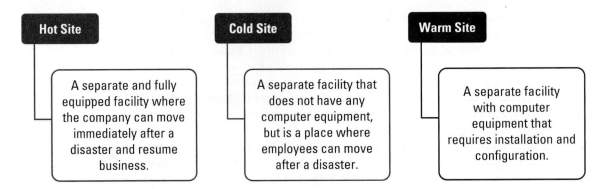

Hot Site	Cold Site	Warm Site
A separate and fully equipped facility where the company can move immediately after a disaster and resume business.	A separate facility that does not have any computer equipment, but is a place where employees can move after a disaster.	A separate facility with computer equipment that requires installation and configuration.

FIGURE B4.3

Sites to Support Disaster Recovery

A *cold site* is a separate facility that does not have any computer equipment but is a place where employees can move after a disaster. A *warm site* is a separate facility with computer equipment that requires installation and configuration. Figure B4.3 outlines these resources that support disaster recovery.

A disaster recovery plan usually has a disaster recovery cost curve to support it. A *disaster recovery cost curve* charts (1) the cost to the company of the unavailability of information and technology and (2) the cost to the company of recovering from a disaster over time. Figure B4.4 displays a disaster recovery cost curve and shows that the best recovery plan in terms of cost and time is where the two lines intersect. Creating such a curve is no small task. Managers must consider the cost of losing information and technology within each department or functional area, and across the whole company. During the first few hours of a disaster, those costs may be low, but they rise over time. With those costs in hand, a company must then determine the costs of recovery.

On April 18, 1906, San Francisco was rocked by an earthquake that destroyed large sections of the city and claimed the lives of more than 3,000 inhabitants. More than a century later, a rebuilt and more durable San Francisco serves as a central location for major MIS corporations as well as a major world financial center. Managers of these corporations are well aware of the potential disasters that exist along the San Andreas Fault and actively update their business continuity plans anticipating such issues as earthquakes and floods. The Union Bank of California is located in the heart of downtown San Francisco and maintains a highly detailed and well-developed business continuity plan. The company employs hundreds of business professionals scattered around the world that coordinate plans for addressing the potential loss of a facility, business professionals, or critical systems so that the company can continue to operate if a disaster happens. Its disaster recovery plan includes hot sites where staff can walk in and start working exactly as if they were in their normal location. It would be a matter of minutes, not hours, for the Union Bank of California to be up and running again in the event of a disaster.[1]

FIGURE B4.4

Disaster Recovery Cost Curve

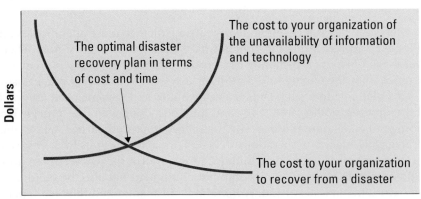

Time from Disaster to Recovery

BUSINESS CONTINUITY PLAN

An ***emergency*** is a sudden, unexpected event requiring immediate action due to potential threat to health and safety, the environment, or property. ***Emergency preparedness*** ensures a company is ready to respond to an emergency in an organized, timely, and effective manner. Natural disasters and terrorist attacks are on the minds of business professionals who take safeguarding their information assets seriously. Disaster recovery plans typically focus on systems and data, ignoring cross-functional and intraorganizational business processes that can be destroyed during an emergency. For this reason many companies are turning to a more comprehensive and all-encompassing emergency preparedness plan known as ***business continuity planning (BCP),*** which details how a company recovers and restores critical business operations and systems after a disaster or extended disruption. BCP includes such factors as identifying critical systems, business processes, departments, and the maximum amount of time the business can continue to operate without functioning systems. BCP contains disaster recovery plans along with many additional plans, including prioritizing business impact analysis, emergency notification plans, and technology recovery strategies (see Figure B4.5).

Business Impact Analysis

A ***business impact analysis*** identifies all critical business functions and the effect that a specific disaster may have upon them. A business impact analysis is primarily used to ensure a company has made the right decisions about the order of recovery priorities and strategies. For example, should the accounting department have its systems up and running before the sales and marketing departments? Will email be the first system for recovery to ensure employees can communicate with each other and outside stakeholders such as customers, suppliers, and partners? The business impact analysis is a key part of BCP as it details the order in which functional areas should be restored, ensuring the most critical are focused on first.

Emergency Notification Services

A business continuity plan typically includes an ***emergency notification service***, that is, an infrastructure built for notifying people in the event of an emergency. Radio stations' occasional tests of the national Emergency Alert System are an example of a very

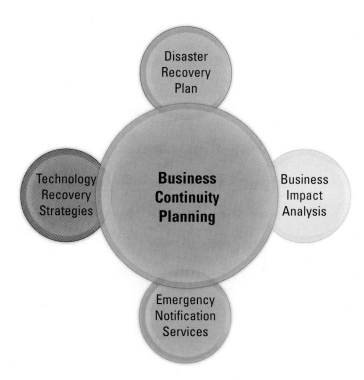

FIGURE B4.5

Business Continuity Planning Focus Areas

large-scale emergency notification system. A firm will implement an emergency notification service to warn employees of unexpected events and provide them with instructions about how to handle the situation. Emergency notification services can be deployed through the firm's own infrastructure, supplied by an outside service provider on company premises, or hosted remotely by an outside service provider. All three methods provide notification using a variety of methods such as email, voice notification to a cell phone, and text messaging. The notifications can be sent to all the devices selected, providing multiple means in which to get critical information to those who need it.

Technology Recovery Strategies

Companies create massive amounts of data vital to their survival and continued operations. A ***technology failure*** occurs when the ability of a company to operate is impaired because of a hardware, software, or data outage. Technology failures can destroy large amounts of vital data, often causing ***incidents***, unplanned interruption of a service. An ***incident record*** contains all of the details of an incident. ***Incident management*** is the process responsible for managing how incidents are identified and corrected. ***Technology recovery strategies*** focus specifically on prioritizing the order for restoring hardware, software, and data across the organization that best meets business recovery requirements. A technology recovery strategy details the order of importance for recovering hardware, software, data centers, and networking (or connectivity). If one of these four vital components is not functioning, the entire system will be unavailable, shutting down cross-functional business processes such as order management and payroll. Figure B4.6 displays the key areas a company should focus on when developing technology recovery strategies.

LO 3. Describe the characteristics of an agile MIS infrastructure.

Supporting Change: Agile MIS Infrastructure

Agile MIS infrastructure includes the hardware, software, and telecommunications equipment that, when combined, provides the underlying foundation to support the organization's goals. If a company grows by 50 percent in a single year, its infrastructure and systems must be able to handle a 50 percent growth rate. If they cannot, they can severely hinder the company's ability not only to grow but also to function.

The future of a company depends on its ability to meet its partners, suppliers, and customers any time of the day in any geographic location. Imagine owning an ebusiness and everyone on the Internet is tweeting and collaborating about how great your business idea is and how successful your company is going to be. Suddenly, you have 5 million global customers interested in your website. Unfortunately, you did not anticipate this many customers so quickly, and the system crashes. Users typing in your URL find a blank message stating the website is unavailable and to try back soon. Or even worse, they can get to your website but it takes three minutes to reload each time they click on a button. The buzz soon dies about your business idea as some innovative web-savvy

FIGURE B4.6

Key Areas of Technology Recovery Strategies

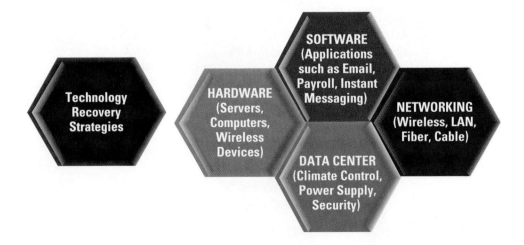

fast follower quickly copies your idea and creates a website that can handle the massive number of customers. The characteristics of agile MIS infrastructures can help ensure your systems can meet and perform under any unexpected or unplanned changes. Figure B4.7 lists the seven abilities of an agile infrastructure.

ACCESSIBILITY

Accessibility refers to the varying levels that define what a user can access, view, or perform when operating a system. Imagine the people at your college accessing the main student information system. Each person that accesses the system will have different needs and requirements; for example, a payroll employee will need to access vacation information and salary information, or a student will need to access course information and billing information. Each system user is provided with an access level that details which parts of the system the user can and cannot access and what the user can do when in the system. For example, you would not want your students to be able to view payroll information or professor's personal information; also, some users can only view information and are not allowed to create or delete information. Top-level MIS employees require ***administrator access,*** or unrestricted access to the entire system. Administrator access can perform functions such as resetting passwords, deleting accounts, and shutting down entire systems.

Tim Berners-Lee, W3C director and inventor of the World Wide Web, stated, "the power of the web is in its universality. Access by everyone regardless of disability is an essential aspect." ***Web accessibility*** means that people with disabilities, including visual, auditory, physical, speech, cognitive, and neurological disabilities, can use the web. The ***web accessibility initiative (WAI)*** brings together people from industry, disability organizations, government, and research labs from around the world to develop guidelines and resources to help make the web accessible to people with disabilities, including auditory, cognitive, neurological, physical, speech, and visual disabilities. The goal of WAI is to allow people to access the full potential of the web, enabling people with disabilities to participate equally. For example, Apple includes screen magnification and VoiceOver on its iPhone, iPad, and iPod, which allows the blind and visually impaired to use the devices.

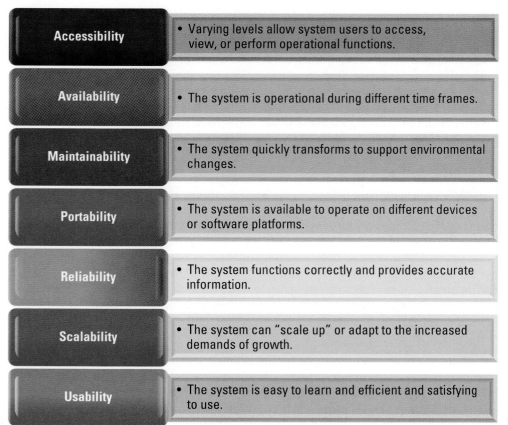

FIGURE B4.7

Agile MIS Infrastructure Characteristics

Accessibility
- Varying levels allow system users to access, view, or perform operational functions.

Availability
- The system is operational during different time frames.

Maintainability
- The system quickly transforms to support environmental changes.

Portability
- The system is available to operate on different devices or software platforms.

Reliability
- The system functions correctly and provides accurate information.

Scalability
- The system can "scale up" or adapt to the increased demands of growth.

Usability
- The system is easy to learn and efficient and satisfying to use.

AVAILABILITY

In a 24/7/365 ebusiness environment, business professionals need to use their systems whenever they want from wherever they want. *Availability* refers to the time frames when the system is operational. A system is called *unavailable* when it is not operating and cannot be used. *High availability* occurs when a system is continuously operational at all times. Availability is typically measured relative to "100 percent operational" or "never failing." A widely held but difficult-to-achieve standard of availability for a system is known as "five 9s" (99.999 percent) availability. Some companies have systems available around the clock to support ebusiness operations, global customers, and online suppliers.

Sometimes systems must be taken down for maintenance, upgrades, and fixes, which are completed during downtime. One challenge with availability is determining when to schedule system downtime if the system is expected to operate continuously. Performing maintenance during the evening might seem like a great idea, but evening in one city is morning somewhere else in the world, and business professionals scattered around the globe may not be able to perform specific job functions if the systems they need are unavailable. This is where companies deploy failover systems so they can take the primary system down for maintenance and activate the secondary system to ensure continuous operations.

MAINTAINABILITY

Companies must watch today's needs, as well as tomorrow's, when designing and building systems that support agile infrastructures. Systems must be flexible enough to meet all types of company changes, environmental changes, and business changes. *Maintainability* (or *flexibility*) refers to how quickly a system can transform to support environmental changes. Maintainability helps to measure how quickly and effectively a system can be changed or repaired after a failure. For example, when starting a small business you might not consider that you will have global customers, a common mistake. When building your systems, you might not design them to handle multiple currencies and different languages, which might make sense if the company is not currently performing international business. Unfortunately, when the first international order arrives, which happens easily with ebusiness, the system will be unable to handle the request because it does not have the flexibility to be easily reconfigured for a new language or currency. When the company does start growing and operating overseas, the system will need to be redeveloped, which is not an easy or cheap task, to handle multiple currencies and different languages.

Building and deploying flexible systems allow easy updates, changes, and reconfigurations for unexpected business or environmental changes. Just think what might have happened if Facebook had to overhaul its entire system to handle multiple languages. Another social networking business could easily have stepped in and become the provider of choice. That certainly would not be efficient or effective for business operations.

PORTABILITY

Portability refers to the ability of an application to operate on different devices or software platforms, such as different operating systems. Apple's iTunes is readily available to users of Mac computers and also users of PC computers, smartphones, iPods, iPhones, iPads, and so on. It is also a portable application. Because Apple insists on compatibility across its products, both software and hardware, Apple can easily add to its product, device, and service offerings without sacrificing portability. Many software developers are creating programs that are portable to all three devices—the iPhone, iPod, and iPad—which increases their target market and they hope their revenue.

RELIABILITY

Reliability (or *accuracy*) ensures a system is functioning correctly and providing accurate information. Inaccuracy can occur for many reasons, from the incorrect entry of information to the corruption of information during transmissions. Many argue that the information contained in Wikipedia is unreliable. Because the Wikipedia entries can be edited by any user, there are examples of rogue users inaccurately updating information. Many users skip over Google search findings that correlate to Wikipedia for this reason. Housing unreliable information on a website can put a company at risk of losing customers, placing inaccurate supplier orders, or even making unreliable business decisions. A *vulnerability* is a system weakness, such as a password that is never changed or a system left on while an employee goes to lunch, that can be exploited by a threat. Reliable systems ensure that vulnerabilities are kept at a minimum to reduce risk.

SCALABILITY

Estimating company growth is a challenging task, in part because growth can occur in a number of different forms—the firm can acquire new customers, new product lines, or new markets. *Scalability* describes how well a system can scale up, or adapt to the increased demands of growth. If a company grows faster than anticipated, it might experience a variety of problems, from running out of storage space to taking more time to complete transactions. Anticipating expected, and unexpected, growth is key to building scalable systems that can support that development.

Performance measures how quickly a system performs a process or transaction. Performance is a key component of scalability as systems that can't scale suffer from performance issues. Just imagine your college's content management system suddenly taking five minutes to return a page after a button is pushed. Now imagine if this occurs during your midterm exam and you miss the two-hour deadline because the system is so slow. Performance issues experienced by firms can have disastrous business impacts causing loss of customers, loss of suppliers, and even loss of help-desk employees. Most users will wait only a few seconds for a website to return a request before growing frustrated and either calling the support desk or giving up and moving on to another website.

Capacity represents the maximum throughput a system can deliver; for example, the capacity of a hard drive represents its size or volume. *Capacity planning* determines future environmental infrastructure requirements to ensure high-quality system performance. If a company purchases connectivity software that is outdated or too slow to meet demand, its employees will waste a great deal of time waiting for systems to respond to user requests. It is cheaper for a company to design and implement agile infrastructure that envisions growth requirements than to update all the equipment after the system is already operational. If a company with 100 workers merges with another company and suddenly there are 400 people using the system, performance time could suffer. Planning for increases in capacity can ensure systems perform as expected. Waiting for a system to respond to requests is not productive.

Web 2.0 is a big driver for capacity planning to ensure agile infrastructures can meet the business's operational needs. Delivering videos over the Internet requires enough bandwidth to satisfy millions of users during peak periods such as Friday and Saturday evenings. Video transmissions over the Internet cannot tolerate packet loss (blocks of data loss), and allowing one additional user to access the system could degrade the video quality for every user.

USABILITY

Usability is the degree to which a system is easy to learn and efficient and satisfying to use. Providing hints, tips, shortcuts, and instructions for any system, regardless of its ease of use, is recommended. Apple understood the importance of usability when it designed the first iPod. One of the iPod's initial attractions was the usability of the click wheel. One simple and efficient button operates the iPod, making it usable for all ages. And to ensure ease of use, Apple also made the corresponding iTunes software intuitive and easy to use. *Serviceability* is how quickly a third party can change a system to ensure it meets user needs and the terms of any contracts, including agreed levels of reliability, maintainability, or availability. When using a system from a third party, it is important to ensure the right level of serviceability for all users, including remote employees.

An MIS infrastructure is dynamic; it continually changes as the business needs change. Each time a new form of Internet-enabled device, such as an iPhone or BlackBerry, is created and made available to the public, a firm's MIS infrastructure must be revised to support the device. This moves beyond just innovations in hardware to include new types of software and network connectivity. The three primary areas where enterprise architects focus when maintaining a firm's MIS infrastructure are as follows:

- *Supporting operations:* Information MIS infrastructure identifies where and how important information, such as customer records, is maintained and secured.

- *Supporting change:* Agile MIS infrastructure includes the hardware, software, and telecommunications equipment that, when combined, provide the underlying foundation to support the organization's goals.

- *Supporting the environment:* Sustainable MIS infrastructure identifies ways that a company can grow in terms of computing resources while simultaneously becoming less dependent on hardware and energy consumption.

Accessibility, 387
Administrator access, 387
Agile MIS infrastructure, 381
Availability, 388
Backup, 382
Business continuity planning (BCP), 385
Business impact analysis, 385
Capacity, 389
Capacity planning, 389
Client, 380
Cold site, 384
Disaster recovery cost curve, 384
Disaster recovery plan, 383
Emergency, 385
Emergency notification service, 385
Emergency preparedness, 385

Enterprise architect, 381
Failback, 383
Failover, 383
Fault tolerance, 382
Hardware, 380
High availability, 388
Hot site, 383
Incident, 386
Incident management, 386
Incident record, 386
Information MIS infrastructure, 381
Maintainability (or flexibility), 388
MIS infrastructure, 380
Network, 380
Performance, 389
Portability, 388
Recovery, 382

Reliability (or accuracy), 388
Scalability, 389
Server, 380
Serviceability, 389
Software, 380
Sustainable MIS infrastructure, 381
Technology failure, 386
Technology recovery strategy, 386
Unavailable, 388
Usability, 389
Vulnerability, 389
Warm site, 384
Web accessibility, 387
Web accessibility initiative (WAI), 387

Chicago Tribune's Server Consolidation a Success

The *Chicago Tribune* is the seventh-largest newspaper in the country. Overhauling its data center and consolidating servers was a difficult task; however, the payoff was tremendous. The *Chicago Tribune* successfully moved its critical applications from a mishmash of mainframes and older Sun Microsystems servers to a new dual-site enterprise architecture, which has resulted in lower costs and increased reliability throughout the company.

The paper's new enterprise architecture clustered its servers over a two-mile distance, lighting up a 1 Gbps dark-fiber link—an optical fiber that is in place but not yet being used—between two data centers. This architecture lets the newspaper spread the processing load between the servers while improving redundancy and options for disaster recovery.

The transfer to the new architecture was not smooth. A small piece of software written for the transition contained a coding error that caused the *Tribune*'s editorial applications to experience intermittent processing failures. As a result, the paper was forced to delay delivery to about 40 percent of its 680,000 readers and cut 24 pages from a Monday edition, costing the newspaper nearly $1 million in advertising revenue.

After editorial applications were stabilized, the *Tribune* proceeded to migrate applications for operations—the physical production and printing of the newspaper—and circulation to the new enterprise architecture. "As we gradually took applications off the mainframe, we realized that we were incurring very high costs in maintaining underutilized mainframes at two different locations," says Darko Dejanovic, vice president and CTO of the Tribune Co., which owned the *Chicago Tribune,* the *Los Angeles Times,* Long Island's *Newsday,* and about a dozen other metropolitan newspapers. "By moving from two locations to one, we've achieved several million dollars in cost savings. There's no question that server consolidation was the right move for us."

The company is excited about its new enterprise architecture and is looking to consolidate software across its newspapers. Currently, each newspaper maintains its own applications for classified advertising and billing, which means the parent company must support about 10 billing packages and the same number of classified-ad programs. Most of the business processes can be standardized. So far, the company has standardized about 95 percent of classified-ad processes and about 90 percent of advertising-sales processes. Over three years, the company will replace the disparate billing and ad applications with a single package that will be used by all business units. The different newspapers will not necessarily share the same data, but they will have the same processes and the same systems for accessing them. Over time, that will allow some of the call centers to handle calls for multiple newspapers; East Coast centers will handle the early-morning calls and West Coast centers the late-day and evening calls.

The company is looking at a few additional projects including the implementation of hardware that will allow its individual applications to run on partial CPUs, freeing up processor power and making more efficient use of disk space.

Questions

1. Review the five characteristics of infrastructure architecture and rank them in order of their potential impact on the Tribune Co.'s business.
2. What is the disaster recovery cost curve? Where should the Tribune Co. operate on the curve?
3. Define backups and recovery. What are the risks to the Tribune Co.'s business if it fails to implement an adequate backup plan?
4. Why is a scalable and highly available enterprise architecture critical to current operations and future growth?
5. Identify the need for information security at the Tribune Co.
6. How could the Tribune Co. use a classified ad web service across its different businesses?

✱ CLOSING CASE TWO

Fear the Penguin

Linux has proved itself the most revolutionary software of the past decade. Spending on Linux was reported to reach $280 million by 2006. Linus Torvalds, who wrote the kernel (the core) of the Linux operating system at age 21, posted the operating system on the Internet and invited other programmers to improve his code and users to download his operating system for free. Since then, tens of thousands of people have, making Linux perhaps the single largest collaborative project in the planet's history.

Today, Linux, if not its penguin mascot, is everywhere. You can find Linux inside a boggling array of computers, machines, and devices. Linux is robust enough to run the world's most powerful supercomputers, yet sleek and versatile enough to run inside consumer items like TiVo, cell phones, and handheld portable devices. Even more impressive than Linux's increasing prevalence in living rooms and pockets is its growth in the market for corporate computers.

Since its introduction in 1991, no other operating system in history has spread as quickly across such a broad range of systems as Linux, and it has finally achieved critical mass. According to studies by market research firm IDC, Linux is the fastest-growing server operating system, with shipments expected to grow by 34 percent per year over the next four years. With its innovative open source approach, strong security, reliability, and scalability, Linux can help companies achieve the agility they need to respond to changing consumer needs and stay ahead of the game.

Thanks to its unique open source development process, Linux is reliable and secure. A "meritocracy," a team specifically selected for their competence by the technical developer community, governs the entire development process. Each line of code that makes up the Linux kernel is extensively tested and maintained for a variety of different platforms and application scenarios.

This open collaborative approach means the Linux code base continually hardens and improves itself. If vulnerabilities appear, they get the immediate attention of experts from around the world, who quickly resolve the problems. According to Security Portal, which tracks vendor response times, it takes an average of 12 days to patch a Linux bug compared to an average of three months for some proprietary platforms. With the core resilience and reliability of Linux, businesses can minimize downtime, which directly increases their bottom line.

The Spread of Open Systems

Businesses and governments are opting for open source operating systems like Linux instead of Windows. One attendee at the Linux Desktop Consortium in 2004 was Dr. Martin Echt, a cardiologist from Albany, New York. Dr. Echt, chief operating officer of Capital Cardiology Associates, an eight-office practice, discussed his decision to shift his business from Microsoft's Windows to Linux. Dr. Echt is not your typical computer geek or Linux supporter, and he is not the only one switching to Linux.

The State Council in China has mandated that all ministries install the local flavor of Linux, dubbed Red Flag, on their PCs. In Spain, the government has installed a Linux operating system that incorporates the regional dialect. The city of Munich, despite a personal visit from Microsoft CEO Steve Ballmer, is converting its 14,000 PCs from Windows to Linux.

"It's open season for open source," declared Walter Raizner, general manager of IBM Germany. One of the biggest corporate backers of Linux, IBM has more than 75 government customers worldwide, including agencies in France, Spain, Britain, Australia, Mexico, the United States, and Japan.

The move toward Linux varies for each country or company. For Dr. Echt, it was a question of lower price and long-term flexibility. In China, the government claimed national security as a reason to move to open source code because it permitted engineers to make sure there were no security leaks and no spyware installed on its computers. In Munich, the move was largely political. Regardless of the reason, the market is shifting toward Linux.

Microsoft versus Linux

Bill Gates has openly stated that Linux is not a threat to Microsoft. According to IDC analysts, Microsoft's operating systems ship with 93.8 percent of all desktops worldwide. Ted Schadler, IDC research principal analyst, states that despite the push of lower cost Linux players into the market, Microsoft will maintain its desktop market share for the following three reasons:

1. Linux adds features to its applications that most computer users have already come to expect.
2. Linux applications might not be compatible with Microsoft applications such as Microsoft Word or Microsoft Excel.

3. Microsoft continues to innovate, and the latest version of Office is beginning to integrate word processing and spreadsheet software to corporate databases and other applications.

The Future of Linux

IDC analyst Al Gillen predicts that an open source operating system will not enjoy explosive growth on the desktop for at least six or eight years. Still, even Gillen cannot deny that Linux's penetration continues to rise, with an estimated 18 million users. Linux's market share increased from 1.5 percent at the end of 2000 to 4.2 percent at the beginning of 2004. According to IDC, by the end of 2005 it surpassed Apple's Mac OS, which has 2.9 percent of the market, as the second most popular operating system. Gartner Dataquest estimates Linux's server market share will grow seven times faster than Windows.

Questions

1. How does Linux differ from traditional software?
2. Should Microsoft consider Linux a threat? Why or why not?
3. How is open source software a potential trend shaping organizations?
4. How can you use Linux as an emerging technology to gain a competitive advantage?
5. Research the Internet and discover potential ways that open source software might revolutionize business in the future.

 MAKING BUSINESS DECISIONS

1. Planning for Disaster Recovery

You are the new senior analyst in the IT department at Beltz, a large snack food manufacturing company. The company is located on the beautiful shoreline in Charleston, North Carolina. The company's location is one of its best and also worst features. The weather and surroundings are beautiful, but the threat of hurricanes and other natural disasters is high. Compile a disaster recovery plan that will minimize any risks involved with a natural disaster.

2. Comparing Backup and Recovery Systems

Research the Internet to find three different vendors of backup and recovery systems. Compare and contrast the three systems and determine which one you would recommend if you were installing a backup and recovery system for a medium-sized business with 3,500 employees that maintains information on the stock market. Compile your findings in a presentation that you can give to your class that details the three systems' strengths and weaknesses, along with your recommendation.

3. Ranking the -ilities

In a group, review the MIS infrastructure characteristics and rank them in order of their impact on an organization's success. Use a rating system of 1 to 7, where 1 indicates the biggest impact and 7 indicates the least impact.

4. Designing an Enterprise Architecture

Components of a solid enterprise architecture include everything from documentation to business concepts to software and hardware. Deciding which components to implement and how to implement them can be a challenge. New IT components are released daily, and business needs continually change. An enterprise architecture that meets your organization's needs today may not meet those needs tomorrow. Building an enterprise architecture that is scalable, flexible, available, accessible, and reliable is key to your organization's success.

You are the enterprise architect (EA) for a large clothing company called Xedous. You are responsible for developing the initial enterprise architecture. Create a list of questions you will need answered to develop your architecture. Below is an example of a few of the questions you might ask.

- What are the company's growth expectations?
- Will systems be able to handle additional users?
- How long will information be stored in the systems?
- How much customer history must be stored?
- What are the organization's business hours?
- What are the organization's backup requirements?

Networks and Telecommunications

LO 1. Compare LANs, WANs, and MANs.

Introduction

Change is everywhere in the information technology domain, but nowhere is change more evident and more dramatic than the realm of networks and telecommunications. Most management information systems today rely on digital networks to communicate information in the form of data, graphics, video, and voice. Companies large and small from all over the world are using networks and the Internet to locate suppliers and buyers, to negotiate contracts with them, and to provide bigger, better, and faster services than ever before. **Telecommunication systems** enable the transmission of data over public or private networks. A **network** is a communications system created by linking two or more devices and establishing a standard methodology by which they can communicate. The world's largest and most widely used network is the Internet. The Internet is a global "network of networks" that uses universal standards to connect millions of different networks around the world. Telecommunication systems and networks are traditionally complicated and historically inefficient. However, businesses can benefit from today's network infrastructures that provide reliable global reach to employees and customers.

Network Basics

Networks range from small two-computer networks to the biggest network of all, the Internet. A network provides two principle benefits: the ability to communicate and the ability to share.

Today's corporate digital networks include a combination of local area networks, wide area networks, and metropolitan area networks. A **local area network (LAN)** is designed to connect a group of computers in proximity to each other such as in an office building, a school, or a home. A LAN is useful for sharing resources such as files, printers, games, or other applications. A LAN in turn often connects to other LANs, and to the Internet or wide area networks. A *wide area network (WAN)* spans a large geographic area, such as a state, province, or country. WANs often connect multiple smaller networks, such as local area networks or metropolitan area networks. The world's most popular WAN is the Internet. A *metropolitan area network (MAN)* is a large computer network usually spanning a city. Figure B5.1 highlights the three different types of networks, and Figure B5.2 illustrates each network type.

Direct data communication links between a company and its suppliers or customers, or both, have been successfully used to give the company a strategic advantage. The SABRE airline reservation system is a classic example of a strategic management information system that depends upon communication provided through a network. SABRE Airline Solutions pioneered technological advances for the industry in areas such as revenue management, pricing, flight scheduling, cargo, flight operations, and crew scheduling. In addition, not only did SABRE help invent ecommerce for the travel industry, the company holds claim to progressive solutions that defined—and continue to revolutionize—the travel and transportation marketplace.

A network typically includes four things (besides the computers themselves):

1. **Protocol**—a set of communication rules to make sure that everyone speaks the same language.

2. **Network interface card (NIC)**—card that plugs into the back (or side) of your computers and lets them send and receive messages from other computers.

3. **Cable**—the medium to connect all of the computers.

4. **Hub (switch or router)**—hardware to perform traffic control.

We will continue to define many of these terms and concepts in the sections that follow.
Networks are differentiated by the following:

- Architecture—peer-to-peer, client/server.

- Topology—bus, star, ring, hybrid, wireless.

- Protocols—Ethernet, transmission control protocol/Internet protocol (TCP/IP).

- Media—coaxial, twisted-pair, fiber-optic.

Architecture

The two primary types of network architectures are peer-to-peer networks and client/server networks.

LO 2. **Compare the two types of network architectures.**

FIGURE B5.1

Network Types

Network Types	
Local area network (LAN)	Designed to connect a group of computers in proximity to each other such as in an office building, a school, or such as a home. A LAN is useful for sharing resources such as files, printers, games, or other applications. A LAN in turn often connects to other LANs, and to the Internet or wide area networks.
Wide area network (WAN)	Spans a large geographic area, such as a state, province, or country. WANs often connect multiple smaller networks, such as local area networks (LANs) or metropolitan area networks (MANs).
Metropolitan area network (MAN)	A large computer network usually spanning a city. Most colleges, universities, and large companies that span a campus use an infrastructure supported by a MAN.

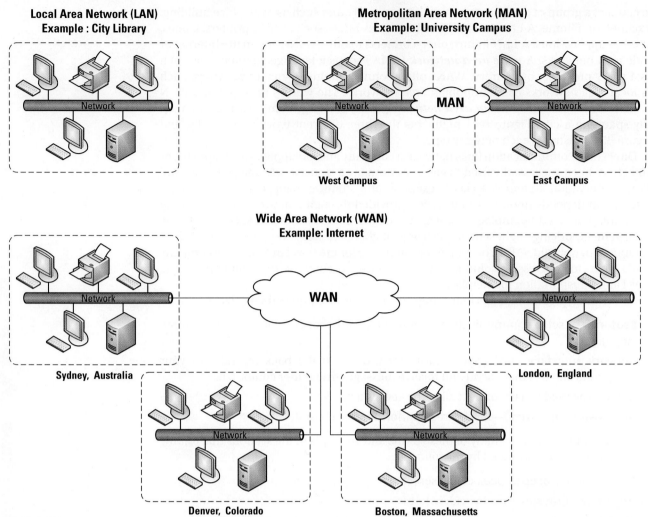

FIGURE B5.2

LAN, WAN, and MAN

PEER-TO-PEER NETWORKS

A ***peer-to-peer (P2P) network*** is a computer network that relies on the computing power and bandwidth of the participants in the network rather than a centralized server, as illustrated in Figure B5.3. Each networked computer can allow other computers to access its files and use connected printers while it is in use as a workstation without the aid of a server.

FIGURE B5.3

Peer-to-Peer Networks

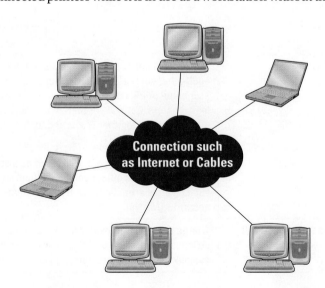

While Napster may be the most widely known example of a P2P implementation, it may also be one of the most narrowly focused since the Napster model takes advantage of only one of the many capabilities of P2P computing: file sharing. The technology has far broader capabilities, including the sharing of processing, memory, and storage, and the supporting of collaboration among vast numbers of distributed computers such as grid computing. Peer-to-peer computing enables immediate interaction among people and computer systems.[1]

CLIENT/SERVER NETWORKS

A *client* is a computer designed to request information from a server. A *server* is a computer dedicated to providing information in response to requests. A *client/server network* is a model for applications in which the bulk of the back-end processing, such as performing a physical search of a database, takes place on a server, while the front-end processing, which involves communicating with the users, is handled by the clients (see Figure B5.4). A *network operating system (NOS)* is the operating system that runs a network, steering information between computers and managing security and users. The client/server model has become one of the central ideas of network computing. Most business applications written today use the client/server model.

A fundamental part of client/server architecture is packet-switching. *Packet-switching* occurs when the sending computer divides a message into a number of efficiently sized units of data called packets, each of which contains the address of the destination computer. Each packet is sent on the network and intercepted by routers. A *router* is an intelligent connecting device that examines each packet of data it receives and then decides which way to send it onward toward its destination. The packets arrive at their intended destination, although some may have actually traveled by different physical paths, and the receiving computer assembles the packets and delivers the message to the appropriate application.

Topology

LO 3. Explain topology and the different types found in networks.

Networks are assembled according to certain rules. Cables, for example, have to be a certain length; each cable strand can support only a certain amount of network traffic. A *network topology* refers to the geometric arrangement of the actual physical organization of the computers (and other network devices) in a network. Topologies vary depending on cost and functionality. Figure B5.5 highlights the five common topologies used in networks, and Figure B5.6 displays each topology.

Protocols

LO 4. Describe protocols and the importance of TCP/IP.

A *protocol* is a standard that specifies the format of data as well as the rules to be followed during transmission. Simply put, for one computer (or computer program) to talk to another computer (or computer program) they must both be talking the same language, and this language is called a protocol.

FIGURE B5.4

Client/Server Network

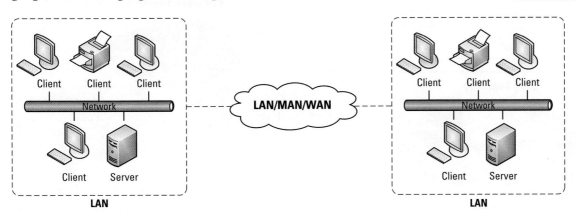

Network Topologies	
Bus	All devices are connected to a central cable, called the bus or backbone. Bus networks are relatively inexpensive and easy to install for small networks.
Star	All devices are connected to a central device, called a hub. Star networks are relatively easy to install and manage, but bottlenecks can occur because all data must pass through the hub.
Ring	All devices are connected to one another in the shape of a closed loop, so that each device is connected directly to two other devices, one on either side of it. Ring topologies are relatively expensive and difficult to install, but they offer high bandwidth and can span large distances.
Hybrid	Groups of star-configured workstations are connected to a linear bus backbone cable, combining the characteristics of the bus and star topologies.
Wireless	Devices are connected by signals between access points and wireless transmitters within a limited range.

A protocol is based on an agreed-upon and established standard, and this way all manufacturers of hardware and software that are using the protocol do so in a similar fashion to allow for interoperability. **Interoperability** is the capability of two or more computer systems to share data and resources, even though they are made by different manufacturers. The most popular network protocols used are Ethernet and transmission control protocol/Internet protocol (TCP/IP).

ETHERNET

Ethernet is a physical and data layer technology for LAN networking (see Figure B5.7). Ethernet is the most widely installed LAN access method, originally developed by Xerox

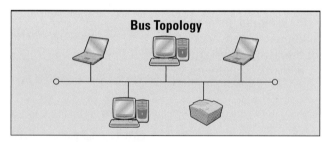

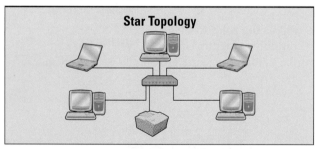

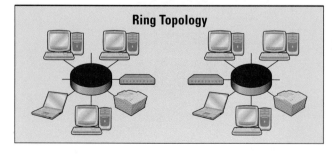

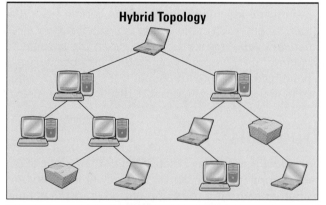

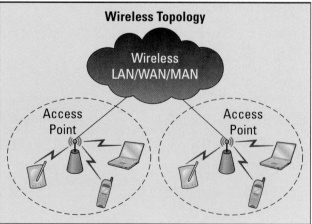

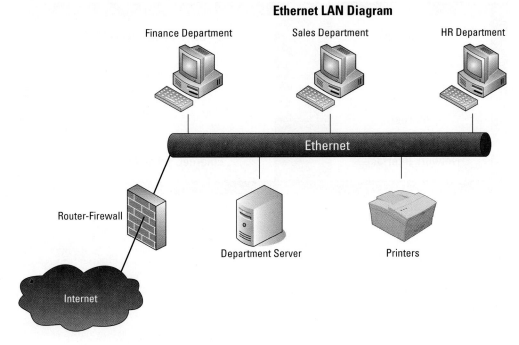

Ethernet LAN Diagram

Finance Department   Sales Department   HR Department

Ethernet

Router-Firewall

Department Server   Printers

Internet

and then developed further by Xerox, Digital Equipment Corporation, and Intel. When it first began to be widely deployed in the 1980s, Ethernet supported a maximum theoretical data transfer rate of 10 megabits per second (Mbps). More recently, Fast Ethernet has extended traditional Ethernet technology to 100 Mbps peak, and Gigabit Ethernet technology extends performance up to 1,000 Mbps.

Ethernet is one of the most popular LAN technologies for the following reasons:

- Is easy to implement, manage, and maintain.
- Allows low-cost network implementations.
- Provides extensive flexibility for network installation.
- Guarantees interoperability of standards-compliant products, regardless of manufacturer.[2]

TRANSMISSION CONTROL PROTOCOL/ INTERNET PROTOCOL

The most common telecommunication protocol is transmission control protocol/ Internet protocol (TCP/IP), which was originally developed by the Department of Defense to connect a system of computer networks that became known as the Internet. *Transmission control protocol/Internet protocol (TCP/IP)* provides the technical foundation for the public Internet as well as for large numbers of private networks. The key achievement of TCP/IP is its flexibility with respect to lower-level protocols. TCP/IP uses a special transmission method that maximizes data transfer and automatically adjusts to slower devices and other delays encountered on a network. Although more than 100 protocols make up the entire TCP/IP protocol suite, the two most important of these are TCP and IP. **TCP** provides transport functions, ensuring, among other things, that the amount of data received is the same as the amount transmitted. **IP** provides the addressing and routing mechanism that acts as a postmaster. Figure B5.8 displays TCP/IP's four-layer reference model:

- Application layer—serves as the window for users and application processes to access network services.
- Transport layer—handles end-to-end packet transportation.

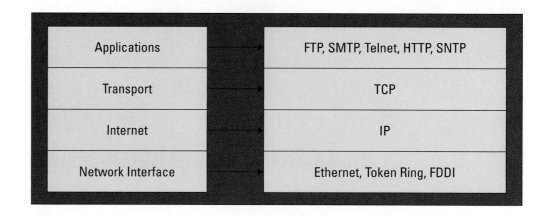

TCP/IP Applications	
File Transfer Protocol (FTP)	Allows files containing text, programs, graphics, numerical data, and so on to be downloaded off or uploaded onto a network.
Simple Mail Transfer Protocol (SMTP)	TCP/IP's own messaging system for email.
Telnet Protocol	Provides terminal emulation that allows a personal computer or workstation to act as a terminal, or access device, for a server.
Hypertext Transfer Protocol (HTTP)	Allows web browsers and servers to send and receive web pages.
Simple Network Management Protocol (SNMP)	Allows the management of networked nodes to be managed from a single point.

OSI Model
7. Application
6. Presentation
5. Session
4. Transport
3. Network
2. Data Link
1. Physical

- Internet layer—formats the data into packets, adds a header containing the packet sequence and the address of the receiving device, and specifies the services required from the network.

- Network interface layer—places data packets on the network for transmission.[3]

For a computer to communicate with other computers and web servers on the Internet, it must have a unique numeric IP address. IP provides the addressing and routing mechanism that acts as a postmaster. An IP address is a unique 32-bit number that identifies the location of a computer on a network. It works like a street address—as a way to find out exactly where to deliver information.

When IP addressing first came out, everyone thought that there were plenty of addresses to cover any need. Theoretically, you could have 4,294,967,296 unique addresses. The actual number of available addresses is smaller (somewhere between 3.2 and 3.3 billion) due to the way that the addresses are separated into classes, and some addresses are set aside for multicasting, testing, or other special uses.[4]

With the explosion of the Internet and the increase in home networks and business networks, the number of available IP addresses is simply not enough. The obvious solution is to redesign the address format to allow for more possible addresses. *Internet protocol version 6 (IPv6)* is the "next generation" protocol designed to replace the current version Internet protocol, IP version 4 (IPv4). However, IPv6 will take several years to implement because it requires modification of the entire infrastructure of the Internet. The main change brought by IPv6 is a much larger address space that allows greater flexibility in assigning addresses. IPv6 uses a 128-bit addressing scheme that produces 3.4×10^{38} addresses.[5]

The TCP/IP suite of applications includes five protocols—file transfer, simple mail transfer, telnet, hypertext transfer, and simple network management (see Figures B5.9 and B5.10).[6]

Media

Network transmission media refers to the various types of media used to carry the signal between computers. When information is sent across the network, it is converted into electrical signals. These signals are generated as electromagnetic waves (analog signaling) or as a sequence of voltage pulses (digital signaling). To be sent from one location to another, a signal must travel along a physical path. The physical path that is used to carry a signal between a signal transmitter and a signal receiver is called the transmission media. The two types of transmission media are wire (guided) and wireless (unguided).

WIRE MEDIA

Wire media are transmission material manufactured so that signals will be confined to a narrow path and will behave predictably. The three most commonly used types of guided media are (see Figure B5.11):

- Twisted-pair cable
- Coaxial cable
- Fiber-optic cable

Twisted-Pair Cable

Twisted-pair cable refers to a type of cable composed of four (or more) copper wires twisted around each other within a plastic sheath. The wires are twisted to reduce outside electrical interference. Twisted-pair cables come in shielded and unshielded varieties. Shielded cables have a metal shield encasing the wires that acts as a ground for electromagnetic interference. Unshielded twisted-pair (UTP) is the most popular and is generally the best option for LAN networks. The quality of UTP may vary from telephone-grade wire to high-speed cable. The cable has four pairs of wires inside the jacket. Each pair is twisted with a different number of twists per inch to help eliminate interference from adjacent pairs and other electrical devices. The connectors (called RF-45) on twisted-pair cables resemble large telephone connectors.[7]

Coaxial Cable

Coaxial cable is cable that can carry a wide range of frequencies with low signal loss. It consists of a metallic shield with a single wire placed along the center of a shield and isolated from the shield by an insulator. Coaxial cable is similar to that used for cable television. This type of cable is referred to as coaxial because it contains one copper wire (or physical data channel) that carries the signal and is surrounded by another concentric

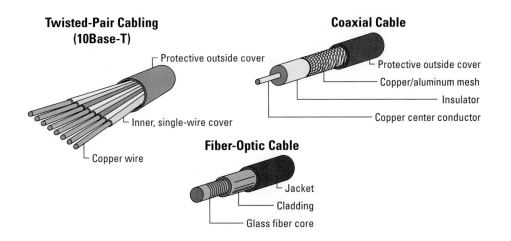

Twisted-Pair Cabling (10Base-T)
- Protective outside cover
- Inner, single-wire cover
- Copper wire

Coaxial Cable
- Protective outside cover
- Copper/aluminum mesh
- Insulator
- Copper center conductor

Fiber-Optic Cable
- Jacket
- Cladding
- Glass fiber core

FIGURE B5.11

Twisted-Pair, Coaxial Cable, and Fiber-Optic

physical channel consisting of a wire mesh. The outer channel serves as a ground for electrical interference. Because of this grounding feature, several coaxial cables can be placed within a single conduit or sheath without significant loss of data integrity.[8]

Fiber-Optic Cable

Fiber optic (or *optical fiber*) refers to the technology associated with the transmission of information as light impulses along a glass wire or fiber. Fiber-optic cable is the same type used by most telephone companies for long-distance service. Fiber-optic cable can transmit data over long distances with little loss in data integrity. In addition, because data are transferred as a pulse of light, fiber optical is not subject to interference. The light pulses travel through a glass wire or fiber encased in an insulating sheath.[9]

Fiber optic's increased maximum effective distance comes at a price. Optical fiber is more fragile than wire, difficult to split, and labor intensive to install. For these reasons, fiber optics is used primarily to transmit data over extended distances where the hardware required to relay the data signal on less expensive media would exceed the cost of fiber-optic installation. It is also used where large amounts of data need to be transmitted on a regular basis.

WIRELESS MEDIA

Wireless media are natural parts of the Earth's environment that can be used as physical paths to carry electrical signals. The atmosphere and outer space are examples of wireless media that are commonly used to carry these signals. Today, technologies for wireless data transmission include microwave transmission, communication satellites, (see Figure B5.12) mobile phones, personal digital assistants (PDAs), personal computers (e.g., laptops), and mobile data networks.

Network signals are transmitted through all media as a type of waveform. When transmitted through wire and cable, the signal is an electrical waveform. When transmitted through fiber-optic cable, the signal is a light wave, either visible or infrared light. When transmitted through the Earth's atmosphere, the signal can take the form of waves in the radio spectrum, including microwaves, infrared, or visible light.

FIGURE B5.12

Communication Satellite Example

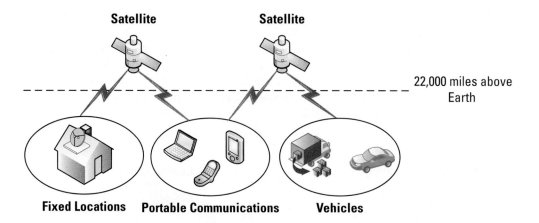

Networks come in all sizes, from two computers connected to share a printer, to the Internet, which is the largest network of all, joining millions of computers of all types all over the world. In between are business networks, which vary in size from a dozen or fewer computers to many thousands. There are three primary types of networks: local area network (LAN), wide area network (WAN), and metropolitan area network (MAN). The following differentiate networks:

- Architecture—peer-to-peer, client/server.
- Topology—bus, star, ring, hybrid, wireless.
- Protocols—Ethernet, Transmission Control Protocol/Internet Protocol (TCP/IP).
- Media—coaxial, twisted-pair, fiber-optic.

Client, 399
Client/server network, 399
Coaxial cable, 403
Ethernet, 400
Fiber optic (or optical fiber), 404
Internet protocol version 6 (IPv6), 402
Interoperability, 400
Local area network (LAN), 396
Metropolitan area network (MAN), 397

Network, 396
Network operating system (NOS), 399
Network topology, 399
Network transmission media, 403
Packet-switching, 399
Peer-to-peer (P2P) network, 398
Protocol, 399
Router, 399

Server, 399
Telecommunication system, 396
Transmission control protocol/Internet protocol (TCP/IP), 401
Twisted-pair cable, 403
Wide area network (WAN), 397
Wire media, 403
Wireless media, 404

Watching Where You Step—Prada

Prada estimates its sales per year at $22 million. The luxury retailer recently spent millions on IT for its futuristic "epicenter" store—but the flashy technology turned into a high-priced hassle. The company needed to generate annual sales of $75 million by 2007 to turn a profit on its new high-tech investment.

When Prada opened its $40 million Manhattan flagship, hotshot architect Rem Koolhaas promised a radically new shopping experience. And he kept the promise—though not quite according to plan. Customers were soon enduring hordes of tourists, neglected technology, and the occasional thrill of getting stuck in experimental dressing rooms. A few of the problems associated with the store:

1. **Fickle fitting rooms**—Doors that turn from clear to opaque confuse shoppers and frequently fail to open on cue.
2. **Failed RFID**—Touch screens meant to spring to life when items are placed in the RFID "closets" are often just blank.
3. **Pointless PDAs**—Salesclerks let the handheld devices gather dust and instead check the stockroom for inventory.
4. **Neglected network**—A lag between sales and inventory systems makes the wireless network nearly irrelevant.

This was not exactly the vision for the high-end boutique when it debuted in December 2001. Instead, the 22,000-square-foot SoHo shop was to be the first of four "epicenter" stores around the world that would combine cutting-edge architecture and 21st century technology to revolutionize the luxury shopping experience. Prada poured roughly 25 percent of the store's budget into IT, including a wireless network to link every item to an Oracle inventory database in real-time using radio frequency identification (RFID) tags on the clothes. The staff would roam the floor armed with PDAs to check whether items were in stock, and customers could do the same through touch screens in the dressing rooms.

But most of the flashy technology today sits idle, abandoned by employees who never quite embraced computing chic and are now too overwhelmed by large crowds to assist shoppers with handhelds. On top of that, many gadgets, such as automated dressing-room doors and touch screens, are either malfunctioning or ignored. Packed with experimental technology, the clear-glass dressing-room doors were designed to open and close automatically at the tap of a foot pedal, then turn opaque when a second pedal sent an electric current through the glass. Inside, an RFID-aware rack would recognize a customer's selections and display them on a touch screen linked to the inventory system.

In practice, the process was hardly that smooth. Many shoppers never quite understood the pedals and disrobed in full view, thinking the door had turned opaque. That is no longer a problem, since staff members usually leave the glass opaque, but often the doors get stuck. Some of the chambers are open only to VIP customers during peak traffic times.

With the smart closets and handhelds out of commission, the wireless network in the store is nearly irrelevant, despite its considerable expense. As Prada's debt reportedly climbed to around $1 billion in late 2001, the company shelved plans for the fourth epicenter store, in San Francisco. A second store opened in Tokyo to great acclaim, albeit with different architects in a different market. Though that store incorporates similar cutting-edge concepts, architect Jacques Herzog emphasized that avant-garde retail plays well only in Japan. "This building is clearly a building for Tokyo," he told *The New York Times.* "It couldn't be somewhere else."

The multimillion-dollar technology is starting to look more like technology for technology's sake than an enhancement of the shopping experience, and the store's failings have prompted Prada to reevaluate its epicenter strategy.

Questions

1. Explain how Prada was anticipating using its wireless network to help its stores operate more efficiently. What prevented the system from working correctly?

2. What could Prada have done to help its employees embrace the wireless network?

3. Would Prada have experienced the same issues if it had used a wire (guided) network instead of a wireless (unguided) network?

4. What security issues would Prada need to be aware of concerning its wireless network?

5. What should Prada do differently when designing its fourth store to ensure its success?

 CLOSING CASE TWO

Banks Banking on Network Security

Bank of America, Commerce Bancorp, PNC Financial Services Group, and Wachovia were victims of a crime involving a person trying to obtain customer data and sell it to law firms and debt-collection agencies. New Jersey police seized 13 computers from the alleged mastermind with 670,000 account numbers and balances. There is no indication the data were used for identity theft, but it highlights how increasingly difficult it is to protect information against such schemes as the market value of personal information grows. In the past, banks were wary of the cost or customer backlash from adopting network security technologies. Today, banks are beefing up network security as more customers begin to view security as a key factor when choosing a bank.

Bank of America

Bank of America is moving toward a stronger authentication process for its 13 million online customers. Bank of America's new SiteKey service is designed to thwart scams in which customers think they are entering data on the bank's website, when they are actually on a thief's site built to steal data. This occurs when a worm tells a computer to reroute the bank's URL into a browser to another site that looks exactly like the bank's.

SiteKey offers two-factor authentication. When enrolling in SiteKey, a customer picks an image from a library and writes a brief phrase. Each time the customer signs on, the image and phrase are displayed, indicating that the bank recognizes the computer the customer is using and letting the customer know that he or she is at the bank's official website. The customer then enters a password and proceeds. When signing on from a different computer than usual, the customer must answer one of three prearranged questions.

Wells Fargo & Company

"Out-of-wallet" questions contain information that is not found on a driver's license or ATM card. Wells Fargo is implementing a security strategy that operates based on "out-of-wallet" questions as a second factor for network password enrollment and maintenance. It is also offering network security hardware such as key fobs that change passwords every 60 seconds. Last fall It launched a two-factor authentication pilot in which small businesses making electronic funds transfers need a key fob to complete transactions.

E*Trade Financial Corporation

E*Trade Financial Corporation provides customers holding account balances of more than $50,000 with a free Digital Security ID for network authentication. The device displays a new six-digit code every 60 seconds, which the customer must use to log on. Accounts under $50,000 can purchase the Digital Security ID device for $25.

Barclays Bank

Barclays Bank instituted online-transfer delays of between several hours and one day. The delays, which apply the first time a transfer is attempted between two accounts, are intended to give the bank time to detect suspicious activity, such as a large number of transfers from multiple accounts into a single account. The online-transfer delay was adopted in response to a wave of phishing incidents in which thieves transferred funds from victims' bank accounts into accounts owned by "mules." Mules are people who open bank accounts based on email solicitations, usually under the guise of a business proposal. From the mule accounts, the thieves withdraw cash, open credit cards, or otherwise loot the account.

Barclays also offers account monitoring of customers' actions to compare them with historical profile data to detect unusual behavior. For instance, the service would alert the bank to contact the customer if the customer normally logs on from England and suddenly logs on from New York and performs 20 transactions.

Questions

1. What reason would a bank have for not wanting to adopt an online-transfer delay policy?
2. Why is network security critical to financial institutions?
3. Explain the differences between the types of network security offered by the banks in the case. Which bank would you open an account with and why?
4. What additional types of network security, not mentioned in the case, would you recommend a bank implement?
5. Identity three policies a bank should implement to help it improve network information security.

1. Secure Access

Organizations that have traditionally maintained private, closed systems have begun to look at the potential of the Internet as a ready-made network resource. The Internet is inexpensive and globally pervasive: Every phone jack is a potential connection. However, the Internet lacks security. What obstacles must organizations overcome to allow secure network connections?

2. Rolling Out with Networks

As organizations begin to realize the benefits of adding a wireless component to their network, they must understand how to leverage this emerging technology. Wireless solutions have come to the forefront for many organizations with the rollout of more standard, cost-effective, and secure wireless protocols. With wireless networks, increased business agility may be realized by continuous data access and synchronization. However, with the increased flexibility comes many challenges. Develop a report detailing the benefits an organization could obtain by implementing wireless technology. Also, include the challenges that a wireless network presents along with recommendations for any solutions.

3. Wireless Fitness

Sandifer's Fitness Club is located in beautiful South Carolina. Rosie Sandifer has owned and operated the club for 20 years. The club has three outdoor pools, two indoor pools, 10 racquetball courts, 10 tennis courts, an indoor and outdoor track, along with a four-story exercise equipment and massage therapy building. Rosie has hired you as a summer intern specializing in information technology. The extent of Rosie's current technology includes a few PCs in the accounting department and two PCs with Internet access for the rest of the staff. Your first assignment is to create a report detailing networks and wireless technologies. The report should explain how the club could gain a business advantage by implementing a wireless network. If Rosie likes your report, she will hire you as the full-time employee in charge of information technology. Be sure to include all of the different uses for wireless devices the club could implement to improve its operations.

4. Network Analysis

Global Manufacturing is considering a new technology application. The company wants to process orders in a central location and then assign production to different plants. Each plant will operate its own production scheduling and control system. Data on work in process and completed assemblies will be transmitted back to the central location that processes orders. At each plant, Global uses personal computers that perform routine tasks such as payroll and accounting. The production scheduling and control systems will be a package program running on a new computer dedicated to this application.

The MIS personnel at Global have retained you as a consultant to help with further analysis. What kind of network configuration seems most appropriate? How much bandwidth is needed? What data should be collected? Prepare a plan showing the information Global must develop to establish this network system. Should Global use a private network or can it accomplish its objectives through the Internet?

5. Telecommunications Options

Research the telecommunications options that currently exist for you to link to the Internet from where you live. Prepare a list of criteria on which to compare the different technologies, such as price (is there tiered pricing depending on speed and amount you can download?), start-up cost (do you need to buy a special modem, or is there an installation fee), maximum data transfer rate, and so on. Compare your responses with several classmates, and then develop a summary of all telecommunications options that you identified, including the criteria and your group comparison based on the criteria.

6. Frying Your Brains?

Radio waves, microwaves, and infrared all belong to the electromagnetic radiation spectrum used. These terms reference ranges of radiation frequencies we use every day in our wireless networking environments. However, the very word *radiation* strikes fear in many people. Cell towers have sprouted from fields all along highways. Tall rooftops harbor many more cell stations in cities. Millions of cell phone users place microwave transmitters/receivers next to their heads each time they make a call. With all this radiation zapping around, should we be concerned? Research the Internet to find out what the World Health Organization (WHO) has had to say about this.

7. Home Network Experience

If you maintain a home computer network (or have set one up in the past), create a document that describes the benefits that the network provides along with the difficulties that you have experienced. Include in your document a network topology, a detailed description of the type of network you have and the equipment you use. If you have no experience with home networking, interview someone who does, and write up his or her comments. Compare this with several classmates, and discuss the benefits and challenges.

Information Security

1. Describe the relationships and differences between hackers and viruses.
2. Describe the relationship between information security policies and an information security plan.
3. Provide an example of each of the three primary information security areas: (1) authentication and authorization, (2) prevention and resistance, and (3) detection and response.

LO 1. Describe the relationships and differences between hackers and viruses.

Security Threats Caused by Hackers and Viruses

Hackers are experts in technology who use their knowledge to break into computers and computer networks, either for profit or just motivated by the challenge. Smoking is not just bad for a person's health; it seems it is also bad for company security as hackers regularly use smoking entrances to gain building access. Once inside they pose as employees from the MIS department and either ask for permission to use an employee's computer to access the corporate network, or find a conference room where they simply plug-in their own laptop. *Drive-by hacking* is a computer attack where an attacker accesses a wireless computer network, intercepts data, uses network services, and/or sends attack instructions without entering the office or organization that owns the network. Figure B6.1 lists the various types of hackers for organizations to be aware of, and Figure B6.2 shows how a virus is spread.

FIGURE B6.1

Types of Hackers

Common Types of Hackers
▨ **Black-hat hackers** break into other people's computer systems and may just look around or may steal and destroy information.
▨ **Crackers** have criminal intent when hacking.
▨ **Cyberterrorists** seek to cause harm to people or to destroy critical systems or information and use the Internet as a weapon of mass destruction.
▨ **Hactivists** have philosophical and political reasons for breaking into systems and will often deface the website as a protest.
▨ **Script kiddies** or **script bunnies** find hacking code on the Internet and click-and-point their way into systems to cause damage or spread viruses.
▨ **White-hat hackers** work at the request of the system owners to find system vulnerabilities and plug the holes.

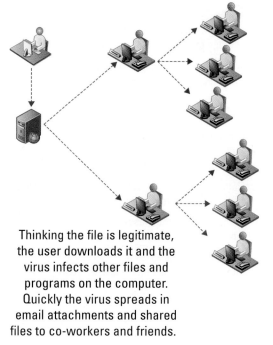

A hacker creates a virus and attaches it to a program, document, or website.

Thinking the file is legitimate, the user downloads it and the virus infects other files and programs on the computer. Quickly the virus spreads in email attachments and shared files to co-workers and friends.

One of the most common forms of computer vulnerabilities is a virus. A *virus* is software written with malicious intent to cause annoyance or damage. Some hackers create and leave viruses causing massive computer damage. Figure B6.3 provides an overview of the most common types of viruses. Two additional computer vulnerabilities include adware and spyware. *Adware* is software that, while purporting to serve some useful function and often fulfilling that function, also allows Internet advertisers to display advertisements without the consent of the computer user. *Spyware* is a special class of adware that collects data about the user and transmits it over the Internet without the user's knowledge or permission. Spyware programs collect specific data about the user, ranging from general demographics such as name, address, and browsing habits to credit card numbers, Social Security numbers, and user names and passwords. Not all adware programs are spyware and used correctly it can generate revenue for a company allowing users to receive free products. Spyware is a clear threat to privacy. Figure B6.4 displays a few additional weapons hackers use for launching attacks.[1]

Organizational information is intellectual capital. Just as organizations protect their tangible assets—keeping their money in an insured bank or providing a safe working

FIGURE B6.3

Common Forms of Viruses

Backdoor programs open a way into the network for future attacks.
Denial-of-service attack (DoS) floods a website with so many requests for service that it slows down or crashes the site.
Distributed denial-of-service attack (DDoS) attacks from multiple computers that flood a website with so many requests for service that it slows down or crashes. A common type is the Ping of Death, in which thousands of computers try to access a website at the same time, overloading it and shutting it down.
Polymorphic viruses and worms change their form as they propagate.
Trojan-horse virus hides inside other software, usually as an attachment or a downloadable file.
Worm spreads itself, not only from file to file, but also from computer to computer. The primary difference between a virus and a worm is that a virus must attach to something, such as an executable file, to spread. Worms do not need to attach to anything to spread and can tunnel themselves into computers.

Elevation of privilege is a process by which a user misleads a system into granting unauthorized rights, usually for the purpose of compromising or destroying the system. For example, an attacker might log onto a network by using a guest account and then exploit a weakness in the software that lets the attacker change the guest privileges to administrative privileges.

Hoaxes attack computer systems by transmitting a virus hoax, with a real virus attached. By masking the attack in a seemingly legitimate message, unsuspecting users more readily distribute the message and send the attack on to their co-workers and friends, infecting many users along the way.

Malicious code includes a variety of threats such as viruses, worms, and Trojan horses.

Packet tampering consists of altering the contents of packets as they travel over the Internet or altering data on computer disks after penetrating a network. For example, an attacker might place a tap on a network line to intercept packets as they leave the computer. The attacker could eavesdrop or alter the information as it leaves the network.

A **sniffer** is a program or device that can monitor data traveling over a network. Sniffers can show all the data being transmitted over a network, including passwords and sensitive information. Sniffers tend to be a favorite weapon in the hacker's arsenal.

Spoofing is the forging of the return address on an email so that the message appears to come from someone other than the actual sender. This is not a virus but rather a way by which virus authors conceal their identities as they send out viruses.

Splogs (spam blogs) are fake blogs created solely to raise the search engine rank of affiliated websites. Even blogs that are legitimate are plagued by spam, with spammers taking advantage of the Comment feature by posting comments with links to spam sites.

Spyware is software that comes hidden in free downloadable software and tracks online movements, mines the information stored on a computer, or uses a computer's CPU and storage for some task the user knows nothing about.

FIGURE B6.4

Hacker Weapons

LO 2. Describe the relationship between information security policies and an information security plan.

environment for employees—they must also protect their intellectual capital, everything from patents to transactional and analytical information. With security breaches and viruses on the rise and computer hackers everywhere, an organization must put in place strong security measures to survive.

The First Line of Defense—People

Organizations today are able to mine valuable information such as the identity of the top 20 percent of their customers, who usually produce 80 percent of revenues. Most organizations view this type of information as intellectual capital and implement security measures to prevent it from walking out the door or falling into the wrong hands. At the same time, they must enable employees, customers, and partners to access needed information electronically. Organizations address security risks through two lines of defense; the first is people, the second technology.

Surprisingly, the biggest problem is people as the majority of information security breaches result from people misusing organizational information. **Insiders** are legitimate users who purposely or accidentally misuse their access to the environment and cause some kind of business-affecting incident. For example, many individuals freely give up their passwords or write them on sticky notes next to their computers, leaving the door wide open for hackers. Through **social engineering,** hackers use their social skills to trick people into revealing access credentials or other valuable information. **Dumpster diving,** or looking through people's trash, is another way hackers obtain information.

Information security policies identify the rules required to maintain information security, such as requiring users to log off before leaving for lunch or meetings, never sharing passwords with anyone, and changing passwords every 30 days. An **information security plan** details how an organization will implement the information security policies. The best way a company can safeguard itself from people is by implementing and communicating its information security plan. This becomes even more important with Web 2.0 and as the use of mobile devices, remote workforce, and contractors are growing. A few details managers should consider surrounding people and information security policies include defining the best practices for[2]

- Applications allowed to be placed on the corporate network, especially various file sharing applications (Kazaz), IM software, and entertainment or freeware created by unknown sources (iPhone applications).

- Corporate computer equipment used for personal reason on personal networks.
- Password creation and maintenance including minimum password length, characters to be included while choosing passwords, and frequency for password changes.
- Personal computer equipment allowed to connect to the corporate network.
- Virus protection including how often the system should be scanned and how frequently the software should be updated. This could also include if downloading attachments is allowed and practices for safe downloading from trusted and untrustworthy sources.

The Second Line of Defense—Technology

LO 3. Provide an example of each of the three primary information security areas: (1) authentication and authorization, (2) prevention and resistance, and (3) detection and response.

Once an organization has protected its intellectual capital by arming its people with a detailed information security plan, it can begin to focus on deploying technology to help combat attackers. **Destructive agents** are malicious agents designed by spammers and other Internet attackers to farm email addresses off websites or deposit spyware on machines. Figure B6.5 displays the three areas where technology can aid in the defense against attacks.

PEOPLE: AUTHENTICATION AND AUTHORIZATION

Identity theft is the forging of someone's identity for the purpose of fraud. The fraud is often financial, because thieves apply for and use credit cards or loans in the victim's name. Two means of stealing an identity are phishing and pharming. **Information secrecy** is the category of computer security that addresses the protection of data from unauthorized disclosure and confirmation of data source authenticity. **Phishing** is a technique to gain personal information for the purpose of identity theft, usually by means of fraudulent emails that look as though they came from legitimate businesses. The messages appear to be genuine, with official-looking formats and logos, and typically ask for verification of important information such as passwords and account numbers, ostensibly for accounting or auditing purposes. Since the emails look authentic, up to one in five recipients responds with the information and subsequently becomes a victim of identity theft and other fraud. Figure B6.6 displays a phishing scam attempting to gain information for Bank of America; you should never click on emails asking you to verify your identity as companies will never contact you directly asking for your user name or password.[3] **Phishing expedition** is a masquerading attack that combines spam with spoofing. The perpetrator sends millions of spam emails that appear to be from a respectable company. The emails contain a link to a website that is designed to look exactly like the company's website. The victim is encouraged to enter his or her username, password, and sometimes credit card information. **Spear phishing** is a phishing expedition in which

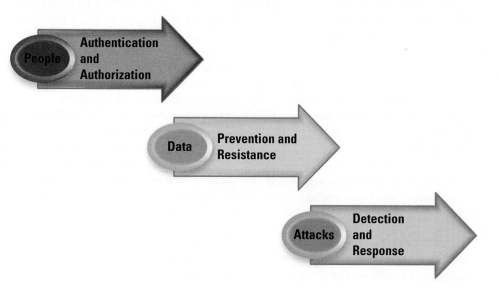

FIGURE B6.5

Three Areas of Information Security

From:	Bank of America Online [ealert@replies.em.bankofamerica.com]
Subject:	Customer Alert: Your Account was been Attended

> The sooner you sign in to Online Banking,
> the simpler your life will get.

Important Notification

Dear **Valued Customer**,

As part of Bank of America Online commitment to provide you with exceptional service, Bank of America Online is taking additional steps to ensure that your account data is secure.

Therefore, we are sending you this e-mail as a security precaution to confirm to you the Inability to accurately verify your account information due to an internal error within server

You are required to confirm your account information to forestall a re-occurence of any future attention with your online banking.

However, failure to update your account information might result in your account being suspended.. Click below to get started.

Get Started

Thank you,
Bank of America Online Banking.

----

* Please do not respond to this email as your reply will not be received.

Bank of America Email, 8th Floor, 101 South Tryon St., Charlotte, NC 28255-0001

the emails are carefully designed to target a particular person or organization. ***Vishing*** (or ***voice phishing***) is a phone scam that attempts to defraud people by asking them to call a bogus telephone number to "confirm" their account information.

Pharming reroutes requests for legitimate websites to false websites. For example, if you were to type in the URL to your bank, pharming could redirect to a fake site that collects your information. A ***zombie*** is a program that secretly takes over another computer for the purpose of launching attacks on other computers. Zombie attacks are almost impossible to trace back to the attacker. A ***zombie farm*** is a group of computers on which a hacker has planted zombie programs. A ***pharming attack*** uses a zombie farm, often by an organized crime association, to launch a massive phishing attack.

Authentication and authorization technologies can prevent identity theft, phishing, and pharming scams. ***Authentication*** is a method for confirming users' identities. Once a system determines the authentication of a user, it can then determine the access privileges (or authorization) for that user. ***Authorization*** is the process of providing a user with permission including access levels and abilities such as file access, hours of access, and amount of allocated storage space. Authentication and authorization techniques fall into three categories; the most secure procedures combine all three:

1. Something the user knows, such as a user ID and password.
2. Something the user has, such as a smart card or token.
3. Something that is part of the user, such as a fingerprint or voice signature.

Something the User Knows Such as a User ID and Password

The first type of authentication, using something the user knows, is the most common way to identify individual users and typically consists of a unique user ID and password. However, this is actually one of the most *ineffective* ways for determining authentication because passwords are not secure. All it typically takes to crack one is enough time. More than 50 percent of help-desk calls are password related, which can cost an organization significant money, and a social engineer can coax a password from almost anybody.

Something the User Has Such as a Smart Card or Token

The second type of authentication, using something the user has, offers a much more effective way to identify individuals than a user ID and password. Tokens and smart cards are two of the primary forms of this type of authentication. *Tokens* are small electronic devices that change user passwords automatically. The user enters his or her user ID and token-displayed password to gain access to the network. A *smart card* is a device about the size of a credit card, containing embedded technologies that can store information and small amounts of software to perform some limited processing. Smart cards can act as identification instruments, a form of digital cash, or a data storage device with the ability to store an entire medical record.

Something That Is Part of the User Such as a Fingerprint or Voice Signature

The third kind of authentication, something that is part of the user, is by far the best and most effective way to manage authentication. *Biometrics* (narrowly defined) is the identification of a user based on a physical characteristic, such as a fingerprint, iris, face, voice, or handwriting. Unfortunately, biometric authentication can be costly and intrusive.

DATA: PREVENTION AND RESISTANCE

Prevention and resistance technologies stop intruders from accessing and reading data by means of content filtering, encryption, and firewalls. *Time bombs* are computer viruses that wait for a specific date before executing their instructions. *Content filtering* occurs when organizations use software that filters content, such as emails, to prevent the accidental or malicious transmission of unauthorized information. Organizations can use content filtering technologies to filter email and prevent emails containing sensitive information from transmitting, whether the transmission was malicious or accidental. It can also filter emails and prevent any suspicious files from transmitting such as potential virus-infected files. Email content filtering can also filter for spam, a form of unsolicited email.

Encryption scrambles information into an alternative form that requires a key or password to decrypt. If there were a security breach and the stolen information were encrypted, the thief would be unable to read it. Encryption can switch the order of characters, replace characters with other characters, insert or remove characters, or use a mathematical formula to convert the information into a code. Companies that transmit sensitive customer information over the Internet, such as credit card numbers, frequently use encryption. To *decrypt* information is to decode it and is the opposite of *encrypt*. *Cryptography* is the science that studies encryption, which is the hiding of messages so that only the sender and receiver can read them. The National Institute of Standards and Technology (NIST) introduced an *advanced encryption standard (AES)* designed to keep government information secure.

Some encryption technologies use multiple keys. *Public key encryption (PKE)* uses two keys: a public key that everyone can have and a private key for only the recipient (see Figure B6.7). The organization provides the public key to all customers, whether end consumers or other businesses, who use that key to encrypt their information and send it via the Internet. When it arrives at its destination, the organization uses the private key to unscramble it.

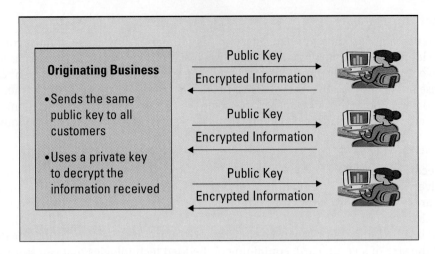

Originating Business

• Sends the same
public key to all
customers

• Uses a private key
to decrypt the
information received

Public Key

Encrypted Information

Public Key

Encrypted Information

Public Key

Encrypted Information

Public keys are becoming popular to use for authentication techniques consisting of digital objects in which a trusted third party confirms correlation between the user and the public key. A *certificate authority* is a trusted third party, such as VeriSign, that validates user identities by means of digital certificates. A *digital certificate* is a data file that identifies individuals or organizations online and is comparable to a digital signature.

A *firewall* is hardware and/or software that guard a private network by analyzing incoming and outgoing information for the correct markings. If they are missing, the firewall prevents the information from entering the network. Firewalls can even detect computers communicating with the Internet without approval. As Figure B6.8 illustrates, organizations typically place a firewall between a server and the Internet. Think of a firewall as a gatekeeper that protects computer networks from intrusion by providing a filter and safe transfer points for access to and from the Internet and other networks. It screens all network traffic for proper passwords or other security codes and allows only authorized transmissions in and out of the network.

Firewalls do not guarantee complete protection, and users should enlist additional security technologies such as antivirus software and antispyware software. *Antivirus software* scans and searches hard drives to prevent, detect, and remove known viruses, adware, and spyware. Antivirus software must be frequently updated to protect against newly created viruses.

FIGURE B6.8

Sample Firewall
Architecture Connecting
Systems Located in
Chicago, New York, and
Boston

ATTACK: DETECTION AND RESPONSE

Cyberwar is an organized attempt by a country's military to disrupt or destroy information and communication systems for another country. *Cyberterrorism* is the use

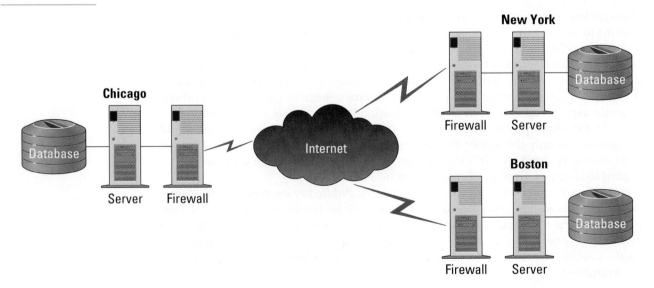

New York

Chicago

Database   Server   Firewall

Internet

Firewall   Server   Database

Boston

Firewall   Server   Database

of computer and networking technologies against persons or property to intimidate or coerce governments, individuals, or any segment of society to attain political, religious, or ideological goals. With so many intruders planning computer attacks, it is critical that all computer systems are protected. The presence of an intruder can be detected by watching for suspicious network events such as bad passwords, the removal of highly classified data files, or unauthorized user attempts. ***Intrusion detection software (IDS)*** features full-time monitoring tools that search for patterns in network traffic to identify intruders. IDS protects against suspicious network traffic and attempts to access files and data. If a suspicious event or unauthorized traffic is identified, the IDS will generate an alarm and can even be customized to shut down a particularly sensitive part of a network. After identifying an attack, an MIS department can implement response tactics to mitigate the damage. Response tactics outline procedures such as how long a system under attack will remain plugged in and connected to the corporate network, when to shut down a compromised system, and how quickly a backup system will be up and running.

Guaranteeing the safety of organization information is achieved by implementing the two lines of defense: people and technology. To protect information through people, firms should develop information security policies and plans that provide employees with specific precautions they should take in creating, working with, and transmitting the organization's information assets. Technology-based lines of defense fall into three categories: authentication and authorization; prevention and resistance; and detection and response.

Implementing information security lines of defense through people first and through technology second is the best way for an organization to protect its vital intellectual capital. The first line of defense is securing intellectual capital by creating an information security plan detailing the various information security policies. The second line of defense is investing in technology to help secure information through authentication and authorization, prevention and resistance, and detection and response.

✳ KEY TERMS

Advanced encryption
   standard (AES), 415
Adware, 411
Antivirus software, 416
Authentication, 414
Authorization, 414
Biometrics, 415
Certificate authority, 416
Content filtering, 415
Cryptography, 415
Cyberterrorism, 416
Cyberwar, 416
Decrypt, 415
Destructive agents, 413
Digital certificate, 416

Dumpster diving, 412
Drive-by hacking, 410
Encryption, 415
Firewall, 416
Hackers, 410
Identity theft, 413
Information secrecy, 413
Information security plan, 412
Information security
   policies, 412
Insiders, 412
Intrusion detection software
   (IDS), 417
Pharming, 414
Pharming attack, 414

Phishing, 413
Phishing expedition, 413
Public key encryption
   (PKE), 415
Smart card, 415
Social engineering, 412
Spear phishing, 413
Spyware, 411
Time bombs, 415
Tokens, 415
Virus, 411
Vishing (or voice
   phishing), 414
Zombie, 414
Zombie farm 414

✳ CLOSING CASE ONE

Thinking Like the Enemy

David and Barry Kaufman, the founders of the Intense School, recently added several security courses, including the five-day "Professional Hacking Boot Camp" and "Social Engineering in Two Days."

Information technology departments must know how to protect organizational information. Therefore, organizations must teach their IT personnel how to protect their systems, especially in light of the many new government regulations, such as the Health Insurance Portability and Accountability Act (HIPAA), that demand secure systems. The concept of sending IT professionals to a hacking school seems counterintuitive; it is somewhat similar to sending accountants to an Embezzling 101 course. The Intense School does not strive to breed the next generation of hackers, however, but to teach its students how to be "ethical" hackers: to use their skills to build better locks, and to understand the minds of those who would attempt to crack them.

The main philosophy of the security courses at the Intense School is simply "To know thy enemy." In fact, one of the teachers at the Intense School is none other than Kevin Mitnick, the famous hacker who was imprisoned from 1995 to 2000. Teaching security from the hacker's perspective, as Mitnick does, is more difficult than teaching hacking itself: A hacker just needs to know one way into a system, David Kaufman notes, but a security professional needs to know *all* of the system's vulnerabilities. The two courses analyze those vulnerabilities from different perspectives.

The hacking course, which costs $3,500, teaches ways to protect against the mischief typically associated with hackers: worming through computer systems through vulnerabilities that are susceptible to technical, or computer-based, attacks. Mitnick's $1,950 social engineering course, by contrast, teaches the more frightening art of worming through the vulnerabilities of the people using and maintaining systems—getting passwords and access through duplicity, not technology. People that take this class, or read Mitnick's book, *The Art of Deception,* never again think of passwords or the trash bin the same way.

So how does the Intense School teach hacking? With sessions on dumpster diving (the unsavory practice of looking for passwords and other bits of information on discarded papers), with field trips to case target systems, and with practice runs at the company's in-house "target range," a network of computers set up to thwart and educate students.

One feature of the Intense School that raises a few questions is that the school does not check on morals at the door: Anyone paying the tuition can attend the school. Given the potential danger that an unchecked graduate of a hacking school could represent, it is surprising that the FBI does not collect the names of the graduates. But perhaps it gets them anyhow—several governmental agencies have sent students to the school.[4]

Questions

1. How could an organization benefit from attending one of the courses offered at the Intense School?

2. What are the two primary lines of security defense and how can organizational employees use the information taught by the Intense School when drafting an information security plan?

3. Determine the differences between the two primary courses offered at the Intense School, "Professional Hacking Boot Camp" and "Social Engineering in Two Days." Which course is more important for organizational employees to attend?

4. If your employer sent you to take a course at the Intense School, which one would you choose and why?

5. What are the ethical dilemmas involved with having such a course offered by a private company?

✱ CLOSING CASE TWO

Hacker Hunters

Hacker hunters are the new breed of crime-fighter. They employ the same methodology used to fight organized crime in the 1980s—informants and the cyberworld equivalent of wiretaps. Daniel Larking, a 20-year veteran who runs the FBI's Internet Crime Complaint Center, taps online service providers to help track down criminal hackers. Leads supplied by the FBI and eBay helped Romanian police round up 11 members of a gang that set up fake eBay accounts and auctioned off cell phones, laptops, and cameras they never intended to deliver.

On October 26, 2004, the FBI unleashed Operation Firewall, targeting the ShadowCrew, a gang whose members were schooled in identity theft, bank account pillage, and selling illegal goods on the Internet. ShadowCrew's 4,000 gang members lived in a dozen countries and across the United States. For months, agents had been watching their every move through a clandestine gateway into their website, shadowcrew.com. One member turned informant called a group meeting, ensuring the members would be at home on their computers during a certain time. At 9 p.m. the Secret Service issued orders to move in on the gang. The move was synchronized around the globe to prevent gang members from warning each other via instant messages. Twenty-eight gang members in eight states and six countries were arrested, most still at their computers. Authorities seized dozens of computers and found 1.7 million credit card numbers and more than 18 million email accounts.

ShadowCrew's Operations

The alleged ringleaders of ShadowCrew included Andres Mantovani, 23, a part-time community college student in Arizona, and David Appleyard, 45, a former New Jersey mortgage broker. Mantovani and Appleyard allegedly were administrators in charge of running the website and recruiting members. The site created a marketplace for over 4,000 gang members who bought and sold hot information and merchandise. The website was open for business 24 hours a day, but since most of the members held jobs, the busiest time was from 10 p.m. to 2 a.m. on Sundays. Hundreds of gang members would meet online to trade credit card information, passports, and even equipment to make fake identity documents. Platinum credit cards cost more than gold ones and discounts were offered for package deals. One member known as "Scarface" sold 115,695 stolen credit card numbers in a single trade. Overall, the gang made more than $4 million in credit card purchases over two years. ShadowCrew was equivalent to an eBay for the underworld. The site even posted crime tips on how to use stolen credit cards and fake IDs at big retailers.

The gang stole credit card numbers and other valuable information through clever tricks. One of the favorites was sending millions of phishing emails—messages that appeared to be from legitimate companies such as Yahoo!—designed to steal passwords and credit card numbers. The gang also hacked into corporate databases to steal account data. According to sources familiar with the investigation, the gang cracked the networks of 12 unidentified companies that were not even aware their systems had been breached.

Police Operations

Brian Nagel, an assistant director at the Secret Service, coordinated the effort to track the ShadowCrew. Allies included Britain's National High-Tech Crimes unit, the Royal Canadian Mounted Police, and the Bulgarian Interior Ministry. Authorities turned one of the high-ranking members of the gang into a snitch and had the man help the Secret Service set up a new electronic doorway for ShadowCrew members to enter their website. The snitch spread the word that the new gateway was a more secure way to the website. It was the first-ever tap of a private computer network. "We became shadowcrew.com," Nagel said.[5]

Questions

1. What types of technology could big retailers use to prevent identity thieves from purchasing merchandise?

2. What can organizations do to protect themselves from hackers looking to steal account data?

3. Authorities frequently tap online service providers to track down hackers. Do you think it is ethical for authorities to tap an online service provider and read people's email? Why or why not?

4. Do you think it was ethical for authorities to use one of the high-ranking members to trap other gang members? Why or why not?

5. In a team, research the Internet and find the best ways to protect yourself from identity theft.

✱ MAKING BUSINESS DECISIONS

1. Firewall Decisions

You are the CEO of Inverness Investments, a medium-sized venture capital firm that specializes in investing in high-tech companies. The company receives more than 30,000 email messages per year. On average, there are two viruses and three successful hackings against the company each year, which result in losses to the company of about $250,000. Currently, the company has antivirus software installed but does not have any firewalls.

Your CIO is suggesting implementing 10 firewalls for a total cost of $80,000. The estimated life of each firewall is about three years. The chances of hackers breaking into the system with the firewalls installed are about 3 percent. Annual maintenance costs on the firewalls are estimated around $15,000. Create an argument for or against supporting your CIO's recommendation to purchase the firewalls.

2. Drafting an Information Security Plan

Making The Grade is a nonprofit organization that helps students learn how to achieve better grades in school. The organization has 40 offices in 25 states and more than 2,000 employees. The company is currently building a website to offer its services online. You have recently been hired by the CIO as the director of information security. Your first assignment is to develop a document discussing the importance of creating information security policies and an information security plan. Be sure to include the following:

- The importance of educating employees on information security.
- A few samples of employee information security policies.
- Other major areas the information security plan should address.
- Signs the company should look for to determine if the new site is being hacked.
- The major types of attacks the company should expect to experience.

3. Discussing the Three Areas of Security

Great Granola Inc. is a small business operating out of northern California. The company specializes in selling unique homemade granola, and its primary sales vehicle is through its website. The company is growing exponentially and expects its revenues to triple this year to $12 million. The company also expects to hire 60 additional employees to support its growing number of customers. Joan Martin, the CEO, is aware that if her competitors discover the recipe for her granola, or who her primary customers are, it could easily ruin her business. Joan has hired you to draft a document discussing the different areas of information security, along with your recommendations for providing a secure ebusiness environment.

4. College Security

Computer and online security is a growing concern for businesses of all sizes. Computer security issues range from viruses to automated Internet attacks to outright theft, the result of which is lost information and lost time. Security issues pop up in news articles daily, and most business owners understand the need to secure their businesses. Your college is no different from any other business when it comes to information security. Draft a document identifying the questions you should ask your college's CIO to ensure information security across your campus.

Ethics

1. Explain the ethical issues in the use of information technology.
2. Identify the six epolicies organizations should implement to protect themselves.

LO 1. Explain the ethical issues in the use of information technology.

Information Ethics

Ethics and security are two fundamental building blocks for all organizations. In recent years, enormous business scandals along with 9/11 have shed new light on the meaning of ethics and security. When the behavior of a few individuals can destroy billion-dollar organizations, the value of ethics and security should be evident.

Copyright is the legal protection afforded an expression of an idea, such as a song, book, or video game. *Intellectual property* is intangible creative work that is embodied in physical form and includes copyrights, trademarks, and patents. A *patent* is an exclusive right to make, use, and sell an invention and is granted by a government to the inventor. As it becomes easier for people to copy everything from words and data to music and video, the ethical issues surrounding copyright infringement and the violation of intellectual property rights are consuming the ebusiness world. Technology poses new challenges for our *ethics*—the principles and standards that guide our behavior toward other people.

The protection of customers' privacy is one of the largest, and murkiest, ethical issues facing organizations today. *Privacy* is the right to be left alone when you want to be, to have control over your personal possessions, and not to be observed without your consent. Privacy is related to *confidentiality,* which is the assurance that messages and information remain available only to those authorized to view them. Each time employees make a decision about a privacy issue, the outcome could sink the company.

Trust among companies, customers, partners, and suppliers is the support structure of ebusiness. Privacy is one of its main ingredients. Consumers' concerns that their privacy will be violated because of their interactions on the web continue to be one of the primary barriers to the growth of ebusiness.

Information ethics govern the ethical and moral issues arising from the development and use of information technologies, as well as the creation, collection, duplication, distribution, and processing of information itself (with or without the aid of

| Individuals copy, use, and distribute software. |
| Employees search organizational databases for sensitive corporate and personal information. |
| Organizations collect, buy, and use information without checking the validity or accuracy of the information. |
| Individuals create and spread viruses that cause trouble for those using and maintaining IT systems. |
| Individuals hack into computer systems to steal proprietary information. |
| Employees destroy or steal proprietary organization information such as schematics, sketches, customer lists, and reports. |

computer technologies). Ethical dilemmas in this area usually arise not as simple, clear-cut situations but as clashes among competing goals, responsibilities, and loyalties. Inevitably, there will be more than one socially acceptable or "correct" decision. The two primary areas concerning software include pirated software and counterfeit software. ***Pirated software*** is the unauthorized use, duplication, distribution, or sale of copyrighted software. ***Counterfeit software*** is software that is manufactured to look like the real thing and sold as such. ***Digital rights management*** is a technological solution that allows publishers to control their digital media to discourage, limit, or prevent illegal copying and distribution. Figure B7.1 contains examples of ethically questionable or unacceptable uses of information technology.[1]

Unfortunately, few hard and fast rules exist for always determining what is ethical. Many people can either justify or condemn the actions in Figure B7.1, for example. Knowing the law is important but that knowledge will not always help, because what is legal might not always be ethical, and what might be ethical is not always legal. For example, Joe Reidenberg received an offer for AT&T cell phone service. AT&T used Equifax, a credit reporting agency, to identify potential customers such as Joe Reidenberg. Overall, this seemed like a good business opportunity between Equifax and AT&T wireless. Unfortunately, the Fair Credit Reporting Act (FCRA) forbids repurposing credit information except when the information is used for "a firm offer of credit or insurance." In other words, the only product that can be sold based on credit information is credit. A representative for Equifax stated, "As long as AT&T Wireless (or any company for that matter) is offering the cell phone service on a credit basis, such as allowing the use of the service before the consumer has to pay, it is in compliance with the FCRA." However, the question remains—is it ethical?[2]

Figure B7.2 shows the four quadrants where ethical and legal behaviors intersect. The goal for most businesses is to make decisions within quadrant I that are both legal and ethical. There are times when a business will find itself in the position of making a decision in quadrant III, such as hiring child labor in foreign countries, or in quadrant II where a business might pay a foreigner who is in the process of getting her immigration

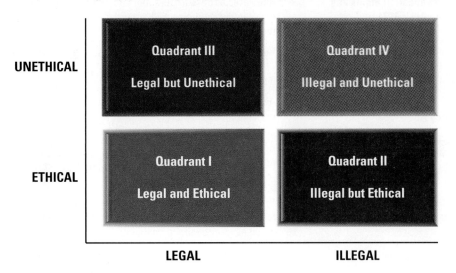

UNETHICAL

Quadrant III

Legal but Unethical

Quadrant IV

Illegal and Unethical

ETHICAL

Quadrant I

Legal and Ethical

Quadrant II

Illegal but Ethical

LEGAL

ILLEGAL

status approved because the company is in the process of hiring the person. A business should never find itself operating in quadrant IV. Ethics are critical to operating a successful business today.

INFORMATION DOES NOT HAVE ETHICS, PEOPLE DO

Information itself has no ethics. It does not care how it is used. It will not stop itself from spamming customers, sharing itself if it is sensitive or personal, or revealing details to third parties. Information cannot delete or preserve itself. Therefore, it falls to those who own the information to develop ethical guidelines about how to manage it. *Information management* examines the organizational resource of information and regulates its definitions, uses, value, and distribution ensuring it has the types of data/information required to function and grow effectively. *Information governance* is a method or system of government for information management or control. *Information compliance* is the act of conforming, acquiescing, or yielding information. *Information property* is an ethical issue that focuses on who owns information about individuals and how information can be sold and exchanged. A few years ago the ideas of information management, governance, and compliance were relatively obscure. Today, these concepts are a must for virtually every company, both domestic and global, primarily due to the role digital information plays in corporate legal proceedings or litigation. Frequently, digital information serves as key evidence in legal proceedings and it is far easier to search, organize, and filter than paper documents. Digital information is also extremely difficult to destroy, especially if it is on a corporate network or sent via email. In fact, the only reliable way to truly obliterate digital information is to destroy the hard drives where the file was stored. *Ediscovery* (or *electronic discovery*) refers to the ability of a company to identify, search, gather, seize, or export digital information in responding to a litigation, audit, investigation, or information inquiry. As the importance of ediscovery grows, so does information governance and information compliance. The *Child Online Protection Act (COPA)* was passed to protect minors from accessing inappropriate material on the Internet. Figure B7.3 provides an overview of some of the important laws individuals and firms must follow in managing and protecting information.[3]

FIGURE B7.3

Established Information-Related Laws

	Established Information-Related Laws
Privacy Act—1974	Restricts what information the federal government can collect; allows people to access and correct information on themselves; requires procedures to protect the security of personal information; and forbids the disclosure of name-linked information without permission.
Family Education Rights and Privacy Act—1974	Regulates access to personal education records by government agencies and other third parties and ensures the right of students to see their own records.
Cable Communications Act—1984	Requires written or electronic consent from viewers before cable TV providers can release viewing choices or other personally identifiable information.
Electronic Communications Privacy Act—1986	Allows the reading of communications by a firm and says that employees have no right to privacy when using their companies' computers.
Computer Fraud and Abuse Act—1986	Prohibits unauthorized access to computers used for financial institutions, the U.S. government, or interstate and international trade.
The Bork Bill (officially known as the Video Privacy Protection Act, 1988)	Prohibits the use of video rental information on customers for any purpose other than that of marketing goods and services directly to the customer.

(Continued)

Established Information-Related Laws	
Communications Assistance for Law Enforcement Act—1994	Requires that telecommunications equipment be designed so that authorized government agents are able to intercept all wired and wireless communications being sent or received by any subscriber. The act also requires that subscriber call-identifying information be transmitted to a government when and if required.
Freedom of Information Act—1967, 1975, 1994, and 1998	Allows any person to examine government records unless it would cause an invasion of privacy. It was amended in 1974 to apply to the FBI, and again in 1994 to allow citizens to monitor government activities and information gathering, and once again in 1998 to access government information on the Internet.
Health Insurance Portability and Accountability Act (HIPAA)—1996	Requires that the health care industry formulate and implement regulations to keep patient information confidential.
Identity Theft and Assumption Deterrence Act—1998	Strengthened the criminal laws governing identity theft making it a federal crime to use or transfer identification belonging to another. It also established a central federal service for victims.
USA Patriot Act—2001 and 2003	Allows law enforcement to get access to almost any information, including library records, video rentals, bookstore purchases, and business records when investigating any act of terrorist or clandestine intelligence activities. In 2003, Patriot II broadened the original law.
Homeland Security Act—2002	Provided new authority to government agencies to mine data on individuals and groups including emails and website visits; put limits on the information available under the Freedom of Information Act; and gave new powers to government agencies to declare national health emergencies.
Sarbanes-Oxley Act—2002	Sought to protect investors by improving the accuracy and reliability of corporate disclosures and requires companies to (1) implement extensive and detailed policies to prevent illegal activity within the company, and (2) to respond in a timely manner to investigate illegal activity.
Fair and Accurate Credit Transactions Act—2003	Included provisions for the prevention of identity theft including consumers' right to get a credit report free each year, requiring merchants to leave all but the last five digits of a credit card number off a receipt, and requiring lenders and credit agencies to take action even before a victim knows a crime has occurred when they notice any circumstances that might indicate identity theft.
CAN-Spam Act—2003	Sought to regulate interstate commerce by imposing limitations and penalties on businesses sending unsolicited email to consumers. The law forbids deceptive subject lines, headers, return addresses, etc., as well as the harvesting of email addresses from websites. It requires businesses that send spam to maintain a do-not-spam list and to include a postal mailing address in the message.

FIGURE B7.3

(Continued)

Developing Information Management Policies

LO 2. Identify the six epolicies organizations should implement to protect themselves.

Treating sensitive corporate information as a valuable resource is good management. Building a corporate culture based on ethical principles that employees can understand and implement is responsible management. Organizations should develop written policies establishing employee guidelines, employee procedures, and organizational rules for information. These policies set employee expectations about the organization's

practices and standards and protect the organization from misuse of computer systems and IT resources. If an organization's employees use computers at work, the organization should, at a minimum, implement epolicies. *Epolicies* are policies and procedures that address information management along with the ethical use of computers and the Internet in the business environment. Figure B7.4 displays the epolicies a firm should implement to set employee expectations.

ETHICAL COMPUTER USE POLICY

In a case that illustrates the perils of online betting, a leading Internet poker site reported that a hacker exploited a security flaw to gain an insurmountable edge in high-stakes, no-limit Texas hold-'em tournaments—the ability to see his opponents' hole cards. The cheater, whose illegitimate winnings were estimated at between $400,000 and $700,000 by one victim, was an employee of AbsolutePoker.com and hacked the system to show that it could be done. Regardless of what business a company operates—even one that many view as unethical—the company must protect itself from unethical employee behavior. *Cyberbullying* includes threats, negative remarks, or defamatory comments transmitted via the Internet or posted on the website. A *threat* is an act or object that poses a danger to assets. *Click-fraud* is the abuse of pay-per-click, pay-per-call, and pay-per-conversion revenue models by repeatedly clicking on a link to increase charges or costs for the advertiser. *Competitive click-fraud* is a computer crime where a competitor or disgruntled employee increases a company's search advertising costs by repeatedly clicking on the advertiser's link.

Cyberbullying and click-fraud are just a few examples of the many types of unethical computer use found today.

One essential step in creating an ethical corporate culture is establishing an ethical computer use policy. An *ethical computer use policy* contains general principles to guide computer user behavior. For example, it might explicitly state that users should refrain from playing computer games during working hours. This policy ensures the users know how to behave at work and the organization has a published standard to deal with infractions. For example, after appropriate warnings, the company may terminate an employee who spends significant amounts of time playing computer games at work.

Organizations can legitimately vary in how they expect employees to use computers, but in any approach to controlling such use, the overriding principle should be informed consent. The users should be *informed* of the rules and, by agreeing to use the system on that basis, *consent* to abide by them.

Managers should make a conscientious effort to ensure all users are aware of the policy through formal training and other means. If an organization were to have only one epolicy, it should be an ethical computer use policy because that is the starting point and the umbrella for any other policies the organization might establish.

INFORMATION PRIVACY POLICY

An organization that wants to protect its information should develop an *information privacy policy,* which contains general principles regarding information privacy. Visa created Inovant to handle all its information systems including its coveted customer information, which details how people are spending their money, in which stores, on which days, and even at what time of day. Just imagine what a sales and marketing department could do if it gained access to this information. For this reason, Inovant bans the use of Visa's customer information for anything outside its intended purpose—billing. Innovant's privacy specialists developed a strict credit card information privacy policy, which it follows.

Now Inovant is being asked if it can guarantee that unethical use of credit card information will never occur. In a large majority of cases, the unethical use of information happens not through the malicious scheming of a rogue marketer, but rather unintentionally. For instance, information is collected and stored for some purpose, such as record keeping or billing. Then, a sales or marketing professional figures out another way to use it internally, share it with partners, or sell it to a trusted third party. The information is "unintentionally" used for new purposes. The classic example of this type of unintentional information reuse is the Social Security number, which started simply as a way to identify government retirement benefits and then was used as a sort of universal personal ID, found on everything from drivers' licenses to savings accounts.

ACCEPTABLE USE POLICY

An *acceptable use policy (AUP)* requires a user to agree to follow it to be provided access to corporate email, information systems, and the Internet. *Nonrepudiation* is a contractual stipulation to ensure that ebusiness participants do not deny (repudiate) their online actions. A nonrepudiation clause is typically contained in an acceptable use policy. Many businesses and educational facilities require employees or students to sign an acceptable use policy before gaining network access. When signing up with an email provider, each customer is typically presented with an AUP, which states the user agrees to adhere to certain stipulations. Users agree to the following in a typical acceptable use policy:

- Not using the service as part of violating any law.
- Not attempting to break the security of any computer network or user.
- Not posting commercial messages to groups without prior permission.
- Not performing any nonrepudiation.

Some organizations go so far as to create a unique information management policy focusing solely on Internet use. An *Internet use policy* contains general principles to guide the proper use of the Internet. Because of the large amounts of computing resources that Internet users can expend, it is essential that such use be legitimate. In addition, the Internet contains numerous materials that some believe are offensive, making regulation in the workplace a requirement. *Cybervandalism* is the electronic defacing of an existing website. *Typosquatting* is a problem that occurs when someone registers purposely misspelled variations of well-known domain names. These variants sometimes lure consumers who make typographical errors when entering a URL. *Website name stealing* is the theft of a website's name that occurs when someone, posing as a site's administrator, changes the ownership of the domain name assigned to the website to another website owner. These are all examples of unacceptable Internet use. *Internet censorship* is government attempts to control Internet traffic, thus preventing some material from being viewed by a country's citizens. Generally, an Internet use policy:

- Describes the Internet services available to users.
- Defines the organization's position on the purpose of Internet access and what restrictions, if any, are placed on that access.
- Describes user responsibility for citing sources, properly handling offensive material, and protecting the organization's good name.
- States the ramifications if the policy is violated.

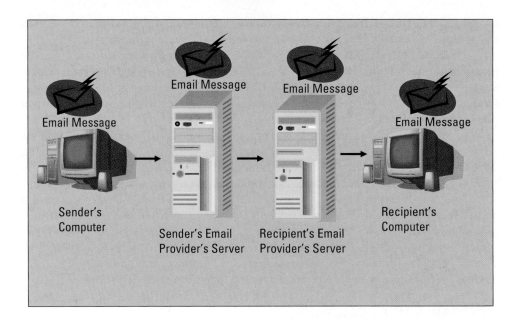

EMAIL PRIVACY POLICY

An *email privacy policy* details the extent to which email messages may be read by others. Email is so pervasive in organizations that it requires its own specific policy. Most working professionals use email as their preferred means of corporate communications. While email and instant messaging are common business communication tools, there are risks associated with using them. For instance, a sent email is stored on at least three or four computers (see Figure B7.5). Simply deleting an email from one computer does not delete it from the others. Companies can mitigate many of the risks of using electronic messaging systems by implementing and adhering to an email privacy policy.

One major problem with email is the user's expectations of privacy. To a large extent, this expectation is based on the false assumption that email privacy protection exists somehow analogous to that of U.S. first-class mail. Generally, the organization that owns the email system can operate the system as openly or as privately as it wishes. Surveys indicate that the majority of large firms regularly read and analyze employees' email looking for confidential data leaks such as unannounced financial results or the sharing of trade secrets that result in the violation of an email privacy policy and eventual termination of the employee. That means that if the organization wants to read everyone's email, it can do so. Basically, using work email for anything other than work is not a good idea. A typical email privacy policy:

- Defines legitimate email users and explains what happens to accounts after a person leaves the organization.

- Explains backup procedure so users will know that at some point, even if a message is deleted from their computer, it is still stored by the company.

- Describes the legitimate grounds for reading email and the process required before such action is performed.

- Discourages sending junk email or spam to anyone who does not want to receive it.

- Prohibits attempting to mail bomb a site. A *mail bomb* sends a massive amount of email to a specific person or system that can cause that user's server to stop functioning.

- Informs users that the organization has no control over email once it has been transmitted outside the organization.

Spam is unsolicited email. It plagues employees at all levels within an organization, from receptionist to CEO, and clogs email systems and siphons MIS resources away from legitimate business projects. An **anti-spam policy** simply states that email users will not send unsolicited emails (or spam). It is difficult to write anti-spam policies, laws, or software because there is no such thing as a universal litmus test for spam. One person's spam is another person's newsletter. End users have to decide what spam is, because it can vary widely not just from one company to the next, but from one person to the next. A user can **opt out** of receiving emails by choosing to deny permission to incoming emails.

Teergrubing is an antispamming approach where the receiving computer launches a return attack against the spammer, sending email messages back to the computer that originated the suspected spam.

SOCIAL MEDIA POLICY

Did you see the YouTube video showing two Domino's Pizza employees violating health codes while preparing food by passing gas on sandwiches? Millions of people did and the company took notice when disgusted customers began posting negative comments all over Twitter. Not having a Twitter account, corporate executives at Domino's did not know about the damaging tweets until it was too late. The use of social media can contribute many benefits to an organization, and implemented correctly it can become a huge opportunity for employees to build brands. But there are also tremendous risks as a few employees representing an entire company can cause tremendous brand damage. Defining a set of guidelines implemented in a social media policy can help mitigate that risk. Companies can protect themselves by implementing a **social media policy** outlining the corporate guidelines or principles governing employee online communications. Having a single social media policy might not be enough to ensure the company's online reputation is protected. Additional, more specific, social media policies a company might choose to implement include:[4]

- Employee online communication policy detailing brand communication.
- Employee blog and personal blog policies.
- Employee social network and personal social network policies.
- Employee Twitter, corporate Twitter, and personal Twitter policies.
- Employee LinkedIn policy.
- Employee Facebook usage and brand usage policy.
- Corporate YouTube policy.

Organizations must protect their online reputations and continuously monitor blogs, message boards, social networking sites, and media sharing sites. However, monitoring the hundreds of different social media sites can quickly become overwhelming. To combat these issues, a number of companies specialize in online social media monitoring; for example, Trackur.com creates digital dashboards allowing executives to view at a glance the date published, source, title, and summary of every item tracked. The dashboard not only highlights what's being said, but also the influence of the particular person, blog, or social media site.

WORKPLACE MONITORING POLICY

Increasingly, employee monitoring is not a choice; it is a risk-management obligation. Michael Soden, CEO of the Bank of Ireland, issued a mandate stating that company employees could not surf illicit websites with company equipment. Next, he hired Hewlett-Packard to run the MIS department and illicit websites were discovered on Soden's own computer, forcing Soden to resign. Monitoring employees is one of the biggest challenges CIOs face when developing information management policies.[5]

Physical security is tangible protection such as alarms, guards, fireproof doors, fences, and vaults. New technologies make it possible for employers to monitor many aspects of their employees' jobs, especially on telephones, computer terminals, through

Common Internet Monitoring Technologies	
Key logger, or key trapper, software	A program that records every keystroke and mouse click.
Hardware key logger	A hardware device that captures keystrokes on their journey from the keyboard to the motherboard.
Cookie	A small file deposited on a hard drive by a website containing information about customers and their web activities. Cookies allow websites to record the comings and goings of customers, usually without their knowledge or consent.
Adware	Software that generates ads that install themselves on a computer when a person downloads some other program from the Internet.
Spyware (sneakware or stealthware)	Software that comes hidden in free downloadable software and tracks online movements, mines the information stored on a computer, or uses a computer's CPU and storage for some task the user knows nothing about.
Web log	Consists of one line of information for every visitor to a website and is usually stored on a web server.
Clickstream	Records information about a customer during a web surfing session such as what websites were visited, how long the visit was, what ads were viewed, and what was purchased.

electronic and voice mail, and when employees are using the Internet. Such monitoring is virtually unregulated. Therefore, unless company policy specifically states otherwise (and even this is not assured), your employer may listen, watch, and read most of your workplace communications. ***Workplace MIS monitoring*** tracks people's activities by such measures as number of keystrokes, error rate, and number of transactions processed (see Figure B7.6 for an overview). The best path for an organization planning to engage in employee monitoring is open communication including an ***employee monitoring policy*** stating explicitly how, when, and where the company monitors its employees. Several common stipulations an organization can follow when creating an employee monitoring policy include:

- Be as specific as possible stating when and what (email, IM, Internet, network activity, etc.) will be monitored.
- Expressly communicate that the company reserves the right to monitor all employees.
- State the consequences of violating the policy.
- Always enforce the policy the same for everyone.

Many employees use their company's high-speed Internet access to shop, browse, and surf the web. Most managers do not want their employees conducting personal business during working hours, and they implement a Big Brother approach to employee monitoring. Many management gurus advocate that organizations whose corporate cultures are based on trust are more successful than those whose corporate cultures are based on mistrust. Before an organization implements monitoring technology, it should ask itself, "What does this say about how we feel about our employees?" If the organization really does not trust its employees, then perhaps it should find new ones. If an organization does trust its employees, then it might want to treat them accordingly. An organization that follows its employees' every keystroke might be unwittingly undermining the relationships with its employees, and it might find the effects of employee monitoring are often worse than lost productivity from employee web surfing.

Advances in technology have made ethics a concern for many organizations. Consider how easy it is for an employee to email large amounts of confidential information, change electronic communications, or destroy massive amounts of important company information all within seconds. Electronic information about customers, partners, and employees has become one of corporate America's most valuable assets. However, the line between the proper and improper use of this asset is at best blurry. Should an employer be able to search employee files without employee consent? Should a company be able to sell customer information without informing the customer of its intent? What is a responsible approach to document deletion?

The law provides guidelines in many of these areas, but how a company chooses to act within the confines of the law is up to the judgment of its officers. Since CIOs are responsible for the technology that collects, maintains, and destroys corporate information, they sit smack in the middle of this potential ethical quagmire.

One way an organization can begin dealing with ethical issues is to create a corporate culture that encourages ethical considerations and discourages dubious information dealings. Not only is an ethical culture an excellent idea overall, but it also acts as a precaution, helping prevent customer problems from escalating into front-page news stories. The establishment of and adherence to well-defined rules and policies will help organizations create an ethical corporate culture. These policies include:

- Ethical computer use policy.
- Information privacy policy.
- Acceptable use policy.
- Email privacy policy.
- Social media policy.
- Workplace monitoring policy.

Acceptable use policy (AUP), 427
Anti-spam policy, 429
Child Online Protection Act (COPA), 424
Click-fraud, 426
Competitive click-fraud, 426
Confidentiality, 422
Copyright, 422
Counterfeit software, 423
Cyberbullying, 426
Cybervandalism, 427
Digital rights management, 423
Ediscovery (or electronic discovery), 424
Email privacy policy, 428

Employee monitoring policy, 430
Epolicies, 426
Ethical computer use policy, 426
Ethics, 422
Information compliance, 424
Information ethics, 422
Information governance, 424
Information management, 424
Information privacy policy, 426
Information property, 424
Intellectual property, 422
Internet censorship, 427
Internet use policy, 427
Mail bomb, 428

Nonrepudiation, 427
Opt out, 429
Patent, 422
Physical security, 429
Pirated software, 423
Privacy, 422
Social media policy, 429
Spam, 428
Teergrubing, 429
Threat, 426
Typosquatting, 427
Website name stealing, 427
Workplace MIS monitoring, 430

Sarbanes-Oxley: Where Information Technology, Finance, and Ethics Meet

The Sarbanes-Oxley Act (SOX) of 2002 was enacted in response to the high-profile Enron and WorldCom financial scandals to protect shareholders and the general public from accounting errors and fraudulent practices by organizations. One primary component of the Sarbanes-Oxley Act is the definition of which records are to be stored and for how long. For this reason, the legislation not only affects financial departments, but also IT departments whose job it is to store electronic records. The Sarbanes-Oxley Act states that all business records, including electronic records and electronic messages, must be saved for "not less than five years." The consequences for noncompliance are fines, imprisonment, or both. The following are the three rules of Sarbanes-Oxley that affect the management of electronic records.

1. The first rule deals with destruction, alteration, or falsification of records and states that persons who knowingly alter, destroy, mutilate, conceal, or falsify documents shall be fined or imprisoned for not more than 20 years or both.

2. The second rule defines the retention period for records storage. Best practices indicate that corporations securely store all business records using the same guidelines set for public accountants, which state that organizations shall maintain all audit or review work-papers for a period of five years from the end of the fiscal period in which the audit or review was concluded.

3. The third rule specifies all business records and communications that need to be stored, including electronic communications. IT departments are facing the challenge of creating and maintaining a corporate records archive in a cost-effective fashion that satisfies the requirements put forth by the legislation.

Essentially, any public organization that uses IT as part of its financial business processes will find that it must put in place IT controls in order to be compliant with the Sarbanes-Oxley Act. The following are a few practices you can follow to begin to ensure organizational compliance with the Sarbanes-Oxley Act.

- Overhaul or upgrade your financial systems in order to meet regulatory requirements for more accurate, detailed, and speedy filings.

- Examine the control processes within your IT department and apply best practices to comply with the act's goals. For example, segregation of duties within the systems development staff is a widely recognized best practice that helps prevent errors and outright fraud. The people who code program changes should be different from the people who test them, and a separate team should be responsible for changes in production environments.

- Homegrown financial systems are fraught with potential information-integrity issues. Although leading ERP systems offer audit-trail functionality, customizations of these systems often bypass those controls. You must work with internal and external auditors to ensure that customizations are not overriding controls.

- Work with your CIO, CEO, CFO, and corporate attorneys to create a document-retention-and-destruction policy that addresses what types of electronic documents should be saved, and for how long.

Ultimately, Sarbanes-Oxley compliance will require a great deal of work among all of your departments. Compliance starts with running IT as a business and strengthening IT internal controls.[6]

Questions

1. Define the relationship between ethics and the Sarbanes-Oxley Act.
2. Why is records management an area of concern for the entire organization?
3. What are two policies an organization can implement to achieve Sarbanes-Oxley compliance? Be sure to elaborate on how these policies can achieve compliance.
4. Identify the biggest roadblock for organizations that are attempting to achieve Sarbanes-Oxley compliance.
5. What types of information systems might facilitate SOX compliance?
6. How will electronic monitoring affect the morale and performance of employees in the workplace?
7. What do you think an unethical accountant or manager at Enron thought were the rewards and responsibilities associated with his or her job?

 CLOSING CASE TWO

Invading Your Privacy

Can your employer invade your privacy through monitoring technologies? Numerous lawsuits have been filed by employees who believed their employer was wrong to invade their privacy with monitoring technologies. Below are a few cases highlighting lawsuits over employee privacy and employer rights to monitor.

Smyth versus Pillsbury Company

An employee was terminated for sending inappropriate and unprofessional messages over the company's email system. The company had repeatedly assured its employees that email was confidential, that it would not be intercepted, and that it would not be used as a basis for discipline or discharge. Michael Smyth retrieved, from his home computer, email sent from his supervisor over Pillsbury's email system. Smyth allegedly responded with several comments concerning the sales management staff, including a threat to "kill the backstabbing bastards" and a reference to an upcoming holiday party as "the Jim Jones Kool-aid affair." Pillsbury intercepted the email and terminated Smyth, who then sued the company for wrongful discharge and invasion of privacy.

The court dismissed the case in 1996, finding that Smyth did not have a reasonable expectation of privacy in the contents of his email messages, despite Pillsbury's assurances, because the messages had been voluntarily communicated over the company's computer system to a second person. The court went on to find that, even if some reasonable expectation of privacy existed, that expectation was outweighed by Pillsbury's legitimate interest in preventing inappropriate or unprofessional communications over its email system.

Bourke versus Nissan Motor Corporation

While training new employees on the email system, a message sent by Bonita Bourke was randomly selected and reviewed by the company. The message turned out to be a personal email of a sexual nature. Once Bourke's email was discovered, the company decided to review the emails of the rest of Bourke's workgroup. As a result of this investigation, several other personal emails were discovered. Nissan gave the employees who had sent the personal messages written warnings for violating the company's email policy.

The disciplined employees sued Nissan for invasion of privacy. The employees argued that although they signed a form acknowledging the company's policy that company-owned hardware and software was restricted for company business use only, their expectation of privacy was reasonable because the company gave the plaintiffs passwords to access the computer system and told them to guard their passwords. However, a California court in 1993 held that this was not an objectively reasonable expectation of privacy because the plaintiffs knew that email messages "were read from time to time by individuals other than the intended recipient."

McLaren versus Microsoft Corporation

The Texas Court of Appeals in 1999 dismissed an employee's claim that his employer's review and dissemination of email stored in the employee's workplace personal computer constituted an invasion of privacy. The employee argued that he had a reasonable expectation of privacy because the email was kept in a personal computer folder protected by a password. The court found this argument unconvincing because the email was transmitted over his employer's network.

However, according to a news account of one case, a court held that an employer's use of a supervisor's password to review an employee's email may have violated a Massachusetts state statute against interference with privacy. In that case, Burk Technology allowed employees to use the company's email system to send personal messages, but prohibited "excessive chatting." To use the email system, each employee used a password. The employer never informed employees that their messages would or could be monitored by supervisors or the company president. The president of the company reviewed the emails of two employees who had referred to him by various nicknames and discussed his extramarital affair. The two employees were fired by the company president, who claimed the terminations were for their excessive email use and not because of the messages' content. The court denied the company's attempt to dismiss the suit and allowed the matter to be set for trial on the merits. The court focused on the fact that the employees were never informed that their email could be monitored.

This case illustrates the importance of informing employees that their use of company equipment to send email and to surf the Internet is subject to monitoring to prevent subsequent confusion, and a possible future defense, on the part of employees.[7]

Questions

1. Pick one of the preceding cases and create an argument on behalf of the employee.
2. Pick one of the preceding cases and create an argument against the employee.
3. Pick one of the preceding cases and create an argument on behalf of the employer's use of monitoring technologies.
4. Pick one of the preceding cases and create an argument against the employer's use of monitoring technologies.

✱ MAKING BUSINESS DECISIONS

1. Information Privacy

A study by the Annenberg Public Policy Center at the University of Pennsylvania shows that 95 percent of people who use the Internet at home think they should have a legal right to know everything about the information that websites collect from them. Research also shows that 57 percent of home Internet users incorrectly believe that when a website has an information privacy policy it will not share personal information with other websites or companies. In fact, the research found that after showing the users how companies track, extract, and share website information to make money, 85 percent found the methods unacceptable, even for a highly valued site. Write a short paper arguing for or against an organization's right to use and distribute personal information gathered from its website.

2. Acting Ethically

Describe how you would react to the following scenarios:

- A senior marketing manager informs you that one of her employees is looking for another job and she wants you to give her access to look through her email.

- A vice president of sales informs you that he has made a deal to provide customer information to a strategic partner and he wants you to burn all of the customer information onto a CD.

- You start monitoring one of your employees' email and discover that he is having an affair with one of the other employees in the office.

- You install a video surveillance system in your office and discover that employees are taking office supplies home with them.

3. Spying on Email

Technology advances now allow individuals to monitor computers that they do not even have physical access to. New types of software can capture an individual's incoming and outgoing email and then immediately forward that email to another person. For example, if you are at work and your child is home from school and she receives an email from John at 3:00 p.m., at 3:01 p.m. you will receive a copy of that email sent to your email address. A few minutes later, if she replies to John's email, within seconds you will again receive a copy of what she sent to John. Describe two scenarios (other than the above) for the use of this type of software: (1) where the use would be ethical, (2) where the use would be unethical.

4. Stealing Software

The issue of pirated software is one that the software industry fights on a daily basis. The major centers of software piracy are in places like Russia and China where salaries and disposable income are comparatively low. People in developing and economically depressed countries will fall behind the industrialized world technologically if they cannot afford access to new generations of software. Considering this, is it reasonable to blame someone for using pirated software when it could potentially cost him or her two months' salary to purchase a legal copy? Create an argument for or against the following statement: "Individuals who are economically less fortunate should be allowed access to software free of charge in order to ensure that they are provided with an equal technological advantage."

Operations Management

1. Explain operations management's role in business.
2. Describe the correlation between operations management and information technology.
3. Describe the five characteristics of competitive priorities.

LO 1. Explain operations management's role in business.

Introduction

Production is the creation of goods and services using the factors of production: land, labor, capital, entrepreneurship, and knowledge. Production has historically been associated with manufacturing, but the nature of business has changed significantly in the last 20 years. The service sector, especially Internet services, has grown dramatically. The United States now has what is called a service economy—that is, one dominated by the service sector.

Organizations that excel in operations management, specifically supply chain management, perform better in almost every financial measure of success, according to a report from Boston-based AMR Research Inc. When supply chain excellence improves operations, companies experience a 5 percent higher profit margin, 15 percent less inventory, 17 percent stronger "perfect order" ratings, and 35 percent shorter cycle times than their competitors. "The basis of competition for winning companies in today's economy is supply chain superiority," said Kevin O'Marah, vice president of research at AMR Research. "These companies understand that value chain performance translates to productivity and market-share leadership. They also understand that supply chain leadership means more than just low costs and efficiency: It requires a superior ability to shape and respond to shifts in demand with innovative products and services."

Operations Management Fundamentals

Books, DVDs, downloaded MP3s, and dental and medical procedures are all examples of goods and services. ***Production management*** describes all the activities managers do to help companies create goods. To reflect the change in importance from manufacturing to services, the term *production* often has been replaced by operations to reflect the manufacturing of both goods and services. ***Operations management (OM)*** is the management of systems or processes that convert or transform resources (including human resources) into goods and services. Operations management is responsible for managing the core processes used to manufacture goods and produce services.

Essentially, the creation of goods or services involves transforming or converting inputs into outputs. Various inputs such as capital, labor, and information are used to create goods or services using one or more transformation processes (e.g., storing, transporting, and cutting). A ***transformation process*** is often referred to as the technical core, especially in manufacturing organizations, and is the actual conversion of inputs to outputs. To ensure that the desired outputs are obtained, an organization takes measurements at various points in the transformation process (feedback) and then compares them with previously established standards to determine whether corrective action is needed (control). Figure B8.1 depicts the conversion system.

Figure B8.2 displays examples of inputs, transformation processes, and outputs. Although goods and services are listed separately in Figure B8.1 it is important to note that goods and services often occur jointly. For example, having the oil changed in a car is a service, but the oil that is delivered is a good. Similarly, house painting is a service, but the paint is a good. The goods–service combination is a continuum. It ranges from primarily goods with little service to primarily service with few goods (see Figure B8.3). There are relatively few pure goods or pure services; therefore, organizations typically sell product packages, which are a combination of goods and services. This makes managing operations more interesting, and also more challenging.

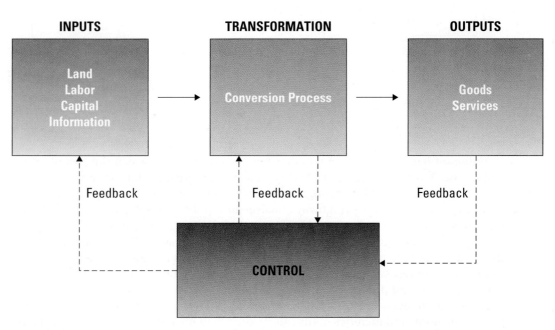

FIGURE B8.1

Operations Involves the Conversion of Inputs into Outputs

Inputs	Transformation	Outputs
Restaurant inputs include hungry customers, food, wait staff	Well-prepared food, well served: agreeable environment	Satisfied customers
Hospital inputs include patients, medical supplies, doctors, nurses	Health care	Healthy individuals
Automobile inputs include sheet steel, engine parts, tires	Fabrication and assembly of cars	High-quality cars
College inputs include high school graduates, books, professors, classrooms	Imparting knowledge and skills	Educated individuals
Distribution center inputs include stock keeping units, storage bins, workers	Storage and redistribution	Fast delivery of available products

FIGURE B8.3

The Goods–Service
Continuum: Most Products
Are a Bundle of Goods
and Services

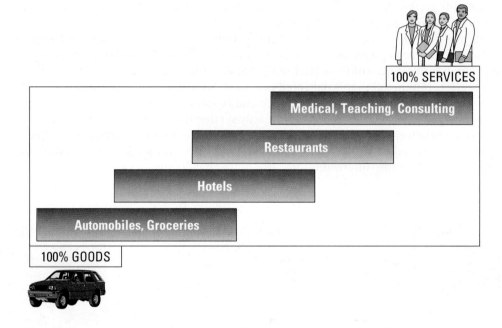

Value-added is the term used to describe the difference between the cost of inputs and the value of price of outputs. OM is critical to an organization because of its ability to increase value-added during the transformation process. In nonprofit organizations, the value of outputs (highway construction, police, and fire protection) is their value to society; the greater the value-added, the greater the effectiveness of the operations. In for-profit organizations, the value of outputs is measured by the prices that customers are willing to pay for those goods or services. Firms use the money generated by value-added for research and development, investment in new facilities and equipment, worker salaries, and profits. Consequently, the greater the value-added, the greater the amount of funds available for these important activities. The scope of OM ranges across the organization and includes many interrelated activities, such as forecasting, capacity planning, scheduling, managing inventories, assuring quality, motivating employees, deciding where to locate facilities, and more.

Reviewing the activities performed in an airline company makes it easy to understand how a service organization's OM team adds value. The company consists of the airplanes, airport facilities, and maintenance facilities, and typical OM activities include:

- **Forecasting:** Estimating seat demand for flights, weather and landing conditions, and estimates for growth or reduction in air travel are all included in forecasting.

- **Capacity planning:** This is the key essential metric for the airline to maintain cash flow and increase revenues. Underestimating or overestimating flights will hurt profits.

- **Scheduling:** The airline operates on tight schedules that must be maintained including flights, pilots, flight attendants, ground crews, baggage handlers, and routine maintenance.

- **Managing inventory:** Inventory of such items as foods, beverages, first-aid equipment, in-flight magazines, pillows, blankets, and life jackets is essential for the airline.

- **Assuring quality:** Quality is indispensable in an airline where safety is the highest priority. Today's travelers expect high-quality customer service during ticketing, check-in, curb service, and unexpected issues where the emphasis is on efficiency and courtesy.

- **Motivating and training employees:** Airline employees must be highly trained and continually motivated, especially when dealing with frustrated airline travelers.

- **Locating facilities:** Key questions facing airlines include which cities to offer services, where to host maintenance facilities, and where to locate major and minor hubs.

Opposite from an airline is a bike factory, which is typically an assembly operation: buying components such as frames, tires, wheels, gears, and other items from suppliers, and then assembling bicycles. A bike factory also does some of the fabrication work itself, forming frames and making the gears and chains. Obviously, an airline company and a bike factory are completely different types of operations. One is primarily a service operation, the other a producer of goods. Nonetheless, these two operations have much in common. The same as the airline, the bike factory must schedule production, deal with components, order parts and materials, schedule and train employees, ensure quality standards are met, and above all satisfy customers. In both organizations, the success of the business depends on short- and long-term planning and the ability of its executives and managers to make informed decisions.

IT's Role in OM

LO 2. Describe the correlation between operations management and information technology.

Managers can use IT to heavily influence OM decisions including productivity, costs, flexibility, quality, and customer satisfaction. One of the greatest benefits of IT on OM is in making operational decisions because operations management exerts considerable influence over the degree to which the goals and objectives of the organization are realized. Most OM decisions involve many possible alternatives that can have varying impacts on revenues and expenses. OM information systems are critical for managers to be able to make well-informed decisions.

Decision support systems and *executive information systems* can help an organization perform what-if analysis, sensitivity analysis, drill-down, and consolidation. Numerous managerial and strategic key decisions are based on OM information systems that affect the entire organization, including:

- **What:** What resources will be needed, and in what amounts?

- **When:** When will each resource be needed? When should the work be scheduled? When should materials and other supplies be ordered? When is corrective action needed?

- **Where:** Where will the work be performed?
- **How:** How will the product or service be designed? How will the work be done (organization, methods, equipment)? How will resources be allocated?
- **Who:** Who will perform the work?

OM STRATEGIC BUSINESS SYSTEMS

UPS uses package flow information systems at each of its locations. The custom-built systems combine operations strategy and mapping technology to optimize the way boxes are loaded and delivered. The goal is to use the package flow software to cut the distance that delivery trucks travel by more than 100 million miles each year. The project will also help UPS streamline the profitability of each of its facility locations.

Operations strategy is concerned with the development of a long-term plan for determining how to best utilize the major resources of the firm so that there is a high degree of compatibility between these resources and the firm's long-term corporate strategy. Operations strategy addresses very broad questions about how these major resources should be configured to achieve the desired corporate objectives. Some of the major long-term issues addressed in operations strategy include:

- How big to make the facilities?
- Where to locate the facilities?
- When to build additional facilities?
- What type of process(es) to install to make the products?

Each of these issues can be addressed by OM decision support systems. In developing an operations strategy, management needs to consider many factors. These include (*a*) the level of technology that is or will be available, (*b*) the required skill levels of the workers, and (*c*) the degree of vertical integration, in terms of the extent to which outside suppliers are used.

Today, many organizations, especially larger conglomerates, operate in terms of ***strategic business units (SBUs),*** which consist of several stand-alone businesses. When companies become really large, they are best thought of as being composed of a number of businesses (or SBUs). As displayed in Figure B8.4, operations strategy supports the long-range strategy developed at the SBU level.

FIGURE B8.4

Hierarchy of Operational Planning

Type of Planning	Time Frame	Issues	Decisions	Systems
Strategic Planning	Long range	Plant size, location, type of processes	How will we make the products? Where do we locate the facility or facilities? How much capacity do we require? When should we add additional capacity?	Materials requirement planning (MRP) systems
Tactical Planning	Intermediate range	Workforce size, material requirements	How many workers do we need? When do we need them? Should we work overtime or put on a section shift? When should we have material delivered? Should we have a finished goods inventory?	Global inventory management systems
Operational Planning and Control (OP&C)	Short range	Daily scheduling of employees, jobs, and equipment, process management, inventory management	What jobs do we work on today or this week? To whom do we assign what tasks? What jobs have priority?	Inventory management and control systems, transportation planning systems, distribution management systems

Decisions at the SBU level focus on being effective, that is, "on doing the right things." These decisions are sometimes referred to as **strategic planning,** which focuses on long-range planning such as plant size, location, and type of process to be used. The primary system used for strategic planning is a materials requirement planning system. **Materials requirement planning (MRP) systems** use sales forecasts to make sure that needed parts and materials are available at the right time and place in a specific company. The latest version of MRP is enterprise resource planning.

Strategic decisions impact intermediate-range decisions, often referred to as tactical planning, which focuses on being efficient, that is, "doing things right." **Tactical planning** focuses on producing goods and services as efficiently as possible within the strategic plan. Here the emphasis is on producing quality products, including when material should be delivered, when products should be made to best meet demand, and what size the workforce should be. One of the primary systems used in tactical planning includes global inventory management. **Global inventory management systems** provide the ability to locate, track, and predict the movement of every component or material anywhere upstream or downstream in the production process. This allows an organization to locate and analyze its inventory anywhere in its production process.

Finally, **operational planning and control (OP&C)** deals with the day-to-day procedures for performing work, including scheduling, inventory, and process management. **Inventory management and control systems** provide control and visibility to the status of individual items maintained in inventory. The software maintains inventory record accuracy, generates material requirements for all purchased items, and analyzes inventory performance. Inventory management and control software provides organizations with the information from a variety of sources including:

- Current inventory and order status.
- Cost accounting.
- Sales forecasts and customer orders.
- Manufacturing capacity.
- New-product introductions.

Two additional OP&C systems are transportation planning and distribution management. **Transportation planning systems** track and analyze the movement of materials and products to ensure the delivery of materials and finished goods at the right time, the right place, and the lowest cost. **Distribution management systems** coordinate the process of transporting materials from a manufacturer to distribution centers to the final customers. Transportation routes directly affect the speed and cost of delivery. An organization will use these systems to help it decide if it wants to use an effectiveness route and ship its products directly to its customers or use an efficiency route and ship its products to a distributor that ships the products to customers.

Competitive OM Strategy

The key to developing a competitive OM strategy lies in understanding how to create value-added goods and services for customers. Specifically, value is added through the competitive priority or priorities that are selected to support a given strategy. Five key competitive priorities translate directly into characteristics that are used to describe various processes by which a company can add value to its OM decisions:

1. Cost
2. Quality
3. Delivery
4. Flexibility
5. Service

LO 3. Describe the five characteristics of competitive priorities.

COST

Every industry has low-cost providers. However, being the low-cost producer does not always guarantee profitability and success. Products sold strictly on the basis of cost are typically commodity-like products including such goods as flour, petroleum, and sugar. In other words, customers cannot distinguish the products made by one firm from those of another. As a result, customers use cost as the primary determinant in making a purchasing decision.

Low-cost market segments are frequently very large, and many companies are lured by the potential for significant profits, which are associated with large unit volumes of product. As a consequence, the competition in this segment is exceedingly fierce—and so is the failure rate. After all, there can be only one lowest-cost producer, and that firm usually establishes the selling price in the market.

QUALITY

Quality can be divided into two categories—product quality and process quality. Product quality levels vary as to the particular market that it aims to serve. For example, a generic bike is of significantly different quality than the bike of a world-class cyclist. Higher quality products command higher prices in the marketplace. Organizations must establish the "proper level" of product quality by focusing on the exact requirements of their customers. Overdesigned products with too much quality will be viewed as being prohibitively expensive. Underdesigned products, on the other hand, will lose customers to products that cost a little more but are perceived by the customers as offering greater value.

Process quality is critical in every market segment. Regardless of whether the product is a generic bike or a bike for an international cyclist, customers want products without defects. Thus, the primary goal of process quality is to produce error-free products. The investment in improving quality pays off in stronger customer relationships and higher revenues. Many organizations use modern quality control standards, including:

- **Six sigma quality:** The goal is to detect potential problems to prevent their occurrence and achieve no more than 3.4 defects per million opportunities. That is important to companies like Bank of America, which makes 4 million transactions a day.

- **Malcolm Baldrige National Quality Awards:** In 1987 in the United States, a standard was set for overall company quality with the introduction of the Malcolm Baldrige National Quality Awards, named in honor of the late U.S. secretary of commerce. Companies can apply for these awards in each of the following areas: manufacturing, services, small businesses, education, and health care. To qualify, an organization has to show quality in seven key areas: leadership, strategic planning, customer and market focus, information and analysis, human resources focus, process management, and business results.

- **ISO 900:** The common name given to quality management and assurance standards comes from the ***International Organization for Standardization (ISO),*** a nongovernmental organization established in 1947 to promote the development of world standards to facilitate the international exchange of goods and services. ISO is a worldwide federation of national standards bodies from more than 140 countries. ISO 900 standards require a company to determine customer needs, including regulatory and legal requirements. The company must also make communication arrangements to handle issues such as complaints. Other standards involve process control, product testing, storage, and delivery.

- **ISO 14000:** This collection of the best practices for managing an organization's impact on the environment does not prescribe specific performance levels, but establishes environmental management systems. The requirements for certification include having an environmental policy, setting specific improvement targets, conducting audits of environmental programs, and maintaining top management review of processes. Certification in ISO 14000 displays that a firm has a world-class management system in both quality and environmental standards.

- **CMMI:** Capability Maturity Model Integration is a framework of best practices. The current version, CMMI-DEV, describes best practices in managing, measuring, and monitoring software development processes. CMMI does not describe the processes themselves; it describes the characteristics of good processes, thus providing guidelines for companies developing or honing their own sets of processes.

DELIVERY

Another key factor in purchasing decisions is delivery speed. The ability of a firm to provide consistent and fast delivery allows it to charge a premium price for its products. George Stalk, Jr., of the Boston Consulting Group, has demonstrated that both profits and market share are directly linked to the speed with which a company can deliver its products relative to its competition. In addition to fast delivery, the reliability of the delivery is also important. In other words, products should be delivered to customers with minimum variance in delivery times.

FLEXIBILITY

Flexibility, from a strategic perspective, refers to the ability of a company to offer a wide variety of products to its customers. Flexibility is also a measure of how fast a company can convert its process(es) from making an old line of products to producing a new product line. Product variety is often perceived by the customers to be a dimension of quality.

The flexibility of the manufacturing process at John Deere's Harvester Works in Moline, Illinois, allows the firm to respond to the unpredictability of the agricultural industry's equipment needs. By manufacturing such small-volume products as seed planters in "modules," or factories within a factory, Deere can offer farmers a choice of 84 different planter models with such a wide variety of options that farmers can have planters virtually customized to meet their individual needs. Its manufacturing process thus allows Deere to compete on both speed and flexibility.

Currently, there appears to be a trend toward offering environmentally friendly products that are made through environmentally friendly processes. As consumers become more aware of the fragility of the environment, they are increasingly turning toward products that are safe for the environment. Several flexible manufacturers now advertise environmentally friendly products, energy-efficient products, and recycled products.

SERVICE

With shortened product life cycles, products tend to migrate toward one common standard. As a consequence, these products are often viewed as commodities in which price is the primary differentiator. For example, the differences in laptops offered among PC manufactures are relatively insignificant so price is the prime selection criterion. For this reason, many companies attempt to place an emphasis on high-quality customer service as a primary differentiator. Customer service can add tremendous value to an ordinary product.

Businesses are always looking toward the future to find the next competitive advantage that will distinguish their products in the marketplace. To obtain an advantage in such a competitive environment, firms must provide "value-added" goods and services, and the primary area where they can capitalize on all five competitive priorities is in the supply chain.

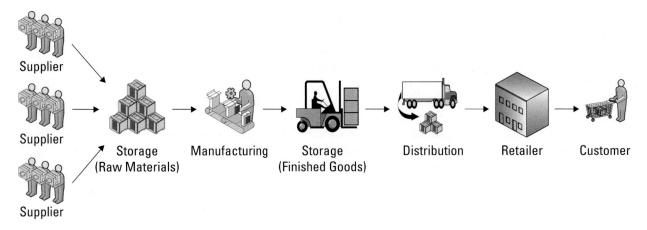

FIGURE B8.5

A Typical Manufacturing
Supply Chain

OM and the Supply Chain

A *supply chain* consists of all parties involved, directly or indirectly, in the procurement of a product or raw material. *Supply chain management (SCM)* involves the management of information flows between and among stages in a supply chain to maximize total supply chain effectiveness and profitability. SCM software can enable an organization to generate efficiencies within these steps by automating and improving the information flows throughout and among the different supply chain components. Figures B8.5 and B8.6 display the typical supply chains for goods and services.

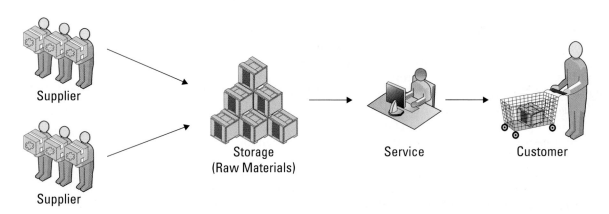

FIGURE B8.6

A Typical Service Supply Chain

This plug-in introduced the concept of operations management, showcasing how information technology can be used to improve fundamental business processes. Operations management exists across a variety of sectors and industries. Various examples were given showcasing information technology's ability to help organizations improve their interactions with suppliers, manufacturers, distributors, warehouses, and customers.

As a business student, you should understand this pivotal role that information technology plays in facilitating operations management and in supporting the basic infrastructure and coordination needed for core business operations to function.

 KEY TERMS

Distribution management
    system, 441
Global inventory management
    system, 441
International Organization for
    Standardization (ISO), 442
Inventory management and
    control system, 441
Materials requirement planning
    (MRP) systems, 441

Operational planning and
    control (OP&C), 441
Operations management
    (OM), 437
Production, 436
Production management, 437
Strategic business unit
    (SBU), 440
Strategic planning, 441
Supply chain, 444

Supply chain management
    (SCM), 444
Tactical planning, 441
Transformation process, 437
Transportation planning
    system, 441
Value-added, 438

CLOSING CASE ONE

How Levi's Got Its Jeans into Walmart

People around the world recognize Levi's as an American icon, the cool jeans worn by movie stars James Dean and Marilyn Monroe. However, the company failed to keep up with the fast-changing tastes of American teenagers. In particular, it missed the trend to baggy jeans that caught hold in the mid-1990s. Sales plummeted from $7.1 billion in 1996 to $4.1 billion in 2003, and Levi's U.S. market share dropped from 18.7 percent in 1997 to 12 percent in 2003, a huge decline of almost one-third in both dollars and market share.

Analyzing and Responding to What Happened

Competition hit Levi Strauss on both the high and low ends. Fashion-conscious buyers were drawn to high-priced brands like Blue Cult, Juicy, and Seven, which had more fashion cachet than Levi's. On the low end, parents were buying Wrangler and Lee jeans for their kids because on average they cost about $10 less than Levi's Red Tab brand. Wrangler and Lee were also the brands they found at discount retailers such as Walmart, Target, and T. J. Maxx. David Bergen, Levi's chief information officer (CIO), described the company as "getting squeezed," and "caught in the jaws of death."

Levi Strauss's new CEO, Philip A. Marineau, came to the company from PepsiCo in 1999, a year after he helped PepsiCo surpass Coca-Cola in sales for the first time. Marineau recruited Bergen in 2000 from Carstation.com. Marineau quickly realized that turning Levi

Strauss around would entail manufacturing, marketing, and distributing jeans that customers demanded, particularly customers at the low end where the mass market was located.

Bergen was eager to join Marineau's team because of his background in clothing, retailing, and manufacturing with companies such as The Gap and Esprit de Corps in the 1980s. He knew that Marineau's plan to anticipate customer wants would require up-to-date IT applications such as data warehousing, data mining, and customer relationship management (CRM) systems. He also knew that selling to mass market retailers would require upgrades to the supply chain management (SCM) systems, and he understood that globalization would necessitate standardized enterprise resource planning (ERP) systems. Overall, it was a challenge any ambitious CIO would covet. After all, designing and installing IT systems that drive and achieve key business initiatives is what it is all about.

Joining Walmart

Walmart was a pioneer in supply chain management systems, having learned early on that driving costs out of the supply chain would let it offer products to customers at the lowest possible prices, while at the same time assuring that products the customers demanded were always on store shelves. Becoming one of Walmart's 30,000 suppliers is not easy. Walmart insists that its suppliers do business using up-to-date IT systems to manage the supply chain—not just the supply chain between Walmart and its suppliers, but the supply chains between the suppliers and their suppliers as well. Walmart has strict supply chain management system requirements that its business partners must meet.

Walmart's requirements presented Levi Strauss with a serious hurdle to overcome because its supply chain management systems were in bad shape. Levi Strauss executives did not even have access to key information required to track where products were moving in the supply chain. For example, they did not know how many pairs of jeans were in the factory awaiting shipment, how many were somewhere en route, or how many had just been unloaded at a customer's warehouse. According to Greg Hammann, Levi's U.S. chief customer officer, "Our supply chain could not deliver the services Walmart expected."

Bergen created a cross-functional team of key managers from IT, finance, and sales to transform Levi Strauss's systems to meet Walmart's requirements. Their recommendations included network upgrades, modifications to ordering and logistics applications, and data warehouse improvements, among others. Although Bergen realized that about half the changes required to current IT systems to accommodate the state-of-the-art demands of Walmart would be a waste of resources since these systems were being replaced by a new SAP enterprise software system over the next five years, Levi Strauss could not wait for the SAP installation if it wanted Walmart's business now, so it decided to move forward with the changes to the current systems.

The successful transformation of its supply chain management system allowed the company to collaborate with Walmart. The company introduced its new signature line at Walmart, which sells for around $23 and has fewer details in the finish than Levi's other lines, no trademark pocket stitching or red tab, for example. Walmart wants big-name brands to lure more affluent customers into its stores, while still maintaining the low price points all Walmart customers have come to expect. Walmart Senior Vice President Lois Mikita noted that Walmart "continues to tailor its selection to meet the needs of customers from a cross section of income levels and lifestyles." She also stated she is impressed with the level of detail Levi Strauss has put into its systems transformation efforts to "make the execution of this new launch 100 percent."

Achieving Business Success through IT

Bergen's changes were a success and the percentage of products delivered on time quickly rose from 65 percent to 95 percent primarily because of the updated supply chain management system. Levi's total sales were also up in the third and fourth quarters of 2003, for the first time since 1996. NPD Group's Fashionworld is a research group that tracks apparel and footwear market trends. In 2003, Levi's appeared on NPD Fashionworld's top 10 list of brands preferred by young women, ending an absence of several years. Marshall Cohen, a senior industry analyst at NPD Fashionworld, noted that Levi's "hadn't been close to that for a while. Teens hadn't gravitated toward Levi's in years. That was incredible. A lot of that has to do with having the right style in the right place at the right time." The improved systems, Cohen noted, also helped the company get the right sizes to the right stores.

Another highly successful IT system implemented by Levi Strauss is a digital dashboard that executives can display on their PC screens. The dashboard lets an executive see the status of a product as it moves from the factory floor to distribution centers to retail stores. For example, the dashboard can display how Levi's 501 jeans are selling at an individual Kohl's store compared to forecasted sales. "When I first got here I didn't see anything," Hammann said. "Now I can drill down to the product level."

The digital dashboard alerts executives to trends that under the previous systems would have taken weeks to detect. For example, in 2003 Levi Strauss started to ship Dockers Stain Defender pants. Expected sales for the pants were around 2 million pairs. The digital dashboard quickly notified key executives that the trousers were selling around 2.5 million pairs. This information enabled them to adjust production upward in time to ship more pants, meet the increased demand, and avoid lost sales. Levi Strauss also uses the systems to control supply during key seasonal sales periods such as back-to-school and Christmas.

"If I look overconfident, I'm not," Bergen said. "I'm very nervous about this change. When we trip, we have to stand up real quick and get back on the horse, as they say." As if to reinforce Bergen's point, Gib Carey, a supply chain analyst at Bain, noted, "The place where companies do fail is when they aren't bringing anything new to Walmart. Walmart is constantly looking at 'How can I get the same product I am selling today at a lower price somewhere else?'"

Questions

1. How did Levi Strauss achieve business success through the use of supply chain management?
2. What might have happened to Levi Strauss if its top executives had not supported investments in SCM?
3. David Bergen, Levi's CIO, put together a cross-functional team of key managers from IT, finance, and sales to transform Levi's systems to meet Walmart's requirements. Analyze the relationships between these three business areas and OM. How can OM help support these three critical business areas?
4. Describe the five basic SCM components in reference to Walmart's business model.
5. Explain the future trends of SCM and provide an example of how Levi Strauss could use these technologies to streamline its business operations.
6. Identify any security and ethical issues that might occur for a company doing business with Walmart.

 CLOSING CASE TWO

The Digital Hospital

For years, health care has missed the huge benefits that information technology has bestowed upon the rest of the economy. During the 1990s, productivity in health care services declined, according to estimates from Economy.com Inc. That is a huge underachievement in a decade of strong gains from the overall economy. This is beginning to change as hospitals, along with insurers and the government, are stepping up their IT investments. Hospitals are finally discarding their clumsy, sluggish first-generation networks and are beginning to install laptops, software, and Internet technologies.

Hackensack University Medical Center's IT Projects

- Patients can use 37-inch plasma TVs in their rooms to surf the Internet for information about their medical conditions. They can also take interactive classes about their condition and find out how to take care of themselves after discharge.

- From virtually anywhere in the world, physicians can make their hospital rounds with the help of a life-size robot, Mr. Rounder. Using laptops with joysticks and web links, doctors drive the robot around the hospital to confer by remote video with patients and other doctors. When a blizzard prevented Dr. Garth Ballantynes from reaching the hospital, he used Mr. Rounder to make his rounds from his home 82 miles away.

- Pocket-sized PCs that hook wirelessly into the hospital's network allow doctors the freedom to place pharmacy orders and pull up medical records from anywhere in the hospital.

- Nurses use wireless laptops to record patients' vitals signs, symptoms, and medications. Doctors can sign into the same central system from the laptops to order prescriptions and lab tests and read their patient's progress.

- The hospital's internal website stores all of its medical images. Doctors can view crystal-clear digital versions of their patients' X-rays, MRIs, and CT scans from any computer in or out of the hospital.

- A giant robot named Robbie, equipped with arms, reads prescriptions entered into the hospital's computer system and then grabs medications stored on pegs on the wall. The pills are then dropped into containers that are marked for each patient.

Hackensack University Medical Center in Hackensack, New Jersey, is one of the nation's most aggressive technology adopters, investing $72 million in IT projects. The IT investments are paying off for the hospital with patient mortality rates decreasing—down 16 percent in four years—and quality of care and productivity increasing. The most important piece of Hackensack's digital initiatives is the networked software that acts as the hospital's central nervous system. Using wireless laptops, nurses log in to the system to record patient information and progress. Doctors tap into the network via wireless devices to order prescriptions and lab tests. Everything is linked, from the automated pharmacy to the X-ray lab, eliminating the need for faxes, phone calls, and other administrative hassles. Figure B8.7 displays the hospital's IT systems development projects.

More important than saving money is saving lives. Poor information kills some 7,000 Americans each year just by missing drug-interaction problems, according to the National Academy of Sciences Institute of Medicine. Hospital errors result in 100,000 deaths annually. Early evidence indicates that proper technology can reduce this amount. Hospitals using electronic prescription systems have seen 80 percent fewer prescription errors.

Questions

1. How would operations management be a critical component to a hospital?
2. How would a hospital use each of the three OM planning strategies to improve its operations?
3. How might a hospital use each of the five competitive priorities to increase value to its goods and services?

1. Operational Mowing

Mary Lou has worked for the same Fortune 500 company for almost 15 years. Although the company had gone through some tough times, things were starting to turn around. Customer orders were up, and quality and productivity had improved dramatically from what they had been only a few years earlier due to a companywide quality improvement program. So it came as a real shock to Mary Lou and about 400 of her co-workers when they were suddenly terminated following the new CEO's decision to downsize the company.

After recovering from the initial shock, Mary Lou tried to find employment elsewhere. Despite her efforts, after eight months of searching she was no closer to finding a job than the day she started. Her funds were being depleted and she was getting more discouraged. There was one bright spot, though: She was able to bring in a little money by mowing lawns for her neighbors. She got involved quite by chance when she heard one neighbor remark that now that his children were on their own, nobody was around to cut the grass. Almost jokingly, Mary Lou asked him how much he'd be willing to pay. Soon Mary Lou was mowing the lawns of 10 neighbors. Other neighbors wanted her to work on their lawns, but she did not feel that she could spare any more time from her job search.

However, as the rejection letters began to pile up, Mary Lou knew she had to make a decision if she would go into business for herself or continue her job search.

By the end of her first year in business, Mary Lou was easily earning a good living. She began performing other services such as fertilizing lawns, weeding gardens, trimming shrubs, and installing sprinkler systems. Business was so good that Mary Lou hired several employees to assist her and believed she could further expand her business. As Mary Lou begins to plan her expansion, she needs your assistance in answering the following questions:

1. In what ways are Mary Lou's customers most likely to judge the quality of her lawn care services?

2. Mary Lou is the operations manager of her business. Among her responsibilities are forecasting, inventory management, scheduling, quality assurance, and maintenance.

   1. What kinds of things would likely require forecasts?
   2. What inventory items does Mary Lou probably have? Name one inventory decision she has to make periodically.
   3. What scheduling must she do? What things might occur to disrupt schedules and cause Mary Lou to reschedule?
   4. How important is quality assurance to Mary Lou's business?

3. What are some of the trade-offs that Mary Lou probably considered relative to:

   1. Working for a company instead of for herself?
   2. Expanding the business?
   3. Launching a website?

4. The town is considering an ordinance that would prohibit grass clippings at the curb for pickup because local landfills cannot handle the volume. What options might Mary Lou consider if the ordinance is passed?

5. Mary Lou decided to offer her employees a bonus of $250 for ideas on how to improve the business, and they provided several good ideas. One idea that she initially rejected now appears to hold great promise. The employee who proposed the idea has left the company and is currently working for a competitor. Should Mary Lou send the employee a check for the idea?

2. Total Recall

In mid-2000, the Firestone Tire Company issued a recall of some of its tires—those mounted on certain sport-utility vehicles (SUV) of the Ford Motor Company. This was done in response to reports that tire treads on some SUVs separated in use, causing accidents, some of which involved fatal injuries as vehicles rolled over.

At first, Firestone denied there was a problem with its tires, but it issued the recall under pressure from consumer groups and various government agencies. All of the tires in question were produced at the same tire plant, and there were calls to shut down that facility. Firestone suggested that Ford incorrectly matched the wrong tires with its SUVs. There were also suggestions that the shock absorbers of the SUVs were rubbing against the tires, causing or aggravating the problem.

Both Ford and Firestone denied that this had been an ongoing problem. However, there was a public outcry when it was learned that Firestone had previously issued recalls of these tires in South America, and the companies had settled at least one lawsuit involving an accident caused by tread separation several years earlier.

This case raises a number of issues, some related to possible causes and others to ethics. Discuss each of these factors and their actual or potential relevance to what happened:

1. Product
2. Quality control
3. Ethics

Sustainable MIS Infrastructures

LEARNING OUTCOMES

1. Identify the environmental impacts associated with MIS.
2. Explain the three components of a sustainable MIS infrastructure along with their business benefits.

LO 1. Identify the environmental impacts associated with MIS.

MIS and the Environment

The general trend in MIS is toward smaller, faster, and cheaper devices. Gordon Moore, co-founder of Intel, the world's largest producer of computer chips or microprocessors, observed in 1965 that continued advances in technological innovation made it possible to reduce the size of a computer chip (the brains of a computer, or even a cell phone now) while doubling its capacity every two years. His prediction that this trend would continue has come to be known as *Moore's Law,* which refers to the computer chip performance per dollar doubles every 18 months. Although Moore originally assumed a two-year period, many sources today refer to the 18-month figure.

Moore's Law is great for many companies as they can acquire large amounts of MIS equipment for cheaper and cheaper costs. As ebusinesses continue to grow, companies equip their employees with multiple forms of electronic devices ranging from laptops to cell phones to iPads. This is great for supporting a connected corporation, significant unintended side effects include our dependence upon fossil fuels and increased need for safe disposal of outdated computing equipment. Concern about these side effects has led many companies to turn to an ecological practice known as sustainable MIS. *Sustainable, or green, MIS* describes the production, management, use, and disposal of technology in a way that minimizes damage to the environment. Sustainable MIS is a critical part of *corporate social responsibility*, that is, companies' acknowledged responsibility to society. Building sustainable MIS infrastructures is a core initiative and critical success factor for socially responsible corporations. Figure B9.1 displays the three primary side effects of businesses' expanded use of technology.

INCREASED ELECTRONIC WASTE

Moore's Law has made technological devices smaller, cheaper, and faster, allowing more people from all income levels to purchase computing equipment. This increased demand is causing numerous environmental issues. *Ewaste* refers to discarded, obsolete, or broken electronic devices. Ewaste includes CDs, DVDs, thumb drives, printer cartridges, cell phones, iPods, external hard drives, TVs, VCRs, DVD players, microwaves, and so on. Some say one human year is equivalent to seven years of technological advancements. A personal computer has a life expectancy of only three to five years and a cell phone is less than two years.

Sustainable MIS disposal refers to the safe disposal of MIS assets at the end of their life cycle. It ensures that ewaste does not end up in landfills causing environmental issues. A single computer contains more than 700 chemicals; some are toxic, such as mercury, lead, and cadmium. If a computer ends up in a landfill, the toxic substances it contains can leach into our land, water, and air. Recycling costs from $15 to $50 for a monitor or computer. Many companies, including public schools and universities, simply can't afford the recycling costs.[1]

Ewaste also occurs when unused equipment stored in attics, basements, and storage facilities never reaches a recycling center. Retrieving the silver, gold, and other valuable metals from these devices is more efficient and less environmentally harmful than removing it from its natural environment.

Currently, less than 20 percent of ewaste in the United States is recycled; however, even recycling does not guarantee the equipment is disposed of safely. While some recyclers process the material ethically, others ship it to countries such as China and India, where environmental enforcement is weak. This action poses its own global environmental problems.

INCREASED ENERGY CONSUMPTION

Energy consumption is the amount of energy consumed by business processes and systems. Huge increases in technology use have greatly amplified energy consumption. The energy consumed by a computer is estimated to produce as much as 10 percent of the amount of carbon dioxide produced by an automobile. Computer servers in the United States account for about 1 percent of the total energy needs of the country. Put in perspective, this is roughly equivalent to the energy consumption of Mississippi.

Computers consume energy even when they are not being used. For convenience and to allow for automatic updates and backup, the majority of computer equipment is never completely shut down. It draws energy 24 hours a day.

INCREASED CARBON EMISSIONS

The major human-generated greenhouse gases, such as carbon emissions from energy use, are very likely responsible for the increases in climatic temperature over the past half a century. Additional temperature increases are projected over the next hundred years, with serious consequences for Earth's environment, if *carbon emissions*, including the carbon dioxide and carbon monoxide produced by business processes and systems, are not reduced.

In the United States, coal provides more than 50 percent of electrical power. When left on continuously, a single desktop computer and monitor can consume at least 100 watts of power per hour. To generate that much energy 24 hours a day for a year would require approximately 714 pounds of coal. When that coal is burned, it releases on average 5 pounds of sulfur dioxide, 5 pounds of nitrogen oxides, and 1,852 pounds (that is almost a ton) of carbon dioxide.[2]

Supporting the Environment: Sustainable MIS Infrastructure

Combating ewaste, energy consumption, and carbon emissions requires a firm to focus on creating sustainable MIS infrastructures. A sustainable MIS infrastructure identifies ways that a company can grow in terms of computing resources while simultaneously

Increased Electronic Waste

Increased Energy Consumption

Increased Carbon Emissions

FIGURE B9.1

Three Pressures Driving Sustainable MIS Infrastructures

LO 2. Explain the three components of a sustainable MIS infrastructure along with their business benefits.

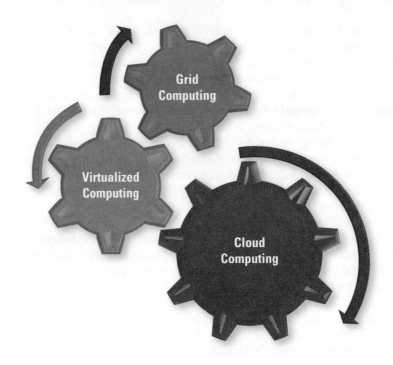

becoming less dependent on hardware and energy consumption. The components of a sustainable MIS infrastructure are displayed in Figure B9.2.

GRID COMPUTING

When a light is turned on, the power grid delivers exactly what is needed, instantly. Computers and networks can now work that way using grid computing. ***Grid computing*** is a collection of computers, often geographically dispersed, that are coordinated to solve a common problem. With grid computing a problem is broken into pieces and distributed to many machines, allowing faster processing than could occur with a single system (see Figure B9.3). Computers typically use less than 25 percent of their processing power, leaving more than 75 percent available for other tasks. Innovatively, grid computing takes advantage of this unused processing power by linking thousands of individual computers around the world to create a "virtual supercomputer" that can process intensive tasks. Grid computing makes better use of MIS resources, allowing greater scalability as systems can easily grow to handle peaks and valleys in demand, become more cost efficient, and solve problems that would be impossible to tackle with a single computer (see Figures B9.4 and B9.5).

The uses of grid computing are numerous, including the creative environment of animated movies. DreamWorks Animation used grid computing to complete many of its hit films including *Antz, Shrek, Madagascar,* and *How to Train Your Dragon.* The third *Shrek* film required more than 20 million computer hours to make (compared to 5 million for the first *Shrek* and 10 million for the second). At peak production times, DreamWorks dedicated more than 4,000 computers to its *Shrek* grid, allowing it to complete scenes in days and hours instead of months. With the increased grid computing power, the DreamWork's animators were able to add more realistic movement to water, fire, and magic scenes (see Figure B9.6). With grid computing a company can work faster or more efficiently, providing a potential competitive advantage and additional cost savings.

Solving the Energy Issue with Smart Grids

A ***smart grid*** delivers electricity using two-way digital technology. It is meant to solve the problem of the world's outdated electrical grid, making it more efficient and reliable by adding the ability to remotely monitor, analyze, and control the transmission of

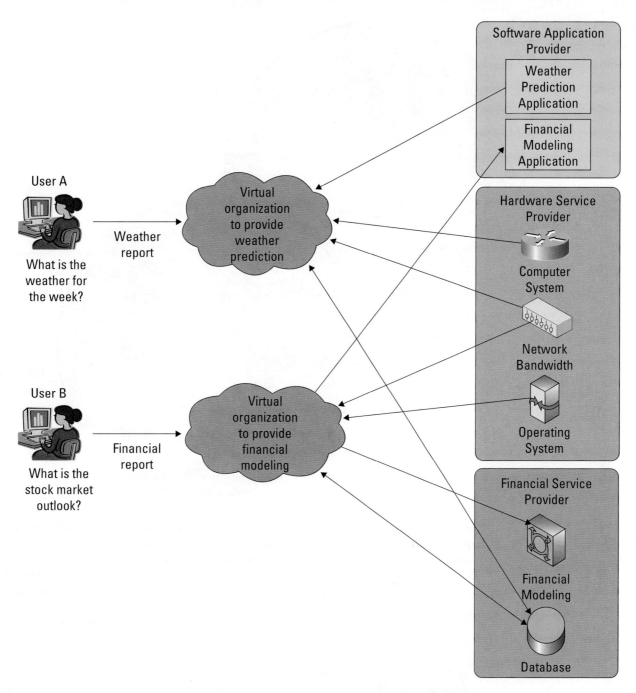

User A

What is the
weather for
the week?

Weather
report

Virtual
organization
to provide
weather
prediction

User B

What is the
stock market
outlook?

Financial
report

Virtual
organization
to provide
financial
modeling

Software Application
Provider

Weather
Prediction
Application

Financial
Modeling
Application

Hardware Service
Provider

Computer
System

Network
Bandwidth

Operating
System

Financial Service
Provider

Financial
Modeling

Database

FIGURE B9.3

Virtual Organizations
Using Grid Computing

power. The current U.S. power grid is said to have outlived its life expectancy by as much as 30 years. Smart grids provide users with real-time usage monitoring, allowing them to choose off-peak times for noncritical or less urgent applications or processes. Residents of Boulder, Colorado, can monitor their use of electricity and control appliances remotely due to the city's large-scale smart grid system. Xcel Energy has installed 21,000 smart grid meters since the $100 million program started several years ago. Energy use by early adopters is down as much as 45 percent.[3]

VIRTUALIZED COMPUTING

Most computers and even servers typically run only one operating system, such as Windows or Mac OS, and only one application. When a company invests in a large system such as inventory management, it dedicates a single server to house the system. This ensures the system has enough capacity to run during peak times and to scale to meet demand.

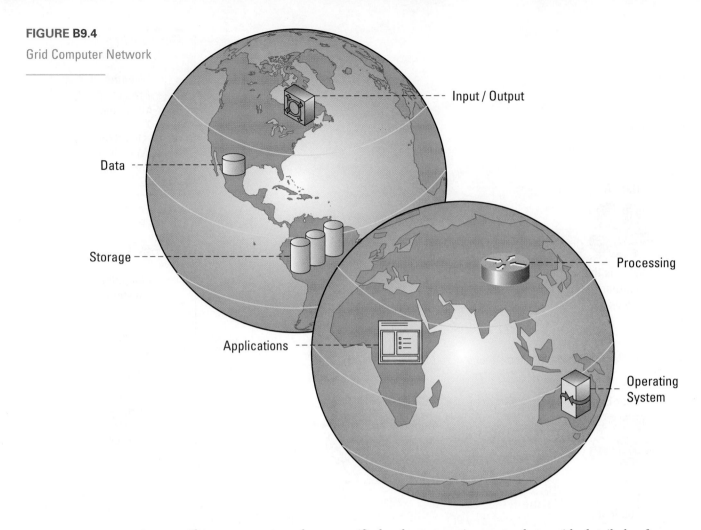

Input / Output

Data

Storage

Processing

Applications

Operating System

FIGURE B9.5

Grid Computing Example

Also, many systems have specific hardware requirements along with detailed software requirements, making it difficult to find two systems with the same requirements that could share the same machine. Through the use of virtualization, computers can run multiple operating systems along with multiple software applications—all at the same time.

Virtualization creates multiple "virtual" machines on a single computing device. A good analogy is a computer printer. In the past you had to purchase a fax machine, copy machine, answering machine, and computer printer separately. This was expensive, required enough energy to run four separate machines, not to mention created additional amounts of ewaste. Today, you can buy a virtualized computer printer that functions as a fax machine, answering machine, and copy machine all on one physical machine, thereby reducing costs, power requirements, and ewaste. Virtualization is essentially a form of consolidation that can benefit sustainable MIS infrastructures in a variety of ways, for example:

■ By increasing availability of applications that can give a higher level of performance depending on the hardware used.

■ By increasing energy efficiency by requiring less hardware to run multiple systems or applications.

■ By increasing hardware usability by running multiple operating systems on a single computer.

How Grid Computing **Works**
Here's how DreamWorks Animation uses technologies to create films such as *Shrek 2* and *Shark Tale*.

1 Artists create digital 3-D characters and scenes on graphics work-stations. These can handle design, but not the heavy data-crunching needed to flesh out the figures.

2 Grid software deals out the animations in bite-size pieces to a cluster of server computers in DreamWorks data centers. These add color, texture, and lighting.

3 If more computing is needed, work is farmed out to more computers at a Hewlett-Packard data center. When all the pieces are complete, they are reassembled for editing.

FIGURE B9.6

Making *Shrek 2* with Grid Computing

Originally, computers were designed to run a single application on a single operating system. This left most computers vastly underutilized (as mentioned earlier, 75 percent of most computing power is available for other tasks). Virtualization allows multiple virtual computers to exist on a single machine, which allows it to share its resources, such as memory and hard disk space, to run different applications and even different operating systems. Mac computers have the ability to run both the Apple operating system and the Windows PC operating system, with the use of virtualization software (see Figure B9.7). Unfortunately, virtualization, at least at the moment, is not available for a PC to run Mac software.

Virtualization is also one of the easiest and quickest ways to achieve a sustainable MIS infrastructure because it reduces power consumption and requires less equipment that needs to be manufactured, maintained, and later disposed of safely. Managers no longer have to assign servers, storage, or network capacity permanently to single applications. Instead, they can assign the hardware resources when and where they are needed, achieving the availability, flexibility, and scalability a company needs to thrive and grow. Also, by virtually separating the operating system and applications from the hardware, if there is a disaster or hardware failure, it is easy to port the virtual machine to a new physical machine allowing a company to recovery quickly from disasters. One of the primary uses of virtualization is for performing backup, recovery, and disaster recovery. Using virtual servers or a virtualization service provider, such as Google, Microsoft, or Amazon, to host disaster recovery is more sustainable than a single company incurring the expense of having redundant physical systems. Also, these providers' data centers are built to withstand natural disasters and are typically located far away from big cities (see Figure B9.8).

System virtualization is the ability to present the resources of a single computer as if it is a collection of separate computers ("virtual machines"), each with its own virtual CPUs, network interfaces, storage, and operating system.

Virtual machine technology was first implemented on mainframes in the 1960s to allow the expensive systems to be partitioned into separate domains and used more efficiently by more users and applications. As standard PC servers became more powerful in the past decade, virtualization has been brought to the desktop and notebook processors to provide the same benefits.

FIGURE B9.7

Virtualization Allows an Apple Macintosh Computer to Run OS X and Windows 8

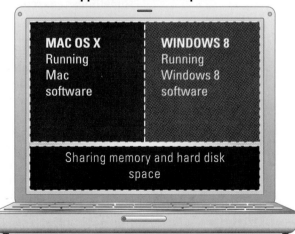

Apple Macintosh Computer

| MAC OS X Running Mac software | WINDOWS 8 Running Windows 8 software |

Sharing memory and hard disk space

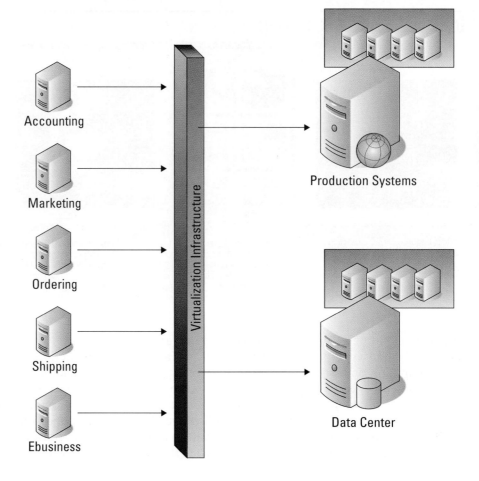

Virtual machines appear both to the user within the system and the world outside as separate computers, each with its own network identity, user authorization and authentication capabilities, operating system version and configuration, applications, and data. The hardware is consistent across all virtual machines: While the number or size of them may differ, devices are used that allow virtual machines to be portable, independent of the actual hardware type on the underlying systems. Figure B9.9 shows an overview of what a system virtualization framework looks like.

Virtual Data Centers

A *data center* is a facility used to house management information systems and associated components, such as telecommunications and storage systems. Data centers, sometimes referred to as server farms, consume power and require cooling and floor space while working to support business growth without disrupting normal business operations and the quality of service. The amount of data a data center stores has grown exponentially over the years as our reliance on information increases. Backups, graphics, documents, presentations, photos, audio and video files all contribute to the ever-expanding information footprint that requires storage. One of the most effective ways to limit the power consumption and cooling requirements of a data center is to consolidate parts of the physical infrastructure, particularly by reducing the number of physical servers through virtualization. For this reason, virtualization is having a profound impact on data centers as the sheer number of servers a company requires to operate decreases, thereby boosting growth and performance while reducing environmental impact, as shown in Figure B9.10. Google, Microsoft, Amazon, and Yahoo! have all created data centers along the Columbia River in the northwestern United States. In this area, each company can benefit from affordable land, high-speed Internet access, plentiful water for cooling, and even more important, inexpensive electricity. These factors are critical

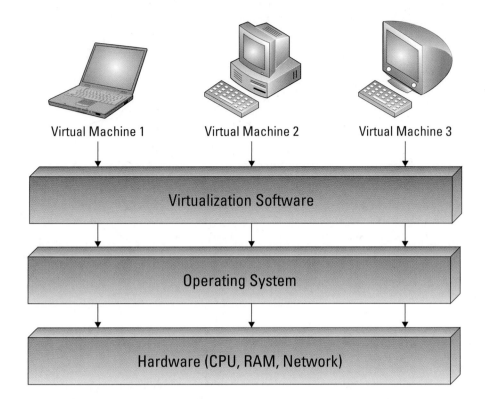

Virtual Machine 1   Virtual Machine 2   Virtual Machine 3

Virtualization Software

Operating System

Hardware (CPU, RAM, Network)

to today's large-scale data centers, whose sheer size and power needs far surpass those of the previous generation. Microsoft's data center in Quincy, Washington, is larger than 10 football fields and is powered entirely by hydroelectricity, power generated from flowing water rather than from the burning of coal or other fossil fuel.

If we take a holistic and integrated approach to overall company growth, the benefits of integrating information MIS infrastructures, environmental MIS infrastructures, and sustainable MIS infrastructures become obvious. For example, a company could easily create a backup of its software and important information in one or more geographically dispersed locations using cloud computing. This would be far cheaper than building its own hot and cold sites in different areas of the country. In the case of a security breach, failover can be deployed as a virtual machine in one location of the cloud can be shut down as another virtual machine in a different location on the cloud comes online.

CLOUD COMPUTING

Imagine a cyclical business that specializes in Halloween decorations and how its sales trends and orders vary depending on the time of year. The majority of sales occur in September and October, and the remaining 10 months have relatively small sales and small system usage. The company does not want to invest in massive expensive servers that sit idle 10 months of the year just to meet its capacity spikes in September and October. The perfect solution for this company is cloud computing, which makes it

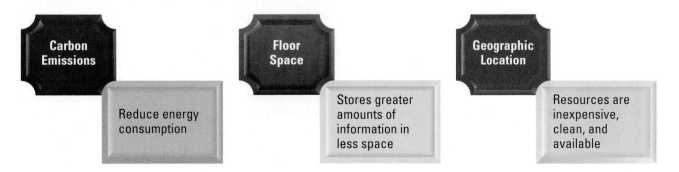

Carbon Emissions	Floor Space	Geographic Location
Reduce energy consumption	Stores greater amounts of information in less space	Resources are inexpensive, clean, and available

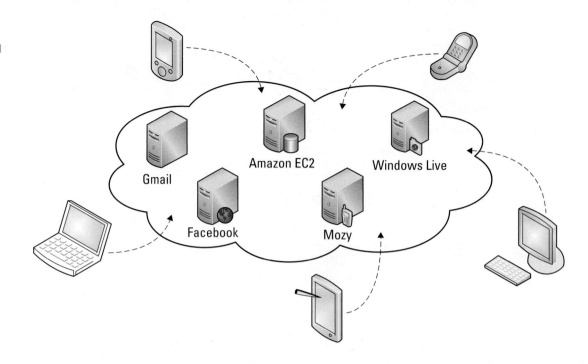

easier to gain access to the computing power that was once reserved for large corporations. Small to medium-size companies no longer have to make big capital investments to access the same powerful systems that large companies run.

According to the National Institute of Standards and Technology (NIST) **cloud computing** is a model for enabling ubiquitous, convenient, on-demand network access to a shared pool of configurable computing resources (e.g., networks, servers, storage, applications, and services) that can be rapidly provisioned and released with minimal management effort or service provider interaction. Cloud computing offers new ways to store, access, process, and analyze information and connect people and resources from any location in the world where an Internet connection is available. As shown in Figure B9.11, users connect to the cloud from their personal computers or portable devices using a client, such as a web browser. To these individual users, the cloud appears as their personal application, device, or document. It is like storing all of your software and documents "in the cloud," and all you need is a device to access the cloud. No more hard drives, software, or processing power—that is all located in the cloud, transparent to the users. Users are not physically bound to a single computer or network; they can access their programs and documents from wherever they are, whenever they need to. Just think of having your hard drive located in the sky and you can access your information and programs using any device from wherever you are. The best part is that even if your machine crashes, is lost, or is stolen, the information hosted in the cloud is safe and always available.

Multi-tenancy in the cloud means that a single instance of a system serves multiple customers. In the cloud, each customer is called a tenant and multiple tenants can access the same system. Multi-tenancy helps to reduce operational costs associated with implementing large systems as the costs are dispersed across many tenants as opposed to **single-tenancy,** in which each customer or tenant must purchase and maintain an individual system. With a multi-tenancy cloud approach, the service provider only has one place to update its system. With a single-tenancy cloud approach, the service provider would have to update its system in every company where the software was running. The **cloud fabric** is the software that makes possible the benefits of cloud computing, such as multi-tenancy. A **cloud fabric controller** is an individual who monitors and provisions cloud resources, similar to a server administrator at an individual company. Cloud fabric controllers provision resources, balance loads, manage servers, update systems, and ensure all environments are available and operating correctly. Cloud fabric is the

| ON-DEMAND SELF-SERVICE Users can increase storage and processing power as needed | BROAD NETWORK ACCESS All devices can access data and applications | MULTI-TENANCY Customers share pooled computing resources |

| RAPID ELASTICITY Storage, network bandwidth, and computing capacity can be increased or decreased immediately, allowing for optimal scalability | MEASURED SERVICE Clients can monitor and measure transactions and use of resources |

FIGURE B9.12

Benefits of Cloud Computing

primary reason cloud computing promotes all of the seven abilities, allowing a business to make its data and applications accessible, available, maintainable, portable, reliable, scalable, and usable. Figure B9.12 displays the benefits of cloud computing.

The cloud offers a company higher availability, greater reliability, and improved accessibility—all with affordable high-speed access. For flexibility, scalability, and cost efficiency, cloud computing is quickly becoming a viable option for companies of all sizes. With the cloud, you could simply purchase a single license for software such as Microsoft Office or Outlook at a far discounted rate and not worry about the hassle of installing and upgrading the software on your computer. No more worries that you don't have enough memory to run a new program because the hardware is provided in the cloud, along with the software. You simply pay to access the program. Think of this the same way you do your telephone service. You simply pay to access a vendor's service, and you do not have to pay for the equipment required to carry the call around the globe. You also don't have to worry about scalability because the system automatically handles peak loads, which can be spread out among the systems in the cloud.

Because additional cloud resources are always available, companies no longer have to purchase systems for infrequent computing tasks that need intense processing power, such as preparing tax returns during tax season or increased sales transactions during certain holiday seasons. If a company needs more processing power, it is always there in the cloud—and available on a cost-efficient basis.

With cloud computing, individuals or businesses pay only for the services they need, when they need them, and where, much as we use and pay for electricity. In the past, a company would have to pay millions of dollars for the hardware, software, and networking equipment required to implement a large system such as payroll or sales management. A cloud computing user can simply access the cloud and request a single license to a payroll application. The user does not have to incur any hardware, software, or networking expenses. As the business grows and the user requires more employees to have access to the system, the business simply purchases additional licenses. Rather than running software on a local computer or server, companies can now reach to the cloud to combine software applications, data storage, and considerable computing power. *Utility computing* offers a pay-per-use revenue model similar to a metered service such as gas or electricity. Many cloud computing service providers use utility computing cloud infrastructures.

SERVICE ORIENTED ARCHITECTURES

Service oriented architecture (SOA) supports organizational computing needs with utility-based computing concepts. Service oriented architecture begins with a service—an SOA *service* being simply a business task, such as checking a potential customer's credit rating when opening a new account. It is important to stress that this is part of a business process (see Figure B9.13). Services are "like" software products; however,

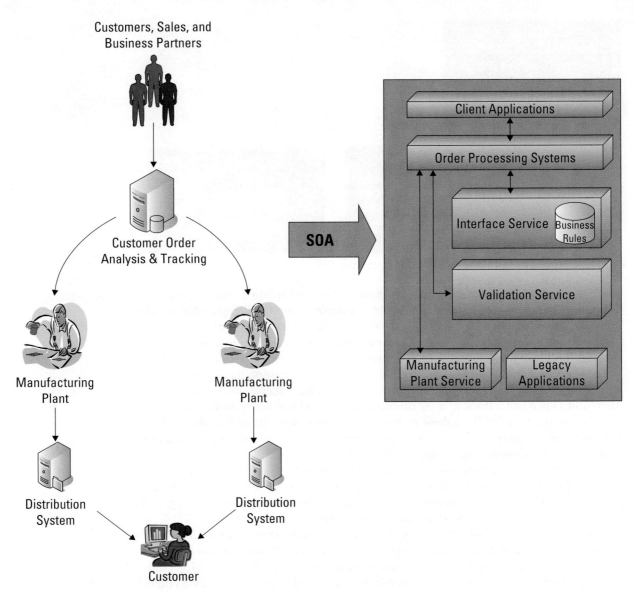

FIGURE B9.13

SOA Integration

when describing SOA, do not think about software or IT. Think about what a company does on a day-to-day basis, and break up those business processes into repeatable business tasks or components.

SOA provides the technology underpinnings for working with services that are not just software or hardware, but rather business tasks. It is a pattern for developing a more flexible kind of software application that can promote loose coupling among software components while reusing existing investments in technology in new, more valuable ways across the organization. SOA is based on standards that enable interoperability, business agility, and innovation to generate more business value for those who use these principles.

SOA helps companies become more agile by aligning business needs and the IT capabilities that support these needs. Business drives requirements for IT; SOA enables the IT environment to effectively and efficiently respond to these requirements. SOA is about helping companies apply reusability and flexibility that can lower cost (of development, integration, maintenance), increase revenue, and obtain sustainable competitive advantage through technology.

It is very important to note that SOA is an evolution. Although its results are revolutionary, it builds on many technologies used in the marketplace, such as web services, transactional technologies, information-driven principles, loose coupling, components, and object-oriented design. The beauty of SOA is that these technologies exist together in SOA through standards, well-defined interfaces, and organizational commitments to reuse key services instead of reinventing the wheel. SOA is not just about technology, but about how technology and business link themselves for a common goal of business flexibility.

Businesses have become increasingly complex over the past couple of decades. Factors such as mergers, regulations, global competition, outsourcing, and partnering have resulted in a massive increase in the number of applications any given company might use. These applications were implemented with little knowledge of the other applications with which they would be required to share information in the future. As a result, many companies are trying to maintain IT systems that coexist but are not integrated.

SOA can help provide solutions to companies that face a variety of business issues; Figure B9.14 lists some of those. Figure B9.15 displays the three primary types of SOA utility-based computing models.

Infrastructure as a Service (IaaS)

Infrastructure as a Service (IaaS) delivers hardware networking capabilities, including the use of servers, networking, and storage, over the cloud using a pay-per-use revenue model. With IaaS the customer rents the hardware and provides its own custom applications or programs. IaaS customers save money by not having to spend a large amount of capital purchasing expensive servers, which is a great business advantage considering some servers cost more than $100,000. The service is typically paid for on a usage basis, much like a basic utility service such as electricity or gas. IaaS offers a cost-effective solution for companies that need their computing resources to grow and shrink as business demand changes. This is known as *dynamic scaling,* which means the MIS infrastructure can be automatically scaled up or down based on needed requirements.

Business Issues	SOA Solutions
■ Agents unable to see policy coverage information remotely ■ Calls/faxes used to get information from other divisions ■ Clinical patient information stored on paper ■ Complex access to supplier design drawings	Integrate information to make it more accessible to employees.
■ High cost of handling customer calls ■ Reconciliation of invoice deductions and rebates ■ Hours on hold to determine patient insurance eligibility ■ High turnover leading to excessive hiring and training costs	Understand how business processes interact to better manage administrative costs.
■ Decreasing customer loyalty due to incorrect invoices ■ Customers placed on hold to check order status ■ Inability to quickly update policy endorsements ■ Poor service levels	Improve customer retention and deliver new products and services through reuse of current investments.
■ Time wasted reconciling separate databases ■ Manual processes such as handling trade allocations ■ Inability to detect quality flaws early in cycle ■ High percentage of scrap and rework	Improve people productivity with better business integration and connectivity.

FIGURE B9.14

Business Issues and SOA Solutions

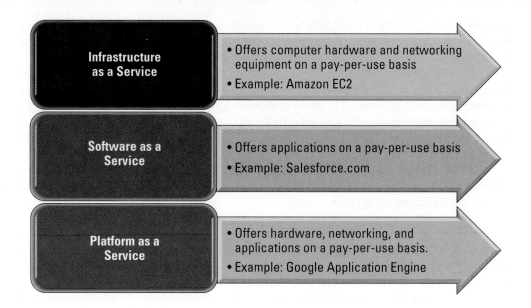

Currently the most popular IaaS operation is Amazon's Elastic Compute Cloud, generally known as Amazon EC2, or simply EC2. EC2 provides a web interface through which customers can load and run their own applications on Amazon's computers. Customers control their own operating environment, so they can create, run, and stop services as needed, which is why Amazon describes EC2 as *elastic*. IaaS is a perfect fit for companies with research-intensive projects that need to process large amounts of information at irregular intervals, such as those in the scientific or medical fields. Cloud computing services offer these companies considerable cost savings where they can perform testing and analysis at levels that are not possible without access to additional and very costly computing infrastructure.

Software as a Service (SaaS)

Software as a Service (SaaS) delivers applications over the cloud using a pay-per-use revenue model. Before its introduction, companies often spent huge amounts of money implementing and customizing specialized applications to satisfy their business requirements. Many of these applications were difficult to implement, expensive to maintain, and challenging to use. Usability was one of the biggest drivers for creating interest in and success for cloud computing service providers.

SaaS offers a number of advantages; the most obvious is tremendous cost savings. The software is priced on a per-use basis with no up-front costs, so companies get the immediate benefit of reducing capital expenditures. They also get the added benefits of scalability and flexibility to test new software on a rental basis.

Salesforce.com is one of the most popular SaaS providers. Salesforce.com built and delivered a sales automation application, suitable for the typical salesperson, that automates functions such as tracking sales leads and prospects and forecasting. Tapping the power of SaaS can provide access to a large-scale, secure infrastructure, along with any needed support, which is especially valuable for a start-up or small company with few financial resources.

Platform as a Service (PaaS)

Platform as a Service (PaaS) supports the deployment of entire systems including hardware, networking, and applications using a pay-per-use revenue model. PaaS is a perfect solution for a business as it passes on to the service provider the headache and challenges of buying, managing, and maintaining web development software. With PaaS the development, deployment, management, and maintenance is based entirely in the cloud and performed by the PaaS provider, allowing the company to focus resources on its core initiatives. Every aspect of development, including the software needed to create it and the hardware to run it, lives in the cloud. PaaS helps companies minimize operational costs and increase productivity by providing all the following without up-front investment:

- Increased security.
- Access to information anywhere and anytime.
- Centralized information management.
- Easy collaboration with partners, suppliers, and customers.
- Increased speed to market with significantly less cost.

One of the most popular PaaS services is Google's Application Engine, which builds and deploys web applications for a company. Google's Application Engine is easy to build, easy to maintain, and easy to scale as a company's web-based application needs grow. Google's Application Engine is free and offers a standard storage limit and enough processing power and network usage to support a web application serving about 5 million page views a month. When a customer scales beyond these initial limits, it can pay a fee to increase capacity and performance. This can turn into some huge costs savings for a small business that does not have enough initial capital to buy expensive hardware and software for its web applications. Just think, a two-person company can access the same computing resources as Google. That makes good business sense. Regardless of which cloud model a business chooses, it can select from four different cloud computing environments—public, private, community, and hybrid (see Figure B9.16).

Public Cloud

Public cloud promotes massive, global, and industrywide applications offered to the general public. In a public cloud, customers are never required to provision, manage, upgrade, or replace hardware or software. Pricing is utility-style and customers pay only for the resources they use. A few great examples of public cloud computing include Amazon Web Services (AWS), Windows Azure, and Google Cloud Connect.

Private Cloud

Private cloud serves only one customer or organization and can be located on the customer's premises or off the customer's premises. A private cloud is the optimal solution for an organization such as the government that has high data security concerns and values information privacy. Private clouds are far more expensive than public clouds because costs are not shared across multiple customers.

Community Cloud

Community cloud serves a specific community with common business models, security requirements, and compliance considerations. Community clouds are emerging in highly regulated industries such as financial services and pharmaceutical companies.

FIGURE B9.16

Cloud Computing Environments

Hybrid Cloud

Hybrid cloud includes two or more private, public, or community clouds, but each cloud remains separate and is only linked by technology that enables data and application portability. For example, a company might use a private cloud for critical applications that maintain sensitive data and a public cloud for nonsensitive data applications. The usage of both private and public clouds together is an example of a hybrid cloud. **Cloud bursting** is when a company uses its own computing infrastructure for normal usage and accesses the cloud when it needs to scale for peak load requirements, ensuring a sudden spike in usage does not result in poor performance or system crashes.

Deploying an MIS infrastructure in the cloud forever changes the way an organization's MIS systems are developed, deployed, maintained, and managed. Moving to the cloud is a fundamental shift from moving from a physical world to a logical world, making irrelevant the notion of which individual server applications or data reside on. As a result, organizations and MIS departments need to change the way they view systems and the new opportunities to find competitive advantages.

Organizations pay special attention to computing basics since these form the underlying foundation that supports a firm's information systems. A solid underlying infrastructure is a necessity for ensuring the security, reliability, quality, and responsiveness of a firm's information systems. These systems are the tools that companies utilize and heavily rely upon to run their businesses and compete in today's competitive environment. As a business student, it is important that you understand the components and activities underpinning an organization's computing infrastructure so that you may be attuned to what is involved and be able to take steps to ensure this infrastructure is kept up-to-date and running as smoothly as possible.

＊ **KEY TERMS**

Carbon emissions, 453	Grid computing, 454	Single-tenancy, 460
Cloud bursting, 466	Hybrid cloud, 466	Smart grid, 454
Cloud computing, 460	Infrastructure as a	Software as a Service
Cloud fabric, 460	Service (IaaS), 463	(SaaS), 464
Cloud fabric controller, 460	Moore's Law, 452	Sustainable, or green,
Community cloud, 465	Multi-tenancy, 460	MIS, 452
Corporate social	Platform as a Service (PaaS), 464	Sustainable MIS
responsibility, 452	Private cloud, 465	disposal, 453
Data center, 458	Public cloud, 465	System virtualization, 457
Dynamic scaling, 463	Service, 461	Utility computing, 461
Energy consumption, 453	Service oriented architecture	Virtualization, 456
Ewaste, 452	(SOA), 461	

＊ **CLOSING CASE ONE**

UPS Invests $1 Billion to Go Green

United Parcel Service (UPS) will make about $1 billion in technology investments to improve the efficiency of its operations, with the goal of cutting billions more from its costs over the long term. One of its main goals is to improve the speed and efficiency of its delivery operations. To achieve that, UPS is equipping its vans with sensors that allow it to collect data about things such as fuel consumption, chosen routes, and how much time its engines spend idling. Reducing fuel consumption will help UPS not only to cut costs, but also to be more environmentally responsible. A big portion of the company's costs comes from transporting packages by air. In fact, UPS is the world's ninth-largest airline, so it is trying to conserve aircraft fuel as well by lowering flight speeds and better planning to avoid duplication of routes. But a lot of fuel is also burned by its trucks, and the sensors being implemented there could save the company millions of dollars.

UPS is installing about 200 sensors in its vehicles—in the brakes, engine box, and on the exterior—to collect data and pinpoint opportunities where drivers can adjust their driving to maximize fuel efficiency. The company wants to reduce idle time of its delivery trucks, as each hour spent idling burns about a gallon of fuel.

The company is also installing equipment to track the routes drivers take to deliver packages. Every morning the drivers are briefed on the data captured by the sensors and how they could drive differently to save fuel. UPS wants to optimize the number of times a vehicle has to start, stop, reverse, turn, or back up.

Green Data Center

The company is also investing in more efficient cooling technologies at its two data centers, which are in Mahwah, New Jersey, and Alpharetta, Georgia. During the winter, the company can shut off its chiller equipment and use outside air for cooling.

The Alpharetta data center has a 650,000-gallon water tank outside for cooling and a heat exchanger to faster dissipate the heat captured in the fluid. The water flows in a circular motion around the data center, cooling the equipment, and the heat exchanger helps lower the temperature of the hot exhaust water more quickly.

UPS is also investing in faster server processors, allowing it to consolidate existing servers through virtualization. That helps lower energy costs and also reduces the physical footprint of its servers. And the company has been consolidating smaller server rooms that were scattered around the world. These changes are saving UPS around $400,000 each year.[4]

Questions

1. Why do you think UPS is embracing sustainable technologies?
2. How is UPS developing a sustainable MIS infrastructure?
3. What business benefits will UPS gain from virtualization?
4. How could UPS benefit from cloud or grid computing?

 CLOSING CASE TWO

Turning Ewaste into Gold

During the 2010 Winter Olympic Games in Vancouver, champions were not just taking home gold, silver, or bronze medals—they were also playing a role in reducing electronic waste. For the first time in Olympic history, each medal, more than 1,000 of them, was made with a tiny bit of the more than 140,000 tons of ewaste that otherwise would have been sent to landfills. The medals are the first containing metal salvaged from televisions, circuit boards, computer monitors, and electronic waste. The so-called urban ore was supplied by Teck Resources Ltd., Canada's largest base-metals producer, which provided gold, silver, and copper used to make the medals. Historically, Olympic medals have been made from mined mineral deposits; this is the first time that recycled materials have been added to them. First-place winners get gold-plated medals that are 92.5 percent silver. The second-place prizes are also 92.5 percent silver, while the third-place bronze medals are mostly copper.

All the medals have some ewaste materials from Teck's electronic recycling program located in Trail, British Columbia. Teck mixed gold, silver, and copper from the program with metals mined from the ground. The company said it couldn't provide the exact percentage of mined versus recycled material in the finished medals. Each gold medal contained a little more than 1.5 percent of ewaste materials, while each copper medal contained just over 1 percent, and the silver medals contained only small pieces. The ewaste came from old computer monitor's glass, various computer parts, and other surplus or discarded technologies.

Several different processing methods were used to extract the materials. First, the company shredded the equipment to separate out the various metals, glass, and other usable parts. To remove the metals that could not be recovered by the shredding process, the parts were fed into a furnace operating at a temperature greater than 2,000 degrees (Fahrenheit). The materials were then combined with other metals to create the medals. Each medal was hand-cropped, ensuring no two are alike, another first in Olympic history. The medals, designed by Canadian artist Corrine Hunt, were also the first nonflat medals made for the Games, with a wavy form to represent the ocean and mountain snowdrifts, both characteristic of Vancouver's environment. In addition to representing the athletes' outstanding achievements, the 2010 Olympic medals gave new life to the precious metals recoverable from ewaste.[5]

Questions

1. Why would the Olympics benefit from creating a strong environmental MIS infrastructure?
2. How can the Olympics help support ethical ewaste initiatives?
3. Why would a sporting event like the Olympics be concerned with reducing its carbon footprint?
4. What could the Olympics do to help shed light on global environmental MIS issues?
5. How could Moore's Law enable future Olympic medals to be made from more ewaste?

MAKING BUSINESS DECISIONS

1. Universities Are Switching to Gmail

Schools around the world are moving to cloud computing applications such as Google Docs & Spreadsheets and Google Calendar. Yale had planned to move from its own email system to Google Mail, but at the last minute decided to cancel the project. The reason was because school administrators and faculty members did not believe the move could support their business requirements. Do you agree or disagree that Google Gmail would be unable to replace a university's private email system? What are the advantages and disadvantages of a private email system? What are the advantages and disadvantages of using a cloud application such as Google Gmail? What choice would you make if you were the primary decision maker for choosing your school's email system?[6]

2. Desktop Virtualization

Every day users are becoming more comfortable with accessing and storing information in the cloud. This creates increased demand on MIS personnel to help manage, control, and provide access to that information—not just on company-issued computers, but on any number of devices, including personal ones. More and more employees want to be able to utilize their own computing devices—cell phones, netbooks, laptops—instead of company-issued ones. For instance, many students graduating from college have been exposed to Macs and may even own one, yet they are finding PCs as the standard computer of choice for most companies. Do you think it is a good business practice to allow your employees to use their personal devices for work-related business? What are the challenges of allowing users to port business applications to their personal devices? What are the challenges of allowing users to connect to corporate systems with personal devices?

3. iTunes in the Cloud

Apple is considering a cloud version of its iTunes software that could possibly provide a host of new services for its users as they would no longer be required to save iTunes to their computers as it would reside in the cloud. With cloud computing, the software for iTunes would reside in centralized servers in data centers, rather than on a specific user computer. What would be the benefits to customers if they could host iTunes in the clouds and access it using a variety of devices? What would be your fears if you were to use iTunes in the cloud?

4. Sustainable Departments

Energy prices and global warming are discussed daily in the news as the environmental impact of ewaste is just beginning to be recognized. Sustainability and corporate social responsibility need to be taken seriously by all managers as everyone should take an active role in helping to preserve the environment. List the different departments in a business and the types of environmental issues they typically encounter. Which department do you think creates the most ewaste? Which department uses the greatest amount of electricity or has the largest carbon footprint? What can each department do to help combat its environmental issues? Why do all managers, and for that matter all employees, need to be aware of environmental issues and ways they can create sustainable MIS infrastructures?

5. Making the Smart Grid Smart

ISO, a regional electricity company in New England, has launched an $18 million project in part because of an $8 million three-year federal grant. The project is designed to speed up the installation of 30 smart-grid devices covering every state in New England. The smart-grid devices will provide control room operators at ISO with enhanced tools to monitor and measure performance of the region's electrical grid, allowing the company to improve its ability to detect and address problems on the system. System status information coming into ISO will increase from once every four seconds to 30 times per second. Would you invest in ISO if you had the chance? Why or why not? If you were awarded an $8 million three-year federal grant, what type of sustainable infrastructure would you create?[7]

6. Box.net in the Cloud

Box.net was started by two college students, Aaron Levie and Dylan Smith, who needed a secure place to collaborate on group projects. The two immediately understood the value of cloud computing, and they created Box.net to allow them to share ideas and collaborate on documents in a virtual work space located in the cloud. They knew the cloud would allow them to access their documents from anywhere and on any device and that there was no chance of their papers being stolen or accidently destroyed. Levie and Smith recognized the business opportunity of their site and jumped at turning Box.net into a real business. Explain how Box.net could help you if you were working on a project with four other students. What would be the challenges of using Box.net?[8]

Business Intelligence

1. Compare tactical, operational, and strategic BI.
2. Explain the three common forms of data mining.
3. Describe the four categories of BI business benefits.

LO 1. Compare tactical, operational, and strategic BI.

Operational, Tactical, and Strategic BI

Claudia Imhoff, president of Intelligent Solutions, believes it is useful to divide the spectrum of data mining analysis and business intelligence into three categories: operational, tactical, and strategic. Two trends are displayed when viewing the spectrum from operational through tactical to strategic. First, the analysis becomes increasingly complex and ad hoc. That is, it is less repetitive, less predictable, and it requires varying amounts and types of data. Second, both the risks and rewards of the analysis increase. That is, the often time-consuming, more strategic queries produce value less frequently but, when they do, the value can be extraordinary. Figure B10.1 illustrates the differences among operational, tactical, and strategic BI.

These three forms are not performed in isolation from each other. It is important to understand that they must work with each other, feeding results from strategic to tactical to promote better operational decision making. Figure B10.2 demonstrates this synergy. In this example, strategic BI is used in the planning stages of a marketing campaign.

FIGURE B10.1

Operational, Tactical, Strategic BI

	Operational BI	Tactical BI	Strategic BI
Business focus	Manage daily operations, integrate BI with operational systems	Conduct short-term analysis to achieve strategic goals	Achieve long-term organizational goals
Primary users	Managers, analysts, operational users	Executives, managers	Executives, managers
Time frame	Intraday	Day(s) to weeks to months	Months to years
Data	Real-time metrics	Historical metrics	Historical metrics

The results of these analytics form the basis for the beginnings of a new campaign, targeting specific customers or demographics, for example. The daily analyses of the campaign are used by the more tactical form of BI to change the course of the campaign if its results are not tracking where expected.

For example, perhaps a different marketing message is needed, or the inventory levels are not sufficient to maintain the current sales pace so the scope of marketing might be changed. These results are then fed into the operational BI for immediate actions—offering a different product, optimizing the sale price of the product, or changing the daily message sent to selected customer segments.

For this synergy to work, the three forms of BI must be tightly integrated with each other. Minimal time should be lost transporting the results from one technological environment to another. Seamlessness in terms of data and process flow is a must. TruServ, the parent company of True Value Hardware, has used BI software to improve efficiency of its distribution operations and reap a $50 million reduction in inventory costs. The marketing department uses BI to track sales promotion results such as which promotions were most popular by store or by region. Now that TruServ is building promotion histories in its databases, it can ensure all stores are fully stocked with adequate inventory. TruServ was able to achieve a positive return on investment in about five to six months.

BI'S OPERATIONAL VALUE

A leading risk insurance company allows customers to access account information over the Internet. Previously, the company sent paper reports and diskettes to all of its customers. Any errors in the reports would take one to two months to correct because customers would first have to receive the report, catch the mistake, and then notify the company of the error. Now customers spot the errors in real time and notify the insurance company directly through an extranet, usually within a couple of days.

Richard Hackathorn of Bolder Technologies developed an interesting graph to demonstrate the value of operational BI. Figure B10.3 shows the three latencies that impact the speed of decision making. These are data, analysis, and decision latencies.

- **Data latency** is the time duration to make data ready for analysis (i.e., the time for extracting, transforming, and cleansing the data) and loading the data into the database. All this can take time depending on the state of the operational data to begin with.

- **Analysis latency** is the time from which data are made available to the time when analysis is complete. Its length depends on the time it takes a business to do analysis. Usually, we think of this as the time it takes a human to do the analysis, but this can be decreased by the use of automated analytics that have thresholds. When the thresholds are exceeded, alerts or alarms can be issued to appropriate personnel, or they can cause exception processes to be initiated with no human intervention needed.

FIGURE B10.3

The Latency between a
Business Event and an
Action Taken

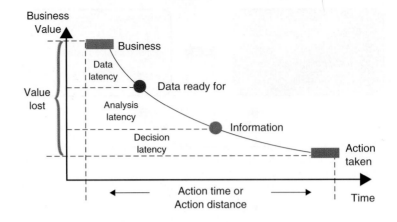

- **Decision latency** is the time it takes a human to comprehend the analytic result and determine an appropriate action. This form of latency is very difficult to reduce. The ability to remove the decision-making process from the human and automate it will greatly reduce the overall decision latency. Many forward-thinking companies are doing just that. For example, rather than send a high-value customer a letter informing him of a bounced check (which takes days to get to the customer), an automated system can simply send an immediate email or voice message informing the customer of the problem.

The key is to shorten these latencies so that the time frame for opportunistic influences on customers, suppliers, and others is faster, more interactive, and better positioned. As mentioned above, the best time to influence customers is not after they have left the store or the website. It is while they are still in the store or still wandering around the website.

For example, a customer who is searching a website for travel deals is far more likely to be influenced by appropriate messaging actions then and there. Actions taken immediately, while customers are still in the site, might include:

- Offering customers an appropriate coupon for the trip they showed interest in while searching for cheap airfares.

- Giving customers information about their current purchase such as the suggestion that visas are needed.

- Congratulating them on reaching a certain frequent-buyer level and giving them 10 percent off an item.

A website represents another great opportunity to influence a customer, if the interactions are appropriate and timely. For example:

- A banner could announce the next best product to offer right after the customer puts an item in her basket.

- The customer could receive an offer for a product he just removed from his shopping basket.

- Appropriate instructions for the use of a product could come up on the customer's screen; perhaps warning a parent that the product should not be used by children under three.

LO 2. Explain the three common forms of data mining.

Data Mining

At the center of any strategic, tactical, or operational BI effort is data mining. Ruf Strategic Solutions helps organizations employ statistical approaches within a large data warehouse to identify customer segments that display common traits. Marketers can then target these segments with specially designed products and promotions. **Data mining** is the process of analyzing data to extract information not offered by the raw data alone. Data mining can also begin at a summary information level (coarse granularity) and progress through increasing levels of detail (drilling down), or the reverse (drilling up). Data mining is the primary tool used to uncover business intelligence in vast amounts of data.

To perform data mining, users need data-mining tools. **Data-mining tools** use a variety of techniques to find patterns and relationships in large volumes of information and infer rules from them that predict future behavior and guide decision making. Data mining uses specialized technologies and functionalities such as query tools, reporting tools, multidimensional analysis tools, statistical tools, and intelligent agents. Data mining approaches decision making with basically a few different activities in mind including:

- **Classification**—assign records to one of a predefined set of classes.
- **Estimation**—determine values for an unknown continuous variable behavior or estimated future value.
- **Affinity grouping**—determine which things go together.
- **Clustering**—segment a heterogeneous population of records into a number of more homogeneous subgroups.

Sega of America, one of the largest publishers of video games, uses data mining and statistical tools to distribute its advertising budget of more than $50 million a year. Using data mining, product line specialists and marketing strategists "drill" into trends of each retail store chain. Their goal is to find buying trends that help them determine which advertising strategies are working best and how to reallocate advertising resources by media, territory, and time.

Data-mining tools apply algorithms to information sets to uncover inherent trends and patterns in the information, which analysts use to develop new business strategies. Analysts use the output from data-mining tools to build models that, when exposed to new information sets, perform a variety of information analysis functions. The analysts provide business solutions by putting together the analytical techniques and the business problem at hand, which often reveals important new correlations, patterns, and trends. The more common forms of data-mining analysis capabilities include:

- Cluster analysis
- Association detection
- Statistical analysis

CLUSTER ANALYSIS

Cluster analysis is a technique used to divide an information set into mutually exclusive groups such that the members of each group are as close together as possible to one another and the different groups are as far apart as possible. Cluster analysis is frequently used to segment customer information for customer relationship management systems to help organizations identify customers with similar behavioral traits, such as clusters of best customers or onetime customers. Cluster analysis also has the ability to uncover naturally occurring patterns in information (see Figure B10.4).

Data-mining tools that "understand" human language are finding unexpected applications in medicine. IBM and the Mayo Clinic unearthed hidden patterns in medical records, discovering that infant leukemia has three distinct clusters, each of which probably benefits from tailored treatments. Caroline A. Kovac, general manager of IBM Life Sciences, expects that mining the records of cancer patients for clustering patterns will turn up clues pointing the way to "tremendous strides in curing cancer."

A great example of cluster analysis occurs when attempting to segment customers based on zip codes. Understanding the demographics, lifestyle behaviors, and buying patterns of the most profitable segments of the population at the zip code level is key to a

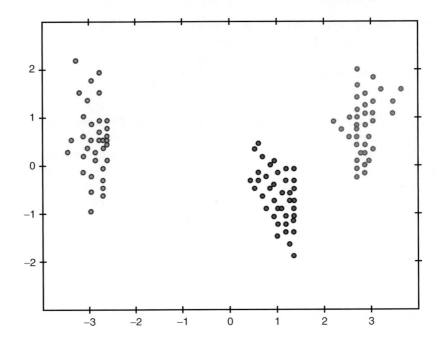

successful target marketing strategy. Targeting only those who have a high propensity to purchase products and services will help a high-end business cut its sales and marketing costs tremendously. Understanding each customer segment by zip code allows a business to determine the importance of each segment.

ASSOCIATION DETECTION

Whirlpool Corporation, a $4.3 billion home and commercial appliance manufacturer, employs hundreds of R&D engineers, data analysts, quality assurance specialists, and customer service personnel who all work together to ensure that each generation of appliances is better than the previous generation. Whirlpool is an example of an organization that is gaining business intelligence with association detection data-mining tools.

Association detection reveals the degree to which variables are related and the nature and frequency of these relationships in the information. Whirlpool's warranty analysis tool, for instance, uses statistical analysis to automatically detect potential issues, provide quick and easy access to reports, and perform multidimensional analysis on all warranty information. This association detection data-mining tool enables Whirlpool's managers to take proactive measures to control product defects even before most of its customers are aware of the defect. The tool also allows Whirlpool personnel to devote more time to value-added tasks such as ensuring high quality on all products rather than waiting for or manually analyzing monthly reports.

Many people refer to association detection algorithms as *association rule generators* because they create rules to determine the likelihood of events occurring together at a particular time or following each other in a logical progression. Percentages usually reflect the patterns of these events; for example, "55 percent of the time, events A and B occurred together," or "80 percent of the time that items A and B occurred together, they were followed by item C within three days."

One of the most common forms of association detection analysis is market basket analysis. *Market basket analysis* analyzes such items as websites and checkout scanner information to detect customers' buying behavior and predict future behavior by identifying affinities among customers' choices of products and services (see Figure B10.5). Market basket analysis is frequently used to develop marketing campaigns for cross-selling products and services (especially in banking, insurance, and finance) and for inventory control, shelf-product placement, and other retail and marketing applications.

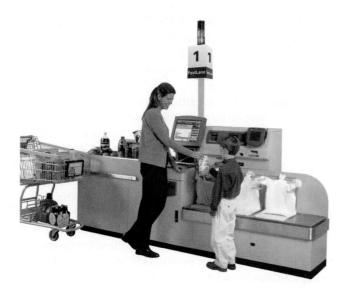

STATISTICAL ANALYSIS

Statistical analysis performs such functions as information correlations, distributions, calculations, and variance analysis. Data-mining tools offer knowledge workers a wide range of powerful statistical capabilities so they can quickly build a variety of statistical models, examine the models' assumptions and validity, and compare and contrast the various models to determine the best one for a particular business issue.

Kraft is the producer of instantly recognizable food brands such as Oreo, Ritz, DiGiorno, and Kool-Aid. The company implemented two data-mining applications to assure consistent flavor, color, aroma, texture, and appearance for all of its food lines. One application analyzed product consistency and the other analyzed process variation reduction (PVR).

The product consistency tool, SENECA (Sensory and Experimental Collection Application), gathers and analyzes information by assigning precise definitions and numerical scales to such qualities as chewy, sweet, crunchy, and creamy. SENECA then builds models, histories, forecasts, and trends based on consumer testing and evaluates potential product improvements and changes.

The PVR tool ensures consistent flavor, color, aroma, texture, and appearance for every Kraft product since even small changes in the baking process can result in huge disparities in taste. Evaluating every manufacturing procedure, from recipe instructions to cookie dough shapes and sizes, the PVR tool has the potential to generate significant cost savings for each product. Using these types of data-mining techniques for quality control and cluster analysis makes sure that the billions of Kraft products that reach consumers annually will continue to taste great with every bite.

Forecasting is a common form of statistical analysis. Formally defined, ***forecasts*** are predictions made on the basis of time-series information. ***Time-series information*** is time-stamped information collected at a particular frequency. Examples of time-series information include web visits per hour, sales per month, and calls per day. Forecasting data-mining tools allow users to manipulate the time series for forecasting activities.

When discovering trends and seasonal variations in transactional information, use a time-series forecast to change the transactional information by units of time, such as transforming weekly information into monthly or seasonal information or hourly information into daily information. Companies base production, investment, and staffing decisions on a host of economic and market indicators in this manner. Forecasting models allow organizations to consider all sorts of variables when making decisions.

Nestlé Italiana is part of the multinational giant Nestlé Group and currently dominates Italy's food industry. The company improved sales forecasting by 25 percent with its data-mining forecasting solution that enables the company's managers to make objective decisions based on facts instead of subjective decisions based on intuition.

Determining sales forecasts for seasonal confectionery products is a crucial and challenging task. During Easter, Nestlé Italiana has only four weeks to market, deliver, and sell its seasonal products. The Christmas time frame is a little longer, lasting from six to eight weeks, while other holidays such as Valentine's Day and Mother's Day have shorter time frames of about one week.

The company's data-mining solution gathers, organizes, and analyzes massive volumes of information to produce powerful models that identify trends and predict confectionery sales. The business intelligence created is based on five years of historical information and identifies what is important and what is not important. Nestlé Italiana's sophisticated data-mining tool predicted Mother's Day sales forecasts that were 90 percent accurate. The company has benefited from a 40 percent reduction in inventory and a 50 percent reduction in order changes, all due to its forecasting tool. Determining sales forecasts for seasonal confectionery products is now an area in which Nestlé Italiana excels.

Today, vendors such as Business Objects, Cognos, and SAS offer complete data-mining decision-making solutions. Moving forward, these companies plan to add more predictive analytical capabilities to their products. Their goal is to give companies more "what-if" scenario capabilities based on internal and external information.

Business Benefits of BI

LO 3. Describe the four categories of BI business benefits.

Rapid innovations in systems and data-mining tools are putting operational, tactical, and strategic BI at the fingertips of executives, managers, and even customers. With the successful implementation of BI systems an organization can expect to receive the following:

- **Single Point of Access to Information for All Users.** With a BI solution, organizations can unlock information held within their databases by giving authorized users a single point of access to data. Wherever the data reside, whether stored in operational systems, data warehouses, data marts and/or enterprise applications, users can prepare reports and drill deep down into the information to understand what drives their business, without technical knowledge of the underlying data structures. The most successful BI applications allow users to do this with an easy-to-understand, nontechnical, graphical user interface.

- **BI across Organizational Departments.** There are many different uses for BI and one of its greatest benefits is that it can be used at every step in the value chain. All departments across an organization from sales to operations to customer service can benefit from the value of BI.

  Volkswagen AG uses BI to track, understand, and manage data in every department—from finance, production, and development, to research, sales and marketing, and purchasing. Users at all levels of the organization access supplier and customer reports relating to online requests and negotiations, vehicle launches, and vehicle capacity management and tracking.

- **Up-to-the-Minute Information for Everyone.** The key to unlocking information is to give users the tools to quickly and easily find immediate answers to their questions. Some users will be satisfied with standard reports that are updated on a regular basis, such as current inventory reports, sales per channel, or customer status reports. However, the answers these reports yield can lead to new questions. Some users will want dynamic access to information. The information that a user finds in a report will trigger more questions, and these questions will not be answered in a prepackaged report.

  While users may spend 80 percent of their time accessing standard or personalized reports, for 20 percent of their tasks, they need to obtain additional information not available in the original report. To address this need and to avoid frustration (and related report backlog for the IT team), a BI system should let users autonomously make ad hoc requests for information from corporate data sources.

For merchants of MasterCard International, access to BI offers the opportunity to monitor their businesses more closely on a day-to-day basis. Advertising agencies are able to use information from an extranet when developing campaigns for merchants. On the authorization side, a call center can pull up cardholder authorization transactions to cut down on fraud. MasterCard expects that in the long term and as business partners increasingly demand access to system data, the system will support more than 20,000 external users.

CATEGORIES OF BI BENEFITS

Management is no longer prepared to sink large sums of money into IT projects simply because they are the latest and greatest technology. Information technology has come of age, and it is expected to make a significant contribution to the bottom line.

When looking at how BI affects the bottom line, an organization should analyze not only the organizationwide business benefits, but also the various benefits it can expect to receive from a BI deployment. A practical way of breaking down these numerous benefits is to separate them into four main categories:

1. Quantifiable benefits.
2. Indirectly quantifiable benefits.
3. Unpredictable benefits.
4. Intangible benefits.

Quantifiable Benefits

Quantifiable benefits include working time saved in producing reports, selling information to suppliers, and so on. A few examples include:

- Moët et Chandon, the famous champagne producer, reduced its IT costs from approximately 30 cents per bottle to 15 cents per bottle.

- A leading risk insurance company provides customers with self-service access to their information in the insurance company's database and no longer sends paper reports. This one benefit alone saves the organization $400,000 a year in printing and shipping costs. The total three-year ROI for this BI deployment was 249 percent.

- Ingram Micro, a wholesale provider of high-tech goods and technology solutions providers, is working to create a new BI extranet to deliver advanced information to the company's suppliers and business partners. Says Ingram Micro CIO Guy Abramo, "Today it's incumbent on us to provide our partners with sell-through information so they can see what happened once their PCs hit distribution. That's critical for them to do inventory planning and manufacturing planning—helping them to understand what products are selling to what segments of the marketplace."

Indirectly Quantifiable Benefits

Indirectly quantifiable benefits can be evaluated through indirect evidence—improved customer service means new business from the same customer, and differentiated service brings new customers. A few examples include:

- A customer of Owens & Minor cited extranet access to the data warehouse as the primary reason for giving the medical supplies distributor an additional $44 million in business.

- "When salespeople went out to visit TaylorMade's customers at golf pro shops and sporting goods retail chains, they didn't have up-to-date inventory reports. The sales reps would take orders for clubs, accessories, and clothing without confidence that the goods were available for delivery as promised," Tom Collard, information systems director with TaylorMade, said. "The technology has helped TaylorMade not only reduce costs by eliminating the reporting backlog . . . it has eliminated a lot of wasted effort that resulted from booking orders that it couldn't fill."

Unpredictable Benefits

Unpredictable benefits are the result of discoveries made by creative users; a few examples include:

- Volkswagen's finance BI system allowed an interesting discovery that later resulted in significant new revenue. The customers of a particular model of the Audi product line had completely different behaviors than customers of other cars. Based on their socioeconomic profiles, they were thought to want long lease terms and fairly large up-front payments. Instead, the information revealed that Audi customers actually wanted shorter leases and to finance a large part of the purchase through the lease. Based on that insight, the company immediately introduced a new program combining shorter length of lease, larger up-front payments, and aggressive leasing rates, especially for that car model. The interest in the new program was immediate, resulting in over $2 million in new revenue.

- Peter Blundell, former knowledge strategy manager for British Airways, and various company executives had a suspicion that the carrier was suffering from a high degree of ticket fraud. To address this problem, Blundell and his team rolled out business intelligence. "Once we analyzed the data, we found that this ticket fraud was not an issue at all. What we had supposed was fraud was in fact either data quality issues or process problems," Blundell said. "What it did was give us so many unexpected opportunities in terms of understanding our business." Blundell estimated that the BI deployment has resulted in around $100 million in cost savings and new revenues for the airline.

Intangible Benefits

Intangible benefits include improved communication throughout the enterprise, improved job satisfaction of empowered users, and improved knowledge sharing. A few examples include:

- The corporate human resources department at ABN AMRO Bank uses BI to gain insight into its workforce by analyzing information on such items as gender, age, tenure, and compensation. Thanks to this sharing of intellectual capital, the HR department is in a better position to demonstrate its performance and contribution to the business successes of the corporation as a whole.

- Ben & Jerry's uses BI to track, understand, and manage information on the thousands of consumer responses it receives on its products and promotional activities. Through daily customer feedback analysis, Ben & Jerry's is able to identify trends and modify its marketing campaigns and its products to suit consumer demand.

Most corporations today are inundated with data—from their own internal operational systems, their vendors, suppliers, and customers and from other external sources such as credit bureaus or industry sales data. The problem with understanding where your company is going is not in the amount of data coming into it. The problem is that this tidal wave of data is not in a form that can easily be digested, comprehended, or even accessed. Ask simple questions like who are your best customers or what are your most profitable products and you will most likely get as many answers as there are employees. Not a comforting position to have in today's era of economic stress.

This is where business intelligence or BI comes in. The goal of BI is to provide the enterprise with a repository of "trusted" data—data that can be used in a multitude of applications to answer the questions about customers, products, supply and demand chains, production inefficiencies, financial trends, fraud, and even employees. It can be used to flag anomalies via alerts, provide visualization and statistical models, and understand the cause and effects of decisions upon the enterprise. Just about every aspect of an enterprise's business can benefit from the insights garnered from BI.

You, as a business student, must understand how technology can help you make intelligent decisions. But at the end of the day, how you interact with a customer face-to-face is the real test of your ability to foster and promote healthy customer relations.

* KEY TERMS

* CLOSING CASE ONE

Intelligent Business: Is It an Oxymoron?

In a pilot program by the State of New York, suburban Rockland County announced that it had uncovered $13 million in improper Medicaid claims made over a 21-month period. Because the problems were discovered before the reimbursements were made, Rockland saved itself the headaches it would have faced if it had paid out the money first and asked questions later.

The credit goes not to a crew of hardworking sleuths but to search and analysis software created by IBM that automatically sorted through thousands of forms, plucked out key bits of information, and sized them up against Medicaid rules. Government officials believe that if the program were to be applied statewide, it could deliver $3.8 billion in savings per year. "This may change the Medicaid industry in New York," said Rockland County Supervisor C. Scott Vanderhoef.

This is just one example of a change in the way corporations and governments find and use information. Data are becoming much easier to access and vastly more useful.

Better Understanding

Organizations have huge amounts of data that pass through their computer systems as they place orders, record sales, and otherwise transact business. Much of this information is stored for future use and analysis. But advances in software and hardware make it easier for companies to analyze data in real time—when the data are first whizzing through their computers—and make them available to all kinds of employees.

Technological innovations also make it possible to analyze unstructured data, such as Rockland County's Medicaid claims, that do not easily fit into the tables of a traditional database. The result of all these changes: It is now possible for companies to understand what is happening in their businesses in a detailed way and quickly take actions based on that knowledge.

These improvements have come largely as a result of advances in business intelligence software. This software—a $3 billion segment growing at about 7 percent a year—gathers information in data warehouses where it can easily be reviewed, analyzes the data, and presents reports to decision makers. In the past, the reports had to be painstakingly assembled by tech-savvy business analysts and were typically made available only to top-tier people.

Personal Google

Information easily available to anybody in an organization is a phenomenon industry folks have dubbed "pervasive business intelligence." Companies are moving from a place where only the more technical people had access to information to more of a self-service situation. People can get information themselves, said Christina McKeon, global business intelligence strategist for software maker SAS Institute, based in Cary, North Carolina.

SAS and other BI software makers are reaching out to the masses in a variety of ways. Several of them have hooked up with search leader Google to give businesspeople easier access to those data warehouses via the familiar Google search bar. They have redesigned their business intelligence web portals so people who do Google searches get not only documents that include their keywords, but also others that are thematically related.

For instance, if a business-unit leader searches for first-quarter financial results, he might also get reports on the 10 largest customers in the quarter and the customers who deliver the most profits. "The data warehouse is starting to go mainstream," said analyst Mark Beyer of tech market researcher Gartner.

Directing Traffic

Business intelligence is also being added to other standard run-the-business applications, such as order fulfillment, logistics, inventory management, and the like. Consider a busy warehouse with a limited number of loading docks. Trucking companies do not want their rigs to wait in line for hours, so some of them charge fees for waiting time at the warehouse.

To avoid those costs, companies can build business intelligence into their logistics planning systems that lets them know when trucks are stacking up and directs supervisors in the warehouse to load the trucks that charge waiting fees before those that do not. The supervisors get this information via their PCs or handhelds on the warehouse floor. People are receiving the benefit of business intelligence without knowing it, said Randy Lea, vice president for product and services marketing at Teradata, a division of NCR, a leader in data warehousing software.

This kind of real-time, behind-the-curtains intelligence is even becoming available to end customers. Travelocity, one of the leading travel websites, has long used business intelligence software to help it analyze buying trends and segment customer types so new services can be tailored for them. Now it has rigged its vast data warehouse directly to its consumer website so it can gather and analyze information about what is going on as it is happening.

Computer Intuition

Travelocity links the profile of individual customers who are on the site to a monitor of their current activity and to information about available airplane flights, rental cars, and vacation packages. If a customer begins asking about flights to Orlando over the Fourth of July weekend, Travelocity's system will understand that the customer is probably planning a family vacation and will place advertisements that are relevant to that kind of trip and even pitch special travel promotions. "If we want to, we could give every customer a custom offer," said Mark Hooper, Travelocity's vice president for product development.

What is next in easy-to-use business intelligence? Gartner has a concept it calls "Biggle"—the intersection of BI and Google. The idea is that the data warehousing software will be so sophisticated that it understands when different people use different words to describe the same concepts or products. It creates an index of related information—á là Google—and dishes relevant results out in response to queries.

In computer science, they refer to this capability as non-obvious relationship awareness. "Nobody's doing this yet," said Gartner's Beyer. Judging from the speed of recent advances in business intelligence, though, it may not be long before companies add the term "Biggling" to their tech lexicon.

Questions

1. What is the problem of gathering business intelligence from a traditional company? How can BI solve this problem?
2. Choose one of the three common forms of data-mining analysis and explain how Travelocity could use it to gain BI.
3. How will tactical, operational, and strategic BI be different when applied to personal Google?
4. How is IBM's search and analysis software an example of BI?
5. What does the term *pervasive business intelligence* mean?
6. How could any business benefit from technology such as personal Google?
7. How could a company use BI to improve its supply chain?
8. Highlight any security and ethical issues associated with Biggle.

✳ CLOSING CASE TWO

The Brain behind the Big, Bad Burger and Other Tales of Business Intelligence

Jay Leno, the *New York Times,* and health nutrition advocacy groups have commented on the newest Hardee's fast-food item "The Monster Thickburger," which consists of:

- Two charbroiled 100 percent Angus beef patties, each weighing in at a third of a pound (150 grams)
- Three slices of processed cheese
- Four crispy strips of bacon
- Dollop of mayonnaise
- Toasted butter sesame seed bun

The Monster Thickburger sounds like a hungry person's dream and the dieter's worst nightmare. Yes, this delicious sounding burger nirvana contains 1,420 calories (5945 kilojoules) and an artery-clogging 107 grams of fat. Even though the Monster Thickburger is one of the most fattening burgers on the market—not to mention that most people add a coke and fries to their order—it is selling like crazy, according to Jeff Chasney, CIO and executive vice president of strategic planning at CKE Restaurants, the company that owns and operates Hardee's.

With the national diet obsession and health-related warnings concerning obesity, most fast-food companies probably would never have even put the Monster Thickburger on the menu. CKE confidently introduced the Monster Thickburger nationwide convinced that the product would sell based on intelligence the company obtained from its business intelligence (BI) system. CKE's BI system—known ironically inside the company as CPR (CKE Performance Reporting)—monitored the performance of burger sales in numerous test markets to determine the monster burger's increase to sales and ensure it was not simply cannibalizing other burger sales. CKE monitored several variables including menu mixes, production costs, Thickburger sales, overall burger sales, profit increases, and Thickburger's contribution to the stores' bottom-line. Using its BI system CKE quickly determined that the production costs of the Thickburger were minimal compared to the increase in sales. Armed with burger intelligence CKE confidently paid $7 million in advertising and successfully released the burger nationwide. In its first quarter sales of the burger exceeded CKE's expectations and the company knew the $7 million it paid in advertising was a smart investment.

Hardee's, Wendy's, Ruby Tuesday, T.G.I. Friday's and others are heavy users of BI software. Many of the big chains have been using BI for the past 10 years, according to Chris Hartmann, managing director of technology strategies at HVS International, a restaurant and hospitality consultancy. The restaurants use operational BI to determine everything from which menu items to add and remove to which locations to close. They use tactical BI for renegotiating contracts and identifying opportunities to improve inefficient processes. BI is an essential tool for operational-driven restaurants and if implemented correctly they can highlight operational efficiency and effectiveness such as:

- Carlson Restaurants Worldwide (T.G.I. Friday's, Pick Up Stix) saved $200,000 by renegotiating contracts with food suppliers based on discrepancies between contract prices and the prices suppliers were actually charging restaurants. Carlson's BI system, which at the time was from Cognos, had identified these discrepancies.

- Ruby Tuesday's profits and revenue have grown by at least 20 percent each year as a result of the improvements the chain has made to its menu and operations based on insights provided by its BI infrastructure, which consists of a data warehouse, analytical tools from Cognos and Hyperion, and reporting tools from Microsoft.

- CPR helped CKE, which was on the brink of bankruptcy, increase sales at restaurants open more than a year, narrow its overall losses and even turn a profit in 2003. A home-grown proprietary system, CPR consists of a Microsoft SQL server database and uses Microsoft development tools to parse and display analytical information.

- In June 2003, Wendy's decided to accept credit cards in its restaurants based on information it got from its BI systems. Because of that decision, Wendy's restaurants have boosted sales; customers who use a credit card spend an average of 35 percent more per order than those who use cash, according to Wendy's executive vice president and CIO John Deane.

Other industries could learn a great deal about BI by analyzing such strategic use of BI. "Most BI implementations fall below the midpoint on the scale of success," says Ted Friedman, an analyst with Gartner. It appears that the restaurant industry has avoided the three common barriers to BI success by cleansing voluminous amounts of irrelevant data, ensuring high-data quality, and decreasing user resistance.

Questions

1. What does business intelligence really mean to a business? How did CPR save millions for CKE?
2. What are the negative impacts of CKE's business intelligence?
3. Explain the three forms of data-mining analysis and explain how CKE can use it to gain BI.
4. How can CKE use tactical, operational, and strategic BI?
5. What types of ethical and security issues could CKE face from CPR?

1. Gaining Business Intelligence from Strategic Initiatives

You are a new employee in the customer service department at Premier One, a large pet food distributor. The company, founded by several veterinarians, has been in business for three years and focuses on providing nutritious pet food at a low cost. The company currently has 90 employees and operates in seven states. Sales over the past three years have tripled, and the manual systems currently in place are no longer sufficient to run the business. Your first task is to meet with your new team and create a presentation for the president and chief executive officer describing tactical, operational, and strategic business intelligence. The presentation should highlight the main benefits Premier One can receive from business intelligence along with any additional added business value that can be gained from the systems.

2. Second Life BI

The virtual world of Second Life could become the first point of contact between companies and customers and could transform the whole customer experience. Since it began hosting the likes of Adidas, Dell, Reuters, and Toyota, Second Life has become technology's equivalent of India or China—everyone needs an office and a strategy involving it to keep their shareholders happy. But beyond opening a shiny new building in the virtual world, what can such companies do with their virtual real estate?

Like many other big brands, PA Consulting has its own offices in Second Life and has learned that simply having an office to answer customer queries is not enough. Real people, albeit behind avatars, must be staffing the offices—in the same way having a website is not enough if there is not a call center to back it up when a would-be customer wants to speak to a human being. The consultants believe call centers could one day ask customers to follow up a phone call with them by moving the query into a virtual world.

Unlike many corporate areas in the virtual world, the National Basketball Association incorporates capabilities designed to keep fans coming back, including real-time 3-D diagrams of games as they are being played.

You are the executive director of BI at StormPeak, an advanced AI company that develops robots. You are in charge of overseeing the first virtual site being built in Second Life. Create a BI strategy for gathering information in a virtual world. Here are a few questions to get you started:

- How will gathering BI for a business be different in a virtual world?
- How can BI help a business become more efficient in a virtual world?
- How will supporting BI in Second Life differ from supporting BI in a traditional company?
- What BI security issues might you encounter in Second Life?
- What BI ethical issues might you encounter in Second Life?

3. Searching for BI

Imagine being able to Google customer phone requests for information, sort through the recorded files of customer complaint calls, or decipher the exact moment when an interaction between a customer and store employee went awry. Being able to query voice records using the same methods as querying textual ones would open up boundless areas of business opportunity. Web surfers can already search audio files and audio/video feeds, but now enterprises can use this technology to help employees search voice mails or recorded calls for keywords and phrases, and, in the end, to decode important customer concerns.

You have recently started your own marketing firm. You have built a BI tool that allows customers to query all of their unique data stores. Now all you need is to prepare your marketing materials to send to potential customers. Create a marketing pitch that you will deliver to customers detailing the business opportunities they could uncover if they purchase your product. Your marketing pitch can be a one-page document, a catchy tune, a video, or a PowerPoint presentation.

4. Mining Physician Data

NPR recently released a story discussing how large pharmaceutical companies are mining physician data. Thousands of pharmaceutical drug company sales representatives visit doctors and try to entice them to prescribe their company's newest drugs. The pharmaceutical companies buy prescription information from pharmacies all over the country describing which drugs are prescribed by which doctors. There is no patient information in the data. The sales representatives receive this BI from their companies and can tailor their sales pitch based on what that particular doctor has been prescribing to patients. Many doctors do not even realize that the sales representatives have this information and know exactly what drugs each individual doctor prescribes. The drug companies love mining data, but critics contend it is an invasion of privacy and drives up the cost of health care. Maine has just become the third state to pass a measure limiting access to the data.

You are working for your state government and your boss has asked you to create an argument for or against pharmaceutical data mining of physician data in your state. A few questions to get you started:

Do you agree that mining physician data should be illegal? Why or why not?

As a patient how do you feel about pharmaceutical companies mining your doctor's data?

As an employee of one of the pharmaceutical companies how do you feel about mining physician data?

5. The Value of Plastic

Accepting credit cards at Wendy's restaurants was a big decision facing corporate executives in early 2003. There was no doubt that customers would appreciate the convenience of plastic, but could this option hurt overall sales? Wendy's executives decided that the best way to determine the value of plastic was to test it at several stores. The BI system was set to monitor how a credit card purchase affects sales, service speed, and cash sales. The intelligence gained from the system told executives that plastic sales were typically 35 percent higher than cash sales. Cash sales typically include a value meal—great for the customer but less profitable for the store. Plastic customers showed a trend of purchasing a la carte items generating a higher bill. Armed with BI, Wendy's introduced credit card readers nationally in June 2003.

You are the vice president of BI for McDonald's restaurants. The board of directors would like you to generate a report discussing the details of how you can use BI to analyze sales trends of menu items for all of its restaurants, including international locations. Identify several different variables you would monitor to determine menu item sales trends.

PLUG-IN
B11

Global Information Systems

1. Explain the cultural, political, and geoeconomic challenges facing global businesses.
2. Describe the four global IT business drivers that should be included in all IT strategies.
3. Describe governance and compliance and the associated frameworks an organization can implement.
4. Identify why an organization would need to understand global enterprise architectures when expanding operations abroad.
5. Explain the many different global information issues an organization might encounter as it conducts business abroad.
6. Identify global system development issues organizations should understand before building a global system.

Introduction

Whether they are in Berlin or Bombay, Kuala Lumpur or Kansas City, San Francisco or Seoul, organizations around the globe are developing new business models to operate competitively in a digital economy. These models are structured, yet agile; global, yet local; and they concentrate on maximizing the risk-adjusted return from both knowledge and technology assets.

Globalization and working in an international global economy are integral parts of business today. Fortune 500 companies to mom-and-pop shops are now competing globally, and international developments affect all forms of business.

LO 1. Explain the cultural, political, and geoeconomic challenges facing global businesses.

Globalization

According to Thomas Friedman, the world is flat! Businesses are strategizing and operating on a global playing field. Traditional forms of business are simply not good enough in a global environment. Recall the way the Internet is changing business

Industry	Business Changes Due to Technology
Travel	Travel site Expedia.com is now the biggest leisure-travel agency, with higher profit margins than even American Express. Thirteen percent of traditional travel agencies closed in 2002 because of their inability to compete with online travel.
Entertainment	The music industry has kept Napster and others from operating, but $35 billion annual online downloads are wrecking the traditional music business. U.S. music unit sales are down 20 percent since 2000. The next big entertainment industry to feel the effects of ebusiness will be the $67 billion movie business.
Electronics	Using the Internet to link suppliers and customers, Dell dictates industry profits. Its operating margins rose from 7.3 percent in 2002 to 8 percent in 2003, even as it took prices to levels where rivals couldn't make money.
Financial services	Nearly every public efinance company remaining makes money, with online mortgage service LendingTree growing 70 percent a year. Processing online mortgage applications is now 40 percent cheaper for customers.
Retail	Less than 5 percent of retail sales occur online, but eBay was on track in 2003 to become one of the nation's top 15 retailers, and Amazon.com will join the top 40. Walmart's ebusiness strategy is forcing rivals to make heavy investments in technology.
Automobiles	The cost of producing vehicles is down because of SCM and web-based purchasing. Also, eBay has become the leading U.S. used-car dealer, and most major car sites are profitable.
Education and training	Cisco saved $133 million in 2002 by moving training sessions to the Internet, and the University of Phoenix online college classes please investors.

by reviewing Figure B11.1. To succeed in a global business environment, cultural, political, and geoeconomic (geographic and economic) business challenges must be confronted.

CULTURAL BUSINESS CHALLENGES

Cultural business challenges include differences in languages, cultural interests, religions, customs, social attitudes, and political philosophies. Global businesses must be sensitive to such cultural differences. McDonald's, a truly global brand, has created several minority-specific websites in the United States: McEncanta for Hispanics, 365Black for African Americans, and i-am-asian for Asians. But these minority groups are not homogenous. Consider Asians: There are East Asian, Southeast Asian, Asian Indian, and, within each of these, divisions of national, regional, and linguistic nature. No company has the budget to create a separate website for every subsegment, but to assume that all Asian Americans fit into a single room—even a virtual room—risks a serious backlash. A company should ask a few key questions when creating a global website:

- Will the site require new navigational logic to accommodate cultural preferences?
- Will content be translated? If so, into how many languages?
- Will multilingual efforts be included in the main site or will it be a separate site, perhaps with a country-specific domain?
- Which country will the server be located in to support local user needs?
- What legal ramifications might occur by having the website targeted at a particular country, such as laws on competitive behaviors, treatment of children, or privacy?

FIGURE B11.2

Global IT Business
Management Areas

POLITICAL BUSINESS CHALLENGES

Political business challenges include the numerous rules and regulations surrounding data transfers across national boundaries, especially personal information, tax implications, hardware and software importing and exporting, and trade agreements. The protection of personal information is a real concern for all countries. For example, evidence from a national survey about citizen satisfaction with the Canadian government online services speaks to the importance of paying attention to privacy concerns. This highly publicized survey, known as Citizens First, was administered by the Institute for Citizen-Centered Service (ICCS) and the Institute for Public Administration in Canada (IPCA). Results from the survey indicate that although other factors help promote citizen satisfaction with the Internet, such as ease of finding information, sufficient information, site navigation, and visual appeal, the key driver that directly impacts whether citizens will conduct online transactions is their concerns over information security and privacy.

For security, there are high levels of concerns over information storage, transmission, and access and identity verification. For privacy and the protection of personal information, there are even stronger concerns about consolidation of information, unauthorized access, and sharing without permission.

GLOBAL GEOECONOMIC BUSINESS CHALLENGES

Geoeconomic refers to the effects of geography on the economic realities of international business activities. Even with the Internet, telecommunications, and air travel, the sheer physical distances across the globe make it difficult to operate multinational business. Flying IT specialists into remote sites is costly, communicating in real-time across the globe's 24 time zones is challenging, and finding quality telecommunication services in every country is difficult. Skilled labor supplies, cost of living, and labor costs also differ among the various countries. When developing global business strategies, all of these geoeconomic challenges must be addressed.

Understanding the cultural, political, and geoeconomic business challenges is a good start to understanding global business, but the problems facing managers run far deeper. The remainder of this plug-in focuses on business management issues that are central to all global business. Business managers must understand four primary areas—global IT business strategies, global enterprise architectures, global information issues, and global systems development—when running multinational companies (see Figure B11.2).

LO 2. Describe the four global IT business drivers that should be included in all IT strategies.

Global IT Business Strategies

Global IT business strategies must include detailed information on the application of information technology across the organization. IT systems depend on global business drivers such as the nature of the industry, competitive factors, and environmental forces. For example, airlines and hotels have global customers who travel extensively and expect the same service regardless of location. Organizations require global IT systems that can provide fast, convenient service to all international employees who are servicing these customers. When a high-end hotel customer checks into a hotel in Asia she expects to receive the same high-end service as when she is checking into a hotel in Chicago or London. Figure B11.3 displays the global IT business drivers that should be included in all IT strategies.

Many global IT systems, such as finance, accounting, and operations management, have been in operation for years. Most multinational companies have global financial

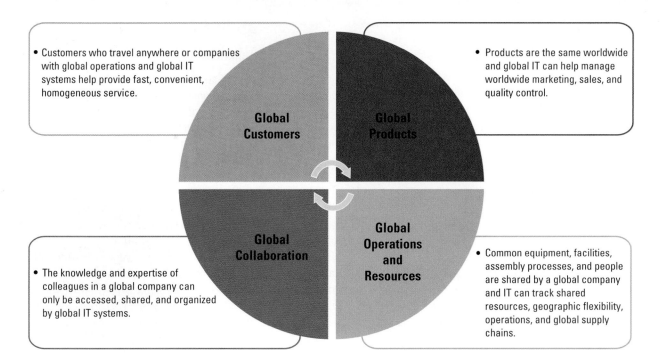

Customers who travel anywhere or companies with global operations and global IT systems help provide fast, convenient, homogeneous service.

Global Customers

Global Products

Products are the same worldwide and global IT can help manage worldwide marketing, sales, and quality control.

Global Collaboration

Global Operations and Resources

The knowledge and expertise of colleagues in a global company can only be accessed, shared, and organized by global IT systems.

Common equipment, facilities, assembly processes, and people are shared by a global company and IT can track shared resources, geographic flexibility, operations, and global supply chains.

FIGURE B11.3

Global IT Business Drivers

budgeting and cash management. As global operations expand and global competition heats up, pressure increases for companies to install global ebusiness applications for customers, suppliers, and employees. Examples include portals and websites geared toward customer service and supply chain management. In the past, such systems relied almost exclusively on privately constructed or government-owned telecommunications networks. But the explosive business use of the Internet, intranets, and extranets for electronic commerce has made such applications more feasible for global companies.

GOVERNANCE AND COMPLIANCE

LO 3. Describe governance and compliance and the associated frameworks an organization can implement.

One fast-growing key area for all global business strategies is governance and compliance. *Governance* is a method or system of government for management or control. *Compliance* is the act of conforming, acquiescing, or yielding. A few years ago the ideas of governance and compliance were relatively obscure. Today, the concept of formal IT governance and compliance is a must for virtually every company, both domestic and global. Key drivers for governance and compliance include financial and technological regulations as well as pressure from shareholders and customers.

Organizations today are subject to many regulations governing data retention, confidential information, financial accountability, and recovery from disasters. By implementing IT governance, organizations have the internal controls they need to meet the core guidelines of many of these regulations, such as the Sarbanes-Oxley Act of 2002.

IT governance essentially places structure around how organizations align IT strategy with business strategy, ensuring that companies stay on track to achieve their strategies and goals, and implementing good ways to measure IT's performance. Governance makes sure that all stakeholders' interests are considered and that processes provide measurable results. IT governance should answer key questions including how the IT department is functioning overall, what key metrics management requires, and what return the business is getting from its IT investment. Figure B11.4 displays the five key areas of focus according to the IT Governance Institute.

Organizations can follow a few different IT governance frameworks, including:

- **CoBIT:** *Information Systems Audit and Control Association (ISACA)* is a set of guidelines and supporting tools for IT governance that is accepted worldwide and generally used by auditors and companies as a way to integrate technology to implement controls and meet specific business objectives.

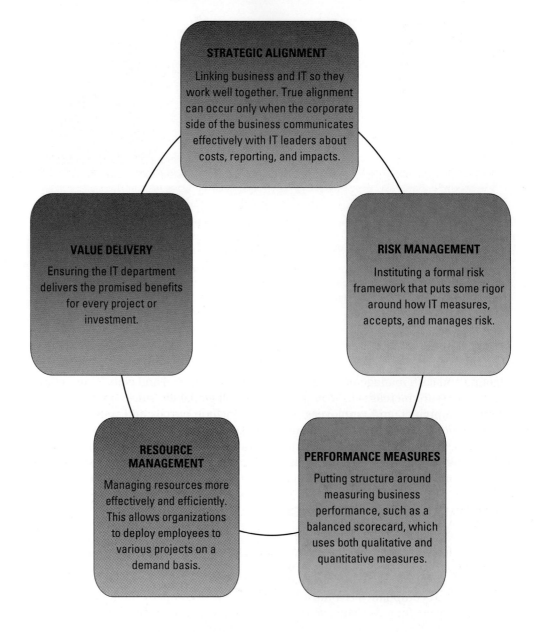

STRATEGIC ALIGNMENT

Linking business and IT so they work well together. True alignment can occur only when the corporate side of the business communicates effectively with IT leaders about costs, reporting, and impacts.

- **ITIL:** The *Information Technology Infrastructure Library (ITIL)* is a framework provided by the government of the United Kingdom and offers eight sets of management procedures: (1) service delivery, (2) service support, (3) service management, (4) Information and Communication Technology (ICT) infrastructure management, (5) software asset management, (6) business perspective, (7) security management, and (8) application management. ITIL is a good fit for organizations concerned about operations.

- **COSO:** The framework developed by the *Committee of Sponsoring Organizations (COSO)* is key for evaluating internal controls such as human resources, logistics, information technology, risk, legal, marketing and sales, operations, financial functions, procurement, and reporting. This is a more business-general framework that is less IT-specific.

- **CMMI:** Created by a group from government, industry, and Carnegie Mellon's Software Engineering Institute, the *Capability Maturity Model Integration method (CMMI)* is a process improvement approach that contains 22 process areas. It is divided into appraisal, evaluation, and structure. CMMI is particularly well-suited to organizations that need help with application development, life cycle issues, and improving the delivery of products throughout the life cycle.

Global Enterprise Architectures

LO 4. Identify why an organization would need to understand global enterprise architectures when expanding operations abroad.

An *enterprise architecture* includes the plans for how an organization will build, deploy, use, and share its data, processes, and IT assets. An organization must manage its global enterprise architecture to support its global business operations. Management of a global enterprise architecture not only is technically complex, but also has major political and cultural implications. For example, hardware choices are difficult in some countries because of high prices, high tariffs, import restrictions, long lead times for government approvals, lack of local service or replacement parts, and lack of documentation tailored to local conditions. Software choices also present issues; for example, European data standards differ from American or Asian standards, even when purchased from the same vendor. Some software vendors also refuse to offer service and support in countries that disregard software licensing and copyright agreements.

The Internet and the World Wide Web are critical to international business. This interconnected matrix of computers, information, and networks that reaches tens of millions of users in hundreds of countries is a business environment free of traditional boundaries and limits. Linking to online global businesses offers companies unprecedented potential for expanding markets, reducing costs, and improving profit margins at a price that is typically a small percentage of the corporate communications budget. The Internet provides an interactive channel for direct communication and data exchange with customers, suppliers, distributors, manufacturers, product developers, financial backers, information providers—in fact, with all parties involved in an international organization.

The Paris-based organization Reporters Without Borders notes that 45 countries restrict their citizens' access to the Internet. "At its most fundamental, the struggle between Internet censorship and openness at the national level revolves around three main means: controlling the conduits, filtering the flows, and punishing the purveyors. In countries such as Burma, Libya, North Korea, Syria, and the countries of Central Asia and the Caucasus, Internet access is either banned or subject to tight limitations through government-controlled ISPs. These countries face a lose-lose struggle against the information age. By denying or limiting Internet access, they stymie a major engine of economic growth. But by easing access, they expose their citizenry to ideas potentially destabilizing to the status quo. Either way, many people will get access to the electronic information they want. In Syria, for example, people go to Lebanon for the weekend to retrieve their email," said Virgini Locussol, Reporters Without Borders desk officer for the Middle East and North Africa.

Figure B11.5 displays the top 10 international telecommunication issues as reported by the IT executives at 300 Fortune 500 multinational companies. Political issues dominate the listing over technology issues, clearly emphasizing their importance in the management of global enterprise architectures.

Estimating the operational expenses associated with international IT operations is another global challenge. Companies with global business operations usually establish or contract with systems integrators for additional IT facilities for their subsidiaries in other countries. These IT facilities must meet local and regional computing needs, and even help balance global computing workloads through communications satellite links. However, offshore IT facilities can pose major problems in headquarters' support, hardware and software acquisition, maintenance, and security. This is why many global companies prefer to outsource these facilities to application service providers or systems integrators such as IBM or Accenture to manage overseas operations. Managing global enterprise architectures, including Internet, intranet, extranet, and other telecommunication networks, is a key global IT challenge for the 21st century.

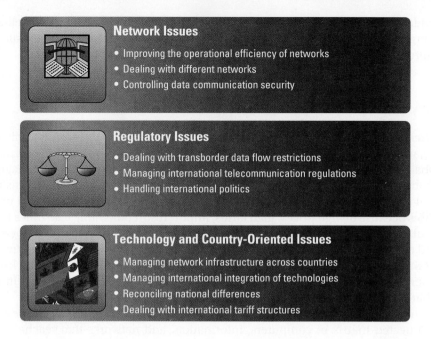

Network Issues

- Improving the operational efficiency of networks
- Dealing with different networks
- Controlling data communication security

Regulatory Issues

- Dealing with transborder data flow restrictions
- Managing international telecommunication regulations
- Handling international politics

Technology and Country-Oriented Issues

- Managing network infrastructure across countries
- Managing international integration of technologies
- Reconciling national differences
- Dealing with international tariff structures

LO 5. Explain the many different global information issues an organization might encounter as it conducts business abroad.

Global Information Issues

While many consumer gadgets and software applications can benefit a company—for instance, by helping employees get their jobs done more efficiently—the security implications are legion, said Ken Silva, chief security officer at VeriSign, which specializes in network security software. "When we bolt those things onto corporate networks, we open up holes in the environment." Drugmaker Pfizer found this out the hard way. An employee's spouse loaded file-sharing software onto a Pfizer laptop at home, creating a security hole that appears to have compromised the names and Social Security numbers of 17,000 current and former Pfizer employees, according to a letter Pfizer sent to state attorneys general. Pfizer's investigation showed that 15,700 of those employees actually had their data accessed and copied.

Rather than fight the trend, some companies are experimenting with giving employees more choice regarding the technology they use—so long as they accept more responsibility for it. In 2005, BP began a pilot project that gives employees about $1,000 to spend on productivity-enhancing tools in addition to standard-issue equipment, according to a report from the Leading Edge Forum. But before they can participate, employees must pass a test of their computer literacy skills.

The company takes other steps to give employees free rein while mitigating risk. BP cordons off its network by letting employees link to the Internet via consumer connections, from outside the firewall, in the case of its 18,000 laptops. At the same time it beefs up security on those machines. This lets employees safely experiment with software such as Amazon's on-demand computing and storage services.

Deperimeterization occurs when an organization moves employees outside its firewall, a growing movement to change the way corporations address technology security. In a business world where many employees are off-site or on the road, or where businesses increasingly must collaborate with partners and customers, some say it's not practical to rely on a hardened perimeter of firewalls. Instead, proponents of deperimeterization say companies should focus on beefing up security in end-user devices and organizations' critical information assets.

INFORMATION PRIVACY

For many years, global data access issues have been the subject of political controversy and technology barriers in global business environments. These issues have become more prevalent with the growth of the Internet and the expansion of ebusinesses. *Transborder data flows (TDF)* occur when business data flows across international boundaries over the telecommunications networks of global information systems. Many countries view TDF as violating their national sovereignty because transborder data flows avoid customs duties and regulations for the import or export of goods and services. Others view transborder data flows as violating their laws to protect the local IT industry from competition or their labor regulations from protecting local jobs. In many cases, the data flow issues that seem particularly politically sensitive are those that affect the movement out of a country of personal data in ebusiness and human resource applications.

Many countries, especially those in the European Union (EU), may view transborder data flows as a violation of their privacy legislation since, in many cases, data about individuals are being moved out of the country without stringent privacy safeguards. Figure B11.6 highlights the key provisions of a data privacy agreement between the United States and the European Union. The agreement exempts U.S. companies engaging in international ebusiness from EU data privacy sanctions if they join a self-regulatory program that provides EU consumers with basic information about, and control over, how their personal data are used. Thus, the agreement is said to provide a "safe harbor" for such companies from the requirements of the EU's Data Privacy Directive, which bans the transfer of personal information on EU citizens to countries that do not have adequate data privacy protection.

Information privacy concerns the legal right or general expectation of individuals, groups, or institutions to determine for themselves when and to what extent information about them is communicated to others. In essence, information privacy is about how personal information is collected and shared. To facilitate information privacy, many countries have established legislation to protect the collection and sharing of personal information. However, this legislation varies greatly around the globe.

EUROPE

On one end of the spectrum lie European nations with their strong information privacy laws. Most notably, all member countries of the European Union adhere to a directive on the protection of personal data. A directive is a legislative act of the European Union that requires member states to achieve a particular result without dictating the means of how to achieve that result.

The directive on the protection of personal data grants European Union members the following rights:

■ The right to know the source of personal data processing and the purposes of such processing.

■ The right to access and/or rectify inaccuracies in one's own personal data.

■ The right to disallow the use of personal data.

These rights are based on key principles pertaining to the collection or storage of personal data. The directive defines personal data to cover both facts and opinions about an individual. Any organization processing personal data of a person living in the European Union must comply with these key principles as outlined in the directive; these state that the data must be:

■ Fairly and lawfully processed.

■ Processed for limited purposes.

■ Adequate, relevant, and not excessive.

■ Accurate.

FIGURE B11.6

U.S.–EU Data Privacy Requirements

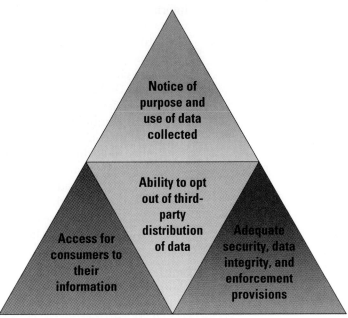

- Not kept longer than necessary.
- Processed in accordance with the data subject's rights.
- Not transferred to countries without adequate protection.

This last right restricts the flow of personal information outside the European Union by permitting its transfer to only countries that provide an "adequate" level of privacy protection—adequate in the sense that these other countries have to offer a level of privacy protection equivalent to that of the European Union. When first implemented, this part of the directive caused some concerns since countries outside the EU had much weaker privacy protection laws. Organizations in the United States were greatly concerned because they were at a legal risk if the personal data of EU citizens were transferred to computer servers in the United States—a likely scenario in today's global world of ebusiness. This led to extensive negotiations. The result was the establishment of a "safe harbor" program in the United States. This program provides a framework for U.S. organizations to show evidence of compliance with the EU directive. In this way, American companies can self-declare their compliance with the key principles of the directive and do business with EU nations without worrying about EU citizens suing them.

THE UNITED STATES

On the other end of the spectrum lies the United States. Information privacy is not highly legislated or regulated. There is no all-encompassing law that regulates the use of personal data or information. In many cases, access to public information is considered culturally acceptable, such as obtaining credit reports for employment or housing purposes. The reason for this may be historical. In the United States, the first amendment protects free speech, and in many instances the protection of privacy might conflict with this amendment.

There are some exceptions. Though very few states recognize an individual's right to privacy, California's constitution protects an inalienable right to privacy. The California legislature has enacted several pieces of legislation aimed at protecting citizen information privacy. For example, California's Online Privacy Protection Act, established in 2003, requires commercial websites or online services that collect personal information of California residents to clearly post a privacy policy on the website or online service and to comply with this policy. Other nationwide exceptions include the Children's Online Privacy Protection Act (COPPA) and the Health Insurance Portability and Accountability Act (HIPAA).

COPPA is a federal law established in 1998 that applies to the collection of personal information from American children who are under 13 years of age. The act outlines what a website should include in its privacy policy, how to seek consent from a parent or guardian, and the responsibilities a website operator has to protect children's online safety and privacy. This law applies to any website that is perceived to be targeting American children. For example, if a toy company established in Canada wanted to sell toys in the United States, the company's website should have to comply with the collection and use of information as outlined in COPPA. To show compliance requires a substantial amount of paperwork. As a result, many websites disallow underage users to join online communities and websites. Not complying with COPPA can be costly. In September 2006, the website Xanga, an online community, was fined $1 million for violating COPPA legislation.

HIPAA was enacted by the U.S. Congress in 1996. Provisions in HIPPA establish national standards for the electronic data interchange of health care-related transactions between health care providers, insurance plans, and employers. Embedded in these standards are rules for the handling and protection of personal health care information.

CANADA

Canada's privacy laws follow very closely the European model. Canada as a nation is quite concerned about protecting the personal information of its citizens. Its primary privacy law is the Personal Information Protection and Electronic Document Act (PIPEDA). The purpose of PIPEDA is to provide Canadians with a right of privacy with respect to how their personal information is collected, used, or disclosed by an organization. This is most important today, especially in the private sector, when information technology increasingly facilitates the collection and free flow of information.

Its precursor was the Privacy Act established in 1983 that restricted the handling of personal information within federal government departments and agencies only. This information concerned such things as pension and employment insurance files, medical records, tax records, and military records.

PIPEDA took effect in January 2001 and, like the Privacy Act, applied only to federally regulated organizations. By January 2004, PIPEDA's reach extended beyond government borders and applied to all other types of organizations, including commercial businesses. By doing so, Canada's PIPEDA law brought Canada into compliance with the European Union's directive on the protection of personal data. Hence, since January 2004, Canada no longer needed to implement safe harbor provisions for organizations wishing to collect and store personal information on European Union citizens.

Global Systems Development

LO 6. Identify global system development issues organizations should understand before building a global system.

It is extremely difficult to develop a domestic information system, but the added complexity of developing a global information system quadruples the effort. Global information systems must support a diverse base of customers, users, products, languages, currencies, laws, and so on. Developing efficient, effective, and responsive information systems for multiple countries, differing cultures, and global ebusinesses is an enormous challenge for any organization. Managers should expect conflicts over local versus global system requirements and difficulties agreeing on common system features. For the project to succeed, the development environment should promote involvement and ownership by all local system users.

One of the most important global information systems development issues is the global standardization of data definitions. Common data definitions are necessary for sharing information among the parts of an international business. Differences in language, culture, and technology platforms can make global data standardization quite difficult. For example, what Americans call a "sale" may be called "an order booked" in the United Kingdom, an "order scheduled" in Germany, and an "order produced" in France. These are all referring to the exact same business event, but could cause problems if global employees have different versions of the data definition. Businesses are moving ahead to standardize data definitions and business processes. Many organizations are implementing corporate wikis where all global employees can post and maintain common business definitions.

Organizations can use several strategies to solve some of the problems that arise in global information systems development. First is transforming and customizing an information system used by the home office into a global application. This ensures the system uses the established business processes and supports the primary needs of the end users. Second is setting up a multinational development team with key people from several subsidiaries to ensure that the system design meets the needs of all local sites as well as corporate headquarters. Third, an organization could use centers of excellence where an entire system might be assigned for development to a particular subsidiary based on its expertise in the business or technical dimensions needed for successful development. A final approach that has rapidly become a major development option is to outsource the development work to global or offshore development countries that have the required skills and experience to build global information systems. All of these approaches require development team collaboration and managerial oversight to meet the global needs of the business.

PLUG-IN SUMMARY

W hether you aspire to be an entrepreneur, manager, or other type of business leader, it is increasingly important to think globally in planning your career. As this plug-in points out, global markets offer many opportunities yet are laced with significant challenges and complexities including cultural, political, and geoeconomic issues, such as:

- Global business strategies.
- Global enterprise architectures.
- Global information issues.
- Global systems development.

KEY TERMS

CLOSING CASE ONE

Tata's Nano $2,500 Car

The announcement by Tata Motors of its newest car, the Nano, priced at $2,500, was revealing on many levels. The announcement generated extensive coverage and commentary, but just about everyone missed the Nano's real significance, which goes far beyond the car itself.

At about $2,500 retail, the Nano is the most inexpensive car in the world. Its closest competitor, the Maruti 800, made in India by Maruti Udyog, sells for roughly twice as much. To put this in perspective, the price of the entire Nano car is roughly equivalent to the price of a DVD player option in a luxury Western car. The low price point has left other auto companies scrambling to catch up.

Thinking Outside the Patent Box

How could Tata Motors make a car so inexpensively? It started by looking at everything from scratch, applying what some analysts have described as "Gandhian engineering" principles—deep frugality with a willingness to challenge conventional wisdom. A lot of features that Western consumers take for granted—air conditioning, power brakes, radios, etc.—are missing from the entry-level model.

More fundamentally, the engineers worked to do more with less. The car is smaller in overall dimensions than the Maruti, but it offers about 20 percent more seating capacity as a result of design choices such as putting the wheels at the extreme edges of the car. The Nano is also much lighter than comparable models as a result of efforts to reduce the amount of steel in the car (including the use of an aluminum engine) and the use of lightweight steel where possible. The car currently meets all Indian emission, pollution, and safety standards, though it only attains a maximum speed of about 65 mph. The fuel efficiency is attractive—50 miles to the gallon.

Hearing all this, many Western executives doubt that this new car represents real innovation. Too often, when they think of innovation, they focus on product innovation using breakthrough technologies; often, specifically, on patents. Tata Motors has filed for 34 patents associated with the design of the Nano, which contrasts with the roughly 280 patents awarded to General Motors (GM) every year. Admittedly that figure tallies all of GM's research efforts, but if innovation is measured only in terms of patents, no wonder the Nano is not of much interest to Western executives. Measuring progress solely by patent creation misses a key dimension of innovation: Some of the most valuable innovations take existing, patented components and remix them in ways that more effectively serve the needs of large numbers of customers.

A Modular Design Revolution

But even this broader perspective fails to capture other significant dimensions of innovation. In fact, Tata Motors itself did not draw a lot of attention to what is perhaps the most innovative aspect of the Nano: its modular design. The Nano is constructed of components that can be built and shipped separately to be assembled in a variety of locations. In effect, the Nano is being sold in kits that are distributed, assembled, and serviced by local entrepreneurs. As Ratan Tata, chairman of the Tata group of companies, observed in an interview with *The Times* of London: "A bunch of entrepreneurs could establish an assembly operation and Tata Motors would train their people, would oversee their quality assurance and they would become satellite assembly operations for us. So we would create entrepreneurs across the country that would produce the car. We would produce the mass items and ship it to them as kits. That is my idea of dispersing wealth. The service person would be like an insurance agent who would be trained, have a cell phone and scooter and would be assigned to a set of customers."

In fact, Tata envisions going even further, providing the tools for local mechanics to assemble the car in existing auto shops or even in new garages created to cater to remote rural customers. With the exception of Manjeet Kripalani, *BusinessWeek*'s India bureau chief, few have focused on this breakthrough element of the Nano innovation.

This is part of a broader pattern of innovation emerging in India in a variety of markets, ranging from diesel engines and agricultural products to financial services. While most of the companies pursuing this type of innovation are Indian, the U.S. engineering firm Cummins (CMI) demonstrates that Western companies can also harness this approach and apply it effectively. In 2000 Cummins designed innovative "gensets" (generation sets) to enter the lower end of the power generator market in India. These modular sets were explicitly designed to lower distribution costs and make it easy for distributors and customers to tailor the product for highly variable customer environments. Using this approach, Cummins captured a leading position in the Indian market and now actively exports these new products to Africa, Latin America, and the Middle East.

Lessons Executives Should Learn

What are the broader lessons that Western executives should learn from this innovation story? Emerging markets are a fertile ground for innovation. The challenge of reaching dispersed, low-income consumers in emerging markets often spurs significant innovation. Western executives should be careful about compartmentalizing the impact of these innovations on the edge of the global economy. These innovations will become the basis for "attacker" strategies that can be used to challenge incumbents in more developed economies. What is initially on the edge soon comes to the core.

- Find ways to help customers and others on the edge to tinker with your products. Modular and open product designs help engage large numbers of motivated users in tailoring and pushing the performance boundaries of your products, leading to significant insight into unmet customer needs and creative approaches to addressing those needs.

Pay attention to institutional innovation. Western executives often become too narrowly focused on product or process innovation. Far higher returns may come from investing in institutional innovation—redefining the roles and relationships that bring together independent entities to deliver more value to the market. Tata is innovating in all three dimensions simultaneously.

 Rethink distribution models. In our relentless quest for operating efficiency, we have gone for more standardization and fewer business partners in our efforts to reach customers. As customers gain more power, they will demand more tailoring and value-added service to meet their needs. Companies that innovate on this dimension are likely to be richly rewarded.

Questions

1. How can cultural and political issues affect Tata Motors' Nano car?
2. How would governance and compliance affect Tata Motors?
3. Identify the different global system development issues Tata Motors might encounter as it deploys its Nano.

✳ CLOSING CASE TWO

Global Governance

Tarun Khanna, a Harvard professor, states that Indian companies exhibit corporate governance superior to their Chinese rivals. Khanna has just released a new book, *Billions of Entrepreneurs: How China and India Are Reshaping Their Future and Yours.* However, Khanna believes that Chinese organizations might not require world-class governance to emerge as fierce competitors. Here are edited excerpts from a recent conversation between Khanna and *BusinessWeek*'s William J. Holstein:

Much as their societies and political systems are different, are Indian and Chinese companies complete opposites when it comes to corporate governance?
Absolutely. Indian companies are so much better governed. India is sort of a noisier version of the U.S. system, which is that you have to be accountable to shareholders and all the other stakeholders. The principles are the same, but the information acquisition is a little bit more problematic in India compared to the U.S. It's not so easy to figure out everything you need to. But there's a very vibrant, credible business media. No opinion is forbidden to be expressed. Information is noisy and unbiased—no one is willfully distorting the truth.

China is the opposite—it is noise-free but biased. You get a clean story but the story is not always right. There are views that cannot be expressed.

Which country has more independent boards of directors?
In India, there is a spectrum of companies, such as Infosys, which on some dimensions is better governed than companies in the West in terms of how quickly it discloses things and how quickly it complies with Nasdaq norms. At the other end of the spectrum you have companies that are still the fiefdoms of families, many of which are badly governed. But even those companies are accountable to the market. Market pressures will force them to clean up their act to some extent. The equity markets function so well that it's hard to believe you could be a continuous violator of norms of good governance and still have access to the equity markets.

In China, none of that matters because the financial markets still do not work in the sense that we think of them working in the U.S. In China, all stock prices move together. They move up on a given day or they move down. There is no company-specific information embodied in the stock price. You cannot possibly decide that a company is good or bad because the market isn't working in that sense. What you see is aggregate enthusiasm, or lack thereof, for China Inc. The market is not putting pressure on managers to behave in ways that approximate corporate governance in the West.

Are companies in India and China making progress in developing talent in the same way that Western multinationals do?

They are both making progress. But Indian companies are significantly further along, partly because India never had a Cultural Revolution as China did, which wiped out much of the business class. It had a residue of corporations already in existence. Some companies are 100 or 150 years old and they have an established way of doing things.

Where are the Chinese when it comes to managing multiculturally?

Utterly zero. It is hard to blame them because there is a language barrier also. A lot of the internal tensions were about language and cultural barriers, and questions like, Can a Frenchman report to a Chinese? And what if the French guy makes more than the Chinese guy?

How do companies of the two countries compare when it comes to corruption?

Here, I am not positive on India at all. Transparency International puts out these indices, and India and China are both close to the bottom of that list. China does a little bit better than India. In China, there is corruption, but it is constructive corruption. You, as a bureaucrat, get to be corrupt but only after you generate some value for society. You get a piece of it.

In India, there is corruption but it is not constructive. You are not fostering new bridges or highways. It is just shuffling stuff back and forth. I do not think we have cracked that in India at all. I am very sorry about that.

In the final analysis, does it matter that Indian companies, on the whole, have an edge over the Chinese in reaching international standards of governance? The Chinese have huge capital at their disposal because of their $1.5 trillion in foreign exchange reserves. Could not they still be fearsome competitors?

I think that is right. Corporate governance matters because you want to reassure the providers of inputs—whether it is time and talent, or ideas, or capital—that their rights will be respected and they will get a return on it. But if you are already sitting on hundreds of billions of dollars of capital, and you do not need to reassure anybody else because you already have your capital, why have good corporate governance?

The reason the Chinese feel less pressured to do something about it is not because they do not know how to do it—far from it, they have the best technical help from Hong Kong and other places. It is because they make a reasoned judgment that it is not worth their while.

Questions

1. Explain governance and compliance and why they are important to any company looking to perform global business.
2. How can an organization use governance and compliance to help protect itself from global security breaches?
3. If you were choosing between outsourcing to India or China, based on this case, which country would you choose and why?
4. What types of ethical dilemmas might an organization face when dealing with IT governance in India or China?

1. Transforming an Organization

Your college has asked you to help develop the curriculum for a new course titled "Building a 21st Century Organization." Use the materials in this text, the Internet, and any other resources to outline the curriculum that you would suggest the course cover. Be sure to include your reasons why the material should be covered and the order in which it should be covered.

2. Connecting Components

Components of a solid enterprise architecture include everything from documentation to business concepts to software and hardware. Deciding which components to implement and how to implement them can be a challenge. New IT components are released daily, and business needs continually change. An enterprise architecture that meets your organization's needs today may not meet those needs tomorrow. Building an enterprise architecture that is scalable, flexible, available, accessible, and reliable is key to your organization's success.

You are the enterprise architect for a large clothing company called Xedous. You are responsible for developing the initial enterprise architecture. Create a list of questions you will need answered to develop your architecture. Below is an example of a few questions you might ask.

- What are the company's growth expectations?
- Will systems be able to handle additional users?
- How long will information be stored in the systems?
- How much customer history must be stored?
- What are the organization's business hours?
- What are the organization's backup requirements?

3. IT Gets Its Say

CIOs need to speak the language of business to sell IT's strategic benefits. It is no secret that the most successful companies today are the ones that deliver the right products and services faster, more efficiently, more securely, and more cost-effectively than their competitors, and the key to that is a practical implementation of enterprise technology to improve business performance. IT executives and managers therefore must speak the language of business to articulate how technology can solve business problems.

CIOs of tomorrow will focus on a number of changing dynamics: enabling the business to grow versus just optimizing performance, saying yes instead of no; allowing open innovation rather than closed, traditional R&D practices; creating a culture of strategic growth and innovation; and empowering the customer to make decisions that drive a heightened value proposition for both the customer and supplier. You have been charged with creating a slogan for your company that explains the correlation of business and IT. A few examples include:

- IT should no longer be viewed as just an enabler of somebody else's business strategy.
- The distinction between technology and business is antediluvian — it's gone.

Create a slogan that you can use to explain to your employees the importance of business and IT.

4. Mom-and-Pop Multinationals

Global outsourcing is no longer just for big corporations as small businesses jump into the multisourcing game. Increasingly, Main Street businesses from car dealers to advertising agencies are finding it easier to farm out software development, accounting, support services, and design work to distant lands. For example, Randy and Nicola Wilburn run a micro-multinational organization right from their home. The Wilburns run real estate, consulting, design, and baby food companies from their home by taking outsourcing to the extreme. Professionals from around the globe are at their service. For $300, an Indian artist designed the cute logo of an infant peering over the words "Baby Fresh Organic Baby Foods" and Nicola's letterhead. A London freelancer wrote promotional materials. Randy has hired "virtual assistants" in Jerusalem to transcribe voice mail, update his website, and design PowerPoint graphics. Retired brokers in Virginia and Michigan handle real estate paperwork.

Elance, an online-services marketplace, boasts 48,500 small businesses as clients—up 70 percent in the past year—posting 18,000 new projects a month. Other online-services marketplaces such as Guru.com, Brickwork India, DoMyStuff.com, and RentACoder also report fast growth. You have decided to jump in the micro-multinational game and start your own online-services marketplace. Research the following as you compile your start-up business plan.

1. To compete in this market what types of services would you offer?
2. What types of cultural, political, and geoeconomic challenges would your business experience?
3. How would governance and compliance fit into your business strategy?
4. What types of global information issues might your company experience?
5. What types of customers would you want to attract and what vehicle would you use to find your customers?
6. What types of global systems development issues would your company experience?
7. What types of information security and ethical dilemmas should you anticipate?

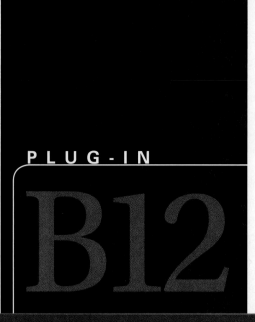

PLUG-IN
B12

Global Trends

LEARNING OUTCOMES

1. Identify the trends that will have the greatest impact on future business.
2. Identify the technologies that will have the greatest impact on future business.
3. Explain why understanding trends and new technologies can help an organization prepare for the future.

Introduction

The core units brought out how important it is for organizations to anticipate and prepare for the future by studying emerging trends and new technologies. Having a broad view of emerging trends and new technologies as they relate to business can provide an organization with a valuable strategic advantage. Those organizations that can most effectively grasp the deep currents of technological evolution can use their knowledge to protect themselves against sudden and fatal technological obsolescence.

This plug-in identifies several emerging trends and new technologies that can help an organization prepare for future opportunities and challenges.

Reasons to Watch Trends

LO 1. Identify the trends that will have the greatest impact on future business.

Organizations anticipate, forecast, and assess future events using a variety of rational, scientific methods including:

- **Trend analysis:** A trend is examined to identify its nature, causes, speed of development, and potential impacts.

- **Trend monitoring:** Trends viewed as particularly important in a specific community, industry, or sector are carefully monitored, watched, and reported to key decision makers.

- **Trend projection:** When numerical data are available, a trend can be plotted to display changes through time and into the future.

- **Computer simulation:** Complex systems, such as the U.S. economy, can be modeled by means of mathematical equations and different scenarios can be run against the model to conduct "what if" analysis.

Top Reasons to Study Trends	
1. Generate ideas and identify opportunities	Find new ideas and innovations by studying trends and analyzing publications.
2. Identify early warning signals	Scan the environment for potential threats and risks.
3. Gain confidence	A solid foundation of awareness about trends can provide an organization with the confidence to take risks.
4. Beat the competition	Seeing what is coming before others can give an organization the lead time it requires to establish a foothold in the new market.
5. Understand a trend	Analyzing the details within a trend can help separate truly significant developments from rapidly appearing and disappearing fads.
6. Balance strategic goals	Thinking about the future is an antidote to a "profit now, worry later" mentality that can lead to trouble in the long term.
7. Understand the future of specific industries	Organizations must understand everything inside and outside their industry.
8. Prepare for the future	Any organization that wants to compete in this hyperchanging world needs to make every effort to forecast the future.

- **Historical analysis:** Historical events are studied to anticipate the outcome of current developments.

   Foresight is one of the secret ingredients of business success. Foresight, however, is increasingly in short supply because almost everything in our world is changing at a faster pace than ever before. Many organizations have little idea what type of future they should prepare for in this world of hyperchange. Figure B12.1 displays the top reasons organizations should look to the future and study trends.

Trends Shaping Our Future

LO 2. Identify the technologies that will have the greatest impact on future business.

According to the World Future Society, the following trends have the potential to change our world, our future, and our lives.

- The world's population will double in the next 40 years.
- People in developed countries are living longer.
- The growth in information industries is creating a knowledge-dependent global society.
- The global economy is becoming more integrated.
- The economy and society are dominated by technology.
- The pace of technological innovation is increasing.
- Time is becoming one of the world's most precious commodities.

THE WORLD'S POPULATION WILL DOUBLE IN THE NEXT 40 YEARS

The countries that are expected to have the largest increases in population between 2000 and 2050 are:

- Palestinian Territory—217 percent increase.
- Niger—205 percent increase.
- Yemen—168 percent increase.

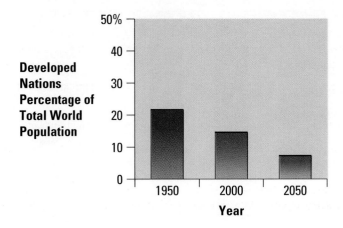

- Angola—162 percent increase.
- Democratic Republic of the Congo—161 percent increase.
- Uganda—133 percent increase.

In contrast, developed and industrialized countries are expected to see fertility rates decrease below population replacement levels, leading to significant declines in population (see Figure B12.2).

Potential Business Impact

- Global agriculture will be required to supply as much food as has been produced during all of human history to meet human nutritional needs over the next 40 years.
- Developed nations will find that retirees will have to remain on the job to remain competitive and continue economic growth.
- Developed nations will begin to increase immigration limits.

PEOPLE IN DEVELOPED COUNTRIES ARE LIVING LONGER

New pharmaceuticals and medical technologies are making it possible to prevent and cure diseases that would have been fatal to past generations. This is one reason that each generation lives longer and remains healthier than the previous generation. On average, each generation in the United States lives three years longer than the previous. An 80-year-old in 1950 could expect to live 6.5 years longer today. Many developed countries are now experiencing life expectancy over 75 years for males and over 80 years for females (see Figure B12.3).

Rising Life Expectancy in Developed Countries		
Country	Life Expectancy (Born 1950–1955)	Life Expectancy (Born 1995–2000)
United States	68.9	76.5
United Kingdom	69.2	77.2
Germany	67.5	77.3
France	66.5	78.1
Italy	66.0	78.2
Canada	69.1	78.5
Japan	63.9	80.5

Potential Business Impact

- Global demand for products and services for the elderly will grow quickly in the coming decades.
- The cost of health care is destined to skyrocket.
- Pharmaceutical companies will be pushed for advances in geriatric medicine.

THE GROWTH IN INFORMATION INDUSTRIES IS CREATING A KNOWLEDGE-DEPENDENT GLOBAL SOCIETY

Estimates indicate that 90 percent of American management personnel will be knowledge workers by 2008. Estimates for knowledge workers in Europe and Japan are not far behind. Soon, large organizations will be composed of specialists who rely on information from co-workers, customers, and suppliers to guide their actions. Employees will gain new power as they are provided with the authority to make decisions based on the information they acquire.

Potential Business Impact

- Top managers must be computer-literate to retain their jobs and achieve success.

- Knowledge workers are generally higher paid and their proliferation is increasing overall prosperity.

- Entry-level and unskilled positions are requiring a growing level of education.

- Information now flows from front-office workers to higher management for analysis. Thus, in the future, fewer midlevel managers will be required, flattening the corporate pyramid.

- Downsizing, restructuring, reorganization, outsourcing, and layoffs will continue as typical large organizations struggle to reinvent and restructure themselves for greater flexibility.

THE GLOBAL ECONOMY IS BECOMING MORE INTEGRATED

International outsourcing is on the rise as organizations refuse to pay high salaries for activities that do not contribute directly to the bottom line. The European Union has relaxed its borders and capital controls making it easier for companies to outsource support functions throughout the continent.

The Internet is one of the primary tools enabling our global economy. One of the primary reasons for the increase in Internet use is the increase in connectivity technology. India's Internet users reached 50 million in 2005 (see Figure B12.4 for India's statistics). The increase in Internet use is increasing revenues for ebusinesses.

FIGURE B12.4

Growth of Internet Users in India

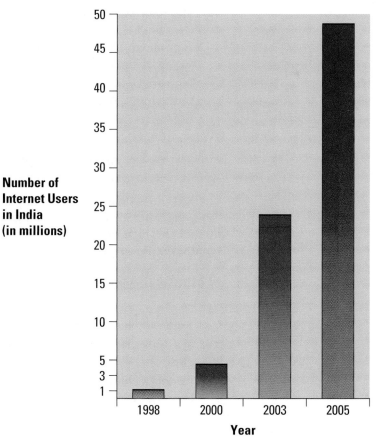

Potential Business Impact

- Demand for personnel in distant countries will increase the need for foreign-language training, employee incentives suited to other cultures, and many other aspects of performing business globally.

- The growth of ebusiness and the use of the Internet to shop globally for raw materials and supplies will reduce the cost of doing business.

- The Internet will continue to enable small companies to compete with worldwide giants with relatively little investment.

- Internet-based operations require sophisticated knowledge workers and thus people with the right technical skills will be heavily recruited over the next 15 years.

THE ECONOMY AND SOCIETY ARE DOMINATED BY TECHNOLOGY

Computers are becoming a part of our environment. Mundane commercial and service jobs, environmentally dangerous jobs, standard assembly jobs, and even the repair of inaccessible equipment such as space stations will be increasingly performed by robots. Artificial intelligence and expert systems will help most companies and government agencies assimilate data and solve problems beyond the range of today's computers including energy prospecting, automotive diagnostics, insurance underwriting, and law enforcement.

Superconductors operating at economically viable temperatures are expected to be in commercial use by 2015. Products eventually will include supercomputers the size of a three-pound coffee can, electronic motors 75 percent smaller and lighter than those in use today, and power plants.

Potential Business Impact

- New technologies provide dozens of new opportunities to create businesses and jobs.
- Automation will continue to decrease the cost of products and services, making it possible to reduce prices while improving profits.
- The Internet is expected to push prices of most products to the commodity level.
- The demand for scientists, engineers, and technicians will continue to grow.

PACE OF TECHNOLOGICAL INNOVATION IS INCREASING

Technology is advancing at a phenomenal pace. Medical knowledge is doubling every eight years. Half of what students learn in their freshman year of college about innovative technology is obsolete, revised, or taken for granted by their senior year. In fact, all of today's technical knowledge will represent only 1 percent of the knowledge that will be available in 2050.

Potential Business Impact

- The time to get products and services to market is being shortened by technology. Products must capture their market quickly before the competition can copy them. During the 1940s the average time to get a product to market was 40 weeks. Today, a product's entire life cycle seldom lasts 40 weeks.
- Industries will face tighter competition based on new technologies. Those who adopt state-of-the-art technology first will prosper, while those who ignore it eventually will fail.

TIME IS BECOMING ONE OF THE WORLD'S MOST PRECIOUS COMMODITIES

In the United States, workers today spend around 10 percent more time on the job than they did a decade ago. European executives and nonunionized workers face the same trend. This high-pressure environment is increasing the need for any product or service that saves time or simplifies life.

Potential Business Impact

- Companies must take an active role in helping their employees balance their time at work with their family lives and need for leisure.
- Stress-related problems affecting employee morale and wellness will continue to grow.
- As time for shopping continues to evaporate, Internet and mail-order marketers will have a growing advantage over traditional stores.

Technologies Shaping Our Future

LO 3. Explain why understanding trends and new technologies can help an organization prepare for the future.

The following technologies are changing our world, our future, and our lives.

- Digital ink
- Digital paper
- Teleliving
- Alternative energy sources
- Autonomic computing

DIGITAL INK

Digital ink (or ***electronic ink***) refers to technology that digitally represents handwriting in its natural form (see Figure B12.5). E Ink Corporation, headquartered in Cambridge, Massachusetts, has developed a proprietary technology called electronic ink, which provides significant advantages over other display technologies. E Ink was founded in 1997 to advance electronic ink, develop applications, and create markets for displays based on this unique technology.

FIGURE B12.5

Digital Ink

Potential Business Impact

- Digital ink has broad usage in many applications, from point-of-sale signs in retail stores, to next generation displays in mobile devices and PDAs, to thin, portable electronic books and newspapers. E Ink has collaborated with various companies like Lucent Technologies to produce reusable paper with digital ink.

- The ultimate dream of E Ink is ***RadioPaper,*** a dynamic high-resolution electronic display that combines a paperlike reading experience with the ability to access information anytime, anywhere. RadioPaper will be thin and flexible and could be used to create an electronic book or newspaper with real pages.

DIGITAL PAPER

Digital paper (or ***electronic paper***) is any paper that is optimized for any type of digital printing. In some ways, digital paper is produced much like a sheet of paper. It comes from a pulp and the finished product has the flexibility to be rolled into scrolls of "paper." However, the major difference between paper produced from a tree and paper produced in a laboratory is that information on a digital paper sheet can be altered thousands of times and not degrade over time (see Figure B12.6). Digital paper offers excellent resolution and high contrast under a wide range of viewing angles, requires no external power to retain its image, is extremely lightweight, costs less, and is remarkably flexible, unlike computer displays.

Macy's department store was the first company to experiment by placing digital paper signs in the children's section at a New Jersey store. As the company spends more than $250,000 a week changing its in-store signs, such renewable signage could prove highly desirable. A networked programmable sign will run for two years on three AA batteries (see Figure B12.7).

As a laboratory prototype, digital ink and digital paper have been around for some time with demonstration of the technologies often leading to wild predictions about ebooks and enewspapers (see Figure B12.8).

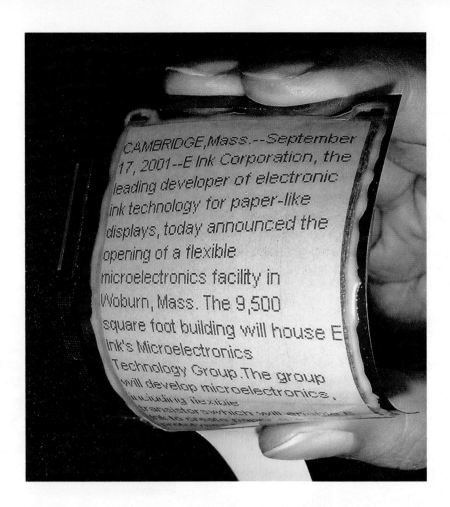

Date	Technology
April 1996	MIT's Media Lab starts work on electronic paper prototype.
April 1997	E Ink is founded to commercialize MIT's electronic paper displays.
May 1999	E Ink debuts Immedia electronic paper display products.
November 2000	E Ink and Lucent Technologies demonstrate first flexible electronic products.
December 2000	Gyricon Media is spun off from Xerox PARC.
February 2001	E Ink teams with Philips Components to develop a high-resolution display for smart handhelds.
March 2001	Gyricon introduces digital paper technology.
June 2001	Macy's is scheduled to test digital paper for in-store signage use.
Late 2001	E Ink/Philips handheld prototype is delivered.
2004/2005	E Ink electronic paper handheld devices becomes available to users.
Mid-2000s	Possible debut of E Ink's RadioPaper wireless electronic publishing technology.

Potential Business Impact

■ Digital paper is driving a new wave of innovation in the content distribution field. Paperlike displays will replace newspapers, magazines, and books since they will be almost as manageable as paper and allow display resolution close to print.

■ The concept of a reusable paper product is an environmentally sound idea considering that a major portion of the world's paper goes to printing newspapers, magazines, pamphlets, and so on.

TELELIVING

Lifestyle changes will emerge as computers develop capabilities that are more sophisticated. *Teleliving* refers to using information devices and the Internet to conduct all aspects of life seamlessly. This can include such things as shopping, working, learning, playing, healing, and praying. Even today, homes, autos, and work environments are wired into intelligent networks that interact with one another. Each year, 4 billion chips are embedded in everything from coffeemakers to Cadillacs.

Potential Business Impact

■ In the future, people will move through a constant stream of information summoned at the touch of a finger. They will interact with life-size images, data, and text in homes and offices. The days of hunching over a computer will be gone.

■ The *virtual assistant (VA)* will be a small program stored on a PC or portable device that monitors emails, faxes, messages, and phone calls. Virtual assistants will help individuals solve problems in the same way a real assistant would. In time, the VA will take over routine tasks such as writing a letter, retrieving a file, and making a phone call.

■ Robotic salespeople will take on human appearances and have the ability to perform all tasks associated with a sales job.

FIGURE B12.9

Wind Power—An
Alternative Energy Source

ALTERNATIVE ENERGY SOURCES

By the end of the decade, wind, geothermal, hydroelectric, solar, and other alternative energy sources will increase from their present level of 10 percent of all energy use to about 30 percent. Worldwide wind-power generating capacity grew by 6,500 megawatts in 2003, the fastest rate of growth yet recorded and 50 percent more than the previous year (see Figure B12.9). Nuclear plants supply 16 percent of the energy in Russia and Eastern Europe. New sources of carbon fuels are frequently being discovered and more-powerful extraction methods are being developed, thereby keeping supply up and costs down.

Potential Business Impact

- China, Asia, India, South America, and Russia are modernizing their economies, which increasingly use large amounts of energy.

- The cost of alternative energy sources is dropping with technical advances. This growing competition from other energy sources will help limit the price of oil.

- The imminent deregulation of the energy industry is expected to create a huge spurt of innovative entrepreneurship, fostering a wide variety of new energy sources.

- Oil will remain the world's most important energy resource. However, in two or three decades a declining reliance on oil will help reduce air and water pollution. By 2060, a costly but pollution-free hydrogen economy may become possible.

AUTONOMIC COMPUTING

Autonomic computing is a self-managing computing model named after, and patterned on, the human body's autonomic nervous system. Autonomic computing is one of the building blocks of widespread computing, an anticipated future computing model in which small—even invisible—computers will be all around us, communicating through increasingly interconnected networks. Many industry leaders, including IBM, HP, Sun, and Microsoft, are researching various components of autonomic computing. However, autonomic computing is not an overnight revolution in which systemwide, self-managing environments suddenly appear. As described in Figure B12.10, autonomic computing is a gradual evolution that delivers new technologies that are adopted and implemented at various stages and levels.

Potential Business Impact

- The complex IT infrastructures of the future will require more computer automation than ever before. Autonomic computing will be used in a variety of areas that include security, storage, network management, and new redundancy and fail-over capabilities.

- Autonomic computers will continuously seek out ways to optimize computing. In the autonomic environment, computers will monitor components and fine-tune workflows to achieve system performance goals.

- Autonomic computers will be able to "self-heal." In the event of a component failure, an autonomic computer will be able to diagnose the failure and develop a workaround that allows the computer to continue with its functions.

- Autonomic computers will be able to "self-protect." Protection for computing resources primarily takes the form of fighting off invasive viruses and security intrusion attempts.

Level	Technologies Implemented
Level 1: Basic	The starting point where most systems are today, this level represents manual computing in which all system elements are managed independently by an extensive, highly skilled IT staff. The staff sets up, monitors, and eventually replaces system elements.
Level 2: Managed	Systems management technologies can be used to collect and consolidate information from disparate systems onto fewer consoles, reducing administrative time. There is greater system awareness and improved productivity.
Level 3: Predictive	The system monitors and correlates data to recognize patterns and recommends actions that are approved and initiated by the IT staff. This reduces the dependency on deep skills and enables faster and better decision making.
Level 4: Adaptive	In addition to monitoring and correlating data, the system takes action based on the information, thereby enhancing IT agility and resiliency with minimal human interaction.
Level 5: Autonomic	Fully integrated systems and components are dynamically managed by business rules and policies, enabling IT staff to focus on meeting business needs with true business agility and resiliency.

FIGURE B12.10

Evolutionary Process of Autonomic Computing

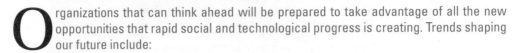
Organizations that can think ahead will be prepared to take advantage of all the new opportunities that rapid social and technological progress is creating. Trends shaping our future include:

- The world's population will double in the next 40 years.
- People in developed countries are living longer.
- The growth in information industries is creating a knowledge-dependent global society.
- The global economy is becoming more integrated.
- The economy and society are dominated by technology.
- The pace of technological innovation is increasing.
- Time is becoming one of the world's most precious commodities.

Technologies shaping our future include:

- Digital ink
- Digital paper
- Teleliving
- Alternative energy sources
- Autonomic computing

✳ KEY TERMS

Autonomic computing, 512
Computer simulation, 504
Digital ink (or electronic ink), 509

Digital paper (or electronic paper), 509
Historical analysis, 505
RadioPaper, 509
Teleliving, 511

Trend analysis, 504
Trend monitoring, 504
Trend projection, 504
Virtual assistant (VA), 511

✳ CLOSING CASE ONE

Autonomic Railways

Canadian Pacific Railway (CPR), based in Calgary, Alberta, Canada, is one of the largest railway systems in North America. With more than 14,400 miles of rail line in Canada and the United States, this $2.6 billion (U.S.) transportation company serves virtually every major industry, from the resource-based industries of the West to the manufacturing bases and consumer markets in central Canada and the northern United States.

Shippers expect fast, reliable services and on-time delivery of goods. As a result, CPR designed many programs—from improving asset management, to strengthening service reliability, to accounting for fluctuating costs—to help it respond to market forces with agility and ease. Val King, manager of IT security for CPR, explains that security management is an essential element in the delivery of these on-demand services. King said, "We must protect our operations from technology attacks, while providing our customers easy, reliable access to information and services online."

The goal of the company's IT security team is simple: minimize risk while optimizing user satisfaction. Yet the team's greatest challenges are lack of resources and tight budgets. "We had to look to technology to help us accomplish our goals," explained King. CPR collaborated with IBM to deliver solutions that are both automated (they can control a defined process without human intervention) and autonomic (they can sense and respond to conditions in accordance with business policies). As a result, IT employees can deliver consistent, reliable service levels at reduced costs since they collaborated with IBM using autonomic computing resources such as Tivoli Risk Manager, Tivoli Access Manager, Tivoli Identity Manager, and Tivoli Decision Support. "The automation of processes through the intelligent self-managing features of Tivoli software can help companies respond to threats more quickly," King said. "The benefit is that organizations can strengthen the resiliency of their environments even as the number of security events increases."

CPR is realizing measurable results from its implementation of Tivoli Security Management solutions and King sees the already-realized benefits as only the "tip of the iceberg." Some of the notable ROI from CPR's investment in Tivoli Security Management solutions include:

1. **Improved productivity**—The IT security team spends less time managing security incidents with Tivoli Risk Manager. The IT staff also expects to spend less time on reporting because data from the various security monitors will be integrated.

2. **Reduced costs**—The application development team estimates that a centralized security model helps accelerate development time. The help desk organization reports a reduction in user calls, due to the password-reset capabilities of Tivoli Identity Manager.

3. **Increased business resiliency**—Using Tivoli Risk Manager, Tivoli Enterprise Console, Tivoli Decision Support, and Tripwire, a data integrity assurance solution from Tripwire, Inc., CPR tests show that if an attack shuts down a service, administrators can get systems back online much faster.

4. **Improved audit compliance**—Before the implementation of Tivoli Access Manager for ebusiness, security staff would need to look at each system or application to see if it properly applied security policy. Now, security policies are consistent enterprisewide.

Questions

1. Which of the trends shaping our future discussed in this plug-in will have the greatest impact on CPR's business?
2. Which of the trends will have the least impact on CPR's business?
3. How are the functions of autonomic computing providing CPR with a competitive advantage?
4. How can CPR take advantage of other technological advances to improve security?

✳ CLOSING CASE TWO

Wireless Progression

Progressive Corporation is the fourth-largest automobile insurer in the United States with more than 8 million policyholders and net premiums of $6.1 billion. Progressive offers wireless web access to holders of its auto insurance policies, a move that analysts have said fits the company's reputation as a technology leader in the insurance industry and its emphasis on customer service.

Customers can use their web-enabled phones to get price quotes, report claims, locate nearby independent agents by ZIP code, and access real-time account information through the company's website. Progressive also has the ability to push time-sensitive data to policyholders via wireless connections, instantly delivering information about an auto-recall notice to a customer's cell phone.

As a cost-saving measure, and in keeping with a corporate tradition of internal development, Ohio-based Progressive decided to build its own wireless applications. Policyholders simply have to type Progressive's web address into their phones or connect to the site through search engines that specialize in wireless ebusiness.

Stephen Williams, president of the Insurance Institute of Indiana, a nonprofit trade association that represents insurers in that state, said it's "not uncommon for Progressive to be on the cutting edge with its use of technology." If Progressive is starting to take advantage of the wireless web, other companies could follow its lead, he added. Jeffrey Kagan, an Atlanta-based wireless technology analyst, called Progressive "the Nordstrom's of insurance because of its emphasis on customer service." The addition of wireless access to its website "is a simple but smart way to use technology" to further improve the company's service, Kagan said. Progressive.com leads the insurance industry in consumer-friendly innovations. It was the first auto insurance website (1995), first to offer online quoting and comparison rates (1996), first to offer instantaneous online purchase of an auto policy (1997), and first to offer after-the-sale service (1998).

The Progressive.com website leads the insurance industry in consumer-friendly innovations and functionality. Progressive.com was recognized as one of the "top 10 websites that work" by *InfoWeek Magazine* and was named to the Smart Business 50 by *Smart Business Magazine* for successful use of the Internet to enhance and expand its business.

Questions

1. Which of the trends shaping our future discussed in this plug-in will have the greatest impact on Progressive's business?

2. Which of the trends will have the least impact on Progressive's business?

3. What other forms of advanced technology would you expect Progressive to deploy in the near future?

✷ MAKING BUSINESS DECISIONS

1. Identifying and Following Trends

What's Hot.com is a new business that specializes in helping companies identify and follow significant trends in their industries. You have recently been hired as a new business analyst and your first task is to highlight current trends in the ebusiness industry. Using the Internet and any other resources you have available, highlight five significant trends not discussed in this text. Prepare a PowerPoint presentation that lists the trends and discusses the potential business impacts for each trend.

2. Reading the Ink on the Wall

IPublish.com is an ebook-only imprint publisher. While large publishers find that ebooks are not selling as expected, IPublish.com continues to report positive growth. However, IPublish.com feels threatened by digital ink and digital paper inventions that seem to be revolutionizing the publishing environment and endangering the global paper industry. You have been hired by IPublish.com to develop a strategy to embrace this new technology. Create a detailed report listing the reasons IPublish.com needs to support these two new technologies.

3. Pen Pal

StyleUs is a digital pen that writes on ordinary paper printed with a unique dot pattern almost invisible to the naked eye. A tiny camera in the pen registers the pen's movement across a printed grid and stores it as a series of map coordinates. These coordinates correspond to the exact location of the page that is being written on. The dot pattern makes up a huge map of tiny distinctive squares, so small portions of it can also be given specific functions, such as "send," "store," or "synchronize." When a mark is made in the send box with the digital pen, it is instructed to send the stored sequence of map coordinates, which are translated into an image. The result is an exact copy of the handwriting displayed on the computer, mobile phone, or received as a fax anywhere in the world.

Analyze this new technology and identify how it might affect the digital ink or digital paper market. Be sure to include a Porter's Five Forces analysis of the market.

4. Less Is More

Your organization is teetering on the edge of systems chaos. Your systems administrator is stressed beyond tolerance by too many systems, too many applications, too few resources, and too little time. The scope, frequency, and diversity of demand are causing greater risk than anyone dares to admit. Automating (and reducing complexity of) the operating environment is critical for your business to survive. Research autonomic computing and write a report discussing how this technology can help an organization gain control over its systems.

5. Fly Pentop Computer

BusinessED specializes in creating new and innovative software for education in the business market. Danny Henningson, founder and president of BusinessED, is interested in developing educational products using digital paper and digital ink. Danny has hired you as the vice president of research and development and is excited to hear your ideas for new products. Your first assignment is to study the Fly Pentop computer (www.flypentop.com) and decide how you can apply this type of technology to the business arena.

6. Alternative Energy

With energy costs on the rise, many U.S. homes are turning to homegrown energy solutions. Your friend Cole Lazarus has decided to start a business offering such solutions. Cole would like your help developing his business. Begin by researching the Internet and find different ways that you could design a home with its own energy sources. Create a document listing the different sources along with advantages and disadvantages of each source.

Apply Your Knowledge Project Overview

Project Number	Project Name	Project Type	Plug-In	Focus Area	Project Level	Skill Set	Page Number
1	Financial Destiny	Excel	T2	Personal Budget	Introductory	Formulas	AYK.4
2	Cash Flow	Excel	T2	Cash Flow	Introductory	Formulas	AYK.4
3	Technology Budget	Excel	T1, T2	Hardware and Software	Introductory	Formulas	AYK.4
4	Tracking Donations	Excel	T2	Employee Relationships	Introductory	Formulas	AYK.4
5	Convert Currency	Excel	T2	Global Commerce	Introductory	Formulas	AYK.5
6	Cost Comparison	Excel	T2	Total Cost of Ownership	Introductory	Formulas	AYK.5
7	Time Management	Excel or Project	T12	Project Management	Introductory	Gantt Charts	AYK.6
8	Maximize Profit	Excel	T2, T4	Strategic Analysis	Intermediate	Formulas or Solver	AYK.6
9	Security Analysis	Excel	T3	Filtering Data	Intermediate	Conditional Formatting, Autofilter, Subtotal	AYK.7
10	Gathering Data	Excel	T3	Data Analysis	Intermediate	Conditional Formatting	AYK.8
11	Scanner System	Excel	T2	Strategic Analysis	Intermediate	Formulas	AYK.8
12	Competitive Pricing	Excel	T2	Profit Maximization	Intermediate	Formulas	AYK.9
13	Adequate Acquisitions	Excel	T2	Break-Even Analysis	Intermediate	Formulas	AYK.9
14	Customer Relations	Excel	T3	CRM	Intermediate	PivotTable	AYK.9
15	Assessing the Value of Information	Excel	T3	Data Analysis	Intermediate	PivotTable	AYK.10
16	Growth, Trends, and Forecasts	Excel	T2, T3	Data Forecasting	Advanced	Average, Trend, Growth	AYK.11
17	Shipping Costs	Excel	T4	SCM	Advanced	Solver	AYK.12
18	Formatting Grades	Excel	T3	Data Analysis	Advanced	If, LookUp	AYK.12

(Continued)

Project Number	Project Name	Project Type	Plug-In	Focus Area	Project Level	Skill Set	Page Number
19	Moving Dilemma	Excel	T2, T3	SCM	Advanced	Absolute vs. Relative Values	AYK.13
20	Operational Efficiencies	Excel	T3	SCM	Advanced	PivotTable	AYK.14
21	Too Much Information	Excel	T3	CRM	Advanced	PivotTable	AYK.14
22	Turnover Rates	Excel	T3	Data Mining	Advanced	PivotTable	AYK.15
23	Vital Information	Excel	T3	Data Mining	Advanced	PivotTable	AYK.15
24	Breaking Even	Excel	T4	Business Analysis	Advanced	Goal Seek	AYK.16
25	Profit Scenario	Excel	T4	Sales Analysis	Advanced	Scenario Manager	AYK.16
26	Electronic Résumés	HTML	T9, T10, T11	Electronic Personal Marketing	Introductory	Structural Tags	AYK.17
27	Gathering Feedback	Dreamweaver	T9, T10, T11	Data Collection	Intermediate	Organization of Information	AYK.17
28	Daily Invoice	Access	T5, T6, T7, T8	Business Analysis	Introductory	Entities, Relationships, and Databases	AYK.17
29	Billing Data	Access	T5, T6, T7, T8	Business Intelligence	Introductory	Entities, Relationships, and Databases	AYK.19
30	Inventory Data	Access	T5, T6, T7, T8	SCM	Intermediate	Entities, Relationships, and Databases	AYK.20
31	Call Center	Access	T5, T6, T7, T8	CRM	Intermediate Entities, Relationships, and	Databases	AYK.21
32	Sales Pipeline	Access	T5, T6, T7, T8	Business Intelligence	Advanced	Entities, Relationships, and Databases	AYK.23
33	Online Classified Ads	Access	T5, T6, T7, T8	Ecommerce	Advanced	Entities, Relationships, and Databases	AYK.23

NOTE: Many of the Excel projects support multiple data files. Therefore the naming convention that you see in the text may not be the same as what you see in a data folder. As an example, in the text we reference data files as AYK1_Data.xlsx; however, you may see a file named AYK1_Data_Version_1.xlsx, or AYK1_Data_Version_2.xlsx.

Project 1:
Financial Destiny

You have been introduced to Microsoft Excel and are ready to begin using it to help track your monthly expenses and take charge of your financial destiny. The first step is to create a personal budget so you can see where you are spending money and if you need to decrease your monthly expenses or increase your monthly income.

Project Focus

Create a template for a monthly budget of your income and expenditures, with some money set aside for savings (or you can use the data file, AYK1_Data.xlsx, we created). Create variations of this budget to show how much you could save if you cut back on certain expenses, found a roommate, or got a part-time job. Compare the costs of a meal plan to costs of groceries. Consider how much interest would be earned if you saved $100 a month, or how much debt paid on student loans or credit card bills. To expand your data set, make a fantasy budget for 10 years from now, when you might own a home, have student loan payments, and have a good salary.

Data File: AYK1_Data.xlsx

Project 2:
Cash Flow

Gears is a five-year-old company that specializes in bike components. The company is having trouble paying for its monthly supplies and would like to perform a cash flow analysis so it can understand its financial position. Cash flow represents the money an investment produces after subtracting cash expenses from income. The statement of cash flows summarizes sources and uses of cash, indicates whether enough cash is available to carry on routine operations, and offers an analysis of all business transactions, reporting where the firm obtained its cash and how it chose to allocate the cash. The cash flow statement shows where money comes from, how the company is going to spend it, and when the company will require additional cash. Gears would like to project a cash flow statement for the next month.

Project Focus

Using the data file AYK2_Data.xlsx complete the cash flow statement for Gears using Excel. Be sure to create formulas so the company can simply input numbers in the future to determine cash flow.

Data File: AYK2_Data.xlsx

Project 3:
Technology Budget

Tally is a start-up website development company located in Seattle, Washington. The company currently has seven employees and is looking to hire six new employees in the next month.

Project Focus

You are in charge of purchasing for Tally. Your first task is to purchase computers for the new employees. Your budget is $250,000 to buy the best computer systems with a scanner, three color printers, and business software. Use the web to research various products and calculate the costs of different systems using Excel. Use a variety of Excel formulas as you analyze costs and compare prices. Use the data file AYK3_Data.xlsx as a template.

Data File: AYK3_Data.xlsx

Project 4:
Tracking Donations

Lazarus Consulting is a large computer consulting company in New York. Pete Lazarus, the CEO and founder, is well known for his philanthropic efforts. Pete knows that most of his employees contribute to nonprofit organizations and wants to reward them for their efforts while encouraging others to contribute to charities. Pete began a program that matches 50 percent of each employee donation. The only stipulations are that the charity must be a nonprofit organization and the company will match only up to $2,000 per year per employee.

Project Focus

Open the data file AYK4_Data.xlsx and determine the following:

- What was the total donation amount per organization?
- What were the average donations per organization?

   Data File: AYK4_Data.xlsx

Project 5:
Convert Currency

You have decided to spend the summer traveling abroad with your friends. Your trip is going to take you to France, England, Italy, Switzerland, Germany, Norway, and Ireland. You want to use Excel to convert currencies as you travel around the world.

Project Focus

Locate one of the exchange rate calculators on the Internet (www.xe.com or www.x-rates. com). Find the exchange rates for each of the countries listed above and create formulas in Excel to convert $100, $500, and $1,000. Use the data file AYK5_Data.xlsx as a template.

   Data File: AYK5_Data.xls

Project 6:
Cost Comparison

You are thinking about purchasing a new computer because the machine you are using now is four years old, slow, not always reliable, and does not support the latest operating system. Your needs for the new computer are simple: anti-virus software, email, web browsing, word processing, spreadsheet, database, iTunes, and some lightweight graphical tools. Your concern is what the total cost of ownership will be for the next three years. You have to factor in a few added costs beyond just the initial purchase price for the computer itself, such as: added hardware (this could include a new printer, docking station, or scanner), software (purchase of a new operating system), training (you're thinking about pursuing web training to get an internship next term), subsequent software upgrades, and maintenance.

Project Focus

- It is useful to think about costs over time—both direct as well as indirect costs. Part of the reason this distinction is important is that a decision should rest not on the nominal sum of the purchase, but rather on the present value of the purchase.

	A	B	C	D	E	F
1	COST OF NEW COMPUTER					
2	Discount Rate	1	0.9325	0.9109	0.7051	
3		Time 0	Year 1	Year 2	Year 3	Present Value Costs
4	Computer					
5	Software					
6	Additional Hardware					
7	Training					
8	Software upgrades					
9	Maintenance					
10						
11	Total Costs					
12						

FIGURE AYK.1

Sample Layout of New Computer Spreadsheet

- A dollar today is worth more than a dollar one year from now.
- The relevant discount rate (interest rate) is your marginal cost of capital corresponding to a level of risk equal with the purchase.
- Use the data file AYK6_Data.xlsx as a template.

Data File: AYK6_Data.xlsx

Project 7:
Time Management

You have just been hired as a business analyst by a new start-up company called Multi-Media. Multi-Media is an interactive agency that constructs phased and affordable website marketing, providing its clients with real and measurable solutions that are supported by easy-to-use tools. Because the company is very new to the business arena, it needs help in creating a project management plan for developing its own website. The major tasks for the development team have been identified but you need to create the timeline.

Project Focus

1. The task names, durations, and any prerequisites are:

   - Analyze and plan—two weeks. Cannot start anything else until done.
   - Create and organize content—four weeks. Can start to develop "look and feel" before this is done.
   - Develop the "look and feel"—four weeks. Start working on graphics and HTML at the same time.
   - Produce graphics and HTML documents—two weeks. Create working prototype after the first week.
   - Create a working prototype—two weeks. Give to test team when complete.
   - Test, test, test—four weeks.
   - Upload to a web server and test again—one week.
   - Maintain.

2. Using Microsoft Excel or Microsoft Project, create a Gantt chart using the information provided above.

Project 8:
Maximize Profit

Books, Books, Books is a wholesale distributor of popular books. The business buys over-stocked books and sells them for a discount of more than 50 percent to local area bookstores. The owner of the company, BK Kane, would like to determine the best approach to boxing books so he can make the most profit possible. The local bookstores accept all shipments from Books, Books, Books because of BK's incredibly low prices. BK can order as many overstocked books as he requires, and this week's options include:

Title	Weight	Cost	Sale Price
Harry Potter and the Deathly Hallows, J. K. Rowling	5 lb	$9	$17
The Children of Húrin, J. R. R. Tolkien	4 lb	$8	$13
The Time Traveler's Wife, Audrey Niffenegger	3.5 lb	$7	$11
The Dark River, John Twelve Hawks	3 lb	$6	$ 9
The Road, Cormac McCarthy	2.5 lb	$5	$ 7
Slaughterhouse-Five, Kurt Vonnegut	1 lb	$4	$ 5

Project Focus

When packing a single box, BK must adhere to the following:

- 20 books or less.
- Books by three different authors.
- Between four and eight books from each author.
- Weight equal to or less than 50 pounds.

BK has come to you to help him determine which books he should order to maximize his profit based on the above information. Using the data file AYK8_Data.xlsx, determine the optimal book order for a single box of books.

Data File: AYK8_Data.xlsx

Project 9:
Security Analysis

SecureWorks Inc. is a small computer security contractor that provides computer security analysis, design, and software implementation for the U.S. government and commercial clients. SecureWorks competes for both private and U.S. government computer security contract work by submitting detailed bids outlining the work the company will perform if awarded the contracts. Because all of the work involves computer security, a highly sensitive area, almost all of SecureWorks tasks require access to classified material or company confidential documents. Consequently, all of the security engineers (simply known as "engineers" within the company) have U.S. government clearances of either Secret or Top Secret. Some have even higher clearances for the 2 percent of SecureWorks work that involves so-called "black box" security work. Most of the employees also hold clearances because they must handle classified documents.

Leslie Mamalis is SecureWorks' human resources (HR) manager. She maintains all employee records and is responsible for semiannual review reports, payroll processing, personnel records, recruiting data, employee training, and pension option information. At the heart of an HR system are personnel records. Personnel record maintenance includes activities such as maintaining employee records, tracking cost center data, recording and maintaining pension information, and absence and sick leave record keeping. While most of this information resides in sophisticated database systems, Leslie maintains a basic employee worksheet for quick calculations and ad hoc report generation. Because SecureWorks is a small company, Leslie can take advantage of Excel's excellent list management capabilities to satisfy many of her personnel information management needs.

Project Focus

Leslie has asked you to assist with a number of functions (she has provided you with a copy of her "trusted" personnel data file, AYK9_Data.xlsx):

1. Copy the worksheet Data to a new worksheet called Sort. Sort the employee list in ascending order by department, then by last name, then by first name.

2. Copy the worksheet Data to a new worksheet called Autofilter. Using the Autofilter feature, create a custom filter that will display employees whose birth date is greater than or equal to 1/1/1965 and less than or equal to 12/31/1975.

3. Copy the worksheet Data to a new worksheet called Subtotal. Using the subtotal feature create a sum of the salary for each department.

4. Copy the worksheet Data to a new worksheet called Formatting. Using the salary column, change the font color to red if the cell value is greater than or equal to 55000. You must use the conditional formatting feature to complete this step.

Data File: AYK9_Data.xlsx

Project 10:

Gathering Data

You have just accepted a new job offer from a firm that has offices in San Diego, Los Angeles, and San Francisco. You need to decide which location to move to. Because you have not visited any of these three cities and want to get in a lot of golf time, you determine that the main factor that will affect your decision is weather.

Go to www.weather.com and locate the box in which you can enter the city or zip code for which you want information. Enter San Diego, CA, and when the data appear, click the Averages and Records tab. Print this page and repeat this for Los Angeles and San Francisco. You will want to focus on the Monthly Average and Records section on the top of the page.

Project Focus

1. Create a spreadsheet to summarize the information you find.
2. Record the temperature and rainfall in columns, and group the cities into four groups of rows labeled Average High, Average Low, Mean, and Average Precipitation.
3. Fill in the appropriate data for each city and month.
4. Because rain is your greatest concern, use conditional formatting to display the months with an average precipitation below 2.5 inches in blue and apply boldface.
5. You also want to be in the warmest weather possible while in California. Use conditional formatting to display the months with average high temperatures above 65 degrees in green and apply an italic font face.
6. Looking at the average high temperatures above 65 degrees and average precipitation below two inches, to which city do you think you should relocate? Explain your answer.

Project 11:

Scanner System

FunTown is a popular amusement park filled with roller coasters, games, and water features. Boasting 24 roller coasters, 10 of which exceed 200 feet and 70 miles per hour, and five water parks, the park's attendance remains steady throughout the season. Due to the park's popularity, it is not uncommon for entrance lines to exceed one hour on busy days. FunTown would like your help to find a solution to decrease park entrance lines.

Project Focus

FunTown would like to implement a handheld scanner system that can allow employees to walk around the front gates and accept credit card purchases and print tickets on the spot. The park anticipates an overall increase in sales of 4 percent per year with online ticketing, with an expense of 6 percent of total sales for the scanning equipment. FunTown has created a data file for you to use, AYK11_Data.xlsx, that compares scanning sales and traditional sales. You will need to create the necessary formulas to calculate all the assumptions including:

- Tickets sold at the booth.
- Tickets sold by the scanner.
- Revenues generated by booth sales.
- Revenues generated by scanner sales.
- Scanner ticket expense.
- Revenue with and without scanner sales.
- Three year row totals.

Data File: AYK11_Data.xlsx

Project 12:

Competitive Pricing

Bill Schultz is thinking of starting a store that specializes in handmade cowboy boots. Bill is a longtime rancher in the town of Taos, New Mexico. Bill's reputation for honesty and integrity is well-known around town, and he is positive that his new store will be highly successful.

Project Focus

Before opening his store, Bill is curious about how his profit, revenue, and variable costs will change depending on the amount he charges for his boots. Bill would like you to perform the work required for this analysis and has given you the data file AYK12_Data.xlsx. Here are a few things to consider while you perform your analysis:

- Current competitive prices for custom cowboy boots are between $225 and $275 a pair.
- Variable costs will be either $100 or $150 a pair depending on the types of material Bill chooses to use.
- Fixed costs are $10,000 a month.

  Data File: AYK12_Data.xlsx

Project 13:

Adequate Acquisitions

XMark.com is a major Internet company specializing in organic food. XMark.com is thinking of purchasing GoodGrow, another organic food Internet company. GoodGrow has current revenues of $100 million, with expenses of $150 million. Current projections indicate that GoodGrow's revenues are increasing at 35 percent per year and its expenses are increasing by 10 percent per year. XMark.com understands that projections can be erroneous, however; the company must determine the number of years before GoodGrow will return a profit.

Project Focus

You need to help XMark.com determine the number of years required to break even, using annual growth rates in revenue between 20 percent and 60 percent and annual expense growth rates between 10 percent and 30 percent. You have been provided with a template, AYK13_Data.xlsx, to assist with your analysis.

  Data File: AYK13_Data.xlsx

Project 14:

Customer Relations

Schweizer Distribution specializes in distributing fresh produce to local restaurants in the Chicago area. The company currently sells 12 different products through the efforts of three sales representatives to 10 restaurants. The company, like all small businesses, is always interested in finding ways to increase revenues and decrease expenses.

The company's founder, Bob Schweizer, has recently hired you as a new business analyst. You have just graduated from college with a degree in marketing and a specialization in customer relationship management. Bob is eager to hear your thoughts and ideas on how to improve the business and help the company build strong lasting relationships with its customers.

Project Focus

Bob has provided you with last year's sales information in the data file AYK14_Data.xlsx. Help Bob analyze his distribution company by using a PivotTable to determine the following:

1. Who is Bob's best customer by total sales?
2. Who is Bob's worst customer by total sales?

3. Who is Bob's best customer by total profit?

4. Who is Bob's worst customer by total profit?

5. What is Bob's best-selling product by total sales?

6. What is Bob's worst-selling product by total sales?

7. What is Bob's best-selling product by total profit?

8. What is Bob's worst-selling product by total profit?

9. Who is Bob's best sales representative by total profit?

10. Who is Bob's worst sales representative by total profit?

11. What is the best sales representative's best-selling product (by total profit)?

12. Who is the best sales representative's best customer (by total profit)?

13. What is the best sales representative's worst-selling product (by total profit)?

14. Who is the best sales representative's worst customer (by total profit)?

Data File: AYK14_Data.xlsx

Project 15:

Assessing the Value of Information

Recently Santa Fe, New Mexico, was named one of the safest places to live in the United States. Since then, housing development projects have been springing up all around Santa Fe. Six housing development projects are currently dominating the local market—Pinon Pine, Rancho Hondo, Creek Side, Vista Del Monte, Forest View, and Santa Fe South. These six projects each started with 100 homes, have sold all of them, and are currently developing phase two.

As one of the three partners and real estate agents of Affordable Homes Real Estate, it is your responsibility to analyze the information concerning the past 600 home sales and choose which development project to focus on for selling homes in phase two. Because your real estate firm is so small, you and your partners have decided that the firm should focus on selling homes in only one of the development projects.

From the New Mexico Real Estate Association you have obtained a spreadsheet file that contains information concerning each of the sales for the first 600 homes. It contains the following fields:

Column	Name	Description
A	LOT #	The number assigned to a specific home within each project.
B	PROJECT #	A unique number assigned to each of the six housing development projects (see table on the next page).
C	ASK PRICE	The initial posted asking price for the home.
D	SELL PRICE	The actual price for which the home was sold.
E	LIST DATE	The date the home was listed for sale.
F	SALE DATE	The date on which the final contract closed and the home was sold.
G	SQ. FT.	The total square footage for the home.
H	# BATH.	The number of bathrooms in the home.
I	# BDRMS	The number of bedrooms in the home.

The following numbers have been assigned to each of the housing development projects:

Project Number	Project Name
23	Pinon Pine
47	Rancho Hondo
61	Creek Side
78	Vista Del Monte
92	Forest View
97	Santa Fe South

It is your responsibility to analyze the sales list and prepare a report that details which housing development project your real estate firm should focus on. Your analysis should be from as many angles as possible.

Project Focus

1. You do not know how many other real estate firms will also be competing for sales in each of the housing development projects.

2. Phase two for each housing development project will develop homes similar in style, price, and square footage to their respective first phases.

3. As you consider the information provided to you, think in terms of what information is important and what information is not important. Be prepared to justify how you went about your analysis.

4. Upon completing your analysis, please provide concise, yet detailed and thorough, documentation (in narrative, numeric, and graphic forms) that justifies your decision.

Data file: AYK15_Data.xlsx

Project 16:
Growth, Trends, and Forecasts

Founded in 2002, Analytics Software provides innovative search software, website accessibility testing software, and usability testing software. All serve as part of its desktop and enterprise content management solutions for government, corporate, educational, and consumer markets. The company's solutions are used by website publishers, digital media publishers, content managers, document managers, business users, consumers, software companies, and consulting services companies. Analytics Software solutions help organizations develop long-term strategies to achieve web content accessibility, enhance usability, and comply with U.S. and international accessibility and search standards.

You manage the customer service group for the company and have just received an email from CIO Sue Downs that the number of phone calls from customers having problems with one of your newer applications is on the increase. This company has a 10-year history of approximately 1 percent in turnover a year, and its focus had always been on customer service. With the informal motto of "Grow big, but stay small," it takes pride in 100 percent callbacks in customer care, knowing that its personal service was one thing that made it outstanding.

The rapid growth to six times its original customer-base size has forced the company to deal with difficult questions for the first time, such as, "How do we serve this many customers?"

One option might be for the company to outsource its customer service department. Before deciding to do that, Analytics Software needs to create a growth, trend, forecast analysis for future predictions.

Project Focus

1. Create a weekly analysis from the data provided in AYK16_Data.xlsx.

2. The price of the products, the actual product type, and any warrantee information is irrelevant.

3. Develop a growth, trend, and forecast analysis. You should use a three-day moving average; a shorter moving average might not display the trend well, and a much longer moving average would shorten the trend too much.

4. Upon completing your analysis, please provide concise yet detailed and thorough documentation (in narrative, numeric, and graphic forms) that justifies your recommendations.

Data File: AYK16_Data.xlsx

Project 17:

Shipping Costs

One of the main products of the Fairway Woods Company is custom-made golf clubs. The clubs are manufactured at three plants (Denver, Colorado; Phoenix, Arizona; and Dallas, Texas) and are then shipped by truck to five distribution warehouses in Sacramento, California; Salt Lake City, Utah; Chicago, Illinois; Albuquerque, New Mexico; and New York City, New York. Because shipping costs are a major expense, management has begun an analysis to determine ways to reduce them. For the upcoming golf season, the output from each manufacturing plant and how much each warehouse will require to satisfy its customers have been estimated.

The CIO from Fairway Woods Company has created a data file for you, AYK17_Data.xlsx, of the shipping costs from each manufacturing plant to each warehouse as a baseline analysis. Some business rules and requirements you should be aware of include:

- The problem presented involves the shipment of goods from three plants to five regional warehouses.

- Goods can be shipped from any plant to any warehouse, but it costs more to ship goods over long distances than over short distances.

Project Focus

1. Your goal is to minimize the costs of shipping goods from production plants to warehouses, thereby meeting the demand from each metropolitan area while not exceeding the supply available from each plant. To complete this project it is recommended that you use the Solver function in Excel to assist with the analysis.

2. Specifically you want to focus on:

- Minimizing the total shipping costs.
- Total shipped must be less than or equal to supply at a plant.
- Total shipped to warehouses must be greater than or equal to the warehouse demand.
- Number to ship must be greater than or equal to 0.

Data File: AYK17_Data.xlsx

Project 18:

Formatting Grades

Professor Streterstein is a bit absentminded. His instructor's grade book is a mess, and he would like your help cleaning it up and making it easier to use. In Professor Streterstein's course, the maximum possible points a student can earn is 750. The following table displays the grade equivalent to total points for the course.

Total Points	Calculated Grade
675	A
635	A–
600	B
560	B–
535	C
490	C–
450	D
0	F

Project Focus

Help Professor Streterstein rework his grade book. Open the data file AYK18_Data.xlsx and perform the following:

1. Reformat the workbook so it is readable, understandable, and consistent. Replace column labels, format and align the headings, add borders and shading as appropriate.

2. Add a column in the grade book for final grade next to the total points earned column.

3. Use the VLookup Function to automatically assess final grades based on the total points column.

4. Using the If Function, format the workbook so each student's grade shows a pass or fail—P for pass, F for fail—based on the total points.

   Data File: AYK18_Data.xlsx

Project 19:
Moving Dilemma

Pony Espresso is a small business that sells specialty coffee drinks at office buildings. Each morning and afternoon, trucks arrive at offices' front entrances, and the office employees purchase various beverages such as Java du Jour and Café de Colombia. The business is profitable. Pony Espresso offices, however, are located north of town, where lease rates are less expensive, and the principal sales area is south of town. This means the trucks must drive across town four times each day.

The cost of transportation to and from the sales area plus the power demands of the trucks' coffee brewing equipment are a significant portion of variable costs. Pony Espresso could reduce the amount of driving and, therefore, the variable costs, if it moved the offices closer to the sales area.

Pony Espresso presently has fixed costs of $10,000 per month. The lease of a new office, closer to the sales area, would cost an additional $2,200 per month. This would increase the fixed costs to $12,200 per month.

Although the lease of new offices would increase the fixed costs, a careful estimate of the potential savings in gasoline and vehicle maintenance indicates that Pony Espresso could reduce the variable costs from $0.60 per unit to $0.35 per unit. Total sales are unlikely to increase as a result of the move, but the savings in variable costs should increase the annual profit.

Project Focus

Consider the information provided to you from the owner in the data file AYK19_Data.xlsx. Especially look at the change in the variability of the profit from month to month. From

November through January, when it is much more difficult to lure office workers out into the cold to purchase coffee, Pony Espresso barely breaks even. In fact, in December, the business lost money.

1. Develop the cost analysis on the existing lease information using the monthly sales figures provided to you in the data file.

2. Develop the cost analysis from the new lease information provided above.

3. Calculate the variability that is reflected in the month-to-month standard deviation of earnings for the current cost structure and the projected cost structure.

4. Do not consider any association with downsizing such as overhead—simply focus on the information provided to you.

5. You will need to calculate the EBIT (earnings before interest and taxes).

   Data File: AYK19_Data.xlsx

Project 20:
Operational Efficiencies

Hoover Transportation Inc. is a large distribution company located in Denver, Colorado. The company is currently seeking to gain operational efficiencies in its supply chain by reducing the number of transportation carriers that it is using to outsource. Operational efficiencies for Hoover Transportation, Inc., suggest that reducing the number of carriers from the Denver distribution center to warehouses in the selected states will lead to reduced costs. Brian Hoover, the CEO of Hoover Transportation, requests that the number of carriers transporting products from its Denver distribution center to wholesalers in Arizona, Arkansas, Iowa, Missouri, Montana, Oklahoma, Oregon, and Washington be reduced from the current five carriers to two carriers.

Project Focus

Carrier selection should be based on the assumptions that all environmental factors are equal and historical cost trends will continue. Review the historical data from the past several years to determine your recommendation for the top two carriers that Hoover Transportation should continue to use.

1. Analyze the last 24 months of Hoover's Transportation carrier transactions found in the data file AYK20_Data.xlsx.

2. Create a report detailing your recommendation for the top two carriers with which Hoover Transportation should continue to do business. Be sure to use PivotTables and PivotCharts in your report. A few questions to get you started include:

   ◼ Calculate the average cost per carrier.
   ◼ Calculate the total shipping costs per state.
   ◼ Calculate the total shipping weights per state.
   ◼ Calculate the average shipping costs per pound.
   ◼ Calculate the average cost per carrier.

   Data File: AYK20_Data.xlsx

Project 21:
Too Much Information

You have just landed the job of vice president of operations for The Pitt Stop Restaurants, a national chain of full-service, casual-themed restaurants. During your first week on the job, Suzanne Graham, your boss and CEO of the company, has asked you to provide an analysis of how well the company's restaurants are performing. Specifically, she would like to know which units and regions are performing extremely well, which are performing moderately well, and which are underperforming. Her goal is to identify where to spend time and focus efforts to improve the overall health of the company.

Project Focus

Review the data file AYK21_Data.xlsx and determine how best to analyze and interpret the data. Create a formal presentation of your findings. A few things to consider include:

- Should underperforming restaurants be closed or sold?
- Should high-performing restaurants be expanded to accommodate more seats?
- Should the company spend more or less on advertising?
- In which markets should the advertising budget be adjusted?
- How are The Pitt Stop Restaurants performing compared to the competition?
- How are units of like size performing relative to each other?

   Data File: AYK21_Data.xlsx

Project 22:

Turnover Rates

Employee turnover rates are at an all-time high at Gizmo Manufacturing's plants. The company is experiencing severe worker retention issues, which are leading to productivity and quality control problems. The majority of the company's workers perform a variety of tasks and are paid by the hour. The company currently tests potential applicants to ensure they have the skills necessary for the intense mental concentration and dexterity required to fill the positions. Because significant costs are associated with employee turnover, Gizmo Manufacturing wants to find a way to predict which applicants have the characteristics of being a short-term versus a long-term employee.

Project Focus

1. Review the information that Gizmo Manufacturing has collected from two of its different data sources. The first data file, AYK22_Data_A.xlsx, contains information regarding employee wages. The second data file, AYK22_Data_B.xlsx, contains information regarding employee retention.

2. Using Excel analysis functions, determine the employee characteristics that you would recommend Gizmo Manufacturing look for when hiring new personnel. It is highly recommended that you use PivotTables as part of your analysis.

3. Prepare a report based on your findings (which should include several forms of graphical representation) for your recommendations.

   Data Files: AYK22_Data_A.xlsx and AYK22_Data_B.xlsx

Project 23:

Vital Information

Martin Resorts Inc. owns and operates four Spa and Golf resorts in Colorado. The company has five traditional lines of business: (1) golf sales, (2) golf lessons, (3) restaurants, (4) retail and rentals, and (5) hotels. David Logan, director of marketing technology at Martin Resorts Inc., and Donald Mayer, the lead strategic analyst for Martin Resorts, are soliciting your input for their CRM strategic initiative.

Martin Resorts' IT infrastructure is pieced together with various systems and applications. Currently, the company has a difficult time with CRM because its systems are not integrated. The company cannot determine vital information such as which customers are golfing and staying at the hotel or which customers are staying at the hotel and not golfing.

For example, the three details that the customer Diego Titus (1) stayed four nights at a Martin Resorts' managed hotel, (2) golfed three days, and (3) took an all-day spa treatment the first day are discrete facts housed in separate systems. Martin Resorts hopes that by using data warehousing technology to integrate its data, the next time Diego reserves lodging for another trip, sales associates may ask him if he would like to book a spa treatment as well, and even if he would like the same masseuse that he had on his prior trip.

Martin Resorts is excited about the possibility of taking advantage of customer segmentation and CRM strategies to help increase its business.

Project Focus

The company wants to use CRM and data warehouse technologies to improve service and personalization at each customer touch point. Using a data warehousing tool, important customer information can be accessed from all of its systems either daily, weekly, monthly, or once or twice per year. Analyze the sample data in AYK23_Data.xlsx for the following:

1. Currently, the quality of the data within the above disparate systems is low. Develop a report for David and Donald discussing the importance of high-quality information and how low-quality information can affect Martin Resorts' business.

2. Review the data that David and Donald are working with from the data warehouse in the data file AYK23_Data.xlsx.

   a. Give examples from the data showing the kind of information Martin Resorts might be able to use to gain a better understanding of its customers. Include the types of data quality issues the company can anticipate and the strategies it can use to help avoid such issues.

   b. Determine who are Martin Resorts' best customers, and provide examples of the types of marketing campaigns the company should offer these valuable customers.

   c. Prepare a report that summarizes the benefits Martin Resorts can receive from using business intelligence to mine the data warehouse. Include a financial analysis of the costs and benefits.

   Data File: AYK23_Data.xlsx

Project 24:
Breaking Even

Mountain Cycle specializes in making custom mountain bikes. The company founder, PJ Steffan, is having a hard time making the business profitable. Knowing that you have great business knowledge and solid financial sense, PJ has come to you for advice.

Project Focus

PJ would like you to determine how many bikes Mountain Cycle needs to sell per year to break even. Using Goal Seek in Excel solve using the following:

- Fixed cost equals $65,000
- Variable cost equals $1,575
- Bike price equals $2,500

Project 25:
Profit Scenario

Murry Lutz owns a small shop, Lutz Motors, that sells and services vintage motorcycles. Murry is curious how his profit will be affected by his sales over the next year.

Project Focus

Murry would like your help creating best, worst, and most-likely scenarios for his motorcycle sales over the next year. Using Scenario Manager, help Murry analyze the information in the data file AYK25_Data.xlsx.

Data File: AYK25_Data.xlsx

Project 26:
Electronic Résumés

Résumés are the currency of the recruitment industry. They are the cornerstone of communication between candidates, recruiters, and employers. Technology is automating elements of the recruitment process, but a complete solution requires proper handling of the actual development of all the pieces and parts that comprise not just a résumé, but also an erésumé. Electronic résumés, or erésumés, have moved into the mainstream of today's job market at lightning speed. Erésumés have stepped up the efficiency of job placement to such a point that you could get a call from a recruiter just hours after submitting your erésumé. With this kind of opportunity, you cannot afford to be left in the dark ages of using only a paper résumé.

Project Focus

In the text or HTML editor of your choice, write your résumé as though you were really putting it online and inviting prospective employers to see it. We recommend typing in all the text and then later adding the HTML tags (rather than trying to type in the tags as you go).

Use the following checklist to make sure you're covering the basics. You do not need to match it exactly; it just shows what can be done.

- Add structural tags.
- Add paragraphs and headings.
- Find an opportunity to include a list.
- Add inline styles.
- Play with the alignment of elements.
- Add appropriate font selection, font size, and color.

Project 27:
Gathering Feedback

Gathering feedback from a website's visitors can be a valuable way of assessing a site's success, and it can help build a customer or subscriber database. For example, a business could collect the addresses of people who are interested in receiving product samples, email newsletters, or notifications of special offers.

Project Focus

Adding form elements to a web page is simple: They are created using a set of HTML form tags that define menus, text fields, buttons, and so on. Form elements are generally used to collect information from a web page.

In the text or HTML editor of your choice, create a web page form that would collect information for a customer ordering a customized bicycle. Use proper web page design and HTML tools to understand the process and function of form elements. Be sure to pay attention to:

- Form layout and design.
- Visual elements, including labels, alignment, font selection, font size, color.
- Required versus nonrequired fields.
- Drop-down boxes, text fields, and radio buttons.

Project 28:
Daily Invoice

Foothills Animal Hospital is a full-service small animal veterinary hospital located in Morrison, Colorado, specializing in routine medical care, vaccinations, laboratory testing, and surgery. The hospital has experienced tremendous growth over the past six months due to customer referrals. While Foothills Animal Hospital has typically kept its daily service records in a workbook format, it feels the need to expand its reporting capabilities to develop a relational database as a more functional structure.

Foothills Animal Hospital needs help developing a database, specifically:

- Create a customer table—name, address, phone, and date of entrance.
- Create a pet table—pet name, type of animal, breed, gender, color, neutered/spayed, weight, and comments.
- Create a medications table—medication code, name of medication, and cost of medication.
- Create a visit table—details of treatments performed, medications dispensed, and date of the visit.
- Produce a daily invoice report.

Figure AYK.2 displays a sample daily invoice report that the Foothills Animal Hospital accountants have requested. Foothills Animal Hospital organizes its treatments using the codes displayed in Figure AYK.3. The entities and primary keys for the database have been identified in Figure AYK.4.

The following business rules have been identified:

1. A customer can have many pets but must have at least one.
2. A pet must be assigned to one and only one customer.
3. A pet can have one or more treatments per visit but must have at least one.
4. A pet can have one or more medications but need not have any.

Project Focus

Your job is to complete the following tasks:

1. Develop and describe the entity-relationship diagram.
2. Use normalization to assure the correctness of the tables (relations).

FIGURE AYK.2

Foothills Animal Hospital Daily Invoice Report

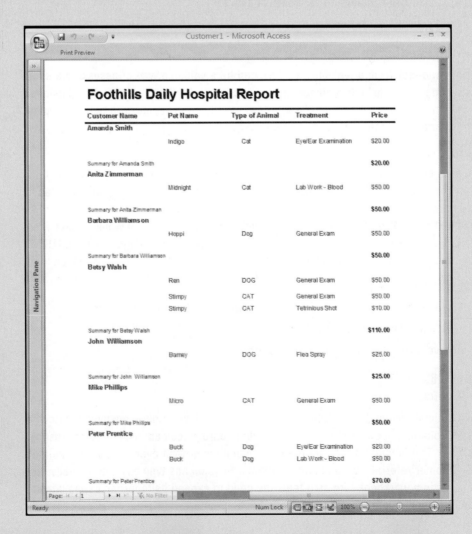

FIGURE AYK.3

Treatment Codes, Treatments, and Price Descriptions

Treatment Code	Treatment	Price
0100	Tetrinious Shot	$10.00
0201	Rabonius Shot	$20.00
0300	General Exam	$50.00
0303	Eye/Ear Examination	$20.00
0400	Spay/Neuter	$225.00
0405	Reset Dislocation	$165.00
0406	Amputation of Limb	$450.00
0407	Wrap Affected Area	$15.00
0408	Cast Affected Area	$120.00
1000	Lab Work—Blood	$50.00
1003	Lab Work—Misc	$35.00
2003	Flea Spray	$25.00
9999	Other Not Listed	$10.00

FIGURE AYK.4

Entity Names and Primary Keys Foothills Animal Hospital

Entity	Primary Key
CUSTOMER	Customer Number
PET	Pet Number
VISIT	Visit Number
VISIT DETAIL	Visit Number and Line Number (a composite key)
TREATMENT	Treatment Code
MEDICATION	Medication Code

3. Create the database using a personal DBMS package (preferably Microsoft Access).

4. Use the data in Figure AYK.3 to populate your tables. Feel free to enter your own personal information.

5. Use the DBMS package to create the basic report in Figure AYK.2.

Project 29:
Billing Data

On-The-Level Construction Company is a Denver-based construction company that specializes in subcontracting the development of single-family homes. In business since 1998, On-The-Level Construction has maintained a talented pool of certified staff and independent consultants providing the flexibility and combined experience required to meet the needs of its nearly 300 completed projects in the Denver metropolitan area. The field of operation methods that On-The-Level Construction is responsible for includes structural development, heating and cooling, plumbing, and electricity.

The company charges its clients by billing the hours spent on each contract. The hourly billing rate is dependent on the employee's position according to the field of operations (as noted above). Figure AYK.5 shows a basic report that On-The-Level Construction foremen would like to see every week concerning what projects are being assigned, the overall assignment hours, and the charges for the assignment. On-The-Level Construction organizes its internal structure in four different operations—Structure (500), Plumbing (501), Electrical (502), and Heating and Ventilation (503). Each of these operational departments can and should have many subcontractors who specialize in that area. On-The-Level Construction has decided to implement a relational database model to track project details according to project name, hours assigned, and charges per hour for each job description. Originally, On-The-Level Construction decided to let one of its employees handle the construction of the database. However, that employee has not had the time to completely implement the project. On-The-Level Construction has asked you to take over and complete the development of the database.

The entities and primary keys for the database have been identified in Figure AYK.6.

The following business rules have been identified:

1. A job can have many employees assigned but must have at least one.

2. An employee must be assigned to one and only one job number.

ON-THE-LEVEL CONSTRUCTION PROJECT DETAIL

PROJECT NAME	ASSIGN DATE	EMPLOYEE LAST NAME	FIRST NAME	JOB DESCRIPTION	ASSIGN HOUR	CHARGE/HOUR
Chatfield						
	6/10/2011	Olenkoski	Glenn	Structure	2.1	$35.75
	6/10/2011	Sullivan	David	Electrical	1.2	$105.00
	6/10/2011	Ramora	Anne	Plumbing	2.6	$96.75
	6/11/2011	Frommer	Matt	Plumbing	1.4	$96.75
Summary of Assignment Hours and Charges					7.30	$588.08
Evergreen						
	6/10/2011	Sullivan	David	Electrical	1.8	$105.00
	6/10/2011	Jones	Anne	Heating and Ventalation	3.4	$84.50
	6/11/2011	Frommer	Matt	Plumbing	4.1	$96.75
	6/16/2011	Bawangi	Terry	Plumbing	4.1	$96.75
	6/16/2011	Newman	John	Electrical	1.7	$105.00
Summary of Assignment Hours and Charges					15.10	$1,448.15
Roxborough						
	6/10/2011	Washberg	Jeff	Plumbing	3.9	$96.75
	6/10/2011	Ramora	Anne	Plumbing	2.6	$96.75
	6/11/2011	Smithfield	William	Structure	2.4	$35.75
	6/11/2011	Bawangi	Terry	Plumbing	2.7	$96.75
	6/16/2011	Johnson	Peter	Electrical	5.2	$105.00
	6/16/2011	Joen	Denise	Plumbing	2.5	$96.75
Summary of Assignment Hours and Charges					19.30	$1,763.78

Entity	Primary Key
PROJECT	Project Number
EMPLOYEE	Employee Number
JOB	Job Number
ASSIGNMENT	Assignment Number

3. An employee can be assigned to work on one or more projects.

4. A project can be assigned to only one employee but need not be assigned to any employee.

Project Focus

Your job is to complete the following tasks:

1. Develop and describe the entity relationship diagram.

2. Use normalization to assure the correctness of the tables (relations).

3. Create the database using a personal DBMS package (preferably Microsoft Access).

4. Use the DBMS package to create the basic report in Figure AYK.5.

5. You may not be able to develop a report that looks exactly like the one in Figure AYK.5. However, your report should include the same information.

6. Complete personnel information is tracked by another database. For this application, include only the minimum: employee number, last name, and first name.

7. Information concerning all projects, employees, and jobs is not readily available. You should create information for several fictitious projects, employees, and jobs to include in your database.

Project 30:

Inventory Data

An independent retailer of mobile entertainment and wireless phones, iToys.com has built its business on offering the widest selection, expert advice, and outstanding customer service. However, iToys.com does not use a formal, consistent inventory tracking system. Periodically, an iToys.com employee visually checks to see what items are in stock. Although iToys.com does try to keep a certain level of each "top seller" in stock, the lack of a formal inventory tracking system has led to the overstocking of some items and understocking of other items. On occasion, a customer will request a hot item, and it is only then that iToys.com realizes that the item is out of stock. If an item is not available, iToys.com risks losing a customer to a competitor.

Lately, iToys.com has become concerned with its inventory management methods. The owner of iToys.com, Dan Connolly, wants to better manage his inventory. The company receives orders by mail, by telephone, or through its website. Regardless of how the orders are received, Dan needs a database to automate the inventory checking and ordering process.

Project Focus

Dan has provided you with a simplified version of the company's current system (an Excel workbook) for recording inventory and orders in an Excel spreadsheet data file AYK30_Data.xlsx.

1. Develop an ERD diagram before you begin to create the database. You will need to use the information provided here as well as the data given in the Excel workbook.

2. Create the database using a personal DBMS package (preferably Microsoft Access) that will track items (i.e., products), orders, order details, categories, suppliers, and shipping methods.

3. In addition to what is mentioned above, the database needs to track the inventory levels for each product, according to a reorder level and lead time.

4. At this time, Dan does not need information stored about the customer; he simply needs you to focus on the inventory structure.

5. Develop a query that will display the products that need to be ordered from their supplier. To complete this, you will want to compare a reorder level with how many units are in stock.

6. Develop several reports that display:

   a. Each product ordered by its supplier. The report should include the product name, quantity on hand, and reorder level.

   b. Each supplier ordered by shipping method.

   c. Each product that requires more than five days lead time. (Hint: You will want to create a query for this first).

   d. Each product ordered by category.

7. Here are some additional business rules to assist you in completing this task:

   a. An order must have at least one product, but can contain more than one product.

   b. A product can have one or more orders, but need not have any orders.

   c. A product must belong to one and only one category, but a category may contain many different products.

   d. A product can only be stocked by one supplier, but a supplier can provide more than one product.

   e. A supplier will use one type of shipping method, but shipping methods can be used by more than one supplier.

   Data File: AYK30_Data.xlsx

Project 31:
Call Center

A manufacturing company, Teleworks, has been a market leader in the wireless telephone business for the past 10 years. Other firms have imitated its product with some degree of success, but Teleworks occupies a dominant position in the marketplace because it has a first-mover advantage with a quality product.

Recently Teleworks began selling a new, enhanced wireless phone. This new phone does not replace its current product, but offers additional features, greater durability, and better performance for a somewhat higher price. Offering this enhanced phone has established a new revenue stream for the company.

Many sales executives at Teleworks seem to subscribe to the-more-you-have, the-more-you-want theory of managing customer data. That is, they believe they can never accumulate too much information about their customers, and that they can do their jobs more effectively by collecting infinite amounts of customer details. Having a firm grasp on a wide range of customer-focused details—specifically reports summarizing call center information—can be critical in enabling your company to successfully manage a customer relationship management (CRM) solution that creates a positive impact.

To continue to provide excellent customer support, and in anticipation of increased calls due to the release of its new product, Teleworks needs a database that it can use to record, track, and query call center information. Teleworks CIO KED Davisson has hired you to develop this database.

Project Focus

1. Teleworks has provided you with a data file AYK31_Data.xlsx; its current approach for recording cell center information is a spreadsheet file.

2. Develop an ERD diagram before you begin to create the database.

3. Create the database using a personal DBMS package (preferably Microsoft Access) that will allow data analysts to enter call center data according to the type of issue and the customer, assign each call to a consultant, and prioritize the call.

4. Develop a query that will display all issues that are "open."

5. Develop a screen form to browse all issues.

6. Develop several reports that display:

    a. All closed issues.

    b. Each issue in detail ordered by issue ID.

    c. Each issue in detail ordered by consultant.

    d. Each issue in detail ordered by category.

    e. Each issue in detail ordered by status.

7. Here are some additional business rules to assist you in completing this task:

    a. An issue must have at least one customer.

    b. A customer can have more than one issue.

    c. Each issue must be assigned to one consultant.

    d. Each consultant can be assigned to more than one issue.

    e. An issue can only belong to one category.

    f. An issue must be assigned only one status code.

    g. An issue must be assigned a priority code.

8. Priorities are assigned accordingly:

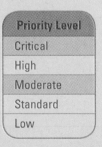

Priority Level
Critical
High
Moderate
Standard
Low

9. Status is recorded as either open or closed.

10. The categories of each issue need to be recorded as:

Category
Hardware/Phone
Software/Voice mail
Internet/Web

Data File: AYK31_Data.xlsx

Project 32:

Sales Pipeline

Sales drive any organization. This is true for every for-profit business irrespective of size or industry type. If customers are not buying your goods or services, you run the risk of not having a business. This is when tough decisions have to be made like whether to slash budgets, lay off staff, or seek additional financing.

Unfortunately, you do not wield ultimate power over your customers' buying habits. While you can attempt to influence buying behavior through strategic marketing, smart businesses remain one step ahead by collecting and analyzing historical and current customer information from a range of internal and external sources to forecast future sales. In other words, managing the sales pipeline is an essential ingredient to business success.

You have recently been hired by RealTime Solutions, a new company that collects information to understand, manage, and predict specific sales cycle (including the supply chain and lead times) in the automobile business. Having an accurate forecast of future sales will allow the company to increase or decrease the production cycle as required and manage personnel levels, inventory, and cash flow.

Project Focus

Using a personal DBMS package (preferably Microsoft Access) create a sales pipeline database that will:

1. Track opportunities from employees to customers.
   - Opportunities should have a ranking, category, source of opportunity, open date, closed date, description.
2. Create a form for inputting customer, employee, and opportunity data.
3. Create a few reports that display:
   - All open opportunities, including relevant customer and employee information.
   - Closed opportunities, including relevant customer and employee information.
   - All customers.
4. Create your own data to test the integrity of the relationships. Use approximately 10 records per table.

Project 33:

Online Classified Ads

With the emergence of the Internet as a worldwide standard for communicating information, *The Morrison Post,* a medium-size community newspaper in central Colorado, is creating an electronic version of its paper-based classified ads.

Advertisers can place a small ad that lists items that they wish to sell and provide a means (e.g., telephone number and email) by which prospective buyers can contact them.

The nature of a sale via the newspaper's classified system goes as follows:

- During the course of the sale, the information flows in different directions at different stages.
- First, there is a downstream flow of information (from seller to buyer): the listing in print in the newspaper. (Thus, the classified ad listing is just a way of bringing a buyer and seller together.)
- When a potential purchaser's interest has been raised, then that interest must be relayed upstream, usually by telephone or by email.
- Finally, a meeting should result that uses face-to-face negotiation to finalize the sale, if the sale can be agreed.

By placing the entire system on the Internet, the upstream and downstream communications are accomplished using a web browser. The sale becomes more of an auction, because many potential buyers, all with equal status, can bid for the same item. So it is fairer for all purchasers and gets a better deal for the seller.

Any user who is trying to buy an item can:

- View items for sale.
- Bid on an item they wish to purchase.

Any user who is trying to sell an item can:

- Place a new item for sale.
- Browse a list of the items that he or she is trying to sell, and examine the bids that have been made on each of those items.
- Accept a bid on an item that he or she is selling.

Your job is to complete the following:

1. Develop and describe the entity-relationship diagram for the database that will support the listed activities.
2. Use normalization to ensure the correctness of the tables.
3. Create the database using a personal DBMS package.
4. Use Figure AYK.7 as a baseline for your database design.

   Data File: AYK33_Data.xlsx

FIGURE AYK.7

The Morrison Post Classified Section
New User Registration

In order to bid on existing "for-sale" items, or sell your own items, you need to register first. Once you have done that, you will have full access to the system.

E-Mail Address:	
First Name:	
Last Name:	
Address:	
City:	
State:	
Postal Code:	
Country:	
Password:	
Verify Password:	

Submit   Reset

3G A service that brings wireless broadband to mobile phones.

A

acceptable use policy (AUP) A policy that a user must agree to follow in order to be provided access to a network or to the Internet.

access point (AP) The computer or network device that serves as an interface between devices and the network.

accessibility Refers to the varying levels that define what a user can access, view, or perform when operating a system.

accounting and finance ERP component Manages accounting data and financial processes within the enterprise with functions such as general ledger, accounts payable, accounts receivable, budgeting, and asset management.

accounting department Provides quantitative information about the finances of the business including recording, measuring, and describing financial information.

accounting Analyzes the transactional information of the business so the owners and investors can make sound economic decisions.

active RFID tags Have their own transmitter and a power source (typically a battery).

adaptive computer device Input devices designed for special applications for use by people with different types of special needs.

administrator access Unrestricted access to the entire system.

advanced encryption standard (AES) Introduced by the National Institute of Standards and Technology (NIST), AES is an encryption standard designed to keep government information secure.

adware Software that generates ads that install themselves on a computer when a person downloads some other program from the Internet.

affinity grouping Determine which things go together.

agile methodology Aims for customer satisfaction through early and continuous delivery of useful software components developed by an iterative process with a design point that uses the bare minimum requirements.

agile MIS infrastructure Includes the hardware, software, and telecommunications equipment that, when combined, provides the underlying foundation to support the organization's goals.

alpha testing Assess if the entire system meets the design requirements of the users.

analysis latency The time from which data are made available to the time when analysis is complete.

analysis phase Analyzing end-user business requirements and refining project goals into defined functions and operations of the intended system.

analytical CRM Supports back-office operations and strategic analysis and includes all systems that do not deal directly with the customers.

analytical information Encompasses all organizational information, and its primary purpose is to support the performing of managerial analysis tasks.

analytics The science of fact-based decision making.

anti-spam policy States that email users will not send unsolicited emails (or spam).

antivirus software Scans and searches hard drives to prevent, detect, and remove known viruses, adware, and spyware.

application architecture Determines how applications integrate and relate to each other.

application programming interface (API) A set of routines, protocols, and tools for building software applications.

application service provider license Specialty software paid for on a license basis or per-use basis or usage-based licensing.

application software Used for specific information processing needs, including payroll, customer relationship management, project management, training, and many others.

arithmetic/logic unit (ALU) Performs all arithmetic operations (for example, addition and subtraction) and all logic operations (such as sorting and comparing numbers).

artificial intelligence (AI) Simulates human intelligence such as the ability to reason and learn.

As-Is process model Represents the current state of the operation that has been mapped, without any specific improvements or changes to existing processes.

asset Anything owned that has value or earning power.

asset tracking Occurs when a company places active or semipassive RFID tags on expensive products or assets to gather data on the items' location with little or no manual intervention.

association detection Reveals the degree to which variables are related and the nature and frequency of these relationships in the information.

asynchronous communication Communication such as email in which the message and the response do not occur at the same time.

attribute Characteristics or properties of an entity class.

augmented reality The viewing of the physical world with computer-generated layers of information added to it.

authentication A method for confirming users' identities.

authorization The process of giving someone permission to do or have something.

automatic vehicle location (AVL)   Uses GPS tracking to track vehicles.

autonomic computing   A self-managing computing model named after, and patterned on, the human body's autonomic nervous system.

availability   Addresses when systems can be accessed by employees, customers, and partners.

B

backup   An exact copy of a system's information.

backward integration   Takes information entered into a given system and sends it automatically to all upstream systems and processes.

balance sheet   Gives an accounting picture of property owned by a company and of claims against the property on a specific date.

balanced scorecard   A management system that enables organizations to clarify their vision and strategy and translate them into action.

bandwidth   The difference between the highest and the lowest frequencies that can be transmitted on a single medium; a measure of the medium's capacity.

benchmark   Baseline values the system seeks to attain.

benchmarking   The process of continuously measuring system results, comparing those results to optimal system performance (benchmark values), and identifying steps and procedures to improve system performance.

best practices   The most successful solutions or problem-solving methods that have been developed by a specific organization or industry.

biometrics   The identification of a user based on a physical characteristic, such as a fingerprint, iris, face, voice, or handwriting.

blog   Website in which items are posted on a regular basis and displayed in reverse chronological order.

Bluetooth   An omnidirectional wireless technology that provides limited-range voice and data transmission over the unlicensed 2.4-GHz frequency band, allowing connections with a wide variety of fixed and portable devices that normally would have to be cabled together.

bookkeeping   The actual recording of the business's transactions, without any analysis of the information.

brainstorming   A technique for generating ideas by encouraging participants to offer as many ideas as possible in a short period of time without any analysis until all the ideas have been exhausted.

break-even point   The point at which revenues equal costs.

bug   Defects in the code of an information system.

bullwhip effect   Occurs when distorted product demand information passes from one entity to the next throughout the supply chain.

business continuity planning (BCP)   A plan for how an organization will recover and restore partially or completely interrupted critical function(s) within a predetermined time after a disaster or extended disruption.

business impact analysis   A process that identifies all critical business functions and the effect that a specific disaster may have upon them.

business intelligence (BI)   Refers to applications and technologies that are used to gather, provide access to, and analyze data and information to support decision-making efforts.

business intelligence dashboard   Tracks corporate metrics such as critical success factors and key performance indicators and includes advanced capabilities such as interactive controls, allowing users to manipulate data for analysis.

business model   A plan that details how a company creates, delivers, and generates revenues.

business process management (BPM)   Integrates all of an organization's business processes to make individual processes more efficient.

business process management tool   Used to create an application that is helpful in designing business process models and also helpful in simulating, optimizing, monitoring, and maintaining various processes that occur within an organization.

business process model   A graphic description of a process, showing the sequence of process tasks, which is developed for a specific purpose and from a selected viewpoint.

business process modeling (or mapping)   The activity of creating a detailed flow chart or process map of a work process showing its inputs, tasks, and activities, in a structured sequence.

business process reengineering (BPR)   The analysis and redesign of workflow within and between enterprises.

business process   A standardized set of activities that accomplish a specific task, such as processing a customer's order.

business requirement   The detailed set of business requests that the system must meet in order to be successful.

business rule   Defines how a company performs a certain aspect of its business and typically results in either a yes/no or true/false answer.

business strategy   A leadership plan that achieves a specific set of goals or objectives.

business-critical integrity constraint   Enforces business rules vital to an organization's success and often requires more insight and knowledge than relational integrity constraints.

business-facing process   Invisible to the external customer but essential to the effective management of the business and includes goal setting, day-to-day planning, performance feedback, rewards, and resource allocation.

business-to-business (B2B)   Applies to businesses buying from and selling to each other over the Internet.

business-to-consumer (B2C)   Applies to any business that sells its products or services to consumers over the Internet.

buyer power   Is assessed by analyzing the ability of buyers to directly impact the price they are willing to pay for an item.

byte   Group of eight bits represents one natural language character.

C

cache memory   A small unit of ultra-fast memory that is used to store recently accessed or frequently accessed data so that the CPU does not have to retrieve this data from slower memory circuits such as RAM.

capability maturity model integration method (CMMI)   A process improvement approach that contains 22 process areas.

capacity   Represents the maximum throughput a system can deliver; for example, the capacity of a hard drive represents the size or volume.

capacity planning   Determines the future IT infrastructure requirements for new equipment and additional network capacity.

capital   Represents money whose purpose is to make more money, for example, the money used to buy a rental property or a business.

carbon emission   Includes the carbon dioxide and carbon monoxide in the atmosphere, produced by business processes and systems.

cartography   The science and art of making an illustrated map or chart.

central processing unit (CPU) (or **microprocessor**)   The actual hardware that interprets and executes the program (software) instructions and coordinates how all the other hardware devices work together.

certificate authority   A trusted third party, such as VeriSign, that validates user identities by means of digital certificates.

chief information officer (CIO)   Responsible for (1) overseeing all uses of information technology and (2) ensuring the strategic alignment of IT with business goals and objectives.

chief knowledge officer (CKO)   Responsible for collecting, maintaining, and distributing the organization's knowledge.

chief privacy officer (CPO)   Responsible for ensuring the ethical and legal use of information within an organization.

chief security officer (CSO)   Responsible for ensuring the security of IT systems and developing strategies and IT safeguards against attacks from hackers and viruses.

chief technology officer (CTO)   Responsible for ensuring the throughput, speed, accuracy, availability, and reliability of an organization's information technology.

Child Online Protection Act (COPA)   A law that protects minors from accessing inappropriate material on the Internet.

chipless RFID tags   Use plastic or conductive polymers instead of silicon-based microchips, allowing them to be washed or exposed to water without damaging the chip.

classification   Assigns records to one of a predefined set of classes.

click-fraud   The abuse of pay-per-click, pay-per-call, and pay-per-conversion revenue models by repeatedly clicking on a link to increase charges or costs for the advertiser.

clickstream data   Exact pattern of a consumer's navigation through a site.

client/server network   A model for applications in which the bulk of the back-end processing, such as performing a physical search of a database, takes place on a server, while the front-end processing, which involves communicating with the users, is handled by the clients.

client   Computer that is designed to request information from a server.

cloud bursting   When a company uses its own computing infrastructure for normal usage and accesses the cloud when it needs to scale for high/peak load requirements, ensuring a sudden spike in usage does not result in poor performance or system crashes.

cloud computing   Refers to resources and applications hosted remotely as a shared service over the Internet.

cloud fabric   The software that makes the benefits of cloud computing possible, such as multi-tenancy.

cloud fabric controller   An individual who monitors and provisions cloud resources similar to a server administrator at an individual company.

cluster analysis   A technique used to divide an information set into mutually exclusive groups such that the members of each group are as close together as possible to one another and the different groups are as far apart as possible.

clustering   Segmenting a heterogeneous population of records into a number of more homogeneous subgroups.

coaxial cable   Cable that can carry a wide range of frequencies with low signal loss.

cold site   A separate facility that does not have any computer equipment, but is a place where employees can move after a disaster.

collaboration system   An IT-based set of tools that supports the work of teams by facilitating the sharing and flow of information.

collaborative demand planning   Helps organizations reduce their investment in inventory, while improving customer satisfaction through product availability.

collaborative engineering   Allows an organization to reduce the cost and time required during the design process of a product.

collective intelligence   Collaborating and tapping into the core knowledge of all employees, partners, and customers.

Committee of Sponsoring Organizations (COSO)   Key for evaluating internal controls such as human resources, logistics, information technology, risk, legal, marketing and sales, operations, financial functions, procurement, and reporting.

communication device   Equipment used to send information and receive it from one location to another.

community cloud   Serves a specific community with common business models, security requirements, and compliance considerations.

competitive advantage   A product or service that an organization's customers place a greater value on than similar offerings from a competitor.

competitive click-fraud   A computer crime where a competitor or disgruntled employee increases a company's search advertising costs by repeatedly clicking on the advertiser's link.

competitive intelligence   The process of gathering information about the competitive environment, including competitors' plans, activities, and products, to improve a company's ability to succeed.

complex instruction set computer (CISC) chip   Type of CPU that can recognize as many as 100 or more instructions, enough to carry out most computations directly.

compliance   The act of conforming, acquiescing, or yielding.

computer   Electronic device operating under the control of instructions stored in its own memory that can accept, manipulate, and store data.

computer simulation   Complex systems, such as the U.S. economy, can be modeled by means of mathematical equations and different scenarios can be run against the model to determine "what if" analysis.

computer-aided software engineering (CASE)   Software suites that automate systems analysis, design, and development.

confidentiality   The assurance that messages and information are available only to those who are authorized to view them.

consolidation   Involves the aggregation of information and features simple roll-ups to complex groupings of interrelated information.

consumer-to-business (C2B)   Applies to any consumer that sells a product or service to a business over the Internet.

consumer-to-consumer (C2C)   Applies to sites primarily offering goods and services to assist consumers interacting with each other over the Internet.

content creator   The person responsible for creating the original website content.

content editor   The person responsible for updating and maintaining website content.

content filtering   Occurs when organizations use software that filters content to prevent the transmission of unauthorized information.

content management system (CMS)   Provides tools to manage the creation, storage, editing, and publication of information in a collaborative environment.

continuous process improvement model   Attempts to understand and measure the current process, and make performance improvements accordingly.

control objectives for information and related technologies (COBIT)   A set of best practices that helps an organization to maximize the benefits of an information system, while at the same time establishing appropriate controls to ensure minimum errors.

control panel   A Windows feature that provides a group of options that sets default values for the Windows operating system.

control unit   Interprets software instructions and literally tells the other hardware devices what to do, based on the software instructions.

conversion   The process of transferring information from a legacy system to a new system.

copyright   The legal protection afforded an expression of an idea, such as a song, video game, and some types of proprietary documents.

core ERP component   Traditional components included in most ERP systems and they primarily focus on internal operations.

corporate social responsibility   Companies' acknowledged responsibility to society.

corporation (also called organization, enterprise, or business)   An artificially created legal entity that exists separate and apart from those individuals who created it and carry on its operations.

counterfeit software   Software that is manufactured to look like the real thing and sold as such.

course management software   Contains course information such as a syllabus and assignments and offers drop boxes for quizzes and homework along with a grade book.

critical path   A path from the start to the finish that passes through all the tasks that are critical to completing the project in the shortest amount of time.

critical success factor (CSF)   A factor that is critical to an organization's success.

CRM analysis technologies   Help organizations segment their customers into categories such as best and worst customers.

CRM predicting technologies   Help organizations make predictions regarding customer behavior such as which customers are at risk of leaving.

CRM reporting technologies   Help organizations identify their customers across other applications.

crowdsourcing   Refers to the wisdom of the crowd.

cryptography   The science that studies encryption, which is the hiding of messages so that only the sender and receiver can read them.

cube   The common term for the representation of multidimensional information.

customer metric   Assesses the management of customer relationships by the organization.

customer relationship management (CRM)   Involves managing all aspects of a customer's relationship with an organization to increase customer loyalty and retention and an organization's profitability.

customer-facing process   Results in a product or service that is received by an organization's external customer.

cyberbullying   Threats, negative remarks, or defamatory comments transmitted via the Internet or posted on a website.

cybermediation   Refers to the creation of new kinds of intermediaries that simply could not have existed before the advent of ebusiness.

cyberterrorism   Seeks to cause harm to people or to destroy critical systems or information and use the Internet as a weapon of mass destruction.

cybervandalism   The electronic defacing of an existing website.

cyberwar   An organized attempt by a country's military to disrupt or destroy information and communication systems for another country.

D

data   Raw facts that describe the characteristics of an event.

data center   A facility used to house management information systems and associated components, such as telecommunications and storage systems.

data dictionary   Compiles all of the metadata about the data elements in the data model.

data element (or data field)   The smallest or basic unit of information.

data flow diagram (DFD)   Illustrates the movement of information between external entities and the processes and data stores within the system.

data latency   The time duration to make data ready for analysis (i.e., the time for extracting, transforming, and cleansing the data) and loading the data into the database.

data mart   Contains a subset of data warehouse information.

data mining   The process of analyzing data to extract information not offered by the raw data alone.

data model   A formal way to express data relationships to a database management system (DBMS).

data visualization   Describes technologies that allow users to "see" or visualize data to transform information into a business perspective.

data visualization tools Moves beyond Excel graphs and charts into sophisticated analysis techniques such as pie charts, controls, instruments, maps, time-series graphs, etc.

data warehouse A logical collection of information—gathered from many different operational databases—that supports business analysis activities and decision-making tasks.

data-driven website An interactive website kept constantly updated and relevant to the needs of its customers through the use of a database.

data-mining tool Uses a variety of techniques to find patterns and relationships in large volumes of information and infer rules from them that predict future behavior and guide decision making.

database Maintains information about various types of objects (inventory), events (transactions), people (employees), and places (warehouses).

database management system (DBMS) Software through which users and application programs interact with a database.

decision latency The time it takes a human to comprehend the analytic result and determine an appropriate action.

decision support system (DSS) Models information to support managers and business professionals during the decision-making process.

decrypt Decodes information and is the opposite of encrypted.

demand planning software Generates demand forecasts using statistical tools and forecasting techniques.

dependency A logical relationship that exists between the project tasks, or between a project task and a milestone.

deperimeterization Occurs when an organization moves employees outside its firewall, a growing movement to change the way corporations address technology security.

design phase Involves describing the desired features and operations of the system including screen layouts, business rules, process diagrams, pseudo code, and other documentation.

destructive agents Malicious agents designed by spammers and other Internet attackers to farm email addresses off websites or deposit spyware on machines.

development phase Involves taking all of the detailed design documents from the design phase and transforming them into the actual system.

development testing Programmers test the system to ensure it is bug-free.

digital certificate A data file that identifies individuals or organizations online and is comparable to a digital signature.

digital Darwinism Organizations that cannot adapt to the new demands placed on them for surviving in the information age are doomed to extinction.

digital dashboard Integrates information from multiple components and tailors the information to individual preferences.

digital ink (or **electronic ink**) Technology that digitally represents handwriting in its natural form.

digital paper (or **electronic paper**) Any paper that is optimized for any type of digital printing.

digital rights management A technological solution that allows publishers to control their digital media to discourage, limit, or prevent illegal copying and distribution.

disaster recovery cost curve Charts (1) the cost to the organization of the unavailability of information and technology and (2) the cost to the organization of recovering from a disaster over time.

disaster recovery plan A detailed process for recovering information or an IT system in the event of a catastrophic disaster such as a fire or flood.

discovery prototyping Builds a small-scale representation or working model of the system to ensure it meets the user and business requirements.

disintermediation Occurs when a business sells direct to the customer online and cuts out the intermediary.

disruptive technology A new way of doing things that initially does not meet the needs of existing customers.

distribution management system Coordinates the process of transporting materials from a manufacturer to distribution centers to the final customer.

dividend A distribution of earnings to shareholders.

drill-down Enables users to get details, and details of details, of information.

drive-by hacking A computer attack where an attacker accesses a wireless computer network, intercepts data, uses network services, and/or sends attack instructions without entering the office or organization that owns the network.

dual boot Provides the user with the option of choosing the operating system when the computer is turned on.

dumpster diving Looking through people's trash, another way hackers obtain information.

dynamic catalog An area of a website that stores information about products in a database.

dynamic information Includes data that change based on user actions.

dynamic scaling Means that the MIS infrastructure can be automatically scaled up or down based on needed requirements.

E

ebook An electronic book that can be read on a computer or special reading device.

ebusiness model An approach to conducting electronic business on the Internet.

ebusiness The conducting of business on the Internet, not only buying and selling, but also serving customers and collaborating with business partners.

ecommerce The buying and selling of goods and services over the Internet.

edge matching (**warping, rubber sheeting**) Occurs when paper maps are laid edge to edge, and items that run across maps but do not match are reconfigured to match.

ediscovery (or **electronic discovery**) Refers to the ability of a company to identify, search, gather, seize, or export digital information in responding to a litigation, audit, investigation, or information inquiry.

effectiveness MIS metric Measures the impact IT has on business processes and activities including customer satisfaction, conversion rates, and sell-through increases.

efficiency MIS metric Measures the performance of the IT system itself including throughput, speed, and availability.

egovernment Involves the use of strategies and technologies to transform government(s) by improving the delivery of services and enhancing the quality of interaction between the citizen-consumer within all branches of government.

elogistics Manages the transportation and storage of goods.

email privacy policy Details the extent to which email messages may be read by others.

emall Consists of a number of eshops; it serves as a gateway through which a visitor can access other eshops.

embedded operating system Used for a single purpose in computer appliances and special-purpose applications, such as an automobile, ATM, or media player.

emergency A sudden, unexpected event requiring immediate action due to potential threat to health and safety, the environment, or property.

emergency notification service An infrastructure built for notifying people in the event of an emergency.

emergency preparedness Ensures a company is ready to respond to an emergency in an organized, timely, and effective manner.

employee monitoring policy States how, when, and where the company monitors its employees.

employee relationship management (ERM) Provides employees with a subset of CRM applications available through a web browser.

encryption Scrambles information into an alternative form that requires a key or password to decrypt the information.

energy consumption The amount of energy consumed by business processes and systems.

enterprise application integration (EAI) middleware Represents a new approach to middleware by packaging together commonly used functionality, such as providing prebuilt links to popular enterprise applications, which reduces the time necessary to develop solutions that integrate applications from multiple vendors.

enterprise architect (EA) Person grounded in technology, fluent in business, a patient diplomat, and provides the important bridge between IT and the business.

enterprise architecture Includes the plans for how an organization will build, deploy, use, and share its data, processes, and IT assets.

enterprise resource planning (ERP) Integrates all departments and functions throughout an organization into a single IT system (or integrated set of IT systems) so that employees can make decisions by viewing enterprisewide information on all business operations.

entity-relationship diagram (ERD) A technique for documenting the relationships between entities in a database environment.

entity In the relational database model, a person, place, thing, transaction, or event about which information is stored.

entry barrier A product or service feature that customers have come to expect from organizations in a particular industry and must be offered by an entering organization to compete and survive.

epolicies Policies and procedures that address the ethical use of computers and Internet usage in the business environment.

eprocurement The B2B purchase and sale of supplies and services over the Internet.

eshop (estore or etailer) A version of a retail store where customers can shop at any hour of the day without leaving their home or office.

estimated time enroute (ETE) The time remaining before reaching a destination using the present speed; typically used for navigation applications.

estimated time of arrival (ETA) The time of day of an expected arrival at a certain destination; typically used for navigation applications.

estimation Determine values for an unknown continuous variable behavior or estimated future value.

ethernet A physical and data layer technology for LAN networking.

ethical computer use policy Contains general principles to guide computer user behavior.

ethics Principles and standards that guide our behavior toward other people.

ewaste Old computer equipment, does not end up in a landfill, where the toxic substances it contains can leach into groundwater, among other problems.

executive information system (EIS) A specialized DSS that supports senior level executives within the organization.

executive sponsor The person or group who provides the financial resources for the project.

expense Refers to the costs incurred in operating and maintaining a business.

expert system Computerized advisory programs that imitate the reasoning processes of experts in solving difficult problems.

explicit knowledge Consists of anything that can be documented, archived, and codified, often with the help of IT.

extended ERP component The extra components that meet the organizational needs not covered by the core components and primarily focus on external operations.

extraction, transformation, and loading (ETL) A process that extracts information from internal and external databases, transforms the information using a common set of enterprise definitions, and loads the information into a data warehouse.

extreme programming (XP) methodology Breaks a project into tiny phases, and developers cannot continue on to the next phase until the first phase is complete.

F

fact The confirmation or validation of an event or object.

failback Occurs when the primary machine recovers and resumes operations, taking over from the secondary server.

failover Backup operational mode in which the function of a computer component (such as a processor, server, network, or database) is assumed by secondary system components when the primary component becomes unavailable through either failure or scheduled down time.

fair use doctrine In certain situations, it is legal to use copyrighted material.

fault tolerance A computer system designed so that in the event a component fails, a backup component or procedure can immediately take its place with no loss of service.

feasibility Determines if the proposed solution is feasible and achievable from a financial, technical, and organizational standpoint.

feedback Information that returns to its original transmitter (input, transform, or output) and modifies the transmitter's actions.

fiber optic (optical fiber)   The technology associated with the transmission of information as light impulses along a glass wire or fiber.

finance   Deals with the strategic financial issues associated with increasing the value of the business while observing applicable laws and social responsibilities.

financial accounting   Involves preparing financial reports that provide information about the business's performance to external parties such as investors, creditors, and tax authorities.

financial quarter   A three-month period (four quarters per year).

financial statement   Written records of the financial status of the business that allow interested parties to evaluate the profitability and solvency of the business.

firewall   Hardware and/or software that guards a private network by analyzing the information leaving and entering the network.

first-mover advantage   An organization can significantly impact its market share by being first to market with a competitive advantage.

flash memory   A special type of rewriteable read-only memory (ROM) that is compact and portable.

folksonomy   Similar to taxonomy except that crowdsourcing determines the tags or keyword-based classification system.

for profit corporations   Primarily focus on making money and all profits and losses are shared by the business owners.

forecast   Predictions made on the basis of time-series information.

foreign key   A primary key of one table that appears as an attribute in another table and acts to provide a logical relationship between the two tables.

forward integration   Takes information entered into a given system and sends it automatically to all downstream systems and processes.

fourth-generation language (4GL)   Programming languages that look similar to human languages.

fuzzy logic   A mathematical method of handling imprecise or subjective information.

G

Gantt chart   A simple bar chart that depicts project tasks against a calendar.

genetic algorithm   An artificial intelligence system that mimics the evolutionary, survival-of-the-fittest process to generate increasingly better solutions to a problem.

geocache   A GPS technology adventure game that posts on the Internet the longitude and latitude location of an item for users to find.

geocoding   Spatial databases in a coding process that takes a digital map feature and assigns it an attribute that serves as a unique ID (tract number, node number) or classification (soil type, zoning category).

geocoin   A round, coin-sized object that is uniquely numbered and hidden in geocache.

geoeconomic   Refers to the effects of geography on the economic realities of international business activities.

geographic information system (GIS)   Designed to work with information that can be shown on a map.

gigabyte (GB)   Roughly 1 billion bytes.

gigahertz (GHz)   The number of billions of CPU cycles per second.

GIS map automation   Links business assets to a centralized system where they can be tracked and monitored over time.

global inventory management system   Provides the ability to locate, track, and predict the movement of every component or material anywhere upstream or downstream in the supply chain.

global positioning system (GPS)   A device that determines current latitude, longitude, speed, and direction of movement.

goal-seeking analysis   Finds the inputs necessary to achieve a goal such as a desired level of output.

goods   Material items or products that customers will buy to satisfy a want or need. Clothing, groceries, cell phones, and cars are all examples of goods that people buy to fulfill their needs.

governance   Method or system of government for management or control.

granularity   Refers to the level of detail in the model or the decision-making process.

graphical user interface (GUI)   The interface to an information system.

grid computing   An aggregation of geographically dispersed computing, storage, and network resources, coordinated to deliver improved performance, higher quality of service, better utilization, and easier access to data.

H

hacker   People very knowledgeable about computers who use their knowledge to invade other people's computers.

hard drive   Secondary storage medium that uses several rigid disks coated with a magnetically sensitive material and housed together with the recording heads in a hermetically sealed mechanism.

hardware   Consists of the physical devices associated with a computer system.

help desk   A group of people who respond to internal system user questions.

high availability   Refers to a system or component that is continuously operational for a desirably long length of time.

historical analysis   Historical events are studied to anticipate the outcome of current developments.

hot site   A separate and fully equipped facility where the company can move immediately after a disaster and resume business.

hotspots   Designated locations where Wi-Fi access points are publicly available.

human resource ERP component   Tracks employee information including payroll, benefits, compensation, and performance assessment, and assures compliance with the legal requirements of multiple jurisdictions and tax authorities.

human resources (HR)   Includes the policies, plans, and procedures for the effective management of employees (human resources).

hybrid cloud   Includes two or more private, public, or community clouds, but each cloud remains separate and is only linked by technology that enables data and application portability.

hypertext markup language (HTML)   Links documents allowing users to move from one to another simply by clicking on a hotspot or link.

I

identity theft   The forging of someone's identity for the purpose of fraud.

IEEE 802.11n (or **Wireless-N**)   The newest standard for wireless networking.

implementation phase   Involves placing the system into production so users can begin to perform actual business operations with the system.

in-sourcing (in-house development)   A common approach using the professional expertise within an organization to develop and maintain the organization's information technology systems.

incident   Unplanned interruption of a service.

incident management   The process responsible for managing how incidents are identified and corrected.

incident record   Contains all of the details of an incident.

income statement (also referred to as **earnings report, operating statement,** and **profit-and-loss (P&L) statement**)   Reports operating results (revenues minus expenses) for a given time period ending at a specified date.

infographics (information graphics)   Displays information graphically so it can be easily understood.

information   Data converted into a meaningful and useful context.

information architecture   Identifies where and how important information, like customer records, is maintained and secured.

information cleansing or scrubbing   A process that weeds out and fixes or discards inconsistent, incorrect, or incomplete information.

information compliance   The act of conforming, acquiescing, or yielding information.

information ethics   Govern the ethical and moral issues arising from the development and use of information technologies, as well as the creation, collection, duplication, distribution, and processing of information itself (with or without the aid of computer technologies) .

information governance   Refers to the overall management of the availability, usability, integrity, and security of company data.

information granularity   Refers to the extent of detail within the information (fine and detailed or "coarse" and abstract information).

information inconsistency   Occurs when the same data element has different values.

information integrity   A measure of the quality of information.

information management   Examines the organizational resource of information and regulates its definitions, uses, value, and distribution ensuring it has the types of data/information required to function and grow effectively.

information MIS infrastructure   Identifies where and how important information, such as customer records, is maintained and secured.

information privacy policy   Contains general principles regarding information privacy.

information privacy   Concerns the legal right or general expectation of individuals, groups, or institutions to determine for themselves when and to what extent information about them is communicated to others.

information property   An ethical issue that focuses on who owns information about individuals and how information can be sold and exchanged.

information redundancy   The duplication of data, or the storage of the same data in multiple places.

information richness   Refers to the depth and breadth of information transferred between customers and businesses.

information secrecy   The category of computer security that addresses the protection of data from unauthorized disclosure and confirmation of data source authenticity.

information security plan   Details how an organization will implement the information security policies.

information security policy   Identifies the rules required to maintain information security.

information security   A broad term encompassing the protection of information from accidental or intentional misuse by persons inside or outside an organization.

Information Systems Audit and Control Association (ISACA)   A set of guidelines and supporting tools for IT governance that is accepted worldwide and generally used by auditors and companies as a way to integrate technology to implement controls and meet specific business objectives.

Information Technology Infrastructure Library (ITIL)   A framework provided by the government of the United Kingdom that offers eight sets of management procedures.

informing   Accessing large amounts of data from different management information systems.

Infrastructure as a Service (IaaS)   The delivery of computer hardware capability, including the use of servers, networking, and storage, as a service.

infrastructure   Includes the hardware, software, and telecommunications equipment that, when combined, provide the underlying foundation to support the organization's goals.

input device   Equipment used to capture information and commands.

insider   Legitimate users who purposely or accidentally misuse their access to the environment and cause some kind of business-affecting incident.

instant messaging (IM or **IMing)**   A type of communications service that enables someone to create a kind of private chat room with another individual in order to communicate in real-time over the Internet.

Institute of Electrical and Electronics Engineers (IEEE)   An organization that researches and institutes electrical standards for communication and other technologies.

intangible benefits   Difficult to quantify or measure.

integration   Allows separate systems to communicate directly with each other.

integration testing   Verifies that separate systems can work together passing data back and forth correctly.

integrity constraint   The rules that help ensure the quality of information.

intellectual property   Intangible creative work that is embodied in physical form.

intelligent agent   A special-purpose knowledge-based information system that accomplishes specific tasks on behalf of its users.

intelligent system   Various commercial applications of artificial intelligence.

interactive voice response (IVR)   Directs customers to use touch-tone phones or keywords to navigate or provide information.

interactivity   Measures the visitor interactions with the target ad.

intermediary   Agent, software, or business that brings buyers and sellers together to provide a trading infrastructure to enhance ebusiness.

International Organization for Standardization (ISO)   A nongovernmental organization established in 1947 to promote the development of world standards to facilitate the international exchange of goods and services.

Internet   A global public network of computer networks that pass information from one to another using common computer protocols.

Internet censorship   Government attempts to control Internet traffic, thus preventing some material from being viewed by a country's citizens.

Internet protocol version 6 (IPv6)   Distributes digital video content using IP across the Internet and private IP networks.

Internet service provider (ISP)   A company that provides individuals and other companies access to the Internet along with additional related services, such as website building.

Internet use policy   Contains general principles to guide the proper use of the Internet.

interoperability   Capability of two or more computer systems to share data and resources, even though they are made by different manufacturers.

intrusion detection software (IDS)   Searches out patterns in information and network traffic to indicate attacks and quickly responds to prevent any harm.

inventory management and control system   Provides control and visibility to the status of individual items maintained in inventory.

IT infrastructure   Includes the hardware, software, and telecommunications equipment that, when combined, provide the underlying foundation to support the organization's goals.

iterative development   Consists of a series of tiny projects.

J

joint application development (JAD)   A session where employees meet, sometimes for several days, to define or review the business requirements for the system.

K

key performance indicator (KPI)   Measures that are tied to business drivers.

kill switch   A trigger that enables a project manager to close the project prior to completion.

knowledge   Skills, experience, and expertise coupled with information and intelligence that creates a person's intellectual resources.

knowledge management (KM)   Involves capturing, classifying, evaluating, retrieving, and sharing information assets in a way that provides context for effective decisions and actions.

knowledge management system (KMS)   Supports the capturing, organization, and dissemination of knowledge (i.e., know-how) throughout an organization.

knowledge workers   Individuals valued for their ability to interpret and analyze information.

L

latitude   Represents a north/south measurement of position.

legacy system   An old system that is fast approaching or beyond the end of its useful life within an organization.

liability   An obligation to make financial payments.

limited liability   Means that the shareholders are not personally liable for the losses incurred by the corporation.

limited liability corporation (LLC)   A hybrid entity that has the legal protections of a corporation and the ability to be taxed (one time) as a partnership.

limited partnership   Much like a general partnership except for one important fundamental difference; the law protects the limited partner from being responsible for all of the partnership's losses.

local area network (LAN)   Computer network that uses cables or radio signals to link two or more computers within a geographically limited area, generally one building or a group of buildings.

location-based services (LBS)   Wireless mobile content services that provide location-specific information to mobile users moving from location to location.

logical view   Focuses on how users logically access information to meet their particular business needs.

long tail   Referring to the tail of a typical sales curve.

longitude   Represents an east/west measurement of position.

loss   Occurs when businesses sell products or services for less than they cost to produce.

loyalty program   Rewards customers based on the amount of business they do with a particular organization.

M

magnetic medium   Secondary storage medium that uses magnetic techniques to store and retrieve data on disks or tapes coated with magnetically sensitive materials.

magnetic tape   Older secondary storage medium that uses a strip of thin plastic coated with a magnetically sensitive recording medium.

mail bomb   Sends a massive amount of email to a specific person or system resulting in filling up the recipient's disk space, which, in some cases, may be too much for the server to handle and may cause the server to stop functioning.

maintainability (or flexibility)   Refers to how quickly a system can transform to support environmental changes.

maintenance phase   Involves performing changes, corrections, additions, and upgrades to ensure the system continues to meet the business goals.

management information systems (MIS)   A general name for the business function and academic discipline covering the application of people, technologies, and procedures—collectively called information systems—to solve business problems.

managerial accounting   Involves analyzing business operations for internal decision making and does not have to follow any rules issued by standard-setting bodies such as GAAP.

managerial level   Employees are continuously evaluating company operations to hone the firm's abilities to identify, adapt to, and leverage change.

market basket analysis Analyzes such items as websites and checkout scanner information to detect customers' buying behavior and predict future behavior by identifying affinities among customers' choices of products and services.

market segmentation The division of a market into similar groups of customers.

market share Calculated by dividing the firm's sales by the total market sales for the entire industry.

marketing The process associated with promoting the sale of goods or services.

marketing communication Seeks to build product or service awareness and to educate potential consumers on the product or service.

marketing mix Includes the variables that marketing managers can control in order to best satisfy customers in the target market.

mashup A website or web application that uses content from more than one source to create a completely new product or service.

mashup editor WYSIWYGs (What You See Is What You Get) for mashups that provide a visual interface to build a mashup, often allowing the user to drag and drop data points into a web application.

mass customization Ability of an organization to give its customers the opportunity to tailor its products or services to the customers' specifications.

materials requirement planning (MRP) system Sales forecasts to make sure that needed parts and materials are available at the right time and place in a specific company.

megabyte (MB or M or Meg) Roughly 1 million bytes.

megahertz (MHz) The number of millions of CPU cycles per second.

memory card Contains high-capacity storage that holds data such as captured images, music, or text files.

memory stick Provides nonvolatile memory for a range of portable devices including computers, digital cameras, MP3 players, and PDAs.

metadata Details about data.

methodology A set of policies, procedures, standards, processes, practices, tools, techniques, and tasks that people apply to technical and management challenges.

metrics Measurements that evaluate results to determine whether a project is meeting its goals.

metropolitan area network (MAN) A computer network that provides connectivity in a geographic area or region larger than that covered by a local area network, but smaller than the area covered by a wide area network.

microblogging The practice of sending brief posts (140 to 200 characters) to a personal blog, either publicly or to a private group of subscribers who can read the posts as IMs or as text messages.

middleware Different types of software that sit in the middle of and provide connectivity between two or more software applications.

MIS infrastructure Includes the plans for how a firm will build, deploy, use, and share its data, processes, and MIS assets.

mobile business (mcommerce or mbusiness) The ability to purchase goods and services through a wireless Internet-enabled device.

model A simplified representation or abstraction of reality.

Moore's Law Refers to the computer chip performance per dollar doubling every 18 months.

multi-tenancy A single instance of a system serves multiple customers.

multiple in/multiple out (MIMO) technology Multiple transmitters and receivers allow sending and receiving greater amounts of data than traditional networking devices.

multitasking Allows more than one piece of software to be used at a time.

mutation The process within a genetic algorithm of randomly trying combinations and evaluating the success (or failure) of the outcome.

N

nearshore outsourcing Contracting an outsourcing agreement with a company in a nearby country.

net income The amount of money remaining after paying taxes.

network A communications, data exchange, and resource-sharing system created by linking two or more computers and establishing standards, or protocols, so that they can work together.

network effect Describes how products in a network increase in value to users as the number of users increases.

network operating system (NOS) The operating system that runs a network, steering information between computers and managing security and users.

network topology Refers to the geometric arrangement of the actual physical organization of the computers (and other network devices) in a network.

network transmission media Various types of media used to carry the signal between computers.

network user license Enables anyone on the network to install and use the software.

neural network (artificial neural network) A category of AI that attempts to emulate the way the human brain works.

nonrepudiation A contractual stipulation to ensure that ebusiness participants do not deny (repudiate) their online actions.

nonvolatile Does not require constant power to function.

not for profit (or nonprofit) corporation Usually exists to accomplish some charitable, humanitarian, or educational purpose, and the profits and losses are not shared by the business owners.

O

object-oriented languages Languages that group data and corresponding processes into objects.

off-the-shelf application Supports general business processes and does not require any specific software customization to meet the organization's needs.

offshore outsourcing Using organizations from developing countries to write code and develop systems.

online analytical processing (OLAP) The manipulation of information to create business intelligence in support of strategic decision making.

online training Runs over the Internet or off a CD-ROM.

online transaction processing (OLTP) The capturing of transaction and event information using technology to (1) process the information according to defined business rules, (2) store the information, and (3) update existing information to reflect the new information.

onshore outsourcing The process of engaging another company within the same country for services.

open source Refers to any software whose source code is made available free for any third party to review and modify.

open system A broad term that describes nonproprietary IT hardware and software made available by the standards and procedures by which their products work, making it easier to integrate them.

operating system software Controls the application software and manages how the hardware devices work together.

operational CRM Supports traditional transactional processing for day-to-day front-office operations or systems that deal directly with the customers.

operational level Employees develop, control, and maintain core business activities required to run the day-to-day operations.

operational planning and control (OP&C) Deals with the day-to-day procedures for performing work, including scheduling, inventory, and process management.

operations management (OM) The management of systems or processes that convert or transform resources (including human resources) into goods and services.

opt out Customer specifically chooses to deny permission of receiving emails.

optimization analysis An extension of goal-seeking analysis, finds the optimum value for a target variable by repeatedly changing other variables, subject to specified constraints.

output device Equipment used to see, hear, or otherwise accept the results of information processing requests.

outsourcing An arrangement by which one organization provides a service or services for another organization that chooses not to perform them in-house.

owner's equity The portion of a company belonging to the owners.

P

packet-switching Occurs when the sending computer divides a message into a number of efficiently sized units called packets, each of which contains the address of the destination computer.

paradigm shift Occurs when a new radical form of business enters the market that reshapes the way companies and organizations behave.

parallel implementation Uses both the legacy system and new system until all users verify that the new system functions correctly.

partner relationship management (PRM) Focuses on keeping vendors satisfied by managing alliance partner and reseller relationships that provide customers with the optimal sales channel.

partnership Similar to sole proprietorships, except that this legal structure allows for more than one owner.

partnership agreement A legal agreement between two or more business partners that outlines core business issues.

passive RFID tags Do not have a power source.

patent An exclusive right to make, use, and sell an invention granted by a government to the inventor.

pay-per-call Generates revenue each time users click on a link that takes them directly to an online agent waiting for a call.

pay-per-click Generates revenue each time a user clicks on a link to a retailer's website.

pay-per-conversion Generates revenue each time a website visitor is converted to a customer.

peer-to-peer (P2P) network Any network without a central file server and in which all computers in the network have access to the public files located on all other workstations.

performance Measures how quickly a system performs a certain process or transaction.

personalization Occurs when a website can know enough about a person's likes and dislikes that it can fashion offers that are more likely to appeal to that person.

personal area network (PAN) Provide communication over a short distance that is intended for use with devices that are owned and operated by a single user.

personal information management (PIM) software Software handles contact information, appointments, task lists, and email.

PERT (Program Evaluation and Review Technique) chart A graphical network model that depicts a project's tasks and the relationships between those tasks.

pharming Reroutes requests for legitimate websites to false websites.

pharming attack Uses a zombie farm, often by an organized crime association, to launch a massive phishing attack.

phased implementation Installs the new system in phases (for example, by department) until it is verified that it works correctly.

phishing Technique to gain personal information for the purpose of identity theft, usually by means of fraudulent email.

phishing expedition A masquerading attack that combines spam with spoofing.

physical security Tangible protection such as alarms, guards, fireproof doors, fences, and vaults.

physical view The physical storage of information on a storage device such as a hard disk.

pilot implementation A small group uses the new system until it is verified that it works correctly, then the remaining users migrate to the new system.

pirated software The unauthorized use, duplication, distribution, or sale of copyrighted software.

planning phase Involves establishing a high-level plan of the intended project and determining project goals.

Platform as a Service (PaaS) Supports the deployment of entire systems including hardware, networking, and applications using a pay-per-use revenue model.

plunge implementation Discards the legacy system and immediately migrates all users to the new system.

podcasting Distribution of audio or video files, such as radio programs or music videos, over the Internet to play on mobile devices and personal computers.

portability Refers to the ability of an application to operate on different devices or software platforms, such as different operating systems.

preventive maintenance Makes system changes to reduce the chance of future system failure.

primary key A field (or group of fields) that uniquely identifies a given entity in a table.

primary storage Computer's main memory, which consists of the random access memory (RAM), cache memory, and read-only memory (ROM) that is directly accessible to the CPU.

primary value activities Found at the bottom of the value chain, these include business processes that acquire raw materials and manufacture, deliver, market, sell, and provide after-sales services.

privacy The right to be left alone when you want to be, to have control over your own personal possessions, and not to be observed without your consent.

private cloud Serves only one customer or organization and can be located on the customer's premises or off the customer's premises.

process modeling Involves graphically representing the processes that capture, manipulate, store, and distribute information between a system and its environment.

product differentiation An advantage that occurs when a company develops unique differences in its products with the intent to influence demand.

product life cycle Includes the four phases a product progresses through during its life cycle including introduction, growth, maturity, and decline.

production The creation of goods and services using the factors of production: land, labor, capital, entrepreneurship, and knowledge.

production and materials management ERP component Handles the various aspects of production planning and execution such as demand forecasting, production scheduling, job cost accounting, and quality control.

production management Describes all the activities managers do to help companies create goods.

productivity The rate at which goods and services are produced based upon total output given total inputs.

profit Occurs when businesses sell products or services for more than they cost to produce.

project A temporary endeavor undertaken to create a unique product or service.

project assumption Factor that is considered to be true, real, or certain without proof or demonstration.

project constraint Specific factor that can limit options.

project deliverable Any measurable, tangible, verifiable outcome, result, or item that is produced to complete a project or part of a project.

project management The application of knowledge, skills, tools, and techniques to project activities in order to meet or exceed stakeholder needs and expectations from a project.

project management office (PMO) An internal department that oversees all organizational projects.

project management software Supports the long-term and day-to-day management and execution of the steps in a project.

project manager An individual who is an expert in project planning and management, defines and develops the project plan, and tracks the plan to ensure all key project milestones are completed on time.

project milestone Represents key dates when a certain group of activities must be performed.

project objective Quantifiable criteria that must be met for the project to be considered a success.

project plan A formal, approved document that manages and controls project execution.

project requirements document Defines the specifications for product/output of the project and is key for managing expectations, controlling scope, and completing other planning efforts.

project risk An uncertain event or condition that, if it occurs, has a positive or negative effect on a project objective(s).

project scope Defines the work that must be completed to deliver a product with the specified features and functions.

project scope statement Links the project to the organization's overall business goals.

project stakeholders Individuals and organizations actively involved in the project or whose interests might be affected as a result of project execution or project completion.

protocol A standard that specifies the format of data as well as the rules to be followed during transmission.

prototype A smaller-scale representation or working model of the user's requirements or a proposed design for an information system.

public cloud Promotes massive, global, industrywide applications offered to the general public.

public key encryption (PKE) Encryption system that uses two keys: a public key that everyone can have and a private key for only the recipient.

Q

query-by-example (QBE) tool Helps users graphically design the answer to a question against a database.

R

radio frequency identification (RFID) Technologies using active or passive tags in the form of chips or smart labels that can store unique identifiers and relay this information to electronic readers.

RadioPaper A dynamic high-resolution electronic display that combines a paper-like reading experience with the ability to access information anytime, anywhere.

random access memory (RAM) The computer's primary working memory, in which program instructions and data are stored so that they can be accessed directly by the CPU via the processor's high-speed external data bus.

rapid application development (RAD) (also called rapid prototyping) methodology Emphasizes extensive user involvement in the rapid and evolutionary construction of working prototypes of a system to accelerate the systems development process.

rational unified process (RUP) methodology Provides a framework for breaking down the development of software into four gates.

read-only memory (ROM) The portion of a computer's primary storage that does not lose its contents when one switches off the power.

real simple syndication (RSS)   Family of web feed formats used for web syndication of programs and content.

real-time communication   Occurs when a system updates information at the same rate it receives it.

real-time information   Immediate, up-to-date information.

real-time system   Provides real-time information in response to query requests.

record   A collection of related data elements.

recovery   The ability to get a system up and running in the event of a system crash or failure and includes restoring the information backup.

reduced instruction set computer (RISC) chip   Limits the number of instructions the CPU can execute to increase processing speed.

reintermediation   Using the Internet to reassemble buyers, sellers, and other partners in a traditional supply chain in new ways.

relational database management system   Allows users to create, read, update, and delete data in a relational database.

relational database model   A type of database that stores information in the form of logically related two-dimensional tables.

relational integrity constraint   The rules that enforce basic and fundamental information-based constraints.

reliability (or accuracy)   Ensures all systems are functioning correctly and providing accurate information.

requirements definition document   Contains the final set of business requirements, prioritized in order of business importance.

requirements management   The process of managing changes to the business requirements throughout the project.

response time   The time it takes to respond to user interactions such as a mouse click.

responsibility matrix   Defines all project roles and indicates what responsibilities are associated with each role.

return on investment (ROI)   Indicates the earning power of a project.

revenue   Refers to the amount earned resulting from the delivery or manufacture of a product or from the rendering of a service.

RFID reader (RFID interrogator)   A transmitter/receiver that reads the contents of RFID tags in the area.

RFID tag   Contains a microchip and an antenna, and typically works by transmitting a serial number via radio waves to an electronic reader, which confirms the identity of a person or object bearing the tag.

RFIS accelerometer   A device that measures the acceleration (the rate of change of velocity) of an item and is used to track truck speeds or taxi cab speeds.

rivalry among existing competitors   High when competition is fierce in a market and low when competition is more complacent.

router   An intelligent connecting device that examines each packet of data it receives and then decides which way to send it onward toward its destination.

S

safe mode   Occurs if the system is failing and will load only the most essential parts of the operating system and will not run many of the background operating utilities.

sales   The function of selling a good or service that focuses on increasing customer sales, which increases company revenues.

satellite   A big microwave repeater in the sky; it contains one or more transponders that listen to a particular portion of the electromagnetic spectrum, amplifying incoming signals, and retransmitting them back to Earth.

scalability   Refers to how well a system can adapt to increased demands.

scripting language   A programming method that provides for interactive modules to a website.

scrum methodology   Uses small teams to produce small pieces of deliverable software using sprints, or 30-day intervals, to achieve an appointed goal.

search engine   Website software that finds other pages based on keyword matching.

search engine optimization (SEO)   Set of methods aimed at improving the ranking of a website in search engine listings.

search engine ranking   Evaluates variables that search engines use to determine where a URL appears on the list of search results.

secondary storage   Consists of equipment designed to store large volumes of data for long-term storage.

selling chain management   Applies technology to the activities in the order life cycle from inquiry to sale.

semantic web   An evolving extension of the World Wide Web in which web content can be expressed not only in natural language, but also in a format that can be read and used by software agents, thus permitting them to find, share, and integrate information more easily.

semi-passive RFID tags   Include a battery to run the microchip's circuitry, but communicate by drawing power from the RFID reader.

semistructured decisions   Occurs in situations in which a few established processes help to evaluate potential solutions, but not enough to lead to a definite recommended decision.

sensitivity analysis   The study of the impact that changes in one (or more) parts of the model have on other parts of the model.

server   Computer that is dedicated to providing information in response to external requests.

service-oriented architecture (SOA)   A collection of services that communicate with each other, for example, passing data from one service to another or coordinating an activity between one or more services.

service   A business task.

serviceability   How quickly a third party or vendor can change a system to ensure it meets user needs and the terms of any contracts, including agreed levels of reliability, maintainability, or availability.

shareholder   Another term for business owners.

shopping bot   Software that will search several retailer websites and provide a comparison of each retailer's offerings including price and availability.

sign-off   The system users' actual signatures indicating they approve all of the business requirements.

single-user license   Restricts the use of the software to one user at a time.

site license   Enables any qualified users within the organization to install the software, regardless of whether the computer is on a network. Some employees might install the software on a home computer for working remotely.

slice-and-dice   The ability to look at information from different perspectives.

smart card   A device that is around the same size as a credit card, containing embedded technologies that can store information and small amounts of software to perform some limited processing.

smart grid   Delivers electricity using two-way digital technology.

smartphone   Combines the functions of a cellular phone and a PDA in a single device.

social bookmarking   Allows users to share, organize, search, and manage bookmarks.

social engineering   Using one's social skills to trick people into revealing access credentials or other information valuable to the attacker.

social media   Refers to websites that rely on user participation and user-contributed content.

social media policy   Outlines the corporate guidelines or principles governing employee online communications.

social network   An application that connects people by matching profile information.

social networking   The practice of expanding your business and/or social contacts by constructing a personal network.

social networking analysis (SNA)   Maps group contacts, identifying who knows each other and who works together.

social tagging   Describes the collaborative activity of marking shared online content with keywords or tags as a way to organize it for future navigation, filtering, or search.

software   The set of instructions that the hardware executes to carry out specific tasks.

Software as a Service (SaaS)   A model of software deployment where an application is licensed for use as a service provided to customers on demand.

software customization   Modifies software to meet specific user or business requirements.

software engineering   A disciplined approach for constructing information systems through the use of common methods, techniques, or tools.

software updates (software patch)   Occurs when the software vendor releases updates to software to fix problems or enhance features.

software upgrade   Occurs when the software vendor releases a new version of the software, making significant changes to the program.

sole proprietorship   A business form in which a single person is the sole owner and is personally responsible for all the profits and losses of the business.

solvency   Represents the ability of the business to pay its bills and service its debt.

source code   Contains instructions written by a programmer specifying the actions to be performed by computer software.

source document   Describes the basic transaction data such as its date, purpose, and amount and includes cash receipts, canceled checks, invoices, customer refunds, employee time sheet, etc.

spam   Unsolicited email.

spatial data (geospatial data or geographic information)   Identifies the geographic location of features and boundaries on Earth, such as natural or constructed features, oceans, and more.

spear phishing   A phishing expedition in which the emails are carefully designed to target a particular person or organization.

spyware   Software that comes hidden in free downloadable software and tracks online movements, mines the information stored on a computer, or uses a computer's CPU and storage for some task the user knows nothing about.

statement of cash flow   Summarizes sources and uses of cash, indicates whether enough cash is available to carry on routine operations, and offers an analysis of all business transactions, reporting where the firm obtained its cash and how it chose to allocate the cash.

statement of owner's equity (also called the **statement of retained earnings** or **equity statement**) Tracks and communicates changes in the shareholder's earnings.

static information   Includes fixed data that are not capable of change in the event of a user action.

statistical analysis   Performs such functions as information correlations, distributions, calculations, and variance analysis.

status report   Periodic reviews of actual performance versus expected performance.

strategic business units (SBUs)   Consists of several stand-alone businesses.

strategic level   Managers develop overall business strategies, goals, and objectives as part of the company's strategic plan.

strategic planning   Focuses on long-range planning such as plant size, location, and type of process to be used.

streaming   A method of sending audio and video files over the Internet in such a way that the user can view the file while it is being transferred.

structured decisions   Involves situations where established processes offer potential solutions.

structured query language   Users write lines of code to answer questions against a database.

stylus   A pen-like device used to tap the screen to enter commands.

supplier power   High when one supplier has concentrated power over an industry.

supplier relationship management (SRM)   Focuses on keeping suppliers satisfied by evaluating and categorizing suppliers for different projects, which optimizes supplier selection.

supply chain event management (SCEM)   Enables an organization to react more quickly to resolve supply chain issues.

supply chain execution (SCE) software   Automates the different steps and stages of the supply chain.

supply chain management (SCM)   Involves the management of information flows between and among stages in a supply chain to maximize total supply chain effectiveness and profitability.

supply chain planning (SCP) software   Uses advanced mathematical algorithms to improve the flow and efficiency of the supply chain while reducing inventory.

supply chain visibility   The ability to view all areas up and down the supply chain.

supply chain   Consists of all parties involved, directly or indirectly, in the procurement of a product or raw material.

support value activities   Found along the top of the value chain and includes business processes, such as firm infrastructure, human resource management, technology development, and procurement that support the primary value activities.

sustainable MIS disposal   Refers to the safe disposal of IT assets at the end of their life cycle.

sustainable MIS infrastructure   Identifies ways that a company can grow in terms of computing resources while simultaneously becoming less dependent on hardware and energy consumption.

sustainable, or "green," MIS   Describes the manufacture, management, use, and disposal of information technology in a way that minimizes damage to the environment, which is a critical part of a corporation's responsibility.

sustaining technology   Produces an improved product customers are eager to buy, such as a faster car or larger hard drive.

switching cost   The costs that can make customers reluctant to switch to another product or service.

synchronous communication   Communications that occur at the same time such as IM or chat.

system   A collection of parts that link to achieve a common purpose.

system availability   Number of hours a system is available for users.

system clock   Works like a wristwatch and uses a battery mounted on the motherboard to provide power when the computer is turned off.

system restore   Enables a user to return to the previous operating system.

system software   Controls how the various technology tools work together along with the application software.

system testing   Verifies that the units or pieces of code function correctly when integrated.

system virtualization   The ability to present the resources of a single computer as if it is a collection of separate computers ("virtual machines"), each with its own virtual CPUs, network interfaces, storage, and operating system.

systems development life cycle (SDLC)   The overall process for developing information systems from planning and analysis through implementation and maintenance.

systems thinking   A way of monitoring the entire system by viewing multiple inputs being processed or transformed to produce outputs while continuously gathering feedback on each part.

T

tacit knowledge   The knowledge contained in people's heads.

tactical planning   Focuses on producing goods and services as efficiently as possible within the strategic plan.

tags   Specific keywords or phrases incorporated into website content for means of classification or taxonomy.

tangible benefits   Easy to quantify and typically measured to determine the success or failure of a project.

taxonomy   The scientific classification of organisms into groups based on similarities of structure or origin.

technology failure   Occurs when the ability of a company to operate is impaired because of a hardware, software, or data outage.

technology recovery strategy   Focus specifically on prioritizing the order for restoring hardware, software, and data across the organization that best meets business recovery requirements.

teergrubbing   Anti-spamming approach where the receiving computer launches a return attack against the spammer, sending email messages back to the computer that originated the suspected spam.

telecommunication system   Enables the transmission of data over public or private networks.

teleliving   Using information devices and the Internet to conduct all aspects of life seamlessly.

terabyte (TB)   Roughly 1 trillion bytes.

test condition   The detailed steps the system must perform along with the expected results of each step.

testing phase   Involves bringing all the project pieces together into a special testing environment to test for errors, bugs, and interoperability and verify that the system meets all of the business requirements defined in the analysis phase.

threat   An act or object that poses a danger to assets.

threat of new entrants   High when it is easy for new competitors to enter a market and low when there are significant entry barriers to entering a market.

threat of substitute products or services   High when there are many alternatives to a product or service and low when there are few alternatives from which to choose.

time bombs   Computer viruses that wait for a specific date before executing instructions.

time-series information   Time-stamped information collected at a particular frequency.

To-Be process model   Shows the results of applying change improvement opportunities to the current (As-Is) process model.

token   Small electronic devices that change user passwords automatically.

transaction processing system (TPS)   The basic business system that serves the operational level (analysts) in an organization.

transaction speed   Amount of time a system takes to perform a transaction.

transactional information   Encompasses all of the information contained within a single business process or unit of work, and its primary purpose is to support the performing of daily operational tasks.

transaction   Exchange or transfer of goods, services, or funds involving two or more people.

transborder data flows (TDF)   When business data flows across international boundaries over the telecommunications networks of global information systems.

transformation process   The technical core, especially in manufacturing organizations; the actual conversion of inputs to outputs.

Transmission Control Protocol/Internet Protocol (TCP/IP)   Provides the technical foundation for the public Internet as well as for large numbers of private networks.

transportation planning system   Tracks and analyzes the movement of materials and products to ensure the delivery of materials and finished goods at the right time, the right place, and the lowest cost.

trend analysis   A trend is examined to identify its nature, causes, speed of development, and potential impacts.

trend monitoring   Trends viewed as particularly important in a specific community, industry, or sector are carefully monitored, watched, and reported to key decision makers.

trend projection   When numerical data are available, a trend can be plotted to display changes through time and into the future.

twisted-pair cable   A type of cable composed of four (or more) copper wires twisted around each other within a plastic sheath.

typosquatting   A problem that occurs when someone registers purposely misspelled variations of well-known domain names.

U

unavailable   When a system is not operating or cannot be used.

unit testing   Testing individual units or pieces of code for a system.

universal resource locator (URL)   The address of a file or resource on the web such as www.apple.com.

unstructured decisions   Occurs in situations in which no procedures or rules exist to guide decision makers toward the correct choice.

usability   The degree to which a system is easy to learn, efficient, and satisfying to use.

user acceptance testing (UAT)   Determines if the system satisfies the user and business requirements.

user documentation   Highlights how to use the system.

user-contributed content (user-generated content)   Content created and updated by many users for many users.

utility computing   Offers a pay-per-use revenue model similar to a metered service such as gas or electricity.

utility software   Provides additional functionality to the operating system.

V

value chain analysis   Views a firm as a series of business processes that each add value to the product or service.

value-added   The term used to describe the difference between the cost of inputs and the value of price of outputs.

variable   A data characteristic that stands for a value that changes or varies over time.

virtual assistant (VA)   A small program stored on a PC or portable device that monitors emails, faxes, messages, and phone calls.

virtual reality   A computer-simulated environment that can be a simulation of the real world or an imaginary world.

virtualization   Protected memory space created by the CPU allowing the computer to create virtual machines.

virus   Software written with malicious intent to cause annoyance or damage.

vishing (or **voice phishing**)   A phone scam that attempts to defraud people by asking them to call a bogus telephone number to "confirm" their account information.

volatile   Must have constant power to function; contents are lost when the computer's electric supply fails.

volatility   Refers to RAM's complete loss of stored information if power is interrupted.

vulnerability   A system weakness that can be exploited by a threat; for example, a password that is never changed or a system left on while an employee goes to lunch.

W

war chalking   The practice of tagging pavement with codes displaying where Wi-Fi access is available.

war driving   Deliberately searching for Wi-Fi signals from a vehicle.

warm site   A separate facility with computer equipment that requires installation and configuration.

waterfall methodology   A sequential, activity-based process in which each phase in the SDLC is performed sequentially from planning through implementation and maintenance.

Web 1.0   Refers to the World Wide Web during its first few years of operation between 1991 and 2003.

Web 2.0 (or Business 2.0)   A set of economic, social, and technology trends that collectively form the basis for the next generation of the Internet—a more mature, distinctive medium characterized by user participation, openness, and network effects.

web accessibility   Means that people with disabilities—including visual, auditory, physical, speech, cognitive, and neurological disabilities—can use the web.

web accessibility initiative (WAI)   Brings together people from industry, disability organizations, government, and research labs from around the world to develop guidelines and resources to help make the web accessible to people with disabilities, including auditory, cognitive, neurological, physical, speech, and visual disabilities.

web browser   Allows users to access the WWW.

web conferencing (webinar)   Blends audio, video, and document-sharing technologies to create virtual meeting rooms where people "gather" at a password-protected website.

web log   Consists of one line of information for every visitor to a website and is usually stored on a web server.

website bookmark   A locally stored URL or the address of a file or Internet page saved as a shortcut.

website name stealing   The theft of a website's name that occurs when someone, posing as a site's administrator, changes the ownership of the domain name assigned to the website to another website owner.

what-if analysis   Checks the impact of a change in an assumption on the proposed solution.

Wi-Fi Protected Access (WPA)   A wireless security protocol to protect Wi-Fi networks.

wide area network (WAN)   Computer network that provides data communication services for business in geographically dispersed areas (such as across a country or around the world).

wiki   Web-based tools that make it easy for users to add, remove, and change online content.

wire media   Transmission material manufactured so that signals will be confined to a narrow path and will behave predictably.

wired equivalent privacy   An encryption algorithm designed to protect wireless transmission data.

wireless access point (WAP)   Enables devices to connect to a wireless network to communicate with each other.

wireless fidelity (Wi-Fi)   A means of linking computers using infrared or radio signals.

wireless LAN (WLAN)   A local area network that uses radio signals to transmit and receive data over distances of a few hundred feet.

wireless MAN (WMAN)   A metropolitan area network that uses radio signals to transmit and receive data.

wireless media   Natural parts of the Earth's environment that can be used as physical paths to carry electrical signals.

wireless WAN (WWAN)   A wide area network that uses radio signals to transmit and receive data.

workflow   Defines all the steps or business rules, from beginning to end, required for a business process.

workplace MIS monitoring   Tracks people's activities by such measures as number of keystrokes, error rate, and number of transactions processed.

workshop training   Set in a classroom-type environment and led by an instructor.

World Wide Web (WWW)   A global hypertext system that uses the Internet as its transport mechanism.

Worldwide Interoperability for Microwave Access (WiMAX)   A telecommunications technology aimed at providing wireless data over long distances in a variety of ways, from point-to-point links to full mobile cellular type access.

Z

zombie   A program that secretly takes over another computer for the purpose of launching attacks on other computers.

zombie farm   A group of computers on which a hacker has planted zombie programs.

NOTES

CHAPTER 1

1. "Apple Profit Surges 95 Percent on iPod Sales," *Yahoo! News,* http://news.yahoo.com/s/afp/20060118/bs_afp/uscompanyearningsit_060118225009, accessed January 2010; "Apple's IPod Success Isn't Sweet Music for Record Company Sales," *Bloomberg.com,* http://quote.bloomberg.com/apps/news?pid=nifea&&sid=aHP5Ko1 pozM0, accessed November 2010; Peter Burrows, "How Apple Could Mess Up Again," *BusinessWeek Online,* http://yahoo.businessweek.com/technology/content/jan2006/tc20060109_432937.htm, accessed January 2011; www.apple.com/iphone, accessed June 2011; *news.com.com* NikeiPodaisesRFIDprivacyconcerns/2100-1029_3-6143606.html, accessed June 2011.

2. Interesting Facts, www.interestingfacts.org, accessed June 2012.

3. Thomas L. Friedman, *The World Is Flat* (New York: Farrar, Straus & Giroux, 2005); Thomas Friedman, "The World Is Flat," www.thomaslfriedman.com, accessed June 2010; Thomas L. Friedman, "The Opinion Pages," *The New York Times,* topics.nytimes.com/top/opinion/editorialsandoped/oped/columnists/thomaslfriedman, accessed June 2012.

CHAPTER 2

1. Ina Fried, "Apple Earnings Top Estimates," *CNET News,* October 11, 2005, http://news.cnet.com/Appleearnings-topestimates/2100-1041_3-5893289.html?tag=lia;rcol, accessed July 2012.

2. Frederic Paul, "Smart Social Networking for Your Small Business," Forbes.com, www.forbes.com/2009/06/05/social-networkinginterop-entrepreneurs-technology-bmighty.html, accessed July 2012.

3. Michael E. Porter, "The Five Competitive Forces That Shape Strategy," The Harvard Business Review Book Series, *Harvard Business Review,* January 2008; Michael E. Porter, "Competitive Strategy: Techniques for Analyzing Industries and Competitors," *Harvard Business Review,* January 2002; Michael E. Porter, "On Competition," *The Harvard Business Review Book Series* (Boston: Harvard Business School Publishing, 1985); Harvard Institute for Strategy and Competitiveness, www.isc.hbs.edu/, accessed June 2012.

4–15. Ibid.

CHAPTER 3

1. Christopher Koch, "The ABC's of Supply Chain Management," www.cio.com, accessed October 2012.

2. "Customer Success Stories," www.siebel.com, accessed October 2012.

3. "Kaiser's Diabetic Initiative," www.businessweek.com, accessed October 2012.

4. "Integrated Solutions—The ABCs of CRM," www.integratedsolutionsmag.com, accessed November 2012.

5. Chi-Chu Tschang, "Contaminated Milk Sours China's Dairy Business," *Bloomberg Businessweek,* September 2008, www.businessweek.com/globalbiz/content/sep2008/gb20080926_543133.htm.

CHAPTER 4

1. Peter Drucker, "The Man Who Invented Management: Why Peter Drucker's Ideas Still Matter," www.businessweek.com/magazine/content/05_48/b3961001.htm, accessed October 2010.

2. Neustar Webmetrics, www.webmetrics.com/, accessed April 2012.

3. Ibid.

4. Ibid.

5. The Balanced Scorecard, www.balancedscorecard.org, accessed February 2010.

6. Clive Thompson, "Do You Speak Statistics?" *Wired,* May 2010, p. 36.

CHAPTER 5

1. "IT Master of the Senate," *CIO Magazine Online,* www.cio.com/archive/050104/tl_govt.html, accessed May 2012.

2. Michael Schrage, "Rebuilding the Business Case," *CIO Magazine Online,* www.cio.com, accessed November 2012.

3. "Integrating Information at Children's Hospital," *KMWorld,* www.kmworld.com/Articles/ReadArticle.aspx, accessed April 2012.

4. Scott Berianato, "Take the Pledge," *CIO Magazine Online,* www.cio.com, accessed November 2012.

5. "2009 CSI/FBI Computer Crime and Security Survey," www.usdoj.gov/criminal/cybercrime/FBI2009.pdf, accessed February 2009.

6. Notes 6–9. Ibid.

10. Schrage, "Rebuilding the Business Case."

11. Ibid.

12. www.norcrossgroup.com/casestudies.html, accessed October 2010.

13. Nick Leiber, Sommer Saadi, Victoria Stilwell, Joel Stonington, John Tozzi, and Venessa Wong, "2011 Finalists: America's Best Young Entrepreneurs," *Bloomberg Businessweek,* September 20, 2011.

14. "Bad Business Decisions," *Business 2.0,* December 2003, pp. S1–S5.

15. Thomas L. Friedman, *Hot, Flat, and Crowded: Why We Need a Green Revolution—and How It Can Renew America* (New York: Farrar, Straus, Giroux, 2008).

16. "Salary Survey," Special Report Staff and Entry Level Salary Comparison, *ComputerWorld,* www.computerworld.com/s/salary-survey/breakdown/2009/job_level/3, accessed June 2010.

17. Ina Fried, "Adobe to Buy Omniture for $1.8 Billion, *CNET News,* September 15, 2009, http://news.cnet.com/8301-13860_3-10353733-56.html.

18. Streeter Seidell, "10 Best Things We'll Say to Our Grand-kids," *Wired,* September, 21, 2009, www.wired.com/culture/culturereviews/magazine/17-10/st_best#ixzz0s65fFq1t.

19. Thomas L. Friedman, *The World Is Flat* (New York: Farrar, Straus & Giroux, 2005); Thomas Friedman, "The World Is Flat," www.thomaslfriedman.com, accessed June 2010; Thomas L. Friedman, "The Opinion Pages," *The New York Times,* topics.nytimes.com/top/opinion/editorialsandoped/oped/columnists/thomaslfriedman, accessed June 2012.

20. J. R. Raphel, "The 15 Biggest Wiki Blunders," *PC World,* August 26, 2009.

21. Peter S. Green, "Merrill's Thain Said to Pay $1.2 Million to Decorator," *Bloomberg Businessweek,* January 23, 2009, www.bloomberg.com/apps/news?sid=aFcrG8er4FRw&pid=newsarchive, accessed April 17 2010.

22. "TED: Ideas Worth Spreading," www.ted.com/pages/view/id/5, accessed June 21, 2012.

CHAPTER 6

1. www.webdesignerdepot.com, accessed April 2012; flowingdata.com/2011/12/21/the-best-data-visualization-projects-of-2011/ , accessed April 2012.

2. Julia Kiling, "OLAP Gains Fans among Data-Hungry Firms," *ComputerWorld,* January 8, 2001, p. 54.

3. Stephen Baker, "What Data Crunchers Did for Obama," *Bloomberg Businessweek,* January 2009.

CHAPTER 7

1. Jim Giles, "Data Sifted from Facebook Wiped after Legal Threats," *NewScientist,* March 31, 2010, www.newscientist.com/article/dn18721-data-sifted-from-facebook-wiped-after-legal-threats.html.

2. www.ellisisland.com, accessed June 2013.

3. "Data, Data Everywhere," *The Economist,* www.economist.com/specialreports/displayStory.cfm?story_id 5 15557443.

4. Michael S. Malone, "IPO Fever," *Wired,* March 2004; "Cyber Bomb—Search Tampering," *BusinessWeek,* March 2009; "Google Knows Where You Are," *BusinessWeek,* February 2009; www.google.com, accessed September 13, 2003.

CHAPTER 8

1. Kathleen Melymuka, "Premier 100: Turning the Tables at Applebee's," *ComputerWorld,* www.computerworld.com, accessed February 2007; Barbara DePompa Reimers, "Too Much of a Good Thing," *ComputerWorld,* April 2007.

2. Alice LaPante, "Big Things Come in Smaller Packages," *ComputerWorld,* June 1996, pp. DW/6–7.

3. Nikhil Hutheesing, "Surfing with Sega," *Forbes,* November 2007.

4. Ibid.

5. Julia Kiling, "OLAP Gains Fans among Data-Hungry Firms," *ComputerWorld,* January 2010.

6. Steve Hamm, "Business Intelligence Gets Smarter," *BusinessWeek,* May 15, 2006.

7. Julie Schlosser, "Looking for Intelligence in Ice Cream," *Fortune,* March 2009; Leslie Goff, "Summertime Heats Up IT at Ben & Jerry's," *ComputerWorld,* July 2010; Customer Success Stories, www.cognos.com, accessed January 2012

8. Maria Popova, "Data Visualization: Stories for the Information Age," *Bloomberg Businessweek,* April 2011.

9. Prashant Gopal, "Zillow Opens Online Mortgage Market-place," *Bloomberg Businessweek,* April 3, 2009.

10. Katie Cassidy, "Barack Obama: "iPad Distracts from the Mes-sage," *Sky News,* May 10, 2010.

11. Ericka Chickowski, "Goldman Sachs Sued for Illegal Database Access," *Security Darkreading.com,* May 2010.

12. U.S. Bureau of Labor Statistics, www.bls.gov/, accessed April 2012.

CHAPTER 9

1. www.actionaly.com, accessed April 2012; www.socialmedia.biz/2011/01/12/top-20-social-media-monitoring-vendors-for-business, accessed April 2012; www.radian6.com, accessed April 2012; www.collectiveintellect.com, accessed April 2012.

2. Tom Davenport, "Tom Davenport: Back to Decision-Making Basics," *Bloomberg Businessweek,* March 2008.

3. "What Is Systems Thinking," *SearchCIO.com,* http://searchcio.tech.

4. Rachel King, "Soon That Nearby Worker Might Be a Robot," *Bloomberg Businessweek,* June 1, 2010, www.businessweek.com/technology/content/jun2010/tc2010061_798891.htm.

5. Sharon Begley, "Software au Natural"; Neil McManus, "Robots at Your Service"; Santa Fe Institute, www.dis.anl.gov/abms/, accessed June 24, 2007; Michael A. Arbib (Ed.), *The Handbook of Brain Theory and Neural Networks* (MIT Press, mitpress.mit.edu, 1995); L. Biacino and G. Gerla, "Fuzzy Logic, Continuity and Effectiveness," Archive for Mathematical Logic.

6. "Darpa Grand Challenge," www.darpa.mil/grandchallenge/, accessed September 1, 2012.

CHAPTER 10

1. Frank Quinn, "The Payoff Potential in Supply Chain Manage-ment," www.ascet.com, accessed June 15, 2012. Jennifer Bresnahan, "The Incredible Journey," *CIO Enterprise,* www.cio.com, accessed March 12, 2012.

2. "The Visionary Elite," *Business 2.0,* pp. S1–S5; money.cnn.com/magazines/business2/, accessed July 2012.

3. Beth Bacheldor, "Steady Supply," *InformationWeek,* www.informationweek.com, accessed June 2012.

4. "Success Story," www.perdue.com, accessed June 2012.

5. Mohsen Attaran, "RFID: An Enabler of Supply Chain Operations," *Supply Chain Management: An International Journal* 12 (2007), pp. 249–57, www.emeraldinsight.com, accessed February 2010.

CHAPTER 11

1. Timothy Keiningham and Lerzan Aksoy "When Customer Loyalty Is a Bad Thing," *Bloomberg Businessweek,* May 8, 2009, www.businessweek.com/managing/content/may2009/ca2009058_567988.htm.

CHAPTER 12

1. "Case Study: IBM Helps Shell Canada Fuel New Productivity with PeopleSoft EnterpriseOne," August 8, 2005, validated February 5, 2007, www.306.ibm.com/software/success/cssdb.nsf.

2. Timothy Keiningham and Lerzan Aksoy, "When Customer Loyalty Is a Bad Thing," *Bloomberg Businessweek,* May 8, 2009, www.businessweek.com/managing/content/may2009/ca2009058_567988.htm.

3. Leroy Zimdars, "Supply Chain Innovation at Harley-Davidson: An Interview with Leroy Zimdars," April 15, 2010, www.ascet.com/authors.asp?a_id=68; "Harley-Davidson: Ride Your Heritage," Fast Company, August 2004, p. 44; "Harley-Davidson on the Path to Success," www.peoplesoft.com/media/success, accessed June 2010.

CHAPTER 13

1. Ingrid Lunden, "Pinterest Updates Terms of Service as It Preps an API and Private Pinboards: More Copyright Friendly," *Tech Crunch,* April 2012; Chad McCloud, "What Pinterest Teaches Us About Innovation in Business," *Bloomberg Businessweek,* May 2012; Courteney Palis, "Pinterest Traffic Growth Soars to New Heights: Experian Report," *The Huffington Post,* April 6, 2012.

2. "Polaroid Files for Bankruptcy Protection," www.dpreview.com/news/0110/01101201polaroidch11.asp, accessed July 2012.

3. Clayton Christensen, *The Innovator's Dilemma* (Boston: Harvard Business School, 1997); Adam Lashinsky, "The Disrupters," *Fortune,* August 11, 2003, pp. 62–65.

4. Ibid.

5. Ibid.

6. Internet World Statistics, www.internetworldstats.com, January 2012.

7. info.cern.ch, accessed June 2010.

8. Brier Dudley, "Changes in Technology Almost Too Fast To Follow," *The Seattle Times,* October 13, 2005.

9. Timothy Mullaney, "Netflix," *Bloomberg Businessweek,* www.businessweek.com/smallbiz/, accessed June 2010.

10. "Disintermediation," *TechTarget,* http://whatis.techtarget.com/defition.html, accessed April 2010.

11. Ibid.

12. Scott McCartney, "You Paid What for That Flight?" *The Wall Street Journal,* August 26, 2010, http://online.wsj.com/article.

13. "A Site Stickier than a Barroom Floor," *Business 2.0,* June 2005, p. 741; www.emarketer.com, accessed January 2010.

14. Ibid.

15. Paul Ormerod, *Why Most Things Fail: Evolution, Extinction, and Economics* (Hoboken, NJ: John Wiley & Sons, 2005).

CHAPTER 14

1. www.google.com, accessed September 2012.

2. Ibid.

3. "The Complete Web 2.0 Directory," www.go2web20.net/, accessed June 2012 "Web 2.0 for CIOs," www.cio.com/article/16807; www.emarketer.com, accessed January 2012.

4. "Internet Pioneers," www.ibiblio.org/pioneers/andreesen.html, accessed June 2012.

CHAPTER 15

1. "The Complete Web 2.0 Directory," www.go2web20.net/, accessed June 24, 2007; "Web 2.0 for CIOs," www.cio.com/article/16807; www.emarketer.com, accessed January 2010; Daniel Nations, "What Is Social Bookmarking," *About.com,* "Web Trends," http://webtrends.about.com/od/socialbookmarking101/p/aboutsocialtags.htm, accessed April 5, 2010.

2. Notes 2–11. Ibid.

12. Tim Berners-Lee, "Semantic Web Road Map," October 14, 1998, www.w3.org/DesignIssues/Semantic.html, accessed April 12, 2012.

13. Douglas MacMillan, "Social Media: The Ashton Kutcher Effect," *Bloomberg Businessweek,* May 3, 2009, www.businessweek.com/technology/content/may2009/tc2009053_934757.htm.

CHAPTER 16

1. "How Do Cellular Devices Work," www.cell-phone101.info/devices.php, accessed February 9, 2008.

2. Ibid.

3. Deepak Pareek, *WiMAX: Taking Wireless to the MAX* (Boca Raton, FL: CRC Press, 2006), pp. 150–51; V. C. Gungor and F. C. Lambert, "A Survey on Communication Networks for Electric System Automation, Computer Networks," *International Journal of Computer and Telecommunications Networking,* May 15, 2006, pp. 877–97.

Notes 4–8. Ibid.

9. "RFID Privacy and You," www.theyaretrackingyou.com/rfid-privacy-and-you.html, accessed February 12, 2012. "RFID Roundup," www.rfidgazette.org, accessed February 10, 2012. "Security-Free Wireless Networks," www.wired.com, accessed February 11, 2012.

10. Ibid.

11. Damian Joseph, "The GPS Revolution," *Bloomberg Businessweek,* May 27, 2009, www.businessweek.com/innovate/content/may2009/id20090526_735316.htm.

12. Natasha Lomas, "Location Based Services to Boom in 2008," *Bloomberg Businessweek,* February 11, 2008, www.businessweek.com/globalbiz/content/feb2008/gb20080211_420894.htm.

13. V. C. Gungor and F. C. Lambert, "A Survey on Communication Networks for Electric System Automation, Computer Networks," *International Journal of Computer and Telecommunications Networking,* May 15, 2006, pp. 877–97.

14. Natasha Lomas, "Location Based Services to Boom in 2008."

15. "Rip Curl Turns to Skype for Global Communications," www.voipinbusiness.co.uk/rip_curl_turns_to_skype_for_gl.asp, July 7, 2006, accessed January 21, 2008; "Navigating the Mobility Wave," www.busmanagement.com, accessed February 2012; "Sprint Plans Launch of Commercial WiMAX Service in Q2 2008," www.intomobile.com, accessed February 2012; Deepak Pareek, *WiMAX: Taking Wireless to the MAX* (Boca Raton, FL: CRC Press, 2006), pp. 150–93; wimax.com, accessed February 2012.

16. Ibid.

17. Ibid.

18. Paul Hochman, "Wireless Electricity is Here," *Fast Company,* February 1, 2009, www.fastcompany.com/magazine/132/brilliant.html.

19. Tim Ferguson, "BBC Taps Web 3.0 for New Music Site," *Bloomberg Businessweek,* April 7, 2009, www.businessweek.com/globalbiz/content/apr2009/gb2009047_713777.htm.

20. "What Is Social Networking," www.socialnetworking.com, accessed June 2010.

CHAPTER 17

1. Charles Bryant, "Top 10 Things You Should Not Share on Social Networks," *Howstuffworks,* howstuffworks.com, accessed May 2012.

2. "Overcoming Software Development Problems," www.samspublishing.com, accessed October 2005.

CHAPTER 18

1. "Four Steps to Getting Things on Track," *Bloomberg Businessweek,* July 7, 2010, www.businessweek.com/idg/2010-07-07/project-management-4-steps-to-getting-things-on-track.html.

CHAPTER 19

1. *CIO Magazine,* June 1, 2006; "The Project Manager in the IT Industry," www.standishgroup.com; Jim Johnson, *My Life Is Failure* (Boston: Standish Group International, 2006); Gary McGraw, "Making Essential Software Work," *Software Quality Management,* April 2003, www.sqmmagazine.com, accessed November 14, 2003.

2. Edward Yourdon, Death March: The Complete Software Developer's Guide to Surviving "Mission Impossible" Projects (Upper Saddle River, NJ: Prentice Hall PTR, 1999).

CHAPTER 20

1. "Baggage Handling System Errors," www.flavors.com, accessed November 16, 2003.

2. www.twitter.com, accessed June 2010.

3. Lynne Johnson, Ellen McGirt, and Sherri Smith, "The Most Influential Women in Technology," *Fast Company,* January 14, 2009, www.fastcompany.com/magazine/132/the-mostinfluential-women-in-technology.html.

PLUG-IN B1

- Adrian Danescu, "Save $55,000," *CIO Magazine,* December 15, 2004, p. 70.

- Alison Overholdt, "The Housewife Who Got Up Off the Couch," *Fast Company,* September 2004, p. 94.

- *Business Dictionary,* www.glossarist.com/glossaries/business/, accessed December 15, 2003.

- "Can the Nordstroms Find the Right Style?" *BusinessWeek,* July 30, 2001.

- "From the Bottom Up," *Fast Company,* June 2004, p. 54.

- Geoff Keighley, "Will Sony's PSP Become the iPod of Gaming Devices?" *Business 2.0,* May 2004, p. 29.

- *Glossary of Business Terms,* www.powerhomebiz.com/Glossary/glossary-A.htm, accessed December 15, 2003.

- *Glossary of Business Terms,* www.smallbiz.nsw.gov.au/smallbusiness/, accessed December 15, 2003.

- *Glossary of Financial Terms,* www.nytimes.com/library/financial/glossary/bfglosa.htm, accessed December 15, 2003.

- "Harley-Davidson: Ride Your Heritage," *Fast Company,* August 2004, p. 44.

- "Ford on Top," *Fast Company,* June 2004, p. 54.

- "Innovative Managers," *BusinessWeek,* April 24, 2005.

- Julie Schlosser, "Toys 'R' Us Braces for a Holiday Battle," *Money,* December 22, 2003.

- "Mastering Management," *Financial Times,* www.ft.com/pp/mfm, accessed December 15, 2003.

- Michael Hammer, *Beyond Reengineering: How the Process-Centered Organization Is Changing Our Work and Our Lives* (New York: HarperCollins Publishers, 1997).

- "Progressive Insurance," *BusinessWeek,* March 13, 2004.

- "Toy Wars," www.pbs.org, accessed December 23, 2003.

PLUG-IN B2

- Bjorn Andersen, *Business Process Improvement Toolbox* (Milwaukee, WI: ASQ Quality Press, 1999).

- "BPR Online," www.prosci.com/mod1.htm, accessed October 10, 2005.

- "Business Process Reengineering Six Sigma," www.sixsigma.com/me/bpr/, accessed October 10, 2005.

- "Customer Success Stories: Adidas," www.global360.com/collateral/Adidas_Case_History.pdf, accessed October 10, 2005.

- *Government Business Process Reengineering (BPR) Readiness Assessment Guide,* General Services Administration (GSA), 1996.

- H. James Harrington, *Business Process Improvement Workbook: Documentation, Analysis, Design, and Management of Business Process Improvement* (New York: McGraw-Hill, 1997).

- H. James Harrington, *Business Process Improvement: The Breakthrough Strategy for Total Quality, Productivity, and Competitiveness* (New York: McGraw-Hill, 1991).

- Michael Hammer and James Champy, "Reengineering the Corporation: A Manifest for Business Revolution," *HarperBusiness,* January 1, 1994.

- Michael Hammer, *Beyond Reengineering: How the Process-Centered Organization Is Changing Our Work and Our Lives* (New York: HarperCollins, 1996).

- Richard Chang, "Process Reengineering in Action: A Practical Guide to Achieving Breakthrough Results (Quality Improvement Series)," 1996.

- "Savvion Helps 3Com Optimize Product Promotion Processes," www.savvion.com/customers/marketing_promotions.php, accessed October 10, 2005.

- SmartDraw.com, www.smartdraw.com/, accessed October 11, 2005.

- "What Is BPR?" searchcio.techtarget.com/sDefinition/0,,sid182_gci536451,00.html, accessed October 10, 2005.

PLUG-IN B3

- Aaron Ricadela, "Seismic Shift," *Information Week,* March 14, 2005.

- Denise Brehm, "Sloan Students Pedal Exercise," www.mit.edu, accessed May 5, 2003.

- "Electronic Breaking Points," *PC World,* August 2005.

- Hector Ruiz, "Advanced Micro Devices," *BusinessWeek,* January 10, 2005.

- Margaret Locher, "Hands That Speak," *CIO Magazine,* June 1, 2005.

- "The Linux Counter," counter.li.org, accessed October 2005.

- Tom Davenport, "Playing Catch-Up," *CIO Magazine,* May 1, 2001.

- www.mit.com, accessed October 2005.

- www.needapresent.com, accessed October 2005.

- www.powergridfitness.com, accessed October 2005.

PLUG-IN B4

- Agam Shah, "UPS Invests $1 Billion in Technology to Cut Costs," www.businessweek.com/idg/2010-03-25/ups-invests-1-billion-intechnology-to-cut-costs.html, accessed April 4, 2010.

- Goodwill Industries International, "Dell and Goodwill Expand Free Recycling Program to Include Microsoft Product," April 21, 2010, www.goodwill.org/press-releases/dell-goodwill-expandfree-consumer-recycling-program-to-include-microsoft-products/, accessed June 3, 2010.

- *Google Docs,* docs.google.com, accessed June 4, 2010.

- Martin LaMonica, "The Journey of Juice, Inside the Electric Grid," *CNET News,* August 24, 2010, http://news.cnet.com/8301-11128_3-20014393-54.html.

- "Moore's Law," www.intel.com/technology/mooreslaw, accessed April 2, 2010; Electronics TakeBack Coalition, "Facts and Figures on E-Waste and Recycling," www.electronicstakeback.com, accessed April 3, 2010; "EPA Report to Congress on Server and Data Center Energy Efficiency," www.energystar.gov/ia/partners/prod_development/downloads/EPA_Report_Exec_Summary_Final.pdf, accessed January 23, 2008.

- "Olympic Medals Made from E-Waste," news.discovery.com/tech/olympic-medals-made-from-e-waste.html, accessed April 4, 2010; Rob Delaney, "Olympic Champs Wear Old Trinitrons as Teck Turns Junk to Medals," *Bloomberg Businessweek,* February 3, 2010, www.bloomberg.com/apps/news?pid 5 newsarchive&sid 5az0yJ8scpCqQ.

- Rich Miller, "Google Data Center FAQ," www.datacenterknowledge.com/archives/2008/03/27/google-data-center-faq/, accessed April 1, 2010.

- Switch on the Benefits of Grid Computing," h20338.www2.hp.com/enterprise/downloads/7_Benefits%20of%20grid%20computing.pdf, accessed April 2, 2010; "Talking to the Grid," www.technologyreview.com/energy/23706/, accessed April 3, 2010; "Tech Update: What's All the Smart Grid Buzz About?" www.fieldtechnologiesonline.com/download.mvc/Whats-All-The-Smart-Grid-Buzz-About-0001, accessed April 3, 2010.

- "The Great 1906 San Francisco Earthquake," *USGS,* http://earthquake.usgs.gov/regional/nca/1906/18april/index.php, accessed July 14, 2010.

- "VMware-History of Virtualization," www.virtualizationworks.com/Virtualization-History.asp, accessed January 23, 2008.

- www.box.net, accessed April 2, 2010.

PLUG-IN B5

- Andy Patrizio, "Peer-to-Peer Goes Beyond Napster," *Wired,* February, 14, 2001, www.wired.com/science/discoveries/news/2001/02/41768, accessed January 2009.

- Cisco, "Network Media Types," www.ciscopress.com/articles/article.asp?p 5 31276, accessed January 2009.

- Cisco, "TCP/IP Overview," www.cisco.com/en/US/tech/tk365/technologies_white_paper09186a008014f8a9.shtml, accessed January 2009.

- Cisco, "TCP/IP Overview."

- Intel in Communications, "10 Gigabit Ethernet Technology Overview," www.intel.com/network/connectivity/resources/doc_library/white_papers/pro10gbe_lr_sa_wp.pdf, accessed January 2009.

- "IPv6," www.ipv6.org, accessed January 2009.

PLUG-IN B6

- Daniel Schorn, "Whose Life Is It Anyway?" *CBS News,* www.cbsnews.com/stories/2005/10/28/60minutes/main990617.shtml, February 2009.

- FTC Spam, www.ftc.gov/bcp/edu/microsites/spam/, accessed June 2013.

- www.ftc.gov/ogc/coppa1.htm, accessed April 2013

- Jon Perlow, "New in Labs: Stop Sending Mail You Later Regret," gmailblog.blogspot.com/2008/10/new-inlabs-stop-sending-mail-you-later.html, accessed June 2013.

- "Kiva—Loans That Change Lives," www.kiva.org, accessed April 2013.

- Michael Schrage, "Build the Business Case," *CIO Magazine,* www.cio.com/article/31780/Build_the_Business_Case_Extracting_Value_from_the_Customer, March 15, 2003.

- Mike Brunker, "Online Poker Cheating Blamed on Employee," *MSNBC.com,* October 19, 2007, www.msnbc.msn.com/id/21381022/, accessed April 2013.

- Richard Mason, "Four Ethical Issues of the Information Age," *Management Information Systems Quarterly* 10, no. 1 (March 1986), www.misq.org/archivist/vol/no10/issue1/vol10no1mason.html, accessed April 2013.

- Ronald Quinlan, "Ex-banker Urges Former Colleagues to Step Down," www.independent.ie/nationalnews/exbanker-urges-former-colleagues-to-stepdown-1558320.html, November 2008.

PLUG-IN B7

- "CBC Tells Journalists How to Behave on Facebook," *Reportr.net,* August 3, 2007, www.reportr.net/2007/08/03/cbc-tells-journalists-how-to-behave-on-facebook/.

- "Planned and Unplanned Downtime," SAP, http://help.sap.com/saphelp_nw72/helpdata/en/45/17396792ef5d79e10000000a11466f/content.htm.

- AMA Research, "Workplace Monitoring and Surveillance," www.amanet.org, accessed March 1, 2004; "2005 CSI/FBI Computer Crime and Security Survey," www.gocsi.com, accessed February 20, 2006.

- Andy McCue, "Bank Boss Quits after Porn Found on PC," www.businessweek.com, accessed June 2004.

- Brian Womack, "Google Ends Self-Censorship, Defies China Government (Update4)," *Bloomberg Businessweek*, March 23, 2010, www.bloomberg.com/apps.

- Daniel Schorn "Whose Life Is It Anyway?" *CBS News 60 Minutes,* July 16, 2006, www.cbsnews.com/stories/2005/10/28/60minutes/main990617.shtml.

- Extracting_Value_from_the_Customer, accessed April 17, 2010.

- Michael Schrage, "Build the Business Case," *CIO Magazine*, March 15, 2003, www.cio.com/article/31780/Build_the_Business_Case_

- Mike Brunker, "Online Poker Cheating Blamed on Employee," MSNBC.com, October 19, 2007, www.msnbc.msn.com/id/21381022/, accessed April 15, 2010.

- Peter S. Green, "Take the Data Pledge," *Bloomberg Businessweek*, April 23, 2009.

- Raymund Flandez, "Domino's Response Offers Lessons in Crisis Management," *The Wall Street Journal*, April 20, 2009, http://blogs.wsj.com/independentstreet/2009/04/20/dominos-response-offers-lessons-in-crisis-management/

- Richard Mason, "Four Ethical Issues of the Information Age," *Management Information Systems Quarterly* 10, no. 1 (March 1986), www.misq.org/archivist/vol/no10/issue1/vol10no1mason.html, accessed April 15, 2010.

- Scott Berinato, "The CIO Code of Ethical Data Management," *CIO Magazine,* July 1, 2002, www.cio.com, accessed April 17, 2010.

- Thomas Claburn, "Web 2.0. Internet Too Dangerous for Normal People," *InformationWeek*, April 1, 2009, www.informationweek.com/news/.

PLUG-IN B8

- Aaron Bernstein, "Backlash: Behind the Anxiety of Globalization," *BusinessWeek,* April 24, 2006, pp. 36–42.

- Andrew Binstock, "Virtual Enterprise Comes of Age*," Information Week,* November 6, 2004.

- Bill Breen, "Living in Dell Time," *Fast Company,* November 2004, p. 86.

- Christopher A. Bartlett and Sumantra Ghoshal, "Going Global: Lessons from Late Movers," *Harvard Business Review,* March–April 2000, pp. 132–34.

- Creating a Value Network," *Wired,* September 2003, p. S13.

- Terry Hill, *Manufacturing Strategy: Text and Cases,* 3rd ed. (New York: McGraw-Hill, 2000).

PLUG-IN B9

- Agam Shah, "UPS Invests $1 Billion in Technology to Cut Costs," *BusinessWeek,* www.businessweek.com/idg/2010-03-25/ups-invests-1-billion-intechnology-to-cut-costs.html, accessed April 4, 2010.

- "Center Energy Efficiency," www.energystar.gov/ia/partners/prod_development/downloads/EPA_Report_Exec_Summary_Final.pdf, accessed January 23, 2008.

- *Google Docs,* docs.google.com, accessed June 4, 2010.

- Martin LaMonica, "The Journey of Juice, Inside the Electric Grid," *CNET News,* August 24, 2010, http://news.cnet.com/8301-11128_3-20014393-54.html.

- "Moore's Law," www.intel.com/technology/mooreslaw, accessed April 2, 2010; Electronics TakeBack Coalition, "Facts and Figures on E-Waste and Recycling," www.electronic-stakeback.com, accessed April 3, 2010; "EPA Report to Congress on Server and Data."

- "Olympic Medals Made from E-Waste," news.discovery.com/tech/olympic-medals-made-from-e-waste.html, accessed April 4, 2010; Rob Delaney, "Olympic Champs Wear Old Trinitrons as Teck Turns Junk to Medals," *Bloomberg Businessweek,*

- Rich Miller, "Google Data Center FAQ," www.datacenter-knowledge.com/archives/2008/03/27/google-data-center-faq/, accessed April 1, 2010.

- "Switch on the Benefits of Grid Computing," h20338.www2.hp.com/enterprise/downloads/7_Benefits%20of%20grid%20computing.pdf, accessed April 2, 2010; "Talking to the Grid," www.technologyreview.com/energy/23706/, accessed April 3, 2010; "Tech Update: What's All the Smart Grid Buzz About?" www.fieldtechnologiesonline.com/download.mvc/

Whats-All-The-Smart-Grid-Buzz-About-0001, accessed April 3, 2010.

- "The Great 1906 San Francisco Earthquake," *USGS,* http://earthquake.usgs.gov/regional/nca/1906/18april/index.php, accessed July 14, 2010.
- "VMware-History of Virtualization," www.virtualizationworks.com/Virtualization-History.asp, accessed January 23, 2008.
- www.box.net, accessed April 2, 2010.

PLUG-IN B10

- Emanuel Rosen, *The Anatomy of Buzz* (New York: Doubleday, 2000).
- "Enterprise Business Intelligence," May 2006. Used with permission: Dr. Claudia Imhoff, Intelligent Solutions.
- Frederick F. Reichheld, *Loyalty Rules* (Bain and Company, 2001).
- Jill Dyche, "The Business Case for Data Warehousing," 2005. Used with permission.
- Meridith Levinson, "The Brain Behind the Big Bad Burger and Other Tales of Business Intelligence," *www.cio.com,* May 15, 2007, www.cio.com/article/109454/The_Brain_Behind_the_Big_Bad_Burger_and_Other_Tales_of_Business_Intelligence.
- "Second Life," www.secondlife.org, accessed March 2008.
- Steve Hamm, "Business Intelligence Gets Smarter," *BusinessWeek,* May 15, 2006.
- "The Critical Shift to Flexible Business Intelligence." Used with Permission: Dr. Claudia Imhoff, Intelligent Solutions, Inc.
- "What Every Marketer Wants—And Needs—From Technology." Used with Permission: Dr. Claudia Imhoff, Intelligent Solutions, Inc.

PLUG-IN B11

- Brian Grow, Keith Epstein, and Chi-Chu Tschang, "E-Spionage," *BusinessWeek,* April 10, 2008.
- "Innovation," *BusinessWeek,* www.businessweek.com/innovate/, accessed February 15, 2008.
- David Bornstein, *How to Change the World,* updated edition (New York: Oxford University Press, 2007).

- Harold Sirkin, "Tata's Nano: An Ingenious Coup," *BusinessWeek,* February 14, 2008.
- Heather Green and Kerry Capell, "Carbon Confusion," *BusinessWeek,* March 6, 2008.
- Jeffrey Hollender and Stephen Fenichell, *What Matters Most: The Future of Corporate Social Responsibility* (New York: Basic Books, 2006).
- Kerry Capell, "Building Expertise through Collective Innovation," *BusinessWeek,* March 5, 2008.
- Peter F. Drucker Foundation, *The Leader of the Future: Visions, Practices, and Strategies for a New Era,* www.peterdrucker.com, accessed 2010.
- Peter F. Drucker, *Management Challenges for the 21st Century* (New York: Collins Business, 2001).
- William J. Holstein, "Corporate Governance in China and India," *BusinessWeek Online,* March 6, 2008, www.businessweek.com/managing/content/mar2008/ca2008036_282896.htm.

PLUG-IN B12

- Denise Dubie, "Tivoli Users Discuss Automation," *Network World,* April 14, 2003.
- Marvin Cetron and Owen Davies, "50 Trends Shaping the Future," *2003 World Future Society Special Report,* April 2004.
- Penelope Patsuris, "Marketing Messages Made to Order," *Forbes,* August 2003.
- "Progressive Receives Applied Systems' 2003 Interface Best Practices Award," www.worksite.net/091203tech.htm, accessed June 18, 2004.
- Stacy Crowley, "IBM, HP, MS Discuss Autonomic Computing Strategies," *Infoworld,* May 19, 2004.
- "The Art of Foresight," *The Futurist,* May–June 2004, pp. 31–35.
- William Halal, "The Top 10 Emerging Technologies," *The Futurist Special Report,* July 2004.

CHAPTER 1

Page 3 (left): © The McGraw-Hill Companies, Inc./Jill Braaten, photographer; p. 3 (center): © The McGraw-Hill Companies, Inc./Lars A. Niki, photographer; p. 3 (right): © The McGraw-Hill Companies, Inc./Christopher Kerrigan, photographer.

CHAPTER 5

Page 63 (left): © Exactostock/SuperStock; p. 63 (center): © Ariel Skelley/Blend Images LLC; p. 63 (right): © Vico Collective/Erik Palmer/Blend Images LLC; p. 65 (left): © The McGraw-Hill Companies, Inc./John Flournoy, photographer; p. 65 (center): © Bloomberg via Getty Images; p. 65 (right): © B Christopher/Alamy; p. 72 (top left): © Hyundai Motor America; p. 72 (top right): © Audi of America, Inc.; p. 72 (bottom left): © Courtesy, Kia Motors America, Inc.; p. 72 (bottom right): © Getty Images.

CHAPTER 6

Page 81 (left): © Image Source/Getty Images RF; p. 81 (center): © Maciej Frolow/Getty Images RF; p. 81 (right): © C. Zachariasen/PhotoAlto; p. 84: © Digital Vision/Getty Images.

CHAPTER 8

Page 115 (left): © Roz Woodward/Getty Images; p. 115 (center): © Getty Images/Digital Vision; p. 115 (right): © Epoxy/Getty Images; p. 116 (left): © C. Borland/PhotoLink/Getty Images; p. 116 (center): © Fuse/Getty Images; p. 116 (right): © NPS photo by Jim Peaco.

CHAPTER 9

Page 129 (left): © JGI/Blend Images/Getty Images RF; p. 129 (center): © Steve Cole/Getty Images RF; p. 129 (right): © Steve Cole/Getty Images RF.

CHAPTER 12

Page 178 (left): © C. Sherburne/PhotoLink/Getty Images; p. 178 (center): © Digital Vision/Getty Images; p. 178 (right): © Ryan McVay/Getty Images; p. 179 (left): © AP/The Paducah Sun, Stephen Lance Dennee; p. 179 (center): © Scott Olson/Getty Images; p. 179 (right): © PRNewsFoto/Harley-Davidson.

CHAPTER 13

Page 191 (left): © John Lund/Marc Romanelli/Blend Images LLC RF; p. 191 (center): © Courtesy of Pinterest.com; p. 191 (right): © AFP/Getty Images; p. 195: © Digital Vision/PunchStock.

CHAPTER 15

Page 217: © Punchstock/Digital Vision; p. 219: © Radius Images/Corbis.

CHAPTER 16

Page 246 (left): © Photodisc/Getty Images; p. 246 (center): © Image Source/Getty Images; p. 246 (right): © Tetra Images/Getty Images; p. 247 (left): © Thinkstock/SuperStock; p. 247 (center): © Getty Images/Blend Images; p. 247 (right): © BananaStock/PictureQuest.

CHAPTER 17

Page 263 (left): © Bernhard Lang/Getty Images; p. 263 (center): © Comstock/Jupiterimages RF; p. 263 (right): © altrendo images/Getty Images RF; p. 267 © PhotoDisc Imaging/Getty Images.

CHAPTER 20

Page 303 (left): © Tetra Images/Getty Images; p. 303 (center): © The McGraw-Hill Companies, Inc./Lars A. Niki, photographer; p. 303 (right): © The McGraw-Hill Companies, Inc./Christopher Kerrigan, photographer, p. 305 (left): © Getty Images/Blend Images: p. 305 (center): © Stockbyte/Getty Images: p. 305 (right): © Ingram Publishing/AGE Fotostock.

PLUG-IN B3

Page 364 (left): © Royalty-Free/Corbis; p. 364 (right): © Stockbyte/Punchstock Images; p. 365 (clockwise, starting left to right): © Royalty-Free/Corbis, © Stockbyte/PunchStock Images, © Nick Rowe/Getty Images, © Digital Vision/Getty Images, © Image Club, © Royalty-Free/Corbis, © Getty Images/Photodisc, © Daisuke Morita/Getty Images, © Don Bishop/Photodisc/Getty Images/RF, © Stockbyte/PunchStock Images, © Stockbyte/PunchStock Images; p. 366 (top): © Nick Rowe/Getty Images; p. 366 (bottom): © Don Bishop/Photodisc/Getty Images/RF; p. 367 (top): © Daisuke Morita/Getty Images; p. 367 (bottom left): © Stockbyte/PunchStock Images; p. 367 (bottom right): © Stockbyte/PunchStock Images; p. 369 (top left): © Digital Vision/Getty Images; p. 369 (top right): © Image Club; p. 369 (bottom): © Royalty-Free/Corbis; p. 370: © Digital Vision/Getty Images.

PLUG-IN B10

Page 477: NCR FastLane™ self-checkout solution.

PLUG-IN B12

Page 509 & 510: Courtesy of E Ink Corporation; p. 512: © Russell Illig/Getty Images.

INDEX

A

Abandoned registrations, 48
Abandoned shopping carts, 48
ABN AMRO Bank, 480
Abramo, Guy, 479
AbsolutePoker.com, 426
AcceleGlove, 369
Accenture, 493
Acceptable use policy (AUP), 427
Access points (APs), 228
Accessibility (MIS infrastructure), 387
Accountability, for data security, 102–103
Accounting, 325
Accounting and finance ERP components, 172
Accounting business processes, 344
Accounting department, 325–328
Accuracy (MIS infrastructure), 388–389
Actionly.com, 129–131
Active RFID tags, 233
Active Software, 170
Adams, Douglas, 77
Adaptec Inc., 148
Address, home, 265
Adidas, 188, 356
Adidas-Salomon, 356–357
Administrator access, 387
Adobe, 69, 374
Advanced encryption standard (AES), 415
Advanced Micro Devices (AMD), 363, 372
Advertising, online, 202–203
Adware, 411
AdWords (Google), 208
ADY (American Dairy), 41
AES (advanced encryption standard), 415
Affiliate programs, 202
Affinity grouping (data), 475
Agent-based modeling systems, 145
Aggregation, data, 105
Agile methodologies, 281–283
Agile MIS infrastructure, 386–389
Agile organizations, methodologies for supporting, 280–283
AI (artificial intelligence), 142–146, 508
Airbus, 154
Airline industry, 22–23, 439
Aksoy, Lerzan, N3
Albertson's, 22
Alpha testing, 275
AltaVista, 205
Altec Lansing Technologies, 3
Alternative energy sources, 512
ALU (arithmetic-logic unit), 363, 365
Amazon, 7–8, 22, 66, 91, 102, 160, 195, 200, 207, 208, 216, 221, 247, 296, 457, 458, 464, 489
Amazon Elastic Compute Cloud (Amazon EC2), 464
Amazon Web Services (AWS), 465
Ambiguous requirements, 278
AMD (Advanced Micro Devices), 363, 372
America Online (AOL), 65, 209, 247
American Dairy (ADY), 41

American Express, 199, 234, 296, 489
The American Family Immigration History Center, 96
American Sign Language (ASL) translator, 369
American Society of Composers, 63
AMR Research Inc., 436
Analysis latency, 473
Analysis phase (SDLC), 270–271
Analytical CRM, 159
Analytical information, 85–87
    defined, 86
    for managerial support, 138–139
Andersen, Bjorn, N5
Anderson, Chris, 200, 252
Anderson, Tom, 8
Android, 4
Annenberg Public Policy Center, 434
Ansari X, 147
Anti-spam policy, 429
Antispyware software, 416
Antivirus software, 416
AOL; *see* America Online
API (application programming interface), 221
Apple (Apple Computer Inc.), 3–5, 19, 66, 197, 231, 388, 389, 393, 457, 469
Apple Macintosh computer, 457
Apple Newton PDA, 204
Applebee's Neighborhood Grill & Bar, 104
Appleton Learning, 64
Appleyard, David, 420
Appliances, 370
Application Engine (Google), 465
Application programming interface (API), 221
Application service provider licenses, 374
Application software, 373–374
The Apprentice, 66
APs (access points), 228
Arbib, Michael A., N2
Architecture, 397–399
Aristotle, 211
Arithmetic-logic unit (ALU), 363, 365
Army (UK), 99–100
Arnold, Thelma, 65
ARPANET, 48
The Art of Deception (Kevin Mitnick), 419
The Art of War (Sun Tzu), 110
Artificial intelligence (AI), 142–146, 508
Artificial neural networks, 143–144
As-Is process models, 347–349
Ascential Software, 108
ASL (American Sign Language) translator, 369
Asset tracking, 233–234
Assets
    defined, 326
    intellectual, 58–59
Associate programs, 202
Association detection, 476
Association rule generators, 476
Asynchronous communications, 218
Atari, 204, 330
ATMs (automated teller machines), 44
AT&T, 63, 209, 231, 371, 373, 423

G